The SAGE International Handbook *of* Educational Evaluation

The SAGE International Handbook *of* Educational Evaluation

Editors

Katherine E. Ryan

University of Illinois at Urbana-Champaign

J. Bradley Cousins

University of Ottawa

Los Angeles | London | New Delhi
Singapore | Washington DC

For information:

SAGE Publications, Inc.
2455 Teller Road
Thousand Oaks, California 91320
E-mail: order@sagepub.com

SAGE Publications India Pvt. Ltd.
B 1/I 1 Mohan Cooperative
  Industrial Area
Mathura Road, New Delhi 110 044
India

SAGE Publications Ltd.
1 Oliver's Yard
55 City Road
London EC1Y 1SP
United Kingdom

SAGE Publications Asia-Pacific Pte Ltd
33 Pekin Street #02-01
Far East Square
Singapore 048763

Printed in the United States of America

Library of Congress Cataloging-in-Publication Data

Ryan, Katherine.
The SAGE international handbook of educational evaluation/Katherine
Ryan, J. Bradley Cousins.
    p. cm.
Includes bibliographical references and index.
ISBN 978-1-4129-4068-9 (cloth : alk. paper)
    1. Educational evaluation—Handbooks, manuals, etc. I. Cousins, J. Bradley. II. Title.

LB2822.75.R9 2009
379.1′58—dc22   2009003451

This book is printed on acid-free paper.

09   10   11   12   13   10   9   8   7   6   5   4   3   2   1

Acquisitions Editor:	Vicki Knight
Associate Editor:	Sean Connelly
Editorial Assistant:	Lauren Habib
Production Editor:	Catherine M. Chilton
Copy Editor:	Heather Jefferson
Typesetter:	C&M Digitals (P) Ltd.
Proofreader:	Annette R. Van Deusen
Indexer:	Diggs Publication Services
Cover Designer:	Glenn Vogel
Marketing Manager:	Stephanie Adams

Contents

Introduction

Katherine E. Ryan and J. Bradley Cousins

Volume Overview

Educational evaluation is at the same time similar and different from evaluation in other domains of human service practice (e.g., health, justice, social service). Moreover, educational evaluation is subject to similar policy and governance structures as might be found across different human service practice domains. Yet educational evaluation is unique in remarkable ways. For instance, the evaluation and assessment of student progress toward valued goals is an integral part of the core business of education—teaching and learning. A corollary is that there exists in education a longstanding tradition of psychometric testing—predominantly achievement testing—that is unparalleled in other domains of human service practice.

The goal of all educational evaluation is to enable programs and policies to improve student learning. There are longstanding tensions resulting in dialogue and discussion about what kinds of educational evaluation families or genres (e.g., science-based approaches involving experimental methods, participatory approaches) are best for accomplishing this goal (Campbell & Stanley, 1963; Cook, 2002; Cronbach et al., 1980; Eisner, 1994; Guba, 1969; Stake, 1984). In contemporary society, broader forces such as globalization[1] are seen as a major factor in the enactment of international and national policies for educational evaluation, assessment, and testing, as well as curriculum and instruction (Burbules & Torres, 2000; Gardner, 2004).

Globalization, to be sure, is a contested and contentious term, one that carries a variety of meanings for different people. The emergence of *new public management* (NPM) as the dominant governance paradigm concerning educational policy and practice and *neoliberalism* as the overarching political theory in contemporary governance are central constructs. The globalization notion is intended to capture the political, economic, and social forces that have converged over the past 30 years. There are different views about what globalization refers to, including the impact of global economic processes (e.g., production, consumption), the decline in the nation-state system, the emergence of new global media and information technologies that permit the circulation of ideas, resources, and even individuals across boundaries, and the decline of local traditions and values (Burbules & Torres, 2000; Rizvi, 2004; Stein, 2001).

Globalization is characterized by values such as efficiency, entrepreneurship, market-based reform, rational management, and performance-based accountability (Burbules, 2002). At the same time, the rise of neoliberal ideologies[2] has taken place. With neoliberalism, the state role is to create an appropriate market and one that creates an individual that is enterprising and entrepreneurial (Biesta, 2004). In contrast, within a liberal democracy, the government is constituted as delegated, institutional power structures administering the interests of society. A neoliberal democracy that focuses on appropriate markets aimed at creating enterprising and entrepreneurial individuals signals different arrangements.

Globalization and Education

Globalization is demanding more of education as markets have shifted from industrial production to one of service, with information technology receiving more attention (Gardner, 2004; Stein, 2001; Teachers College Annual Report, 2004). Within the knowledge-based economy, intellectual resources and knowledge, instead of natural resources and industrial labor, are critical assets for continuing economic growth. Educational evaluation is playing a key role in this shift to a knowledge-based society, which demands that students be educated for the new world order to remain competitive in the global economy.

Nations now vie for highly competitive positions within the global marketplace (Anderson, 2005). As a consequence, governments are paying increasing attention to the performance of their educational systems—the outcomes of education. Although student learning continues to be paramount, part of this changing contemporary society involves extending learning beyond traditional boundaries to the notion of life-long learning. The life-long learning framework includes learning throughout the life course from birth onward in a wide variety of learning environments, such as formal, nonformal, and informal pathways.[3] Improved student learning is therefore the *raison d'être* for all educational evaluation, with the understanding that "Who is the student?" is changing.

Further, there is a fundamental tension between improving educational achievement and the amount and kinds of resources available for realizing these improvements. Historically, increased demands on education have been supported with increases in resources. However, a defining feature of globalization is the commitment to the notion that growth can be achieved through increased production and efficiency (Lundgren, 2003; Stein, 2001). At the same time, the economic gap between the rich and the poor has increased within the United States and globally. There are also persistent educational achievement gaps between low-income, racial, ethnic, and linguistic minority students and their peers (Baker & LeTendre, 2005; National Center for Educational Statistics, 2005; Organisation for Economic Co-operation and Development, 2003).

Concerns about quality and the resources directed to education are increasing demands for information about school performance. These demands are being addressed with the (a) implementation of performance measurement systems (e.g., high-stakes educational tests) and (b) development of science-based research and evidence-based policy that is intended to distinguish between "what works" from what does not in improving education. Together, performance-based, accountability-based NPM[4] (Behn, 2001), and evidence-based policy (EBP) result in a potentially powerful mechanism for steering educational policy.

Performance Measurement Systems

According to Nevo (2002), external educational evaluations were always intended as a form of control. Today, the steering of educational policy is reflected in increasing governmental oversight and control of curriculum, instruction, pedagogy, and evaluation in the international arena. For instance, Argentina, Chile, other Latin American countries, France, Australia, England, the United States, and others have implemented large-scale assessments to monitor school quality. Test results are used for such diverse purposes as providing resources to or to publicize poorly performing schools, identify school system inefficiencies, and assess the extent to which students learned the prescribed curriculum and others.

Large-scale assessment use in the United States illustrates this kind of policy steering. For example, the 2001 No Child Left Behind (2002) legislation institutionalizes the reliance on high-stakes tests (performance indicators) as a key mechanism for improving student achievement reflecting NPM (Behn, 2001). When schools and districts do not show adequate annual yearly progress (AYP)[5] for more than 2 years, a summative evaluative judgment is triggered—a school is judged as "unsuccessful" with no other information. Instead, students then may legally enroll in another school, a policy reflecting a free market approach to improving student learning.

Student achievement is also ranked and compared on international assessments such as the Third International Mathematics Science and Math Study (TIMSS) and Programme for International Student Assessment (PISA), which are used to examine cross-curricular competences (Stronach, 1999; Stronach, Halsall, & Hustler, 2002). These cross-country assessment comparisons are linked to economic performance in these countries in the global economy (Stronach et al., 2002). Quantitative performance indicators have come to represent and communicate quality and quantity of education (Carnoy, 1999). There is an assumption that increases from this kind of quantitative measurement represent more and better education. This is essentially an efficiency model that uses indicators of productivity (gains in achievement test scores) to represent increased school productivity. The Organisation for Economic Co-operation and Development, the International Education Association, and the National Center for Educational Statistics have contributed to developing this view through their respective policy efforts.

"What Works"

In addition, within No Child Left Behind (2002), *scientifically based research* is defined as "rigorous, systematic, and objective procedures to obtain valid knowledge that is evaluated using experimental or quasi-experimental design." The U.S. Coalition for Evidence-Based Policy (EBP) defines evidence-based policy as based on research that has been proven effective by randomized controlled experiments replicated on a large scale (Coalition for Evidence-Based Policy, 2002). There are many brokerage agencies that have been established worldwide aimed at building capacity to produce EBP. The agencies (a) establish criteria for conducting and evaluating science-based educational research, and (b) house a database of "what works." Examples of national and international brokerage agencies include Evidence for Policy and Practice Information and Co-ordinating (Centre United Kingdom) (http://eppi.ioe.ac.uk), Iterative Best Evidence Synthesis Programme (New Zealand) (www.minedu.govt.nz), What Works Clearinghouse (USA) (www.whatworks.ed.gov), and the Campbell Collaboration (www.campbellcollab oration.org), an international nonprofit organization. In effect, evidence-based policy changes what kind of evidence matters for determining educational program effectiveness.

Educational Evaluation for Learning and Accountability?

At the same time, the notion of evaluation as learning is becoming increasingly attractive with both proponents of educational evaluation for improvement and educational evaluation for accountability staking claims to this notion. Single, stand-alone educational evaluations reflecting responsive evaluation roots aimed at learning and discovery at the local program level are under some duress—either being supplemented or supplanted by outcome indicators (Dahler-Larsen, 2006; Mayne & Rist, 2006). Meanwhile, despite known conceptual complexities (e.g., divergent evaluation purposes), performance monitoring is identified as one evaluation approach aimed at practice improvement and organization learning (Rogers & Williams, 2006). Although performance monitoring's historical role in holding individuals and organizations accountable is recognized, performance monitoring is becoming known as a means to improve programs, services, and practices, effectively blurring foundational evaluation purposes.

Globalizing Evaluation

Educational evaluation, in this sense, is being "globalized." Evaluation theories and practices are being influenced and are influenced by the movement of ideas across national boundaries. How and the extent to which educational evaluation theories and practices are changing in response to globalization and other political and social changes has not been examined. In the literature, the ideology of globalization is often portrayed as an inevitable consequence of market forces that results in a top-down homogenization effecting social, political, and cultural changes (Carnoy, 1999; Lingard, 2000). Nevertheless, globalization scale (e.g., global, regional, national, state, and local levels) effects are just beginning to be considered. For instance, how globalization effects influence or interact with the local level and the relationships between the local and global are not well understood. (This is also the case for other levels, such as regional, state, etc.). In the educational evaluation context, the extent to which globalization effects influence how educational evaluation theories and practices are instantiated locally or at other levels is not clear. Local and national politics and social relations can mediate or moderate the effects of globalization on the local or other levels (Lingard, 2000). Politics, local histories, and cultures will influence how these educational evaluation approaches actually play out at the local and other levels.

Volume Aims and Perspectives

The volume aim is to address the challenges, tensions, and issues within and across educational evaluation genres in response to an increasingly globalized society. Contributors from various theoretical and practice perspectives examined whether and how educational evaluation is being redefined by the changing circumstances of globalization. How to address the challenges, tensions, and issues within and across educational evaluation perspectives in response to an increasingly globalized society was considered.

We examined these globalization effects vis-à-vis a comparative examination of various educational evaluation genres or families. Although there are many possibilities, we conceptualize the genres or families as follows. The *role of science in educational evaluation* includes approaches emphasizing science characterized by measurement and design. *Educational evaluation, capacity building, and monitoring* involve educational evaluation theories and practices that assume improved organizations, management, and programs will improve student learning. The third genre, *educational evaluation as learning* reflects educational evaluation theories and practices that emphasize attention to understanding of program contexts in general and from stakeholders' views, stakeholder participation in evaluation, and value pluralism with a preference for qualitative or mixed methods. *Educational evaluation in a political world* incorporates educational evaluation (a) oriented around a set of values or ideology and (b) presupposes educational programs and what works is best understood in relationship to the political currents that influence them.

This kind of comparative analysis of evaluation families or genres is one approach to understanding evaluation (e.g., Cook, 2002; Greene, 1994; House, 1978; Shadish, Leviton, & Cook, 1991). We make no special claim that representing the field according to these specific families of evaluation theory and practice is authoritative in describing evaluation as a domain of inquiry. Further, we acknowledge that there are a variety of perspectives that could be utilized as a framework for this kind of project. As one critical friend notes, examining specific educational practices such as evaluation in higher education, the evaluation of school effectiveness, and the like could serve as a framework for this kind of endeavor that would yield an interesting set of chapters. There are other important educational evaluation issues such as classroom assessment and evaluation and teacher evaluation beyond the scope of the *Handbook.* Rather, our intentional focus was on the evaluation of educational programs, policies, organizations, or systems.

Yet we do assert that this framework adequately captures the range of evaluation perspectives that exist in contemporary society. Despite spillage from one family to the next, the categories are sufficiently meaningful and discernable as to warrant their use as an organizing structure. On this point, our editorial board agreed.

At this juncture, we would like to acknowledge our wise and wonderful international editorial board composed of acclaimed educational evaluation scholars. The *Handbook* editorial board members were tireless in providing excellent advice in all matters of the volume. They served in several capacities involving a variety of tasks, including peer reviews for the chapters, critical and generous feedback on the volume framework, identification and recruitment of chapter authors, and guidance about critical topics and controversies. In particular, there were significant efforts devoted to recruiting educational evaluation scholars across the world to prepare chapters for this volume. We achieved only modest success in this area even with help from the *Handbook* editorial board and board members from evaluation societies. Although we are delighted to have successfully recruited chapter authors from Australia, Europe, Middle East, North America, and Latin America, we know there are other notable educational evaluation perspectives that would have enhanced the volume.

Volume Organization

This volume is organized in six parts. In addition to parts structured around the educational evaluation genres, we included an introductory part on the *context for educational evaluation* (Part I) and a concluding part on *opportunities and new dilemmas* (Part VI). Part I articulates the volume framework describing the current educational evaluation context, including globalization definitions and changing educational policies, foundations, and historic evaluation dilemmas.

The chapters in Parts II through V of the volume each takes up a particular educational evaluation perspective or genre (e.g., educational evaluation as science) in relationship to the changing circumstances of globalization. Within genre parts, we recruited authors to write chapters about either theory associated with the genre, methods specific to it, or exemplary case exemplars of work in the area. In each part, two evaluation theory and method chapters, representing the particular genre, are examined. The theories and their respective methodologies are defined and then examined in relationship to the questions focusing the volume. Both the theory and methods chapters are intended to illustrate a defining educational evaluation genre feature or tension (e.g., mixed methods), rather than be exhaustive. The case study chapters illustrate how the respective theories translate to practice in a globalized society, including, for example, what counts as knowledge, stakeholder representation, and how student achievement is represented. In some cases, exemplars were positive manifestations or success stories, whereas other revealed challenges, unintended processes or consequences, and/or practical departures from planned directions. The critical appraisal chapter in each part describes how the genre contributes to improving educational policy and practices by providing a critical analysis of the merits and shortcomings of this approach for shaping educational policy and serving educational public interests in a globalized society. The chapters in Part VI focus on educational evaluation issues in contemporary society, including educational evaluation and educational policy, the effects of technology, and serving the public interests. The final chapter is by the editors and the focus is on continuing educational evaluation dilemmas (e.g., evaluator role). In this final chapter, we endeavored to look across the many contributions in the handbook with an eye to synthesis and integration about educational evaluation in a globalized society.

Notes

1. We acknowledge that *globalization* is a contested term. For the purposes of this book, we incorporate multiple views of globalization, including (a) the integration of markets and production through large multinational corporations based on the notion of efficiency (Burbules & Torres, 2000; Stein, 2001); (b) the transmission of products, technology, ideas, and cultures across national boundaries (Burbules & Torres, 2000; Suarez-Orozco & Qin-Hilliard, 2004); and (c) others.

2. How or whether these ideological shifts are intertwined with these economic changes is the subject of substantial discussion and debate (Biesta, 2004; Burbules & Torres, 2000; Carnoy, 1999).

3. Retrieved from http://74.125.95.132/search?q=cache:KT02QVGARtcJ:www1.world bank.org/education/lifelong_learning/ World Bank, 2005.

4. NPM is an array of strategies designed to regulate individuals and organizations through auditable performance standards (Power, 1997). These standards are aimed at increasing performance and to make these kinds of improvements transparent and public. Performance is represented by reductions, efficiency, and effectiveness.

5. AYP is (a) the percentage of reading and math scores that meet or exceed standards, compared with the annual state targets; and (b) the participation rate of students in taking the state tests, which must meet or exceed 95%.

References

Anderson, J. A. (2005). *Accountability in education*. Paris: UNESCO, International Institute for Educational Planning.

Baker, D. P., & LeTendre, G. K. (2005). *National differences, global similarities: World culture and the future of schooling*. Stanford, CA: Stanford Social Sciences Press.

Behn, R. D. (2001) *Rethinking democratic accountability*. Washington, DC: Brookings Institution Press.

Biesta, G. J. (2004). Education, accountability, and the ethical demand: Can the democratic potential of accountability be regained? *Educational Theory, 54*(3), 233–250.

Burbules, N. C. (2002). The global context of educational research. In L. Bresler & A. Ardichvili (Eds.), *Research in international education: Experience, theory, and practice* (pp. 157–170). New York: Peter Lang.

Burbules, N. C., & Torres, C. A. (Eds.). (2000). *Globalization and education: Critical perspectives*. New York: Routledge.

Campbell, D. T., & Stanley, J. (1963). *Experimental and quasi-experimental designs for research.* Chicago: Rand-McNally.

Carnoy, M. (1999). *Globalization and educational reform: What planners need to know.* Paris: UNESCO, International Institute for Educational Planning.

Coalition for Evidence-Based Policy. (2002, November). *Bringing evidence-driven progress to education: A recommended strategy for the U.S. Department of Education.* Available at http://www.excelgov.org/usermedia/images/uploads/PDFs/coalitionFinRpt.pdf

Cook, T. D. (2002). Randomized experiments in educational policy research: A critical examination of the reasons the educational evaluation community has offered for not doing them. *Educational Evaluation and Policy Analysis, 24*(3), 175–199.

Cronbach, L. J., Ambron, S. R., Dornbusch, S. M., Hess, R. D., Hornik, R. C., Phillips, D. C., Walker, D. F., & Weiner, S. S. (1980). *Toward a reform of program evaluation: Aims, methods, and institutional arrangements.* San Francisco, CA: Jossey-Bass.

Dahler-Larsen, P. (2006). Evaluation after disenchantment? Five issues shaping the role of evaluation in society. In I. Shaw, M. M. Mark, & J. Greene (Eds.), *The Sage handbook of evaluation* (pp. 141–160). Thousand Oaks, CA: Sage.

Eisner, E. W. (1994). *The educational imagination* (3rd ed.). Upper Saddle River, NJ: Prentice-Hall.

Gardner, H. (2004). How science changes: Considerations of history, science, and values. In M. Suarez-Orozco & D. M. Qin-Hillard (Eds.), *Globalization: Culture and education in the new millennium* (pp. 235–258). Berkeley: University of California Press.

Greene, J. C. (1994). Qualitative program evaluation: Practice and promise. In N. Denzin & Y. Lincoln (Eds.), *Handbook of qualitative inquiry* (1st ed., pp. 530–544). Thousand Oaks, CA: Sage.

Guba, E. (1969). The failure of educational evaluation. *Educational Technology, 9*(5), 29–38.

House, E. R. (1978). Assumptions underlying evaluation models. *Educational Researcher, 1*(3), 4–12.

Lingard, B. (2000). It is and it isn't: Vernacular globalization, educational policy, and restructuring. In N. Burbules & C. Torres (Eds.), *Globalization and education: Critical perspectives* (pp. 125–134). New York: Routledge.

Lundgren, U. P. (2003). The political governing (governance) of education and evaluation. In P. Haug & T. A. Schwandt (Eds.), *Evaluating educational reforms: Scandinavia perspectives* (pp. 99–110). Greenwich, CT: InfoAge.

Mayne, J., & Rist, R. C. (2006). Studies are not enough: The necessary transformation of evaluation. *Canadian Journal of Program Evaluation, 21*(3), 93–120.

National Center for Educational Statistics. (2005). *The condition of education, 2005* (NCES Publication 2005-094). Washington, DC: U.S. Government Printing Office.

Nevo, D. (2002). Dialogue evaluation: Combining internal and external evaluation. In D. Nevo (Ed.), *School-based evaluation: An international perspective* (pp. 3–16). Kidlington, Oxford: Elsevier Science.

No Child Left Behind Act of 2001 (2002). Pub. L. No. 107th Cong., 110 Cong. Rec. 1425. 115 Stat.

Organisation for Economic Co-operation and Development. (2003). *Where immigrant students succeed: A comparative review of performance and engagement.* Paris: Author.

Power, M. (1997). *The audit society.* New York: Oxford University Press.

Rizvi, F. (2004, September). *Higher education from a global perspective.* Paper presented at the Higher Education Collaborative, University of Illinois, Urbana, IL.

Rogers, P. J., & Williams, B. (2006). Evaluation for practice improvement and organizational learning. In I. Shaw, M. M. Mark, & J. Greene (Eds.), *The Sage handbook of evaluation* (pp. 76–97). Thousand Oaks, CA: Sage.

Ryan, K. E. (2004). Serving the public interests in educational accountability. *American Journal of Evaluation, 25*(4), 443–460.

Shadish, W., Leviton, L., & Cook, T. (1991). *Foundations of program evaluation: Theories of practice.* Thousand Oaks, CA: Sage.

Stake, R. E. (1984). Program evaluation, particularly responsive evaluation. In G. F. Madaus, M. Scriven, & D. L. Stufflebeam (Eds.), *Evaluation models* (pp. 287–310). Boston: Kluwer-Nijhoff.

Stein, J. G. (2001). *The cult of efficiency.* Toronto, ON: House of Anansi Press, Ltd.

Stronach, I. (1999). Shouting theatre in a crowded fire: Educational effectiveness as cultural performance. *Evaluation, 5*(2), 173–193.

Stronach, I., Halsall, R., & Hustler, D. (2002). Future imperfect: Evaluation in dystopian times. In K. Ryan & T. Schwandt (Eds.), *Exploring evaluator role and identity* (pp. 167–192). Greenwich, CT: InfoAge.

Suarez-Orozco, M., & Qin-Hilliard, D. M. (2004). *Globalization: Culture and education in the new millennium.* Berkeley: University of California Press.

Teachers College Annual Report. (2004). *New rules, old responses.* Retrieved October 1, 2004, from http://www.tc.columbia.edu/news/article.htm?id=4741

Acknowledgments

We had the great and good fortune to be advised by many individuals and groups who generously provided wise counsel and thoughtful advice throughout all phases of this *Handbook*. As we mentioned earlier, first and foremost, our authors and editorial board individually and collectively freely shared vital intellectual capital that is woven into all the chapters, sections, and the overall project. Students in our evaluation courses provided helpful feedback as they read the project prospectus and chapter drafts taking up the issues addressed in the handbook in their own intellectual projects. We thank them for their excitement about the project and their thoughtful reflections.

With unfailing good humor and efficiency, Nora Gannon, one of our students, provided support throughout the project, including the coordination of e-mail invitations, file management, author timetables, and many other matters. We are deeply grateful for her help. We also acknowledge our wonderful publishers and editors, Lisa Cuevas Shaw, Vicki Knight, Sean Connelly, the Sage editorial support and production team Catherine Chilton and Heather Jefferson, and many others. They managed to be patient, supportive, and encouraging while urging us to stay close to the timelines— a daunting task to be sure.

Further, we are grateful to our respective departments, colleges, and universities— the Department of Educational Psychology in the College of Education at the University of Illinois and the Faculty of Education at the University of Ottawa. We are fortunate indeed to be in the kind of academic environment that is supportive of this kind of intellectual endeavor. We extend a special thank you to our partners, Norman Denzin and Danielle Delorme, who listened to what we had to say, encouraged us to stay the course, and were so helpful in a variety of other ways. We greatly appreciate their unstinting support and patience.

Sage Publications would like to thank the following reviewers:

Karen L. Alderete
Austin Independent School District

Kathy Garvin-Doxas
University of Colorado

Thomas E. Grayson
University of Illinois at Urbana-Champaign

William H. Rickards
Alverno College

Roger A. Rennekamp
University of Kentucky

PART I

The Educational Evaluation Context

The chapters in Part I provide the context for the volume, including a sense of the current milieu surrounding educational evaluation in an increasingly globalized society. Moreover, critical concepts and issues involving the volume's framework, such as globalization, educational evaluation foundations, and how globalization may be influencing historical evaluation dilemmas (e.g., evaluator identity and role), are addressed.

In Chapter 1, Rizvi presents a sweeping overview of how current educational policy research, and in turn educational evaluation, is being changed by globalization. Among other matters, he briefly reviews various meanings of *globalization* and proposes that a transnational framework is essential for an examination of these changing national and international educational policy processes. In Chapter 2, Schwandt addresses educational evaluation inquiry foundations, including philosophical, ethical, and political assumptions and how they are being influenced by globalization discourses and practices. Notably, he begins with a critical examination of the definitions of *educational evaluation*—a concept that is characterized by multiple meanings. After analyzing challenges to the Western evaluation identity posed by globalization, Schwandt concludes that these challenges can be viewed productively by turning the tensions to opportunities for reexamination of educational evaluation aims. In the last chapter in Part I, Smith (Chapter 3) proposes historical evaluation dilemmas (e.g., what is acceptable evidence?) as a lens for considering how educational evaluation is changing in response to the circumstances of globalization. After elaborating a variety of definitions of the *globalization of evaluation* (e.g., globalization as spread), Smith proposes that educational evaluation theories and practices will need to become more flexible and accommodating around global issues. Such issues include, for instance, the value of written versus oral communication and individual versus group interests.

CHAPTER 1

Globalization and Policy Research in Education

Fazal Rizvi

This chapter explores some of the ways in which policy research in education—conceived broadly to include studies of the context in which policy options are explored, the political dynamics associated with policy development and implementation, and the issues surrounding policy and program evaluation—is affected by the contemporary processes of globalization. It suggests that globalization has destabilized the traditional conception of policy research as territorially bounded. Public policy research in particular can no longer take for granted the exclusive link between a given territory, such as the state, and its political authority (Sassen, 2007). The globalization of economy and various transnational political and cultural forces have altered both state and non-state institutions. The state has become a fragmented policy arena, permeated by policy networks that are both domestic and transnational, whereas the work of non-state institutions is no longer confined to national boundaries, but potentially stretches across the globe.

These transformations demand a new perspective on educational policy research, including educational evaluation. In evaluating policies and programs, for example, we need to examine how they are now produced and legitimated within a broader transnational framework, and how they are steered by the global forces of capital, various corporate interests, as well as transnational relations of more informal kinds. We need to ask how global policy networks affect and are utilized in the processes of policy development and evaluation. From a broader perspective, we need to consider the ways in which these transnational dynamics have possibly created conditions for the global convergence of educational policies.

Within this shifting context, this chapter suggests that globalization has led to the production of a new *social imaginary* of education, created as a result of the growing pressure on states for more market-friendly policies, better aligned to the requirements of the global knowledge economy. There is, however, nothing inevitable about this social imaginary of education. If it expresses values that are not in line with the popular sentiments for democracy and social justice, and specific national interests, then it is argued in

3

this chapter that a major contemporary task of educational evaluation is to "name" this contradiction and suggest alternatives that contest the dominant neoliberal policy discourses now circulating around the world.

The argument in this chapter is structured around a number of steps. First, it shows how the nature and sources of authority underlying public policy in education is changing. Second, it suggests that these changes are influenced by the contemporary processes of globalization. It is argued that globalization can be viewed both as an objective and subjective phenomenon, and that, as a subjective phenomenon, it describes how policy authority is institutionalized through the "work of social imagination" (Appadurai, 1996). Third, this chapter shows how recent processes of globalization have thus steered educational systems around the world toward a particular social imaginary of education, predicated on a range of neoliberal assumptions. However, this imaginary has emerged in neither a spontaneous nor a deterministic fashion, but through processes that are inherently political and work in various locally contingent ways. The final section of this chapter discusses some of the implications of this argument for the theory and practice of educational evaluation.

Public Policy and the Sources of Its Authority

It is now more than 50 years since David Easton, regarded by many as one of the architects of the field of study we now call "policy research," provided a most succinct definition of the concept of *policy*. Easton (1954) argued that policies expressed "authoritative allocation of values." Policies are always normative: They presuppose certain values and direct people toward action, but in ways that are authoritative. Their legitimacy is derived from an authority, be it a government, a corporation, or a social institution such as a school system or church. Easton's definition has been highly influential; it has been assumed by policy researchers working within

the positivist and rationalist traditions, and it has formed the basis of interpretive and critical approaches.

Stephen Ball (1994), for example, regards an exploration of the nature and scope of authority to be a central task of policy research. Policy research, he argues, involves an examination of three key aspects of policy: texts, discourses, and effects. Policies, he suggests, are always contested, value-laden, and dynamic, and they are a product of various compromises. They are encoded in representations of what is mandated and what should be done. They are often expressed in a textual form, but within the framework of a broader discourse. Policy analysis thus involves the decoding of texts, in relation to both the context in which they are embedded and the effects they have.

If Easton's definition provides a basic framework for interpreting and analyzing policies, then the questions arise as to where the authority underpinning a policy comes from and how authority is exercised through that policy. With respect to public policies in education, the answer to the first of these questions would appear to be the state. Without the authority of the state, public policies can neither be supported with public funds nor have the symbolic value to guide action. But how does the state allocate its authority through policy, seeking to manage community expectations and to develop subjects who are sufficiently vested in its political priorities? How do certain values become authoritative? Expressed in these terms, the idea of authority would appear to be central to the notion of policy. Yet few policy researchers address it explicitly. So, for example, although Ball's discussion of the idea of policy highlights the complexities of the various ways in which policies are constructed and interpreted, it does not problematize issues surrounding the nature of policy authority itself.

Like most other theorists of policy, Ball assumes policy authority to be located within the structures of the state, from where policy texts and discourses get their purchase. Indeed, public policies in education have traditionally been thought to emanate from a national government and its agencies, designed by the state to deliver educational provision in a most effective and efficient, and sometimes equitable, manner. Not surprisingly, therefore, most policy researchers assume state authority to be sovereign. This assumption is based on a Westphalian understanding about the nature of political authority (Krasner, 2000), which includes the view that authority can only be exercised by a state over a defined geographical territory, that each state has the autonomy to develop its own policies, and that no external actor can direct that state's priorities.

Modern states are assumed to hold ultimate territorial jurisdiction, organized around a specific set of administrative functions. This assumption of the taken-for-grantedness of territoriality can be found in the work of most 20th-century social theorists and policy researchers. Indeed, it has been considered a fundamental feature of modernity on which the political architecture of the modern state system is based (Mann, 2000). The modern state is represented as a kind of container that separates an "inside" of domestic political interactions from an "outside" of international or interstate relations (Brenner, Jessop, Jones, & Macleod, 2003). The state is thus given an authoritative monopoly over the subjects and institutions located within its territory, allocated through a system of international relations.

However, this conception of authority, involving the institutional, territorial, and centralized nature of the state, cannot be sustained without popular consent. It requires a "social imaginary" (Taylor, 2004) concerning the nature and scope of the state's political authority. It demands people's consent to view national formations as inevitable, timeless and natural, territorially bounded, and entirely legitimate. This view is in line with Anderson's (1991) contention that nations are "imagined communities" that were brought into existence in the early modernization processes initially by intellectuals, artists, political leaders, and others and only later became infiltrated into the whole

society through myths, stories, songs, and the like. Processes of formal schooling played a major role in developing and sustaining national imaginaries. Assumptions surrounding national authority came to be widely accepted, sometimes through the exercise of violence, but mostly through the inculcation of a social imaginary without which people could not even conceive how things could be otherwise. Most policy research in education continues to operate within this Westphalian framework.

Globalization has destabilized this framework. In what follows, I argue that even if the authority of the state has not entirely declined, and even if many states remain influential and strong, its nature and functions are changing. The state is no longer the only site of policy development and source of political legitimacy; transnational processes intersect in a variety of complex ways with the mechanisms of policy development, dissemination, and evaluation at the national level. If the assumption that policy authority is always located within the structures of the state can no longer be taken for granted, then it follows that, in analyzing the ways in which values are allocated in and through policy, we can no longer merely attend to issues internal to the state, but also need to ask how the interior of the state is being reconstituted by forces emanating from outside its borders, becoming "relativized" (Waters, 1995) by the processes of globalization.

Globalization

In less than two decades, the idea of globalization has become ubiquitous, widely used around the world in policy and popular discourses alike. It is used to describe the various ways in which the world is becoming increasingly interconnected and interdependent, referring to a set of social processes that imply "inexorable integration of markets, nation-states and technologies to a degree never witnessed before—in a way that is enabling individuals, corporations and nation-states to reach round the world farther, faster, deeper and cheaper than ever before"

(Friedman, 2000, p. 7). Such integration is far from complete and clearly benefits some communities more than others. This suggests that globalization is not experienced and interpreted in the same way everywhere.

Not surprisingly, therefore, globalization is a highly contested notion. Historically, it is articulated with a range of colonial practices (Rizvi, 2007). But its more recent forms are associated with technological revolutions in transport, communication, and data processing. These developments have transformed the nature of economic activity, changing the modes of production and consumption. Harvey (1989) provides perhaps one of the best descriptions of economic globalization. He argues that globalization describes "an intense period of time-space compression that has had a disorienting and disruptive impact on political-economic practices, the balance of class power, as well as upon cultural and social life" (p. 9). In this new era, global capitalism has become fragmentary as time and space are rearranged by the dictates of multinational capital.

Improved systems of communication and information flows and rationalization in the techniques of distribution have enabled capital and commodities to be moved through the global market with greater speed.

At the same time, there has been a shift away from an emphasis on goods to greater trade in services—in business, educational, and health services, as well as entertainment and lifestyle products. The rigidities of Fordism have been replaced by a new organizational ideology that celebrates flexibility as a foundational value, expressed most explicitly in ideas of subcontracting, outsourcing, vertically disintegrated forms of administration, just-in-time delivery systems, and the like. In the realm of commodity production, argues Harvey, the primary effect of this transformation has been an increased emphasis on virtues of speed and instantaneity.

Considerable significance is now attached to information and global networks. According to Castells (2000) the new economy is knowledge-based, postindustrial, and service-oriented.

Cultural and political meanings, Castells argues, are now under siege by global economic and technological restructuring. He speaks of an "informational mode of development" through which global financial and informational linkages are accelerated: They convert places into spaces and threaten to dominate local processes of cultural meanings. According to Castells (2000), networks constitute "the new social morphology of our societies"; and the diffusion of networking logic, substantially modifying "the operation and outcomes in the processes of production, experience, power and culture." The new economy, he maintains, is "organized around global networks of capital, management, and information, whose access to technological know-how is at the roots of productivity and competitiveness" (p. 82). This view implies, then, that states are no longer the only or even the major drivers of the global economy.

Within the system of modern states, considerable cultural importance was attached to education. Educational systems carried the narratives of the nation. As Gellner (1983) points out, it was the mass educational systems that provided a common framework of understanding, which enhanced the processes of state-coordinated modernization. Through the diffusion of ideas, meanings, myths, and rituals, citizens were able to "imagine" the nation and filter conceptions of their "other." Although education continues to serve this function, according to many globalization theorists (e.g., Steger, 2003), the nation-state can now be imagined in a number of different ways, and the lives of its citizens are now inextricably linked to cultural formations that are produced in far-away places.

Under the conditions of globalization, then, the assumption of discrete national cultural formations can no longer be taken for granted because there is now an ever-increasing level of cultural interactions across national and ethnic communities. With the sheer scale, intensity, speed, and volume of global cultural communication, the traditional link between territory and social identity appears to have been broken, as people can more readily choose to detach their identities from particular time, place, and traditions. The media and the greater transnational mobility of people have had a "pluralizing" impact on identity formation, producing a variety of hyphenated identities that are less "fixed or unified." This has led to the emergence of a "global consciousness," which may represent the cultural basis of an "incipient civil society" (Hall, 1996).

The Transformed State

These economic and cultural developments have seriously challenged the Westphalian conception of the nation-state, including the nature and scope of its authority. Throughout the 1990s, much of the literature on globalization suggested that the exclusive link between the nation-state and political authority was being broken. It suggested that sovereign states could no longer claim exclusive authority over their citizens. It was argued that changes in international law, regional political associations, the structure of global economy and institutions, as well as shifts produced by the globalization of economy and culture had altered the fundamental constitution of the state system. Writers such as Held and McGrew (2000) maintained that the idea of state sovereignty was on the edge of a major transformation, if not extinction. In her highly influential book, *The Retreat of the State*, Strange (1996) went so far as to argue that governments had lost much of their authority: "the impersonal forces of world market, integrated over the postwar period more by private enterprise in finance, industry and trade than by cooperative decisions of governments, are now more powerful than states" (p. 13).

Over the past decade, and especially since September 11, 2001, however, these claims about the imminent demise of the system of nation-states have been shown to be grossly exaggerated (Rizvi, 2003). Indeed, against a new discourse of security, it has become clear that many powerful nation-states have reasserted their authority, and that their authority is indispensable in coordinating

and controlling global mobility, interactions, and institutions. It has become equally clear that this new discourse of security is linked inextricably to the imperatives of global capitalism. Evidently, without global security, the structures of global capitalism cannot be sustained. But if capitalist and security imperatives now work off each other, then they need, more than ever before, a system of nation-states. As Wood (2003) has argued, "The more universal capitalism has become, the more it has needed an equally universal system of reliable local states" (p. 152).

The need for nation-states can also be demonstrated by looking at the recent rhetoric of the "war on terrorism." It has been suggested that the war on terrorism is a war without borders because the terrorists work across national boundaries. However, as we have seen, the main target of this war are nation-states, albeit weak ones such as Afghanistan. This is so because it is assumed that it is the weak states that inevitably harbor terrorists. Stronger states, in contrast, can more readily control their movements and actions. Both global security and capitalism thus need strong reliable states, which do not pose great risks to global economic activity, but can influence and coordinate the behavior of their citizens. In this context, nation-states are even able to exercise considerable coercive power so long as it is conducive in producing social conditions necessary for capital accumulation.

Wood (2003) maintains that "globalization has certainly been marked by a withdrawal of the state from its social welfare and ameliorative functions; and, for many observers, this has more than anything else created an impression of the state's decline" (p. 140). But this impression is misleading because it is impossible for global capitalism to dispense with many of the social functions performed by the state, such as security, social stability, and infrastructural provisions that have proved essential for economic success. Global capitalism depends more than ever then on "a system of multiple and more or less sovereign states." Wood (2003) insists that "The very fact that 'globalization' has extended capital's purely economic powers far beyond the range of any single nation state means that global capital requires many nation states to perform the administrative and coercive functions that sustain the system of property and provide the kind of day-to-day regularity, predictability, and legal order that capitalism needs more than any other social form" (p. 141).

Over the past decade in particular, these functions have included controlling the movement of people. One of the most cherished beliefs of many globalization theorists in the 1990s concerned the increased movement of people across national boundaries. According to Cohen (1997), a globalizing economy, characterized by a new international division of labor, the activities of transnational corporations, and the effects of liberal trade and capital flow policies, together with better communication and cheaper transport, led inevitably to a greater number of people crossing national borders. New forms of transnational mobility emerged through contractual relationships of work, family visits, international education, intermittent stays abroad, and sojourning.

During the 1990s, bilateral agreements permitting dual, and even multiple, citizenships became commonplace. The intensification of interactions among different sectors of the world economy led to the development of "global cities," "whose significance resides more in their global, rather than in their national role" (Cohen, 1997, p. 157). However, once the scale of mobility from the developing to developed countries became a major problem for the global cities, it was only the nation-states that had the capacity to control the volume of flows of people and develop policies that encouraged the mobility of global capital and the cosmopolitanization of the city space, on the one hand, but discouraged the unfettered movement of people, especially unskilled workers and refugees, on the other hand.

What this brief discussion shows is that, under the conditions of contemporary globalization, we are not so much experiencing the demise of the system of nation-states as we are its transformation. What is challenged is the traditional conception of the nation-state as a fundamental unit of world order, a unitary phenomenon characterized by its relative homogeneity with a set of singular purposes. This has been replaced by a fragmented policy arena permeated by transnational networks as well as domestic agencies and forces. As Held and McGrew (2005) argue, "the contemporary era has witnessed layers of governance spreading within and across political boundaries" (p. 11) transforming state sovereignty into shared exercise of power. With the emergence of new patterns of political interconnectedness, "the scope of policy choices available to individual governments and the effectiveness of many traditional policy instruments tends to decline" (p. 13). The transformed state is now increasingly located within various webs of global and regional networks that challenge the traditional authority of the state, as well as require the state to perform the new functions of policy coordination and the development and delivery of programs.

A Shifting Imaginary of Education

Educational policy is of course embedded within these transformations. Policy development in education is deeply affected by intergovernmental and transnational forces, pushing it into a certain direction. So, for example, the political dynamics of the global economy has shifted the balance of power between the markets and states and has generated powerful pressures on governments to develop a market-friendly view of education. This has been achieved through the allocation of a new social imaginary in which education policy has become secondary to and an instrument of economic policy. The idea of the need for education to produce individuals and nations that are globally competitive has come to occupy a central place in the new vocabulary of education policy, as have the ideas of knowledge economy and life-long learning. These ideas have become globally distributed, as has their authority.

The concept of life-long learning, for example, is no longer understood in humanist or social democratic terms. It has instead become associated with values that suggest the need to produce flexible, self-actualizing, mobile individuals deemed necessary for the requirements of the new knowledge economy. But with respect to Easton's definition of *policy*, how have these values been allocated across communities, becoming so authoritative? To address this issue, it might be helpful to examine how social imaginaries are formed in the era of globalization and are globally distributed through a range of mechanisms that have led to the extensive penetration of local and national communities by transnational forces; to understand how "new international and transnational institutions have both linked states together and transformed sovereignty into the shared exercise of power" (Held & McGrew, 2005, p. 11).

A "social imaginary" (Taylor, 2004) represents a discourse, or a set of overlapping discourses, that is at once descriptive and prescriptive of conceptions of how practice is best organized around policy, is directed toward certain outcomes, and is organized around a set of norms. For Taylor, the idea of social imaginary involves a complex, unstructured, and contingent mix of the empirical and the affective—not a "fully articulated understanding of our whole situation within which particular features of our world become evident" (Taylor, 2004, p. 21). A social imaginary is a way of thinking that is shared in a society by ordinary people, the common understandings that make everyday practices possible, giving them sense and legitimacy. It is embedded in ideas, practices, and events, and it carries within it deeper normative notions and images, constitutive of a society. It involves:

something much broader and deeper than the intellectual schemes people may entertain when they think about social reality in a disengaged mode. I am thinking, rather, of the ways in which people imagine their social existence, how they fit together with others, how things go on between them and their fellows, the expectations that are normally met, and the deeper normative notions and images that underlie these expectations. (Taylor, 2004, p. 23)

More important, however, a social imaginary is not simply inherited and already determined for us; rather, it is something that is in a constant state of flux. In this way, it is an enabling concept that describes the ways people act as world-making collective agents within a given symbolic matrix that refuses to assume an "ontology of determinism" (Castoriadis, 1987). It is a creative force in the making of social-historical worlds, a force that has to be attentive to the "signs of the time" and interpret all those particular, rather uneven, and emotionally charged events that make up everyday life (Maffesoli, 1993). It is through the collective sense of imagination that discourses and institutional practices are created and given coherence. Social imaginaries are thus created differently, subsist differently, and are transformed differently through the exercise of collective political agency. It follows then that communities interpret and engage with the world outside their borders differently, but always within their always-emerging social imaginary.

Appadurai (1996) has analyzed the role of social imaginary in the formation of subjectivities within the globalizing context in which we now live, a context that is characterized by diffusion of social images, ideas, and ideologies across communities around the world. This diffusion is facilitated by electronic media, mass migration, and the mobility of capital and labor, creating conditions through which most societies around the world have become culturally diverse and hybrid and cannot avoid, in a fundamental sense, engaging with each other transnationally. As Appadurai (1996) puts it, the "system of nation-states is no longer the only game in town" (p. 14), insofar as international governance and transnational economic and political traffic are concerned, but also with respect to cultural formations.

We live in a world in which ideas and ideologies, people and capital, and images and messages are constantly in motion, transforming the vectors of our social imaginaries. We live amid many social imaginaries, in addition to those that are dictated by the dominant national expressions. Each has a different point of origin, a different axis, and each travels through different routes and is constituted by different relationships to institutional structures in different communities and nations. However, any attempt to rethink educational policy research in the era of globalization cannot ignore the facts of policy convergence. To overlook how our social imaginary is being reshaped by global and local processes simultaneously is to fail to critically engage with these processes in order to develop alternatives to the education policies that have become hegemonic.

Neoliberalism and Educational Policy

In the current era, the dominant social imaginary of education policy has been given a name: neoliberalism. As an imaginary, it demands the recasting of educational policy for an era of globalization in ways that would indicate the need to restructure it to meet the requirements of the global economy. Because imaginaries are neither static nor entirely coherent, the neoliberal imaginary too allows for a range of conflicting precepts about the specific implications of globalization for educational policy. However, its tacit assumptions and core images are taken for granted, as is the need to develop a specific attitude to recent economic, political, and cultural transformations.

This attitude is promoted vigorously by many transnational organizations and national governments alike, through both formal and informal means. As a result, there has been an unmistakable trend toward a global policy convergence in dealing with the various pressures that educational systems confront and in articulating a similar conception of educational aims and programs of procedural and organizational

reform. As Schugurensky (1999) points out, this trend toward global convergence is intensifying. What is most striking about the current programs of policy reform in education, he observes, is "the unprecedented scope and depth of changes taking place as well as the similarity of changes occurring in a wide variety of nations having different social, historical and economic characteristics" (Schugurensky, 1999, p. 284). Although the actual dynamics and pace of change vary across national systems, the direction of change appears unmistakably similar, located within the same neoliberal imaginary.

This imaginary represents an almost universal deepening of a shift away from social-democratic orientations. There is enormous pressure on educational systems around the world to increase the amount of formal education young people are now required to have and to align this education to what is widely referred to as the "imperatives of the global economy." As a result, new requirements of policy have emerged, resulting in the corporatization and marketization of education. This has involved new demands for greater accountability, surveillance, and increased bureaucratization of institutions, creating new pressures on teachers' work (see Blackmore, 2005; Luke, 2004). In most Western countries, as public resources for education have declined, there has been a growing emphasis on increasing the role of the private sector. Yet in the midst of all this change, and despite pressure on educational systems around the world to diversify—to meet the diverse needs of the global economy—educational systems have, somewhat paradoxically, tended to mimic each other, pursuing a common set of solutions to their fiscal and organizational problems. Indeed, they have even interpreted the requirements of reform themselves in a broadly similar fashion.

At a general level, a new human capital theory has informed discussions of educational policy. The new human capital theory postulates, as the old theory did (Becker, 1964), that expenditure on training and education is costly, but should be considered an investment because it is undertaken with a view to increasing personal incomes and can be used to explain occupational wage differentials. The neoliberal imaginary extends this claim to the requirements of the global economy, as well as to the competitive advantage of individuals, corporations, and nations within the transnational context. In its popular form, it imagines all human behavior to be based on the economic self-interest of individuals operating within free competitive markets. It assumes economic growth and competitive advantage to be a direct outcome of the levels of investment in developing human capital. It suggests that, in a global economy, performance is increasingly linked to people's knowledge stock, skills level, learning capabilities, and cultural adaptability. Therefore, it demands policy frameworks that enhance labor flexibility through the deregulation of the market, as well as through reform to systems of education and training designed to better align them to the changing nature of economic activity.

In its most radical form then, this new social imaginary requires reform of systems of educational governance and demands a reconceptualization of the purposes of education (Organisation for Economic Co-operation and Development, 2004). It suggests, for example, that the advances in information and communication technologies have so transformed the nature of knowledge production and utilization, the organization of work and labor relations, modes of consumption and trade, and patterns of cultural exchange that education now needs to produce different kinds of subjectivities who are better able to work creatively with knowledge; who are flexible, adaptable, and mobile; who are globally minded and interculturally confident; and who are life-long learners. What this view implies is that learning for learning sake is no longer sufficient, and that education does not have any intrinsic ends as such, but must always be linked to the instrumental purposes of human capital development and economic self-maximization. This should not be taken to mean that ethical and cultural issues are no longer relevant to

education, but that they should be interpreted within the broader framework of education's economic ends. In this way, the neoliberal imaginary rests on what George Soros (1998) has called "economic fundamentalism," a kind of conceptual prism through which even such moral notions as diversity and equity are rearticulated.

Within this imaginary, the idea of knowledge economy features prominently. It suggests that globalization has fundamentally altered the relationship between the production of knowledge and its economic application, and that the emergence of knowledge-intensive activities and the production and diffusion of information technologies have led to the development of new models of work organization (Paul, 2002). It suggests (for a discussion, see Peters & Besley, 2006) that a knowledge-driven economy is one in which the generation and exploitation of knowledge play a predominant part in the creation of wealth. In the industrial era, wealth was created by using machines to replace human labor. In the knowledge economy, in contrast, it suggests, the new quality jobs will be in high-technology industries such as telecommunications and financial services. This view of the relationship between economy and educational aims has now become commonplace around the world (see Rizvi, 2004), from the developed countries to the newly industrializing countries of Asia, such as Singapore and India, to countries such as China and Vietnam, where the communist parties remain in control.

Everywhere it is assumed that the knowledge economy will require a larger proportion of workers to be prepared for highly skilled jobs, workers who have competencies linked to both their ability to use new technologies and their cultural attitudes toward change, even if most of the new jobs are in low-paid and highly casualized service industries. In a rapidly changing world, it is believed, these competencies must involve certain behavioral features such as adaptability, organizational loyalty and integrity, and the ability to work in culturally diverse contexts and provide leadership (Organisation for Economic Co-operation and Development, 2004). This conception of education involves a new approach to human capital development, grounded not so much in the amount of schooling individuals have, but in the learning attributes they are able to develop, with which to deal effectively and creatively with unfamiliar and constantly changing conditions of work. It emphasizes the development of broad generic skills such as communication, problem solving, and the ability to work independently and under pressure, take responsibility for decisions, and quickly and efficiently obtain field-specific knowledge and spot its commercial potential.

The renewed emphasis on the teaching of science and mathematics around the world displays a similar logic. The teaching of these subjects is encouraged not for its own sake or for better understanding the natural world around us, but as a way of better engaging with the knowledge economy. Even more emphatically, the potential of teaching about information and communication technologies in transforming educational practice is stressed not so much as a way of enabling people greater access to each other, but in facilitating educational growth and productivity. Consistent with this view is the assumption around the world that the language of global trade is English. English has become a language, so it is assumed, that provides job opportunities, access to higher education, and a broader flow of information, as well as facilitating diplomatic discussions and business negotiations. Global processes, so it seems, cannot be imagined in any language other than English.

Another imperative for educational reform implied by the neoliberal imaginary is the internationalization of education. Of course, the idea of international education is not new. There has always been international mobility of students and researchers in search of new knowledge, as well as training where this is not available within the nation. There has always been an interest in intercultural knowledge, and in programs in foreign languages and studies, as

a way of enhancing the level of international understanding and cooperation. In the past, the more developed nations sponsored international students with a view to developing skills, attitudes, and knowledge so that, upon their return, graduates can make a robust contribution to national development.

However, the neoliberal imaginary has transformed these sentiments into a new economic discourse of trade, which seeks to redefine the ways in which educational institutions need to engage with the emerging imperatives of globalization (Rizvi, 2005). This discourse points to the commercial opportunities offered by the increasing movement of people, capital, and ideas. It encourages a new kind of knowledge about international relations and programs based on a particular interpretation of the changing nature of the global economy, which is assumed to be knowledge-based and requires increased level of intercultural communication. So, international cooperation and the value of knowledge networks is couched almost exclusively in economic terms because education is commodified and converted into a commercial product for sale.

Processes of Policy Convergence

What this discussion of these shifts in thinking about education shows is that they are constructed around a new social imaginary that is globally distributed. Of course, this discursive transformation has not occurred in an ad hoc or spontaneous manner. Nor is it entirely correct to assume that the neoliberal social imaginary is a function of the structural conditions of globalization. To believe this to be the case is to fail to understand the link between global processes and the ways policy options are interpreted and are taken up at the level of the nation-state in a range of historically specific ways articulated through various power configurations, both global and local. These processes are inherently political and work in various locally contingent ways. It is useful perhaps to look at what some of these processes might be, as I have done in an earlier article (Rizvi, 2004).

The first of these processes relates to the global circulation of ideas and ideologies, increasingly powered by developments in transportation, information, and communication technologies. With these developments, the international mobility of people has never been greater. This mobility has enabled ideas to be exchanged among policymakers and researchers coming together from different countries, even if this exchange is not symmetrical in its power configurations. So, for example, the ideas emanating from Europe and the United States have a greater chance of becoming accepted even if these ideas ultimately prove to be self-serving. Nation-states, however, no longer seek to influence each other directly, but promote their preferred conceptions vigorously through international organizations and the operations of the market, such as those dictated by the World Trade Organization (see Robertson, Bonal, & Dale, 2006).

Under the conditions of globalization, a new global policy space has emerged that allows educational ideas and ideologies to be produced and distributed instantaneously. This space has often been sponsored by intergovernmental organizations such as the Organisation for Economic Co-operation and Development (OECD), United Nations Educational, Scientific and Cultural Organization (UNESCO), and the European Union (EU). Although these organizations often insist that they only seek to provide forums for open and free exploration of educational ideas, they find it hard to hide their own positions committed to neoliberal priorities in education. In recent years, for example, the OECD, which views itself as a site for the free exchange of ideas, has become a major carrier of neoliberal policy imagination: It has become a policy actor in its own right (Rizvi & Lingard, 2006). The educational ideas that it sponsors are distributed widely and often taken up by its members, as well as other countries to which it provides policy advice.

A second set of processes through which the neoliberal imaginary of education has become globally dominant relates to international conventions, embodying consensus among parties. These conventions have invariably led developing countries in particular to accept neoliberal prescription, even if there has been political opposition to them. Examples of such conventions include human rights and democratic elections, as well as modes of governance. The idea of "good governance," for example, has become a Trojan horse around the world. Although conventions around good governance involve formal agreements, they have exposed domestic policy practices to external scrutiny, thus reducing national autonomy. Conventions are supposedly entered into voluntarily, yet there is often a great deal of pressure on nation-states to conform to particular priorities, producing what appears as a neoliberal consensus but masks deep divisions.

Perhaps the best-known recent example of this notion is the Washington Consensus. The term *Washington Consensus* refers to "the lowest common denominator of policy advice addressed by the Washington-based institutions to Latin American countries." According to Williamson (2000), the Washington Consensus is a product of "the intellectual convergence," which is designed to get most of the developing countries to accept a set of common assumptions about economic reform and institutional governance. Although the principles of the Washington Consensus no longer enjoy the appeal they once had, most development institutions, such as the International Monetary Fund (IMF) and the World Bank, continue to adhere to some of its key principles, including the values of macroeconomic discipline, trade openness, market-friendly microeconomic policies, and new public sector management. In the field of education, this implies fiscal discipline about funding, a redirection of public expenditure toward fields offering both high economic returns, but within the context of privatization and deregulation.

A third set of processes that have globally promoted a neoliberal social imaginary of education relates more explicitly to coercive strategies, such as those represented by Structural Adjustment Programs (SAPs), rather than the covert pressures of consensus and conventions. These programs were created ostensibly because developing countries are unable to meet the payment schedules on their debts to international banks such as the World Bank and IMF. However, as Dicken (1998) has shown, before these countries are permitted to renegotiate schedules of debt repayment, they are forced to meet a range of conditions in order to "better manage their economy" and "get their house in order." Although these conditions are often assumed to have the status of contracts, they often are negotiated under coercive demands that require debtor countries to pursue the principles of neoliberalism as a condition of loans. It is often difficult for developing countries to reject the offer of help, yet the conditions attached to the offer often involve implementing alienating and exploitative policies. Ultimately, SAPs require developing countries to concede some of their autonomy and pursue policies designed to create conditions more conducive to international investment than to the improvement of social conditions and educational opportunities.

Of course, the international lending agencies and the transnational corporations (TNCs) offering to invest in developing countries demand neoliberal restructuring of educational systems. The relationship between TNCs and governments is a complex one involving the dynamics of both conflict and cooperation. Dicken (1998) argues that sometimes governments and TNCs appear as rivals, but they collude with one another at the same time. In the global economy, the governments need TNCs to help them in wealth and job creation, whereas TNCs require the nation-states to "provide the necessary supportive infrastructures, both physical and institutional, on the basis of which

they can pursue their strategic objectives" (Dicken, 1998, p. 276).

TNCs and governments are often involved in a bargaining process as each tries to get maximum advantage from the other. As Dicken (1998) observes, "states have become increasingly locked into a cut-throat competitive bidding process for investments, a process which provides TNCs with the opportunity to play off one bidder against another" (p. 281). Some of this bargaining involves demands by TNCs that education be restructured along market lines, with policies more conducive to the creation of a human resource pool to better meet their labor needs. The recent development of Educational Processing Zones (EPZs) in developing countries, such as Vietnam and Cambodia, is in line with these demands (Dicken, 1998). The zones often lie outside the framework of national jurisdiction and are appropriately referred as "transnational spaces."

Finally, a fourth set of processes involves multilateral cooperation among nations. Asia-Pacific Economic Cooperation (APEC) represents one such attempt to pursue multilateralism. Although it has not yet been able to develop initiatives in education similar to those established in Europe, such as the Bologna Declaration (2001), it has committed itself to the development of new processes of quality assurance and the elimination of all barriers to student mobility. Through the Bologna Declaration, European countries have pledged themselves to certain educational reforms designed to enhance the quality of teaching and learning, encourage student mobility, and restructure programs so that credit across countries can be more easily transferred, thus ensuring the employability of graduates within the global economy. Although these arrangements appear consensual, they are informed uniformly by neoliberal assumptions. They are embedded in and promoted a social imaginary of education, which barely hides its more fundamental economic rationale: its preference for the marketization of education. It assumes as unproblematic the global trend toward commodification, privatization, and commercialization of education, effectively sidelining education's traditional commitment to social and cultural development and the public good.

Toward a Global Perspective on Educational Evaluation

I have discussed the ways in which a new social imaginary of education, often referred to as neoliberalism, has emerged globally and how various global processes seem to have contributed to it becoming hegemonic. Everywhere, it seems, policies associated with the neoliberal imaginary of education have become authoritative. It needs to be noted, however, that this authority involves actual human agents, organizations, and governments—with capacity to accept, resist, or reject neoliberal priorities, rather than a function of globalization per se. It is fundamentally misguided to reify globalization and treat it as if it represents an inevitable historical phenomenon, leading invariably to a single and globally uniform perspective on education.

On the contrary, different communities experience, interpret, and respond to global processes differently. Globalization has different consequences for different groups of people and nation-states, with variable capacity to engage with the political dynamics associated with globalization (Smith, 2001). Much depends on national and local systems of communication, political activity, and corporate interests, as well as the level of coercion. In some countries, political systems are robust, whereas in other countries, they are weak and are easily manipulated by outside forces. Some countries enjoy a great deal of policy autonomy. Some are happy to meet the so-called "requirements of globalization" enthusiastically, whereas others resist even under conditions in which transnational forces seem overwhelming. This suggests that global processes affecting education need to be understood against the specific political and historical backdrop relevant to different policy communities,

which allocate different meaning and significance to them (see Cisneros-Cohernour & Grayson, Chapter 13, this volume).

That various global processes now affect all policy communities, albeit in ways that are historically and politically specific, can no longer be denied, however. If this is so, then the question arises as to how should theories and practices of educational evaluation reflect an engagement with global transformations. To begin with, we need to say farewell to what Scholte (2000) refers to as "methodological territorialism." According to Scholte, methodological territorialism has had a pervasive and deep hold on the conventions of social research, so much so that such conventions have meant formulating concepts and questions, constructing hypotheses, gathering and interpreting evidence, and drawing inferences within a territorially spatial framework. Thus, policy researchers, as we have already noted, have automatically treated governance as a territorial question—about how local and national governments develop policies around a set of values, assume their authority to be sovereign, and develop strategies to allocate this authority throughout the community within their jurisdiction, sometimes symbolically, but more often through specific programs.

Evaluators are often engaged to assess these programs, but they mostly perform this assessment within the traditions of "territorialist cartography" (Scholte, 2000, p. 57), providing detailed accounts of how these programs were developed and experienced, what impact they had on the communities for which they were devised, and the extent to which the program objectives were realized. What they do not often do is explore how the communities within which the programs are implemented have become deeply implicated in transnational processes. They are deeply affected by shifting demographic profiles, economic realities, political processes, and communication systems. High levels of immigration, for example, have changed the character of urban communities in particular, requiring an engagement with a new politics of cultural difference. Increasingly, fluid and dynamic economic, political, and cultural borders are changing the way many people think about their senses of belongingness.

Of course, not all communities and people have been transnationalized in the same way and to the same extent. Global cities (Sassen, 1995) such as Chicago and London have become transnationalized to a greater extent than isolated rural communities in Africa, for example. In this sense, transnationalization is more appropriately viewed as an ongoing social process affected by the levels and forms of connectivity between the global and the local, between a community's interior and its exterior. According to Steger (2003), these shifts have involved "the creation of new and the multiplication of existing social networks and activities in recent decades that increasingly overcome traditional political, economic, cultural and geographical boundaries" (p. 9). More significant, these shifts have not occurred merely on the objective and material levels; rather, they have also transformed consciousness about the growing manifestations of social interdependence.

The distinction between the inside of a community and its outside has been central to methodological territorialism. But if this distinction can no longer be assumed, then it raises a range of new questions for the practices of evaluation. The relationship between the evaluator and the people she studied was already complex, but in transnational context, new questions have arisen around such key terms as *othering* and *authorial control*, leading to what Wittel (2000) calls a "crisis in objectification" (p. 1). If a community can no longer be treated as a coherent entity, unique from and unaffected by its engagement with global networks, then an objectivist focus becomes impossible to achieve. Through enhanced mobility of capital, people, and ideas, global interconnectivity has become a norm, leading Clifford (1997) to suggest, for example, that human location is now constituted by displacement as much as it is by statis.

This analysis suggests the need to focus on relational ties and policy networks that span the world. If networks are open structures, able to expand without limits and are highly dynamic, and consist of a set of nodes and connections across the nodes characterized by flows and movement, as Castells (2000) has pointed out, then practices of evaluation cannot afford to ignore how social imaginaries circulate globally, under what condition they become popular and hegemonic, and how policies and programs are constructed around complex information flows across various nodes of networks. If information flows about educational ideas circulate in a global space that is characterized by asymmetry of power, then the question of how do some policies and programs become authoritative must be of more than a cursory interest to evaluators. Indeed, if the questions of transnationality have become central to their work, then it is clear that they need new intellectual resources and methodologies of evaluation that are better able to account for global policy networks and information flows in education, as well as the increasingly shifting social constitution of communities and social identities that are the subject of the policies and programs they are asked to evaluate.

References

Anderson, B. (1991). *Imagined community: Reflections on the origin and spread of nationalism* (rev. ed.). London: Verso.

Appadurai, A. (1996). *Modernity at large: Cultural dimensions of globalization.* Minneapolis: University of Minnesota Press.

Ball, S. (1994). *Education Reform: A critical and post-structural approach.* Buckingham and Philadelphia: Open University Press.

Becker, G. (1964). *Human Capital: A theoretical and empirical analysis, with special reference to education.* New York: Columbia University Press.

Blackmore, J. (2005). Localization/globalization and the midwife state: Strategic dilemmas for state feminism in education? In H. Lauder et al. (Eds.), *Education, globalization, and social change* (pp. 212–227). Oxford: Oxford University Press.

Bologna Declaration on the European Space for Higher Education. (2001). Available at http://ec .europa.eu/education/policies/educ/bologna/bol ogna.pdf

Brenner, N., Jessop, B., Jones, M., & Macleod, G. (Eds.). (2003). *State/space reader*. Oxford: Blackwell.

Castells, M. (2000). *Network society*. Oxford: Blackwell.

Castoriadis, C. (1987). *The imaginary institution of society* (K. Blamey, Trans.). Cambridge, MA: MIT Press.

Clifford, J. (1997). *Routes: Travel and translation in the late twentieth century*. Cambridge, MA: Harvard University Press.

Cohen, R. (1997). *Global diasporas: An introduction*. Seattle: University of Washington Press.

Dicken, P. (1998). *Global shift: Reshaping the global economic map in the 21st century*. New York: Guildford Press.

Easton, D. (1954). *The political system: An inquiry into the state of political change*. New York: Alfred Knopf.

Friedman, T. (2000). *Lexus and the olive tree*. New York: First Anchor Press.

Gellner, E. (1983). *Nations and nationalism*. Oxford: Blackwell.

Hall, S. (1996). *Stuart Hall: Critical dialogues in cultural studies*. London: Routledge.

Harvey, D. (1989). *The condition of postmodernity*. Oxford: Blackwell.

Held, D., & McGrew, A. (Eds.). (2000). *The global transformation reader: An introduction to the globalization debate* (2nd ed.). Cambridge, MA: Polity Press.

Held, D., & McGrew, A. (Eds.). (2005). *The global transformation reader: An introduction to the globalization debate* (3rd ed.). Cambridge, MA: Polity Press.

Krasner, S. (2000). Compromising Westphalia. In D. Held & A. McGrew (Eds.), *The global transformation reader: An introduction to the globalization debate* (2nd ed.). Cambridge, UK: Polity Press.

Luke, A. (2004). Teaching after the market: From commodity to cosmopolitan. *Teacher's College Record, 106*(7), 1422–1443.

Maffesoli, M. (1993). Introduction: The social imaginary. *Current Sociology, 41*(2), 1–7.

Mann, M. (2000). Has globalization ended the rise and rise of the nation-state? In D. Held &

A. McGrew (Eds.), *The global transformations reader* (pp. 136–147). Cambridge, UK: Polity Press.

Organisation for Economic Co-operation and Development. (2004). *Innovation in the knowledge economy: Implications for education and learning* (produced by CERI). Paris: Author.

Paul, J. (2002). University and the knowledge-based economy. In J. Enders & O. Fulton (Eds.), *Higher education in a globalizing world* (pp. 202–221). Dordrecht: Kluwer Academic Publishers.

Peters, M., & Besley, T. (2006). *Building knowledge cultures*. Lanham, MD: Rowman & Littlefield.

Rizvi, F. (2003). Democracy and education after September 11. *Globalization, Societies and Education, 1*(1), 54–69.

Rizvi, F. (2004). Theorizing the global convergence of restructuring policies in education. In S. Lindblad & T. Popkewitz (Eds.), *Educational restructuring: International perspectives on travelling policies*. Greenwich, CT: InfoAge.

Rizvi, F. (2005). Globalization and the dilemmas of internationalization in Australian higher education. *Access: Critical Perspectives on Communication, Cultural and Policy Studies, 24*(1), 86–101.

Rizvi, F. (2007). Postcolonialism and globalization in education. *Cultural Studies ↔ Critical Methodologies, 7*(1).

Rizvi, F., & Lingard, B. (2006). Globalization and the changing nature of the OECD's work. In H. Lauder, P. Brown, J. Dillabough, & A. Halsey (Eds.), *Education, globalization and social change* (pp. 247–260). Oxford: Oxford University Press.

Robertson, S., Bonal, X., & Dale, R. (2006). GATS and the education service industry: The politics of scale and global reterritorialization. In H. Lauder, P. Brown, J. Dillabough, & A. Halsey (Eds.), *Education, globalization and social change* (pp. 228–246). Oxford: Oxford University Press.

Sassen, S. (1995) *The global city: New York, London & Tokyo*. Princeton NJ: Princeton University Press.

Sassen, S. (2007). *Territory, authority rights: From medieval to global assemblages*. Princeton, NJ: Princeton University Press.

Scholte, J. (2000). *Globalization: A critical introduction*. New York: St. Martin's Press.

Schugurensky, D. (1999). Higher education restructuring in the era of globalization: Toward a heteronomous model? In R. Arnove & C. Torres (Eds.), *Comparative education: The dialectic of the global and the local* (pp. 283–304). Lanham, MD: Rowman & Littlefield.

Smith, M. P. (2001). *Transnational urbanism: Locating globalization*. Oxford: Blackwell.

Soros, G. (1998). *The crisis of global capitalism*. Boston: Little, Brown.

Steger, M. (2003). *Globalization: A very short introduction*. Oxford: Oxford University Press.

Strange, S. (1996). *The retreat of the state: The diffusion of power in the world economy*. Cambridge, England: Cambridge University Press.

Taylor, C. (2004). *Modern social imaginaries*. Durham, NC: Duke University Press.

Waters, M. (1995). *Globalization*. London: Routledge.

Williamson, J. (2000). What should the World Bank think about the Washington Consensus? *The World Bank Research Observer, 15*(2), 251–264.

Wittel, A. (2000). *Ethnography on the move: From field to net and Internet*. Retrieved January 2007 from http://qualitative-research.net/fqs

Wood, E. M. (2003). *Empire of capital*. London: Verso.

CHAPTER 2

Globalizing Influences on the Western Evaluation Imaginary

Thomas A. Schwandt

It is something like a fool's errand to accept the invitation to interrogate the field of educational evaluation in order to examine how its philosophical, ethical, and political assumptions are impacted by the discourse and practices of globalization. What makes it so is that neither the field in question nor the globalizing forces impinging, influencing, challenging, or otherwise having some bearing on that field are easily defined. Nonetheless, this chapter aims to tackle this task in a modest way—first, by attempting to characterize generally the field of educational evaluation practice; second, by offering a broad portrayal of the Western social-political imaginary that informs such practice; and third, by pointing to several dimensions in which globalization both troubles and reinforces this imaginary.

Defining Educational Evaluation

To characterize educational evaluation in a straightforward and precise way is nearly impossible for several reasons (Kellaghan, Stufflebeam, & Wingate, 2003; Nevo, 2006). First, although some evaluators aim to distinguish the terms *assessment* (pupil performance), *appraisal* (teacher performance), and *evaluation*, such efforts are not always successful or consistent (e.g., personnel evaluation, teacher assessment) in day-to-day uses of the terms. Thus, the term *evaluation* can encompass a broad range of objects of examination, including, for example, teachers' qualifications; teachers' classroom management, instruction, or pedagogy; students' academic performance; students' conduct;

AUTHOR'S NOTE: My thanks to the editors of this *Handbook*, an anonymous reviewer, and especially Helen Simons and Timothy Cash for their helpful comments on earlier drafts.

administrators' performance; individual school and school system performance; school reform initiatives; curriculum; projects (e.g., evaluating a one-time venture in one school that involves retired persons working with elementary school children on reading skills); programs (e.g., evaluating an after-school intervention adopted across a school district aimed at enhancing math skills in underachieving students); policies; instructional materials; instructional technologies; facilities; and so on. Each of these objects of evaluation has its own literature and special concerns.

Second, any or all of these potential objects of evaluation can be examined in different institutional locations, including, for example, public and private elementary and secondary schools, public and private higher education systems (community colleges, universities), informal education settings (adult learning centers), and educational and training programs in the private sector as well as in government agencies. Moreover, practices and assumptions of educational evaluation vary across the social-political settings or contexts of institutions; for example, Anglo-American societies reflect different concerns about educational evaluation than Latin American and African societies.

Third, the practice (and purpose and means) of educational evaluation can be examined from different social locations. For example, issues surrounding the design and conduct of educational evaluation can be studied from the point of view of individual evaluation researchers (or teams of evaluators) contracting with a client or responding to a tender or request for proposal for a particular study. Educational evaluation could also be investigated in terms of the work and impact of an educational evaluation agency, such as the Danish Evaluation Institute (EVA); a national system of educational evaluation, such as the Office for Standards in Education, Children's Services and Skills (Ofsted); or an evaluation system and technology functioning across an educational sector, such as quality assurance in e-learning (e.g., the United Nations Educational, Scientific and Cultural Organization

[UNESCO] and the Organisation for Economic Co-operation and Development [OECD] 2005 "Guidelines for Quality Provision in Cross-Border Higher Education" or the International Network for Quality Assurance Agencies in Higher Education).

Fourth, there are different and conflicting schools of thought, so to speak, on how to do educational evaluation. As is evident in several of the chapters in this handbook, one (and perhaps the dominant) school of thought growing out of psychometrics in educational psychology associates educational evaluation with assessment, measurement, testing, and, in general, the quantification of educational performances of varying kinds and comparisons of such performances using indicators. Classic examples of evaluations conducted in this tradition are found in the extensive literature on school effectiveness research (e.g., Carney, 2003; Luyten, Visscher, & Witziers, 2005), performance models in higher education (Atkinson-Grosjean & Grosjean, 2000), including the National Assessment of Educational Progress (NAEP) started in the United States in the 1960s (Stake, 2007), the OECD-administered Program for International Student Assessment (PISA), and the World Education Indicator project (WEI), a joint initiative of the World Bank, OECD, and UNESCO begun in the early 1990s. A second approach to evaluation arose in curriculum evaluation in the United States and the United Kingdom in the 1970s largely in opposition to the influence of educational psychology and its almost exclusive focus on evaluation as measurement. It was developed, at least initially, by an informal group of scholars (e.g., Robert Stake, David Hamilton, Barry MacDonald, Rob Walker, and others).[1] This is often referred to as the case study or case and context tradition (Gilligan, 1990; Stevenson & Thomas, 2006), and some of the assumptions of that way of thinking about evaluation were manifest in later approaches to educational evaluation: responsive (Stake, 2004), democratic (Norris, 1990; Simons, 1987), and fourth-generation evaluation

(Guba & Lincoln, 1989). A third school of thought reflects a strong orientation to managerial decision making and is grounded in a simple systems perspective. The most widely known example is the Context, Input, Process, Product (CIPP) model of evaluation developed by Daniel Stufflebeam and colleagues in the 1960s, out of their experience of evaluating education projects for the Ohio Public Schools in the United States. This approach to evaluation aims to provide an analytic and rational basis for program decision making based on a cycle of planning, structuring, implementing, reviewing, and revising *decisions*, each examined through a different aspect of evaluation—context, input, process, and product. Finally, another scheme for educational evaluation present in the United States as early as the 1960s in evaluations of Head Start and other social programs is grounded in an experimentalist tradition arising out of both applied social psychology and sociology. This tradition has experienced something of a revival in recent years, especially given the U.S. Department of Education's Institute for Education Sciences preferences for experimental designs to provide rigorous evidence for educational policy and practice (http://www.ed.gov/about/offices/list/ies/index.html), as well as the growing influence of the worldwide Campbell Collaboration and its Education Coordinating Group (see http://www.campbellcollaboration .org/ and http://www.campbellcollaboration .org/ECG/index.asp).

Fifth, although evaluation is a disciplined—organized, deliberate, methodical, systematic—practice (or, more accurately, a collection of disciplined practices), it is not a professionalized and credentialed practice, at least in the sense of how we understand the professions of medicine, law, and accounting. It does not have what could be readily identified as a proprietary core body of knowledge or a set of techniques, procedures, and investigatory tools that is unique to the practice. Its practitioners are a diverse lot as well. Although perhaps some 10,000 individuals at least nominally self-identify as evaluators and belong to one or more of the many national and international evaluation associations and societies around the world (and only a few of these are specifically concerned with *educational* evaluation), hundreds of thousands of teachers and professors, corporate trainers and human resource professionals, as well as school, university, and college administrators routinely engage in practices of educational evaluation.[2]

Finally, the various practices of evaluation draw on a wide-ranging evaluation discourse, the breadth of which is evident in compendia such as the *Handbook of Evaluation* (Shaw, Greene, & Mark, 2006), the *Encyclopedia of Evaluation* (Mathison, 2005), and the *International Handbook of Educational Evaluation* (Kellaghan & Stufflebeam, 2003), as well as the extensive literature on educational assessment (e.g., Linn, 2004; Pellegrino, Chudowsky, & Glaser, 2001). For example, the practice of curriculum evaluation originating in Ralph Tyler's idea that instruction is related to measurable learning objectives is grounded in the substance (basic concepts, findings) and syntax (methods of discovery) of the Thorndike tradition of educational psychology. An alternative approach to curriculum evaluation known as case study reflects different influences, assumptions, and ideas drawn from Dewey, Schwab, Stenhouse, and others. The classic CIPP model of educational evaluation reflects still other influences from organizational theory and decision management practices. The wide-ranging scene of educational evaluation has not substantially changed since the publication of *Educational Evaluation: Theory and Practice* more than 30 years ago (Worthen & Sanders, 1973) that described the field as characterized by several different conceptions of the meaning of evaluation; its purpose; the duties, authority, and responsibility of evaluators; and its methods and means.

Given this varied and diverse landscape, it can be reasonably argued that, to talk responsibly of the philosophical, ethical, and political foundations of educational evaluation, one would have to develop an account of each of the various practices of educational evaluation and its founding assumptions, central ideas, and ways of proceeding. Or one would have to undertake something like a sociopolitical history of the purpose and use of evaluation in a given educational domain—for example, the evaluation of teacher training programs, higher education institutions, elementary school curriculum, school effectiveness, national educational policy, and so on—and the relationship between ways of conceiving of and conducting evaluation and implicit and explicit theories of education.

In contrast, it is possible to regard evaluation as a distinct and relatively well-defined social undertaking. That is, despite the diversity and scope of what goes on in the name of educational evaluation, from a sociological, pragmatic, and practice perspective, there is a strong sense that evaluation forms some kind of satisfactorily coherent entity.[3] As Dahler-Larsen (2006) explains,

> In practice, the term *evaluation* brings a sufficient number of people together who share enough of the same interests, and who despite confusions and disagreements about vocabulary [and definitions of evaluation], do *evaluation*, attend *evaluation* conferences, and take standpoints on *evaluation standards*. They read some of the same books and journals, interact considerably across paradigms, topical interests, and national and cultural borders and [collectively] position themselves in ways that make sense to others. (p. 142)

The Evaluation Imaginary

Expanding on Dahler-Larsen's view, my thesis in this chapter is that educational evaluation achieves its coherence in part because it rests on a set of taken-for-granted understandings and ways of being in the world that I refer to as the *Western evaluation imaginary*—a term derived, with considerable liberties, from Charles Taylor's (2004) notion of a social imaginary.

Taylor uses the term to refer to the "way we collectively imagine our social life in the contemporary western world" (p. 50). He argues that the notion is not the same as an intellectual scheme that we employ in contemplating social reality at a distance, nor a social theory, but rather refers to the "ways people imagine their social existence, how they fit together with others, how things go on between them and their fellows, the expectations that are normally met, and the deeper normative notions and images that underlie those expectations" (p. 23). In adapting Taylor's ideas for present purposes, I have chosen to use the term descriptively to refer to "that common [i.e., intersubjective or social] understanding that makes possible common practices and a widely shared sense of legitimacy" (p. 23) for contemporary evaluation practices in education. Moreover, that "common understanding" is moral-political: moral in that it reflects ideas of what individuals and societies should do, not simply what they are likely to do, and political in that it concerns ways in which societies make decisions and govern themselves. The way we think about, conduct, and value the practice(s) of evaluation amid a world of other social agents—for example, clients, stakeholders, the general public, and what Cronbach and Associates (1980) called the policy-shaping community—who desire objective, external judgments of the value of social and educational plans and accomplishments is both animated by (and sustains) the evaluation imaginary. It is by virtue of the intersubjective agreements we have in place in the imaginary, so to speak, that evaluation has social purpose and meaning and evaluation knowledge has currency. It is

> Within the folds of a social imaginary [that] we see ourselves as agents who traverse a social space and inhabit a temporal horizon, entertain certain beliefs and norms, engage in and make sense of our practices in terms of purpose, timing, and appropriateness, and exist among other agents. (Gaonkar, 2002, p. 10)

The Western evaluation imaginary has an Enlightenment bias and is thoroughly modernist. In other words, it asserts the ability (indeed, the necessity) of human beings to create, improve, and reshape themselves, their societies, and their environment by means of practical experimentation, scientific knowledge, and effective deployment of technology. In this way of thinking, evaluation is regarded as something both neutral and rational (Wedel, Shore, Feldman, & Lathrop, 2005, make a similar point about the notion of "policy" in the Western imaginary). The imaginary presumes a world of agents sharing core social values, including freedom of choice, the uniqueness of the individual, skepticism, and achievement grounded in merit. In this imaginary, evaluation acquires its currency from the belief that social progress is related to aggressive (empirical and objective) problem solving, reduction of anxiety and risk, and replacement of tradition and prejudice by clear-headed rational thought and change-oriented social institutions (Dahler-Larsen, 2006; House, 1993). Evaluation is what it is because we imagine that it is both possible and worthwhile to define and categorize the constitutive effects of evaluation knowledge on social realities (Dahler-Larsen, 2007). Hence, there is considerable discussion of how evaluation is used or misused, whether its effects are positive or negative, intended or unintended, pathological and dysfunctional or reasonable and salutary, and so on. Evaluation practices have value because it is assumed that the description and judgment of the merit and worth of people and their accomplishments (i.e., their ideas, professional actions, practices, policies, institutions, societies, etc.) is of considerable social consequence.

Within this broad Enlightenment orientation, evaluation is linked to a democratic ideal of the polity via dissimilar and opposing moral-political orientations (that, in part, constitute different social imaginaries). Evaluation practices (and theories) are allied to the state as a geopolitical, political, and cultural space. Within such a space, on the one hand, evaluation is oriented to elites—the executive branch of governments, program managers, program funders, government agency directors, and the like and their need for evaluation information in decision making. Established values and policy objectives are generally taken for granted, and evaluation serves elites by developing both an analytic capacity within government agencies and organizations and a more sophisticated knowledge base that fosters a culture of smarter, more scientifically informed decision making (Chelimsky, 2006). The democratic functions assumed and constituted here by evaluation include rational feedback on actions (e.g., goal-oriented rationality), well-planned social change (e.g., the experimenting society), establishing management efficiency, and exercising control and accountability in service provision (Davies, Newcomer, & Soydan, 2006; Hanberger, 2006). Broadly speaking, evaluation aligned with elitist versions of democracy is often referred to as scientific, rationalistic, and technical-instrumental (Bovens, 'T Hart, & Kuipers, 2006; Squires & Measor, 2005).

On the other hand, evaluation has social currency because of a moral-political orientation focused on the masses, so to speak, on the institutions and organizations of civil society more generally, on program beneficiaries, and the like.[4] Underlying evaluation here are cultural presumptions of the value of an informed citizenry, the right of the public to know, and the active involvement or participation of citizens in decisions about social goods. Understood in this way, evaluation both presumes and contributes to the creation of democratic functions such as enhanced citizen self-determination, improved quality of public debate, and the collective enlightenment of the citizenry (Cronbach & Associates, 1980; Hanberger, 2006). Evaluation envisioned in this orientation is often spoken of as democratic, argumentative, communicative, and participatory.

It is because the Western evaluation imaginary embraces both of these bold moral-political orientations—that we, of necessity, must negotiate and interpret—that it makes any sense at all to debate the merits of different approaches to evaluation, different ways of realizing its modernist aims, its different political orientations, the use of different tools for generating evaluation knowledge, different schemes of evaluation evidence, and so on. The central question addressed in the remainder of this chapter is "What kinds of things are taking place in the discourse and practices of globalization that have some bearing on the Western evaluation imaginary so conceived?"

Defining Globalization

For the purposes of this chapter, the notion of globalization is treated as short hand for what is happening to us (as individuals and our societies, cultures, institutions, etc.) as a consequence of global flows of ideas and ideologies, people and goods, and images and messages. It includes the invention and dissemination of new media and communication technologies that overcome previous boundaries of space, place, and time; make possible the creation and dissemination of new kinds of knowledge; and create new industries and labor markets (Kellner, 1997). It is generally accepted that the acceleration and intensification of interaction, interchange, and integration of individuals and institutions affects individual well-being, the environment, culture, ideas, political systems, and economies. However, as Appadurai (1999) notes, "the various flows we see are not coeval, convergent, isomorphic or spatially consistent" (p. 230). These flows have varied origins and proceed at different speeds and along different pathways, issuing in "different relationships to institutional structures in different regions, nations or societies" (p. 231) and precipitating different kinds of problems and frictions in different local situations.

One obvious global flow has to do with the emergence of the global professional. Lenn and Campos (1997) have argued that we are seeing the emergence of individuals who are qualified to provide professional services in any country around the world. Moreover, in their view, "traditional nationalistic ideas about professionals and the quality of their education will inevitably give way to global definitions founded on common evaluation criteria—education, experience and ethics" (p. 1). In the field of evaluation (not specifically limited to educational evaluation), the emergence and movement of global professionals is evident in the cadres of specialists (economists, psychometricians, etc.) that circulate through evaluation projects around the world that are managed and/or funded by transnational agencies such as the World Bank, OECD, the United Nations Development Program, and large nongovernmental organizations.

Global flows in communication and information technologies are producing fundamental changes in the spatial and temporal contours of human existence, including deterritorialization, interconnectedness, and the acceleration of aspects of social life. This development is variously interpreted, with some scholars focusing on how it undermines or makes irrelevant the importance of local and national boundaries in understanding ideas of identity, citizenship, actions, social practices, ideas, and so on, whereas others see the promise of transnational movements and a global society (Rizvi, Chapter 1, this volume; Scheuerman, 2006).

What is referred to as economic globalization is a flow of prevailing ideas and practices, known as neoliberalism, endorsed by currently dominant economic and political elites. These ideas include policy instruments for the devolution, outsourcing, and privatization of government services, free markets and free trade, minimizing economic regulation, reducing expenditures on public services, and strict controls on organized labor (Falk, 1999; Harvey, 2005; Kettl, 2000; Olssen, 2004). For some scholars, the spread of neoliberal thinking is closely related to institutional globalization, defined by Astiz, Wiseman, and Baker (2002) as

Convergence toward a uniform model of polity and of rationalization. At the heart of this transformation is the convergence of formal institutions within and across nations toward similar goals and operating structures. Cross-national descriptions of schools, health care, social welfare, and justice systems reveal significant trends in this convergence.

This process of institutional convergence is evident in the growing influence of nongovernmental and intergovernmental organizations (e.g., UNESCO, OECD, the World Bank, the European Union [EU]) in creating global uniformity in educational policies, as well as in the establishment of networks of influential policy actors who begin to function as international policy elites with a common agenda. For example, Lawn and Lingard (2002) describe the emergence and role of a new European class of educational system actors that constitute a policy elite shaping the emerging European discourse of educational policy. In 2002, UNESCO convened the Global Forum on Quality Assurance in Higher Education, where influential members of the educational policy communities from 30 countries discussed (among other agenda items) how to develop a framework through which national quality assurance professionals in countries around the world can position themselves to ensure higher education quality internationally (Eaton, 2003). St. Clair (2006) explains how the World Bank works as a major global governance actor, a transnational expertised institution, whose legitimacy and credibility as an expert "is drawn through a circular process between the knowledge it produces and the audiences that legitimize that knowledge" (p. 77).

As Clarke (2004) explains, there are two general views of the worldwide impact and spread of global flows. The often dominant view is apocalyptic and focuses on neoliberal globalization as a "unified, unilinear and monological process" that marks "an inexorable economic transition responsible for undermining nation

states, rendering public spending indefensible, dismantling welfare states and over-riding democratic control" (p. 29). Global flows of ideas, people, products, images, and so on are regarded as a force for homogenization. Another perspective, more in line with Appadurai's views as noted earlier (see also Kellner, 2002), is an unevenness hypothesis. Here, globalization is regarded "in a more differentiated, more uneven, more contradictory and more unfinished way" in which both "contradiction and contestation are integral elements of globalizing processes" (Clarke, 2004, p. 29). In a similar way, Falk (1999) challenges the idea of a predatory globalization from above by arguing for a globalization from below—a view that draws on ideas of citizen activism across borders and notions of cosmopolitan democracy (Benhabib, 2006; Held, 2004).

Challenges to the Western Evaluation Imaginary

Global flows of ideas, practices, ideologies, people, and so on are occasioning several kinds of developments in the understandings and activities that comprise cultures, societies, and institutions throughout the world. These developments are differentially experienced in particular locales as homogenization, contradiction, contestation, confrontation, or opposition. Take, for example, the global flow of ideas and practices surrounding the definition of *education* as the acquisition of skills and knowledge required for employment in the global economy. To fully understand the impact of this global flow on actual educational practices and how evaluation theory and practice are implicated therein would require empirical study of educational evaluation practices in particular arenas of education (higher education, compulsory schooling, teacher preparation, qualification, assessment, etc.) and specific national contexts—a comparative investigation beyond the scope of this chapter.[5] Hence, I have opted for a different kind of investigation—one that is focused at a meta-level. In what follows, I sketch in broad strokes several ways in which the phenomenon of globalization (as defined earlier) challenges the Western evaluation imaginary. Befitting the view that the globalization problematic is characterized by complexity and uncertainty, I have chosen to portray these challenges as tensions "between X and Y" to signify that it is mistaken to talk of a simple unidirectional movement from one state of affairs or way of thinking to another. The poles X and Y identified in each of the tensions identified next represent directions or orientations—and, in some cases, stakeholding audiences as well—that are historically evident as well as emergent in evaluation practices.

Between Serving Governments and Serving Governance

In the Western evaluation imaginary, evaluation practices acquire meaning, in large part, because they are linked to the interests and needs of national democratic governments. These practices, as Chelimsky (2006) argues, serve governments' needs for accountability and a strong knowledge base for policymaking, as well as helping government agencies and ministries develop greater capacity for policy and program planning, implementation, and analysis of results. Independent evaluations of government policies and social interventions are contracted for in the government marketplace, and evaluation functions are built into executive branches of central government as well as agencies and ministries (e.g., in the United States, the Office of Management and Budget, the National Science Foundation, and the National Center for Education Evaluation and Regional Assistance—an arm of the Institute of Education Sciences; in Spain, the National Agency for the Evaluation of Public Policies and Quality of Services). Understood in this way, evaluation functions as one among many policy instruments (others include regulations, economic means, and information) useful in substantiating, implementing, or effecting social change (Vedung, 1998).

However, largely as the outcome of global flows of ideas and practices, evaluation is no longer only a contingent instrument of administration in government, doing its best to inform policy debates and decisions with scientific evidence. It is also now functioning as "a central legitimating device for a new form of politics. . . . Along with audit and performance management, evaluation has become a key entry in the lexicon of new public management and the pursuit of what politicians increasingly frame as 'value-free policy' " (D. Taylor 2005, p. 605). What is emerging here is the idea of governance by evaluation.

Governance refers to patterns of involvement of institutions and actors coordinated through networks and partnerships producing policy outcomes, in which government is but one actor in the process. The World Education Indicator (WEI) project is an example of the participation of educational evaluation in governance. The development of the WEI project exemplifies an emerging multilateralism in both educational policy and in the use of evaluation instruments to determine education success (Rutkowski, 2007). In brief, this multilateralism has a specific content—a neoliberal view of education for economic development—that, in turn, promotes the value of a specific kind of educational knowledge (i.e., indicators) for the comparative analysis of educational systems across countries. The WEI project is but one example of the idea of worldwide governance strategies for national educational systems driven by powerful international actors in which evaluation of educational quality is based on performance and achievement indicators (see, e.g., the report *Governance for Quality of Education* [Gallacher, 2001]—the published proceedings of a conference jointly sponsored by the World Bank Group and the Institute for Educational Policy of the Open Society Institute).

Governance by evaluation can also mean institutionalizing quality assurance systems in local practices. This is the idea behind the clinical governance movement in the health services field (McSherry & Pearce, 2007; Swage, 2004). Clinical governance refers to a system for making health services responsive and accountable to patients and professionals and for reducing variability in practice. Evaluation technologies for monitoring and evaluation (e.g., audit, risk assessment, complaints handling) as well as evaluations of the causal effectiveness of various treatments and health care interventions are key drivers in the system. A parallel idea is evident in the rapid development in recent years of quality assurance networks in education. The International Network of Quality Assurance Agencies in Higher Education, for example, aims to develop guidelines for quality provision in cross-border education. The European Association for Quality Assurance in Higher Education disseminates information, experiences, and good practices to promote convergence on definitions and means of quality assurance among national quality assurance agencies in the signatory states of the Bologna declaration.

Between Aligning With Bureau Professionalism and Aligning With the New Managerialism

In the Western evaluation imaginary, professional practices of evaluation have acquired social currency, in part, because of their alliance with the mix of bureaucratic administration and professionalism known as bureau professionalism.[6] In this organizational settlement, as Clarke and Newman (1997) describe it, the public interest was to be served by a combination of bureaucratic administration that promised predictability, stability, and impartiality in the provision of social welfare and professional knowledge that served as the engine of social progress, promising the use of expert knowledge to enhance the public good. Evaluation was one of many professional undertakings of use to the nation-state, although there were (and continue to be) arguments about the kind of specialized knowledge it brings (and should bring) to the table and how that knowledge is best used in service of social problem solving. For example, Cronbach and Associates'

(1980) *Toward Reform of Program Evaluation*, as well as Shadish, Cook, and Leviton's (1991) often-cited *Foundations of Program Evaluation*, both can be read as history of how evaluators in the United States envisioned the alliance. More recently, Mark, Henry, and Julnes (2000) revisit the union of professional evaluation and administrative decision making through an explanation of how evaluation serves as assisted sense-making in service of the goal of social betterment.

This is not the place to rehearse the history of the partial dismantling of the settlement between bureaucracy and expert knowledge in Western nation-states (see, e.g., Aucoin, 1990; Clarke & Newman, 1997; Gerwitz, Ball, & Bowe, 1995; Pollitt, 1990). It will have to suffice to point out that the machinery of governing the provision of social services underwent significant transformation in the 1980s and 1990s, from being directed by an ideology of bureau professionalism grounded in a public-service ethos to being influenced by the new managerialism, also called the new public management, grounded in a customer-service ethos. Managerialism is a set of beliefs, attitudes, values, and activities that support the view that management is essential to good administration and governance. Management is understood as an approach to problem solving that avoids conflict and argument and focuses on the rational assessment of problems (e.g., gathering information, weighing alternatives, evaluating consequences, and choosing the best course of action). Management framed in this way is grounded in a kind of technicist belief in the power of human mastery—the strength of ability to solve social, economic, and political problems with the use of the right scientific tools and methods and the right technologies (systems, techniques). In managerialism, evaluation is one of the technologies needed for effective management, and in this way evaluation is oriented to elites. That is, evaluation is a technical undertaking that involves the application of tools, systems, or procedures for determining goal attainment, outcomes, or effects of policy and program interventions.

Although far from uniform in its effects on the organization and provision of public services, managerialism has affected the social positioning—the place and power—of evaluation as a professional practice in this provision. Clarke and Newman (1997) explain three types of changes that are unfolding. First, *displacement* refers to processes through which public services are reorganized as regimes. They are "reshaped around a command structure which privileges the calculative framework of managerialism: how to improve efficiency and organisational performance" (p. 76). Second, although complete displacement is rare, a more common change is *subordination*, which "takes the form of framing the exercise of professional judgment by the requirement that it takes account of the 'realities and responsibilities' of budgetary management" (p. 76). The aim here is to discipline what is perceived as the irresponsible exercise of professional judgment by "making it coterminous with the allocation of resources" (p. 76). In the United States, this development is quite obvious in the institutionalization of the Office of Management and Budget's Program Assessment and Review Technique. This evaluation technology is used to identify a program's strengths and weaknesses to simultaneously inform funding and management decisions aimed at making the program more effective (http://www.whitehouse.gov/omb/part/). The kinds of social needs assessments that are typical of efforts to establish criteria in evaluation for judging program value are now "disciplined by a managerial calculus of resources and priorities" (p. 76). Finally, a strategy of *co-option* is evident: "This refers to managerial attempts to colonise the terrain of professional discourse, constructing articulations between professional concerns and languages and those of management" (p. 76). The importation of the language of financial audits into the evaluation of programs is a clear example of this articulation of traditional management concerns with the concerns of professional evaluation (Mayne, 2006; Power, 1997).

As with other globalizing influences, this one has differential effects. An epidemic of education

"quality" and attempts at its systematization and management through the production of indicators, comparative evaluation, and the like is, as Clarke and Newman (1997) point out, an effort to discipline the professional discretion of evaluators to determine quality (see also Stake & Schwandt, 2006). Yet it is mistaken to believe that some kind of complete transformation has occurred in organizational cultures in which evaluation operates. As Simkins (2000) has noted, empirical studies indicate increasingly managerialist patterns of control in education institutions occasioned by pressures on administrators, such as the need to perform in the quasi-market and take a more customer-focused approach to those whom they serve; the need to set and meet demanding targets in terms of measurable performance indicators that are set by central governments or their agents; and the need to exhibit appropriate forms of management and organization that can be inspected and for which institutions can be held to account. On the basis of comparative studies, however, he argues

> It is dangerous . . . to draw sweeping conclusions about the replacement of the traditional bureau-professional organizational order in education by a managerial one. Rather, it is better to view the process as a dynamic one in which growing tensions between the "old" and the "new" are worked out within particular policy and management arenas as different values systems and interests compete for influence. (p. 330)

Between Building and Supporting Technocratic and Human-Centered Knowledge Systems

As noted earlier, the Western evaluation imaginary embraces two moral-political orientations. The longstanding tension between these orientations is exacerbated in view of the global flow of ideas surrounding the development of the knowledge society and the ways in which evaluation practices are implicated in efforts of the public (and private) sector to build capacity to capture the benefits of revolutions in knowledge, innovation, and technology. The significance of this effort to manage and grow a knowledge society is evident in the following excerpt from a United Nations Division for Public Administration and Development Management report:

> The role of knowledge in development and governance is certainly not new. However, knowledge has taken on an even greater degree of relevance and a different shape with the advent and deepening of the knowledge economy and society. There are multiple drivers of this phenomenon, one of them being the way in which society is becoming more complex and unpredictable in both positive and challenging ways. One can point to globalization, the economic value of ideas, global production chains, demographics of youth, challenges to political systems and rapid development in science and technology, including ICTs, as examples of this change. It can be argued that these new imperatives demand responses that are more creative, innovative, smarter, and more active in their use of knowledge. Yet, while we often have an abundance of information, there is equally often a pronounced deficit of knowledge, or at least a deficit in our ability to create, use and apply it meaningfully. (Department of Economic and Social Affairs, 2003, p. 1)

The knowledge systems discussion often unfolds along two different lines of thought (Department of Economic and Social Affairs, 2003). One is a technocentric view in which (a) useful knowledge is defined as either propositional (i.e., knowledge of what, scientific knowledge) or prescriptive (i.e., techniques, instructions, and procedures), (b) technology plays a central shaping role in system design, and (c) convergence on best (knowledge-based)

practices is a major goal. In significant ways, this technocentric view is associated with psychometric, managerialist, and experimentalist approaches to educational evaluation.

Another view is human-centered, placing the mix of human purposes, judgment, beliefs, and knowledge at center stage. It valorizes diversity, interdependence, and tolerance of ambiguity. It emphasizes that knowledge systems must incorporate rich storehouses of tacit and local knowledge and be in service of the various roles that citizens play in shaping their society—actor, participant, interlocutor, mediator, and decision maker. The human-centered view is premised on the notion of an engaged, informed civil society pursuing need-based, purposeful goals and using knowledge of various kinds as a resource in this effort.

Evaluation practices in education align with both of these ways of thinking. On the one hand, they figure prominently in the instrumental logic of the technocentric view in several ways: (a) the use of evaluation to generate an evidence base of what works—a central organizing principle of the Campbell Collaborations, the U.S. Institute of Education Sciences, and the UK Evidence for Policy and Practice Information and Coordinating (EPPI) Centre; (b) the use of evaluation as a decision support system—compiling educational indicators for purposes of country-by-country comparison of educational systems; and (c) the use of evaluation to provide reassurance of conformance to plan and, subsequently, rank performance as evident in the high-stakes testing required under No Child Left Behind (NCLB) legislation in the United States and the higher education research assessment exercises used in the UK, Australia, and New Zealand.

On the other hand, evaluation practices also align with the more political logic of the human-centered view of knowledge systems. They tend to do so, however, on a far more local or community basis, rather than on a broad social level, and these practices are more prominent in the world of development evaluation (with its links to education) than they are in the field of educational evaluation per se. Here evaluation functions less as a kind of assurance of conformance to plan and more as a vehicle for citizen self-determination, social criticism, and resistance to elite rule. Norris (2007) characterizes this kind of evaluation as a source of countervailing authority to the institutionalized evaluative accountability systems characteristic of managerialist and technocentric practices. Reimers (2003), speaking of the situation surrounding educational evaluation in Latin America, summarizes this view:

> The practice of evaluation in Latin America has been shaped by institutional rules that reflect State dominance and elitism. . . . State dominance has depended on coopting international influences and local research communities. The advancement of more democratic education policies will require public ideas that convey the importance [of] ways to strengthen . . . the learning opportunities of marginalized children. These ideas need to reach social movements that can generate political pressure to support progressive policy reform. To contribute to such a debate and democratic process . . . the practice of evaluation will have to be turned on its head and itself become more independent, rigorous, open, and public. (p. 461)

Between Apolitical Assurance and Politically Situated Social Criticism

A related tension arises from the manner in which the relationship between the purpose and politics of evaluation is conceived in the evaluation imaginary. It is widely acknowledged that because evaluation is inextricably tied to institutional structures and practices, it is political in character—as Pawson and Tilley (1997) put it, "the very act of engaging in evaluation constitutes a political statement" (p. 11). However, *political* here is typically taken to mean the discourse of norms, values, power, authority,

influence, and so on that threatens (or at least potentially clashes with) evaluation understood as a *scientific* activity conceived in terms of facts, objectivity, and empirically warranted assertions. In other words, the world of politics is thought to lie outside of the scientific practice of evaluation, and it poses dangers in the form of impediments, constraints, undue influence, or obstructions to the successful conduct of that practice. Given this way of thinking of politics in evaluation, it is not surprising that some evaluators argue that it is precisely the tough, realistic, and uncompromising determination of the *effects* of educational interventions that matter most in policy and practice decisions. The idea of evidence-based practices for education (both teaching and educational management) is framed as an apolitical decision support strategy—that is, knowing what works is all that matters to teachers and administrators as decision makers about effective educational curricula and to parents as consumers of educational services and products for their children.

This view is met by criticism from other evaluators who view the *political* in evaluation in a different way (Greene, 2006; Schwandt, 1997a, 1997b). For them, evaluation in support of generating evidence-based practices and policies (as well as in support of managerialism more generally) is an "attempt to depoliticize the public realm" and to "deny or displace the possibility of policy conflict, choice or decision by not subjecting public issues to alternative 'regimes of truth'" (Clarke, 2004, p. 34). In brief, the kinds of solely technical and pragmatic evaluations that serve as handmaidens to decision makers fail to offer a critical perspective on what is being done, and invariably serve the agenda of those in power (Squires & Measor, 2005). From the perspective of Taylor and Balloch (2005), evaluation as apolitical assurance of performance according to plan or achievement of intended effects ignores the fact "that evaluation operates within discursive systems and its social meaning is preconstituted within wider relations of power independently of any particular use" (p. 2). From the perspective of these critics, evaluation must function as a kind of politically informed social criticism—*politically informed*, in the sense that determining what is in the best of interest of society must be done in an open and deliberative process, both in the planning that precedes decision making and in the appraisal that follows decision making, in which all interests and points of view are represented, scrutinized, and critically appraised (House & Howe, 1999).

Between a National and a Global Focus

As noted earlier, evaluation in the Western imaginary is enfolded in ideas of serving national governments and assumes a particular kind of relation among agents and between agents and institutions in society. The way professional evaluation practices unfold and the manner in which issues of evaluation purpose, meta-evaluation, evaluation ethics, and evaluation governance are understood are tied to this way of thinking and being. Globalizing influences challenge all these self-understandings.

Consider first what is assumed in the Western imaginary about the nature and purpose of evaluation. As Garaway (2003) explains, Western imaginaries assume a particular kind of sociopolitical relationship—one in which society is regarded as dynamic and (relatively) politically decentralized, subordinates do not necessarily consider their superiors to be better than themselves, planning for the future is seen as essential not simply for survival but for social improvement, and wealth and power are (relatively) distributed. In this way of thinking about the relationship between people in a society, evaluation is about judgment, and judgment speaks criticism. Evaluation is about public scrutiny and dialogue and predicated on the value of open communication and interaction. This imaginary is exported, so to speak, in evaluation that is conducted through individual actors, donor agencies, NGOs, and transnational institutions from

the West, whether economists, on the one hand, or participatory evaluators, on the other hand, inspire that evaluation. The globalization of evaluation has meant that this aspect of the imaginary is challenged. Perhaps most obviously, globalization from below has been marked by challenges to the imposition of Western cultural democratic understandings of evaluation on developing countries. Illustrating the challenge, Garaway (2003) (drawing on the work of Etounga-Manguelle) draws attention to how this aspect of the Western evaluation imaginary clashes with the following common ground of shared values, attitudes, and institutions of African culture: subordination of the individual by the community; a resistance to changes in social standing; thought processes that avoid skepticism because it is perceived as a mental endeavor tied to individualism; a high level of acceptance of uncertainty about the future; and a high value placed on social cohesion, sociability, and consensus such that differences in viewpoint are often masked or rejected in an effort to avoid conflict and promote conviviality.

As forms of governance are changing from nation-state to global, to interstate, to nongovernmental, and to private market mechanisms (Olssen, 2004), evaluation is challenged to explore the idea of meta-evaluation—the way in which evaluation practices are monitored, guided, and evaluated. The tension here is manifest in national society versus global society standards for evaluation practice, as well as in conceptions of evaluation governance. In the past 10 years or so, many national evaluation associations and societies have developed their own evaluation standards, often adapting or modifying the standards for evaluation developed by the U.S.-based Joint Committee on Standards for Educational Evaluation (1994). These standards reflect conceptions of professional conduct as well as the sociopolitical realities of conducting evaluations within the geopolitical spaces of particular countries. At the same time, there is a simultaneous movement toward global convergence on what constitutes "good" evaluation, as evidenced, for example, in the endorsement of the value of causal effectiveness studies in development evaluation by the Network of Networks on Impact Evaluation (see http://www.worldbank.org/ieg/nonie/) and the Sourcebook for Evaluating Global and Regional Partnership Programs being developed by the OECD/Development Assistance Committee Network on Development Evaluation (see http://web.worldbank.org/WBSITE/EXTERNAL/EXTOED/EXTGLOREGPARPRO/0,,content MDK:21178261~menuPK:2831800~pagePK:64 168445~piPK:64168309~theSitePK:2831765,00. html). Two challenges are evident: One has to do with whether it is possible and desirable to develop autonomous nation-state standards for evaluation practices that also respect global evaluation engagements. The other challenge concerns the development of standards and guidelines for evaluation governance that reflect the sociopolitical realities underlying the purpose and role of evaluation in different nations—for example, the norms guiding the expectations of roles among evaluation commissioners, evaluators, and participants; appropriate contractual relationships; oversight of self-evaluation by independent evaluation; and "evaluability" norms for program and policy design (Picciotto, 2005).

The global flows of people, deterritorialization, interconnectedness, and challenges to reigning paradigms of international relations governed by a few great national powers are changing the scale of human social organization, such that it no longer corresponds neatly to the nation-state (McGrew; quoted in Olssen, 2004). Hence, as the nation-state ceases to be the sole repository of democratic life, new forms and practices of citizenship and new forms of global democracy, global justice, and global solidarity are taking shape. This represents a significant challenge to practices of evaluation grounded in the Western evaluation imaginary to develop a professional global ethics. There is a strong sense that evaluators, within a nation-state, serve the "public" good. Increasingly, however, evaluators are called on to assess public policies and programs that extend beyond national borders; as a result, a global evaluation community is in the making (Picciotto, 2005). Who does/should evaluation serve in a global context—international or transnational elites or civil society and the public more generally? Who is the public in such a scenario, and how are we to understand the public good? Does taking responsibility for the public good mean that evaluators should act in defense of local cultures and resist the cultural homogenization that results from the globalizing influences of intergovernmental organizations such as OECD, UNESCO, the World Bank, and the EU? Should evaluators who work in the vast terrain of international aid and development adopt a particularly activist global ethic that emphasizes global justice, environmental stewardship, social interdependence, and reverence for place; an ethic that derives its bearings from careful consideration of the problems engendered by the advance of Western science and technology? The Center for Ethics and Values Inquiry at Ghent University in The Netherlands has drawn a distinction between the ethics of globalization and ethics under globalization (see http://www.ceviglobal ethics.ugent.be/ceviglobalethics). The former is concerned with the moral implications of globalizing processes, such as the erosion of the nation-state, the spread of migration, and the growth of media-dictated mass consumption, whereas the latter deals with a widespread moral perplexity about the adequacy of current moral philosophy to deal with the realities of a postindustrial society, a scientistic ideology, the tension between moral universalism and moral particularism, and technological-expertise visions of rationality. These are dimensions of the Western evaluation imaginary that we have only just begun to explore (Schwandt, 2007).

Conclusion

An apocalyptic reading of the effects of globalization on educational evaluation theory and practice regards the ascendancy of the combination of managerialism, audit cultures, new public management, evidence-based thinking, and the neoliberal political economy to be complete. In such a scenario, educational evaluation has been colonized by these ideas and brought within the purview of a broadly evaluative state—a "system orchestrated by the logic of calculation and of measuring outcomes and results"; a state in which "fundamental questions about the purposes and politics of education and its relation to the common good cannot be easily formulated" (Hall, 2005, p. 180); a state in which we have government by professional managers and their experts, rather than a government of citizens. Such a reading aligns with Castoriadis' (referenced in Bauman, 1998) pronouncement that the trouble with the contemporary condition of our modern civilization is that it stopped questioning itself.

Despite the rhetorical and political appeal of such a reading, I do not believe that the empirical evidence of what is transpiring in educational evaluation supports it. No single school of educational evaluation can claim a monopoly on the field of practice. Hence, any apocalyptic reading regarding specifically the effects of globalization and its effects on educational evaluation seems tenuous. What currently seems of utmost importance in the globalization of evaluation is the simultaneous exposing of the strengths and weakness of the Western evaluation imaginary. Globalization is not a homogeneous development, but a heterogeneous one in which the largely taken-for-granted hidden framework of educational (and, more broadly, all social programs) evaluation is more readily exposed and scrutinized. Questions of what constitutes valuable evaluation knowledge and why, as well as who (and what) evaluation is in service of in a global context, are now paramount. This is salutary because it moves the discussion of the significance of evaluation off the tired topics of methods and models and restores a focus on the political and moral orientation of the practice. By the latter I mean more careful and sustained attention to whose interests are being served in the conduct of evaluation, the

social location(s) of evaluation practices, the manner in which such practices acquire social legitimacy, and the built-in assumptions of evaluation practices with respect to legitimate forms of social organization (Schwandt, 1997b). This is a much more difficult discussion to be sure, but one that holds the promise of developing new ideas about what counts as evaluation knowledge and "what communities of judgment and accountability . . . are central in the pursuit of such knowledge" (Appadurai, 1999, p. 237).

Notes

1. At approximately the same time, a parallel development in the UK was unfolding in action research that shared many of the assumptions of a case study approach in evaluation, but was specifically focused on improving educational practice.

2. Dahler-Larsen (2006) reported that as of November 2004, 83 evaluation associations, societies, or networks were located via an Internet search. The count included international, national, and regional organizations, as well as chapters of national associations. Presumably, because the search identified all organizations with the word *evaluation* in their name, the search included testing-oriented associations such as the International Test and Evaluation Association, the International Association for Evaluation of Educational Achievement, and so on.

3. This chapter is primarily concerned with the nature and purpose of the evaluation of educational (and, more broadly, all social) policies and programs. I do not specifically address the shared understandings of educational evaluation as testing and assessment because that topic is well covered elsewhere in this handbook.

4. The term *civil society* is used throughout this chapter in the sense captured in the following working definition from The London School of Economics Centre for Civil Society: "Civil society refers to the arena of uncoerced collective action around shared interests, purposes and values. In theory, its institutional forms are distinct from those of the state, family and market, though in practice, the boundaries between state, civil society, family and market are often complex, blurred and negotiated. Civil society commonly embraces a diversity of spaces, actors, and institutional forms, varying in their degree of

formality, autonomy, and power. Civil societies are often populated by organizations such as registered charities, development non-governmental organizations, community groups, women's organizations, faith-based organizations, professional associations, trade unions, self-help groups, social movements, business associations, coalitions, and advocacy groups." Retrieved July 21, 2008, from http://www.lse.ac.uk/collections/CCS/what_is_civil_society.htm.

5. For one example of this kind of investigation, see the examination of reforms in higher education and higher education evaluation systems across countries in Dodds (2005), Gough (2007), Atkinson-Grosjean and Grosjean (2000), Kells (1999), and Mok (2003).

6. Bureau professionalism, or welfarism, as it is sometimes called, unfolded in different ways in the United States, the UK, and the countries of Western Europe. What is sketched here is a general characterization of this development.

References

Appadurai, A. (1999). Globalization and the research imagination. *International Social Science Journal,* 51(160), 229–238.

Astiz, M. F., Wiseman, A. W., & Baker, D. P. (2002). Slouching towards decentralization: Consequences of globalization for curricular control in national education systems. *Comparative Education Review,* 46(1), 88.

Atkinson-Grosjean, J., & Grosjean, G. (2000). The use of performance models in higher education: A comparative review. *Education Policy Analysis Archives,* 8(30). Available at http://epaa.asu.edu/epaa/v8n30.html

Aucoin, P. (1990). Administrative reform in public management: Paradigms, principles, paradoxes and pendulums. *Governance: An International Journal of Policy and Administration,* 3(2), 115–137.

Bauman, Z. (1998). *Globalization: The human consequences.* New York: Columbia University Press.

Benhabib, S. (2006). *Another cosmopolitanism.* Oxford: Oxford University Press.

Bovens, M., 'T Hart, P., & Kuipers, S. (2006). The politics of policy evaluation. In M. Moran, M. Rein, & R. E. Goodin (Eds.), *The Oxford handbook of public policy* (pp. 317–333). Oxford: Oxford University Press.

Carney, S. (2003). Globalisation, neo-liberalism and the limitations of school effectiveness research in

developing countries: The case of Nepal. *Globalisation, Societies and Education,* 1(1), 87–101.

Chelimsky, E. (2006). The purpose of evaluation in a democratic society. In I. F. Shaw, J. C. Greene, & M. M. Mark (Eds.), *Handbook of evaluation* (pp. 33–55). London: Sage.

Clarke, J. (2004). Dissolving the public realm? The logics and limits of neo-liberalism. *Journal of Social Policy,* 33(1), 27–48.

Clarke, J., & Newman, J. (1997). *The managerial state.* London: Sage.

Cronbach, L. J., & Associates (1980). *Toward reform of program evaluation.* San Francisco, CA: Jossey-Bass.

Dahler-Larsen, P. (2006). Evaluation after disenchantment? Five issues shaping the role of evaluation in society. In I. F. Shaw, J. C. Greene, & M. M. Mark (Eds.), *Handbook of evaluation* (pp. 141–160). London: Sage.

Dahler-Larsen, P. (2007). Constitutive effects of performance indicator systems. In S. Kushner & N. Norris (Eds.), *Dilemmas of engagement: Evaluation and the new public management* (pp. 17–36). Oxford: Elsevier.

Davies, P., Newcomer, K., & Soydan, H. (2006). Government as structural context for evaluation. In I. F. Shaw, J. C. Greene, & M. M. Mark (Eds.), *Handbook of evaluation* (pp. 163–183). London: Sage.

Department of Economic and Social Affairs. (2003). *Expanding public space for the development of the knowledge society* (Report of the Ad Hoc Expert Group Meeting on Knowledge Systems for Development). New York: United Nations, Division for Public Administration and Development Management. Available at upan1.un.org/intradoc/groups/public/documents/UN/UNPAN014138.pdf.

Dodds, A. (2005). British and French evaluation of international higher education issues: An identical political reality? *European Journal of Education,* 40(2), 155–172.

Eaton, J. S. (2003, Winter). The UNESCO Global Forum: Continuing conversations about quality review and higher education. *International Higher Education* newsletter. Retrieved January 3, 2007, from http://www.bc.edu/bc_org/avp/soe/cihe/newsletter/News30/text007.htm.

Falk, R. (1999). *Predatory globalization: A critique.* Cambridge, England: Polity Press.

Gallacher, N. (2001). *Governance for quality in education.* Budapest, Hungary: The Open Society Institute. Available at http://www.soros.org/

initiatives/esp/articles_publications/publications/
governance_20010401.

Gaonkar, D. P. (2002). Toward new imaginaries: An introduction. *Public Culture, 14*(1), 1–19.

Garaway, G. (2003). Evaluating educational programs and projects in the third world. In T. Kellaghan & D. L. Stufflebeam (Eds.), *International handbook of educational evaluation* (pp. 701–720). Dordrecht, The Netherlands: Kluwer.

Gerwitz, S., Ball, S. J., & Bowe, R. (1995). *Markets, choice and equity in education.* Buckingham, England: Open University Press.

Gilligan, C. (1990). A rationale for case study in curriculum evaluation. *Queensland Researcher, 6*(2), 39–51. Available at http://www.iier.org.au/qjer/qr6/gilligan.html.

Gough, N. (2007). Internationalisation, globalization, and quality audits: An empire of the mind? In B. Somekh & T. A. Schwandt (Eds.), *Knowledge production: Research work in interesting times* (pp. 92–107). London: Routledge.

Greene, J. C. (2006). Evaluation, democracy, and social change. In I. F. Shaw, J. C. Green, & M. M. Mark (Eds.), *Handbook of evaluation* (pp. 118–140). London: Sage.

Guba, E. G., & Lincoln, Y. S. (1989). *Fourth generation evaluation.* Newbury Park, CA: Sage.

Hall, K. D. (2005). Science, globalization, and educational governance: The political rationalities of the new managerialism. *Indiana Journal of Global Legal Studies, 12*(1), 153–182.

Hanberger, A. (2006). Evaluations of and for democracy. *Evaluation, 12*(1), 17–37.

Harvey, D. (2005). *A brief history of neoliberalism.* Oxford: Oxford University Press.

Held, D. (2004). *Globalisation: The dangers and the answers.* Retrieved April 21, 2008, from http://www.opendemocracy.net/globalization-vision_reflections/article_1918.jsp.

House, E. R. (1993). *Professional evaluation.* Newbury Park, CA: Sage.

House, E. R., & Howe, K. (1999). *Values in evaluation and social research.* Thousand Oaks, CA: Sage.

Joint Committee on Standards for Educational Evaluation. (1994). *The program evaluation standards* (2nd ed.). Thousand Oaks, CA: Sage.

Kellaghan, T., & Stufflebeam, D. L. (Eds.). (2003). *International handbook of educational evaluation.* Dordrecht, The Netherlands: Kluwer.

Kellaghan, T., Stufflebeam, D. L., & Wingate, L. A. (2003). Introduction. In T. Kellaghan & D. L. Stufflebeam (Eds.), *International handbook of educational evaluation* (pp. 1–6). Dordrecht, The Netherlands: Kluwer.

Kellner, D. (1997). *Globalization and the postmodern turn.* Retrieved April 17, 2008, from http://www.gseis.ucla.edu/courses/ed253a/dk/glopm.htm.

Kellner, D. (2002). Theorizing globalization. *Sociological Theory, 20*(3), 285–305.

Kells, H. R. (1999). National higher education evaluation systems: Methods for analysis and some propositions for the research and policy void. *Higher Education, 38*, 209–232.

Kettl, D. F. (2000). The transformation of governance: Globalization, devolution, and the role of government. *Public Administration Review, 60*(6), 488–497.

Lawn, M., & Lingard, B. (2002). Constructing a European policy space in educational governance: The role of transnational policy actors. *European Educational Research Journal, 1*(2), 290–307.

Lenn, M. P., & Campos, L. (Eds.). (1997). *Globalisation of the professions and the quality imperative.* Madison, WI: Magna Publications.

Linn, R. L. (2004). *Measurement and assessment in teaching* (9th ed.). New York: Prentice-Hall.

Luyten, H., Visscher, A., & Witziers, B. (2005). School effectiveness research: From a review of the criticism to recommendations for further development. *School Effectiveness and School Improvement, 16*(3), 249–279.

Mark, M. M., Henry, G., & Julnes, G. (2000). *Evaluation: An integrated framework for understanding, guiding, and improving policies and programs.* San Francisco, CA: Jossey-Bass.

Mathison, S. (Ed.). (2005). *Encyclopedia of evaluation.* Thousand Oaks, CA: Sage.

Mayne, J. (2006). Audit and evaluation in public management: Challenges, reforms, and different roles. *Canadian Journal of Program Evaluation, 21*(1), 11–45.

McSherry, R., & Pearce, P. (2007). *Clinical governance: A guide to implementation for health care professionals* (2nd ed.). Oxford: Blackwell.

Mok, K. (2003). Similar trends, diverse agendas: Higher education reforms in East Asia. *Globalisation, Societies and Education, 1*(2), 201–221.

Nevo, D. (2006). Evaluation in education. In I. F. Shaw, J. C. Greene, & M. M. Mark (Eds.), *Handbook of evaluation* (pp. 441–460). London: Sage.

Norris, N. (1990). *Understanding educational evaluation.* London: Kogan Page.

Norris, N. (2007). Evaluation and trust. In S. Kushner & N. Norris (Eds.), *Dilemmas of engagement:*

Evaluation and the new public management (pp. 139–153). Boston: Elsevier.

Olssen, M. (2004). Neoliberalism, globalisation, democracy: Challenges for education. *Globalisation, Societies and Education, 2*(2), 231–275.

Pawson, R., & Tilley, N. (1997). *Realistic evaluation.* London: Sage.

Pellegrino, J. W., Chudowsky, N., & Glaser, R. (2001). *Knowing what students know: The science and design of assessment.* Washington, DC: The National Academy Press.

Picciotto, R. (2005). The value of evaluation standards: A comparative assessment. *Journal of Multidisciplinary Evaluation, 2*(3), 60–77.

Pollitt, C. (1990). *Managerialism and the public services: The Anglo-American experience.* Oxford: Basil Blackwell.

Power, M. (1997). *The audit society: Rituals of verification.* Cambridge, England: Oxford University Press.

Reimers, F. (2003). The social context of educational evaluation in Latin America. In T. Kellaghan & D. L. Stufflebeam (Eds.), *International handbook of educational evaluation* (pp. 441–463). Dordrecht, The Netherlands: Kluwer.

Rutkowski, D. (2007). *Toward a new multilateralism: The development of world education indicators.* Unpublished doctoral dissertation, University of Illinois at Urbana-Champaign, Urbana, IL.

Scheuerman, W. (2006, Summer). Globalization. In E. N. Zalta (Ed.), *The Stanford encyclopedia of philosophy.* Available at http://plato.stanford.edu/archives/sum2006/entries/globalization/.

Schwandt, T. A. (1997a). The landscape of values in evaluation: Charted terrain and unexplored territory. In D. J. Rog & D. Fournier (Eds.), Progress and future directions in evaluation: Perspectives on theory, practice, and methods. *New Directions for Evaluation, 76,* 25–39.

Schwandt, T. A. (1997b). Whose interests are being served? Evaluation as a conceptual practice of power. In L. Mabry (Ed.), *Evaluation and the post-modern dilemma* (pp. 89–104). Greenwich, CT: JAI Press.

Schwandt, T. A. (2007). Expanding the conversation on evaluation ethics. *Evaluation and Program Planning, 30,* 400–403.

Shadish, W. R., Cook, T. D., & Leviton, L. C. (1991). *Foundations of program evaluation.* Newbury Park, CA: Sage.

Shaw, I. F., Greene, J. C., & Mark, M. M. (Eds.). (2006). *Handbook of evaluation.* London: Sage.

Simkins, T. (2000). Education reform and managerialism: Comparing the experience of schools and colleges. *Journal of Education Policy, 15*(3), 317–332.

Simons, H. (1987). *Getting to know schools in a democracy: The politics and process of evaluation.* London: Falmer Press.

Squires, P., & Measor, L. (2005). Below the decks on the youth justice flagship: The politics of evaluation. In D. Taylor & S. Balloch (Eds.), *The politics of evaluation* (pp. 21–40). Bristol, England: Polity Press.

St. Clair, A. L. (2006). The World Bank as a transnational expertised institution. *Global Governance, 12,* 77–95.

Stake, R. E. (2004). *Standards-based and responsive evaluation.* Thousand Oaks, CA: Sage.

Stake, R. E. (2007). NAEP, report cards and education: A review essay. *Education Review, 10*(1). Retrieved April 3, 2007, from http://edrev.asu.edu/essays/v10n1index.html.

Stake, R. E., & Schwandt, T. A. (2006). On discerning quality in evaluation. In I. F. Shaw, J. C. Greene, & M. M. Mark (Eds.), *Handbook of evaluation* (pp. 404–418). London: Sage.

Stevenson, J., & Thomas, D. (2006). Intellectual contexts. In I. F. Shaw, J. C. Greene, & M. M. Mark (Eds.), *Handbook of evaluation* (pp. 200–224). London: Sage.

Swage, T. (2004). *Clinical governance in healthcare practice* (2nd ed.). New York: Elsevier.

Taylor, C. (2004). *Modern social imaginaries.* Durham, NC: Duke University Press.

Taylor, D. (2005). Governing through evidence: Participation and power in policy evaluation. *Journal of Social Policy, 34*(4), 601–618.

Taylor, D., & Balloch, S. (2005). The politics of evaluation: An overview. In D. Taylor & S. Balloch (Eds.), *The politics of evaluation* (pp. 1–17). Bristol, England: Polity Press.

Vedung, E. (1998). Policy instruments: Typologies and theories. In M.-L. Bemelmans-Videc, R. C. Rist, & E. Vedung (Eds.), *Carrots, sticks, and sermons: Policy instruments and their evaluations.* New Brunswick, NJ: Transaction Publishers.

Wedel, J. R., Shore, C., Feldman, G., & Lathrop, S. (2005). Toward an anthropology of public policy. *AAPSS, 600,* 30–51.

Worthen, B. R., & Sanders, J. R. (Eds.). (1973). *Educational evaluation: Theory and practice.* Belmont, CA: Wordsworth.

CHAPTER 3

Fundamental Evaluation Issues in a Global Society

Nick L. Smith

Introduction

The world is becoming increasingly globalized, interactive, and interconnected. Economic markets are becoming more integrated and interdependent, mass media are growing with worldwide reach and impact, and we see simultaneous and reciprocal cross-fertilization of ideas, expectations, and influences across multiple national and cultural boundaries.

What are the likely effects of this globalization on evaluation? In ways now only faintly discerned, evaluation is becoming increasingly globalized in that what is done in one setting, nation, or region shapes, and is shaped by, what happens elsewhere. Within the United States, evaluation will also continue to diversify as the U.S. society becomes increasingly multicultural. As a consequence of these forces within and outside the United States, we can expect that evaluation in the United States and the role of U.S.

evaluation worldwide, will continue to change over the coming decades. The evaluation world scene is likely to change dramatically. How do we stay abreast of this shifting evaluation scene, make reasoned responses to emerging changes, and thoughtfully plan for the future?

A means is needed to think about evaluation at a basic level so that as the various forms, theories, methods, and practices of evaluation continue to evolve over time, our essential underlying conceptions can continually be updated to provide a relevant and stable framework within which to consider, react to, and promote change within evaluation. Considering evaluation in terms of underlying fundamental issues is one such means. Fundamental issues are those underlying questions and choices that periodically reemerge as problematic in the conduct of evaluation. Such issues may be settled for a time, but then resurface later as conditions continue to change. Fundamental issues, by their

AUTHOR'S NOTE: Very helpful revisions to prior drafts were suggested by Karen L. Zannini Bull, Ross Conner, Karen E. Kirkhart, Jing Lei, Jim Rugh, Jie Zhang, an anonymous reviewer, and this volume's editors, Katherine E. Ryan and Brad Cousins. My thanks to them. Remaining limitations are, of course, my responsibility.

very nature, are never finally solved, but only temporarily resolved (Smith & Brandon, 2008).

Conceptualizing evaluation in terms of its underlying fundamental issues provides the needed stable reference points for detecting and evaluating changes in evaluation as it becomes increasingly diversified and globalized. Fundamental issues that will underlie the continuing shift in the nature of evaluation worldwide are likely to include such questions as, for example, What is the proper social role for evaluation? What should be the role of government in shaping evaluation policy and practice? Observing how the answers to such questions evolve as the profession becomes more globalized will allow us to chart the shifting nature and direction of evaluation.

First, however, it is helpful to clarify how evaluation is becoming more global. Three alternative views of the globalization of evaluation are considered next, followed by a discussion of how attention to select fundamental issues can assist in understanding and reacting to the changes in the nature of educational evaluation that are sure to come as a result of increasing globalization.

Views of Globalization

As professional evaluation activities around the world become more visible, it is said that evaluation is becoming increasingly globalized. It is often not clear, however, just what is the nature of this globalization. I present here three views of the globalization of evaluation: (a) globalization as Spread—this is primarily a historical account; (b) globalization as Interaction—this reflects, I think, a contemporary and still emerging view of the evaluation profession; and (c) globalization as Ecological Transformation—this view provides a way to envision the multiple possible futures of the evaluation enterprise. These three conceptions are not mutually exclusive, but reflect more a blending over time of the evaluation enterprise, which first spreads to new environments, then interacts with different variations, and subsequently becomes altered in form and

function. Although there are various perspectives from which one could consider the globalization of evaluation (e.g., the practice of individual evaluators), the efforts of national governments (e.g., United States Agency for International Development [USAID]), or the policies of international agencies (e.g., Organisation for Economic Co-operation and Development [OECD], the World Bank), the following review is written largely from the point of view of how globalization is reflected through the growth of professional associations.

Globalization as Spread

Professional educational evaluation has spread and diversified quickly over the past several decades in the United States. The passage of the Elementary and Secondary Education Act of 1965 is often noted as providing a major impetus for the growth of modern program evaluation in U.S. education. Stufflebeam and Shinkfield (2007), in tracing the early development of educational evaluation from about 1930 to the present, note the remarkable progress made by evaluators since the 1970s in professionalizing the field. A number of professional evaluation associations were created in the late 1970s, including the Eastern Evaluation Research Society, the Evaluation Network, and the Evaluation Research Society, the latter two merging in 1986 to form the American Evaluation Association (AEA). At present, the AEA has more than 5,000 members reflecting 41 Topical Interest Groups, as well as an increasing number of international members. Additionally, 24 independent state and regional evaluation groups hold formal affiliation with the AEA (American Evaluation Association, 2008a).

Other professional associations and groups address issues of educational program evaluation in the United States, including the American Educational Research Association, the American Psychological Association, the Campbell Collaboration, the What Works Clearinghouse, and the Society for Research on Educational

Effectiveness, to name just a few. Educational evaluation has grown dramatically in scope, funding, participation, and influence since the late 1960s.

Evaluation of educational programs has spread widely throughout the world as well in recent decades. Bhola (2003a) claims that "educational evaluation, which is an invention of the United States has now been accepted as a normative-professional culture and incorporated in practice by evaluators all around the world" (pp. 392–393). That educational evaluation is an invention solely of the United States is an overstatement. Early forces and important writings leading to our understanding of modern professional evaluation certainly arose in Canada, Europe, Australia, and elsewhere, as well as in the United States. It is probably accurate, however, to claim that Western influence has played a dominant role in creating and shaping the nature of current professional educational evaluation.

For decades, forces such as colonialism, increased economic interdependence, expanding Western technology, and shared professional discourse have contributed to an increasingly globalized, interconnected, and interdependent world. To *globalize* can be taken to mean to become adopted on a global scale (*The American Heritage College Dictionary*, 1997). Thus, we might say that cigarette smoking has become globalized. Bhola (2003b) asserts that the modern globalization of evaluation (i.e., the widespread adoption of evaluation) is largely the result of Western colonialism and its aftermath.

> Educational systems in non-Western countries, almost without exception, were established by the West during the period of colonization, and remain highly congenial to West-driven innovations including planning, management, and evaluation. (Bhola, 2003b, p. 402)

The diffusion and dissemination of the cultural package of professional educational evaluation has been possible through a number of intertwined processes: (i) provision of training of evaluators in non-Western areas; (ii) mandating evaluation of programs and projects supported by Western donors in cooperation with government and non-government agencies around the world; and (iii) promoting professional associations of educational evaluators in non-Western countries. (Bhola, 2003b, p. 404)

Bhola argues that, although the West

> defined and shaped educational evaluation as a discipline ... even more important for inducing and articulating a culture of educational evaluation was the demand by almost all donor agencies, including UNESCO, UNICEF, UNDP, USAID, SIDA, OECD, and the World Bank that governmental and non-governmental agencies, accepting funding from donors, include an evaluation component in the project under negotiation. The evaluations were expected to follow particular models, methods, and formats. (Bhola, 2003b, p. 404)

Thus, a key fundamental issue underlying the spread of evaluation through Western economic influence has been: For whose benefit should evaluation be conducted? Should evaluation promote the interests of international donor agencies or the interests of institutions within recipient nations?

Bhola's account that the globalization of evaluation reflects colonial influences is similar to characterizations of the globalization of other Western professional enterprises (e.g., the global spread of professional psychology).

Professional associations of psychology around the world have had active collaborations since the first International Congress of Psychology in 1889 in Paris. Subsequent meetings of the International Congress led to the establishment in 1951 of the International Union of Psychological Sciences (IUPsyS). Currently with 71 member countries, the IUPsyS promotes international projects worldwide and organizes scientific meetings (International

Union of Psychological Sciences, 2007): The 29th meeting of the International Congress of Psychology was held in July 2008 in Berlin. Cole (2006) notes that "internationalism in psychology has grown enormously over its 125-year history to become more global and more inclusive" (p. 906). But Cole also links the early U.S. and European domination of professional psychology to colonialism:

When the view of the origins of psychology is broadened to include the state of world history as the field was emerging, the domination of Europe and North America in international psychological relations is not difficult to understand. The first congress coincided with the period during which European colonialism reached its high watermark. Several events marked this coincidence. For example, in 1884, 15 European powers (joined by the United States) gathered in Berlin to complete the "scramble for Africa." Colonial powers were officially enjoined to defend and administer the areas they occupied if they wanted other countries to recognize their claims. By 1900, roughly 90% of Africa, 99% of Polynesia, 56% of Asia, and 27% of the Americas were under European colonial rule (and this does not count either Australia or the United States; Sapan, 1906). The United States, in fact, had joined the process of colonial expansion, most notably in the Philippine Islands. (Cole, 2006, p. 905)

In contrast to the long history of the international spread of psychology, it is interesting to note that there currently is no worldwide association for educational research. Professional societies in education appear to be a more recent creation. For example, the American Psychological Association was founded in 1892, while the American Educational Research Association (AERA) was not founded until 1916, and the Australian Council for Educational Research was founded in 1930.

Following meetings in Chicago in April 2007 (American Educational Research Association, 2007) and London in September 2007, representatives of 28 national, regional, and international education research associations met in New York City in March 2008. Having previously approved a resolution to establish a world education research association (WERA), working groups of delegates are presently drafting details of organizational purpose, structure, finance, activities, and representation ("Progress on Establishing," 2008). Important Western influence in the formation of WERA is evident in the selection of the first three meeting sites and the fact that the AERA will continue to provide facilitation and secretariat functions until the organization is formally established ("Progress on Establishing," 2008).

Returning to evaluation, the International Organization for Cooperation in Evaluation (IOCE) was formed as "an organization for evaluation networks and societies that is committed to building a worldwide evaluation community" (International Organization for Cooperation in Evaluation, 2008). Following a joint meeting of the Canadian Evaluation Society and the American Evaluation Association in Vancouver, Canada, in 1995, discussions began concerning the formation of an international evaluation association. Planning continued at the 1998 annual meeting of the American Evaluation Association, with formal presentations by representatives of the African, American, Australasian, Canadian, European, Italian, Malaysian, and United Kingdom associations (Russon & Love, 1999). After additional organizational meetings in Barbados in 2000 and the Dominican Republic in 2002, the inaugural assembly of the IOCE was held in 2003 in Lima, Peru (Russon & Love, 2003).

The IOCE then began a transition period, with an interim board and officers, until 2006. The interim board established operational guidelines and bylaws and held interim board meetings in 2004 in Sao Paulo, Brazil, in conjunction with the launch of the Latin America Evaluation Network; in Kuala Lumpur, Malaysia, at the meeting of the Malaysian Evaluation Society; and in Toronto, Canada, in 2005, when it held its first general meeting and elected its first formal board and officers. IOCE formally began its operation at the beginning of 2006 (International Organization for Cooperation in Evaluation, 2008).

Worldwide professional associations reflect the spread of a professional enterprise such as evaluation, as well as subsequently promote increased global interaction. Thus, one meaning of the globalization of educational evaluation is reflected in its spread and adoption throughout the world, fostered in large part by early Western colonialism and subsequent Western influence on public education in many settings. A second interpretation of the phrase the "globalization of evaluation" suggests its spread around the globe, as well as the increasing interconnectedness and interdependence of its operation. This is more the way we use the term *globalization* when we refer to global warming and the global economy. It is to this latter sense of the globalization of evaluation that I now turn.

Globalization as Interaction

Using the Internet and electronic technologies, professional evaluation organizations are now able to share resources such as journals, presentations, reports, and training and practice materials on a worldwide scale. International communication through e-mail, websites, list-servs, chat rooms, video conferencing, and so on is transforming the nature and amount of interaction among evaluators on a global scale. Geographic distance is no longer a serious barrier; evaluators from around the world can now collaborate on joint projects, serve on editorial boards and professional panels, and participate in professional training (e.g., through online learning courses). In addition, open source technology promises to further reduce financial constraints on professional interactions.

Formal international interactions among professional associations in evaluation have frequently focused on such activities as holding joint meetings (e.g., those between the American Evaluation Association and the Canadian Evaluation Society in 1995 and 2005, as well as recent joint meetings of European evaluation societies). International associations, however, provide additional opportunities for collaborative efforts. For example, the IOCE has compiled 14 case studies of the development and operation of national evaluation organizations and published them as a book (Segone & Ocampo, 2006) as part of a larger collection of materials to support and strengthen evaluation societies. Increasing international interaction is a basic agenda for international associations.

At the core of the IOCE vision is the belief that evaluation as a practice can best be strengthened by the collective and professional efforts of colleagues working together in organized ways. Whether in terms of the development of new knowledge through comparison, reflection and the cross fertilization of ideas; or in terms of the development of skills through training, professional development and the transfer of knowledge, IOCE places at centre stage associations and societies including those fledgling organisations that begin their lives as more informal networks. (Segone & Ocampo, 2006, p. 11)

Another recent example of international collaboration and interaction is the work of the Network of Networks Impact Evaluation (NONIE). NONIE is a coalition of the OECD's Development Assistance Committee's Evaluation Network, the United Nation's Evaluation Group, and the Evaluation Cooperation Group of the international development banks.

Hosted by the World Bank's Independent Evaluation Group, the NONIE coalition is conducting a program of impact evaluation activities aimed at developing a common understanding of the meaning of impact evaluation and approaches to conducting impact evaluation in the promotion of international development effectiveness. (American Evaluation Association, 2008b)

NONIE will be preparing impact evaluation guidelines, developing agreements for collaborative arrangements and identifying resources for impact evaluations. The IOCE has been invited into the process to add developing country and association voices.

As a result of globalization as spread, recent years have evidenced increasing research and evaluation activities that reflect national efforts being expanded into international scope, multinational cooperation, and global efforts by international agencies—globalization as interaction is rapidly expanding.

Bamberger (2000) notes, however, that, despite the rapid growth of international program evaluation, with evaluations of development programs being conducted throughout the world, many U.S. evaluators, for example, are still unfamiliar with how different these international contexts are from the U.S. setting. Further, international development agencies have had a major impact in supporting program evaluation and in developing national evaluation capacity; however,

> International agencies have also had a major influence in the development of evaluation methodologies, many of which may not be culturally appropriate or respond to the information needs of local stakeholders . . . little progress has been made in many countries in developing evaluation methodologies that respond to local cultural conditions and research traditions. (Bamberger, 2001, p. 122)

Smith (1991) has pointed out that, although Western evaluators are increasingly aware of contextual differences in evaluation practices throughout the world, many still seem to believe that some variation of Western approaches can be made to work regardless of the setting.

Ginsberg (1988) has criticized even the U.S. evaluation approaches that emphasize sensitivity to cultural differences on the basis that they treat such differences as if they were simply the same as stakeholder differences in a U.S. evaluation. These authors argue that such a view promotes a Western-based responsive methodology for dealing with differences without recognizing that such differences may reflect fundamentally different belief systems. Ginsberg argues that contextual differences in cross-cultural evaluations require more careful attention than simple modifications to existing Western approaches.

Is it possible or desirable to modify existing Western evaluation approaches to become more responsive to non-Western values and interests or will entirely new perspectives and approaches be needed? How will the evaluation enterprise have to change within the Western contexts as the world becomes more globally interconnected and interdependent? What values will shape evaluation efforts resulting from newly emerging evaluation interactions?

Western values of democracy, accountability, and transparency appear to be promoted by the IOCE. In the IOCE collection of 14 case studies of the development of evaluation organizations, Segone and Ocampo (2006) state:

> Evaluation associations, societies and networks are also a means to ensure the independence and authority of evaluators. Whether in stable or emerging political systems, values of openness, democratic accountability and adaptability—the willingness to learn and improve—must always be cherished and sometimes defended. This is one of the reasons that these case studies often emphasize the importance of democratic organization—the election of board members and officers—and active membership participation in evaluation societies and associations themselves. Evaluators need to demonstrate in their own behaviour the values of democracy and transparency that their work represents. In the IOCE we are aware how important this is to

ensure the growth of successful and vibrant societies. (pp. 11–12)

Viewing globalization as interaction, therefore, also highlights important fundamental issues related to influence and power: Whose values should dominate the formation of organizational structures and policies in collaborative ventures? What is the proper role and level of influence of various constituencies? For example, although financial resources from Western foundations and associations supported early planning efforts of the IOCE, care was taken throughout the formation process that all perspectives were represented and that Western concerns did not dominate the collective agenda. Members of the interim and formal boards represented northern and southern regions, developing and developed countries, and men and women. The first formal IOCE president was a male from a developed country in the north (Ross Conner from the United States and the representative from the American Evaluation Association), and the second president was a woman from a southern developing nation (Oumoul Ba Tall from Mauritania and the representative from the African Evaluation Association).

Although these are the values and procedures currently followed by the IOCE, other international collaborative efforts may view these fundamental issues differently. Another time, another group of international representatives may reach a different resolution, just as governmental policies change with changing administrations.

As evaluation groups interact across regional, national, and cultural boundaries, issues of contextual differences become increasingly explicit and salient. Effective international collaboration requires a sophisticated understanding of contextual differences and the will and means to accommodate radically different forms of knowing and action. International interactions foster the comparative study of contextual differences and the forces that shape evaluation within given contexts. From these clashes of context, fundamental transformations may ultimately arise, and so I now turn to a

consideration of the third form of globalization as ecological transformation.

Globalization as Ecological Transformation

Contextual Forces

Interactions among and across varying contexts may lead to transformations, within those contexts, regionally, and worldwide. This is a view of the globalization of evaluation as the reshaping of professional evaluation resulting from myriad political, economic, and cultural forces interacting reciprocally across national and regional boundaries as a result of the global spread and interaction of evaluation.

If all politics is local, then all evaluation is contextual. As a social enterprise, as well as a profession, evaluation functions across overlapping, complex contexts of operation (Patton, 1985; Smith, 1991, 1995, 1999).

Context matters both in the theory and practice of evaluation. Theory builders and model makers have to realize that their work is context-bound in several ways. First, theory often gets its color from its ideological context. . . . More importantly, and more concretely, theory building and model making are also confined within particular political, economic and cultural contexts (such as England or Indonesia) and are located in differentiated professional cultures (such as education, welfare, or business). . . . Evaluation as practice has to resonate to a multiplicity of layered contexts: the professional culture of evaluators and the institutional culture of the place in which evaluation is [conducted]. (Bhola, 2003a, pp. 391–392)

To understand why and how particular evaluations are conducted, the impact of their results, and their social role in a given setting, it is necessary first to understand the contexts of their operation. It is widely recognized that context shapes evaluation practice (e.g., Russon & Russon, 2000; Smith & Jang, 2002), evaluator training (e.g., Smith, 2002), and professional issues such as the development of standards (e.g., Russon, 2000; Smith, Chircop, & Mukherjee, 1993).

The possible effects of globalization on evaluation can thus be viewed as changes that occur in evaluation as contexts come into contact with each other, changing each other, and creating new contexts that did not exist before. It is important to understand the characteristics of these contexts that are now beginning to intersect.

What have been and are likely to continue as major contextual influences shaping evaluation both within and across regional, national, and cultural boundaries, and how might those influences shape the fundamental issues evaluators will increasingly have to deal with at a local and global level? Major forces that have influenced evaluation around the world include: governmental policies and practices, political ideology, economic stability and pressures, organized religion, military influence, teacher union activities, actions of universities and professional research societies, and funding programs and policies of international agencies, to name a few. Such forces help explain the variety of evaluation forms worldwide; evaluation for improvement in some nations versus evaluation for development or accountability in others, indirect evaluation feedback in settings where public criticism can lead to unacceptable social embarrassment, and gentler forms of evaluation in less judgmental societies. These forces may facilitate or impede mutual adaptation and change as a result of globalization. To the extent that these forces are compatible across different settings, similar evaluation forms may develop; when the history and influences of these forces are disparate across settings, increased spread and interaction are likely to result in transformation.

Although each of the forces listed earlier is important and worthy of extended consideration, such attention is beyond the scope of this chapter. Probably the major influence on the nature of educational evaluation throughout the world has been the role of governmental policies

and practices, from colonialism to the actions of current governments (e.g., in the United States, recent discussions include Berry & Eddy, 2008; Julnes & Rog, 2007; Smith, 2008).

In the United States, Candoli and Stufflebeam (2003) provide a detailed description of the context of educational evaluation, including a review of the basic principles, structure, and governance of U.S. public education. An important influence on the evaluation of educational programs is the fact that the governance of U.S. school districts is largely the responsibility of the states and of locally elected school board officials. Many evaluation and assessment programs are, therefore, initiated at the state level.

> The federal government, in general, has no authority to evaluate the public schools. It acquires control and can initiate evaluations to the extent that school districts violate federal statutes, such as equality of opportunity, and when school districts accept federal grants. (p. 420)

Federal involvement in the evaluation of public education, therefore, arises largely as a result of legislated accountability requirements related to such policies as equal opportunity, desegregation, and affirmative action. Mandated evaluation requirements also accompany federally funded educational reform programs, and thereby the federal government plays a significant role in the evaluation of U.S. public education. See, for example, the insistence by the U.S. Department of Education on the use of randomized control trials in the evaluation of educational programs (Smith, 2008).

In Europe, intergovernmental forces shape evaluation. Karlsson (2003) states that:

> one of the major factors in increasing the use of evaluation on a national basis in Europe has been . . . the European Union's increasingly superior role in governance, which in turn has contributed to the centralization and standardization of evaluation. At the same time, there are forces that

oppose homogenization and wish to guard the right of nation states to carry out evaluations according to their own traditions of public management and control. (p. 432)

Struggles among competing political ideologies that lie behind governmental policies also influence the shape of evaluation. Reimers (2003) argues that educational reform, and consequently educational evaluation, in Latin America in the 20th century was shaped significantly by the struggle between conservatism and progressivism. Karlsson (2003) discusses the tensions in Europe between two political ideologies—new public management, designed to rationalize governmental budget cuts and reduce the public sector; and Democratic evaluation, designed to increase the role of stakeholders in public negotiation and decision making. These ideologies influence governmental policies and are a result, in part, of reduced economic growth and the need to increase effectiveness and reduce public costs. Further, Karlsson suggests that dialogue across growing professional organizations in evaluation nationally and internationally will influence how these ideologies ultimately shape governmental policy. Clearly, the forces influencing evaluation have complex interconnections within and across national and global contexts.

Although globalization as spread can be seen as a form of dissemination, globalization as transformation is reciprocal—the changers become changed. As Western evaluators work abroad, they must accommodate to non-Western contexts. When they return to the West, they bring back non-Western views, approaches, and values. As internationals come to the West to study and stay to work, they gradually reshape Western approaches. When all parties are ultimately reshaped through continued interactions, we have globalization as transformation.

Ecological Transformation

Viewing international collaboration across disparate contexts as depending on negotiated accommodations overlooks the possibility that more subtle changes are likely that will change the fundamental nature of evaluation both within individual contexts and worldwide. That is, future evaluation may become not some variation on an existing form, constructed through extensive deliberations, but a radically new form may emerge, the entire evaluation enterprise may change—globalization may result in ecological transformation.

Such profound changes have occurred in the past:

> Galileo's fateful confrontation with the Holy Office in 1633 is often taken to mark the start of the Scientific Revolution, the moment when a whole new approach to knowledge began to take over the western world. Among the many repercussions of this great epistemological shift was the development of a new "transparent" type of discourse, felt to reflect reality more directly than the elaborate verbal edifices of the Scholastics. Today, the "authoritative plain style", as Lawrence Venuti calls it, is so prevalent in English academic and factual writing that knowledge configured otherwise is rarely allowed past the cultural gatekeepers. (Bennett, 2007, p. 171)

Example: Historical Jamestown. Consider the example of the transformation wrought by the English at Jamestown, Virginia (the following description borrows extensively from Mann, 2007). Although three fourths of the 6,000 people who came to Jamestown between 1607 and 1624 died from disease, hunger, and conflict with the Indians, they eventually managed to establish the first permanent English settlement in North America (Lange, 2007; Mann, 2007). They had settled at the edge of a rapidly expanding Indian empire called Tsenacomoco, ruled by Chief Powhatan, its inhabitants living in villages of a few hundred surrounded by cleared land planted in corn. The English survived not through victory in warfare. They lost most battles, and Powhatan may have decided that the sick and starving invaders would die off soon enough without his intervention. Only repeated arrivals of new settlers kept the settlement viable.

The English eventually managed to supplant the much more successful and thriving Indian society through ecological imperialism. The English replaced or degraded so much of the native ecosystem that they made it harder and harder for the Indians to survive in their native lands. As the colonists bitterly came to realize that Virginia had no gold and that the Indians weren't going to selflessly provide them with all the food they needed, they began to mold the land to their needs. Unable to adapt to this foreign landscape, they transformed it into a place they could understand. In doing so, they unleashed what would become a multilevel ecological assault on North America. Their unlikely weapons in this initial phase of the campaign were tobacco, honeybees, and domestic animals (Mann, 2007).

The English converted much of the land to tobacco production, having replaced the local tobacco with a sweeter variety popular in England that they imported from Trinidad and Venezuela. They imported European honey bees for their honey, and the bees pollinated the new plants the settlers brought with them: peaches, apples, and watermelons. The English fenced the lands that the Indians had kept open for hunting-and-gathering purposes and used it to raise livestock: cattle, sheep, goats, chickens, pigs, and horses. Other than dogs, North America had no large domesticated animals prior to the arrival of the Europeans, and the Indians had no need for fences; now, free-range cows and horses trampled the Indians' corn crops, and feral pigs dug up their underground plants. The forests became more open and dry and lost much of their understory through the inadvertent introduction of earthworms from the plants and ships' ballasts that the English unloaded. Prior to the arrival of the Europeans, northern American forests had no native earthworms—the worms ate the litter under trees that contained needed tree nutrients and changed the nature of the forest.

After 1492, the world's ecosystems collided and mixed as European vessels carried thousands of species to new homes across the oceans. The Columbian exchange . . . is why there are tomatoes in Italy, oranges in Florida, chocolates in Switzerland, and hot peppers in Thailand. It is arguably the most important event in the history of life since the death of the dinosaurs. (Mann, 2007, p. 37)

At Jamestown, the English did not overcome a superior Indian society by force or by the inadvertent introduction of disease, but as a result of their desperate attempts to survive in what was, to them, a hostile environment. The English created an environment suited to their own needs, but one in which the Indians could not sustain their prior lifestyle. The English supplanted the Native American culture, but in ways they could not have foreseen or controlled. "Four centuries ago, the English didn't discover a New World— they created one" (Mann, 2007, p. 53).

Example: Modern China. These examples of Galileo and Jamestown suggest that when disparate contexts clash, the long-term outcomes may reflect radical departures from prior conditions. Further, the complexity of our world suggests that the changing scene is likely to be unpredictable and the process hidden from view except as we are carried along in it.

The growth of education evaluation described earlier, globalization characterized as spread and interaction, evidences an underlying theme of the long-term domination of Western influence in spreading the demand and form of educational evaluation. We know that governmental, economic, political, and myriad other factors influence the nature of evaluation in different international contexts. If Western influence in world economic and political affairs is counterbalanced, or surpassed by say the Eastern influences of China, India, Indonesia, Korea, and Japan, how might those influences reshape the international environment and, subsequently, the nature of educational evaluation? What of the increasing influences of African and South and Central American points of view? Consider just one example, China.

In recent years, China has emerged as a global power and, on many issues, the second most important country in the world. China has the world's longest continuous civilization and largest population—1.3 billion people, or 20% of the world's population. China has between 100 and 160 cities with 1 million or more people, whereas the United States has only 9 cities that size (Dorsch, 2008). In 2007, China contributed more to global growth than the United States; that has not happened since the 1930s, and it became the world's largest consumer, surpassing the United States in four of the five basic food, energy, and industrial commodities (Zakaria, 2008).

The scale and pace of growth in China has been staggering, utterly unprecedented in history—and it has produced equally staggering change. In two decades China has experienced the same degree of industrialization, urbanization and social transformation as Europe did in two centuries. (Zakaria, 2008, p. 38)

China's rapid growth has not been without considerable cost. Cancer, caused by pollution, is now China's leading cause of death (Kahn & Yardley, 2007). Approximately 500 million people lack safe drinking water, and only 1% of the 560 million city dwellers breathe air considered safe by the EU (Kahn & Yardley, 2007). China's pollution problems affect many around the world.

Chinese pollution arrives on the shores of not only Asian countries, but on our western shores, too. Anything that affects China in a major way, now affects the world in a major way. It has one fifth of the world's population and its imprint on everything from the job picture to the environment will be significant in very much the same way that the emergence of the United States affected the whole world in fundamental

ways over the last 100 years. China will be offering a similar story over the next 100 years. (Dorsch, 2008, p. 14)

Such impacts are already being felt. In recent years, the EU, Japan, and the United States have imposed bans on the import of Chinese-produced seafood because of illegal drug residues (Barboza, 2007). There have been similar recalls of other Chinese products, such as toys, pet food, toothpaste, and medical drugs, such as heparin, due to contaminations. Of course, such recalls are common for products produced in other countries as well, including the United States. What makes these stories notable, however, is the global impact of Chinese production. For example, most of the world's supply of the common blood thinner heparin is produced in China (Harris & Bogdanich, 2008; Hooker & Bogdanich, 2008). In the first half of 2007, China exported heparin products to 42 countries and regions (Harris & Bogdanich, 2008). Quality control of Chinese medicines has worldwide implications.

As China works to improve the quality of its products, how will that change the nature of product evaluation as practiced in China and consequently elsewhere? What new forms of environmental evaluation will be needed to help China, and thus the world, with massive pollution problems? In the coming years, China will affect the world not only economically and politically, but also in terms of how evaluation will have to be reshaped and perhaps even transformed in order to solve problems never before dealt with on such a global scale.

Tracking the Globalization of Evaluation

Fundamental Issues as a Conceptual Framework

The globalization of evaluation as spread can be readily documented, globalization as interaction is more complex and difficult to monitor, and globalization as transformation is likely to be impossible to anticipate. How then might we think about evaluation, such that we can understand the forces that are shaping new forms of evaluation and can track them, such as an unseen animal that we know is there, but only by the traces left in its path? I suggest that attention to the fundamental issues that underlie all forms of evaluation is one means of tracking the emerging transformations of evaluation that may arise due to increased globalization.

What Are Fundamental Issues?

In evaluation, fundamental issues are those essential, underlying concerns that shape the function and nature of the evaluation enterprise. Phrased as perennial questions, these issues periodically resurface in need of attention and resolution. Elsewhere (Smith, 2008), I have provided the following examples and description of fundamental issues:

- Why should evaluation be done? To improve programs? To influence decision making? To protect the public? To solve social problems? To promote social diversity?
- What are the proper social roles for the evaluator as a professional? Researcher? Teacher? Advocate? Facilitator? Judge?
- What should we consider acceptable evidence for making evaluative decisions? Causal claims? Moral conclusions? Expert opinion? Aesthetic judgments? Stakeholder consensus?
- How do we arrive at the most valid understandings of quality? Controlled experiments? Moral deliberation? Phenomenological renderings?
- How can stakeholders best be involved in evaluation studies? As served clients? As participants? As collaborators? As empowered citizens?
- What is the most effective way to ensure the quality of evaluation practice? Advanced training? Accreditation and licensing? Consensual professional standards? Mandatory meta-evaluation?

Fundamental issues underlie all areas of evaluation theory, method, practice, and the profession, whether it is communication with clients, ethical dilemmas, cultural differences, preparation of new evaluators, work with special populations, governmental service, methodological difficulties, social justice, evaluation influence, or economic survival as a professional. Fundamental issues are essential considerations of the evaluation enterprise that recur over time. They are periodically encountered, struggled with, and resolved, reflecting contemporary values, technical considerations, political forces, professional concerns, emerging technologies, and available resources. There can never be a final "once-and-for-all" resolution to a fundamental issue. The resolution of such issues is often a point of contention and debate as the profession struggles to shed old ways of dealing with the issue and adopt a newer, more effective position. The attention and effort generated during these struggles attest to the fundamental importance of these concerns to the identity and livelihood of professional evaluation (Smith, 2008).

Fundamental issues are serious underlying concerns or questions, the answers to which shape the form and activities of the evaluation enterprise. As the world changes, the answers to these underlying issues will also continue to change; thus, any contemporary answer to a fundamental issue is only a temporary resolution. The fundamental issue, however, remains.

Possible Fundamental Issues for Global Evaluation

What have been primary fundamental issues of concern among early originators of evaluation thought? A few brief examples suffice as illustrations:

- What are the proper *purposes* of an evaluation study?
- What are the proper *roles* for an *evaluator* in an evaluation study?
- What are the proper *roles* for *stakeholders* in an evaluation study?

- What are the proper *questions to address* in an evaluation study?
- What is the proper *nature of evidence* relevant to an evaluation study?
- What are the proper *methods* relevant to an evaluation study?

Resolutions of such fundamental issues are inextricably interrelated. The selection of proper methods and evidence in a given study is clearly contingent on an understanding of the study's purpose and the questions being addressed. Similarly, the proper role for stakeholders in a study may depend, in part, on the purpose of the study and the role and methods of the evaluator. In other cases, it may be the role of the stakeholders to determine the questions addressed and the methods used. Yet all these issues have to compatibly be resolved in each study if it is to be conducted with structural integrity and impact.

Additional issues arise when we consider the contexts of international collaboration:

- What are the proper models of international collaboration in evaluation? Who controls? Who pays? Who benefits?
- What does is mean to be culturally competent (contextually competent?) in evaluation, to conduct culturally competent evaluation practice? How do we train for and monitor the quality of cross-cultural evaluation? Who does this?

Recognizing that context matters, do we become more explicit in describing in our writings and report the contextual frameworks underpinning the relevance and meaning of our work? Should a description of the context of development and application become a necessary part of every evaluation report, theoretical treatise, and training material? As evaluation becomes more global, should individuals from disparate contexts work together on problems both unique to individual settings and shared across settings? For example, should there be collaborative development of strategies related to such professional issues as ethics, training,

standards, licensure, and certification? Should we search for universal theories or methods of a general form that are adaptable to a variety of contexts, or does this deny the uniqueness of individual contexts?

If globalizing evaluation means decolonializing evaluation so that evaluation approaches based on non-Western models are fully accepted as equally authentic forms of judgment (Kawakami, Aton, Cram, Lai, & Porima, 2008), how might evaluation approaches be developed that reflect such conditions as:

1. power relationships, patterns of information flow, and access to resources that follow familial or tribal lines; for example, in an African context (Chapman, 1992)?

2. group interests that are prioritized over individual rights; for example, in a South Korean context (Smith & Jang, 2002)?

3. greater respect being accorded elders and those with senior authority; for example, in a South Korean context (Smith & Jang, 2002)?

4. the quality of social interaction being viewed as important, or more so, than task completion; for example, in a Cameroonian (Smith, 1991), Caribbean (Cuthbert, 1985), or Maltese (Chircop, 1987) context?

5. written communication that is associated with authority and so used sparingly, with oral communication dominating; for example, in an Egyptian context (Seefeldt, 1985)?

6. ancestry and locating current projects in ancestral place and time being considered important; for example, in a Polynesian context (Kawakami et al., 2008)?

When we consider these non-Western contextual conditions, what resolutions are most appropriate to such fundamental issues as: What is the proper purpose of an evaluation? What are the proper roles for stakeholders? What methods are most appropriate for conducting an evaluation? How will current evaluation theories, methods, and practices need to be transformed to be appropriate to these contexts?

Examining evaluation theory, method, practice, and the profession in terms of fundamental issues provides one mechanism for both charting new variations in evaluation approach and tracking changes in the evaluation enterprise as it becomes increasingly globalized. Whether one views globalization as spread, interaction, or transformation, a posture of flexible responsiveness seems most appropriate as we constantly adapt to local and worldwide changes that will require repeated reworking of our resolutions to these fundamental issues in evaluation.

References

American Educational Research Association. (2007). Inaugural meeting of international educational research associations held in Chicago, April 13–14, 2007. *Educational Researcher, 36*(5), 290–292.

American Evaluation Association. (2008a). *Organization.* Retrieved May 4, 2008, from www .eval.org

American Evaluation Association. (2008b, February). *Impact evaluation: Global networks unite.* AEA Newsletter. Retrieved February 23, 2008, from http://archive.constantcontact.com/fs014/11006 94346064/archive/1101985422983.html

Bamberger, M. (2000). The evaluation of international development programs: A view from the front. *American Journal of Evaluation, 21,* 95–102.

Bamberger, M. (2001). Book Reviews: Evaluation in developing countries: Experience with agricultural research and development. The annotated bibliography of international program evaluation. *American Journal of Evaluation, 22,* 117–122.

Barboza, D. (2007, December 15). *In China, farming fish in toxic waters.* Retrieved December 15, 2007, from www.nytimes.com.

Bennett, K. (2007). Galileo's revenge: Ways of construing knowledge and translation strategies in the era of globalization. *Social Semiotics, 17*(2), 171–193.

Berry, T., & Eddy, R. M. (Eds.). (2008). Consequences of No Child Left Behind for educational evaluation. *New Directions for Evaluation 117.*

Bhola, H. S. (2003a). Introduction. In T. Kellaghan & D. L. Stufflebeam (Eds.), *International handbook of educational evaluation: Part I. Perspectives* (pp. 389–396). Dordrecht: Kluwer.

Bhola, H. S. (2003b). Social and cultural contexts of educational evaluation: A global perspective. In T. Kellaghan & D. L. Stufflebeam (Eds.), *International handbook of educational evaluation: Part I. Perspectives* (pp. 397–416). Dordrecht: Kluwer.

Candoli, C., & Stufflebeam, D. L. (2003). The context of educational program evaluation in the United States. In T. Kellaghan & D. L. Stufflebeam (Eds.), *International handbook of educational evaluation: Part I. Perspectives* (pp. 417–428). Dordrecht: Kluwer.

Chapman, D. (1992). Investigative strategy in international technical assistance projects. In N. L. Smith (Ed.), Varieties of investigative evaluation. *New Directions for Program Evaluation, 53,* 63–74.

Chircop, S. (1987, October). *Evaluation approaches: Utility across cultures?* Paper presented at the meeting of the American Evaluation Association, Boston, MA.

Cole, M. (2006). Internationalism in psychology: We need it now more than ever. *American Psychologist, 61*(8), 902–917.

Cuthbert, M. (1985). Evaluation encounters in third world settings: A Caribbean perspective. In M. Q. Patton (Ed.), Culture and evaluation. *New Directions for Program Evaluation, 25,* 29–35.

Dorsch, M. (2008, February). Why China matters. *State Legislatures,* pp. 12–14.

Ginsberg, P. E. (1988). Evaluation in cross-cultural perspective. *Evaluation and Program Planning, 11*(2), 189–195.

Harris, G., & Bogdanich, W. (2008). *German authorities report problems with blood thinner.* Retrieved March 7, 2008, from www.nytimes.com

Hooker, J., & Bogdanich, W. (2008). *Tainted drugs tied to maker of abortion pill.* Retrieved January 31, 2008, from www.nytimes.com

International Organization for Cooperation in Evaluation. (2008). Retrieved May 17, 2008, from http://ioce.net/index.shtml

International Union of Psychological Sciences. (2007). *History of the IUPsyS.* Retrieved October 10, 2007, from http://www.am.org/iupsys/information/current-history.html

Julnes, G., & Rog, D. J. (Eds.). (2007). Informing federal policies on evaluation methodology: Building the evidence base for method choice in government sponsored evaluation. *New Directions for Evaluation 113.*

Kahn, J., & Yardley, J. (2007, August 26). As China roars, pollution reaches deadly extremes. *The New York Times*, p. 1.

Karlsson, O. (2003). Program evaluation in Europe: Between democratic and new public management evaluation. In T. Kellaghan & D. L. Stufflebeam (Eds.), *International handbook of educational evaluation: Part I. Perspectives* (pp. 429–440). Dordrecht: Kluwer.

Kawakami, A. J., Aton, K., Cram, F., Lai, M. K., & Porima, L. (2008). Improving the practice of evaluation through indigenous values and methods: Decolonizing evaluation practice—Returning the gaze From Hawai'i and Aotearoa. In N. L. Smith & P. R. Brandon (Eds.), *Fundamental issues in evaluation* (pp. 219–242). New York: Guilford.

Lange, K. (2007). Legacy of Jamestown. *National Geographic, 211*(5), 56–66.

Mann, C. C. (2007) Creating America. *National Geographic, 211*(5), 32–55.

Patton, M. Q. (Ed.). (1985). Culture and evaluation. *New Directions for Program Evaluation 25.*

Progress on establishing a world education research association continues at third international meeting. (2008, April). *Educational Researcher, 37*(4), 170–173.

Reimers, F. (2003). The social context of educational evaluation in Latin America. In T. Kellaghan & D. L. Stufflebeam (Eds.), *International handbook of educational evaluation: Part I. Perspectives* (pp. 441–464). Dordrecht: Kluwer.

Russon, C. (Ed.). (2000). *The program evaluation standards in international settings* (Occasional Paper Series, No. 17). Kalamazoo, MI: Western Michigan University Evaluation Center.

Russon, C., & Love, A. (Eds.). (1999). *Creating a worldwide evaluation community* (Occasional Paper Series, No. 15). Kalamazoo, MI: Western Michigan University Evaluation Center.

Russon, C., & Love, A. (2003). *The inaugural assembly of the International Organization for Cooperation in Evaluation* (Occasional Paper Series, No. 20). Kalamazoo, MI: Western Michigan University Evaluation Center.

Russon, C., & Russon, K. (Eds.). (2000). *The annotated bibliography of international program evaluation.* Dordrecht: Kluwer.

Sapan, A. (1906). *Die territoriale Entwicklung der europäischen Kolonien* [*The territorial development of the European colonies*]. Gotha, Germany: J. Perthes.

Seefeldt, F. M. (1985). Cultural considerations for evaluation consulting in the Egyptian context. In M. Q. Patton (Ed.), Culture and evaluation. *New Directions for Program Evaluation, 25,* 69–78.

Segone, M., & Ocampo, A. (Eds.). (2006). *Creating and developing evaluation organizations: Lessons learned from Africa, Americas, Asia, Australasia and Europe.* Lima: Desco.

Smith, N. L. (1991).The context of investigations in cross-cultural evaluations. *Studies in Educational Evaluation, 17,* 3–21.

Smith, N. L. (1995). The influence of societal games on the methodology of evaluative inquiry. In D. M. Fournier (Ed.), *Reasoning in evaluation: Inferential links and leaps* (pp. 5–14). San Francisco, CA: Jossey-Bass.

Smith, N. L. (1999). A framework for characterizing the practice of evaluation, with application to empowerment evaluation [Special Issue]. *The Canadian Journal of Program Evaluation, 14,* 39–68.

Smith, N. L. (2002). International students' reflections on the cultural embeddedness of evaluation theory. *American Journal of Evaluation, 23*(4), 481–492.

Smith, N. L. (2008). Fundamental issues in evaluation. In N. L. Smith & P. R. Brandon (Eds.), *Fundamental issues in evaluation* (pp. 1–23). New York: Guilford.

Smith, N. L., & Brandon, P. R. (Eds.). (2008). *Fundamental issues in evaluation.* New York: Guilford.

Smith, N. L., Chircop, S., & Mukherjee, P. (1993). Considerations on the development of culturally relevant evaluation standards. *Studies in Educational Evaluation, 19*(1), 3–13.

Smith, N. L., & Jang, S. (2002). Increasing cultural sensitivity in evaluation practice: A South Korean illustration. *Studies in Educational Evaluation, 28,* 61–69.

Stufflebeam, D. L., & Shinkfield, A. J. (2007). *Evaluation theory, models, and applications.* San Francisco, CA: Jossey-Bass.

The American Heritage College Dictionary (3rd ed.). (1997). Boston, MA: Houghton Mifflin.

Zakaria, F. (2008, December 31–January 7). The rise of a fierce yet fragile superpower. *Newsweek,* pp. 38–39.

PART II

The Role of Science in Educational Evaluation

Part II, focusing on the *role of science in educational evaluation*, includes evaluation theories and practices emphasizing scientific inquiry. The theories and practices are characterized by rigorous and objective procedures used to obtain valid knowledge that is replicable. Judgments about educational program effects are based on results from experimental and quasi-experimental methods. Theory building and testing complex theoretical relations are studied with causal analysis methods. Such approaches represent the social sciences' cornerstone mode of determining causal attribution or linking observed outcomes to educational policies and programs.

The concept of assisted sensemaking—that evaluation can broaden and extend individuals' natural sensemaking about educational programs and policies—is the organizing concept for Mark's *theory* chapter (Chapter 4). In considering the role of scientific methods in sensemaking, he proposes that experimental methods, quasi-experimental methods, and other variants are one set of pathways to specific evaluation consequences. The two notably different *method*s chapters in this part represent some of the current tensions about what kinds of science-based evaluations yield the best results for educational planning and improving student learning. Steiner, Wroblewski, and Cook (Chapter 5) critically examine both educational experiments and quasi-experiments elaborating on how these methods assess causal efficacy and effectiveness. After considering the role of experiments in evaluating education programs in both the European Union and the United States, they highlight the strengths and weaknesses of the experiment for evaluating educational reform. In contrast, citing the kinds of complex problems, populations, and educational programs currently found in international environments, Chatterji (Chapter 6) calls for a broader science-based evaluation framework—extended-term, mixed-method designs. This science-based framework incorporates a multiphase, multimethod design oriented toward explanatory and confirmatory goals, including the causal contingencies common to complex educational interventions.

The two *case study* chapters exemplify critical tensions surrounding scientific methods in educational evaluation. Henry and Rickman (Chapter 7) illustrate why science-based educational evaluation and evidence-based policymaking is capturing worldwide attention by distinguishing between "what works" from what does not work in early childhood education. Their strong, scientifically grounded design yielded robust findings that illustrate how educational evaluation can influence educational policy. At the same time, Marszalek and Bragg (Chapter 8) show the challenges in implementing science-based methodology such as quasi-experimental designs in complex educational contexts like career and technical education. They identified several obstacles—such as data coordination between agencies with dissimilar cultures, complex legal issues, and the intersection between research and policies—that had an impact on the implementation of their quasi-experimental study on the ground. Datta (Chapter 9) frames her discussion of critical appraisal around her analysis of the notions of consistency and diversity. As she argues, design consistency and uniformity exemplified by science-based educational evaluations are actively promoted by educational policy organizations (e.g., Organisation for Economic Co-operation and Development [OECD]). At the same time, there is a pull toward educational evaluation diversity when considering how to capture the local (e.g., indigenous cultures, Africa). She predicts this tension will lead to changes in science-based educational evaluation and to some evaluation context-appropriate designs used for indigenous populations and elsewhere.

CHAPTER 4

Evaluation, Method Choices, and Pathways to Consequences

Trying to Make Sense of How Evaluation Can Contribute to Sensemaking

Melvin M. Mark

This chapter addresses a pair of related questions. The first, more general question is: What is the role of educational evaluation in a globalized society? A second, more limited question, addressed here in a limited fashion, is: What is the place of scientific methods in the conduct of evaluation? In addressing these two questions, I make several assertions. First, the role of evaluation can largely be captured by the general concept of "evaluation as assisted sensemaking." The basic idea is that evaluation can contribute by extending, enhancing, and checking the natural sensemaking that people engage in about educational policies, programs, and practices. Although this may sound fairly apparent and uncontroversial, commitment to this general idea should help avoid the extreme positions that, as recent controversies have demonstrated, can easily arise in

evaluation theory and practice. Second, evaluation can and, under varying conditions, should have different consequences. That is, the proper role of evaluation is not unidimensional. Third, the road to evaluation's consequences can follow many pathways: By giving more explicit attention to influence pathways, we may be better able to inform research on, theory about, and practice of educational evaluation. A fourth assertion is relevant to much contemporary debate and to the specific question about the place of scientific methods. Specifically, the contention is that one visible form of scientific inquiry—that is, randomized trials and their closest approximations—can play an important role in certain pathways to the desired consequences of evaluation, but that this role is limited in applicability and range, relative to the potential scope of evaluation practice.

Overarching the previous four assertions is a fifth, general assertion—that evaluators' and others' conceptions of evaluation should be a mixture of high aspirations and modest expectations, with less attention given to the individual evaluation than to the integration of the individual evaluation with other evaluations and other reasoning and evidence, with concern about the level of support that evaluation provides for generalizing, and with recognition that there is no single pathway by which evaluation can serve democracy in particular and governance in general—which should not be surprising in the face of the mixed-model governments seen in much of the world.

In the next section, I briefly discuss the concept of globalization, as well as ways that globalization may generally interact with education and educational evaluation. The remainder of the chapter is largely structured around the first four assertions just noted. For each section, a general position is provided (e.g., that the proper role of evaluation is well captured by the idea of evaluation as assisted sensemaking). In addition, in each section, some issues related to globalization are discussed. A final section offers some tentative conclusions and suggestions for further debate and study. In service of truth in advertising, the overall framework and assertions presented here were developed in a Western, predominately U.S. context. Moreover, many of the globalization-related extensions offered here are speculative, without an extensive evidence base. My hope is that, nevertheless, there is some value added in terms of the way evaluators think about the role of evaluation and science-based evidence in their primary practice context and more generally in an increasingly globalized world.

Educational Evaluation in a Global Context

Like evaluation, globalization is a concept about which complete consensus does not exist. Alternative perspectives on globalization focus on the existence and effects of: (a) international or multinational business organizations; (b) supranational forms of governance (e.g., the European Union [EU]); (c) global reach of media, communication technologies, and culture; (d) ideologies of governance shared across many nation-states (such as the new public management); and (e) the use of the construct of globalization as a rhetorical tool (Burbules & Torres, 2000). In this chapter, I do not forge a novel perspective about globalization, nor even seek to stake a strong position about the relative merits of these alternative perspectives on globalization. Rather, I assume that, although globalization is a social construct that can be used to rhetorical and ideological ends, there are real forces underlying the concept. Perhaps at its essence, globalization involves the trend toward institutions, processes, and communication channels that increase interdependence and potential commonalities across traditional nation-states and regions. At the same time, globalization does not preclude national (or other) diversity and specificity; indeed, globalization may engender nationalist or other sentiments (Giddens, 1990; Stern, 2006). In addition, I assume that specific apparent characteristics of globalization at one point in time, such as the diffusion of a particular political management ideology, need not be intrinsic or enduring aspects of globalization per se. For additional discussion of the topic of globalization in the context of educational evaluation, also see this *Handbook*'s introduction, first section, and especially the chapters by Rizvi (Chapter 1), Schwandt (Chapter 2), and Smith (Chapter 3).

Drawing on several sources, especially Stern (2006) and Carnoy (1999), one can suggest that globalization currently has several implications for education (and for other public sectors and types of programs). These include movement toward: (a) decentralization, privatization, and the incorporation of market forces in education; (b) increased demand for educational services and outcomes, based at least in part on concern about labor market needs, but with these increasing demands coming in the face of opposition to increases in public-sector expenditures; and (c) emphasis on outcomes rather than inputs, including cross-national measurement of educational outcomes. Again, at least some of these implications for education may be features of the historical moment, rather than intrinsic and stable characteristics of globalization. For example, moves made to infuse market forces in education may be prevalent at a particular period of time, but could subsequently lose popularity even as globalization proceeds. By way of analogy, deregulation of financial markets has been popular across many countries, but the pendulum could swing away from this trend in response to the economic declines of fall 2008.

Of course, globalization has implications for educational (and other) evaluation, as well as for education itself. Several of these evaluation-related implications correspond to challenges that evaluation has already faced as practiced within single nation-states. Many of the challenges call for a kind of technical response. But other implications of globalization should stimulate consideration of what kind of aspirations we should have for evaluation. As an aside, in addition to thinking about the effects of globalization on evaluation, it is also important to consider evaluation as an increasingly global activity (Donaldson, 2007). In a sense, the forces of globalization have contributed to evaluation being practiced across the globe, and this expanded scope of practice has some notable implications.

Starting with a relatively simple form of potential consequence, globalization may affect the nature of the *evaluand*, the thing that is to be evaluated. For example, if globalization is associated with the spread of school choice policies, then evaluators will increasingly be called on to evaluate such policies. Alternatively, globalization may not lead to a new evaluand, but might lead to alterations of a given evaluand, such as by affecting the *content* of an educational program. In a global world, the study of history may be less homeland-centric than in years past, for instance. Although the emergence of a new evaluand or of new curricular content may make additional work for the evaluator, conceptually

the challenge is familiar and largely involves evaluation design and measurement.

Related to content, globalization can also affect the *criteria or comparison standards* by which educational programs, policies, and practices are to be judged. Rather than judge the merit and worth of a math program in terms of gains relative to an alternative program, for example, stakeholders may be inclined to consider whether the program will help improve the national ranking in math relative to other countries. That is, international competitiveness could increasingly come to replace more local criteria, which could put increased importance on the quality of cross-national assessment regimens. As another example, concepts such as *workforce readiness*, which is meant to represent school graduates' capacity to work in a global economy ("Conference Board," 2006), may increasingly be cited as criteria for educational evaluation. Although shifts in the criteria of merit might seem to complicate the task of reaching summative judgments, the fundamental logic of drawing bottom-line conclusions remains the same (see, e.g., Scriven, 1991).

Globalization may also affect the *context* in which educational policies, programs, and practices are embedded. Evaluators (and evaluation theorists) often refer to "context," although this too often may be done without good theory or a good model that specifies which of the myriad aspects of context matter, in what ways, for particular educational programs. Globalization adds complexity to the mix. Globalization may add factors that become part of the long-term context, such as a focus by policymakers on national competitiveness, as well as more rapid diffusion across nations of trends in governance (e.g., accountability via performance measurement systems). Relatively enduring changes in context can be addressed as long as evaluators recognize the shifts and consider their implications. However, globalization may also contribute new and perhaps more transient forces that interact with educational programs, policies, and practices in ways that modify their implementation and effects. In this way, globalization may tend to shorten the "half life of generalizations"—that is, to reduce the time-frame and scope across which evaluation findings serve as a reasonable guide to action (see Cronbach, 1975, 1982). For example, by leading to more rapid and perhaps more nuanced changes in local labor markets, globalization may make it more tenuous to generalize from a particular evaluation of a nation-state's pilot job training program to the future or to sites not studied. At the same time, globalization may also increase policymakers' and other stakeholders' desires to generalize across nation-states and parts of the globe: If a new style of reading program works in France, they may wonder, why not implement it in New Jersey?

In short, globalization could lead to greater concern about the capacity of evaluations to support *generalizations* to future action at times and locations not examined in the evaluation. Of course, concern about generalization from evaluations is hardly new (Cook & Campbell, 1979; Cronbach, 1982). The point, rather, is that globalization may increase that longstanding concern while making efforts to generalize more challenging. Fortunately, ways to respond to this pressure have already been suggested. House (2001) suggests that early evaluation experiences, including frustrations about evaluation's inability to support generalizations to guide general action, led evaluators to two different kinds of reactions. One was to adopt a more explicitly limited set of aspirations, framing evaluation as a case study intended to enhance local understandings, but not to support enduring generalizations. Stake's (1995) case study approach to evaluation is an exemplar. An alternative response was to infuse program theory into evaluation practice. This led evaluators to conduct empirical tests of the mediators (or underlying processes) through which a program may bring about its effects and of the moderators (or inter-acting factors) that may modify the program's effects (Chen, 1990; see Donaldson, 2007, for a variant). In short, one rationale for program the-ory-driven evaluation is that knowledge about mediators and moderators will provide a firmer

basis for generalization. That is, by identifying how and when a program works, the program theory-driven approach should make it easier for stakeholders to make sensible judgments about whether to apply evaluation findings to new set-tings and in the future.

Globalization may increase the pressure on evaluators to adopt either a case study or a pro-gram theory-driven approach to evaluation, or to explore alternative ways to sensibly limit or sup-port generalizations from evaluation. My specu-lation is that globalization will usually push toward theory-driven approaches given their promise of providing explanatory accounts that enhance one's ability to judge where evaluation findings apply. In contrast, when the forces of globalization inspire nationalization (or other local sentiments), there might be a stronger press toward a case study perspective, with its more cir-cumscribed focus. More generally, globalization could help focus evaluators' attention to the kinds of aspirations we should have for evaluation.

The next section—on evaluation as assisted sensemaking—explicitly addresses the issue of the proper aspirations for evaluation, as does the remainder of the chapter, implicitly. Global-ization may lead to greater diversification of opinions about the proper role of evaluation. Varied opinions already exist partially because different evaluators have drawn on different bases in crafting approaches to evaluation. As Chelimsky (2006) notes, some potential pur-poses or roles of evaluation comport well with classical views about representative democracy. In contrast, other perspectives on the purpose or role of evaluation draw on such sources as con-tinental philosophy and liberation theology (Schwandt & Burgon, 2006). Assuming evalua-tion continues to grow globally, it is likely to draw on even more varied sources to develop practices for varied national and local settings, and to borrow from different spheres of practice that overlap with evaluation. This would seem to suggest the continued emergence of new approaches to evaluation, with different aspira-tions regarding evaluation's role and potential contribution. In contrast, forces of globalization also pull toward sharing and perhaps homogenization. With the ease and frequency of communication and travel across the world, globalization appears to have accelerated interchange among evaluators (and evaluation users) across the world, across more and less developed economies, across centralized and decentralized educational systems, and across older democracies and more recent democracies and nondemocracies. In terms of evaluation, then, globalization seems to be contributing to quicker and expanded conversations about alternative roles for evaluation, both in general and in terms of different national contexts. I return to the topic of alternative, specific roles for evaluation in a subsequent section, following consideration of evaluation's more general role.

Evaluation as Assisted Sensemaking

Humans are natural sensemakers. Indeed, people are so hardwired to look for patterns that they will often see patterns when there are none (Fiske & Taylor, 1991). Making sense of the world also involves making evaluative judgments, which appears to be a natural, often automatic activity for humans (Albarracin, Johnson, & Zanna, 2005). Teachers, students, parents, and other stakeholders do not hold off on making evaluative judgments about educational programs and practices until "the evaluator" arrives. Of course, as considerable research on psychological biases indicates, and as the logic of research design implies, these informal evaluations can be inaccurate. For instance, special education teachers will not see the methodologist's "counterfactual"— that is, they will not be able to observe how well their students would have done in the absence of their special education program. In addition, the teachers' personal investment in the program may lead them to focus on the success cases and to more readily recall these cases when making an evaluative judgment.

In short, although humans fairly naturally make evaluative judgments, these judgments are

susceptible to limited information and potential biases. This observation undergirds a view of the role of evaluation represented by the concept of "evaluation as assisted sensemaking" (Mark, Henry, & Julnes, 2000). The fundamental idea is that evaluation can contribute by extending, enhancing, and checking the natural sensemaking that people engage in about educational policies, programs, and practices. Evaluators have at their disposal a set of tools (e.g., randomized experiments, case studies) and a set of roadmaps to guide them—that is, evaluation theories, approaches, or models (Shadish, Cook, & Leviton, 1991). The tools are human inventions, as are the roadmaps (although one hopes they are inventions whose value has been validated at least by past experience). One metaphor is to eyeglasses, which are a kind of invented tool to aid human vision. A more apt metaphor would involve a set of shops that contain a variety of tools for improving human perception— eyeglasses, telescopes, microscopes, hearing aids, and so on. Evaluation theories or models are kinds of roadmaps intended to help guide the selection of tools for the right purpose. An alternative metaphor, less apt in terms of its connection to human understanding of the world, is of a homebuilder with many tools (including various tools, each for construction, plumbing, electrical work, etc.) and with an architect's blueprint to help guide the selection of tools for specific work in particular places. Thinking about a globalized world adds variations to these metaphors, suggesting, first, that planning may take place for different kinds of buildings in different parts of the world, but, second, that information technologies are leading to rapid exchange of building plans.

What, if any, implications are there of the idea of evaluation as assisted sensemaking? First, it places evaluation practice in the broader context of human judgment and action processes. It readily incorporates the notion that organizational decision making typically is complicated, with information having a limited role relative to values and politics (Weiss, 1988). But it can also accommodate user-focused approaches, in which the evaluator serves the information needs of specific stakeholders motivated to facilitate use (e.g., Patton, 1997). Human sensemaking takes place in a variety of organizational contexts, from strict command and control to the metaphoric sausage-making of democratic governmental processes. This attention to varied contexts is important when considering the role of evaluation within most single nation-states, but even more important when thinking of evaluation as a global enterprise. For example, some parts of the world may be better characterized in terms of command-and-control governance and others less so. In any case, the evaluation as assisted sensemaking approach suggests that evaluation is an aid to judgment rather than a dispensation from it.

Second, the metaphors of tools (created by humans) and roadmaps or blueprints serve as a counter to tendencies that have been demonstrated in past and current controversies in evaluation. Debates too often have focused on gold standards for tools (such as randomized trials), without adequate prior discussion of the more important question of when, why, and how often to use that kind of tool (Mark, 2009). Relatedly, a third potential benefit is that the idea of assisted sensemaking may offer a safe harbor amid any recurrences of the so-called paradigm wars—that is, past debate about the relative merits of qualitative and quantitative approaches to evaluation. Thoughtful humans necessarily (although usually implicitly) demonstrate a combination of realism (e.g., letting someone know whether their paycheck does not come) and constructivism (e.g., recognizing that people have differing views about the priority on financial success), and they realize that action in the world does not require investing heavily in determining the relative priority of these or other philosophy of science positions. If evaluators followed the lead of the people with whom they work in this regard, perhaps excessive recurrences of the paradigm wars could be avoided (Mark, 2003). This could be an even larger contribution amid the increasingly global practice of evaluation—there is likely to be little value in exporting paradigm wars.

The idea of evaluation as assisted sensemaking has several additional implications, beyond the preceding three, for what our aspirations for evaluation should be. Fourth, by seeing evaluation as an aid to, but not a replacement of human judgment, the idea of evaluation as assisted sensemaking argues against the use of evaluation in automatic fashion. This contrasts with the perhaps growing trend for what Weiss, Murphy-Graham, and Birkeland (2005) call mandated or imposed use, in which evaluation findings result in programs being placed on an approved list from which schools or other implementing units can choose. Fifth, direct use of evaluation in decision making is not seen as a good criterion for judging the worth of evaluation. An optician may provide a great set of eyeglasses, with the correct adjustment, comfortable, attractive, and affordable. The optician may even encourage the patient to wear the glasses, noting, for example, the importance for safety while driving. But the patient may not always wear the glasses. Direct use should be the evaluator's aspiration, but not a general expectation. Sixth, the idea of assisted sensemaking suggests sensitivity to stakeholders' natural sensemaking proclivities. Some forms of presentation and certain kinds of information and interaction should connect better with stakeholders' representations and ways of thinking. To take but one important example, program theory-driven tests typically connect better than simpler bottom-line judgments of the merit and worth of a program because the theory-driven evaluation can provide an account as to *why* the program works or not (Donaldson, 2007). More generally, theory-driven accounts offer a form of narrative, an explanatory narrative, which facilitates everyday recall and persistent memory. Consistent with the idea of enlightenment, accounts that are more conceptual may have an advantage over the long haul.

The issue of globalization highlights valuable perspectives and raises interesting questions when applied to the general idea of evaluation as assisted sensemaking. In terms of general perspective, the concept of evaluation as assisted sensemaking can be valuable when evaluation begins as a systematic endeavor in new settings. It helps avoid any tendency to think of evaluation as a technical activity that should replace fallible human judgment. Among the general questions that the concept raises are questions about cultural variations in the ways people make sense of the world around them. For instance, do people in collectivist cultures rely more on interpersonal sources in drawing conclusions about the world, relative to those from individualistic cultures? If such differences exist, how should evaluation practice respond to them? Another question is whether individuals from different kinds of cultures may tend to focus on different sensemaking tasks to which evaluation may contribute. Metaphorically, might those from Western, individualistic societies be more likely to ask the architect to build a new room (e.g., to conduct a summative evaluation of a new program), whereas might those from collectivist societies be more likely to ask for improvements in shared living areas (e.g., to try to improve processes and relationships in existing school settings)? Even simply raising such questions can be valuable because the idea of evaluation as assisted sensemaking provides an overarching framework and rationale for cultural sensitivity, supplementing the contention that cultural sensitivity is good in and of itself. A longer term question involves the extent to which the forces of globalization will tend to reduce any such cultural variations over time— that is, whether globalization will reduce existing differences in preferred evaluation questions and evidence.

Again, the concept of evaluation as assisted sensemaking is not revolutionary. Many practicing evaluators appear to hold to similar views, even if implicitly. Nevertheless, the potential benefits of the position suggest that there may be value in it. As just suggested, one way that the position can help inform our aspirations for evaluation is by the explicit recognition that people interested in educational policies,

programs, and practices have several sensemaking tasks. The needs that evaluation can help meet vary, perhaps across the life cycle of the program (e.g., during initial pilot testing vs. implementation at scale), perhaps as a consequence of the decision making environment (e.g., whether resources and politics allow replacing current programming, whether the culture is collectivist or individualist), and perhaps depending on the person's location in relation to the program (e.g., a parent vs. an Assistant Minister of Education). Accordingly, there is not a single predominant, specific role of evaluation. Rather, in the ideal, evaluators are attuned to a range of potential roles intended to achieve one or more of a set of alternative consequences of evaluation.

Alternative Consequences of Evaluation

The idea that evaluation can have different consequences is a longstanding one, embodied in the evaluation literature in part in the idea of multiple forms of use (Caracelli, 2000; Cousins & Leithwood, 1986). Many evaluators differentiate among direct, conceptual, process, and, perhaps, symbolic use. Early evaluation literature and practice emphasized direct, instrumental use. In the case of direct use, evaluation leads to immediate and specific actions, such as program continuation, expansion, revision, or termination (Caracelli, 2000). Conceptual use, sometimes called *enlightenment* in the evaluation literature (Weiss, 1977), refers instead to more general learning that takes place as a result of evaluation, with stakeholders having an improved understanding of an educational problem or its possible solutions. Symbolic use includes such actions as the use of evaluation to justify a preexisting position or simply to signify the purported rationality of an agency. Concerns about symbolic use were raised in the early use literature; more recently, evaluators have suggested the legitimacy of using evaluation to support an existing position. Process use, a later addition to the literature, refers to use that arises not because of the findings of an evaluation, but as a result of participation in the process of evaluation (Patton, 1997).[1]

In addition to the classic literature on evaluation use, the idea that evaluation can have different consequences has long been addressed in discussions of evaluation *purposes*. The distinction between formative and summative evaluation eventually gave way to the slightly expanded idea that there are three general purposes of evaluation (at least three purposes of evaluation findings, as opposed to process; Patton, 1997): (a) to support policymaking and public accountability, (b) to facilitate program and organizational improvement, and (c) to contribute to knowledge development (Chelimsky, 2006; Patton, 1997). It is possible to connect these ideas of evaluation purpose to the parallel literature on use. That is, policymaking and program improvement represent different forms of instrumental use, whereas knowledge development overlaps with conceptual use. However, a growing set of evaluation theories also suggest other potential purposes for evaluation, which are more difficult to connect with the classic taxonomy of types of use. These include the empowerment of stakeholders, the development of learning organizations, the creation of forums for democratic deliberation, the advancement of social justice, and the enhancement of practical wisdom and good practice judgments. As this list suggests, there is a wide and seemingly growing list of different potential evaluation consequences that evaluators have suggested.

In trying to lay out a framework for tracing the processes through which evaluation can be influential, Henry and Mark (2003), Mark and Henry (2004), and Mark (2006) have attempted to categorize many of the alternative consequences that evaluation may have. The result is a three-by-five classification system, with three "levels of analysis" combined with five "types of consequences." In addition, several specific, potential consequences are laid out in each of the 15 cells of a three-by-five table. Here, selective attention to several of the major categories

suffices, starting with ones that are more familiar in terms of their relationship to the past literature on evaluation use and purposes. Of the five types of evaluation consequences that Mark and Henry note, two correspond to the familiar distinction between conceptual use and instrumental use. In Mark and Henry (2004), "cognitive and affective processes" refer to shifts in thoughts and feelings, such as attitude valence, and correspond to conceptual use. "Behavioral processes," according to Mark and Henry, refer to changes in actions, thus corresponding to instrumental use. Expanding on Henry and Mark (2003), and on the traditional categories of use, Mark and Henry (2004) point out that these two types of evaluation consequences (like the other three mentioned later) can further be differentiated along another dimension. That is, types of evaluation consequences, including cognitive/affect and behavioral consequences, can also be distinguished in terms of three "levels of analysis": individual, interpersonal, and collective. The basic idea is that the consequences of evaluation sometimes involve a change within a particular person (individual), sometimes a change in the interaction between individuals (interpersonal), and sometimes a process at a more macro, organizational unit (collective). For example, the ultimate desired behavioral change from evaluation might involve changes in an individual classroom teacher's instructional practices, the initiation of certain collaborative practices across teachers at the interpersonal level; or the collective-level implementation of a governmental policy change or program-funding decision.

The distinction among these different levels of analysis is not trivial. Evaluators of different stripes often appear to be focusing on different levels of analysis. For example, advocates of randomized trials and meta-analysis appear to focus more on collective change, such as program-funding decisions; in contrast, advocates of alternative evaluation approaches, such as those directed toward lived experience and practitioner judgment, appear to be focusing on the individual (or perhaps interpersonal) levels (see, e.g., Lipsey, 2000a, 2000b; Schwandt, 2000a,

2000b; also see Weiss, 1998, on the distinction between use of evaluation for policy and practice). In addition, as Henry and Mark (2003) suggest, the pathways that lead to individual- or interpersonal-level action may be quite different than the pathways that lead to collective action. Explicit recognition of this perhaps unremarkable assertion might benefit future research and synthesis of studies of evaluation's consequences, as well as contribute to better planning of efforts to try to increase the likelihood that evaluation contributes to action.

Recently, Mark (2006) proposed the addition of another category of evaluation consequences to the Mark and Henry (2004) framework. Mark tentatively labeled this new category as *relational consequences* because it includes efforts by evaluators to modify aspects of ongoing relationships, structures, and organizational processes, rather than behavior or attitude. The relational category includes, for example, such potential consequences as individuals' self-perception of their empowerment (Fetterman, 1996), creation of a democratic forum for deliberation (House & Howe, 1999), and the facilitation of the learning organization (Preskill & Torres, 1998). In general, the evaluation theories (or models) that advocate for such relational consequences generally are more recent, relative to the theories that focus on program-related action and understandings (Alkin, 2004). These newer approaches often tend to view evaluation, not as narrowly concerned with the policy, program, or practice being evaluated; rather, they often treat evaluation, in part, as a vehicle to use to try to bring about other forms of change, such as empowerment or the creation of a learning organization. As a result, many of these approaches may be subject to the criticism (e.g., "But is it evaluation?") from commentators who hold a more traditional definition of evaluation (e.g., Scriven, 1997). They are also subject to questions about whether in practice they achieve their stated relational goal; for example, Miller and Campbell (2006) ask whether evidence indicates that empowerment evaluation actually empowers people. However, these criticisms are not unlike ones that can be applied to traditional views about the intended consequences of evaluation, such as whether classic comparative evaluation designs actually are used in decision making. Although not established in the literature, the relational category or something like it seems useful, in part, because it reminds us that there is a set of potential evaluation consequences that extend beyond the boundaries of the traditional direct and conceptual use.

Globalization suggests some interesting questions that can be related to the Mark (2006) and Mark and Henry (2004) framework of the consequences of evaluation. Many of these have to do with the relative interest in different consequences as a function of the forces of globalization. For instance, the spread of new public management (NPM) would appear to be associated with greater attention to behavioral consequences or, in older language, to direct instrumental use, especially to summative judgment and action. Efficiency is a key value of NPM, after all. Notably, at least some versions of NPM would emphasize the individual level of analysis, in the form of providing information to "consumers" to allow them to make more informed choices. Various versions of school choice policies illustrate this approach, with performance measurement systems that are intended to give information to families, in turn allowing them to choose better rather than poorer schools. Notice that the role of citizens in this model can simply be as consumers who are given information about school performance in order to make better choices. In contrast, other streams within globalization emphasize stakeholder participation. One speculation is that, to the extent that stakeholders are engaged as partners in evaluation, relational consequences may tend to rise in importance. Perhaps this emphasis on relational outcomes would also arise in more collectivist, rather than individualistic, societies. More generally, there is interesting future work to be done about the effects of globalization on, and about cultural variation in, *relative interest* in alternative consequences of evaluation.

Pathways to and Conditions Under Which

As summarized in the preceding section, the potential consequences of evaluation can be extended beyond the cognitive/affective and behavioral to include relational consequences. Mark and Henry (2004) also described two other types of consequences: general influence and motivational processes. However, these two categories differ in an important way from those mentioned in the previous section. As exemplified by the aspirations of various evaluation theories or approaches (Alkin, 2004), evaluation is often undertaken with the objective of influencing cognition/affect, behavior, and relationships. These three are the different, general end-state uses that evaluators (and evaluation sponsors and potential evaluation users) may hope that evaluation will affect.[2] In contrast, general influence and motivational processes are typically of note as the initial or interim steps along a pathway to those targets, rather than as the ultimate target that evaluation is intended to affect.

"General influence processes," according to Mark and Henry (2004), are parts of the "fundamental architecture of change" and "are likely to set into motion some [other] change" (p. 40). For example, at the individual level, the general influence process of "elaboration" refers to a person thinking systematically about an issue. Elaboration is not of interest in and of itself as a consequence of evaluation, but can be quite important as an initial step in generating changes in a person's cognition/affect and, perhaps subsequently, his or her behaviors. As with the other types of consequences, general influence processes can occur at all three levels of analysis. At the interpersonal level, for instance, persuasion attempts are a kind of general influence process. Again, if an evaluation stimulates an interpersonal persuasion attempt, this is not of interest in and of itself, but rather as a possible step toward other change.

Similarly, Mark and Henry (2004) describe "motivational processes" as involving goals and aspirations, as well as human responses to perceived rewards and punishments. Although motivational processes have received limited attention in the evaluation literature, they are likely to be important in pathways to influence practitioner behavior. For example, the theory of change for high-stakes testing regimens, the program theory for charter schools, and efforts to affect classroom teaching by setting or raising standards, all include the presumption that behavioral changes can be stimulated by creating new standards that change the teacher's goals and aspirations.

To summarize the Mark and Henry model of evaluation consequences, it includes five types of evaluation consequences (cognitive/affective, behavioral, relational, general influence, and motivational), each of which can occur at any of three levels of analysis (individual, interpersonal, and collective). One stimulus to the model's development is the idea that the traditional end-state uses—instrumental and conceptual—did not capture the sometime long and complex path through which evaluation comes to have its influence. To take a simplified example, a briefing about evaluation findings might trigger (a) an individual to engage in elaboration of her thoughts about a program, which might in turn (b) lead her to have a more positive attitude toward the program, which might in turn (c) lead her to engage in interpersonal processes such as persuasion to try to affect others, which might (d) eventually contribute to reconsideration of school policy and, ultimately, to (e) collective-level policy change. The metaphor is of a set of dominoes, sitting upright on end, with the first consequence needing to fall and knock down the second, the second to knock down the third, and so on, to reach (or, if the sequence is interrupted without another line of dominoes in the background, to fail to reach) the end-state use, such as instrumental use in policymaking.[3]

The jury is not yet in on whether and how much benefit will accrue from thinking about such "influence pathways." Mark and Henry (2004) suggest, first, that a focus on influence pathways may be a useful guide to new kinds of research on evaluation influence and use; and, second, that consideration of possible influence pathways during evaluation planning might increase the likelihood that evaluation will matter. Thinking about influence pathways could also sharpen our thinking about alternative evaluator roles in facilitating use. For example, an evaluator working for an advocacy group or private foundation might stay involved all along the multiple series of steps in an influence pathway, whereas an evaluator working for an independent government agency might be involved only for a few steps, relying on other actors in the policy process to move beyond the initial steps. There may also be important cultural variation in these norms, such that in one set of countries, government-based evaluations might be expected to stand back after the first step of two in an influence pathway, to facilitate the perception of independence, while in other nations evaluators may have freer range to attempt to persuade. Consideration of influence pathways might also help us think about what might be called *blends*—that is to say, evaluation consequences associated with different evaluation theories that complement each other (Christie & Alkin, 2003), as when certain relational changes facilitated by collaboration enhance the likelihood of behavioral change of the formative evaluation variety (Cousins, 2003).

Attention to globalization suggests several hypotheses that might be tested about pathways to influence in a globalized world. I attempt here to identify four related, but distinctive ways that influence pathways may depend on, or vary across, the globalized world. First, as noted in the previous section, different regions of the world, or different countries, may tend to focus on different potential consequences of evaluation. Imagine, for example, that southern countries may tend to emphasize relational consequences more than northern countries. The existence of different desired end-state uses would imply different likely pathways to them.

Second, the nature of governmental organizations (and other key entities) will require or enable different influence pathways. Nations

with a history of checks and balances between legislative and executive branches offer opportunities for influence that are different than those in countries without such a structure. As another example, informing the public may be more effective in fostering changes in democracies rather than nondemocracies, and perhaps especially in democracies with higher levels of citizen participation. In an example that connects to the view of globalism as involving supranational organizations, entities such as the EU may provide for different pathways to evaluation use than in traditional nation-states. Stame (2008) notes one example, a mix of competition and cooperation, whereby EU member states compete with each other by implementing different educational (or other) policies and programs and then cooperate in terms of the dissemination of the most successful options. More generally, influence pathways likely depend, in part, on the decision-making structure relevant to the policy or program in question. For instance, in so-called development evaluation, a given intervention and, even more so, a given location is likely to receive funding support from multiple donors, including nation-states, supranationals, and private foundations. At the least, this likely complicates the nature of influence pathways.

Third, cultural specifics can greatly affect whether a given influence pathway operates and even what processes exist. As noted previously, collectivist cultures may depend more on interpersonal processes (interpersonal cognition) than on individual consideration (e.g., elaboration) as important general influence processes. In cultures in which face saving is a powerful motive, influence pathways may need to allow for evaluative information to be shared without an implication of blame for any actor. Indeed, a global version of the Mark and Henry (2004) framework might need to be extended to incorporate additional processes that apply in different cultural contexts. Related to this idea, globalization and cultural variation may have important implications for what kind of pathways are and are not effective. For the Maori and many other indigenous peoples, any pathway that does not include intensive Maori input into the evaluation planning is not likely to result in use (Centre for Social Research and Evaluation, 2004). More generally, different localities are likely to have existing practices and networks that afford some pathways to influence and constrain others. At the same time, forces of globalization may lead to greater commonality across sites. For example, the wide availability of web-based information, including information from educational evaluation, could lead to common influence pathways centered on new media. The preceding comments suggest a number of potentially fruitful ways to investigate influence pathways in a comparative fashion. In addition, the current speculations may suffice to indicate that the general idea of influence pathways may serve as an overarching framework for the synthesis of the study of evaluation's consequences across the globe.

In short, evaluation has a varied set of possible intended (and emergent) consequences. These are represented in the classic notions of type of use, the related ideas of alternative purposes of evaluation, and the expanded Mark and Henry (2004) taxonomy of types of evaluation consequences and levels of analysis. In addition, at least in principle, there are many varied pathways by which evaluation may lead (or not) to its ultimate effects. A related notion—that evaluation should have different consequences depending on the circumstances—is not new. Shadish et al. (1991) contended that the third of three stages of evaluation theory consisted of contingency theories—that is, models of evaluation that incorporated alternative approaches to evaluation (as laid out in the prior two theories) and that specified the conditions under which each approach was more appropriate—although one could argue that since 1991, many visible figures in evaluation theory have advocated for the wide use of an evaluation approach, rather than offering increasingly nuanced or empirically tested contingencies.

Nevertheless, most evaluators appear to agree with the idea that the purpose of evaluation

should be contextual depending on the circumstances (Mark, 2009). Different forms of contingency theories exist. For example, some focus on responsiveness to specific stakeholders' information needs (Patton, 1997), others primarily on program stage (Chen, 2005), and others on a kind of policy analytic assessment of the relative likely contribution of different kinds of evaluation (Mark et al., 2000). No single contingency theory is likely to be adequate as a guide to contingent decision making across the diverse circumstances in which evaluation is practiced. A slogan might be, "Even the contingencies are contingent." A worthwhile focus of future evaluation theory development is continued attention to the conditions under which varying evaluation approaches, with different intended consequences, are appropriate. Attention to such questions has largely been within nation or without explicit attention to globalization and cultural variation. Expanding our evaluation theories (or models) to a globalized world and global evaluation practice is a worthwhile effort, assisted perhaps in no small part by the current *Handbook*. In the meantime, however, the general ideas that there are multiple forms of evaluation use and that different intended evaluation consequences are appropriate under varying circumstances serve as a useful backdrop to thinking about the role in evaluation of randomized experiments and their best quasi-experimental evaluations—a notable but certainly not the only kind of method that comes to mind when considering "scientific methods."

Randomized Trials, Debates, and Future Directions

As pointed out in several chapters in this *Handbook*, especially within this section (e.g., Steiner, Wroblewski, & Cook, Chapter 5; Datta, Chapter 9), recent years have seen a growing debate about the proper role of randomized experiments in evaluation, both in education in the United States and in other areas of practice, such as international development. Future historians of evaluation, if such creatures come to exist, will likely ponder the causes and deeper meanings of this debate. They will likely frame it as a specific (if extended) battleground in the longer paradigm wars also known as the qualitative-quantitative debate (on the latter, see, e.g., Reichardt & Rallis, 1994). Future historians of the debate will almost certainly identify as one key stimulus to these battles the decision of the U.S. Department of Education, through its Institute for Education Sciences (IES), to establish a priority for randomized trials in several of its funding programs. In essence, when this priority is used, the rating panels that review proposals give extra points to applicants who propose a randomized experiment. Related to the IES priority, randomized experiments have a special place in the review process at the What Works Clearinghouse (WWC), which is designed to identify educational interventions that have been demonstrated as effective through evaluation studies that pass certain methodological screens (see Gersten & Hitchcock, 2009, for more detail). In education, this emphasis on randomized experiments took place in a historical context that had led some observers to argue strenuously that the field of educational research and evaluation had underutilized randomized trials relative to their potential benefits (e.g., Cook, 2002). The IES priority and the WWC scoring preference for randomized experiments both created considerable controversy (Donaldson, Christie, & Mark, 2009).

Moving beyond the United States, randomized experiments are also the primary method of the evaluations synthesized by members of the Campbell Collaboration. This organization, now headquartered in Oslo, is international in membership. It is designed to prepare and disseminate systematic reviews (primarily meta-analyses or quantitative syntheses) of the evidence about the effectiveness of interventions in the areas of education, criminal justice, and social welfare. As with the WWC, the Campbell Collaboration employs a methodological screen that emphasizes randomized experiments or the closest quasi-experimental approximations. Debates about randomized experiments have also occurred in the context of international development evaluation. For example, the International Initiative for Impact Evaluation (3IE) was created to advocate and guide the conduct of impact evaluations within development evaluation. Although much of 3IE's scope falls outside education, it seems likely that over time a good deal will involve education. Critics of 3IE suggest that it overemphasizes the importance of impact evaluation relative to other forms of evaluation and that it actually is promoting a narrow view of impact evaluation that will give priority to randomized controlled (or clinical) trials, or RCTs (European Evaluation Society, 2007). As the examples of the Campbell Collaboration and 3IE suggest, controversies about RCTs are not limited to the United States. Indeed, rapid transmission of the battle over RCTs could continue and could serve as an example of the increased rapidity with which trends disseminate in a globalized world. In addition, there could be a more specific, globalization-related force at work. Schwandt and Burgon (2006), Greene (2009), and others see connections between support for RCTs (and the more general evidence-based practice movement) and trends in public management, such that the pressure to use RCTs is a manifestation of the globalization of the NPM and neoliberalism. Another way in which the controversy about RCTs connects to the theme of globalization is that we are seeing the creation of notable nongovernmental organizations, such as the Campbell Collaboration and 3IE, designed to advocate for certain approaches to evaluation and to facilitate the use of evaluation results.

Beyond its possible role as an illustration of globalization in relation to evaluation, what is to be made of the continuing and perhaps growing debate about the role of RCTs? First, consider the role of RCTs in relation to the alternative purposes of evaluation and the multiple potential pathways to evaluation making a difference. RCTs are especially valuable for estimating the (relative) effect of a program. For example, experiments are a good technology for estimating the average effect of preschool on school readiness. Such information is most relevant as a guide to action when there is a possible fork in the road. That is, instrumental use of RCTs' findings may arise when the environment is such that there are choices to be made about adopting one program or another. Often these will be collective decisions, such as when a state decides to fund universal preschool or not. Alternatively, they may involve decisions by individual consumers, as when a family chooses to buy a house in one town versus another because of the type of reading curriculum in place at each school district, in conjunction with the family members' understanding of the relative effectiveness of phonics versus whole-language instruction. Whether collective or not, the key point is that RCTs are most relevant when there is a decision to be made about which course of action to adopt.

To better answer the question about the role of this particular scientific method in evaluation, it would be helpful to have a sense of the relative frequency and relative importance of these kinds of "fork-in-the-road" circumstances. Three points seem especially important. First, impressionistically, other potential circumstances for evaluation use seem more common. For example, there may be more opportunities to contribute to improvements of new and ongoing programs than to contribute to decisions about the selection or expansion of new programs or the elimination of an existing program. In education, many policies, programs, and practices will continue for every one being considered for adoption or elimination. Indeed, after a program is adopted, it will likely continue for some time. Evaluation can contribute in many ways in the face of continuing programs, whether in terms of behavioral, conceptual, or relational consequences.

A second point is that the pathway(s) to the use of RCTs may be more treacherous than the pathways to use of other kinds of evaluations. Put differently, when evaluation findings are intended to influence fork-in-the-road decisions (as with RCTs), evaluation may in general be uninfluential, relative to other kinds of uses of

evaluation, such as (modest) program improvement. Again, the pathways whereby RCTs could be influential will often involve a series of steps connecting the evaluation findings to the collective action of a government agency, say, a legislator, ministry of education, or school board. Sometimes, of course, the number of steps along the way will be small, especially in circumstances in which the agency requested the evaluation and has a prior commitment to consider the results. But there will usually be many steps along the way, for example, as the evaluation comes to be known to individuals at some remove from the ultimate decision (e.g., lower level staff members, individuals in the broader education community), and these parties then attempt in a variety of ways to influence those who are more centrally involved in the decision. In any case, especially for fork-in-the-road decisions, decision making is often diffuse, involving multiple parties, and the information from an evaluation may well not hold sway over other important considerations, including values, politics, competition for attention on a limited agenda, and fiscal and other practical constraints (Weiss, 1977, 1988). At other times, the decisions that RCTs are meant to inform are decentralized, as when local school districts rather than a central agency select a kind of program or when evaluation is intended to influence individual consumers' choice. Here the challenges related to the influence pathway involve how to get understandable information to the decentralized decision makers and whether they will use it in their decisions. Limited evidence exists as to how tenuous or robust these pathways are, but at least in one educational programming area (school-based substance abuse prevention programs in the United States), evaluation findings were not generally influential in decentralized decisions in the way that less-thoughtful advocates of RCTs might have wanted (Weiss et al., 2005). An additional complication in the use of RCTs and other impact evaluations relates to the earlier discussion of generalizability. Weiss et al. (2005) found a number of potential evaluation users who felt that the findings wouldn't apply at their school or with their child. In contrast, for at least some other kinds of evaluation, there may often be fewer, smaller steps involved in an influence pathway, and perhaps with less concern about generalizability. This will typically be true, for example, when evaluation is aimed at incremental program improvements and the program staff who would implement the improvements are participants in the evaluation process in their own school.

To summarize, the kind of use to which RCTs are likely to be put may be less frequent than alternative uses, and the pathway to their use may typically be more precarious. A countervailing consideration, however, is that when evaluation does make a difference in fork-in-the-road situations, the contribution can be considerable. It seems likely, for example, that when evaluation aids in the selection of a more effective program (e.g., a better curriculum), greater benefit accrues in terms of children's learning than when evaluation is used to other, more formative or relational ends. Put differently, a kind of risk-reward ratio tradeoff may exist: The likelihood of making a difference is probably lower when RCTs are used in service of fork-in-the-road decisions, but *if* evaluation makes a difference in such cases, the payoff is likely to be greater. In short, the potential role of RCTs and their closest quasi-experimental approximations is limited relative to the entire scope of evaluation practice. But when appropriate, the methods can be quite valuable in providing relatively defensible estimates of average treatment effect (see Donaldson et al., 2009; Julnes & Rog, 2007; Mark, 2009, for discussion of the rationale for RCTs relative to alternative methods for addressing the same questions).

Interestingly, globalization-related forces may be working to try to shorten and pave the pathway from RCTs to use in decision making. It appears that globalization, at least at present, entails a focus on efficiency and on the development of national and supranational organizations that contribute to the infusion of scientific evidence into public decision making. In this context, quasi-independent and international organizations such as the WWC and the Campbell Collaboration, respectively, are intended to hasten the application of RCTs and related methods in policymaking. At the extreme, the idea of mandated use (Weiss et al., 2005) would automate the translation between the findings and the use of experimental evaluations. Mandated use occurs, for example, when potential evaluation users perceive (accurately or not) that they must select approved programs from a list such as that provided by the WWC or from a review such as that provided by the Campbell Collaboration. In an environment in which mandated use could apply, and in which organizations such as the WWC and 3IE are developed to influence evaluation methods and use, concerns about generalization, raised earlier, are especially important.

Looking within the evaluation community, the debate on RCTs also reveals that many evaluators and others involved may far too easily get into debates about methods per se. Elsewhere (Mark, 2009), I address in some detail the desirability of trying to "change the terms of the debate," focusing less directly on methods and more on the underlying assumptions and perhaps more tractable, related questions. Rather than debating about RCTs per se, we might have more productive conversations about such questions as: What is the right evaluation question (or set of questions) in a particular setting? More specifically, what is the potential value of answering the question of a program's average effect? How are the preceding two questions to be answered? In the context of the program and its environment, if the question of the program effects is of interest, how well can the question be answered by RCTs and how well by alternative methods? How does the next evaluation study fit into the broader portfolio of other evaluative work and of relevant research done elsewhere? How are the answers to all of these questions affected by the tradeoffs created by constraints such as budget and timeframe? Expanding on the idea that it would be useful to specify more fully and explicitly the preconditions for the use of RCTs, it may be worth noting that one-size-fits-all approaches rarely work well unless prior work has been done to ensure that all the individual cases being clothed are about the same size. Of course, the recognition that one size does not fit all can be followed quickly by questions about what size fits whom (i.e., which evaluation approach or purposes are most appropriate in which circumstances). No comprehensive response exists, especially for the varied governance and decision settings of a globalized world. But partial efforts exist, including Mark, Henry, and Julnes (2000) and Julnes and Rog (2007).

Thoughtful discussion about the role of RCTs within educational practice would benefit from explicit recognition by evaluators (and others) that there is no single pathway or a single set of evaluation users by which evaluation can serve democracy in particular or good governance in general. This is notable, in part, because advocates of quite different views regarding RCTs cite democratic values in supporting their rather different positions. Henry (2009), a strong advocate of RCTs, cites contemporary theory about representative democracy while describing the benefits that may accrue when democratically elected and appointed officials and voters have access to convincing information about program effects. In contrast, Greene (2009, p. 157), drawing more on a notion of participatory democracy, contends that stakeholders other than policymakers "have other legitimate and important questions" and that the "privileging of the interests of the elite in evaluation and research is radically undemocratic." Rather than advocate for one of these positions or the other, we should perhaps embrace both, in the sense of supporting contingent choices about the best way to contribute to democratic processes in particular circumstances. Notably, most contemporary democracies are mixed model, including both participatory and representative components. Fortunately, there are different possible pathways and alternative possible consequences of evaluation. RCTs may serve some well and others poorly. The hard work is in setting

relative priorities for particular sorts of circumstances. That is a task that involves judgment— judgment that can more thoughtfully be made drawing on the varied perspectives and evaluation approaches represented in this *Handbook*.

Conclusion

This chapter began with two questions: What is the role of educational evaluation in a globalized society? What is the place of scientific methods in the conduct of evaluation? For the first question, I suggest that an answer can be given in a general sense. Evaluation's role is to assist human sensemaking about educational policies, programs, and practices. One hopes that this role is in service of others' capacity to have better understanding, engage in more productive action, make better decisions, and participate in more effective relationships and arrangements. This perspective, although seemingly noncontroversial, can have several benefits. These include serving as a counterweight to rigid and technocratic implementation of evaluation use, contributing another conceptual framework in support of cultural sensitivity (especially in terms of variations of sensemaking goals and practices), and pulling us away from the extremities of gold standard arguments.

A more specific answer to the question of evaluation's role is difficult to give because evaluation can and should play many roles. There are many legitimate "targets" for evaluation to try to hit. Several of these are captured in the classic notions of types of evaluation use and alternative purposes of evaluation. Others have emerged more recently as evaluation theory and practice have expanded. Many of these recent candidates fall in the new category of "relational" consequences. Additional roles can be expected to develop as the practice of evaluation continues and as new lines of thought and lessons from other practice areas are incorporated and adapted into evaluation—a circumstance more likely to occur as globalization speeds the intersection of ideas and actors from around the world. Of course, to say that evaluation can play many legitimate roles may call to mind this question: Under what conditions should each role take priority? I have not attempted to give a detailed answer to this question here. In part, the answer may vary across settings, with different sets of relative priorities in places with different traditions and governance structures. In part, the answer about more detailed evaluation roles is a matter to be resolved, always tentatively and temporarily, by way of the same processes that guide program and policy decisions.

For the second question—What is the place of scientific methods in the conduct of evaluation?—the best answer is somewhat nuanced. This chapter has not attempted to cover the entire range of scientific methods as they apply to evaluation or even to wrestle comprehensively with what *scientific methods* means. Instead, the focus here has been on a particular method, randomized trials, as well as their closest quasi-experimental approximations. RCTs are worth special attention, in that they clearly fall into the category that people have in mind when they refer to scientific methods, and they have been the source of considerable controversy that could continue to spread globally. I have argued that RCTs have a potentially quite valuable contribution to certain potential influence pathways that can be triggered by evaluation; however, these RCT-related pathways are probably in a minority and are often tenuous, relative to the many other varied pathways by which evaluation can contribute to assisted sensemaking and action. A judgment about the sensibility of conducting an RCT in a particular circumstance should be, in the best sense of the term, a judgment based on careful consideration of the potential contribution of this method for evaluation relative to other approaches, in light of the sensemaking needs of various stakeholders that evaluation might assist.

Allegiance to evaluation as an aid to human sensemaking implies a kind of modesty. Humans do not have access to what philosophers sometimes call the God's eye view. Nor do evaluators

have access to a God's eye view of how evaluation should be done. Nor do we have a God's eye view of the future directions of globalization and its longer term effects on education and educational evaluation. Modesty is also called for when we consider the multitude of forces that can affect the attitudes, actions, and relations that evaluation is intended to influence. But modesty in expectations is not the same as limited aspirations. Evaluation aspires to make a difference in the world. This is a noble enterprise even as we move with some degree of uncertainty in our collective efforts to do it better.

Notes

1. Process use can be seen as categorically different from instrumental or conceptual use. Process use is defined by the *source* of evaluation's influence, specifically the process of participating in an evaluation, rather than evaluation findings. However, participation in the evaluation process presumably could contribute to changes in understandings (i.e., conceptual use) or actions (i.e., instrumental use; Henry & Mark, 2003).

2. Although the language here suggests a priori intentionality, such preferences can be emergent, implicit, and subject to dissension.

3. The metaphor of a single string of dominoes is misleading in its simplicity. There may be multiple pathways emanating from a single evaluation, diverging and connecting. In addition, influence pathways related to the evaluation may have other sources. Pathways independent of the evaluation may be operating, including ones going in the opposite direction. Such is the limit of simple metaphors.

References

Albarracin, D., Johnson, B. T., & Zanna, M. P. (2005). *The handbook of attitudes.* New York: Routledge.

Alkin, M. (Ed.). (2004). *Evaluation roots: Tracing theorists' views and influences.* Thousand Oaks, CA: Sage.

Burbules, N. C., & Torres, C. A. (2000). Globalization and education: An introduction. In N. C. Burbules & C. A. Torres (Eds.), *Globalization and education: Critical perspectives* (pp. 1–26). New York: Routledge.

Caracelli, V. J. (2000). Evaluation use at the threshold of the twenty-first century. In V. Caracelli & H. Preskill (Eds.), The expanding scope of evaluation use. *New Directions for Evaluation, 88,* 99–111. San Francisco, CA: Jossey-Bass.

Carnoy, M. (1999). *Globalization and education reform: What planners need to know.* Paris: United Nations Educational, Scientific and Cultural Organization.

Centre for Social Research and Evaluation. (2004). *Guidelines for research and evaluation with Māori.* Wellington, NZ: Ministry for Social Development.

Chelimsky, E. (2006). The purposes of evaluation in a democratic society. In I. F. Shaw, J. C. Greene, & M. M. Mark (Eds.), *The SAGE handbook of evaluation* (pp. 33–55). London: Sage.

Chen, H.-t. (1990). *Theory-driven evaluations.* Thousand Oaks, CA: Sage.

Chen, H.-t. (2005). *Practical program evaluation: Assess and improve planning, implementation, and effectiveness.* Thousand Oaks, CA: Sage.

Christie, C. A., & Alkin, M. C. (2003). The user-oriented evaluator's role in formulating a program theory: Using a theory-driven approach. *American Journal of Evaluation, 24*(3), 373–385.

Conference Board, Partnership for 21st Century Skills, Corporate Voices for Working Families, and Society for Human Resource Management. (2006). *The Workforce Readiness Report Card.* Retrieved September 2008 from http://www.21st centuryskills.org/documents/FINAL_REPORT_ PDF09-29-06.pdf

Cook, T. D. (2002). Randomized experiments in educational policy research: A critical examination of the reasons the educational evaluation community has offered for not doing them. *Educational Evaluation and Policy Analysis, 24,* 175–199.

Cook, T. D., & Campbell, D. T. (1979). *Quasi-experimentation: Design and analysis issues for field settings.* Chicago, IL: Rand McNally.

Cousins, J. B. (2003). Utilization effects of participatory evaluation. In T. Kelligan & D. L. Stufflebeam (Eds.), *International handbook of educational evaluation* (pp. 245–266). Dordrecht: Kluwer.

Cousins, J. B., & Leithwood, K. A. (1986). Current empirical research on evaluation utilization. *Review of Educational Research, 56*(3), 331–364.

Cronbach. L. J. (1975). Beyond the two disciplines of scientific psychology. *American Psychologist, 30,* 116–127.

Cronbach, L. J. (1982). *Designing evaluations of educational and social programs.* San Francisco, CA: Jossey-Bass.

Donaldson, S. I. (2007). *Program theory-driven evaluation science: Strategies and applications.* New York: Routledge.

Donaldson, S. I., Christie, T. C., & Mark, M. M. (Eds.). (2009). *What counts as credible evidence in applied research and evaluation practice?* Thousand Oaks, CA: Sage.

European Evaluation Society. (2007). *EES statement: The importance of a methodologically diverse approach to impact evaluation—specifically with respect to development aid and development interventions.* Retrieved August 1, 2008, at http://www.europeanevaluation.org/down load/?noGzip=1&id=1969403

Fetterman, D. M. (1996). *Foundations of empowerment evaluation.* Thousand Oaks, CA: Sage.

Fiske, S. T., & Taylor, S. E. (1991). *Social cognition* (2nd ed.). New York: Longman.

Gersten, R., & Hitchcock, J. (2009). What is credible evidence in evaluation? The role of the What Works Clearinghouse in informing the process. In S. Donaldson, T. C. Christie, & M. M. Mark (Eds.), *What counts as credible evidence in applied research and evaluation practice?* (pp. 78–95). Thousand Oaks, CA: Sage.

Giddens, A. (1990). *The consequences of modernity.* Cambridge: Polity Press.

Greene, J. C. (2009). Evidence as "proof" and evidence as "inkling." In S. Donaldson, T. C. Christie, & M. M. Mark (Eds.), *What counts as credible evidence in applied research and evaluation practice?* (pp. 153–167). Thousand Oaks, CA: Sage.

Henry, G. T. (2009). When getting it right matters: The case for high quality policy and program impact. In S. Donaldson, T. C. Christie, & M. M. Mark (Eds.), *What counts as credible evidence in applied research and evaluation practice?* (pp. 32–50). Thousand Oaks, CA: Sage.

Henry, G. T., & Mark, M. M. (2003). Beyond use: Understanding evaluation's influence on attitudes and actions. *American Journal of Evaluation, 24,* 294–314.

House, E., & Howe, K. (1999). *Values in evaluation and social research.* Thousand Oaks, CA: Sage.

House, E. R. (2001). Unfinished business: Causes and values. *American Journal of Evaluation, 22,* 309–315.

Julnes, G., & Rog, D. (Eds.). (2007). Informing federal policies on evaluation methodology: Building the evidence base for method choice in government sponsored evaluations. *New Directions for Evaluation*. San Francisco, CA: Jossey-Bass.

Lipsey, M. W. (2000a). Meta-analysis and the learning curve in evaluation practice. *American Journal of Evaluation, 21*, 207–212.

Lipsey, M. W. (2000b). Method and rationality are not social diseases. *American Journal of Evaluation, 21*, 221–223.

Mark, M. M. (2003). Program evaluation. In S. A. Schinka & W. Velicer (Eds.), *Comprehensive handbook of psychology* (Vol. 2, pp. 323–347). New York: Wiley.

Mark, M. M. (2006). *The consequences of evaluation: Theory, research, and practice.* Presidential address at the annual meeting of the American Evaluation Association, Portland, OR.

Mark, M. M. (2009). Credible evidence: Changing the terms of the debate. In S. Donaldson, T. C. Christie, & M. M. Mark (Eds.), *What counts as credible evidence in applied research and evaluation practice?* (pp. 214–238). Thousand Oaks, CA: Sage.

Mark, M. M., & Henry, G. T. (2004). The mechanisms and outcomes of evaluation influence. *Evaluation, 10*(1), 35–57.

Mark, M. M., Henry, G. T., & Julnes, G. (2000). *Evaluation: An integrated framework for understanding, guiding, and improving policies and programs.* San Francisco, CA: Jossey-Bass.

Miller, R. L., & Campbell, R. (2006). Taking stock of empowerment evaluation: An empirical review. *American Journal of Evaluation, 27*, 296–319.

Patton, M. Q. (1997). *Utilization-focused evaluation: The new century text.* Thousand Oaks, CA: Sage.

Preskill, H., & Torres, R. (1998). *Evaluative inquiry for organizational learning.* Thousand Oaks, CA: Sage.

Reichardt, C. S., & Rallis, S. F. (1994). The qualitative-quantitative debate. *New Directions for Program Evaluation 61.* San Francisco, CA: Jossey-Bass.

Schwandt. T. A. (2000a). Further diagnostic thoughts on what ails evaluation practice. *American Journal of Evaluation, 21*, 225–229.

Schwandt, T. A. (2000b). Meta-analysis and everyday life: The good, the bad, and the ugly. *American Journal of Evaluation, 21*, 213–219.

Schwandt, T. A., & Burgon, H. (2006). Evaluation and the study of lived experience. In I. F. Shaw, J. C. Greene, & M. M. Mark (Eds.), *The SAGE handbook of evaluation* (pp. 33–55). London: Sage.

Scriven, M. S. (1991). *Evaluation thesaurus* (4th ed.). Thousand Oaks, CA: Sage.

Scriven, M. S. (1997). Empowerment evaluation revisited. *Evaluation Practice, 18*, 165–175.

Shadish, W. R., Cook, T. D., & Leviton, L. C. (1991). *Foundations of program evaluation: Theories of practice.* Newbury Park, CA: Sage.

Stake, R. E. (1995). *The art of case study research.* Thousand Oaks, CA: Sage.

Stame, N. (2008). *Evaluation and policy implementation in multi-level governance.* Keynote address at the European Evaluation Society meeting, Lisbon, Portugal.

Stern, E. (2006). Contextual challenges for evaluation practice. In I. F. Shaw, J. C. Greene, & M. M. Mark (Eds.), *The SAGE handbook of evaluation* (pp. 292–314). London: Sage.

Weiss, C. H. (Ed.). (1977). *Using social research in public policy making.* Lexington, MA: Lexington Books.

Weiss, C. H. (1988). Evaluation for decisions: Is anybody there? Does anybody care? *Evaluation Practice, 9*(1), 5–20.

Weiss, C. H. (1998). Improving the use of evaluations: Whose job is it anyway? *Advances in Educational Productivity, 7*, 263–276.

Weiss, C. H., Murphy-Graham, E., & Birkeland, S. (2005). An alternative route to policy influence: How evaluations affect D.A.R.E. *American Journal of Evaluation, 26*, 12–30.

CHAPTER 5

Randomized Experiments and Quasi-Experimental Designs in Educational Research

Peter M. Steiner, Angela Wroblewski, and Thomas D. Cook

Introduction

Since the 1960s, nearly all highly industrialized societies have sought to improve the performance of school systems. Measures taken to support that goal are many and diverse, including evaluating what these educational reform efforts have achieved. So causal investigations are central to educational evaluation, and the main issue is: What form should these evaluations take? Are randomized experiments still the gold standard in causal inference and are quasi-experimental designs as good as randomized experiments? This chapter deals mainly with the use of randomized experiments to assess causal efficacy and effectiveness (Flay, 1986), but also considers some of the strongest quasi-experimental designs (Shadish, Cook, & Campbell, 2002). Although quasi-experimental designs are often recommended for educational

evaluations, their empirical justification is inferior to that of the experiment. Within-study comparisons have shown that quasi-experiments regularly fail to reproduce experimental results (Cook, Shadish, & Wong, 2008; Glazerman, Levy, & Myers, 2003) unless the assignment mechanism into treatment is completely known (regression discontinuity design) or extensively and reliably measured. Examples of quasi-experiments meeting this standard include nonequivalent control group designs with plausible theories of selection into treatment versus control states and extensive and reliable measurements of this selection process (Shadish, Clark, & Steiner, 2008; Steiner, Cook, Shadish, & Clark, under review). But even in these cases, randomized experiments are still more efficient and rely on fewer and clearer assumptions than quasi-experimental methods. Policymakers and evaluators in the fields of education are well advised to stick to experiments whenever possible. However, if experiments cannot be conducted, strong quasi-experimental designs are still possible, and we outline the best warranted of them. A slight trend toward quasi-experimental methods has recently been observed. The American Educational Research Association (AERA) has edited a book outlining strong quasi-experiments (Schneider, Carnoy, Kilpatrick, Schmidt, & Shavelson, 2007), and even the Institute for Educational Sciences now supports more use of regression discontinuity and matched group designs. This also holds for the European Union (EU; European Commission, 2004). Finally, the increasing international coordination in educational planning and policy, which has proved so effective in descriptive monitoring like in PISA and TIMMS, will likely be extended to cover summative causal outcome evaluation. This will probably mean closer coordination of experimental and quasi-experimental practices across nations.

The chapter is organized as follows. After a brief description of the underlying concept of causation, the justifications of randomized experiments as well as quasi-experimental designs are discussed. Then we focus on the reasons that experimental designs are relatively rare in educational evaluation. First, we consider the role of experimentation in the context of the evaluation tradition, particularly in the United States and the EU. Then reservations about using experiments in educational evaluations are discussed in some detail, thereby revealing the strengths and limitations of randomized experiments.

Causation

In modern sciences, the notion of causality has been strongly affected by David Hume and John Stuart Mill. Hume discussed three main conditions for causation: (a) The cause and effect have to be in spatial and temporal contiguity, (b) the cause should occur prior to the effect, and (c) the cause and effect are constantly conjoined (i.e., they are perfectly correlated). The dependence of causation on counterfactuals also goes back to

Hume, who asked: What would have happened if the cause had not been there—for instance, how student performance might have been without a specific intervention? The implication is that a causal effect can only be claimed with reference to some kind of a control condition. Mill took up some of the same ideas as Hume, but in a way that pointed more explicitly toward the necessity for linking cause to variation in what happens when a cause is present or absent (hence to control groups) and to the advantages of studying active intrusions into an ongoing process. According to Mill, a causal relationship may exist if (a) the cause precedes the effect, (b) the cause is related to the effect, and (c) no plausible alternative explanation for the effect exists other than the cause (i.e., all other competing causes can be ruled out). Active intrusion helps with the first and last of these conditions.

The clear identification of causal relationships is difficult because a given effect may be produced by different causes or by a complex interplay of multiple causes. It may also depend on specific conditions in the setting where the research takes place. In practice, we cannot identify all of these other causal circumstances especially as concerns how they relate to each other. Therefore, it might be more accurate to refer to the causes that educational evaluators typically study as *inus* conditions—as "an *insufficient* but *nonredundant* part of an *unnecessary* but *sufficient* condition" (Mackie, 1974, p. 62; italics original). To envisage this, consider increasing the number of school days per year (cause) in order to improve student performance (effect). In some applications, more school days can increase performance and so is sufficient for it. But it is not necessary for a performance increase because other mechanisms can achieve this end. Even in a particular application that increases performance, to add days does not by itself cause performance to rise because the children also have to be attentive and the additional time also has to be spent in effective instruction. However, increasing the number of days is not the same as creating attention or having more effective instruction, and so it is a nonredundant part of what is sufficient for increasing performance. The implication here is that a full explanation of any causal relationship is necessarily context-dependent and that many factors are usually required for a given cause-effect relationship to occur. This renders causation a probabilistic rather than a deterministic concept. A cause (i.e., *inus* condition) does not always lead to an effect; it merely increases the probability that it will occur.

During the 20th century, statisticians—with Neyman (1923/1990), Rubin (1974, 1978, 1986), and Holland (1986) at the forefront—developed a formal model of causation that is closely related to experimentation. It is now generally known as the Rubin Causal Model (RCM). Rubin explicitly defined the causal effect as the difference between what would have happened, for instance, to students under the treatment condition and what would have happened to these same students in the counterfactual or control situation (i.e., without intervention, but under identical circumstances). RCM can be characterized by three main characteristics (Holland, 1986). First, it refers to the *effect of a cause* and not to the cause of a given effect. Second, the effect of a cause is always *relative* to another cause—the counterfactual, so that both a treatment and contrast are required to define a cause-effect relation. Third, only *manipulable* events can be a cause ("no causation without manipulation"; Holland, 1986). In this theory, events and attributes that cannot be manipulated in practice or in theory (e.g., weather or student's age and sex) cannot be causes.

This RCM theory leads to a fundamental problem of causal inference: It is not possible to expose a student, class, or school to the treatment and control condition under exactly the same circumstances at exactly the same time. So the most appropriate counterfactual is not possible—the same unit (e.g., the same student) being simultaneously exposed to both the treatment and control condition. Nonetheless, three main research strategies are commonly considered to justify causal inference, although each requires assumptions:

1. Within-subject designs measure each experimental unit under the treatment and control condition, not simultaneously but successively. Unfortunately, within-subject designs are rarely useful in education unless they are linked to other methods for enhancing causal conclusions. This is primarily because students typically mature over time, and this maturation is confounded with treatment effects, particularly when performance is measured only at pretest and again at posttest. Moreover, it is not reasonable to expose someone to a control condition after a treatment one if there is any reason to expect that the original treatment effect will persist over time.

2. Matching designs seek to pair nearly identical units before or after assigning them to the treatment and control conditions. But it has not yet been possible to identify matching techniques that consistently re-create the same results as experiments. This is primarily because of the possibility of unmeasured differences between groups that might be correlated with the outcome (for a summary, see Glazerman et al., 2003).

3. Random assignment seeks to create treatment and control groups that, on average, are identical with respect to all measured and unmeasured variables save the treatment they receive. Randomized experiments, also known as randomized clinical or controlled trial (RCT), have a clear theoretic warrant in statistics, and they are routinely used today in many sectors other than education, in clinical or agricultural research, for instance. If certain transparent assumptions are met, we know that randomized experiments generate unbiased causal inference.

Random assignment entails using the equivalent of a fair coin toss to create two or more initially equivalent groups. The intervention under consideration is then assigned to the treatment group, whereas the control group is exposed to something else—often no explicit treatment, but sometimes a qualitatively different one. Randomization ensures that, prior to treatment, both groups will be on average equal in all measured and unmeasured variables. Consequently, if an experiment is properly implemented initially and then maintained over time, any observed group differences at the end of a study can be reasonably attributed to the intervention; they are not likely to be due to selection, thanks to the random assignment process. But this particular counterfactual is not perfect. *Individual* causal effects cannot be estimated, only *average* ones—thanks to the random assignment equating treatment and control groups on average. In Rubin's conceptualization, the causal effect of an experiment is defined by the difference between the average outcome of the treatment and control groups.

RCM offers us a clear but restrictive formal conceptualization of cause. It focuses solely on causal description (i.e., ascertaining the average effect of a presumed cause). It does not seek to explain any of the causal mechanisms through which cause and effect are related, nor can it deal with a large number of contingency variables that limit the conditions under which a cause and an effect are related. Moreover, cause only refers to potentially manipulable events and excludes non-manipulable ones that are central for causal explanation in some social sciences. Of course, RCM was never intended to be a model of causal explanation, nor was it intended to be so general as to apply to all the everyday life contexts where causation is invoked. Nonetheless, due to its clarity and strength, RCM is the predominant model of causal description. The following discussion of experiments and quasi-experimental designs strongly sticks to this causal model.

Causation and Experiments

Experiments are well suited for inferring causal relationships because (a) the presumed cause (treatment) is manipulated, making it easy to know that the cause precedes the effect in time; (b) covariation between the treatment and outcome can be readily observed; and (c) the treatment and control groups are treated identically in every way other than for treatment assignment, thus ruling out all alternative interpretations when certain assumptions are met. These are quite transparent assumptions because one can readily observe whether the groups were initially similar, whether there has been differential attrition from the study, and whether there is contamination between the treatment and control groups. No nonexperimental method matches the experiment on all of these characteristics that promote stable causal inference.

Some assumptions are crucial even when an experiment is done. The key ones are the following. First, randomization must be successfully implemented. For instance, if members of the administrative staff responsible for the assignment of students, classes, or schools overrule the random process, then a selection bias may emerge that corrupts causal effect estimates by confounding them with a potential selection effect. Second, because randomization equates treatment and control group "on average," detectable group differences may occur within probability limits, particularly when the number of sampled units is low and so unhappy randomization may result even from a proper randomization procedure. Third, random assignment controls for selection, but selection is only one of the many threats to internal validity on Cook and Campbell's (1979) list. So we have to add the further assumption that the treatment and control conditions are treated similarly in all ways other than treatment assignment, particularly in the ways that observation and measurement take place. Fourth, it is assumed that there is no differential attrition between the treatment and control groups. Attrition may occur when parents take their children out of the program or when students change schools. If the pattern of attrition differs by group, then a selection confound is introduced. Finally, neither the random assignment procedure nor the treatment or nontreatment other students (classes, schools) receive should affect a student's outcome. This assumption, often called the stable-unit-treatment-value-assumption (SUTVA), is violated if, for instance, some control students seek to compensate for not receiving the planned treatment or if some intervention students do not faithfully comply with the program details. To achieve SUTVA, it is advisable to implement the experiment in a way such that students and teachers do not become aware of the specific treatment or control condition to which they were not assigned. This can often be achieved by selecting treatment and control classes from different schools and districts.

These assumptions are small in number, testable, and intuitively clear to theorists and practitioners of educational evaluation alike. Moreover, the long tradition of experimentation has led to developing strategies that protect against the violation of assumptions by learning both how to prevent them from occurring and how to deal with them if they should occur and are not extreme (see Cook & Campbell, 1979; Shadish et al., 2002).

Quasi-Experimental Designs

For ethical, practical, legal, or political reasons, randomized experiments are sometimes hard or impossible to implement. Many of the nonexperimental methods are exclusively correlational, making it difficult to know which of the correlated variables is the cause and which is the effect given the ambiguity of temporal precedence. Moreover, correlational relationships may be due to a confounding variable correlated with both the cause and the effect—the reason for the cliché that correlation cannot prove causation. Even the strongest quasi-experimental designs—regression discontinuity designs, interrupted time series analysis, and nonequivalent control group designs, including propensity score matching and selection modeling—are

less well suited for causal inference than experiments (Cook, Shadish, & Wong, 2008; Glazerman et al., 2003). These alternative designs and their linked analyses typically require more numerous and less realistic causal assumptions than the experiment, and the statistical techniques on which they depend for estimating effects require even more and even less transparent assumptions. Also a problem is that statistical tests are less efficient with non- and quasi-experiments than with experiments. However, nonrandomized designs are frequently recommended as good alternatives to randomized experiments (e.g., by AERA; Schneider et al., 2007). Here, we briefly describe the basic settings of the strongest quasi-experimental designs and discuss their warrants (for a general overview, see Shadish et al., 2002; West, Biesanz, & Pitts, 2000).

Regression Discontinuity Designs

Regression discontinuity designs have a long tradition, but have only recently experienced a renaissance (Cook, 2008), including educational evaluation (e.g., Angrist & Lavy, 1999; Barnett, Lamy, & Jung, 2005; Cohen, 2006; Gormley, Gayer, Phillips, & Dawson, 2005; Jackson et al., 2007; Jacob & Lefgren, 2004; Lockwood, Gill, Setodji, & Martorell, 2007; Van der Klaauw, 2002; Wong, Cook, Barnett, & Jung, 2008). The basic regression discontinuity design requires that participants are deterministically assigned to a treatment and control condition on the basis of a quantitative assignment variable (e.g., a student's birthday or a pretest score). There is no necessity that the assignment variable has a clear meaning or is measured without error. The crucial need is that participants with a measure below a fixed cutoff value of the assignment variable are assigned to one condition (treatment or control), whereas those above the cutoff are assigned to the other condition. After treatment, the causal effect on an outcome variable is investigated by regressing the outcome on the quantitative assignment variable and a treatment dummy variable—treated units are coded with 1, and untreated units are coded with 0. The dummy variable models the expected discontinuity in the regression line exactly at the cutoff point and represents the causal effect. Because the treatment effect is estimated via regression, the assignment variable must be quantitative (i.e., a continuous variable). Nominal variables, such as gender or race, cannot be used because no regression line can be estimated—the discontinuity due to the treatment would be confounded with the effect of the dichotomous assignment variable.

Regression discontinuity designs are warranted by the feature that the assignment process into treatment or control conditions is completely known (Goldberger, 1972a, 1972b). For this reason, unbiased treatment effects can be estimated at the cutoff value, but only if assumptions in addition to those for the randomized experiment are met. First, the functional form of the regression equation must be correctly specified; second, there should be no interaction between the treatment and assignment variables. Frequently, a linear relationship between the outcome and assignment variable is assumed. However, curvilinear relationships should be modeled by including higher order polynomial terms of the quantitative assignment variable if substantive theory and data suggest it. Misspecifications of the functional form result in biased estimates of the treatment effect. In practice, the robustness of effect estimates should be checked by using different regression models. The assumption that there is no interaction effect between treatment and assignment variable implies that the regression lines are parallel for the treatment and control group. This means that there is only a discontinuity in the regression line at the cutoff, but no change in the slope. Interpretation complicates when there is a significant change in the slope or, more generally, in the functional form. If there is no discontinuity at the cutoff, but a change in slope, the increased or decreased slope cannot be uniquely attributed to the treatment without further assumptions. This is because the change

may also reflect a nonlinear relationship between the outcome and the assignment variable. If there is a discontinuity at the cutoff in addition to the change in slope, the offset can be interpreted as a causal effect, but at the cutoff point only. The estimation of (nonconstant) treatment effects at other values than the cutoff is only possible if the change in slope was uniquely caused by treatment—alternative explanations, including nonlinear functional forms, must be ruled out.

However, if these additional assumptions hold, regression discontinuity designs are also empirically warranted alternatives to randomized experiments (Cook & Wong, in press). Indeed, at the cutoff point, regression discontinuity designs are equivalent to randomized experiments. But in contrast to randomized experiments, they have considerably lower power (given the same sample sizes). Power mainly depends on the choice of the cutoff value—cutoffs at the extreme ends of the assignment variable should be avoided—and the strength of correlation between the outcome and assignment variable. Even for well-designed regression designs, 2.75 times more observations are necessary to achieve the same power as in a corresponding randomized experiment (Goldberger, 1972a). Moreover, the use of only a single cutoff value restricts the generalization of causal effect estimates because treatment effects can only be interpreted at or close to the cutoff value. However, more complex variants of the basic design can at least partially deal with these restrictions (Judd & Kenny, 1981; Shadish et al., 2002; Trochim, 1984).

The key requirement of the regression discontinuity design is that subjects are assigned to the treatment or control condition solely on the basis of the cutoff of a quantitative assignment variable. This requirement is as strict as random assignment in a randomized experiment. If assignment does not solely take place according to the cutoff, the strength of the regression discontinuity design is corrupted, and biased effect estimates may result. This is the case if administrators or participants override the assignment rule in order to achieve or avoid treatment. For instance, teachers may override the assignment rule for students close to the cutoff value because they think that some of these students do or do not need treatment. If students know in advance about the assignment variable (e.g., a vocabulary pretest) and the cutoff, they may try to manipulate their own pretest score by intentionally producing poor results. Because in such cases assignment is not completely controlled, selection bias may contaminate estimated treatment effects. The same holds if there are treatment crossovers (subjects assigned to treatment do not receive treatment, and subjects assigned to the control condition receive treatment) and attrition from the study.

Interrupted Time Series Designs

Interrupted time series designs are similar to regression discontinuity designs. The quantitative assignment variable is exclusively given by a time variable. The implementation of an intervention at a certain point in time separates an observed time series of the outcome under investigation into two parts: the time series before and the time series after intervention. As with regression discontinuity designs, regression analysis is used to assess potential effects of the intervention. For an effective intervention, one would expect an interruption in the pattern of the observed time series immediately after the intervention point. In the simplest case, this can be either a change in the time series' level, slope, or both.

To achieve unbiased estimates of treatment effects with interrupted time series designs, two assumptions must be met. First, time is the sole variable determining implementation of treatment. If time is not the single factor determining the assignment to the control and treatment condition, treatment effects may be biased. Second, the functional form of the outcome over time must be correctly modeled. That includes the correct specification of the long-term trend, as well as the identification of potential periodic cycles in the time series. Moreover, serial dependencies are likely because observations

close together in time are likely to be not independent of each other. Although misspecifications of long-term trends or periodic cycles result in biased treatment effect estimates, the failure to adequately model serial dependencies leads to biased standard errors and, as a consequence, incorrect statistical inference. The proper specification of a time series typically requires a long time series—100 observations, as a rule of thumb (Velicer & Harrop, 1983). Otherwise long-term and cyclical trends cannot be reasonably estimated. If only short time series are available, competing models may fit the data equally well, but effect estimates may substantially differ. Hence, for short time series, more substantive knowledge or stronger assumptions about the functional form are needed to justify the results from a specific interrupted time series design.

Another problem associated with the interpretation of an interrupted time series design is that an observed change in the level, slope, or both must be uniquely attributable to the intervention. That is, alternative explanations for the interruption in the time series pattern must be ruled out. Particularly, effects of events occurring at approximately the same time as the intervention under investigation may be confounded with the treatment effect. First, other unrelated, competing, or compensating interventions influencing the outcome of interest may have been launched at about the same time. Second, the population under investigation may have changed. This happens if, immediately after the announcement, implementation, or becoming aware of the intervention, subjects start to select themselves into or out of treatment or the measurement framework. In such cases, the interruption in the time series is probably only due to an unintended change in the composition of the population covered by the pre- and postintervention time series. Third, changes in the measurement framework of the outcome (i.e., the reporting, measuring, or recording of the outcome of interest) may have changed over time, particularly simultaneously with the implementation of treatment.

An additional challenge with interrupted time series analyses occurs when interventions do not produce immediate but rather delayed effects. The reason for this may be that interventions are either not immediately and completely implemented, slowly diffuse through the population, or both. Delayed effects are more difficult to interpret unless theoretical justifications exist for explaining the observed delay. The longer the time period between treatment and the first possible effects, the more alternative interpretations are plausible. In particular, with short time series, only immediate effects can be detected. The assessment of delayed effects requires much longer time series. Further, power issues are also important for interrupted time series analysis. If time series are short and show a high amount of unexplained error, weak effects are difficult to prove.

For both the regression discontinuity and the interrupted time series analysis, the major problem is that alternative interpretations for the discontinuity or interruption must be ruled out. If alternative interpretations other than the treatment remain likely, then the observed effect may not be causally attributed to the intervention. To rule out alternative explanations, the basic design can be improved by including nonequivalent control group time series without any treatment or other nonequivalent dependent variables that are not affected by treatment, but would reveal potential threats to the interrupted time series' internal validity. Sometimes it is also possible to show the effect of an intervention not only by introducing it, but also by removing it at a later point in time. Another strategy consists of adding a switching replication of the time series, where an additional group receives treatment at a later point in time (Shadish et al., 2002).

However, if time series are long enough and if the required assumptions hold, then interrupted time series designs are among the strongest quasi-experimental designs. Nonetheless, time series designs in educational evaluations are rare and typically not long (Henry & Rubenstein, 2002; Kearney & Kim, 1990; Lin & Lawrenz, 1999; May & Supovitz, 2006; Moon, Stanley, & Shin, 2005).

Nonequivalent Control Group Designs

The currently most popular quasi-experimental alternative is probably the nonequivalent control group design. As in a randomized experiment, a group of subjects who received treatment is compared to a control group not receiving treatment. But unlike in randomized experiments, treatment is not randomly assigned to participants. Rather, they select themselves or are selected by administrators or third persons (e.g., parents) into treatment. Thus, the selection process into treatment is usually not completely known and measured. Hence, a direct comparison of the treatment and comparison groups cannot yield an unbiased estimate of the treatment effect as long as groups differ prior to treatment with respect to important background characteristics that are related to the outcome under study. Only if treatment and comparison groups can be balanced on all important covariates that are related to both treatment and outcome, effect estimates can be adjusted for pretreatment group differences. In principle, two main strategies for aligning treatment and comparison groups are possible: individual case matching and intact group matching.

Individual Case Matching

With individual case matching treatment and comparison groups are typically balanced on the basis of individual-level covariates, but also group-level covariates may be included for each case. A variety of statistical methods has been suggested to adjust treatment effects for pretreatment group differences in observed covariates (Morgan & Winship, 2007; Rosenbaum, 2002; Rubin, 2006). Among them are covariance adjustment via regression analysis (ANCOVA), econometric selection modeling, as well as stratification, weighting, and matching approaches on the basis of either the originally observed covariates or the propensity score. Propensity scores are currently frequently used in educational evaluations (e.g., Hill, Rubin, & Thomas, 1999; Hong & Raudenbush, 2005, 2006; Morgan, 2001). Propensity scores try to model the unknown selection process and are defined as the conditional probability that subjects received treatment, given all observed background variables (Rosenbaum & Rubin, 1983, 1984). In practical applications, propensity scores are estimated using logistic regression or discriminant analysis with observed covariates as independent variables. If the propensity score model is correctly specified, estimated propensity scores are able to balance pretreatment group differences on observed covariates. Balance in groups can then be achieved by (a) including the propensity score as a predictor into the regression model for the outcome, (b) stratifying observations on the basis of the propensity score, (c) weighting observations with weights derived from the propensity score, or (d) matching individual cases of the treatment and comparison group solely on the basis of propensity scores or together with other covariates.

However, all these methods require a strong assumption to obtain unbiased treatment effects: the assumption of a strongly ignorable treatment assignment, also called selection on observables or unconfoundedness assumption (Rosenbaum & Rubin, 1983). This assumption requires that (a) all important covariates related to treatment and outcome are identified and reliably measured, and (b) sufficient overlap of treatment and comparison group on these covariates is given. The first part of the strong ignorability assumption ensures that all pretreatment group differences that also affect the outcome can be balanced. This is possible only when all these confounding covariates are measured. The second part of the assumption requires that the joint covariate distributions of the treatment and control group completely overlap. This means that for each treated subject with specific background characteristics, a corresponding untreated subject with the same or similar background characteristics should have been observed. If no subjects in the control group share similar characteristics, a lack of overlap is given and treatment effects for this part of the covariate distribution cannot be estimated. The assumption of sufficient overlap can be checked by plotting the treatment and control group's univariate distributions of observed covariates and propensity scores. Unfortunately, an empirical test of the first part of the strong ignorability assumption is not possible. Only substantive theory on determining factors of the actual selection process and their relation to the outcome under investigation may help to justify the assumption. If there are reasonable doubts about whether all covariates related to both treatment selection and outcome have been measured, strong ignorability may not hold, and estimates of the treatment effect may remain considerably biased. For instance, if the most important covariates explaining treatment selection—that is, pretest measures on the same scale as the outcome and motivational factors for choosing or avoiding the treatment under consideration—are not measured, strong ignorability can hardly be assumed (Steiner et al., under review). It is important to note that groups must also be balanced with regard to different maturation rates, which is a major issue in educational evaluations. This can be achieved by considering changes in pretest measures as additional covariates. Even if all covariates required for establishing a strongly ignorable treatment assignment are observed, regression models for the outcome or the propensity score must be correctly specified in order to obtain unbiased effect estimates.

Intact Group Matching

In retrospective studies, which rely on existing databases, not all important covariates related to treatment assignment may be available. Consequently, a strongly ignorable treatment assignment cannot be reasonably assumed, and effect estimates based on individual case matching may be plagued by hidden bias. This is particularly true when national datasets are used to construct matched pairs for a locally implemented intervention. National datasets are not designed to represent the complex selection models operating in local settings with a specific intervention. Within-study comparisons have shown that such retrospective nonequivalent group designs using propensity scores nearly always fail to approximate the results of their experimental benchmarks when treatment and comparison populations are initially very different (Cook et al., 2008; Glazerman et al., 2003). This emphasizes the importance of locally and focally similar comparison groups—groups that come from data samples in the same locale with the same substantive characteristics as the treatment group. Then, even without individual selection modeling, the comparison of well-matched, intact groups can result in pretest means and slopes that are similar for experimentally and nonexperimentally constructed comparisons (Aiken, West, Schwalm, Caroll, & Hsuing, 1998; Bloom, Michaelopoulos, & Hill, 2005). Even if complete bias reduction cannot be achieved with an intact group matching, the greater initial overlap relative to other possible nonequivalent populations is likely to improve bias reduction with adjustment methods such as individual case propensity score matching.

In cases where classrooms or schools are the unit of analysis, one can also take advantage of the fact that school achievement data from prior years are often available. Then multiple comparison schools can be selected by matching on school-level pretest means and slopes over several years.

Experimentation and Evaluation in the United States and Europe

Quasi-experimental designs, although not the strongest ones as described earlier, are dominant in educational evaluation, whereas experimental designs are often an exemption, particularly in Europe. Two main reasons for the marginal role of experimentation in evaluating educational programs can be identified: the historical emergence and tradition of experimentation (described in this section), and reservations about using experiments in educational evaluation (described in the next section).

In the United States, experiments are common for assessing the effectiveness of a program or intervention, although they are relatively rare in education (Cook & Gorard, 2007). In the European countries, experiments are rare except in medicine, psychology, and agriculture. In general, this has to do with the different roles that evaluation plays in the United States and Europe. In the United States, evaluation has a longer tradition and is more institutionalized. According to Rossi, Freeman, and Lipsey (1999), evaluation of social programs has its roots in the United States of the 1930s. A real boom started in the 1960s, when various social welfare programs were launched and their effects had to be assessed. The demand for evaluation exceeded the capacity of the U.S. General Accounting Office, and so evaluation opened up new employment possibilities for the dramatically increasing number of social science doctorates. Two professional evaluation societies also began in the 1970s (Evaluation Research Society and Evaluation Network), and professional journals and standards were not long behind.

In the 1980s, some countries within the Anglo-Saxon tradition started introducing public sector reforms (known as New Public Management). Here, the UK, Australia, and New Zealand were foremost, and some Northern European continental countries (e.g., Sweden) followed. According to Stame (2003), these countries also participated in the Anglo-Saxon debate concerning evaluation methods and techniques. The situation in most European countries has lagged behind this development. The process of professionalism and institutionalization started during the 1990s, thanks to an external push coming from the EU. The EU has developed "a complex system of multi-level governance of which a specific architecture of evaluation is a crucial element" (Stame, 2003, p. 39). This system of multilevel governance is characterized by the following process: The EU establishes general goals and allocates money to the states, the member states establish specific goals and allocate money to regions, and the lower levels decide on programs and interventions. As a consequence, an evaluation hierarchy corresponding to these levels has been institutionalized. Important steps toward professionalism of evaluation were the foundation of the European Evaluation Society (founded in 1994) or the German Association for Evaluation (founded in 1997). The development of methods is characterized by a combination of orientation toward the established standards in the Anglo-Saxon countries and the development of original approaches building on their own cultural traditions.

Although in the United States evaluation emerged from substantive evaluation theory and the general development of social science methods, in Europe evaluation was strongly associated with standards and procedures of accounting. Auditors are much more central in evaluation than social scientists trained in evaluation theory. Not surprisingly, auditors and social scientists have quite different views about evaluation (Cook & Wittmann, 1998). Social scientists translate government programs into theoretical statements about the relationship between inputs and outputs. They are interested in the causal conditions and program factors that lead to a more or less successful implementation of the program. They focus on different levels (e.g., students, classes, schools, regions) and include unintended side effects into their investigations. They use different methods for revealing the truth about the program, including experimental and quasi-experimental designs, econometric models, and qualitative techniques. They are concerned about ethics and values, fearing the limitation to a single perspective, particularly that of a powerful government. In contrast, auditors are more engaged with auditing standards, the monitoring of program implementation according to these standards, and the cost effectiveness of public funds spent for governmental programs. They are less interested in the causal relation between inputs and outputs, and they do not care much about how an effect came about. Likewise, unintended side effects and policy and ethical considerations are of minor relevance to them. Auditing standards mainly focus on the judgment of how well a

program is implemented relative to its goals. In the United States, evaluation is strongly associated with empirically based decision making. In Europe, it is seen as a supportive management tool for an efficient allocation of resources, for further development of programs, and for helping politicians when they argue for or against a program. Hence, European evaluators are generally more sensitive about the political consequences of their work.

The priority of evaluation questions also differs between the United States and European countries. In the United States, evaluation mainly refers to generating and using information on the actual performance of implemented programs. In Europe, evaluation also comprises ex-ante investigations for planning intended programs and assessing effects to be expected in the future. Hence, this kind of ex-ante evaluation strongly depends on the validity of the substantive model and the underlying assumptions, whereas ex-post evaluation—as typical for the United States— relies on demonstrated performance—that is, what happened and not what might happen.

Due to the different perspectives of evaluation, experiments are of higher significance in the United States than in Europe (Cook & Wittmann, 1998). During the 1960s, quantitative methods dominated qualitative techniques in the United States. To investigate the causal effects of programs, experimental methods were clearly preferred to nonexperimental ones, design controls were preferred to statistical controls, and qualitative techniques were downplayed because they are not able to rule out competing causal interpretations. However, in the 1970s and 1980s, qualitative methods became more and more important in education as experience led commentators to believe that large causal effects are rare. In addition, an increasing number of social scientists and scholars thought that quantitative methods—especially experiments—are epistemologically too restricted. Because the development of evaluation in Europe lagged behind the one of the United States, the booming phase of experimentation was basically missed. Instead, European evaluators were more strongly committed to both auditing and qualitative versus quantitative methods. In the latest evaluation guidelines of the European Commission (Directorate-General [DG] Budget, 2004), experimental designs are not even mentioned, although the DG for Employment concluded that quasi-experimental designs constitute the most important way to assess effects of intervention "since perfect experimental comparisons do not exist" (European Commission, 1999, p. 14). For educational evaluation, the EU has not yet formulated explicit evaluation method preferences. However, the number of experiments is low in educational evaluation in both the United States and Europe, and educational evaluators in each setting generally use the same arguments for rejecting experiments in favor of quasi- or nonexperimental investigations. Their reservations to randomized experiments are analyzed in some detail in the remainder of this chapter.

The Validity of Reservations About Using Experiments in Educational Evaluation

The superiority of random assignment for drawing inferences about the consequences of planned interventions is routinely acknowledged in philosophy, medicine, public health, agriculture, statistics, microeconomics, psychology, criminology, prevention research, early childhood education, and marketing. Furthermore, it is also acknowledged in those parts of political science and sociology concerned with improving opinion surveys, as well as in all the elementary education method textbooks we have consulted. However, random assignment is relatively rare in educational evaluation, especially for assessing the impact of educational interventions of obvious policy relevance. Random assignment is also rare in sociology, political science, macroeconomics, and management. Yet causal statements are routinely made in these fields, usually through a process that links substantive theory to various qualitative or quantitative nonexperimental practices.

We do not argue that correct causal conclusions come only from experiments. We argue that experiments provide a better warrant for such conclusions than any quasi-experimental method (see also the series of discussions in the Point/Counterpoint Section of the *Journal of Policy Analysis and Management 27*(2), *27*(3), and *28*(1), with the opening statements in Nathan, 2008). So, if experiments can be conducted in schools, they should be. Not to use them requires a strong justification.

Over the last 30 years, self-ascribed educational evaluators such as Alkin, Cronbach, Eisner, Fetterman, Fullan, Guba, House, Hubermann, Lincoln, Miles, Provus, Sanders, Schwandt, Stake, Stufflebeam, and Worthen have proposed many justifications for not doing experiments (Cook, 2002). These theorists want educational evaluation to pursue goals other than describing what works in schools. Most of them want evaluation to improve the organization and management of individual districts or schools, assuming that this will routinely improve student performance. They examine ways to provide individual schools or district staff with continuous feedback about strategic planning, program implementation, and student or teacher performance monitoring. The expectation is that local officials will immediately use this feedback in their schools and that student performance will consequently improve. This model of research and its connection to organizational change is much like what we find in management consulting in the private sector. Other educational evaluators want evaluation to contribute to developing general theories, especially those that specify the often complex constellation of forces that bring about important school effects. Engaged time on task is such a generative process and, over a broad set of circumstances, enhances academic achievement. It can be instantiated in many different ways—as more days of schooling per year, as longer school days, as more time devoted to the core curriculum, as textbooks that are engaging, as exposure to teachers who know how to motivate students, and so on. Identifying such generative causal mechanisms becomes the paramount goal of evaluation. Unfortunately, neither the management consulting nor the causal mechanism model of evaluation places the premium where experimentation does—on directly observing student change and unambiguously attributing it to a single policy-related treatment. Although the management consulting and causal mechanism approaches may deliver valuable hints and theories for causal inference, they are not able to disentangle the complex and confounded effects on empirically measured student achievements.

The objections to randomized experimentation are manifold. According to Cook (2002), who discusses several reservations to experiments and illustrates them with a lot of examples from the United States, the common arguments put forward can be divided into five main categories: (a) practical arguments, (b) arguments about undesirable trade-offs, (c) arguments that experiments are not necessary because better alternatives exist, (d) arguments that schools will not use experimental results, and (e) philosophical arguments. In the following, we only discuss the first three arguments because they are more strongly related to practical issues and alternative approaches to randomized experiments.

Practical Reasons for Not Doing Experiments

Randomized Experiments Cannot Be Mounted

Opponents of randomized experiments assert a number of reasons that experimentation cannot be implemented, particularly in school research: Many officials do not like the unequal allocation of resources generated by random assignment and fear respective negative reactions from parents and staff. Due to their complexity, educational related topics are not appropriate for experimental investigations. Therefore, other—often less effective and less esteemed—methods are generally preferred to randomized experiments (Cook, 2002). Nevertheless, it is striking that—at least in the United States—experiments in

schools are to be found when the topic is not pedagogic, such as school-based programs to prevent negative behavior (tobacco, drugs, alcohol). They are also common in preschool education. One possible explanation might be the different time requirements associated with the intervention and when it is expected to achieve results. Pedagogical interventions are more likely to be multiyear; they require a change in established routines, and if they are not successful it might threaten a school's local reputation.

Furthermore, the discipline-based difference in the frequency of experiments may also be due to disciplinary culture. Random assignment is common in health sciences, where it is institutionally supported by funding agencies, integrated in graduate training programs, has a long tradition (e.g., clinical trials), and is considered in political discussions.

Cook (2000) argues that the implementation of experimental settings is easier in cases with centralized decision making (e.g., when funding of a program is bound to the use of experiments in evaluation). Furthermore, it is necessary to give an incentive to schools that participate in the control group of an experiment. A motivation for schools to participate without belonging to the treatment group could be the promise that they would be the first to offer the intervention at the study end, by when it might be improved. Last but not least, all these practical challenges indicate that random assignment should be in independent hands and carried out by staff with experience in randomization in complex settings.

Even When Experiments Are Mounted, Many of the Planned Between-Treatment Contrasts Become Compromised

Random assignment leads to treatment and control groups that are equivalent at the pretest prior to treatment. Assuming unchanged circumstances, the treatment effect is defined as the difference in the outcome variable in a posttest. Experiments are likely to be compromised if systematic effects—making groups different—operate. Such effects are differential attrition and treatment crossovers.

Differential attrition occurs if different kinds of students drop out of various treatment groups, resulting in nonequivalent groups and consequently in effect estimates of questionable value. Attrition may be kept at a low rate if school staff can strongly be committed to participation and the acceptance of the random assignment results and if modest payments to the units experiencing less desirable treatments are provided. It is also important that treatment implementation is closely monitored, particularly in order to detect and deal with early dropout trends. However, with long-lasting treatments, some attrition—due to changes in the school management, for instance—cannot be prevented. Nevertheless, units lost to intervention should remain within the measurement framework. Although attrition may never be completely avoided, the resulting bias is likely to be less than the bias due to a complete self-selection of schools or teachers from the start. Statistical selection controls are better the smaller the initial bias and the better selection have been measured (Holland, 1986).

Furthermore, experiments might be compromised by treatment crossover. Although extensive crossovers may be rare, Cook et al. (1999) showed that 3 out of 10 control schools borrowed program elements. This was mainly due to informal communication paths, which facilitated an exchange between units in the treatment and control groups concerning the intervention. Minimizing crossovers requires a well-planned experimental design, including random selection of physically separated units, innovative treatments, and the measurement of treatment fidelity.

Random Assignment Assumes Fixed Program Theory and Standard Implementation, But These Treatment-Specific Assumptions Are Not Valid for School Contexts

The interpretation of experimental results is facilitated when intervention is based on strong substantive theory, when implementation

corresponds with the treatment-specific program theory, and when variation within each treatment implementation is minimal. However, in school research, these conditions are rarely met because schools are complex social organizations faced with conflicting stakeholder goals. Standardized implementation of a reform initiative or total fidelity to program theory is usually not achieved. So, the assumption of treatment homogeneity or invariance of settings in the educational contexts can hardly be justified in experimental investigations.

However, random assignment does not require well-specified program theories, good management, standard implementation, or treatments that exactly correspond to program theory. Experiments primarily protect against bias in causal estimates and only secondarily against imprecision in these estimates resulting from the complexity and heterogeneity of schools. But increasing school sample sizes and measuring school-specific sources of variation to reduce their unwanted influence through statistical control can tackle this. In addition, implementation quality should be studied on its own to learn about which types of schools and teachers implement the program better. It is important to note that only a few educational interventions will be standardized once they are implemented as formal policy. So, why standardize in an experiment? The measurement of sources of implementation variation and their inclusion in the analysis of causal effects is of greater importance than standardization.

Random Assignment Entails Undesirable Trade-Offs

Increasing Internal Validity Decreases External Validity

The strength of experiments is internal validity, the focus on unbiased causal estimates, rather than external validity or causal explanation. Therefore, experiments are clearly limited in time and space. But scientists typically prefer general results—results that are at least more general than those derived from a single experiment of a specifically implemented intervention in a particular sample of schools that volunteered for experimentation. Moreover, educational evaluators seek for general causal agents whose operating mechanisms are fully understood. They place less priority on the effectiveness of a particular implementation of a program in a particular time with a particular group of respondents. This means that they are prepared to tolerate more uncertainty than other scientists who would like to know whether a program works reliably.

One possibility to overcome the limited generalizability of single experiments is to implement experiments in a way that sampling particulars permit tests of generalization across types of students, teachers, settings, and times. With random sampling of these instances, followed by random assignment to treatment, empirical robustness of effects or boundary conditions under which effects occur can hopefully be demonstrated.

However, random sampling is hardly relevant if, for instance, volunteering to be in a study is required or causal relationships may vary by historical period. Further, random sampling cannot be used to select the outcome measures and treatment variants that are used to represent general cause-and-effect constructs. So, a different generalization model is required—one that emphasizes how consistently a causal relationship replicates across multiple sources of heterogeneity (Cook, 1993): Can the same causal relationship be observed across different laboratories, time periods, regions of the country, and ways of operationalizing the cause and effect? This heterogeneity-of-replication model permits purposive instead of random sampling. Only the heterogeneous sampling plan with respect to people, settings, operational definitions, and times are of vital importance. Single experiments rarely produce definitive answers, and, in addition, they are not able to answer all ancillary questions about the contingencies on which a causal relationship depends. In this sense, causal generalization can be understood as an average effect size derived from heterogeneous studies of the same hypothesis. But it can also be seen as an identifying generative causal process. For instance, engaged time on task is presumed to stimulate achievement through activities such as more homework, summer classes, or longer school days. The methods for identifying such explanatory processes place relatively little weight on sampling; instead, they require the measurement of each variable in the presumed generative theory. Fortunately, it is easier to build these explanatory methods into individual experiments than it is to sample at random or to add populations to the sampling design. Hence, experiments could and should be designed to explain the consequences of interventions and not just to describe them. This means adding to an experiment's measurement and sampling plan and abjuring black box experiments.

Prioritizing Scientific Purity Over Utility

Critics frequently argue that experimenters focus only on uncertainty reduction about the cause in order to obtain pure effect estimates, rather than results of more general utility. Some questions may illustrate this point of view. Why not use a more liberal level of significance, say $\alpha = .25$ instead of a conservative $\alpha = .05$? Why include schools defying treatment implementation in the treatment group for the intention-to-treat analysis? Why not investigate unplanned treatment interactions or treatment implementations? Why persist with the original research question if a more useful question has emerged during the study, even if unbiased answers to the new question are not possible? It seems that experiments are only designed for bias reduction and that other types of knowledge are secondary at best. But experiments need not be so rigid. There is no need for stringent alpha rates. One need not be restricted to the intention-to-treat analysis only, although these results should be reported. Also, interaction effects may be investigated, with substantive theory and statistical power in mind. Hence, pure effect estimates can be obtained from experimental data as well as other relevant results, especially if additional ethnographic data are used. Such data are of relevance for understanding issues on implementation, causal mediation, and unintended outcomes and improve each controlled experiment.

Random Assignment Is Not Needed Because Better Alternatives Already Exist

Intensive Case Studies Are More Flexible

Intensive qualitative case studies are often seen as superior alternatives to experiments, mainly due to their greater flexibility. Although an experiment only focuses on a narrow causal aspect, evaluators are convinced that case studies are appropriate for evaluating program theory, assessing implementation, recording program redesign, identifying intended and unplanned effects, detecting contingencies, or assessing the findings relevance for different stakeholder groups. They assert that intensive qualitative case studies are able to reduce the uncertainty about a cause to an acceptable level and sometimes— undoubtedly—even all the uncertainty about a cause. However, it will usually be difficult to know when this happened. Nonetheless, case studies do not reduce as much causal uncertainty as well-executed experiments. The absence of control groups—the causal counterfactual— makes it difficult to know how a treatment group would have changed in the absence of the intervention. If a high standard of uncertainty reduction is prioritized, randomized experiments are indispensable.

However, intensive qualitative case studies complement experiments whenever a causal question is central, but it is not clear how successful program implementation will be, why implementation shortfalls may occur, what unexpected effects are likely to emerge, what the mediating processes are, and so on. Case studies can have a central role within experiments, but are not better alternatives to experiments in causal questions.

Quasi-Experiments Are as Good as Experiments

Quasi-experiments are identical to experiments in purpose and in most structural details, the defining difference being nonrandom assignment. Quasi-experiments use design rather than statistical controls to create the best possible approximation to the missing counterfactual that random assignment would have generated. These design controls include matched comparison groups, age or sibling controls, pretest measures at several times before a treatment begins, interrupted time series assigning units based solely on a quantitative criterion, assigning the same treatment to different groups at different times, and building multiple outcome variables into studies, some of which should theoretically be influenced by a treatment and others not (Corrin & Cook, 1998; Shadish et al., 2002). Quasi-experimental designs are created through a mixing process that tailors the research problem and the resources available to the best design that can be achieved by mixing the previous design elements.

However, strong quasi-experiments with design elements mentioned earlier are rarely found in educational evaluation. In particular, the strongest quasi-experiments—interrupted time series analysis, regression discontinuity analysis, and nonequivalent control group designs with more than one pretest measurement— started to enter educational evaluation only recently (see the section on quasi-experimental designs). Instead, weak quasi-experiments with some form of nonequivalent control groups or some pretreatment observations can be frequently found, but they run the risk of being "generally causally uninterpretable" (Campbell & Stanley, 1963; Cook & Campbell, 1979).

Quasi-experiments are more likely to be biased and inefficient when compared with experimental results. In areas such as education, where few studies exist, randomized experiments are particularly needed. It will take fewer of them to arrive at what might—or might not—be the same answer, and anyway, most scholars trust the answers from experiments more than from quasi-experiments.

Theories of Change

Theories of change are used in evaluations of interventions in complex social settings such as schools or communities (Connell, Kubisch, Schorr, & Weiss, 1995). The theory of change requires a detailed explication of the substantive theory behind a reform initiative and the specification of all flow-through relationships that should occur if the intended intervention is to impact on a major distal outcome such as student achievement. To this end, highly valid measurements of each construct in the substantive theory as well as a valid analysis of multivariate explanatory processes are necessary for assessing whether the postulated relationships have actually occurred in the predicted time sequences. Without using a causal counterfactual (i.e., control or comparison groups), it is assumed that the theory under investigation is proved if the data patterns obtained are congruent with the program theory.

Without a doubt, the extensive use of substantive theory to guide measurement and analysis is of great value for improving causal probes. But the issue is whether such measurement and analysis alone can completely substitute for randomized experiments. There are reasons for skepticism about the validity of using theories of change to support strong causal conclusions (Cook, 2000). They comprise the difficulty with making program theory explicit and unique (competing theories may exist). They also cover problems in specifying the timelines of effects, the linearity in the flow of influence often neglecting reciprocal feedback loops or external contingencies moderating effects, or the difficulty in obtaining valid measurement. In addition, there is usually not only one unique but a set of rather heterogeneous theories of change that all fit to a single pattern of data (Glymour, Scheines, Spirtes, & Kelly 1987). The implication here is that causal modeling is more valid when multiple competing models are

tested against each other, rather than when a single model is tested. As with case studies, the biggest problem with theory-of-change models is the absence of a valid counterfactual that models what would have happened without treatment. As a result, it is impossible to decide whether the observed data result from the intervention or would have occurred anyway. Although theories of change are not an adequate alternative to experiments if causal effects are to be analyzed, they give valuable information about why these effects occurred, as well as the mechanisms behind that. From that point of view, theories of change are—like case studies—no alternative to randomized experiments, but they are a valuable completion.

Conclusion

Within the RCM, random assignment remains the most reliable technique for justifying causal inference. It provides the logically most valid and efficient causal counterfactual. Consequently, results are more credible than those from other quasi- or nonexperimental methods. Moreover, empirical comparisons of experiments and their alternatives suggest (Bloom, Michaelopoulos, Hill, & Lei, 2002; Glazerman et al., 2003; Lipsey & Wilson, 1993) that individual experiments are less biased, and that, as studies on a topic accumulate, they are more efficient about reducing causal uncertainty than quasi-experiments. Therefore, from a pragmatic point of view, experiments have a lower risk of drawing false causal conclusions, and they are probably less expensive in the long run because fewer of them are needed for the same degree of confidence in the causal conclusion drawn.

Although the superiority of randomized experiments is generally known, experimentation is still too rare in research on the effectiveness of school-based strategies to improve student performance. However, random assignment is not at all rare in preschool education or in school research on preventing negative behaviors or feelings. One possible reason is the difference in intellectual culture. Prevention researchers and preschool teachers tend to be trained in fields where random assignment is more esteemed and where funders and journal editors clearly prefer this technique. In contrast, training and professional rewards in educational research set no high value on experimentation. Another reason may be the difference in experiments' scale. Most school-based prevention experiments are typically shorter, implemented by researchers, rather than school staff, and research topics probably involve educators less than issues of school governance or teaching practice. It is true, experimentation is more demanding in school-based research, but it can and should be done, particularly in cooperation with evaluators trained and experienced in randomized experiments.

However, a more successful dissemination of random assignment in school-based research is restrained by the belief of most educational evaluators that experiments are of little value. They believe that the theory of causation underlying experimentation is naïve, that experiments cannot be successfully implemented, and that they require unacceptable trade-offs. They also argue that experiments deliver a kind of information that is rarely used to change policy, and that the information experiments provide can be gained using simpler and more flexible methods. Some of these beliefs are better justified than others. Beliefs about the viability of alternatives to experiments are particularly less strongly warranted because no current quasi-experimental method or other alternative provides as convincing a causal counterfactual as the randomized assignment.

Educational evaluators will not be persuaded to do experiments simply by outlining their advantages and describing newer methods for implementing randomization. Most educational evaluators share some of the reservations outlined earlier. To start a dialogue, advocates of experimentation will need to be more explicit about the method's limit. They will also have to take some of the critics' concerns seriously—especially about program theory, the quality of implementation, the value of qualitative data,

the necessity for analysis of causal contingency, and concern to meet the information needs of school personnel as well as other stakeholders. Finally, they will have to incorporate them into experimental practice.

Strongly warranted quasi-experimental methods—regression discontinuity designs, interrupted time series designs, and nonequivalent control group designs with close matching or sophisticated pattern matching—should be used whenever randomized experiments cannot be conducted. In any case, quasi-experimental investigations can complement findings from randomized experiments and may help in generalizing them. For successful educational planning and policymaking, we need strong causal evidence from both randomized experiments and quasi-experiments.

References

Aiken, L. S., West, S. G., Schwalm, D. E., Caroll, J., & Hsuing, S. (1998). Comparison of a randomized and two quasi-experimental designs in a single outcome evaluation: Efficacy of a university-level remedial writing program. *Evaluation Review, 22*(4), 207–244.

Angrist, J. D., & Lavy, V. (1999). Using Maimonides' rule to estimate the effects of class size on academic achievement. *Quarterly Journal of Economics, 114*(2), 533–576.

Barnett, W. S., Lamy, C., & Jung, K. (2005). *The effects of state prekindergarten programs on young children's school readiness in five states*. New Brunswick, NJ: National Institute for Early Education Research.

Bloom, H. S., Michaelopoulos, C., & Hill, C. J. (2005). Using experiments to assess nonexperimental comparison-group methods for measuring program effects. In H. S. Bloom (Ed.), *Learning more from social experiments* (pp. 173–235). New York: Russell Sage Foundation.

Bloom, H. S., Michaelopoulos, C., Hill, C. J., & Lei, Y. (2002). *Can non-experimental comparison group methods match the findings from a random assignment evaluation of mandatory welfare-to-work programs?* New York: Manpower Demonstration Research Corporation.

Campbell, D. T., & Stanley, J. C. (1963). *Experimental and quasi-experimental designs for research*. Chicago: Rand-McNally.

Cohen, J. L. (2006). *Causes and consequences of special education placement: Evidence from Chicago public schools*. Cambridge, MA: MIT Press.

Connell, J. P., Kubisch, A. C., Schorr, L. B., & Weiss, C. H. (Eds.). (1995). *New approaches to evaluating community initiatives: Concepts, methods and contexts*. Washington, DC: Aspen Institute.

Cook, T. D. (1993). A quasi-sampling theory of the generalization of causal relationships. In L. Sechrest & A. G. Scott (Eds.), *New Directions for Program Evaluation, 57*, 39–82. San Francisco, CA: Jossey-Bass.

Cook, T. D. (2000). The false choice between theory-based evaluation and experimentation. In L. Sechrest & A. G. Scott (Eds.), *New Directions in Evaluation, 87*, 27–34. San Francisco, CA: Jossey-Bass.

Cook, T. D. (2002). Randomized experiments in educational policy research: A critical examination of the reasons the educational evaluation community has offered for not doing them. *Educational Evaluation and Policy Analysis, 24*(3), 175–199.

Cook, T. D. (2008). "Waiting for life to arrive": A history of the regression-discontinuity design in psychology, statistics and economics. *Journal of Econometrics, 142*(2), 636–654.

Cook, T. D., & Campbell, D. T. (1979). *Quasi-experimentation: Design and analysis issues for field settings*. Boston: Houghton Mifflin.

Cook, T. D., & Gorard, S. (2007). Where does good evidence come from? *International Journal of Research and Method in Education, 30*(3), 307–323.

Cook, T. D., Habib, F., Phillips, J., Settersten, R. A., Shagle, S. C., & Degirmencioglu, S. M. (1999). Comer's school development program in Prince George's County, Maryland: A theory-based evaluation. *American Educational Research Journal, 36*(3), 543–597.

Cook, T. D., Shadish, W. R., & Wong, V. C. (2008). Three conditions under which experiments and observational studies produce comparable causal estimates: New findings from within-study comparisons. *Journal of Policy Analysis and Management, 27*(4), 724–750.

Cook, T. D., & Wittmann, W. W. (1998). Lessons learned about evaluation in the United States and some possible implications for Europe.

European Journal of Psychological Assessment, 14(2), 97–115.

Cook, T. D., & Wong, V. C. (in press). Empirical tests of the validity of the regression discontinuity design. *Annales d'Economie et de Statistique*.

Corrin, W. J., & Cook, T. D. (1998). Design elements of quasi-experimentation. *Advances in Educational Productivity, 7*, 35–57.

European Commission. (1999). *Guidelines for systems of monitoring and evaluation of ESF assistance in the period 2000-2006*. DG Employment, Industrial Relations and Social Affairs. Retrieved July 15, 2007, from www.igfse.pt/upload/docs/aval_LP_orientacoes_processo_aval_inter_DGEmprego.pdf.

European Commission. (2004). *Evaluating EU activities. A practical guide for the Commission services*. DG-Budget, Evaluation Unit, Office for Official Publications of the European Communities, Luxemburg.

Flay, B. R. (1986). Efficacy and effectiveness trials (and other phases of research) in the development of health promotion programs. *Preventive Medicine, 15*, 451–474.

Glazerman, S., Levy, D. M., & Myers, D. (2003). Nonexperimental versus experimental estimates of earnings impacts. *The Annals of the American Academy, 589*, 63–93.

Glymour, C., Scheines, R., Spirtes, P., & Kelly, K. (1987). *Discovering causal structure: Artificial intelligence, philosophy of science and statistical modeling*. Orlando, FL: Academic Press.

Goldberger, A. S. (1972a). *Selection bias in evaluating treatment effects: Some formal illustrations*. Unpublished manuscript, Madison, WI.

Goldberger, A. S. (1972b). *Selection bias in evaluating treatment effects: The case of interaction*. Unpublished manuscript, Madison, WI.

Gormley, W. T., Gayer, T., Phillips, D., & Dawson, B. (2005). The effects of universal pre-K on cognitive development. *Developmental Psychology, 41*(6), 872–884.

Henry, G. T., & Rubenstein, R. (2002). Paying for grades: Impact of merit-based financial aid on educational quality. *Journal of Policy Analysis and Management, 21*(1), 93–109.

Hill, J., Rubin, D. B., & Thomas, N. (1999). The design of the New York school choice scholarship program evaluation. In L. Bickman (Ed.), *Research designs: Donald Campbell's legacy* (pp. 155–180). London: Sage.

Holland, P. W. (1986). Statistics and causal inference. *Journal of the American Statistical Association, 81,* 945–970.

Hong, G., & Raudenbush. S. W. (2005). Effects of kindergarten retention policy on children's cognitive growth in reading and mathematics. *Educational Evaluation and Policy Analysis, 27*(3), 205–224.

Hong, G., & Raudenbush, S. W. (2006). Evaluating kindergarten retention policy: A case study of causal inference for multilevel observational data. *Journal of the American Statistical Association, 101,* 901–910.

Jackson, R., McCoy, A., Pistorino, C., Wilkinson, A., Burghardt, J., Clark, M., Ross, C., Schochet, P., Swank, P., & Schmidt, S. R. (2007). *National evaluation of early reading first* (Final Report to Congress). Washington, DC: U.S. Department of Education, Institute of Education Sciences.

Jacob, B., & Lefgren, L. (2004). Remedial education and student achievement: A regression discontinuity analysis. *Review of Economics and Statistics, 86*(1), 226–244.

Judd, C. M., & Kenny, D. A. (1981). *Estimating the effects of social interventions.* New York: Cambridge University Press.

Kearney, C. P., & Kim, T. (1990). Fiscal impacts and redistributive effects of the new federalism on Michigan school districts. *Educational Evaluation and Policy Analysis, 12*(4), 375–387.

Lin, H. S., & Lawrenz, F. (1999). Using time-series design in the assessment of teaching effectiveness. *Science Education, 83*(9), 409–422.

Lipsey, M. W., & Wilson, D. B. (1993). The efficacy of psychological, educational, and behavioral treatment: Confirmation from meta-analysis. *American Psychologist, 48*(12), 1181–1209.

Lockwood, J. R., Gill, B. P., Setodji, M. C., & Martorell, F. (2007, July). *Regression discontinuity analyses of the effects of NCLB accountability provisions on student achievement.* Paper presented at the Joint Statistical meeting, Salt Lake City, UT.

Mackie, J. L. (1974). *The cement of the universe.* Oxford, England: Oxford University Press.

May, H., & Supovitz, J. A. (2006). Capturing the cumulative effects of school reform: An 11-year study of the impacts of America's choice on student achievement. *Educational Evaluation and Policy Analysis, 28*(3), 231–257.

Moon, S., Stanley, R. E., & Shin, J. (2005). Measuring the impact of lotteries on state per pupil expenditures for education: Assessing the national evidence. *Review of Policy Research, 22*(2), 205–220.

Morgan, S. L. (2001). Counterfactuals, causal effect heterogeneity, and the Catholic school effect on learning. *Sociology of Education, 74*(4), 341–374.

Morgan, S. L., & Winship, C. (2007). *Counterfactuals and causal inference: Methods and principles for social research.* Cambridge: Cambridge University Press.

Nathan, R. P. (2008). The role of random assignment in social policy research. *Journal of Policy Analysis and Management, 27*(2), 401–415.

Neyman, J. (1923/1990). On the application of probability theory to agricultural experiments: Essay on principles, Section 9. *Statistical Science, 5*(4), 465–480.

Rosenbaum, P. R. (2002). *Observational studies* (2nd ed.). New York: Springer-Verlag.

Rosenbaum, P. R., & Rubin, D. B. (1983). The central role of the propensity score in observational studies for causal effects. *Biometrika, 70*(1), 41–55.

Rosenbaum, P. R., & Rubin, D. B. (1984). Reducing bias in observational studies using subclassification on the propensity score. *Journal of the American Statistical Association, 79,* 516–524.

Rossi, P. H., Freeman, H. E., & Lipsey, M. W. (1999). *Evaluation. A systematic approach* (6th ed.). Thousand Oaks, CA: Sage.

Rubin, D. B. (1974). Estimation of causal effects of treatments in randomized and nonrandomized studies. *Journal of Educational Psychology, 66*(5), 688–701.

Rubin, D. B. (1978). Bayesian inference for causal effects. *The Annals of Statistics, 6,* 34–58.

Rubin, D. B. (1986). Which ifs have causal answers. *Journal of the American Statistical Association, 81,* 961–962.

Rubin, D. B. (2006). *Matched sampling for causal effects.* Cambridge: Cambridge University Press.

Schneider, B., Carnoy, M., Kilpatrick, J., Schmidt, W. H., & Shavelson, R. J. (2007). *Estimating causal effects using experimental and observational designs* (Report from the Governing Board of the American Educational Research Association Grants Program). Washington, DC: American Educational Research Association.

Shadish, W. R., Clark, M. H., & Steiner, P. M. (2008). Can nonrandomized experiments yield accurate answers? A randomized experiment comparing random to nonrandom assignment. *Journal of the American Statistical Association, 103,* 1334–1343.

Shadish, W. R., Cook, T. D., & Campbell, D. T. (2002). *Experimental and quasi-experimental designs for generalized causal inference.* Boston: Houghton Mifflin.

Stame, N. (2003). Evaluation and the policy context: The European experience. *Evaluation Journal of Australasia, 3*(2), 36–43.

Steiner, P. M., Cook, T. D., Shadish, W. R., & Clark, M. H. (under review). The importance of covariate selection in controlling for selection bias in observational studies.

Trochim, W. M. K. (1984). *Research design for program evaluation.* Beverly Hills, CA: Sage.

Van der Klaauw, W. (2002). Estimating the effect of financial aid offers on college enrollment. A regression-discontinuity approach. *International Economic Review, 43*(4), 1249–1287.

Velicer, W. F., & Harrop, J. W. (1983). The reliability and accuracy of time series model identification. *Evaluation Review, 7*(4), 551–560.

West, S. G., Biesanz, J. C., & Pitts, S. C. (2000). Causal inference and generalization in field settings. Experimental and quasi-experimental designs. In H. T. Reis & C. M. Judd (Eds.), *Handbook of research methods in social and personality psychology* (pp. 40–84). Cambridge: Cambridge University Press.

Wong, V. C., Cook, T. D., Barnett, W. S., & Jung, K. (2008). An effectiveness-based evaluation of five state pre-kindergarten programs. *Journal of Policy Analysis and Management, 27*(1), 1–33.

CHAPTER 6

Enhancing Impact Evidence on How Global Education Initiatives Work

Theory, Epistemological Foundations, and Principles for Applying Multiphase, Mixed Method Designs

Madhabi Chatterji

The term *globalization* today broadly connotes economic, political, and cultural changes affecting the world's peoples in common ways (Spring, 2008; Stromquist, 2002). As a fundamental means for developing human capital, education is central to globalization and national development trends, tied closely to agendas for economic development and progress (Anderson, 2005). Educational evaluation and evidence-based education are two significant movements linked to global development efforts. Correspondingly, one finds a push for higher standards in securing scientific evidence on the effects of educational innovations.

The call for evidence-based practices—the basic principle that interventions, tools, and materials used to educate or provide services are scientifically tested and proven to yield desired results—cuts across multiple professions, including education, public health, and medicine (see Guyatt & Rennie, 2002; Petticrew & Roberts, 2002). Calls for "impact" evidence on educational interventions have spread from the developed world to developing regions in Asia, Africa, and South and Central America today, where innovations are sponsored by international institutions such as the World Bank. School-based programs are just one of many forms of global education.

Education in emerging economies serves as a key to developing individual and national capacities necessary for success on a global plane. It is also viewed as the means for human emancipation from poverty and subjugation (UNICEF, 2007a, 2007b). As a consequence, many international donor-sponsored programs are complex.

Agendas in basic education are combined with poverty alleviation, human rights education, public health promotion, and environmental education goals. Gender equality and women's economic empowerment via education, for example, is a common goal of projects run by the international human rights organization, CARE (www.care.org). Likewise, the United Nation's Millennium Development Goals and Education for All initiatives have parallel programs aiming toward universal primary education, economic development, and public health improvement. While providing access and comparable educational opportunities for girls and boys, these initiatives are also trying to combat child mortality, maternal ill health, and diseases such as malaria and HIV/AIDS (UNICEF, 2007a, 2007b).

Global donors and local stakeholders in these cases seek evidence on how well their education programs and short-term projects work in overseas environments. "Programs" are frequently packaged ideas transferred from more developed nations to developing ones. Local decision making and actions on programs stand to gain when informed by a solid base of evidence. Scaling up, dissemination, continuation, and discontinuation of programs are only a few actions that rely on the availability of sound and systematically gathered information. In an evaluation context, therefore, the following question is not a trivial one: Which scientific frameworks, research methodologies, and tools of inquiry will yield the best evidence on whether complex education initiatives are effective?

Impact evidence refers to evidence of a program's effectiveness in yielding expected outcomes in target populations. Does the program work? (See the What Works Clearinghouse at http://ies.ed.gov/ncee/wwc/). For some time now, there has been a widely disseminated position among high-level policymakers calling for evidence-based practices in the United States and overseas that some research designs are better than others in yielding impact evidence on education programs (No Child Left Behind Act of 2001, 2002; Education Sciences Reform Act [ESRA] of 2002).

Referred to as the "evidence hierarchy" in debates central to science-based approaches to evidence gathering (Petticrew & Roberts, 2002), the policy position places true experiments (i.e., randomized controlled trials [RCTs]) at the topmost rung of the methodological ladder for generating the best evidence on causal effects of interventions. Quasi-experiments (Campbell & Stanley, 1963; Shadish, Cook, & Campbell, 2002) occupy the next rung in the evidence ladder. The hierarchy discounts other research methods, such as nonexperimental (observational), descriptive, and qualitative approaches, as not having the scientific merit necessary for assessing the efficacy of programs and practices (see also Coalition for Evidence-Based Policy).

To what extent is the evidence hierarchy useful to evaluation researchers and users of global education interventions? Are traditionally designed RCTs or quasi-experiments likely to yield best evidence on program effects in global settings? In what ways are assumptions of laboratory-style RCTs tested under global conditions? Given the accumulated knowledge in the evaluation sciences to date, what methodological approaches could enhance the grade of impact evidence on global education efforts?

Purpose

The purpose of this chapter is to delineate the unique characteristics of global education initiatives and offer a countermethodology to traditional RCTs for gathering scientific evidence on their effects. Labeled as extended-term, mixed method (ETMM) designs in recent publications (Chatterji, 2005, 2007), the approach calls for a multiphase research design with exploratory and confirmatory parts. Each phase is guided by hypotheses based on the underlying logical or theoretical framework of a program and factors in the larger environment likely to influence its operation. ETMM designs use quantitative, descriptive, and qualitative evidence in a complementary manner to determine how, why, and under which conditions complex educational interventions work in their natural environments.

Comparative experiments, including RCTs, are not ruled out in ETMM designs. Rather, they are employed when interventions can be effectively manipulated and environments are better understood by researchers. More empirically informed causal hypotheses can thus be tested. When formal experiments cannot be mounted in the confirmatory phases of research, ETMM approaches permit the approximation of causal effects with suitable nonexperimental or quasi-experimental designs, supported with alternate methods and tools. Instead of a limited focus on whether programs work, ETMM designs are aimed at securing a more comprehensive body of evidence useful for informing stakeholder actions.

In arguing for ETMM designs in global environments, the chapter starts by speaking to the epistemological foundations and theoretical ideas on which the approach stands. To demonstrate how ETMM designs offer evaluation researchers several advantages over RCT designs and quasi-experiments employed by themselves, the chapter contrasts assumptions, strengths, and limitations of these traditional methods for impact assessment with the proposed ETMM approach. A hypothetical example of a school-based reading program is used to present six guidelines for application. A discussion of an actual international evaluation follows, showing methodological elements that correspond with ETMM design principles. Potential benefits, in terms of evidence quality, are discussed. The chapter concludes by acknowledging limitations and likely resistances to the ETMM approach and ways to counter the same.

Theoretical and Epistemological Foundations of ETMM Designs

ETMM designs draw on scientific realism as the epistemological base. Ideas about causal designs with context-sensitivity, systemic frameworks,

and built-in learning and confirming phases of research are taken from the writings of Cronbach and associates (1980), House (1991), Saloman (1991), and Reynolds (2005). The complementary use of multiple research methods guided by research purposes and evolutionary stage of a program are taken from Campbell's (1981) later works, as well as documentation of pragmatist evaluation practices (Greene & Caracelli, 1997). Elaborations follow.

Scientific Realist Foundations of ETMM Designs

The quantitative tradition in social science inquiry is based on logical positivism, often referred to as the "standard view" of science (Robson, 2002). The purpose of science, from this perspective, is the pursuit of universal laws that predict cause-and-effect relationships. A basic belief in this tradition is that there is an objective reality outside the researcher that can be investigated. The derivative of positivism is the post-positivistic tradition of inquiry. This view also holds that knowledge gained is objective (separate from the researcher) and value-free, but acknowledges that it can be imperfect and probabilistic.

Both positivistic and post-positivistic traditions hold that knowledge about the objective world is acquired by empirical means using a *scientific method*. Originating in laboratories, this general method involves the use of controlled procedures to collect quantitative data on variables of interest. Observations are tested against a priori hypotheses using deductive logic (Best & Kahn, 2003; Rosenthal & Rosnow, 1991).

Generalizability is central to quantitative hypothesis testing, giving researchers the ability to extrapolate from smaller sample statistics to larger population parameters in probabilistic terms. The main class of research designs for establishing cause-and-effect relationships in this tradition is the comparative experiment. This family of designs includes RCTs and quasi-experiments.

In contrast, scientific realism holds that knowledge about the world is socially and historically constructed. Causation and explanation are viewed as the key tasks of science. Issues of causation are attacked by developing and testing theories using rational criteria grounded in direct knowledge of actual phenomena. Social reality is acknowledged to be complex and layered. Causal inferences are enhanced by uncovering understandings of social structures (Robson, 2002).

In conducting research and evaluation of educational programs in actual field conditions, scientific realist ideas are more useful than positivistic ones. This is because most education and social service interventions are complex social entities. Both social and operational complexities are characteristic particularly of global programs, such as the examples detailed earlier. Programs are typically found in multilevel, open, and dynamic systems where multiple causal agents influence outcomes (House, 1991; Saloman, 1991). Program effects, therefore, are not easy to pin down or monitor. Even when guided by common intents and international standards that aim to homogenize impacts across nations (Steiner-Khamsi, 2004), the educational processes and effects manifest themselves in highly variable ways in different regions, influenced by national, regional, and local factors.

Rigid positivistic views are limiting under such field conditions. Three assumptions that become untenable are (a) causality is based on dependent chains of events (if x, then y), (b) firm controls are possible to institute in field experiments, and (c) predictability is the ultimate test of theory with the aim of all empirical science as prediction.

The more contextualized approach of a scientific realist opens up greater possibilities in understanding causalities surrounding complex social systems that global and local education programs typify. Unrealistic assumptions, about holding constant all other factors in order to study phenomena, are discarded in favor of more systemic and theory-driven research designs. A search for facts divorced from value orientations of society, including values of researchers—is not viewed as an achievable end in the realist framework. Nor is it seen as a barrier.

Saloman (1991) pointed out that "systemic" rather than "analytic" designs are more helpful in capturing the richness of events and actions in classrooms or communities where most education programs tend to be found. The research focus shifts to patterns of relationships among relevant variables, recognizing their interdependencies, inseparability, and transactional relations. When factors are interdependent, the effect of a variable is contingent on another (e.g., the delivery of an education curriculum depending on resource allocation factors). Variable influences may cross different levels of a system, such as, from schools down to classrooms. In other cases, factors that potentially influence outcomes are inseparable in operation—for instance, instructors' teaching styles are confounded with program delivery protocols. In other cases, programs have important transactional assumptions that directly impact outcomes in target populations, such as expected follow-up actions of students after curriculum delivery, which affect learning outcomes.

From a scientific-realist perspective, deeper study of environmental conditions and the phenomenon under study becomes a precondition to making more empirically and substantively guided causal interpretations. Such work can be undertaken during exploratory phases of evaluation research. At the time of confirmatory testing for a program's effects, these systemic influences may be modeled as exogenous factors, mediators, or moderators of effects, or as statistical controls (covariates).

Pragmatic Approach to Using Quantitative and Qualitative Methods

In applying ETMM designs, a pragmatic stance is taken in mixing research methods. The choice of methods is directly influenced by a preference for more nuanced guiding research questions that broadly examine impact issues. Questions ideally account for the complexities in a program's configuration, its developmental stage, and surrounding ecology (Chatterji, 2007, 2008).

The pragmatist views the object of inquiry and the guiding question(s) as paramount; the design and research tools serve as the means to solve the problem at hand and illuminate our understandings of the phenomenon under investigation (Robson, 2002). As such, useful evaluation frameworks must permit researchers to attack novel problems from angles that lie outside any single established methodological tradition. In an earlier publication, Greene and Caracelli (1997) documented three forces that drive a pragmatic use of mixed methods approaches in evaluation research:

1. Triangulation (or the need to establish validity through convergence of findings obtained via different methods)

2. Complementarity (or the need to combine methods to fill gaps in the understanding of a construct)

3. Expansion (or the need to use more than one method to obtain a fuller picture of the object of inquiry)

In the same vein, ETMM designs capitalize on the complementarities found in both quantitative and qualitative methodological traditions in social science research. Methods that on the surface appear *not* to be complementary may also be mixed in the service of enhancing the grade of evidence on programs examined.

Leaning toward scientific realism in later writings, Campbell (1981) recommended that researchers should acknowledge environmental realities in their designs, viewing them as factors that authenticate the research process when appropriately modeled, rather than as limitations. As the pioneering advocate of quasi-experimentation, he later endorsed the use of multiple methods in impact studies, including opinion surveys with multiple social indicators. In his introduction to a textbook on social experimentation, we also find Campbell acknowledging that evaluations of governmental policies inevitably become a political process. Use of more than one method, he states, lends greater validity to results of field experiments despite the added research burden.

Need for Multiphase Designs

ETMM designs, as indicated earlier, call for two or more phases of evaluative research. The early phases are dedicated to formative and exploratory inquiry of new, field-based education interventions, providing an opportunity for researchers to learn about a program and its environment. The early phases are also useful in building treatment fidelity and stability per the underlying "program theory." After exploratory studies, formative feedback can be diverted back toward program delivery personnel and local stakeholders for tightening or modifying a program. In later phases, ETMM designs are dedicated to confirming program effects, with tighter and more informed analytic designs, responsive to environmental conditions (Chatterji, 2005). In a set of historical recommendations, Cronbach & Associates (1980) offered several organizing theses that support the rationale for these design characteristics. Paraphrased, three points follow:

1. A good evaluative study ought to examine a program's underlying plan of operation and actual delivery processes before documenting how subjects ("clients") respond to it (Recommendation #37, p. 5).

2. More accurate outcome assessment is "sensible" only after an intervention is well-developed, supported with earlier "pilot" work (#40, p. 6).

3. There is utility in building in a "before-and-after study" within the overall research plan, where the early study is

dedicated to development work at a few sites; the sample is increased only after pointed, significant questions arise that smaller samples cannot answer. (p. 271)

Strengths and Limiting Assumptions of Experimental and Other Quantitative Designs

Given the previous theoretical rationale for broadening impact evaluation designs, this section now reevaluates the methodological advantages and barriers to using quantitative designs in field settings, starting with experimental designs (after Chatterji, 2007). Not discounting the importance of ethical considerations, the main focus here is on methodological issues.

There could be ethical blocks to mounting and executing field experiments. In high-need populations, for instance, it might be controversial and socially unacceptable to withhold treatment from a designated control group.

Promising new quantitative design options are now available for approximating causal effects of field interventions (see Cook, 2002; Schneider, Carnoy, Kilpatrick, Schmidt, & Shavelson, 2007). However, the argument for ETMM holds. Without a multiphase, mixed methods approach, the impact evidence on most complex education initiatives will fall short.

Utility of Experimental Designs

RCTs, based on the laboratory-style experiment, are appropriate designs when the aim is to establish a causal link between a manipulated intervention (X) on some observable outcome (Y), with all else being equal. Starting with a defined population, the basic RCT design is implemented by initially setting up two or more equivalent groups through random assignment of subjects. For example, students may be assigned to a new program (Treatment, T) and alternate conditions (Control, C). In doing so, RCTs provide researchers with a definitive

strategy to equalize preexisting differences in T and C groups on variables that could eventually affect the outcome, capitalizing on principles of probability and independence of case assignment.

When all relevant extraneous and confounding variables are equalized through randomization, individuals in both groups are expected to display the same average outcome if their group assignment were switched. In summary, if RCT designs meet theoretical expectations, conditions are optimized for making causal inferences between X and Y. Meeting the two assumptions of randomness and independence also creates optimal conditions for making statistical inferences using significance tests, which are also governed by the laws of chance. True experiments, the alias for RCTs, continue to be considered the strongest design option for answering impact evaluation questions.

Two issues need to be balanced in executing field experiments. These are (a) *internal validity*— or strategies for controlling outside factors to establish the link between X and Y, and (b) *external validity*—or evidence to support that the observed effect will generalize to other units in the population.

With socially complex education programs found in the typical contexts described earlier, the assumptions of RCTs are often violated after researchers start with random assignment of subjects to T and C conditions. Threats to external validity occur due to poor sampling of subjects, conditions, or time points when measuring effects. This is often a consequence of very tight experimental controls. Common threats to internal validity include

- Changes in definitions of T and C conditions, including a transference of ideas, materials, and resources among these conditions
- Differential subject attrition from T and C conditions due to openness of systems where programs are located, coupled with population mobility factors

- New and nonrandom additions to the subject pool, also due to mobility in the population
- Multiple variables that cannot be extricated from environmental, control, or treatment conditions
- Multilevel systems, where the independence assumptions are violated due to nesting of subjects in schools, homes, or educational communities
- Direct, mediating, or moderating influences of various factors outside the treatment on the expected outcome that are overlooked in designs

Effects realized thus are typically "gross" rather than "net"—this means that other factors along with X have an effect on Y. But because RCT designs are not equipped to generate information on factors that intervene or that confound the manifested effect, emphasizing instead controlled group differences on average outcomes, the true nature of the effect often remains hidden or misunderstood.

Violations of independence assumptions because of nested structures can be addressed with appropriate multilevel analytic methods. However, without supporting data on context variables, implementation inputs, and delivery processes, effects are difficult to link with a new intervention and often hard to explain.

Quasi-Experimental and Observational Designs

Other quantitative design options are quasi-experiments and nonexperimental, causal-comparative methods. Cook (2002) and Shadish, Cook, and Campbell (2002) identify regression discontinuity, interrupted time series, and matched cohort designs as the strongest alternatives to randomized experiments for making causal inferences. These quasi-experimental design options are intended for particular types of intervention manipulations (West, Biesanz, & Pitts, 2000).

Like RCTs, quasi-experiments allow researchers to manipulate the intervention. If other interfering factors are well controlled, these designs can potentially yield evidence to support a conclusion that a manipulated change in X causes a corresponding change in Y. The dual attributes of comparison and manipulation grant quasi-experiments a design status close to RCTs. However, despite proposed strategies for establishing group equivalence (such as matching or use of covariates), the internal validity of quasi-experiments frequently gets jeopardized because of inhospitable field conditions. Potential threats have been well documented (Cook, 2002; Shadish, Cook, & Campbell, 2002; West, Biesanz, & Pitts, 2000).

Observational (nonexperimental) designs cannot be ruled out as designs for impact studies, because field conditions may not always allow researchers to manipulate the educational treatment. Recently, the grants division of the American Educational Research Association endorsed the usefulness of observational designs for generating tentative causal evidence with large datasets, recommending a range of newer statistical techniques (Schneider et al., 2007). Outside manipulation, research design characteristics that support causal inferences include establishing causal relativity, structural modeling and testing of causal pathways, temporal ordering of variables, and systematic elimination of alternative explanations. To approximate randomization, researchers could also use econometric methods, including the use of instrumental variables and propensity score matching.

As is evident, neither RCTs, quasi-experiments, nor observational designs are enough by themselves to comprehensively ascertain the effectiveness of socially complex interventions. Scaffolded with appropriate forms of descriptive and qualitative methods, evidence on intervention effects may be rendered more meaningful and ecologically valid.

Applying ETMM Designs With School-Based Education Programs: Guiding Principles

How would evaluation researchers conduct ETMM studies? Table 6.1 now offers six general guidelines that build on each other (after Chatterji, 2005). The rationale for each guideline follows, situated in a hypothetical example of a school-based reading program.

Guideline 1: Ask Nuanced Guiding Questions

To start, guiding evaluation questions to properly gauge effects of complex education interventions must be broadened and might follow the example given next:

> WHAT is it about this kind of intervention that works, for WHOM, in what CIRCUM-STANCES, in what RESPECTS, and WHY? (Pawson, Greenhalgh, Harvey, & Walshe, 2005, pp. 29–31; capitalization in original)

In evaluating a novel reading program at a school, for example, the question would not simply be: Does the new program have a statistically significant effect, when compared to an existing one? Instead, we might ask: What are the operational characteristics of the program, *in situ*, when effects are documented in students? In what respects does the program differ from the comparison conditions? To what extent

Table 6.1   Guidelines for Applying ETMM Designs to Evaluate the Impact of Global Education Programs

Guideline	Elaboration of Design Principle
Guideline 1	Ask nuanced guiding questions, examining not just whether a program works, but how, why, and under what circumstances it yield effects.
Guideline 2	Extend timeline to developmentally track a program; plan to study a significant part of the "lifespan" of a program in natural environments.
Guideline 3	Incorporate two or more phases of research that build on each other, have deliberate research goals, and refine the research strategies progressively. • Exploratory phase(s) • Confirmatory phase(s)
Guideline 4	Use contextually based logic models or conceptual frameworks to map expected causal links among variables, frame hypotheses, and develop data collection and analysis plans.
Guideline 5	Delay formal assessment of effects to confirmatory phases of research, when programs can be effectively manipulated and contextual variables appropriately modeled. Consider appropriate quasi-experimental and nonexperimental designs as alternatives when experiments are impossible to mount.
Guideline 6	Combine relevant forms of qualitative and quantitative evidence aligned to questions to draw comprehensive conclusions on causal effects *in situ*; evaluate the meaning and generalizability of effects with stakeholder needs in mind.

does the reading program significantly improve reading skills in children with different mother tongues or from different socioeconomic strata? Under what conditions (classroom, community, and/or home) are program effects maximized (or reduced)? To what extent does the manifested effect of the program generalize to different schools, classrooms, or provinces?

Expanded questions alter the implications for data collection, analysis, and hypothesis testing. They move researchers from looking solely (or mainly) at average outcomes in those who do and do not receive a program to examining what mechanisms of programs lead to outcomes. Forces that mediate, moderate, or work jointly with the program to enhance outcomes are thus incorporated in the study plan.

Guideline 2: Extend Timeline to Developmentally Track a Program

A typical education program has an evolutionary trajectory in given sites that a research and evaluation design must consider. ETMM designs would account for this factor.

As emphasized throughout, the term *field-based* means that school programs are situated in some larger organizational or community unit, and an array of context factors potentially influence how they function and their manifested outcomes. Effects in terms of outcomes cannot be properly gauged until there is relatively stable program delivery, with entities operating per some underlying logical or theoretical plan of operation. This plan is referred to as the *program theory* and is further elaborated in guidelines that follow.

For example, before outcomes of a new reading program can be reasonably examined at a school, or processes meaningfully appraised, the program must mature and settle in its environment per the underlying design of operation. Such a design might specify that teachers and personnel are trained, materials appropriately distributed, and novel programs pilot tested before an impact assessment. A two- or three-phase

evaluation design that accounts for these temporal needs give researchers an advantage over a design that overlooks this aspect.

Guideline 3: Implement Multiphase Design With Exploratory and Confirmatory Studies

The third guideline follows from the second. An extended timeline allows for a multiphase research design with deliberate evaluative goals. Phases of research could build on each other and allow the research strategies to be progressively refined.

Exploratory phases could have formative goals to help stabilize delivery of the intervention and understand environmental dynamics. Confirmatory phases could formally examine effects. Research methods, such as observation and measurement strategies, sample selection, power, and qualitative methods, could also be improved.

In testing for effects of a reading curriculum, for example, the buy-in of a school's leadership to the program, its compatibility with larger school district initiatives, possible turnover in trained teachers and support staff who deliver the program, the composition and mobility of students, are all context factors that would likely influence program outcomes in direct or indirect ways. Exploratory phases could gather evidence on the extent to which these factors will alter outcomes. Confirmatory phases could selectively incorporate such factors in a summative analysis of effects. Methods could be honed along the way.

Guideline 4: Use Contextually Based Logic Models or Conceptual Frameworks in Designs

To attend to field-based complexities, ETMM designs use conceptual frameworks reflecting a program's underlying assumptions and anticipated effects in the typical context. As already suggested, education programs in schools are rarely tightly configured, singular, and discrete entities;

they are made up of complex and multiple components. Although their operation might appear atheoretic and chaotic at first (Byrne, 1998), program components are eventually expected to operate per some underlying plan or theory leading to outcomes. At any point in time or place, the implementation of an education program in field settings is likely to be consistent with the underlying plan to a greater or lesser degree.

The logical plan of program operation is called the *program theory* in the evaluation literature. The assumptions underlying the plan may be depicted graphically in the form of a *program theory model* or *logic model* that shows causal pathways to outcomes (see Bickman, 2000; Weiss, 2000). A program's underlying theory may be founded on a social science idea, such as an empirically tested theory of children's literacy development in a reading program. Alternatively, there could be other logical bases to a program, combining the beliefs, experiences, and both tested and untested ideas held by its users, proponents, and developers.

From a research and evaluation perspective, an analysis of a program's theory and formulation of a contextualized logic model helps reveal the explicit and "hidden" causal pathways by which variables influence a program's workings and effects. Categorization of relevant variables as Context, Input, Process, and Outcome factors (after Stufflebeam, 2000), before portraying possible links and pathways, is one way for researchers to contextualize their logic models. Decisions on variable selection, data collection, measurement, and analysis could flow from such a conceptual model during both exploratory and confirmatory phases of inquiry.

Guideline 5: Delay Formal Assessment of Effects to Confirmatory Phases

If experimental and appropriate quasi-experimental designs can be successfully incorporated in impact evaluations, they should be mounted when the program is effectively manipulated. Delaying formal experiments is helpful in this regard.

It is not enough to introduce an innovation in a new site and assume it is different from the "other" condition. To properly evaluate effects in comparison with a preexisting or control condition, the new program must be operationally distinct and relatively well defined.

For example, a reading innovation may use multicultural literature as the innovative element. If teachers or parents in the control condition are inclined toward reading diverse literature with their children, that context factor would interfere with the "treatment" definition. The manipulation would become diluted. In studying the impact of such a school-based program, there should be formally collected evidence showing its distinctiveness from the other conditions.

In cases where a program cannot be experimentally manipulated, due to practical, ethical, or other barriers, nonexperimental designs with appropriate causal models are useful in tentatively gauging the pattern of effects and associations (Reynolds, 2005; Schneider et al., 2007). Regardless of design choice, delayed assessment of effects enhances an evaluation in several ways.

Guideline 6: Combine Qualitative and Quantitative Evidence to Interpret Effects Comprehensively

ETMM designs use both quantitative and qualitative tools and sources of evidence. This pragmatic strategy aids in drawing firmer conclusions on program effects, shedding more light on the meaning and generalizability of effects across subjects, sites, and time frames sampled. In cases where effects are found (or vice versa) with quantitative methods, qualitative data may suggest reasons for such findings. Researchers select tools guided by questions and issues. If questions change and evolve from exploratory to confirmatory phases, the methods and tools should change in alignment.

A Global Example of a Strategic Impact Inquiry With Elements of ETMM Designs

Although not identified with this specific label, a compelling case for ETMM designs may be found in the global research framework for the Strategic Impact Inquiry (SII) studies of CARE International's women's education and empowerment programs. CARE is a human rights organization dedicated to alleviating poverty, building self-sufficiency, and achieving gender equality among people in developing nations. CARE's programs include several community-based education components.

CARE's SII studies were initiated in 2005 and are being conducted over a multi-year period. They focus on programs underway in Bangladesh, India, and Ecuador. Specifically, the education programs for women provide services in basic literacy, health and nutrition education, development of life skills and awareness of rights, and technical training in small business development. In this sense, the programs may be considered life-long learning programs. A key outcome of interest is women's empowerment. The programs are implemented by international donor-sponsored agencies, in collaboration with different national/local stakeholder groups and participants.

The SII case is now described, showing parallels with several of the ETMM design principles outlined in Table 6.1. The illustrative case shows the complexities of the constructs that define a global education program, the hierarchical and changing configurations of the national environments where the CARE programs are in effect, and research design decisions made by an interdisciplinary team of researchers to address the challenges in documenting program impacts. The information on the SII case was accessed from two sources:

www.csps.emory.edu/CARE%20SII.dwt

www.care.org

ETMM Design Elements in CARE's Global Research Framework

ETMM Guideline 1. Asking Nuanced Guiding Questions. To start, one finds the guiding questions for the early phases of the SII studies to be multi-layered and complex. They are aimed at determining how CARE's education and other interventions are helping poor women in these regions fulfill their needs and rights and become more empowered. Consistent with ETMM principles, the main questions probe not just into the direction, magnitude, or statistical significance of average "effects" but also the nature of the impacts and how they come about. For instance, two sets of questions on their website read as follows:

- Are CARE's programs impacting the underlying causes of poverty and rights denial? If so, how?
- What is CARE's contribution to women's empowerment and gender equity? What evidence exists to establish a link between CARE's approaches and principles and advancement of gender equity?

ETMM Guidelines 2 and 3. Use of Multiphase and Multiyear Studies. Like ETMM designs, the SII studies extend over a 3-year period and use a "learning process" approach. This idea is similar to the exploratory-confirmatory approach in ETMM. Direct learning by the research team through empirical inquiry is expected to inform subsequent phases of the research. The authors state: "The package of methods and three year timeframe were not random choices. They were based on specific design and measurement challenges that an investigation on women's empowerment faces" (see section on Purposes and Principles of SII, p. 2).

ETMM Guideline 4. Use of Contextually Based Logic Models or Conceptual Frameworks. To examine the links between CARE's programs and women's outcomes, the SII research design utilizes a conceptual model that mimics the notion of a "logic model" in ETMM designs. The framework, called the Household Livelihood Security Framework, identifies multiple variables and relationships with empowerment processes and outcomes. The specified paths include the role of enabling environmental factors, resources, and services (including CARE's education programs); access to and flow of opportunities; and women's outcomes mediated by household factors (see The Global Research Framework, SII, June 9, 2005). This framework shows possible exogenous and endogenous variables, along with mediators and moderators of effects.

Aligned with ETMM principles, one finds that the SII breaks down complex social constructs using theoretical frameworks. The key construct of interest in the first phase of the SII research is women's empowerment. The construct is defined both as an outcome and a process for building capacities in women. Per social science theory, empowerment is expected to be manifested via three avenues in women served by CARE's programs: individual agency, social structures, and relationships built by the women.

Also consistent with ETMM design principles, there is a clear acknowledgment of contextual variabilities and hierarchical data structures in the design. Investigators cite literature on possible macro- and microlevel influences within and across projects, localities, and nations that must be modeled to effectively understand and measure program impacts. For example, that women's empowerment levels can be measured in their households, communities, and on national and global levels is recognized. Further, that definitions can be culture-specific is also recognized.

ETMM Guideline 6. Use of Multiple Research Methods and Comprehensive Interpretations. As in ETMM, SII studies employ multiple methods and tools, complementing secondary analysis of quantitative databases with field research, site-based interviews, and surveys with more qualitative participant-oriented methods. A meta-evaluation is also included in the overall design. Experimental

manipulation (see ETMM Guideline 5) of CARE's multipart program was not possible in this case.

The operational definitions of complex social constructs are clarified via a common core of 23 dimensions (such as "knowledge" and "self-respect"), with qualitative and quantitative evidence indicators.

Global aggregation of outcomes against some comparison program or standard is not the stated goal of the impact studies. Rather, the goal is to paint a picture that is more like a mosaic, showing women's empowerment as a process of change as it relates to CARE's programmatic contributions. The analytic framework accounts for national and site-specific factors. The concept of a "global mosaic" is akin to the ETMM ideas that impact evaluations should aim toward drawing a comprehensive picture of the function of a program and a contextualized analysis of the evidence on outcomes.

The global research framework of CARE's education program is a useful illustration because several ETMM design elements are evident in the case. The program is a particularly complex, out-of-school intervention for which effects play out on individual, community, national, and global levels. ETMM designs are intended for programs with similarly complex configurations, whether found in school or community settings.

The SII studies also show how evaluation researchers working in challenging global settings with multiple stakeholders, are automatically drawn to the basic principles and tools of ETMM designs to find meaningful answers to impact questions. Fundamentally, the questions for such studies change; uneven results are expected, conditioned by contextual differences; research tools are selected to capture the context, change processes, and differential outcomes. Stakeholder-utility of findings is placed front and center.

Limitations of and Resistances to ETMM Designs

No design framework is a panacea nor the ultimate solution to all methodological challenges faced in the conduct of impact evaluations. ETMM designs are best suited for particular types of evaluation problems and evaluands. When the aim is to garner a high grade of impact evidence on complex social phenomena that can only be investigated in field settings, they provide much-needed flexibility and several design options to researchers. ETMM design principles may generalize to disciplines outside education, with similarly complex interventions. However, their disadvantages bear acknowledgment.

First, ETMM designs cannot be used to address all evaluation questions. Cost-related, philosophical, or political concerns that often revolve around global policies or programs cannot be addressed with the approach. The following questions are examples of issues that ETMM designs cannot inform: Does this program warrant the expenditures and costs? Is the program worth the disruption or focus away from other goals?

Second, impact researchers could face resistances when opting to use ETMM designs. Funders of research may be skeptical because the methodology appears too new and, on the surface, may seem highly resource-dependent. As demonstrated via the CARE example, elements of ETMM methods may actually be evident in the empirical literature, but not characterized as such (under this label). As more researchers document utility in the principles, future work in the evaluation profession could focus on identifying exemplary studies.

Third, ETMM designs call for sufficient resources to support a long-term and comprehensive project; this factor may be seen as a disadvantage. Cost-benefit studies comparing traditional methods such as RCTs against alternatives such as ETMM designs for the same programs (presently absent in the literature) may be of interest to both funders and the research and evaluation community. The harms of misapplication or an overreliance on RCTs in medicine have been documented through studies on drugs such as Vioxx. Educational studies, likewise, should be appraised from the standpoint of methodological rigor appropriate to field conditions with documentation of loss or harmful side effects that ensue over time for communities served in global arenas.

Other oppositions to ETMM designs may come from the training demands they impose on researchers and consumers of research. Current training in higher education institutions is often polarized to fall under either quantitative or qualitative traditions. Finding researchers and evaluators who are appropriately trained to undertake ETMM designs might pose a considerable challenge. Philosophical opposition to ETMM designs could come from quantitative methodologists trained in psychological methods. They might reject the "softer" qualitative data. Qualitative purists might likewise oppose ETMM concepts, especially when trained in pluralistic and critical-interpretive traditions. In this regard also, CARE's SII case illustrates how multidisciplinary teams of researchers were able to join forces to deliver a series of complex impact analyses on a global education program, complementing each other's diversity in philosophies, training, tools, and ideas.

Finally, other questions may be raised as to "how long" an ideal ETMM study needs to continue and whether such studies fall in the same category as longitudinal studies. The term *extended* in ETMM refers to a *phased* approach. This is a somewhat different connotation from a longitudinal design. In the author's experience and as suggested by the CARE example, a 3-year timeline is minimally needed for education programs that are well developed and supported.

Conclusion

Field-based, socially complex education programs call for a different framework and methodology for evidence gathering, where the rigor in the "science" of investigative processes must be evaluated with a different set of criteria than are traditionally employed with RCTs or quasi-experiments. The need for enhancing educational evaluation methodologies cannot be denied today given global policies calling for documentation, accountability, and evidence-based practices. Websites originating in geographically distant regions attest to the multinational consensus on the need for scientifically credible evidence on the effectiveness of various education initiatives and a shared value for evidence-based education (e.g., Evidence for Policy and Practice Information database in the U.K. and the Iterative Best Evidence Synthesis Programme in New Zealand,).

In looking ahead, future work remains to be undertaken in implementing ETMM designs on a wider scale and in formally developing criteria for evidence appraisal. I applaud the mission to promote education practices and programs worldwide supported with the best research evidence.

References

Anderson, J. A. (2005). *Accountability in education.* Paris: UNESCO, International Institute for Educational Planning.

Best, J. W., & Kahn, J. V. (2003). *Research in education.* Boston, MA: Pearson Education.

Bickman, L. (2000). Summing up program theory. *New Directions in Evaluation, 87,* 103–112.

Byrne, D. (1998). *Complexity theory in the social sciences: An introduction.* New York: Routledge.

Campbell, D. T. (1981). Introduction: Getting ready for the experimenting society. In L. Saxe & M. Fine (Eds.), *Social experiments: Methods for design and evaluation* (pp. 13–18). Beverly Hills, CA: Sage Publications.

Campbell, D. T., & Stanley, J. (1963). *Experimental and quasi-experimental designs for research.* Chicago, IL: Rand McNally.

Chatterji, M. (2004). Evidence of "What Works": An argument for extended-term mixed method (ETMM) evaluation designs. *Educational Researcher, 33*(9), 1–13.

Chatterji, M. (2005). Reprint. *Educational Researcher, 34*(6), 13–24.

Chatterji, M. (2007). Grades of evidence: Variability in quality of findings in effectiveness studies of complex field interventions. *American Journal of Evaluation, 28*(3), 239–255.

Chatterji, M. (2008). Comments on Slavin: Synthesizing evidence from impact evaluations

in education to inform action. *Educational Researcher, 37*(1), 23–26.

Coalition for Evidence-Based Policy. (2002, November). *Bringing evidence-driven progress to education: A recommended strategy for the U.S. Department of Education.* Available at http://www.excelgov.org/usermedia/images/uploads/PDFs/coalitionFinRpt.pdf

Cook, T. D. (2002). Randomized experiments in educational policy research: A critical examination of the reasons the educational evaluation community has offered for not doing them. *Educational Evaluation and Policy Analysis, 24*(3), 175–199.

Cronbach, L. J., & Associates. (1980). *Toward reform in program evaluation.* San Francisco, CA: Jossey-Bass.

Education Sciences Reform Act (ESRA). (2002). H.R. 3801. Education Sciences Reform Act of 2002 (107th Congress).

Greene, J. C., & Caracelli, V. J. (Eds.). (1997). Advances in mixed-method evaluation: The challenges and benefits of integrating diverse paradigms. *New Directions in Evaluation 74.* San Francisco, CA: Jossey-Bass.

Guyatt, G., & Rennie, D. (2002). *Users' guide to the medical literature: A manual for evidence-based clinical practice.* Chicago, IL: American Medical Association Press.

House, E. R. (1991). Realism in research. *Educational Researcher, 20*(6), 2–9.

No Child Left Behind Act of 2001. (2002). Pub. L. No. 107th Cong., 110 Cong. Rec. 1425. 115 Stat.

Pawson, R., Greenhalgh, T., Harvey, G., & Walshe, K. (2005). Realist review: A new method of systematic review designed for complex policy interventions. *Journal of Health Services Research and Policy, 10*(1), 29–34.

Petticrew, M., & Roberts, H. (2002). *Evidence, hierarchies, and typologies: Horses for courses.* Retrieved December, 15, 2006, from www.jech.bmj.com on.

Reynolds, A. J. (2005). Confirmatory program evaluation: Applications to early childhood interventions. *Teachers College Record, 107*(10), 2401–2425.

Robson, C. (2002). *Real world research* (2nd ed.). Malden, MA: Blackwell Publishing.

Rosenthal, R., & Rosnow, R. L. (1991). *Essentials of behavioral research: Methods and data analysis.* New York: McGraw-Hill.

Saloman, G. (1991). Transcending the qualitative-quantitative debate: The analytic and systemic approaches to educational research. *Educational Researcher, 20*(6), 10–18.

Schneider, B., Carnoy, M., Kilpatrick, J., Schmidt, W. H., & Shavelson, R. J. (2007). *Estimating causal effects using experimental and observational designs: A think tank white paper.* Washington, DC: The Governing Board of the American Education Research Association Grants Program.

Shadish, W. R., Cook, T. D., & Campbell, D. T. (2002). *Experimental and quasi-experimental designs for generalized causal inference.* Boston, MA: Houghton Mifflin.

Spring, J. (2008). Research on globalization and education. *Review of Educational Research, 78*(2), 330–363.

Steiner-Khamsi, G. (2004). Blazing a trail for policy theory and practice. In G. Steiner-Khamsi (Ed.), *The global politics of educational borrowing and lending* (pp. 201–220). New York: Teachers College Press.

Stromquist, N. (2002). *Education in a globalized world: The connectivity of economic power, technology and knowledge.* Lanham, MD: Rowman & Littlefield.

Stufflebeam, D. L. (2000). The CIPP model for evaluation. In D.L. Stufflebeam, G.F. Madaus, & T. Kellaghan (Eds.), *Evaluation models: Viewpoints on educational and human services evaluation* (pp. 279–317). Boston, MA: Kluwer Academic.

UNICEF. (2007a). *Millennium development goals: Promote gender equality and empower women.* Retrieved on December 1, 2007, from: http://www.unicef.org/mdg/gender.html.

UNICEF. (2007b). *Basic education and gender equality.* Retrieved on July 20, 2008, from www.unicef.org/girlseducation/index.php.

Weiss, C. H. (2000). Which links in which theories shall we evaluate? *New Directions in Evaluation, 87,* 35–45.

West, S. G., Biesanz, J. C., & Pitts, S. C. (2000). Causal inference and generalization in field settings. In H. T. Reis & C. M. Judd (Eds.), *Handbook of research methods in social and personality psychology.* Cambridge, UK: Cambridge University Press.

CHAPTER 7

The Evaluation of the Georgia Pre-K Program

An Example of a Scientific Evaluation of an Early Education Program

Gary T. Henry and Dana K. Rickman

That was what we meant by science. That both question and answer are tied up with uncertainty, and that they are painful. But that there is no way around them, and that you hide nothing; instead everything is brought out into the open.

—Peter Hoeg (*Borderliners*, 1994)

Introduction

In this chapter, we present an evaluation of the Georgia Pre-K Program as an example of a scientific evaluation of an education program. Perhaps unfortunately, the term *scientific evaluation* or *science-based evaluation* conjures a variety of images depending on who hears it. For some, it means randomized control trials, nothing more and nothing less. For some, the term may represent a means of cutting through conflicting views of educational programs and the uncertainty about their effectiveness. For others, it conveys a waste of resources chasing certainty that can never be attained in a complex world with unparalleled inequalities. For still others, it is a political agenda that slows social progress, restrains innovation, excludes the voices of societies' most vulnerable members, and impedes the development and implementation of public policies that could benefit the poor and disenfranchised. The list of images conjured up by the use of the word

AUTHORS' NOTE: The Early Childhood Study was funded by Bright From the Start: Department of Early Care and Learning and the National Institute for Early Education Research. The chapter represents the views of the authors and not necessarily those of the sponsors.

scientific in conjunction with *evaluation* is longer than we can repeat here, but these examples will do to show the diversity.

We feel that scientific evaluation of public policies and programs is best characterized as a quest for better answers to questions about how social betterment can be achieved, what steps should be taken on behalf of the public good, and what society should do to actually reduce social inequalities—questions for which we currently do not have accurate answers. In straightforward language, the quest most often associated with scientific evaluation is to seek more accurate estimates of the effects of programs. It, therefore, follows from this that the main objective of scientific evaluation is to produce unbiased estimates of the effects of programs, but additional objectives can include producing accurate estimates of differences in outcomes attributable to differences in program implementation and accurate measures of program outcomes (Mark, Henry, & Julnes, 2000).

Datta (Chapter 9, this volume) emphasizes three characteristics of scientific evaluations: (a) they tend to be summative, (b) they use quantitative measures, and (c) they give primacy to methods. Although these are accurate descriptions, other qualities can be stressed as well. For example, scientific evaluations place a premium on knowledge accumulation. Rather than stressing a generic evaluator's toolkit and reliance on stakeholders for deciding on the important questions, scientific evaluators often turn to fundamental issues of program impact on intended beneficiaries and prior research to aid in defining questions. But stakeholders' views, especially in defining the outcomes of greatest importance to them, are often thoughtfully incorporated into scientific evaluation through techniques such as values inquiry (Mark et al., 2000). Use of the prior evaluation and research literature on the intervention is critical to scientific evaluation as well because that literature presents methods used in prior research, which can be used as a basis for identifying methodological weaknesses that can be addressed in evaluations of similar policies in the future.

In part because scientific evaluators place such stock in cumulating knowledge, they also emphasize transparency of procedures and contributing to the research literature. Transparency of procedures is usually considered a requirement for any evaluation that makes judgments or recommendations concerning public policies and programs. But evaluators working in the scientific genre seeking to improve on the accuracy of the findings from earlier evaluations depend on transparency, such as clearly describing procedures used to select study participants (see American Association for Public Opinion Research's reporting standards for response rates as an example), interviewing protocols and other data-collection methods, and the analytical procedures from which the study findings were drawn.

Placing a priority on the dissemination of study findings is not unique to scientific evaluation; they are clearly specified for all evaluations in the American Evaluation Association's Guiding Principles for Evaluators (2008). However, efforts to publish study procedures and findings for other evaluators to review, critique, and set out to improve are extremely important in scientific evaluations. These published reports provide the basis for detecting potential bias in prior studies, at which improvements in future evaluations can be targeted.

The example presented in this chapter, the evaluation of Georgia's Pre-K Program, had as its goal all three of the objectives for scientific evaluations presented earlier: the description of children's development, including those children participating in the program; the assessment of the extent to which children's outcomes were associated with variations in program implementation; and the estimation of the effects of the program on children living in poverty. The evaluation measures presented are primarily quantitative, although mixed methods were used in the evaluation, and a major part of the evaluation employed semi-structured interviews of parents of children living in poverty.

This example also illustrates the cumulative nature of scientific evaluation and the importance of transparency and dissemination. In addition to countless briefings of the study findings to policy (e.g., state legislators and blue ribbon panels appointed to develop state or local Pre-K initiatives), practitioner, and research audiences, to date the results have been published in six refereed journal articles across the fields of policy science, psychology, and education. The findings were widely reported in the media during the lead up to the unsuccessful Pre-K ballot initiative in California, used as a guide for developing the Pre-K Program developed in at least one other state, South Carolina, and presented to the U.S. Senate during hearings on the reauthorization of Head Start. In the description presented in this chapter, we attempt to make the study processes transparent, including both the strengths and weaknesses.

The design, one of Datta's defining characteristics, may be considered the evaluation's major weakness by some because a randomized control trial (RCT) was not used. RCT designs, which are preferred by most of the proponents of scientific evaluation, require the fewest assumptions in inferring a causal effect (Rubin, 1974, 2005). A sophisticated matched sampling design, known as propensity score matching (Rosenbaum, 2002; Rosenbaum & Rubin, 1983), was employed for the assessment of causal impacts. Describing this method does allow us to illustrate the painstaking, but steady, progress being made in the development of alternatives to RCT designs and to bring some of the empirical work assessing these types of methods to bear. Before presenting the example of scientific evaluation, it is important to go beyond some defining characteristics and discuss how scientific evaluations and the specific evaluation of the particular publicly funded preschool program in Georgia can be linked to the broader theme of globalization.

Scientific Evaluation of Education Programs, Pre-K, and Globalization

The theme of globalization establishes a context within which this example of scientific evaluation

can be described and examined for an *international* handbook of *educational evaluation*. For the purposes of this chapter, we use a definition of *globalization* from Gibson-Graham (1996): "a set of processes by which the world is being rapidly integrated into one economic space via increased international trade, the internationalization of production and financial markets, and the internationalization of a commodity culture promoted by an increasingly networked global telecommunication system" (p. 120). Globalism and its impacts have expanded beyond the international or macroeconomic, with ramifications for domestic economies, communication and information technologies, labor forces, multinational political organizations, and multinational corporations, as well as spawning political alliances that link nations for economic and cultural purposes.

The theme of globalization can be related to this chapter's subject—the evaluation of an early education program as an example of scientific evaluation—in three distinct ways: (a) through the focus on public provided early education, (b) the scientific methods used in the evaluation, and (c) the use of competition in the provision of the Pre-K services.

First, early education is receiving significantly expanded public investment throughout the United States (Barnett, Hustedt, Robin, & Schulman, 2004) partially in response to the need to find new and lower cost ways to improve human capital and maintain the competitive edge enjoyed by the U.S. economy. It has become widely recognized that human development occurs most rapidly during early childhood and that skill development is more readily stimulated among the very young than at any other time of life (Heckman, 2006; Shonkoff & Phillips, 2000). Although developing countries are stretching thin resources to move toward universal secondary education and other more developed countries have long since provided universal access to high-quality developmental programs for young children, the United States only recently has begun to rapidly expand the education of its youngest residents. The recent focus on early education and development programs in the United States has been focused primarily on 4-year-olds and is often justified by expected returns to human capital and economic development.

Second, the theme of globalization can be linked to the increased emphasis on scientific evaluation. The adoption of the No Child Left Behind Act of 2001 and supporting legislation, the Education Sciences Reform Act (ESRA) of 2002, in the United States can be viewed as a response to globalization. Specifically, the ESRA, which established the Institute of Education Sciences (IES) within the U.S. Department of Education, emphasizes the scientific evaluation of "the effectiveness of Federal and other education programs" (H.R. 3801, p. 5 Part A, Sec 111). IES is to "conduct and support scientifically valid research activities, including basic research and applied research, statistics activities, scientifically valid education evaluation, development, and wide dissemination" (H.R. 380, p. 6 Part A, Sec 112). The need for this type of evidence is, at least in part, to increase confidence that education programs have payoffs in terms of increasing students' skills and knowledge, which will lead to a more productive work force. Although globalization is neither a necessary nor a sufficient cause of the movement for more scientific evaluation and the need for more accurate information on educational program effectiveness, a linkage between globalization and the emphasis on scientific evaluation is easy to draw.

The third and final way in which globalization can be linked to the scientific evaluation of Georgia's Pre-K program is through the program's reliance on competition as a means of providing efficient and effective services. Economic globalization movements and policies freely embrace Milton Friedman's theory of competition and decreased government involvement in economic policies. Through economic competition that is not overly regulated by individual government involvement, the market is expected to reach its highest production capacity (Stromquist & Monkman, 2000) and maximize efficiency. It is possible that the preference for

open markets expressed in economic policies that have brought about increased globalization has spilled over into other public policy domains, including education in the United States. However, other societal pressures, such as dissatisfaction with academic achievement in U.S. public schools, may have independently contributed to the adoption of market-oriented education policies sometimes referred to as choice or parental choice policies.

The Georgia Pre-K Program was—from its inception—a market-based program. The Georgia Pre-K Program established a market in which parents of 4-year-olds could choose to enroll their children in publicly funded preschool provided by public schools, not-for-profit agencies, and private-for-profit firms at no cost to the parents. Each provider's funding depends on their ability to enroll a sufficient number of children to fill a classroom. An earlier study did provide confidence that the market-based approach produced benefits for the children participating in the programs. Specifically, it showed that greater local competition among the organizations providing Pre-K services raised children's language and math skills and did not increase the likelihood that children would be retained in grade for an extra year (Henry & Gordon, 2006).

In each of these three ways, globalization can be linked to the example evaluation presented in this chapter, but the links were not explicitly drawn when the evaluation began in 2001. When the purposes of this evaluation, the Georgia Early Childhood Study (ECS), were established, two rose to the top: (a) to chart the development of Georgia's 4-year-olds, particularly, but not exclusively, the children participating in the Georgia Pre-K Program; and (b) to assess the effectiveness of the state's early education programs. At that time, Georgia stood at the forefront of the American states in providing nearly universal Pre-K, ranking as second in the nation in terms of providing preschool for its 4-year-olds (Barnett, Hustedt, Robin, & Schulman, 2004). Therefore, assessing the growth and attainment of skills—both cognitive and social emotional—of Georgia's young residents offered an important opportunity to gather evidence to inform policy and program decisions about Pre-K within the state, as well as influence the adoption and implementation of early education policies in other states or jurisdictions.

Among the research questions addressed in the evaluation, we have chosen to highlight four in this chapter:

1. What were the developmental patterns for the children participating in Georgia Pre-K, and was it similar to other children in the state?

2. To what extent do variations in the Georgia Pre-K Program affect children's developmental outcomes?

3. For children living in poverty, how did the outcomes of children served by Georgia Pre-K compare with those of children served by Head Start?

4. How much influence do peers have on the development of other children in their classrooms?

Prior to presenting the answers for each of these four study questions, we turn to the description of the methods to make the study processes as transparent as possible within the constraints of a chapter-length presentation.

Early Childhood Study Design: Sample and Measures

Four Groups of Children in Georgia

In 1995, Georgia became the first state in the country to offer universal (non-means tested) Pre-K to all 4-year-olds whose parents chose to enroll them. By 2001, for example, 63,613 children, or 52% of the estimated population of 4-year-olds in Georgia, participated in the program for that school year. When Head Start's 10,976 spaces for 4-year-olds in 2001 were included, publicly subsidized early childhood

programs were provided for 61.3% of the state's 4-year-olds. In addition to children enrolled in Pre-K and Head Start, a third group included in the original study was 4-year-olds enrolled full time in private preschool programs or center-based child care. A fourth group, children who did not participate in full-time, formal preschool as 4-year-olds, was added to the ECS in 2002.

With publicly subsidized preschool as prevalent as it was in Georgia in 2001, it was difficult to find a group of children in Georgia whose development would be similar to those enrolled in Pre-K, but who did not participate in any preschool program. Even those children who did remain in the care of their family may have experiences, such as a mother who did not work outside the home, which could make their development different from that which Pre-K children would have experienced in the absence of the program. We discuss various ways in which we coped with these issues, especially with respect to answering the third research question comparing the outcomes of children participating in Pre-K and Head Start.

The next four subsections describe the populations from which the four groups of children in the study were drawn—the three groups of preschoolers included in the original study and a fourth group, children who did not participate in full-time preschool as 4-year-olds.

Georgia Pre-K

Funded by earmarked proceeds from the Georgia Lottery, the Georgia Pre-K Program began as a program for children from lower income families in the 1993–1994 school year. Beginning with the 1995–1996 academic year, Georgia became the first state in the nation to offer Pre-K for all 4-year-olds whose parents chose to enroll them—regardless of household means. By 1996–1997, the program served more than 57,000 four-year-olds annually, and in 2001–2002 it had expanded to serve 63,613 children, 25,711 of whom were classified as at risk (Georgia Office of Educational Accountability, 2002). The state expended approximately $216.3 million to operate the program in the 2001–2002 academic year.

The Pre-K Program is administered at the state level, but the providers may be local public schools, not-for-profit organizations, or private for-profit firms. Each provider must receive approval from the state's Bright From the Start: Georgia Department of Early Care and Learning (Bright From the Start, formerly the Office of School Readiness) to offer one or more Pre-K classes. In 2001–2002, four-year-olds could have attended one of the 3,152 Pre-K classes offered by 1,683 providers at no tuition cost to the child's family for the 6.5-hour instructional program. Private-for-profit providers offer the largest number of classes (1,460), but are closely followed by local public school systems (1,325), which together offer 88% of the classrooms. Not-for-profit providers include Head Start agencies (40 classes) and nonsectarian entities operated by faith-based organizations (Bright From the Start, 2005). Each approved class can enroll up to 20 children who receive full-day services (at least 6.5 hours) under the guidance of a lead teacher who must have a college degree (associate's degree or above).

Head Start

Head Start is a national program that provides comprehensive developmental services for low-income preschool children and their families. Currently funded at approximately $6.2 billion nationally, Head Start serves more than 900,000 children and their families each year (Congressional Research Service, 2003). In Georgia, Head Start programs serve nearly 20,000 children ranging from 3 to 5 years old in 33 different programs covering 157 of Georgia's 159 counties (Georgia Head Start Collaboration Office, 2003). During the 2001–2002 school year, Georgia Head Start provided spaces for 10,976 four-year-olds. The program in Georgia is designed to address developmental goals for children, employment and self-sufficiency goals for adults, and support for parents in their work

and in their roles as parents (Bright From the Start, 2005).

Private Preschools

Private preschools, for the purpose of this study, are schools or child-care centers that offer educational and developmental programs for 4-year-olds in exchange for tuition or fees for these services. The families of the children receiving the services usually pay the school or center directly. These preschools include private, not-for-profit programs, such as church-based schools, and private, for-profit programs, such as child-care facilities or private college-preparatory day schools. All of the preschools included as private preschools are licensed by the state. However, the preschools vary in a number of significant ways, including the population of 4-year-olds served and whether the teachers use a specific curriculum in the preschool classrooms. The average socioeconomic status of parents was significantly higher in the private preschools than Georgia Pre-K or Head Start.

Nonpreschool Sample

Throughout the report, children from the previously mentioned three groups are referred to as Georgia preschoolers because these three groups comprise a probability sample of the 4-year-olds in Georgia who attended a formal early education program. In addition to these three groups, a new sample of students was added to the study in the fall of 2002, their kindergarten year.

This new group of students comprises a sample of 4-year-olds in Georgia who did not attend a formal early education program. However, the individual experiences of these children varied, in some cases from day to day. For example, 44% of the sample attended an organized "mother's morning out" program routinely. In addition, 60% spent most of their weekdays at home, with relatives or in family day care. Finally, 4% attended a formal preschool for up to 3 days a week. As these percentages indicate, many children who are classified as receiving informal care had a variety of child-care experiences during the week. For example, some parents reported that their child stayed at home, but that they also attended preschool two or three mornings a week.

Because these children were added to the study after preschool, we did not collect baseline data from the fall in which they turned 4 years old. Therefore, these children are not included in several of the analyses that include baseline measures.

Sample Selection

A probability sample of 4-year-olds receiving instructional and supervisory services under the auspices of Head Start, the Georgia Pre-K Program, and private preschools was selected. For the study, 135 sites were chosen, and 126 agreed to participate. Children were sampled after obtaining parental consent (75% or more consented in most sites). The total sample size for the first year was 630. This includes 353 children

from Georgia Pre-K (56% of the sample), 134 children from Head Start (21% of the sample), and 143 children from private preschool (23% of the sample).

Only those children who had remained in their preschool program for the duration of the 2001–2002 school year (approximately 9 months) were eligible for continuing in the study. Of the 570 children eligible, 449 (79%) were located in a Georgia kindergarten classroom during the fall 2002. In addition, a new sample of 225 children who did not attend formal preschool was selected. These children were sampled at random from the kindergarten classrooms in which the first-year children were currently enrolled.

Table 7.1 provides a breakdown of the number of eligible children included in the study data from the beginning of preschool through the end of first grade. Effective follow-up methods for retaining children from the original sample in the study are extremely important to minimize the effects of attrition. Table 7.1 clearly shows that a high retention rate was achieved, which is important for scientific longitudinal evaluations.

Table 7.1   Number of Children in the Georgia Early Childhood Study per Testing Period

	Preschool		Kindergarten		1st Grade	
	Fall 2001	Spring 2002	Fall 2002	Spring 2003	Fall 2003	Spring 2004
Total	570	570	795*	793**	786**	785**
Tested	570	539	670	661	N/A	670
GA Pre-K	325	311	264	262	N/A	272
Head Start	119	108	92	94	N/A	97
Private	126	120	89	93	N/A	97
Nonpreschool	N/A	N/A	225	212	N/A	204

*In the fall of 2002 (kindergarten), 570 children were eligible to continue the study, and 225 children with no formal preschool experience were added to the study.

**The decreases in the number of eligible students in the spring of 2003, fall of 2003, and spring of 2004 were due to parental or school withdrawal from the study.

For a more complete understanding of the similarities and differences in the four groups of children included in the study, we describe characteristics of the children, their parents, and their families in the next section. For each characteristic, we note differences among any of the groups that are statistically significant.

Characteristics of Study Children

The average age of participants upon their entry into preschool was 4.5 years (Table 7.2). The majority of children enrolled in Head Start (60%) were African American, whereas the majority of children enrolled in private preschools (66%) were White. In Georgia Pre-K, the sample was split more evenly between White and non-White participants. The largest difference between White and non-White participants was found in the nonpreschool sample, with a large majority of White children represented (80%). All four groups of children had similar percentages of Hispanic children

and children grouped in the "Other minorities" category.

The proportions of boys and girls in the study groups differed as well. In Georgia Pre-K, the percentage of males and females was equal. However, in Head Start and private preschools, there were disproportionately more male students than female students.

Parental Characteristics and Interactions

The levels of parental education and other parent characteristics that have been associated with children's development differ significantly across the four groups of children in Georgia (Table 7.3). The average education levels of mothers and fathers of children who attended private preschools or did not attend preschool were significantly higher than those of children enrolled in Georgia Pre-K and Head Start. Furthermore, mothers and fathers of children who attended Head Start had significantly lower levels of education

Table 7.2   Characteristics of Children Participating in the Georgia Early Childhood Study

Demographic Characteristic	Georgia Pre-K (n = 325)	Head Start (n = 119)	Private (n = 126)	Nonpreschool (n = 225)	Overall (n = 795)
Age upon preschool entry (SD)	4.5 (0.29)	4.5 (0.26)	4.5 (0.29)	N/A	4.5 (0.28)
Age upon kindergarten entry (SD)	5.5 (0.29)	5.5 (0.26)	5.5 (0.29)	5.5 (0.27)	5.5 (0.29)
Sex					
% Male	50.8	52.3	59.2	48.0	51.7
% Female	49.2	47.7	40.8	52.0	48.3
Race					
% White[a,b]	50.5	29.8	64.2	76.6	57.7
% African American[a]	39.5	57.0	26.9	16.5	33.0
% Hispanic	2.7	4.1	1.0	5.4	3.6
% Other	7.3	9.0	7.9	2.2	4.9

a. Children from Head Start differ significantly from children who attended Georgia Pre-K, private preschool, and no formal preschool.

b. Children from Georgia Pre-K differ significantly from children who attended Head Start and no formal preschool.

than their counterparts in Georgia Pre-K. Head Start children had the highest proportion of parents with less than a high school diploma. The children who attended Head Start also had the highest proportion of teenage mothers (38%), significantly more than the children enrolled in Georgia Pre-K, private preschools, and the children without a formal preschool experience.

Table 7.3 Parent Characteristics of Children Participating in the Georgia Early Childhood Study

Family Characteristic	Georgia Pre-K (n = 326)	Head Start (n = 119)	Private (n = 126)	Nonpreschool (n = 223)	Overall (n = 794)
Mother's education					
% Less than HS[a]	6	30	1	5	7
% HS degree[e]	63	64	50	53	59
% BA or more[a,b]	29	4	48	40	32
Father's education					
% Less than HS[a]	8	21	3	6	8
% HS Degree	65	66	58	54	62
% BA or more[g]	27	9	38	38	29
Total gross income[f] (1–10 range) (mean)	4.7	2.2	6.7	6.1	5.2
Means tested benefits					
% TANF[a]	4.3	17.0	2.0	3.6	5.7
% Food Stamps[a,e]	18.0	50.7	2.1	10.2	17.9
% SSI	4	4	1	1	3
Unemployment insurance (%)	9.9	12.7	3.2	8.0	8.6
Currently insured[a] (%)	97.0	82.7	97.1	97.1	95.1
Insurance type					
% Medicaid[a]	18.7	59.8	8.1	8.53	20.7
% PeachCare	14.8	15.7	10.8	12.4	13.0
% Employer[a,c]	54.1	20.7	71.2	58.9	53.2
Teenage mother[a] (%)	8.9	19.0	2.6	5.9	8.3
Sufficient food (1–4 range) (mean)	2.9	2.8	3.0	2.9	2.9

a. Children from Head Start differ significantly from children who attended Georgia Pre-K, private preschool, and no formal preschool.

b. Children from private preschool differ significantly from children who attended Georgia Pre-K and Head Start.

c. Children from Pre-K differ significantly from children who attended Head Start, private preschool, and no formal preschool.

d. Children from Head Start differ significantly from children who did not attend formal preschool.

e. Children from Georgia Pre-K differ significantly from private preschool children.

f. All groups differ significantly from each other except children from private preschool and children with no formal preschool.

g. Children from Head Start differ significantly from children who attended private preschool and children who did not attend formal preschool.

Families with children who attended private preschool and with children who did not attend preschool had a significantly higher household income than the families with children enrolled in Georgia Pre-K and Head Start. There was also a significant difference in household income among families with children enrolled in Head Start and the families with children enrolled in Georgia Pre-K. Differences in family economic status were also found to be significant across the four groups, with more children enrolled in Head Start being from families that received benefits such as TANF (21%) and Food Stamps (53%).

Results also indicated that there were children in Georgia Pre-K with family backgrounds similar to children in Head Start and private preschools. For example, the proportion of children who received Medicaid, a means tested federal program, was significantly higher among Head Start children than children enrolled in Georgia Pre-K and private preschools. However, the proportion of children in Head Start who received PeachCare, a state-funded insurance program that subsidized health care costs for low-income families not qualifying for Medicaid, was nearly equal to the proportion of children in Georgia Pre-K who received these benefits.

Measuring Children's Development and Other Child Outcomes

Prior to beginning this study, a values inquiry (Mark, Henry, & Julnes, 2000) was conducted with probability samples of parents, teachers, program administrators, and Georgia residents (Henry, 2002). According to these groups, high-priority objectives for the Georgia Pre-K Program are to prepare each child for success in school and reduce problem behaviors such as dropping out and juvenile crime. Unfortunately, actual success in school and these types of problem behaviors can be assessed only after a number of years. In this study, we have measured numerous indicators of early school success and leading indicators

of later school success, such as promotion to second grade on time. Being prepared for school is a complex process that experts believe requires a mix of cognitive, communication, and social skills, as well as good health and physical well-being (Kagan, Moore, & Bradekamp, 1995). Therefore, the ECS measured multiple outcomes that are considered to be indicators of school success, many of which were measured at preschool entry and at the end of each school year. These data, which cover all of the dimensions that have been identified as important indicators of school readiness, came from several sources, including direct assessments by trained staff, teachers' ratings, and parents' ratings.

Study Measures

The ECS intended to collect developmental outcome information as comprehensively and accurately as possible, while being mindful not to take too much of any individual's time. Measures were taken periodically from the beginning of the children's preschool year (fall 2001) through the completion of first grade (spring 2004).

For comprehensiveness, we measured characteristics in four of the dimensions recommended by the National Education Goals Panel on School Readiness: cognition, language development, social and emotional development, and health and physical well-being (Kagan et al., 1995). For accuracy, we utilized three of the best sources available to assess children's skills at multiple time points:

- Trained professionals to individually administer widely used developmental assessments with each child in the study;
- Parents who provided the researchers with essential family information; and
- Teachers who directly evaluated each child's behavioral, social, communication, and academic skill levels.

The assessment battery was carefully selected to include norm-referenced assessments and other measures of children's skills. The battery provided valid and reliable information about children's cognitive, math, and language skills, including vocabulary, letter and word recognition, expressive language, and phonemic processing. During the first year of the study, children were assessed using a variety of nationally standardized tests that measured basic premath skills (WJ–III; Applied Problems subtest), receptive language (PPVT–III, Form A), expressive language (OWLS), and letter and word recognition (WJ–III Letter-Word Identification subtest). A series of nationally recognized basic mastery skills tests were also administered. Other measures were added during the study to tap emerging skills and attitudes. For example, in spring 2004, the Children's Attitudes Toward School, a new assessment tool, was added to the assessments to measure the children's attitudes toward school and learning (Mashburn & Henry, 2004).

Findings Related to Four Selected Research Questions

Research Question 1. What was the developmental pattern for the children participating in Georgia Pre-K and was it similar to other children in the state?

The interest in this question was motivated to better understand how the development of young children in Georgia compared with the typical development of children across the country. It can be viewed as a needs assessment that can be used to identify groups of children and specific skills that deserve greater attention in the state. The assessments presented in this section have been nationally scaled by age, with a mean of 100. Thus, any average score above 100 indicates that the group of children is performing above the average that is expected for

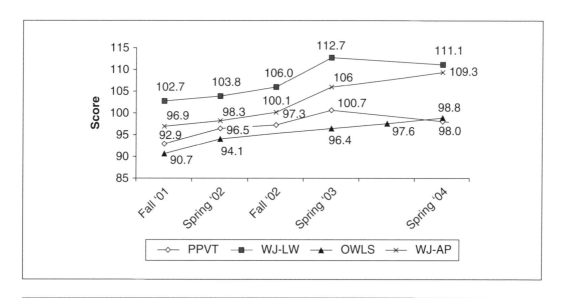

Figure 7.1   Direct Assessments Relative to the National Norm for Georgia's Preschool Students

Note: Average score for GA preschoolers: national norm = 100.

children across the nation. As shown in Figure 7.1, children in Georgia made significant gains from the beginning of preschool to the end of first grade in terms of their skills compared with national samples of children their age. Georgia's preschoolers began that school year significantly behind peers of their age across the nation. However, by the end of kindergarten, they exceeded the national norms on their overall math skills, phonemic awareness, and letter and word recognition, and they had gained significant ground in expressive language skills. During their first-grade year, they lost part of the gains in receptive vocabulary (PPVT) and letter-word recognition (WJ-LW) relative to their peers across the nation, but gained on the other measures, including applied problem-solving skills (WJ-AP).

Program Influences

Children enrolled in the Georgia Pre-K Program gained substantially on their peers nationally on the assessments of language and cognitive skills used throughout this study. They began preschool well

behind the national norms on three of four skill assessments and finished well above the national norms on three and on par with the national norm on the fourth. Pre-K participation was associated with more positive outcomes than other preschool experiences on 11 of 16 measures, but the differences were not statistically significant at the end of the first grade (see Figure 7.2).

The effects of the Georgia Pre-K Program are evident in the increases in skills using age-adjusted scores as displayed in Figure 7.2. It is important to note that Georgia's preschoolers, including those who had been enrolled in Georgia Pre-K, lost ground against the national norms between the end of kindergarten and the end of first grade on two measures of language skills, although their scores remained well above those achieved at the beginning of preschool.

Although comparisons with other programs are informative, the differences between children in different groups cannot be construed as an estimate of the effects of Georgia Pre-K. To the extent that parents made good choices when selecting their

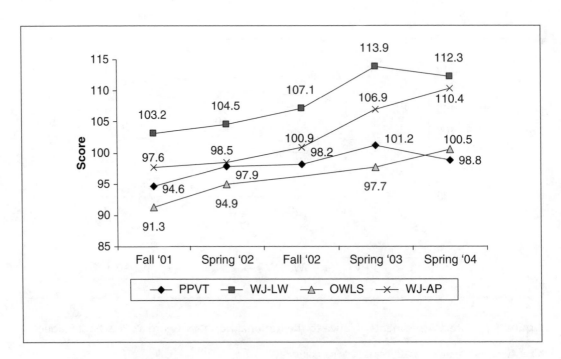

Figure 7.2   Outcomes of Children Enrolled in Georgia Pre-K

Note: Average score for GA pre-K: national norm = 100.

children's preschools, those choices complicate the comparison of differences across programs. We examine this issue in more detail when we present the findings for Research Question 3.

Research Question 2. To what extent do variations in the Georgia Pre-K Program affect children's developmental outcomes?

A primary purpose of many evaluations, including scientific educational evaluations, is to estimate how variations in the ways that programs are implemented can contribute to differences in children's outcomes. These findings can be used by program administrators to improve their programs in ways that are most likely to improve the outcomes of the targeted beneficiaries. Georgia Pre-K Program classrooms differ in several ways, including the teachers' credentials and teaching styles, the curriculum, and the program setting. We addressed each of these sources of variation, and we examined whether these differences are associated with differences in literacy, cognitive, or social skills of the children.

Requiring that teachers have a college degree is one way that Pre-K Programs attempt to control quality and improve children's outcomes. In this study, no differences were found in children's outcomes when taught by teachers with bachelor's degrees when compared with teachers holding associate's degrees or technical diplomas.

Teachers are often characterized in terms of having a "child-centered" teaching style or a more directive, adult-centered approach to teaching. In some cases, teachers fall into a third group that shifts from "child-centered" to "adult-directed" styles. The third group, referred to as "middle of the road" teaching style, was not as positive for children's development as the "child-centered" teaching style. Children who had Pre-K teachers with a middle of the road teaching style were more frequently withdrawn, had a less positive attitude toward school and learning, and performed less well in math than children whose teachers applied a child-centered style. There were no statistical differences between these two

groups in terms of language and literacy skills. The social behaviors of children who had adult-directed teachers in Pre-K were rated lower than those of children in child-centered classes. No other differences were significant, although math scores were slightly lower for the children in classrooms with adult-directed teachers.

On four comparisons of 15, children who attended a Pre-K operated by their local school system performed better than children who attended a Pre-K operated by a private provider. Children in public school Pre-K classes appeared to be less aggressive, perform better on math calculations, and recognize more letters and words. However, children attending public school Pre-K performed less well in terms of expressive language skills.

In 42 out of 45 comparison measures, children taught using the High Reach curriculum performed less well than children taught using other curricula, but only in 13 comparisons were the differences significant. On average, children who were taught using the High/Scope curriculum performed significantly better at the end of kindergarten than children taught using High Reach in nine comparisons (expressive language, letter-word recognition, elision, applied problems, composite math, academic skills ratings, positive attitude toward learning, withdrawn behavior, and behavior ratings); those taught using Creative curriculum performed significantly better than children taught using High Reach in four comparisons (communication ratings, academic skills ratings, positive attitude toward learning, and behavior ratings). There were no statistical differences in children's performance on the 15 outcome measures between children in High Reach classrooms and children in classrooms using "other" curricula.

Research Question 3. For children living in poverty, how did the outcomes of children served by Georgia Pre-K compare with children served by Head Start?

To assess the relative effectiveness of alternative programs, such as Georgia Pre-K and Head

Start, evaluators must control for the differences in program participants. The most difficult difference to adjust for is called *selection bias*, which means differences that are associated with choosing alternative programs (or choosing not to have a child attend preschool), but which can appear to be related to the program. Reducing or eliminating selection bias so that more confident attribution of causal impacts can be estimated is one of the highest priority goals for scientific evaluations of education programs. Random assignment to the alternative programs is widely considered the best option for eliminating selection bias and other sources of differences in children's outcomes, but it was not possible to use random assignment in this evaluation.

Another technique that has been developed in recent years, known as propensity score matching, improves the matching of participants and when baselines scores are available, as is the case in the ECS. Empirical studies show that propensity score matching, when combined with correctly specified

regression adjustments, reduces bias from the non-equivalent-matched comparison groups, quasi-experimental design (Glazerman, Levy, & Myers, 2003). Propensity score matching (Ravallion, 2001; Rosenbaum, 2002; Rosenbaum & Rubin, 1983) provides for independence of assignment to treatment across all covariates, and Rubin (2001) has developed tests for the equivalence of the groups. The technique was applied to the impact evaluation and used to select a group of Georgia Pre-K participants who were eligible for Head Start and similar to the Head Start probability sample in most ways (Henry, Gordon, & Rickman, 2006).

In terms of language development, there were no significant differences between low-income children enrolled in Head Start and low-income children enrolled in Pre-K when entering preschool. However, significant differences did emerge in terms of receptive language (PPVT) and letter-word recognition (WJ-LW) by the end of preschool and into the beginning of kindergarten (Table 7.4). This same pattern is

Table 7.4   Direct Assessment Scores at Fall and Spring of Preschool Year and at Entry to Kindergarten

	Head Start (n = 106)	Pre-K (n = 201)	Difference	Bootstrap Standard Error
PPVT				
Entry to preschool	84.01	88.42	4.41	2.70
End of preschool	85.87	92.93	7.06**	2.96
Entry to kindergarten	90.18	93.54	3.36**	1.89
WJ-LW				
Entry to preschool	97.47	97.68	0.21	3.60
End of preschool	97.85	101.90	4.05*	2.10
Entry to kindergarten	100.02	104.27	4.25**	1.58
WJ-AP				
Entry to preschool	89.49	92.44	2.95	2.32
End of preschool	91.26	94.92	3.66**	1.66
Entry to kindergarten	93.33	97.56	4.23**	1.55
OWLS				
Entry to preschool	83.68	88.68	5.45**	1.72
End of preschool	84.93	91.61	6.69**	1.62

*$p < .10$; **$p < .05$. Tests of significance are indicated next to the differences.

present in terms of the children's problem-solving skills (WJ-AP). However, children who enrolled in Head Start began their preschool significantly behind their Pre-K counterparts in expressive language (OWLS). This difference persisted and increased at their entry into kindergarten.

Research Question 4. How much influence do peers have on the development of other children in their classrooms?

It is quite plausible that the development of individual children in Pre-K classrooms is significantly influenced by the skills of their peers in the class. Children spend substantial amounts of time interacting and playing with other children in Pre-K, perhaps more time than interacting with the adults in these classes. Prior to this study, the effects of peer skills on the

developmental outcomes of children in Pre-K had not been systematically assessed (Henry & Rickman, 2007).

To test the influence of peer skills, we constructed an indicator of peer skills that draws from the entire battery of skills that were directly assessed in the study. The baseline scores for each measure were converted to standardized scores (z scores) and averaged for each child. The average score for the sample of each child's peers within the classroom were averaged and included as the measure of peer ability. After controlling for individual child and family characteristics, baseline scores, classroom composition, and school inputs, children in Pre-K classes with peers who had acquired higher levels of skills were more familiar with print materials, were able to comprehend written materials better, and posted higher problem-solving skills (Table 7.5). It does not appear that peer skills influence children's ability to recognize letters or words, and the findings concerning receptive vocabulary were mixed.

Table 7.5   Kindergarten Outcome Measures

	PPVT	Letter/Word (WJ-LW)		Cognitive Skills (WJ-AP)		Story and Print	
	Fall	Spring	Fall	Spring	Fall	Spring	Fall
Peer Effects							
Class ability score	4.90**	0.71	0.26	−2.27	5.64**	3.84**	0.98**
Class Composition							
% of boys	0.74	2.29	−3.09	−10.51	−1.16	−25.25**	−0.73
% of African-American students	9.19*	0.46	−0.72	−4.32	−1.74	7.82**	0.08
% of Hispanic students	7.34	−3.94	−7.26	−16.51*	−4.67	−1.13	2.36
School Inputs							
Total number of students	0.52**	0.14	−0.17	−0.28	0.09	0.17	0.02
Teacher experience (years teaching)	0.14	0.01	−0.03	−0.26**	−0.10	−0.15	−0.01
Teacher has a bachelor's degree	−1.33	0.18	3.16*	0.59	−1.47	−5.06**	0.18
ECERS-R Rating	2.03	0.03	0.17	0.47	−1.99*	−1.19	−0.08
Time teacher spends on discipline	0.40	−0.49	−0.50	−1.43	−0.14	0.44	0.06

*p < .10; **p < .05. Tests of significance are indicated next to the differences.

Conclusions

As is the case with any evaluation, scientific educational evaluation should ultimately be judged by its outcomes, not process indicators, such as the technical quality of the data or the satisfaction of its sponsors (Henry & Mark, 2003; Mark & Henry, 2004). As we stated earlier in the chapter, we have been actively engaged in both scholarly discussions and policy formulation activities with policy makers, practitioners, other researchers, journalists, and experts on early childhood development. We know that the evidence generated by this evaluation has informed policy choices made for Pre-K programs from Los Angeles to Cleveland to South Carolina, and that it has been used to make improvements in the Georgia Pre-K Program. However, a substantial amount of time can pass before the outcomes of an evaluation are fully understood. At this time, we can point to some evidence-based actions that are taking place through which the evaluation's findings may be positively influencing children's outcomes. We believe that these actions could lead to four pathways to programmatic and policy-relevant improvements that could result in better outcomes for children in the future.

First, the study findings indicated that children gave back part of their previous gains in children's language skills during their first-grade year. This "fade out" appears to be associated with fewer children attaining the higher order skills measured by standardized assessments. This finding is also consistent with earlier studies, which found that cognitive and literacy skills are subject to "fade-out," but that positive effects in social outcomes continue into middle age (Nores, Belfield, & Barnett, 2005). In Georgia, coordination of the early elementary learning objectives and instructional methods across the early education and primary education systems is underway (Bright From the Start, 2007). This process, which may reduce redundancy in instruction across the grades and encourage children to learn higher order skills at an earlier age, began with establishing, disseminating, and training Pre-K

through third-grade teachers on the standards in an effort to increase the rate at which children develop skills in their early years of school.

Second, the study clearly shows that the skill gap appears to have been reduced by Georgia's Pre-K Program, but some children—those from economically disadvantaged families who experience serious skills deficiencies with respect to their peers—need more support. A developmental preschool program for 3-year-olds should be considered for these children. These children may require longer exposure to activities in developmentally oriented classes before they undergo rapid skill acquisition. An additional year of preschool, similar to Pre-K, may substantially reduce the skill gap and later achievement gaps. The state legislature has initiated a review of the feasibility of developing a preschool program or other services for 3-year-olds, but no additional action has occurred to date. Other research and advocacy groups have taken up the issue of intervening with younger children who are likely to experience lags in the development of cognitive and communication skills prior to Pre-K. In fact, the push toward economic competitiveness and enhanced human capital stimulated in part by globalization may raise the priority for investing in the development of our most vulnerable young children.

Third, the study produced additional findings about the benefits for children's development that arise from being in a Pre-K classroom with higher ability children. The abilities of a child's peers were found to be strongly associated with that child's growth in skills during preschool (Henry & Rickman, 2007). This is a strong, evidence-based argument for universal preschool, which allows the incorporation of students with different abilities in the classroom, rather than targeted programs such as Head Start, which concentrate children whose development has fallen below a typical rate. If it becomes evident that preschool peer effects are consistent with those shown in research from K-12 environments, children with lower levels of skills will benefit more from high-ability peers than children of higher levels of skills.

Thus, in terms of policy prescriptions, adoption of universal preschool programs may prove more beneficial than programs targeted only to children from economically disadvantaged families.

Finally, as stated in the preface to this volume, education policy is increasingly being influenced by governmental oversight to monitor student performance and school quality. Large-scale evaluations and high-stakes testing are being implemented to identify poor performing schools and school system shortcomings. The Georgia ECS sought to incorporate the most commonly used and rigorous measures of Pre-K classroom quality to provide information about children's development. However, many quality measures, including those used in this study that have been modified for use in the monitoring efforts of many states, are not associated with children's development (Early et al., 2007). We need better measures of classroom quality or teacher-child interactions that relate to children's skill development, and we need additional careful scientific evaluations to validate these relationships. New classroom and teaching quality measures that have a strong relationship with children's skill development would allow us to revise monitoring instruments to provide greater assistance to Pre-K providers in making quality improvements that will result in even greater skill development.

Each of these four evidence-based actions represents potential pathways, which, if followed, could result in this evaluation influencing children's development in a positive and substantial way. The effects of this evaluation are not direct; any effects will be mediated by the actions of individual practitioners and providers or policymakers and advocates. But all pathways to social betterment from evaluations of any type are likely to mediated (Henry & Mark, 2002; Mark & Henry, 2003). Because scientific evaluation often sets out to evaluate large-scale policies and programs, the potential effects may take longer to occur and may occur on a larger scale.

In closing, we believe that scientific evaluations have an important place in the field of evaluation regardless of whether the current trends toward globalization hold or changes in the environment, cost of transportation, or political winds shift to reverse some aspects of globalization. It remains to be seen if the need for subject matter knowledge and the need for knowledge accumulation for scientific evaluations will cause scientific evaluators to associate with others with similar substantive interests (e.g., early education or environmental programs), rather than the broader community of evaluators. Certainly, there will be a need for summative evaluations that seek to provide unbiased estimates of program effects. Where there is need, there will be researchers who will scientifically evaluate the claims for improved conditions and reduced inequality without regard to whether they label themselves evaluators or identify with a community of evaluators.

References

American Evaluation Association (2008). *American Evaluation Association Guiding Principles for Evaluators.* Available at http://www.eval.org/Publications/GuidingPrinciples.asp.

Barnett, W. S., Hustedt, J., Robin, K., & Schulman, K. (2004). *The state of preschool: 2003 state preschool yearbook.* New Brunswick, NJ: National Institute of Early Education Research.

Bright From the Start: Georgia Department of Education. (2005a). *Georgia's Pre-K Program Content Standards.* Available at http://www.decal.state.ga.us/PreK/PrekServices.aspx?Header=2&SubHeader=21&Position=11&HeaderName=Teachers

Bright From the Start: Georgia Department of Education. (2005b). *Pre-K Program.* Available at http://www.decal.state.ga.us/PreK/PreKMain.aspx

Bright From the Start: Georgia Department of Education. (2007). *Georgia Early Learning Standards.* Retrieved March 16, 2009, from http://www.decal.ga.gov/CCS/CCSMain.aspx

Congressional Research Service. (2003). *Head Start: Background and funding.* Washington, DC: Author.

Early, D. M., Maxwell, K. L., Burchinal, M., Alva, S., Bender, R. H., Bryant, D., et al. (2007). Teachers' education, classroom quality, and young children's academic skills: Results from seven studies of preschool programs. *Child Development, 78,* 558–580.

Georgia Head Start Collaboration Office. (2003). *Georgia Head Start facts and figures.* Available at www.osr.state.ga.us/headstart1.html

Georgia Office of Educational Accountability. (2002). *Report card* [Electronic Version]. Available at www.reportcard.gaosa,org/yr2003.osr.

Gibson-Graham, J. K. (1996). *The end of capitalism (as we knew it).* Oxford: Blackwell.

Glazerman, S., Levy, D. M., & Myers, D. (2003). Nonexperimental versus experimental estimates of earnings impacts. *Annals of the American Academy of Political and Social Science, Misleading Evidence and Evidence-Led Policy: Making Social Science More Experimental, 589,* 63–93.

Heckman, J. J. (2006). Skill formation and the economics of investing in disadvantaged children. *Science, 312*(5782), 1900–1902.

Henry, G. T. (2002). Choosing criteria to judge program success: A values inquiry. *Evaluation, 8*(2), 182–204.

Henry, G. T., & Gordon, C. S. (2006). Competition in the sandbox: A test of the effects of pre-school competition on educational outcomes. *Journal of Policy Analysis and Management, 25*(1), 97–127.

Henry, G. T., Gordon, C. S., & Rickman, D. K. (2006). Early education policy alternatives: Comparing the quality and outcomes of Head Start and state pre-kindergarten. *Educational Evaluation and Policy Analysis, 28*(1), 77–99.

Henry, G. T., Henderson, L. W., Ponder, B. D., Gordon, C. S., Mashburn, A., & Rickman, D. K. (2003). *Report of the findings from the Georgia Early Childhood Study: 2001-2002.* Atlanta, GA: Andrew Young School of Policy Studies, Georgia State University.

Henry, G. T., & Mark, M. M. (2003). Beyond use: Understanding evaluation's influence on attitudes and actions. *American Journal of Evaluation, 24*(3), 293–314.

Henry, G. T., & Rickman, D. K. (2007). Do peers influence children's skill development in preschool? *Economics of Education Review, 26*(1), 100–112.

Hoeg, P. (1994) *Borderliners.* Surry, England: Delta Publishing.

Kagan, S. L., Moore, E., & Bradekamp, S. (1995). *National education goals panel of school readiness.* Washington, DC: National Education Goals Panel.

Mark, M. M., & Henry, G. T. (2004). The mechanisms and outcomes of evaluation influence. *Evaluation, 10*(1), 35–57.

Mark, M. M., Henry, G. T., & Julnes, G. (2000). *Evaluation: An integrated framework for understanding, guiding, and improving policies and programs.* San Francisco, CA: Jossey-Bass.

Mashburn, A., & Henry, G. (2004). Assessing school readiness: Validity and bias in preschool and kindergarten teachers' ratings. *Educational Measurement: Issues and Practice, 23*(4), 16–30.

Nores, M., Belfield, C. R., & Barnett, W. S. (2005). Updating the economic impacts of the High/Scope Perry Preschool Program. *Educational Evaluation and Policy Analysis, 27,* 245–261.

Ravallion, M. (2001). Assessing the poverty impact of an assigned program. In F. Bourguignon & L. Pereira da Silva (Eds.), *The impact of economic policies on poverty and income distribution: Evaluation techniques and tools* (pp. 103–119). Oxford, UK: Oxford University Press.

Rosenbaum, P. R. (2002). Attributing effects to treatment in matched observational studies. *Journal of the American Statistical Association, 97*(457), 183–192.

Rosenbaum, P. R., & Rubin, D. B. (1983). The central role of the propensity score in observational studies for causal effects. *Biometrica, 70,* 41–55.

Rubin, D. B. (1974). Estimating causal effects of treatments in randomized and nonrandomized studies. *Journal of Education Psychology, 66,* 688–701.

Rubin, D. B. (2001). Using propensity scores to help design observational studies: Application to the tobacco litigation. *Health Services and Outcomes Research Methodology, 2,* 169–188.

Rubin, D. B. (2005). Causal inference using potential outcomes: Design, modeling, decisions. *Journal of the American Statistical Association, 100,* 322–331.

Shonkoff, J., & Phillips, D. A. (Eds.). (2000). *From neurons to neighborhoods.* Washington, DC: National Academy of Sciences.

Stromquist, N. P., & Monkman, K. (Eds.). (2000). *Globalization and education: Integration and contestation across cultures.* Lanham, MD: Rowman & Littlefield.

CHAPTER 8

Globalization—Blessing and Bane in Empirical Evaluation

Lessons in Three Acts

Jacob Marszalek and Debra D. Bragg

Prologue

Increasingly, educational policies are driven by global competition, causing tension between perceived needs and willing action. For example, despite criticism of the extreme measures taken by Asian students to perform at high levels on standardized tests and matriculate to the best colleges and universities within and outside their borders, their countries are observed closely throughout the world because of their success in stimulating economic advantages in the global marketplace. By comparison, the United States has fallen in the academic achievement of its students and the strength of its economy. Whereas the exact nature of the relationship between education and the economy is unclear, it is widely recognized that higher education is a major component of economic competitiveness in the knowledge-based global economy, a fact echoed in a major report from the Organisation for Economic Co-operation and Development (OECD;

Santiago, Tremblay, Basri, & Arnal, 2008a, 2008b).

The OECD conducted an international review of converging lines of research concerned with globalization in postsecondary education. Santiago et al. (2008b) synthesized summative findings presented at a recent conference, the scope and comprehensiveness of which make it a rare and uniquely important work to our own study. As such, it forms a major part of our theoretical framework for this chapter. One of its findings was that, relative to students with secondary-only education, students with postsecondary education had much higher rates of employment, earnings, job satisfaction, training, and skill. The challenge for the global economy is moving students from the secondary to the postsecondary level.

However, despite the nationwide commitment of federal reforms associated with No Child Left Behind (NCLB) and the Carl D. Perkins Career and Technical Education

Improvement Act (the bill awarding the largest amount of funds to high schools of any federal legislation), secondary education has limited impact on local economies. Specifically, the Perkins law encouraged the development of new curricula to bridge the gap between academic education and career and technical education (CTE) and prepare more students to transition to college and careers.

Although well intentioned, curriculum development efforts associated with Perkins have faced enormous challenges. Inadequate financial support, limited institutional capacity, and weak commitment to implementation have impeded curriculum reform. Inadequate communication of academic standards between the secondary and postsecondary levels has been a major impediment to facilitating student transition to college (Kirst & Venezia, 2004), a problem not uncommon internationally (Santiago et al., 2008b).

Of all postsecondary institutions, community colleges are arguably the most engaged in curriculum alignment with high schools because of their roots in K-12 education (Orr & Bragg, 2001). For some time, community colleges have emphasized the preparation of employees to fill semiskilled professional and technical positions associated with the global economy (Carnevale & Desrochers, 2002; Jacobs & Grubb, 2002). Their long history of delivering CTE and their open access mission provide the opportunity to enroll substantial numbers of students, including diverse populations that have heretofore had limited experience with higher education. In fact, nearly half of undergraduate students attending public institutions of higher education attend community colleges (Phillippe & Patton, 2000), with CTE being a dominant curricular focus.

Internationally, community colleges are part of a greater trend of diversification in the delivery mechanisms of postsecondary education (Santiago et al., 2008a). By associating with the global economy and globalization (Levin, 2001), community colleges seek to provide opportunities for students to find employment in family-wage-sustaining careers (Alssid et al., 2002) or

through transfer to universities, professional education, and employment options.

Despite obstacles to implementation, CTE programs are attracting more attention nationally (Wood, 2006) and internationally (Santiago et al., 2008a) partly due to their emphasis on easing the transition to college for student populations traditionally underserved by higher education, such as first-generation citizens. Federal legislation focusing on transition, sometimes called *career pathway programs*, attempts to provide students with CTE coursework that is integrated with academic education.

When the Perkins Act was reauthorized in 2006, it emphasized programs of study that facilitate student transition from secondary to postsecondary education and entry into family-wage-sustaining careers, paralleling the development of policy recommendations for similar programs by the Directorate for Education of the OECD (Santiago et al., 2008b). Career pathways are expected to align and articulate curriculum, encouraging students to obtain college (dual) credit while attending high school (Morest & Karp, 2006)—as well as a 2-year college credential—and to enhance transfer opportunities from the 2-year college to the university (Warford, 2006).

In keeping with the trend of greater accountability in educational program implementation both at home (e.g., NCLB) and abroad (e.g., Santiago et al., 2008a), we undertook an evaluation of CTE transition programs. Our study examined secondary and postsecondary CTE transition programs chosen from those that had been examined by the 2000–2002 *Sharing What Works: Exemplary and Promising Career and Technical Education Programs* project funded by the U.S. Department of Education (USDE). The *Sharing What Works* programs were identified as either *exemplary* or *promising* based on scientific criteria associated with high-quality programs, innovative practices, and promising student outcomes—in short, educational effectiveness. Among the CTE transition programs recognized by *Sharing What Works* and included in the current study was a health care-related Emergency

Medical Technology (EMT) program located in the Southeast as promising in 2000 and exemplary in 2002. A second career pathway program was an Information Technology/Computer Information Sciences (IT) program located in the Northwest.

The current evaluation, based on sound social science principles, systematically examined local programs and practices and measured student outcomes by employing two distinct but related parts: (a) a study of high school students during the 12th grade and followed through their first semester of college, and (b) a retrospective study of postsecondary students enrolled in a regional community college that partnered with their high school of attendance where the specified career pathway program was offered. In evaluating students' access and participation, this evaluation helped fill in one of the gaps in the knowledge base that impairs the evaluation of postsecondary education policies around the world (Santiago et al., 2008b).

To examine program effects on students, the level of engagement in CTE transition programs operating within selected secondary schools was documented through qualitative field research. By examining the engagement of programs, our evaluation also helped fill in another gap in the knowledge base—allocation of human and financial resources. Study results documented educational practices associated with the CTE transition programs and how they operate, including how practices influence students' academic achievement; transition to college; and postsecondary placement, persistence, and completion. It is our hope that the results will help address a third gap in the international knowledge base—student completion and outcomes.

This chapter shares the various ways that our current science-based mixed-methods study of two programs was shaped by the promise and pitfalls of globalization, beginning with recognizing that our work was afflicted with impediments shared with other international attempts at filling the gaps in the information base. Such obstacles can be classified in several broad categories: the coordination of data development between agencies separated by geographic, bureaucratic, or professional distance; legal obstacles; disparate timeframes required by science-based research, public policy, and commercial interest; and the nature of the interface between research and policy (Santiago et al., 2008b). These obstacles form the context of our story.

Act I: High Hopes (or the Challenge of Coordination Between Different Areas of Public Authority)

Scene 1: Overcoming a Shallow Interface Between Research and Policy

Applying for scientific grants can hardly be said to be a purely scientific endeavor. Politics often play a role, as happens when resources are finite. We were fortunate enough to receive a grant for our current evaluation to do a "scientific" study of CTE programs in the wake of Debra's long-term involvement with national research centers devoted to CTE, funded by the USDE. Part of Debra's previous involvement was the implementation of *Sharing What Works*, which was a deliberate commitment to blending research, dissemination, and innovative practice to enhance the quality of future CTE programs.

Sharing What Works selected CTE programs across the nation and recognized them as exemplary or promising. The project used a mixed-method design that integrated the judgments of numerous stakeholder groups (i.e., local practitioners, content experts, practitioner experts, experienced evaluators) on theory-to-practice connections, which stimulated innovative practice and enhanced the validity and reliability of local evidence of student outcomes. Despite the systematic design and careful analysis of processes and outcomes, *Sharing What Works* was halted by the federal government due to the lack of results gathered through "experimental" research. This is unfortunate because, in 2008, the OECD called for just such projects to help advance "quality assurance" in postsecondary education worldwide: "An effective, well co-ordinated quality assurance system would need to gather consensus among the different stakeholders based on shared expectations on purposes and outcomes" (Santiago et al., 2008a, p. 9).

Of course, one of the great difficulties in educational research is designing ethical, valid studies that can demonstrate "effects" based on the presence of cause-and-effect relationships. Disappointed but not deterred by *Sharing What Works*, and fully committed to the notion that educational policy can be improved through the careful examination and dissemination of effective practice, we pursued additional federal support to study CTE program, practices, and student outcomes. Debra's leadership of *Sharing What Works* and long-time affiliation with a national research center dedicated to CTE created the opportunity to reformulate it into the current project.

Attempting to address the requirements of the federal government and meet the needs of the field, she proposed a rigorous investigation of a few CTE programs that emerged as most promising in *Sharing What Works*. After proposal submission and a lengthy negotiation, Debra was successful in acquiring a federal grant that was as close as possible to experimentation as was defensible, which meant choosing from a toolbox of alternative nonexperimental designs with varying degrees of investigator control. The new design again emphasized mixed methods, employing a causal-comparative quantitative approach with several qualitative methods, including interviews, questionnaires, and document analysis.

The design attempted several comparisons, including students in CTE and those not in CTE, students in schools with CTE programs and those in schools without them, and variation in CTE focus, health sciences versus information technology (IT). Interestingly, our final technical report noted that we studied these particular technical programs because of their importance to preparing workers in fields critical to the global economy. To protect the anonymity of this work, we do not disclose the exact Internet dissemination site, but it is important to know that the final report is posted on the Web and being distributed worldwide.

Looking back, USDE officials showed enthusiasm for the current study mostly because of their anticipation of more "scientific" evidence than had been generated by *Sharing What Works*. In a sense, they may have been right. It has become popular in recent years in some circles of the U.S. educational system to apply business models (see, e.g., Dew & Nearing, 2004), which often promote the idea of regarding education as an end product. The educational climate brought about by NCLB was much more business model-oriented, meaning there was a great deal of interest in standardizing educational procedures and a growing recognition of the federal priority placed on experimental design, the ultimate "gold" standard. We were aware that such standardization comes about with description of existing procedures as a first step, but then leads to procedural comparisons and, ultimately, procedural choices, and we accepted those assumptions in taking on this new project. Other complexities, imposed by the sponsoring research center, our partners, and ourselves, were less obvious at the beginning, but unfolded as the project evolved.

Scene 2: Miscommunication About Project Design

Despite the universally regarded notion of globalization as, at least in part, the compression of space and time in human intercourse (Scheuerman, 2006), miscommunication was an unfortunate theme in our current project especially because it was conducted at a distance. Our partners in conducting the evaluation with fellow colleagues at the University of Illinois were employed by a large Washington, DC-based firm located more than 700 miles from our campus. The two programs we evaluated were located in different corners of the United States. From our campus, the Southeast site is about 1,000 miles away, and the Northwest site is about 2,000 miles away. Although lacking expertise on CTE specifically, our partners' agency was experienced in secondary education research around the globe, which complemented our experience in postsecondary research in the United States.

A contributor to enthusiasm for the project by our sponsoring research center was the focus on preparing workers for the IT industry, which is a driving force of globalization (telephones, computers, networking, and communications are all salient features). Health care, our other selected technical field of study, is a growing industry with worldwide impact due in part to its interface with IT. Enthusiastic about being chosen for a federally funded study that had the potential to spotlight their college, both community colleges chosen for the study agreed to participate after a site visit where members of our research team articulated the purpose of the study and asked for a commitment. In both cases, local officials signed a data-sharing agreement specifying that the institution would provide requested data on student demographics, participation, and outcomes in accordance with relevant privacy requirements.

On reflection, we were shortsighted in not recognizing at the beginning some of the pitfalls of marrying our university-based research team with a Washington, DC-based consulting firm. With limited firsthand knowledge of the people involved in each organization's work team and no prior experience working together, clear differences in organizational mission, and an unwillingness of the sponsoring research center to designate one of the two organizations as the clear project leader, the project experienced difficulties from the start. Adding the factor of distance to the

equation, the likelihood of miscommunication and misunderstanding was almost certain. The problems inherent in working with partners so far removed from us physically and bureaucratically/professionally, or at least the kinds of problems that might emerge and how quickly they would manifest themselves, are common on a global scale (Santiago et al., 2008b). Due to their experience in secondary education research and our expertise in postsecondary education, our partners were given responsibility for the secondary education component of the study. Their initial charge was to recruit secondary schools and high school seniors currently enrolled in CTE and select a comparison sample. We were given charge of the postsecondary component, in which former CTE students and a comparison sample would be studied.

Almost immediately, disagreement arose regarding the selection of high schools, creating confusion and discontent about a fundamentally important design decision to the entire study.

Because our partners were responsible for the secondary education component, they were entrusted with the selection of high schools. As mentioned earlier, the original study was meant to include a between-schools comparison—high schools with the CTE program of study and schools without it. However, this feature was misunderstood by our partners. A lack of on-the-ground knowledge of CTE led to the selection of only schools that had the CTE program of study, allowing for within-schools comparison of CTE participants and nonparticipants only.

This interpretation was particularly problematic for our Southeast site because there were only two high schools that had the EMT

Table 8.1 Basic Study Design and Research Group Responsibilities

Component	Research Group	CTE Students	Other Students
Secondary	Washington, DC	Current	Current
Postsecondary	Illinois	Both current and graduated	Both current and graduated

program, and it had existed for just 3 years. Other high schools feeding into the same community college had patient care assistant (PCA) programs, so our partners wanted to switch to studying just those high schools. This decision was unsound not only on the basis of the study design, but the PCA programs were not consistent with the notion of CTE "transition" programs that lead from high school to college. PCA programs, in contrast to the selected EMT programs, do not emphasize college transition, but instead award short-term certificates and encourage immediate and relatively low-wage employment. After several rounds of e-mails and phone calls, a compromise was reached: EMT and PCA programs would both be included, and rather than comparing high schools on a participation/nonparticipation basis, they would be classified as high, medium, and low engaged in CTE transition programs.

In the interest of internal validity (to allow for intersite comparisons), this compromise necessitated alteration of the research design for the IT site in the Northwest. At this site, there was not a similar programmatic differentiation among high schools, so we asked a third party to help us categorize the schools as high, medium, and low engaged. This party was the coordinator of a county-wide consortium of high schools, community colleges, and technical schools and had primary responsibility for coordinating administrative services and partnerships supporting CTE transition programs throughout the region. She answered several scaled questions about each high school, which were used to compile an overall school-level engagement score.

To address doubts about the reliability of a single-person measure, we employed another measure of engagement: the number of CTE IT courses offered at each school. By combining these two measures, our team felt we had produced a defensible measure of school-level engagement. Despite our best intentions regarding standardization, our counterparts preferred a qualitative, nuanced measure that relied on researcher judgment of the level of commitment

of school leaders to CTE transition programs based on a face-to-face interview. Our inability to reach a consensus on such a critical variable created an inconsistency that was irreconcilable, to the detriment of the overall study.

Scene 3: Attitudinal Difference in Sites

Differences in CTE program administration were evident between the Southeast and Northwest sites. At the Southeast site, both the EMT and PCA programs were offered at schools in a limited number of school districts, whereas at the Northwest site, the IT programs were offered by high schools from many different districts. Within the Southeast site, the EMT and PCA programs were administered somewhat differently; the PCA program was run through a regional technical center, and the EMT program was offered by high schools affiliated with a regional community college. At the Northwest site, the IT program was administered through four different community and technical colleges and the third-party coordinating agency. This difference is part of a global trend of diversification in the delivery of postsecondary education (Santiago et al., 2008a).

Perhaps related to this difference was a distinct difference in receptivity of the programs to external scrutiny. Programs forming a coalition would naturally need to be open to communication about and coordination and standardization of program features. A program operating by itself would have little need to cultivate the same type of culture among its personnel and runs contrary to a recognized global trend in higher education of increased intensification of interinstitutional networking (Santiago et al., 2008a).

A prime example of the lack of openness, or at least of transparency, was the difficulty we experienced in determining what students had actually completed the EMT program. Our original inquiries led us to program-level leadership that was highly receptive to our inquiries and willing to identify participants and contact information. However, campus administration balked at this action, claiming the request would be overly burdensome (despite our offering to compensate the institution), arguing that a recent changeover from one institutional data system severely diminished the ability to identify participants with certainty, referencing the 1972 Family Educational Rights and Privacy Act (FERPA) as a legal mechanism that prevented data sharing under any circumstances. Our efforts to clarify the intent of FERPA, including consultation with our UIUC campus attorneys, failed to budge the conversation (this issue is detailed later in the chapter). Our experience at the Northwest site seemed much more positive in retrospect because we received, in the main, full cooperation at all levels.

The scientific problem becomes apparent when pondering the generalizability of our evaluation results. Which of our two experiences is typical: the closed attitude of the community college at the Southeast site or the openness of the community college at the Northwest site? Perhaps neither, and most community colleges fall somewhere in between. The differences in site cooperation may be an example of one reason for the difficulty in coordinating data development between different areas of public authority, a global trend of giving more decision-making responsibility to local postsecondary institutions. In 2007, OECD stated that even if particular authorities bought into evidence-based policy, the lack of generalized agreement on policy priorities, possible regional rivalries, and varying willingness to share information "could lead to a situation where policymakers see the pooling of resources required to engage the national research community as a time-consuming and fruitless procedure" (Santiago et al., 2008b, p. 201).

With the help of program leaders, we did eventually identify a list of former students who had graduated from the Southeast health care program (although not of all students who had participated) and key contacts at both the

secondary level and the community college. Those contacts changed over time, which is to be expected, but it was an unwelcome surprise when it happened without follow-up communication. For example, in the midst of our protracted effort to obtain some cooperation in our data collection from the Southeast community college, we were informed that one of our key contacts had left the school some time beforehand. It was a surprise because we had been including that person in our communications with the college throughout the process. Difficulties continued to mount as our contacts moved beyond the program leaders most receptive to the study to the chief institutional research (IR) officer and upper level administrators who were openly skeptical of our research design, disagreeing with the notion of establishing comparable groups and collecting data on students from institution-level IR datasets or from the students themselves.

Scene 4: A Hurricane

Also, during the first few months of contact with the Southeast site, a major hurricane struck the region, which contributed another level of complexity to our communications. The after effects of the hurricane were cited by our initial high school contacts as one reason for an expressed desire to withdraw from the study. Out of sensitivity for the plight of the people there, we refrained from contacting the schools for several weeks, which may explain how certain requests were forgotten. Recovering from a natural disaster may also explain reluctance in participating in a major evaluation effort. However, as the community college administrators reiterated to us as we neared the conclusion of the study, their concern was not with their ability to handle our request, but with the appropriateness of the research design. It seems that, despite federal assertions of the merits of science-based evaluation, campus officials, including the chief IR official, were not convinced of the value of participating in a rigorous study such as ours.

Act II: Where the Rubber Met the Road (or Facing Legal Obstacles in Addressing Data Gaps)

Scene 1: Intransigence of the Southeast Site

We requested data central to our study that we regarded as a mix of *directory* and *nondirectory information*, none of which would be considered problematic in terms of putting student participants at risk of harm in any way. In fact, under FERPA, certain demographic variables of all postsecondary students may be shared with third parties by the institution without consulting the students. Of course, when using ambiguous terms such as *may* in the crafting of a law (U.S. Department of Education, 2007), there is considerable room for interpretation. The community college strongly disagreed with us over the propriety of sharing many different variables (e.g., phone number, address, e-mail) crucial for participant recruitment, slowing us from collecting data from students enrolled in the EMT transition program. In contrast, the Northwest site cooperated fully in our request for both directory and nondirectory (e.g., grades, courses taken) information, interpreting our data request as falling within the FERPA exemption allowing for educational research.

Such variability in legal application is reflective of the global situation regarding postsecondary data collection, with some countries unable to compel individual institutions to respond to data queries and others putting in place legal requirements for postsecondary institutions to provide data on a regular basis (Santiago et al., 2008b). Even in the latter case, however, new data requests may "require a complex process to amend the official data questionnaire [postsecondary institutions] have to fill in" (Santiago et al., 2008b, p. 201). Because of these difficulties, collection of new data, such as student completion rates, often depends on the persuasion of respondents or the goodwill of administrators completing supplementary questionnaires (Santiago et al., 2008b).

In an effort to stimulate data collection with the Southeast site, we sought support from the director of the sponsoring research center to help demonstrate to USDE that every action that could be taken to collect the data and be accountable had been attempted. We also sought legal advice from our own campus attorneys. This decision provided comfort for our research team, in that the campus lawyers confirmed that our directory information request met the letter of the law. The Southeast site, in contrast, lodged even stronger objections, possibly seeing our attempts as strong arming them into participation.

Fortunately, the involvement of the director of the research center helped break the logjam, but only after several weeks of slowly moving up the hierarchy at the community college. The slow climb was necessary because of the intransigence of one influential college official who was decidedly unsympathetic to our cause. This person's claims of the lack of validity of our research design, combined with concerns about the burden of assembling the requested data, dampened our team's enthusiasm and nearly derailed the study altogether.

Although there may have been other stronger reasons for refusing to cooperate (hurricane recovery having already been mentioned), an honestly different interpretation of FERPA seems plausible or at least plausible enough to the community college so as to seem like a good screen. There are those of us who suspect that the college bit off more than it cared to chew when it agreed to participate in the study and accept the monetary compensation we offered.

Scene 2: Mixed Reception at Northwest Site

Contrary to current international trends, we operated with an implicit assumption that legal issues would be nonexistent within the U.S. educational system. The Northwest site, in contrast, anticipated global trends in setting up its coalition of CTE-oriented partner institutions. The coalition is a prime example of widening channels of interaction and encouraging interinstitutional collaboration through flexibility and responsiveness to industry needs in terms of cooperative projects, a recommended policy for aligning postsecondary education delivery with the needs of globalization (Santiago et al., 2008a). It worked well because it had many fewer barriers to exchanges of information than the Southeast site, which claimed a different interpretation of federal law.

The globalization-friendly structure of the Northwest site was advantageous for collecting science-based evidence of educational effectiveness, but there were other challenges presented by globalization. Although we received college records of CTE and non-CTE students who attended the community college, our study design required secondary records of the students, as well as any postsecondary records of theirs at other institutions. For example, some students may have gone on to study at a 4-year institution, or they may have decided to attend one of the other 2-year colleges within the CTE coalition. To obtain those data, we had to ask the students, but globalization can be said to have set up two unintentional obstacles.

Inaccessibility of Students

Of course, it may be the cultural context of globalization (people and systems are essentially the same everywhere, exchange of communications and products will be fast and easy) that led us to expect data collection in the Northwest to be no different than data collection in the Midwest for investigators stationed in the Midwest. Initially, there was no difference. We randomly selected a large sample from a dataset provided by the site and then proceeded to mail out invitations to participate. The format, language, and costs were all the same, but the response rate was not. The initial rate of acceptance was below 1%, which was shocking to us because we were offering $20 in exchange for permission to look at the participant's high school transcripts and take a survey.

One reason for the low response rate was inaccurate contact information; about one in every eight of our letters was returned. This may indicate the first way in which globalization interfered with our evaluation with the Northwest site: Students at the community college were able to physically move easily and quickly. In fact, they may have had to move because jobs can be moved quickly and easily. One example of this is that, during the time of our study, the IT industry experienced a colossal economic downturn following 9/11. Also, a major corporate headquarters moved from the Northwest to the Midwest, a move that surprised many observers in the local media. As individuals and institutions become more mobile, it has become extremely difficult for community colleges and other educational institutions to maintain accurate contact information about their students, which is a trend seen worldwide (Santiago et al., 2008b).

The inaccuracy of the up-to-date records obtained from the community college extended to telephone and e-mail records as well. In light of the low response to our letter, we followed up with telephone calls to each of the potential recruits. This, too, produced limited success, again due to invalid telephone contact information for many students. Often, if the number was still in use by relatives or friends, there was resistance to providing accurate contact information or even taking a message. Perhaps here we run into yet another way in which globalization interfered with our data collection. Because it has become easier and perhaps more effective to solicit people with the advent of new technologies such as e-mail spam and computerized telemarketing, it has also become easier to perpetrate fraud. Globalization helps make this possible by knocking down physical, technological, and legal barriers to economic activities across state, local, and international boundaries. This has led to distrust on the part of many people to any type of unsolicited communication from agencies with which they are unfamiliar or even with which they have no known relationship.

Conflict of Globalization and Confidentiality

Such mistrust may have weakened two important assumptions in human subjects research. The first is the acquisition of a sample representative of the population of interest. One serious limitation to our evaluation is that we had to drop the testing of several hypotheses because we could not generalize the results beyond a narrow subset of the population of community college students, and our hope was that the study would offer generalizable results. The second assumption is more procedural and affects how we tried to ensure a representative sample of observations by ensuring confidentiality.

Confidentiality has been under assault for quite some time in both the academic and business sectors of human subjects research (Doherty & Fulford, 2005). Problems with confidentiality can perhaps be most readily seen in the business world, in which people are often required to sign lengthy disclaimers that allow the sharing of their personal information with third parties. Such disclaimers have also made their way into medical, dental, and mental health offices, which all must share patient information with other professional and sometimes legal agencies. Via these health care practices, disclaimers have also been introduced into the realm of academic research.

Coupled with the practice of sharing confidential information with third parties, whether motivated by ethics or profit, is the increasing practice of storing such data in secure databases for lengthy or indefinite periods. For example, our consent letter stated that we would eventually destroy the data we collected *after a period of 10 years!* This is a common and entirely ethical practice that provides researchers with the flexibility to thoroughly examine study results without the unnecessary pressure of immediate use. Researchers in other fields may keep data for even longer periods, often in the interests of both patient and agency protection, but just as often in the interests of longitudinal tracking for more scientific accuracy and, hence, more

accurate business decisions (i.e., whether to target a particular group or individual with a marketing campaign).

Greater tracking capability backed by cooperation between the state and postsecondary institutions is, in fact, one of the recommended ways to address the gap in knowledge about the performance of graduates in the international labor market (Santiago et al., 2008a, 2008b). The threat to confidentiality in all of this is that the more time you allow a dataset to exist, the greater the probability of a compromise in data security. A prime example of this is the recent compromise of a Veteran's Affairs database, in which a laptop containing the database was misplaced and not found for a month (Stout & Zeller, 2006). Statements by the department that there was no evidence of foul play were hardly reassuring to veterans. If the military (i.e., specialists in secret encoding and high security) can be hacked, who cannot be?

As globalization continues, subject confidentiality will increasingly become dubious due to these two threats of the sharing and long-term storage of information. Globalization makes the sharing of data easier and faster, and it makes certain aspects of data more vulnerable, such as the lack of physical limitations to how much may be stored, secured, and stolen. The increasing lack of security makes it harder for potential research participants to trust guarantees of confidentiality, which in turn hurts recruiting efforts and the likelihood of obtaining a representative sample. The lack of representativeness in a sample hurts its generalizability as well as the replicability of the study, two pillars of science-based evidence. This may well be what hurt our evaluation of the educational effectiveness of CTE transition programs the most.

The Southeast site saw similar problems in obtaining volunteers for the study, but serves as an example of how globalization can provide solutions for challenges of its own making. As mentioned previously, the community college at the Southeast site refused to share contact information about its students. The informal list of students we initially obtained from program leaders did not include contact information, and the institutional research office refused to provide it. Determined to give participants and graduates of the EMT program an opportunity to volunteer for the study, we sought to obtain contact information through Internet searches.

Globalization helped rather than hindered us in this respect due to the existence of international communications and information systems such as the Internet. Although many barriers to long-distance data gathering have been eliminated, and we possessed the tools to take advantage of their absence, our search was largely futile; we received responses from less than 10% of the students. Here, the same difficulties came into play as at the Northwest site: distrust among the population of interest, and a much more mobile population (perhaps especially after the hurricane).

ACT III: From Bad to Worse (or the Difference in Timeframes Among Policymakers, Researchers, and Business)

Scene 1: Southeast Data Collection

Although the college initially refused to release data, it was eventually persuaded to provide the following variables: date of birth, whether a student was enrolled in a particular term during the years of the EMT program, a student's major at the beginning and end of this period, and the degree or certificate that was earned. This dataset allowed a comparison between the approximately 30 students whom we knew to be program participants/graduates and everyone else. To perform the other intended comparisons, we needed to at least know the high school from which each student graduated; after more negotiation, the college agreed to provide this information.

However, by this time, our grant-funding period was drawing to a close, and there was considerable pressure to complete data collection. An internationally recognized challenge to

obtaining postsecondary data is the disconnect in the usual timeframes under which various stakeholders operate: Researchers usually operate over a period of several years, policymakers over election cycles, and commercial interests over months (Santiago et al., 2008b). Our case was no different in that we needed much more time to carry out the collection of science-based evidence, but the funding agency pressed for results. We suspected that the Southeast site was privy to the issue of time and had used stalling as a strategy.

Ultimately, we secured data from the Southeast community college, but not directly. Instead, the institutions' student data files had been outsourced to a company in a neighboring state, which introduced a tighter commercial timeframe to the process. The company would not want to spend more time on the project than was profitable. Additionally, the added layer of bureaucracy contributed to more miscommunication and confusion about our data request. For example, after explaining the request to the agency, we received a dataset that was incomplete; it contained a subset of students who had enrolled for the exact time period of the program, rather than all students who had been enrolled at any time during that period, whether they began earlier or ended later.

Several more rounds of unsuccessful data extractions followed, all of which were unsatisfactory because they failed to include some program students. To minimize sampling bias, our design called for students having any period of enrollment in the program to be included, including students who were enrolled and given credit for the EMT program at the community college. This was a *dual-credit* CTE program, which refers to high school courses in which credit is earned for both high school and college graduation. A dual-credit program requires cooperation from both the student's high school and a college.

Although globalization—in the sense of eliminating legal, economic, and technological obstacles—made this evaluation and the college's outsourcing of data management possible, it proved to be only as beneficial as the people involved could make it. Our ability to take advantage of the benefits of globalization rested on other forms of standardization: business etiquette, language, legal interpretation, and postsecondary data compilation and organization. All of us made implicit assumptions at various points that things worked the same in the Midwest, Southeast, and elsewhere in the United States. Unwarranted assumptions of standardization led to frustration and also may have allowed a temptation to sacrifice rigor for expediency. The final result of our data-collection efforts was, perhaps, just such an occurrence. The database that was sent to us in the end was still missing five students from the EMT program, much to our consternation and the frustration of the database contractors.

Scene 2: Decisions About Data Compilation

Another illustration of the challenge of differing timeframes was begotten from the previously mentioned challenge of coordinating data development between different areas of public authority. Our research partners, who had taken on the task of evaluating high school CTE programs at the same sites, were part of a private, nonprofit organization dependent on soft money. Because their organization was always seeking for the next source of funding, they had a faster timeframe for the project than we, who were not as dependent on grant funding and had a vested interest in producing science-based evidence worthy of scholarly dissemination.

Knowing that a combined analysis of secondary and postsecondary data was the goal of the project, efforts were made to standardize transcript data collection. This may be a story as much about science getting in its own way as it is about addressing the challenges of globalization. Because the different people who would be conducting, managing, and supervising transcript data collection were separated by more than 700 miles, we felt the more standardization of procedure, the better. A database management program was chosen because of its abilities

to provide uniform data entry with limited options for how data would be entered, its centralized method of controlling the data compilation process through the use of "master" and "slave" versions of the database, and its method of relating multiple lines of data (courses) to a single case (the student) through *queries*.

Two main difficulties arose with using the software, one of which was related to communications, the other of which was related to making it work, and both of which were related to human frailty. Having made the decision to use the database program, we had to confront the problem of training the research teams to use it, especially with reference to the data entry interface. So our research partners came to our campus to discuss the project and receive instruction. The assumption was made that everyone involved with the project had a certain baseline comfort and ability to work with computers, but the reality was that there was a wide range of computer literacy in our two groups.

Hands-on training did not cover nearly as much as was initially hoped for a full day of training, but we assumed that what was missed could be communicated effectively over long distance. In hindsight, it may have been better to extend the training to a second day, but time pressures dictated scheduling. Although communication was greatly facilitated by teleconferencing, telephoning, e-mail, and electronic data file sharing, progress was slow and frustrating—so much so that the prudence of using the database rather than a simple spreadsheet was openly questioned.

For our partners, the final straw may have been a meeting between our two teams, this time in their Washington, DC, office, when they requested more hands-on instruction. Although eager to assist, limited time was available on the agenda, and the training was postponed. Shortly thereafter, communication about the new database trickled to an end. It was not until several months afterward that we learned that our partners had reverted back to an old software package already familiar to their staff, with expediency in accomplishing particular demands of the study taking priority over the standardization of data entry.

Similar to earlier differences in carrying out a common sampling plan and site selection, our partner prioritized expediency over comparability. Possibly because of their dependency on grant funding, we speculated that the looming deadline took precedence over the collaborative agreements we had attempted to establish at the start of the project. In a consulting firm such as this, funding drives the bottom line. Like many law firms, employees bill hourly, heightening the importance of producing results before the grant funding ends regardless of whatever challenges arise.

Scene 3: Hitting a Fly With a Sledgehammer

One important reason that we did not press our partners on the issue of using a common data entry system was that the comparability of the secondary and postsecondary transcript datasets had lost importance for us as well. We too experienced trouble in acquiring CTE transcript data (as described previously). One assumption we had when we chose the database software was that there would be many tens, if not a few hundred, participants, and thousands of individual courses to organize and relate. As the reality of our dataset became clearer, our own doubts grew as to the advisability of using such a powerful tool for a small sample especially because many of the procedures began to seem too unwieldy (sort of like using a sledgehammer to kill a fly).

For example, when our first try at recruitment came to an end and we were obviously going to get few volunteers, we were deeply immersed in the entry of hundreds of high school courses into a relational database to be used as a sophisticated drop-down list in our transcript data entry interface. This makes sense if there are hundreds of transcripts and thousands of courses to enter, but not if there are less than 50; the cost-benefit ratio is too inflated. Of course, we still hoped the second attempt at recruitment would be fruitful, and then the third, but the size of the final sample did not

become clear until we had completed that particular task.

Coding Transcripts

One recommendation of the OECD to address policy challenges to meeting the need of globalization is to establish sound instruments for steering postsecondary education (Santiago et al., 2008a). Two methods of accomplishing this are "strengthening credit transfer and articulation arrangements to foster mobility between institutions, and improving the availability of information about quality to prospective students" (Santiago et al., 2008a, p. 6). Our experience in this study suggests a specific way to carry out these methods, increasing standardization.

For example, the U.S. educational system would be served well by increasing standardization for all manner of instruction and assessment, whether it be criteria for certificates and degrees, methodology for reading instruction, or even coding and descriptions for courses. Standardization would eliminate barriers: to students moving from one district to another and from one level of the system to another (most notably in this case from high school to college); to comparing observations of educational phenomena from different parts of the country; and to educators, students, and other stakeholders sharing their own ideas and experiences within the system. However, there is still a long way to go, as we found when attempting to compare courses between students using transcript data.

Although we had access to and used several different coding schemes made available by the USDE for relating courses from disparate school systems, assigning particular courses to specific codes required a lot of subjective judgment. For example, what one high school referred to as Algebra II another might refer to as Algebra A, Algebra B, or College Algebra, all depending on the content of the courses and their place in the mathematics sequence at that particular school. So not only was a standard coding scheme needed, but also standardized procedures for making decisions about the coding and standardized descriptions of the courses them-selves (assuming that the courses were taught in the same way and covered the same material).

As communication about the transcript data organization wore down between our two research teams, communication about the analysis suffered. So the scientific comparability of the secondary and postsecondary transcript results was greatly reduced; we did not know whether we could say that we arrived at our cod-ing decisions in the same way. The original plan was to exchange datasets and check each other's coding by taking a random sample of 10% of the courses and recoding them. We would have then compared the coding results to see how much agreement there was. This plan fell through, in large part, because of time and money con-straints, but perhaps also because of the difficul-ties experienced in trying to coordinate the initial transcript data using the sophisticated database software mentioned previously.

Even within our own postsecondary study, sci-entific comparability among the high schools rep-resented by our small sample of students was in jeopardy because of our difficulties in obtaining current course catalogs. This job had been assigned to our research partners earlier in the project, and communication with the high schools on this issue initially went through them. However, our agen-cies had a mismatch of priorities, and after waiting for several months, we ultimately concluded that we would have to contact the schools ourselves. Even then, we were sometimes provided with cat-alogs that were several years old.

We concluded that not every district issues a new catalog every year (this goes to standardiza-tion of procedure in education), and none had them in electronic form, so we had to adjust to waiting for materials in the mail, rather than instantaneously over the Internet. These were issues inherent in different operational time-frames on several levels. Some of the same diffi-culties applied to the matching of courses on the high school transcripts with those in the com-munity college transcripts, although the consor-tium at the Northwest site had a useful website with cross-tables of relevant courses.

Scene 4: Hidden Gems in the Northwest

One advantage to the lack of standardization in the educational system was that we had an unexpected opportunity to examine a growing form of articulated credit program offered at the Northwest site, but not at the Southeast site. For the CTE programs that we were primarily inter-ested in evaluating, the dual-credit model was in play. In the Southeast site, the preponderance of dual credit was offered to students taking courses in the high school, whereas the Northwest site emphasized high school students taking the coursework on the college campus.

We were able to collect science-based evi-dence for a comparison of these two groups and draw some interesting conclusions about the similarities and differences of educational effec-tiveness. But the fact that we were able to do so highlights the tension between the different timeframes of our two organizations; our research partners did not take advantage of the same opportunity in their analysis of the sec-ondary education component partly due to tim-ing, but also due to the fact that the study of dual credit was not formally articulated in the research proposal that defined our partner's scope of work.

Here, both science and globalization shined in their best and brightest. The opportunity to compare two preexisting groups was an affirma-tion of the value of quasi-experimental tech-niques that are gaining wider acceptance by scientists for their ability to provide unexpected insights into the nature of educational phenom-ena (see Collier, Brady, & Seawright, 2004, for an excellent methodological discussion; Henry, Gordon, & Rickman, 2006, for a current exem-plar). In this case, we were able to discern strengths and weaknesses of the two approaches to CTE transition programs, which will help administrators and policymakers to make informed decisions regarding the implementa-tion of such programs in the future.

Globalization will surely help with the dissem-ination of results of this study (the summative report is posted on the World Wide Web), but also was instrumental in our ability to take advantage of the existence of the new program. First of all, only with rapid long-distance communication could the Northwest site share the information about its dual-credit program with us, and we in turn share it with our investigative partners and conduct further discussion in its regard. Without the technology and standardization inherent in globalization, we would not have been able to take advantage of the opportunity within the timeframe allowed by our funders. Second, only through the sharing of the electronic transcript data were we able to differentiate how the courses were credited. Globalization at its best can facilitate the flexibility sometimes needed in the scientific process to make new discoveries.

Epilogue

Study Results

Ultimately, the study yielded valuable information on the educational experiences and outcomes of student participants in the CTE transition program, particularly in the Northwest site, where we had considerable access to data relative to nonparticipants. Student participants in CTE transition programs showed equivalent academic (college prep) course taking, more CTE courses, and more dual-credit courses than non-CTE student participants. Students enrolled in the CTE transition programs had significantly higher reading test scores (but no difference in mathematics) and higher self-reported confidence in their readiness to transition to college than nonparticipants. Further, a higher proportion of CTE participants transitioned to the community college, earning more college credits while in attendance than nonparticipants.

Results were not uniformly positive for CTE transition program participants, however. A majority of both groups—CTE transition participants and nonparticipants—were required to take at least one remedial course when enrolling at the community college. Although remedial course-taking did not appear to impede college course-taking, the fact that recent high school graduates entered college from high school without having the requisite skills in mathematics and communications was disappointing. Also, due somewhat to the amount of time since high school graduation, but also to part-time enrollment linked to part- or full-time employment and other personal reasons that impede college enrollment, few students reached the point of earning certificates or degrees. Although the numbers were small, dual-credit was associated with a higher likelihood of finishing a college credential, suggesting taking dual-credit courses in association with academics and CTE may be an incentive to college persistence and completion.

These results offered insights and implications not yet reported in the literature that are valuable to educational policy and practice. Specifically, the study informed high school-to-college transition policy and practice pertaining to the implementation of CTE transition programs associated with the federal Perkins legislation, which calls for an expansion of CTE programs of study in high-skill, high-wage, or high-demand occupations. These results suggest that CTE transition programs offer opportunities for high school students to develop academic and CTE skills associated with high-skill, high-wage, and high-demand occupations. In a world increasingly dominated by globalization, whether experienced by students or witnessed by researchers, these outcomes offer promising lessons on all levels.

Lessons to Be Learned

Our study yielded a number of valuable lessons about how to carry out scientific research in our increasingly globalized world. Possibly even more important, the study yielded lessons on what to avoid. Humbling as the hard lessons were to come by, by telling our story, we strive to help educate others about the complexities of evaluating educational programs in an increasingly borderless and yet imperfectly standardized planet. Different understandings, untested assumptions, and failed communications are important themes that shaped the evolving storyline in this chapter. Reflecting on our practice, it is clear now that, despite our best intentions, we ultimately produced research displaying a mix of meaningful as well as meaningless results, particularly if one applies the quintessential gold standard of science-based educational research. Hopefully, the meaningful outweighs the meaningless.

We caution readers not to make the same mistake we did in assuming that different localities are more alike than different. Despite the outward display of uniformity, at a deeper level where phenomena are assigned meaning, the local matters a great deal. Differences in this regard are well documented on an international scale, whether as differences in timeframes used by researchers, policymakers, and commercial interests; differences in law or its interpretation; or the overlap between different areas of public authority.

It is extremely important to avoid making design decisions based on global (or national) assumptions. When this happens, researchers fail to comprehend differences that are integrally tied to the local context. Despite the growing impact of globalization, when it comes to educational systems within or across states, differences in policies, programs, and perspectives can be enormous and present particular obstacles in determining educational effectiveness. Much depends on the depth of the nature and depth of the research and policy interface (Santiago et al., 2008b). Thus, to assume that what works in one locale will work in another mitigates against designing research that is sensitive to the treatment. In the end, research without validity has little value to anyone.

Closely related to our last point, we further emphasize that, despite globalization, there is beauty in the "local flavor" of educational programs and in research designs that are sensitive to local practice. Research designs that mix methods, capitalizing on qualitative and quantitative approaches, seem to produce interesting and innovative options without losing sight of cross-site, cross-cutting practices that may (or may not) relate to student outcomes. In our study, qualitative methods revealed programs and practices at the system and policy levels, whereas quantitative methods helped to discover student outcomes.

Without the mixing of methods, our ability to draw insights about relationships among programs, processes, and outcomes—important elements in determining educational effectiveness—would have been seriously impaired. Thanks to this approach, our attempt to fill gaps in the knowledge base—such as postsecondary education access and participation, completion and participation, and resource allocation—were successful.

Our experience leads us to caution against relying too heavily on technological innovations for either day-to-day communications or larger, longer term facets of the research operation, including storing, cataloguing, or analyzing data. Even with our best intentions to draw on new technologies for communications and data management, lagging capacity to use technologies was at best frustrating and at worst detrimental. Moreover, we experienced difficulties on many levels with the openness, disclosure, and confidentiality with which data were shared, collected, and handled, let alone disseminated. Without intervention by the research sponsor, as well as our campus legal counsel, little quantitative data would have been collected from one of our sites.

We also caution against blind faith in the business model that prizes outcomes (outputs) and minimizes context and process (programs, practices). Without careful attention paid to implementation of each of the CTE transition programs within various high school and community college environments, we would have faced far more difficulty interpreting program implementation and student outcomes than occurred using mixed methods. Analyzing student outcomes was an undeniably important endeavor, but outcomes assessment was only half the picture. Without the mixed approach, we would have little more than a black box, leaving program designers and policymakers with little science-based evidence relevant to determining educational effectiveness.

Finally, despite the widespread adoption of globalization—hence, the reference to *global* or *worldwide* throughout the chapter—our experience with conducting evaluation of a seemingly global aspect of education was fraught with pitfalls. Even when drawing on methods and technologies consistent with educational programs dedicated to preparing workers for an increasingly global economy, we experienced misunderstandings and inconsistencies that limited our ability to employ the scientific method as we originally envisioned and generalizing results in ways we had expected.

References

Alssid, J. L., Gruber, D., Jenkins, D., Mazzeo, C., Roberts, B., & Stanback-Stroud, R. (2002, October). *Building a career pathways system: Promising practices in community college-centered workforce development*. Retrieved November 1, 2006, from http://www.workforcestrategy.org/publications/

Carnevale, A., & Desrochers, D. M. (2002). *The missing middle: Aligning education and the knowledge economy*. Princeton, NJ: Educational Testing Service.

Collier, D., Brady, H. E., & Seawright, J. (2004). Sources of leverage in causal influence: Toward an alternative view of methodology. In H. E. Brady & D. Collier (Eds.), *Rethinking social inquiry* (pp. 229–266). Lanham, MD: Rowman & Littlefield.

Dew, J. R., & Nearing, M. M. (2004). *Continuous quality improvement in higher education*. Westport, CT: American Council on Education/Praeger Publishers.

Doherty, N. F., & Fulford, H. (2005). Do information security policies reduce the incidence of security breaches: An exploratory analysis. *Information Resources Management Journal, 18*(4), 21–39.

Henry, G. T., Gordon, C. S., & Rickman, D. K. (2006). Early education policy alternatives: Comparing quality and outcomes of head start and state prekindergarten. *Educational Evaluation and Policy Analysis, 28*(1), 77–99.

Jacobs, J., & Grubb, N. W. (2002). *Implementing the "education consensus": The federal role in supporting vocational-technical education*. Washington, DC: Office of Vocational and Adult Education. (ERIC Document Reproduction Service No. ED466946)

Kirst, M. W., & Venezia, A. (Eds.). (2004). *From high school to college: Improving opportunities for success in postsecondary education*. San Francisco, CA: Jossey-Bass.

Levin, J. (2001). *Globalizing the community college: Strategies for change in the twenty-first century*. New York: Palgrave.

Morest, V., & Karp, M. (2006). Twice the credit, half the time? The growth of dual-credit in community colleges and high schools. In T. Bailey & V. Morest (Eds.), *Defending the community college equity agenda* (pp. 223–245). Baltimore: Johns Hopkins University Press.

Orr, M. T., & Bragg, D. (2001). Policy directions for K-14 education: Looking to the future. In B. Townsend & S. Twombly (Eds.), *Educational policy in the 21st century: Volume 2. Community colleges: Policy in the future context* (pp. 101–128). Westport, CT: Ablex Publishers.

Phillippe, K. A., & Patton, M. (2000). *National profile of community colleges: Trends & statistics*. Washington, DC: American Association of Community Colleges.

Santiago, P., Tremblay, K., Basri, E., & Arnal, E. (2008a, April). *OECD thematic review of tertiary education: Synthesis report*. Overview. Organisation for Economic Co-operation and Development conference, Tertiary Education for the Knowledge Society, Lisbon, Portugal. Retrieved August 27, 2008, from http://oecd-conference-teks.iscte.pt/documents.html

Santiago, P., Tremblay, K., Basri, E., & Arnal, E. (2008b, April). *OECD thematic review of tertiary education: Synthesis report*. Volume 3. Organisation for Economic Co-operation and Development conference, Tertiary Education for the Knowledge Society, Lisbon, Portugal. Retrieved August 27, 2008, from http://oecd-conference-teks.iscte.pt/documents.html

Scheuerman, W. (2006, Summer). *Globalization. The Stanford encyclopedia of philosophy.* Retrieved August 22, 2007, from http://plato.stanford .edu/archives/sum2006/entries/globalization/

Stout, D., & Zeller, Jr., T. (2006, May 23). *Vast data cache about veterans is stolen.* Available at http://www.nytimes.com

U.S. Department of Education. (2007). *Family Educational Rights and Privacy Act (FERPA).* Retrieved October 23, 2007, from http://www .ed.gov/policy/gen/guid/fpco/ferpa/index.html

Warford, L. J. (2006). College and career transitions initiative: Responding to a quiet crisis. In L. J. Warford (Ed.), *Pathways to student success: Case studies from the College and Careers Transitions Initiative* (pp. 3–14). Phoenix, AZ: League for Innovation in the Community College.

Wood, D. B. (2006, October 12). *Suddenly, vocational training back in vogue.* Retrieved November 12, 2006, at http://www.csmonitor.com/2006/1012/ p01s03-usec.html

Science-Based Educational Evaluation and Student Learning in a Global Society

A Critical Appraisal

Lois-ellin Datta

A Story About a Poor Quality Evaluation. Patton (2007a) writes,

> [This is] is a large and important but controversial project funded by an international agency in a developing county. All sites visited were selected by the host government. Only project participants selected by the host government were interviewed and always with project and/or government people present. Most requested documents and data were "not available." ... Of the several people [on the team] only one had any evaluation background, knowledge, or training ... the project involved issues of life and death for the intended beneficiaries and huge potential embarrassment to the host county.

A Story About a Good Quality Randomized Experiment Evaluation. Boruch (2007) describes

a randomized trial in Mexico of the effectiveness of cash payments to mothers conditional on their children's school enrollment and attendance. The experiment met the five ethical criteria he proposes regarding randomized designs: The social problem is serious, the purported solution is debatable, the randomized trials will yield less equivocal and more unbiased results than alternative approaches, the results will be used, and human rights will be protected. In the Progresa case, cash payments increased school enrollment. "Partly on account of these results," Boruch writes, "the program has continued through at least three government administrations in Mexico. This continuation is remarkable" (p. 58).

A Story About Not-Good Consequences of Science-Based Evaluation. Tracking the effects of science-based evaluation on educational policy in South Africa, Jansen (2002) concludes: "The distance between privileged schools (mainly though not exclusively white) and disadvantaged (mainly black) schools has in fact increased. . . . The massive retrenchment of teachers, justified . . . on the basis of international research on class size and student achievement, has depleted many black schools of teachers." He remains skeptical at best of applications of science-based "international research," when applied in a country such as South Africa, without sensitive, thorough, and widespread consideration of potential perverse effects, as well as the hopes for better outcomes.

The three questions are addressed in this chapter. First, by what theory of action might science-based educational evaluation contribute to improved student learning? Second, what are the strengths and limitations of this educational evaluation genre in relation to evaluation theory, methods, practice, and educational policy, particularly its contribution to student learning? Third, is science-based educational evaluation likely to shape globalization in some way or is globalization likely to change the way we define science-based educational research? By globalization, I mean the process of integrating what is local, regional, and national into a unified or highly interdependent function, be this economic, social, educational, or cultural.

A general theme of the chapter is that educational evaluation globally expresses a tension between consistency and diversity. What can be perceived as the Western-modern-American evaluation approach pulls toward science-based evaluations that are globally consistent in intended use (primarily summative and impact), methods (primacy of randomized designs), and measures (mostly quantitative assessment). Consistency and uniformity in design are being energetically promoted by multiorganizational agreements. Evaluations supported through these organizations will follow a common, science-based framework that is now endorsed by some economists as the newest, best solution to issues such as poverty (Barron, 2007).

Concurrently, developments in African, Alternative Western, and Indigenous evaluations pull toward evaluation diversity, emphasizing situational appropriateness (formative and summative use, context-appropriate designs, and multiple measures). The rapidly expanding national evaluation organizations and some large foundations are turning for their keynote speakers and advisors to evaluators known for their skepticism about feasibility of the randomized design, for encouraging a wide array of approaches and measures, for collaborative and participatory stances, and for their interest in alternative designs.

Looking ahead, it seems likely that some elements of the Western evaluation approach, appealing to global desires for strong policy conclusions and promising more certain estimates of effects of interventions, may penetrate fairly extensively. Many elements of the African, Alternative Western, and Indigenous approaches, however, are likely to appeal to nationalism, to a collaborative, partnership stance with funding organizations, to offer realistic adaptations to field conditions, and may succeed in achieving greater diversity. I do not think the approaches will eat each other up like the Gingham Dog and the Calico Cat, but they seem likely to change each other and both to change and be changed by globalization.

The next sections explore these assertions in more detail. First, however, I offer a brief reminder that our present questions are continuations of centuries of inquiry on student learning and its evaluation.

Past and Present

There has hardly been a time within our historical records without some cross-national, cross-cultural influences. Xenophon's possibly historical, possibly fictional "The Education of Cyrus" (about 400 BCE) sought to influence the purposes and methods of education in the Greek city-states through describing the excellent results of the ways in which a young king of the Persian empire, Cyrus, was educated (Ambles, 2001). A thousand years later, in about 1300 AD, Marco Polo's stories included descriptions of the performance test system for selecting civil servants in China. In words not far from today's, he wrote of how extensively preparation for the career-determining tests influenced the Chinese educational system. Intensive test preparation courses were offered widely. Further, a system of schools focused on readiness for passing these ultra-high-stakes tests had developed as early as the Han Dynasty, between 200 BCE and 20 CE. This testing approach spread to Korea and other Chinese-influenced countries by the 7th century.

One could trace, historically, the rate of global uptake of educational ideas. For example, in 1910, Montessori in Italy described her early childhood program, a program she emphasized was science-based in its concept and in the research she carried out, reporting what still seems astonishing growth of slum children under her tutelage (Lindenfors, Mackinnon, Lillard, & Else-Quest, 2007). Her books sparked a worldwide movement that flourishes today in more than 7,000 certified Montessori schools located in scores of countries. Piaget (1928) in France published exquisitely detailed, brilliantly interpreted observations of the development of one of his children ($N = 1$) and a few other children. Within 10 years, his work on developmental stages and their implications for children's education was well known in Europe, the Americas, and countries as distant from France as India—ideas described as among the most influential of the 20st century in their effect on education. More recently, Freire's (1972) approach to socially just education has had a similar infusion through his books, personal consultations, and inclusion in courses for teachers. The nonformal education programs he developed are still carrying out his principles.

Such educational changes associated with nongovernmental influences may engender considerable research (e.g., Lillard & Else-Quest, 2006). Educational evaluations of approaches spread through nonformal networks do not seem to be undertaken, however, with quite the same vigor as do educational evaluations required or encouraged by more formal funders, such as governments, international organizations, and philanthropic groups. The more formal organizations are adopting as conditions of project funding, including educational projects, what I already have referred to as Western-modern-American approaches to evaluation.

With regard to evaluation stances, some groups such as the Kellogg Foundation, the U.S. National Science Foundation, Heifer International, and the Soros Foundation apply a more nuanced form of the Western frameworks, encouraging the development and field trials of different approaches to impact evaluation and suggesting a variety of approaches to establishing the counterfactual. Others, such as the Center for Global Development, the Organisation for Economic Co-operation and Development, and the U.S. Department of Education, apply a less nuanced form.

With this as context, I turn now to the chapter's three questions regarding science-based evaluation: a theory of action, strengths, and limitations of science-based approaches, and the influences on and by globalization.

Question 1: By what theory of action might science-based educational evaluation contribute to improved student learning in a globalized society?

For self-interest or for humanitarian reasons, many wealthier countries and an array of multinational agencies invest heavily in projects to improve the human condition. The time scales of such agencies can expand to 20-year or more horizons initially, with considerable tolerance for evaluations that are formative, illuminating, and suggestive, rather than summative and conclusive. Time passes, early results may disappoint, new ideas compete for resources, and underlying program assumptions are questioned. Patience ends, and the time scale can compress. When this happens, agencies can shift to a results and accountability "now" frame of mind.

The first story, told by Patton, represents a worst case for project evaluations: so great the human need, so many billions spent, so little credible evidence of consequences, so little improvement over ideology and anecdote, or, at least, so little credible evidence when the only evidence accepted as credible comes from randomized designs. Would evaluations rejected because they do not have experimental designs also be rejected as poor quality studies if standards of excellence for other methods were used (Savedoff, Levine, & Birdsall, 2006)? By any methodological name, studies can be untrustworthy and of poor quality.

What makes science-based educational evaluation attractive can be the promises by its advocates of credibility, certainty, generalizability, and, possibly, the cachet of economists' endorsement. The promise can be expressed as a theory of action.

Such a theory of action may begin with the assertion that evidence-based problem analysis will lead to evidence-based selection of options. Evidence-based planning then will lead to increasing the likelihood of promoting student learning. Use of science-based evaluation will lead to greater certainty about the findings through control of biases and a more complete ruling out of counterfactual interpretations. Greater certainty about findings from a specific project or program strategy will lead to more decisive action. Further, terms such as *bringing rigor, precision*, and *concreteness* will communicate well with economics- and business-oriented institutions such as the International Monetary Fund, the African Bank, and the Bill and Melinda Gates Foundation. Ineffective project-level approaches will drop out, the theory continues. Effective strategic approaches will expand. Where needed, new approaches will be tried out as governments increasingly regard evaluations as part of good management.

Second, the theory of action continues, common use of science-based evaluation in all projects funded in different nations will lead to a common metric, such as effect size for student learning and quantitative indicators such as

graduation rates. A common metric can be used across many evaluations to compare successes. Common metrics also can help establish that a policy isn't working. Further, they can be used to examine factors that may better define what works where and for whom, thus leading to better decisions on whether to expand, change direction, or continue at the policy level.

Science-based has been taken to mean an emphasis on (a) summative intended use; (b) methods intended to establish attribution or causality, particularly the primacy of the randomized control trial method as a way of ruling out alternative explanations of results; and (c) quantitative measurement, particularly tests and numerically derived assessments. Evaluators are advised that "Only studies with acceptable approaches to counter-factuals need apply for inclusion in our data bases on evaluations" (World Bank, 2007).

The passion with which this view is held is well documented. For example:

- Boruch (2007): "The world of domestic and international aid is littered with well-intentioned, failed programs, and there is no shortage of projects that are thought to do good but whose value remains uncertain. Randomized trials are essential to establish that these interventions do work" (p. 71; see also Boruch, 1997).
- Duflo (2005): "People never used to do randomized evaluations of policy programs. It was always referred to as 'the gold standard' but nobody actually did it. The revolution [in the world of economics] is that [the randomized experiment] is no longer the gold standard. It's the standard. If you are in the business of telling people how to do things better, you better make sure it's true."
- Savedoff et al. (2006): "The knowledge gained from rigorous impact studies is in part a public good. . . . Poor quality evaluations are misleading. . . . While it is widely recognized that withholding programs that are known to be beneficial

would be unethical, the implicit corollary—that programs of unknown impact should not be widely replicated without proper evaluation—is frequently dismissed" (pp. 2–30). Following the principles of Savedoff et al., the International Initiative for Impact Evaluation (2008) has been launched to fund studies "contributing to evidence-based policy making in developing countries."

Is the passion justified?

Question 2: What are the strengths and limitations of this educational evaluation genre in theory, methods, practice, and contributions to policy?

Theory and Evaluation Design Issues

Few areas may be more contentious than whether there is a one best approach to be used wherever feasible or whether the gold standard for educational evaluation should be diversity and situationally appropriate use (Lawrenz & Huffman, 2006).

The randomized control trial seeks to promote certainty of conclusions by controlling biases and ruling out counterfactuals subtractively. The evaluands (individuals, schools, communities, and states) are assigned at random to participate or not in the intervention being tested. All other things being equal, differences in outcomes are attributed to the intervention. Lack of differences is interpreted as indicating that the intervention is ineffective or, more appropriately, failing to reject the null hypothesis is expressed as a "no credible evidence" finding.

The science-based approach has important nuances. When the randomized control trial is not possible, according to the criteria for this approach, some quasi-experimental approaches, if carefully implemented, are seen as providing adequate approximations to results from randomized control trials (see Cook, 1985; Shadish, Cook, & Campbell, 2002). As an example,

evaluations admitted to the World Bank (2007) Poverty Impact Evaluations database can use one or more of seven designs: randomized control trials, propensity score matching, pipeline comparisons, simulated counterfactuals, difference in means of single difference, difference in difference or double difference, and instrumental variables. The theory, practice, and results of the randomized control trials remain, however, the benchmark against which other approaches are compared. If a quasi-experimental evaluation and a randomized control trial get different results, the randomized control trial is assumed to be the more valid, when criteria for appropriate use of both approaches are met. That is, the randomized control trial is the gold standard of value.

Among other nuances, incorporating process studies linked to a theory of action can help explain the results. Proper replications and meta-analysis across randomized studies can strengthen generalizability. Shadish et al. (2002) provide an excellent, in-depth source for understanding the claims and methods of the science-based approach. The website files of the Campbell and Cochrane Collaboratives offer extensive examples of the randomized control trial in education and health, respectively.

What are the criteria for selecting a randomized control trial design? When the evaluation question is fairly crisply defined; when the intervention is fairly stable, well bounded, and brief; when a double-blind situation is possible; when the experimental and control groups are passive rather than active; and when the methodological and practical requirements in random assignment are met and ethical considerations can be fulfilled, then randomized control trials can offer quantitative answers presented with assurance (Donaldson & Christie, 2005). The second story (incentive payments in Mexico) illustrates what Boruch believes to be such a situation.

Certain quasi-experimental designs can also offer quantitative answers presented with assurance. Consider a good instance of propensity score use. Henry, Gordon, and Rickman (2006) were asked to find out whether state-managed preschool programs do as well as Head Start in preparing children from low-income families for school. Henry and his colleagues looked at a small, but representative, sample of children from Head Start programs in one state (Georgia), using propensity scores to select a sample of children who actually attended the state-sponsored preschools, but who looked as if they might have selected Head Start. Follow-up showed minor differences between the two groups on measures of reading, writing, and arithmetic. Henry was careful to emphasize that no assessments were made of certain outcomes important to Head Start, such as those involving families, and did not overgeneralize beyond Georgia, but the findings have been regarded as policy-useful (see also Mark, Henry, & Julnes, 2000, on quasi-experimental designs).

A significant instance of meta-analytic use of quasi-experimental as well as available experimental designs is the analysis commissioned by the National Academy of Education (2007) regarding evidence of the value of race-conscious policies for assigning students to schools. The meta-analysts examined the 27 instances in which evaluation data were used in amicus briefs presented to the U.S. Supreme Court. Their report, an exemplar of careful use of diverse designs, concludes, "the overall academic and social effects of increased racial diversity are likely to be positive. Racial diversity per se does not guarantee such positive outcomes, but it provides the necessary conditions under which other educational policies can facilitate improved academic achievement, improved intergroup relations, and positive long-term outcomes" (National Academy of Education, 2007, p. 49).

In countries that are fairly top-down in the development of Terms of Reference for carrying out evaluations and fairly centralized with regard to who initiates, who pays for, and who is the primary evaluation stakeholder, the randomized control trials framework and the use of program logic specifications seem likely to be adopted where an evaluation culture is at least somewhat developed and other conditions are favorable. Indeed, as mentioned, it already has been endorsed by Organisation for Economic

Co-operation and Development, the U.S. Department of Education, the Bill and Melinda Gates Foundation, and the European Union (EU), although more comprehensive discussions of evaluation practice make clear the influences, nation by nation, of historical, cultural, and political circumstances (Furubo, Rist, & Sandahl, 2002; Zajda et al., 2005).

In contrast to enthusiasm by business, banking, and economics-oriented funders for the science-based approach, in countries with a strong indigenous population and with a greater variety of funding agencies for innovative programs and evaluations, an almost equally swift evaluation tide may be rising. This looks at alternative methods and measures; tends to be based on an additive framework, systems, and complexity theories; situates the present in connection to past and future; aims at reducing uncertainty through understanding influences; and aligns with appreciation of the traditional ways of knowing of indigenous peoples, giving appropriate attention to questions other than impact and outcomes.

The sources of these approaches are varied. From New Zealand, Smith's (1999) widely read book *Decolonizing Methodologies* has been highly influential in encouraging indigenous methodologies. Her approach can be seen in practice in the conferences of the Aotearoa Evaluation Association and in the terms of reference for evaluations, particularly in Maori contexts, commissioned by New Zealand educational authorities (Ministry of Education, New Zealand, 2003). Williams in Australia is a leader in the application of systems-based frameworks in evaluation (Williams & Iman, 2006). Pawson and Tilley (1997; Tilley, 2004) in Great Britain developed an iterative, action-research, context-dependent framework for evaluation. Elliott (1999), from Great Britain, offers an important case study of appreciative inquiry. Owen and Rogers (1999) in Australia present internationally practiced approaches to integrating program logic and analysis with multiple designs and measures. In the United States, there is a strong history of evaluation theory and practice grounded in ideals of social justice and cultural competence (Cousins & Earl, 1995; Fetterman, 2005; Patton, 1997; Preskill & Catsambas, 2006), including those articulated by Native Americans and in Canada by First Peoples (see, e.g., Abma, 1999, on narratives in evaluation).

These theorists dispute the primacy of randomized control trials or indeed any single method as the one entitled to be privileged as "science based" on grounds including logic, limited applicability in areas such as human services, and feasibility.

One concern is that the crucial assumption "all things being equal" as a result of randomization is not likely to be true where the control groups are active. Active control groups can make for conservative estimates of program effects due, in part, to increased variability and decreased treatment differentiation as a consequence of treatment/control crossovers (Datta, 2007). Even rigorous efforts, such as the randomized control experiment in India managed by the MIT Poverty Action Laboratory, can encounter postassignment challenges. One of the two experimental sites for an educational intervention ran into "administrative difficulties," and only two thirds of the schools that were assigned special teachers actually received them. These schools were nonetheless included in analyses of the treatment group results by applying heroic statistical adjustments (World Bank, 2007). Perhaps not surprisingly, the results for that site were disappointing.

It would be illuminating to know how many of the randomized control trials cited as evidence of feasibility did not require considerable imputation and adjustments. Each of these adjustments, interpreted carefully, increases reliance on various assumptions regarding random error and decreases the certainty of conclusions. One would expect comparing (a) treatments actually received to (b) treatments actually not received would be a fairer test of concept than comparing (c) treatments actually received plus imaginary (imputed, estimated) treatment results to (d) treatments actually not received plus with similar treatments received under other auspices. As an axiom, the greater the difference between experiences actually received by experimental

and control/comparison groups, the greater the likelihood of detecting treatment effects. Scrupulous evaluators report data on experiences actually received and modulate certainty of conclusions so that among the headlines, the Executive Summary, and the small-print Technical Appendices, there are no royal robings of methodologically modest dress. A small but telling indicator of the value of the treatment as experienced may be the two lead articles of the flagship issue of the *Journal of Research on Educational Effectiveness*, intended to showcase randomized control trial designs. Both had to use variation in degree of implementation (treatment on treated) to demonstrate effect size (Chambers et al., 2008; Sarama, Clements, Starkey, Klein, & Wakeley, 2008).

Further, few educational interventions are developed and tried out as called for in the medical model, which the application of randomized control trials in education emulates. In the archetypical medical model approach, basic research establishes grounds in theory for understanding a situation and predicting what might happen with a theory-derived intervention. This is followed by trying out the intervention on a small scale, looking particularly for side effects and unexpected results. An approach passing this stage then is subject to efficacy trials establishing the results through comparisons. Then, and only then, are randomized trials of effectiveness carried out to test for generalizability in diverse real-world conditions.

This sequence is rarely followed, say the critics, in randomized educational evaluations, and it may not be appropriate even in the medical model from which it is derived. Indeed, some of the more trenchant criticisms of the randomized control trial approach come from the health area (Cundiff, 2007; Sehon & Stanley, 2003). Still further, continue those believing the randomized control trial has beauty, but can be a beast with limited applicability, education is best viewed as a complex system, one quite fluid in most circumstances, and better understood through additive methods, establishing an understanding of what is happening and why.

Critics of the science-based approach are not anti-evaluation. Rather, they consider that rigorous, sound evaluation offering the greatest possible reduction of uncertainty about effects is an essential component of action programs. To them, a better standard—what might be thought of as the platinum standard—would be situationally appropriate evaluation.

The situationally appropriate evaluation concept refers to systematic efforts to document something has happened and to estimate the contribution of the program or other intervention to what has happened, using methods that best fit the circumstances, broadly considered. Such methods can include, in the more quantitative mode, propensity-matching approaches and regression discontinuity designs. In the more qualitative mode, methods can include systematic case studies. In the mixed mode, there are many possible combinations of frameworks, designs, and measures to be selected according to the evaluative questions and conditions. In other words, the starting point would be quasi-experimental designs with randomized approaches used when circumstances support their appropriateness and values (see, e.g., Mark et al., 2000; Patton, 1997, 2007b; Pawson & Tilley, 1997; Stufflebeam & Shinkfield, 2007; Yin & Moore, 1988).

Some theorists supporting randomized control designs resent the implication in these criticisms that they (the theorists) have urged the use of randomized control trials regardless of circumstances. Their resentment is well justified, in that some of the most detailed, hard-hitting, wide-reaching statements of circumstances when the randomized control trial is inappropriate are found in work generally supporting the privileging of randomized experiments in education (Boruch, 2007; Savedoff et al., 2006; Shadish, 2007; Shadish et al., 2002).

The resentment is not justified, however, in that some policymaking bodies, such as the U.S. Department of Education and the U.S. Office of Management and Budget, do regard the randomized control trial as the required standard for evaluation support. These actions seem taken without discernable attention to all the ethics standards and caveats listed by the theorists and without discernable protests by the theorists or initiatives to ensure scrupulous examination of whether the conditions have been met (Datta, 2007).

Fear resulting from the consequences of past inappropriate use can be another source of resistance to both the randomized control trial and quasi-experimental approaches, even when they may be appropriate in new circumstances. Case reports from evaluations in African countries are fairly extensively and richly illustrating the perverse results of inappropriate application of "Western" evaluation approaches and the benefits of local or adapted methods (Jansen & Christie, 1999). Countries highly dependent on grants from multinational and international foundations can feel as if the generally macro-negative results of science-based designs in the complex real world will confirm funder concern that social problems are not solved quickly, even with massive amounts of funds: AIDS may not go away soon, literacy may not rise rapidly, and gender equity may not be achieved quickly.

Ofir (2007), calling to the international community, writes:

> Many of you know that the movement to promote randomized control trials as "the method" has been shifting their efforts very strongly to developing countries. . . . No-one disputes that evaluation in developing countries is in dire need of improvement. But it is exactly because of this that we need to understand and use the rich portfolio of evaluation frameworks and methodologies to suit the nature of what we need to evaluate. . . . The Network of Networks on Impact Evaluation is powerful grouping of around 70 development assistance organizations. . . . One of its working groups has to map and systematize different approaches to impact evaluation . . . and recommend to the Network of Networks on Impact Evaluation what approaches should be used to ensure rigor and quality impact

evaluation work. . . . Please assist us [with] your vast evaluation experience and expertise from all over the world. (see also the Network of Networks on Impact Evaluation, 2007)

When the funders' concerns are confirmed (too much corruption, too much tribalism, and too much of whatever is perceived as obstacles causing the negative results), so the fear runs, two consequences may follow. The first consequence may be concentration of money on what can be tested, proved effective, and provide success stories—not always the most significant problems and not always the most promising approaches. The second consequence, it is feared, may be a redirection of funds into areas other than education and human services.

Measurement and Practice Issues

As stated earlier, the three components of the science-based approach are intended use (primarily summative), consistent method (particularly randomized trials), and quantitative measures (including educational tests). This section briefly discusses national and global aspects of testing and measurement in educational evaluation as part of the science-based approach.

National Assessments of Student Learning

Quantitative assessment has expanded concurrently with the emphasis on experimental methods. Kellaghan (2003) notes,

Most countries in the industrialized world, with the notable exception of Germany, had established national assessment systems by 1990. During the 1990s, capacity to carry out assessment studies developed rapidly in developing countries, particularly in Africa and Latin America. The activity for the most part seems attributable to

the stress in the Declaration of the World Conference on Education for All (United Nations Educational, Scientific, and Cultural Organization, 1990) on the importance of knowing to what extent students were actually learning. (p. 876)

As one might expect, procedures differ from country to country in what is assessed (content), whether the assessment is population or a sample, the grade levels that are assessed, how often the assessments are carried out, whether information is provided at the school level or at higher aggregations, and how the results are used. Kellaghan observes that assessment systems are more elaborated in countries that do not have a national testing system for school leaving or grade advancement purposes.

In the United States, the National Assessment of Educational Progress, proposed in 1964 by Ralph Tyler, continues with primarily illuminative and symbolic use. In contrast, the 2002 No Child Left Behind (NCLB) Act moved the United States toward a national testing system with penetrating consequences. States currently can establish their own performance testing systems, although this may change. Schools failing to meet progress standards must undergo energetic improvement protocols and, in some instances, may lose federal funding (Jones, 2003).

The assessment of the assessment systems has been fairly vigorous. Kellaghan (2003) reports that an 1880s assessment movement in Great Britain stumbled when the validity of the measures was cast into doubt. Contemporary concerns remain focused on the psychometric properties of the tests, particularly when the results are used for decision making, rather than more symbolically.

A vigorous criticism of the NCLB assessments by Nichols and Berliner (2007) begins with an examination of Campbell's Law. As quoted by Nichols and Berliner, Campbell observed in 1975 that "the more any quantitative social indicator is used for social decision-making, the more subject it will be to corruption pressures and the more apt it will be to distort and corrupt the social processes it is intended to monitor" (p. 26). Nichols and Berliner (2007) document, among other concerns, strong evidence of teaching to the test to the exclusion of other learning, cheating through "correcting" tests after the students have taken them, bribery of the children to excel on the test, schemes to avoid having less able children in school on the day of testing, watering down the test items and standards by individual states to scandalously low levels, and draconian pressures on classroom teachers, driving many to leave the profession.

Most crucially, according to Nichols and Berliner (2007), there is no evidence that the NCLB testing improves student learning as measured by less corrupted tests, such as the National Association of Educational Progress. Claims to benefits, these authors conclude, are based on data that do not withstand a close look. They write, "high-stakes testing does not increase achievement (and in some cases may erode it), . . . and unintended outcomes of the high-stakes testing process [are] detrimental to the educational process" (p. xv). It is unclear whether Nichols and Berliner pursued evidence of benefits as vigorously as they pursued evidence of collateral damage. Testing is one part of a complex package; when the whole package is well carried out, what happens? Can the whole package be well carried out at scale? Is there enough political will to pay the true costs, enough infrastructural skill to put concept into action?

A well-regarded report by Lee (2006) concludes there was no evidence that NCLB testing has improved reading and math achievement or has reduced achievement gaps. In this analysis, performance on the uncorrupted (at least relatively) National Assessment of Educational Progress showed no gains comparing (a) the 1990 to 2001, pre-NCLB period to (b) the 2002–2005, post-NCLB period when the state NCLB assessments showed improvements. If the reported NCLB gains from the states were reliable, then the students would be expected to perform similarly on both tests because the same subjects were covered.

Methodologically, NCLB is a uniquely valuable opportunity to use interrupted time series concepts because the intervention (NCLB assessments) was introduced at a specific time, nationally, for a large number of replicated instances. Lee (2006) used a growth curve model for his analyses. His report is worth study in itself as a science-based approach to assessing whether national assessments such as NCLB improve, have no effect on, or are deleterious to student learning.

Although defenders of NCLB testing have criticized the critics or argued for a national test, such as one based on the National Assessment of Educational Progress, whose integrity could be better maintained than the state-level assessments, there does not appear to be a methodologically solid study showing that the testing per se actually is contributing to greater student learning. In time, there may be more indirect benefits, but these have yet to appear. Murray (2006) comments, "Is it too early to tell? The schools our children have attended have turned themselves inside out to try to produce the right test results, with dismaying effects on the content of classroom instruction and devastating effects on teacher morale" (p. 4).

The more qualitative values of assessments for student learning are much discussed and could be considered well documented. They include showing how testing focuses attention on what communities and countries seek as the outcomes of public education, efforts to improve assessment methodologies, examination of the alignments between what is being taught and what is expected to be learned, and use of findings, particularly trends, as benchmarks of progress or problems. This later role has demonstrably been linked to actions in policy and practice, which may have effects on student learning. Issues include whose expectations for learning are assessed, demands for standardization, and requirements for quantification in contrast to more qualitative approaches. Even an area that appears straightforward, such as use of writing samples and student learning portfolios, can erupt with controversy.

International Assessments

Systematic international assessment of student learning began with methodological and feasibility studies launched in the early 1960s. By the 1980s, comparative international studies were proving of much interest to educators and policymakers, particularly when the analyses spoke to determinants of achievement differences and enriched understanding of education in different countries (Plomp, Howie, & McGaw, 2003). As examples,

- The International Association for the Evaluation of Educational Achievement with its more than 55 members has looked at mathematics, science, written comprehension, reading comprehension, foreign languages, and civics education. Results, which have showed (for example) superior mathematics performance in Asian countries, have also proven that the achievement gaps between girls and boys are not a universal, whereas the relation between home environment and achievement apparently is. Grounded in an understanding of curricula as a guide to the assessment items, the international assessments seem particularly helpful where national priorities and curricula are aligned with the measures. Curriculum emphasis reported across countries is convincingly related to assessment outcomes.
- The Organisation for Economic Co-operation and Development (OECD), with its more than 30 members, primarily integrates educational statistics and improves indicators to give a comparative cross-national picture of education. The OECD context is productivity and economic well-being; thus, the data are particularly rich in information about economic, social, and population contexts—resources invested in education, participation rates, processes, and both education and labor market outcomes.

- The Southern Africa Consortium for Monitoring Educational Quality has been working since 1991 on studies of schooling and achievement. Here, each country prepares a report that is brought together with reports from other countries in a meta-analysis. Although the meta-analytic reports are intended for planning purposes, the Southern Africa Consortium has been helpful in identifying differences in achievement across the countries and in stimulating national discussions of improvement.

A notable literature has developed around these and other international comparative studies of student achievement (see Plomp et al., 2003). The methodological issues examined include sampling procedures, response rates, measure development, translation equivalence, cultural biases in response styles, data collection, and data analysis such as computation of equating errors . Knowledge of costs, requirements in planning time and personnel, and approaches to quality assurance demonstrably have benefited from the challenges of undertaking such science-based international comparative studies.

Evidence of the effect on student learning from these evaluations is at best indirect. There is apparently no comparable study to Lee's. Thus, what can be said about the science-based evidence of consequences of this form of educational evaluation on student learning is limited primarily to symbolic, conceptual, and enlightenment aspects of evaluation use. Considerable differences among countries exist not only in how planning and decision making take place but also in the transparency of this process. There are anecdotal instances of consequences (not always benign), rather than more systematic evidence of instrumental use.

Nonetheless, the effect of globalization on educational evaluation is clearly seen in the almost worldwide participation in comparative assessments and in the intense interest when their results are published. The longstanding questions appearing nationally also appear globally: Are those elements of student learning most important to a globalized world being measured? If not, will what is being measured drive out adequate attention to what should be measured? Can international assessments escape Campbell's Law and what Nichols and Berliner have shown can involve harm to the educational process and to students?

Question 3: Is science-based educational evaluation likely to shape or be shaped by globalization?

In this section, I look first at some consequences of educational evaluations and then consider the flows of influences between consistency- and diversity-oriented approaches.

The Belief That Educational Evaluations Are Appropriate and Necessary

Before the current degree of globalization, some countries used evaluations to inform decisions about educational policies and practices. The approaches reflected the diversity of national, county, and local relationships. Education systems are more centralized in countries such as France; they are more decentralized in other nations. Countries such as Australia, Holland, Germany, Sweden, and New Zealand have relied upon an inspectorate of visiting committees. The committees review individual schools in depth against clearly set-out standards; their recommendations have considerable influence on these schools as well as on national policies. Such countries also have looked keenly at results of nationally administered tests not only for individual student recognition but also for what the trends suggest about education programs and policies. These countries also have used formal evaluations, including science-based approaches, to try out new educational ideas.

Other countries did not have such an elaborated experience. In some instances, where the

culture, traditions, and ideologies did not promote evaluation, external pressures have powerfully affected educational evaluation. For instance, O'Hara, McNamara, Boyle, and Sullivan (2007) write,

> [An] evaluation culture in the public sector and particularly education in Ireland [has emerged] over the past three decades . . . the emergence of this culture was strongly influenced by external factors, particularly the EU, and to a lesser but significant degree, the Organisation for Economic Cooperation and Development. Indeed, it can be argued that without these external influences no culture of evaluation would have emerged. (p. 75)

Karimov et al. (2007), writing of the newly independent states of the former Union of Soviet Socialist Republics, says:

> The development of program evaluation as a profession started simultaneously with the appearance of foreign donors at the beginning of 1990s. Evaluation was "imported" together with the project approach as one of the management functions of foreign organizations. . . . By the second half of the 90s, the project approach had been thoroughly studied by the region's non-government organizations . . . with the development of program evaluation proceeding faster in some countries and slower in others. (pp. 84–85)

The meteoric expansion of national and regional evaluation associations indicates that belief in the appropriateness and necessity of formal, science-based evaluation, including educational evaluation, may be close to global, with the exceptions of some of the more war-torn regions and some Middle Eastern countries (see, e.g., the International Organization for Cooperation in Evaluation case studies on the characteristics of evaluation agencies in more than 60 countries; Segone & Ocampo, 2007). Much of this expansion can be and is attributed to external demand from funding agencies during the 1990s for more rigorous and conclusive evaluations; evidence suggests more tentatively a growing internalization of evaluation as good governance and management.

Expansion of Training and Communication

Almost every culture has had some way of finding out the quality of schooling offered to its young and whether the consequences were what they should be. Indeed, the most exhaustive, rigorous, and demanding evaluation of individual learner skills with which I am familiar is reported from Africa in the context of a forest-based, hunter-gatherer community. The skills needed for survival in this environment are many, must be learned to a high level of perfection, and, literally, no child can be left behind. The evaluation approach here is observation and rigorous performance testing. The results affect the individual learner and are the subject of community policy decisions and debates. This instance is highly adapted to local needs and circumstances, not standardized within the area or country. However, data situating local achievement within large political entities are demanded by funders and, through evolution or experience, by nations, in part through considerations of equity and resource allocation.

Approaches that increase standardization, are more quantitative, and involve comparisons across schools and communities call for trained evaluation professionals. Educational evaluation capacity building is encouraged by international organizations requiring these consistency-oriented approaches.

One example is the efforts by the World Bank to train evaluators in every country according to their standards of evaluation quality (Grasso, Wasty, & Waeving, 2003; Kusek & Rist, 2001; Picciotto, 2005). These are far more than fairly brief workshops. The World Bank efforts involve off-site advanced programs taught by

internationally recognized evaluation specialists, creating a university of the world in evaluation. The World Bank's International Program for Development Training is administered in cooperation with Carleton University (International Program for Development Evaluation Training, 2008). About 12,000 evaluators from 21 countries have graduated since 2001 from the 80-hour core program with follow-on workshops.

Another example is the more than 30-year-old international program, led by the U.S. Government Accountability Office, bringing auditors from every country to Washington, DC, for a full year of internships, intense training, academics, and enrichment experiences in auditing, including performance auditing and evaluation. The intent is to raise the status of auditing departments to ensure uniformly high levels of professional skill and to build a worldwide community of expert auditors/evaluators. Because many of these participants are already high-level officials in their country, the leverage of this program is high, wide, and very handsome.

A third example are the many workshops sponsored by groups such as Heifer International, the Soros Foundation, and international agencies bringing renowned evaluators to train recipients of the agencies' grants in how to evaluate the results of their project.

Other instances include the establishment of international journals, the development of evaluation agencies, and the glorious rise of international conferences on evaluation issues, now held almost all over the globe. A development almost as rapid as expansion of national evaluation conferences is the expansion of university-based courses and degree programs in globalization and international education, which include courses in evaluation from a global perspective.

The prominence being given internationally to evaluation as a necessary aspect of good government is leading to development of evaluation capacity worldwide. Of the probable benefits of globalization per se on education and student learning, these are the best documented at present. Other, more downstream benefits on student learning, as predicted by the theory of action, may be hoped for. Science-based evaluation may be part of this if the confident assurances of interpretable, authoritative results offered by its advocates are part of the attraction for governments, legislators, and foundations funding much of the formal training.

Program, Curricular, and Student Learning Consequences

Some benefits of science-based evaluations for student learning can be taken as given. Where reasonably well-grounded, systematic, empirical information replaces ideology and anecdote, better information for decision making is likely to lead to better decision making, as suggested in the theory of action. Where the evaluative framework and evaluative processes are engaged as part of planning, clarification of values, and identification of gaps, process use can be hoped for. Where a community of evaluators can share experiences in similar national circumstances, pitfalls can be avoided and practice better assured. But not always.

On the positive side, there are clearly instances where one raison d'être for the science-based approach—stop wasting money on what doesn't work—has been realized. For instance, some programs that seem consistently ineffective or that present only anecdotal and dubious evidence, such as Drug Abuse Resistance Education (D.A.R.E.), which addresses student behavioral issues including drug use, are overhauled or discontinued (Weiss, Murphy-Graham, & Birkland, 2005). On the negative side, some programs shown through quasi-experimental methods to be effective approaches to student learning are branded as "effectiveness unproven," with chilling effects on funding. Further, new programs that may offer innovative, potentially valuable approaches, but are difficult to evaluate through the randomized control trials, may not get a chance: They may be less competitive for funding.

Garaway (2003) shares what evaluation looks like in some Third World situations. She describes an effort to look at implementation of an initiative to improve rural education. Arriving unannounced, she finds a few children and no teacher. "He often doesn't come," they say. In another site, she can observe teaching and test the children's achievement. Sharing experiences with other evaluators, she and they note that, in the presence of the male authority, the women were silent. The evaluator feels that quantitative information from these sites can be given to the multilateral donor, but the evaluation may have missed the mark. Later, she meets in an urban setting for two focus-group sessions attended by local educational authorities and the nongovernment organization national staff. Here, she finds that, to the participants, she represents the funders, and they plea for continued support without which they cannot continue. Their purpose in attending the focus groups is to discuss funding, not to discuss evaluation.

To Garaway (2003), these and other experiences heighten the dilemmas in connecting local realities with evaluation idealities: shortages of skilled personnel, deflection of funds, disparities between schools, lack of infrastructure and facilities, the "hierarchical distance" in relationships in contrast with a more horizontal society, and, quintessentially, the pervasiveness of our cultural values and expectations: Is wealth the distance from the water tap or is wealth the hut in a lush garden? She writes,

> In terms of impact made by the process, there is on the one hand the unintentional impact related to inappropriate implementation . . . on the other hand are large numbers of appropriately implemented participatory processes that have resulted in learning and tremendous program improvement. (p. 710)

She finds that postevaluation utilization is constrained by barriers to locally and nationally effective communication, with instrumental use more likely by the donor agencies if there is any use at all and likely to be nonsystematic. Lessons learned from her experiences echo those from such international evaluators as Bamberger (2000). She concludes that more than science-based versus other methodologies, sound evaluation requires joint processes in defining aims of the evaluation, greater diversity of measures, integration where possible of the evaluation into a circular program process, and greater alignment of the evaluation with the needs of a particular educational setting.

Despite the challenges, Garaway sees tremendous potential for evaluation as a contribution to educational improvement, seen systemically and seen in student learning.

Jansen (2002) offers a somewhat contrasting view. Speaking of postapartheid education in South Africa, he describes how outcomes-based initiatives were transported from Australia, the United States, New Zealand, Scotland, and other parts of the United Kingdom to The Netherlands, Chile, India, and South Africa. He observes, "International experts, visiting consultancy groups, overseas exchange visits, funded conferences and 'linkage projects' have enabled . . . the . . . transfer of first-world policy experiments within Africa on a scale never before witnessed in post-colonial Africa" (p. 4). The context was fitting a South African national policy emphasis on redistribution within a framework of control and accountability as a means to this end. Such a framework makes for selection of indicators such as gap analyses by ethnicity and economic status in educational quality and, eventually, educational outcomes. The third story with which this chapter begins, from Jansen, documents poor quality education and less student learning as a result of inappropriate use of the science-based evaluation approach.

More industrialized nations can experience these tensions, and they affect postsecondary, technical, and professional education, as well as elementary and secondary areas. For instance, as the EU works toward a common intellectual currency in university education, the various departments, universities, and nations need to decide whether to align their curricula and assessment, their degree-granting requirements, with the EU standards. In some instances, congruence may be

sufficiently high that adjustments would be minimal. In other instances, standardization could chop off, like Procrustes' bed, features that differentiate—for example—how literature is thought about and taught in Prague and Toledo, in Berlin and Athens. Would the distinctive voices that are among the common treasures of the world and the national treasures of each country be amplified or diminished?

As noted earlier, evaluation currents perhaps resemble those of wind and water globally. In these, high-altitude systems can be flowing in one direction; lower altitude, another; or, for oceans, the surface and deeper layers may move in opposite ways. At present, the surface layers of educational evaluation seem to be consistency-oriented and science-based, particularly favoring randomized control trials designs for finding out how effectively different programs and policies promote student achievement (Costas, 2007). These approaches stem from experiences in more Western countries.

The deeper layers (or higher altitude) currents include approaches primarily originating in non-Western traditions of knowledge (epistemology), authenticity of information (such as narratives and storytelling), and knowledge utilization (particularly the importance of face time, trust, and in-depth cultural knowledge). These flows can be traced in books used for evaluator training; the growth of specialized international, regional, and national evaluation journals; and the emergence of cross-national evaluation organizations around themes such as qualitative evaluations (Vulliamy, 2004). The conference agendas from the more than 90 national evaluation associations exemplify this flow and counterflow. For instance, 2007 saw more than 1,000 evaluators from across the globe attend the Third International Conference on Qualitative Evaluation. In the future, some exciting new approaches may emerge from the evaluation efforts and associations in non-Western countries, reversing in some countries the direction of the current tide exemplified in the OECD documents (see Rizvi, 2005; Rizvi & Lingard, 2006).

But these currents can mingle. Increasingly, advocates of a hierarchy beginning with quantitative meta-analyses, continuing to randomized experiments, and ending many steps below this top rung in cases studies and observation-based expert judgment emphasize the understanding necessary for sound use of randomized trials. Boruch (2007), for instance, eloquently writes of four necessary understandings: understanding when randomized trials are ethically acceptable and how to design trials to be ethically acceptable, understanding when and why a nonrandomized trial might generate estimates similar in magnitude and direction to those generated in a randomized trial, understanding how to build cumulative knowledge through prospective and retrospective registers, and understanding how to enhance the quality of reporting on both randomized and nonrandomized trials. Shadish (2007) declares, "Rigor should not be conflated indiscriminately with any one design, particularly in today's rapidly changing world of causal inference, where so many improvements are occurring to how we study cause and effect relationships" (p. 104). Lipsey (2007):

> The more critical question is whether a given methodology is useful (or practical, credible, convincing, suitable, or something else) for answering the kind of question being asked. This is a matter of judgment. . . . Concerns that influence such judgment include prior experience, consideration of the context in which the program or policy questions *is* being asked, and consideration of the audience to be persuaded.

Would a well-planned series of globally attended conferences focused on delineating the understanding or conditions necessary for using each and all of the leading evaluation approaches find much common ground? Could we give equal time to looking at completed evaluations and practice? Could there be much agreement on what further evaluation research would clarify the applicability and benefits? Can we avoid the sometimes discourteous debates impugning other people's motives, virtue, and brains (come

on, colleagues: All the evaluators I know are deeply concerned about making this world a better place, and they aren't in this field to get rich) and whether the evaluation discussions are really neocolonialism through economic globalization under multinational control?

In Summary

I have considered the globalization of science-based educational evaluation as a movement toward consistency characterized by summative, impact questions and summative utilization intent, methodological consistency, the primacy of randomized control trials, and consistency in quantitative assessments. This strenuous effort toward evaluation consistency in design, measures, and standards correlates with such global statements of purposes as the Millennium Goals, coordinating purposes and priorities across many international funding organizations.

Many evaluators have worked hard over many years to improve science-based evaluation and to document its superiority. They have, I believe, demonstrated that science-based evaluation has a role in globalization because in appropriate circumstances it is a superb approach to finding out what works. These circumstances include meeting ethical considerations; programs that are fairly mature, well bounded, and shorter term; situations of high salience where contrasting approaches exist; contexts where crossovers are not likely to diminish notably the distinction between control and experimental treatments as experienced; where double-blindedness is possible; and the absence of other well-known threats to appropriateness in various situations.

Science-based evaluation also has a role in fears. It has been applied without adequate attention to the threats to appropriateness, with too cheerful a view of the robustness of fixes for the problems encountered and too dour a view of the value of alternatives. It has promised answers more quickly than those concerned with understanding educational context know is possible.

In contrast, there is clearly a countercurrent toward diversity: diversity of questions, many forms of evaluation utilization, methodological diversity, and diversity of measurement. Well-stated discussions of the foundations of these stances in evaluation theory abound. Yet it is still true that claims of virtue can outstrip evidence of value when the approaches are carried to national or international scale, although there are some robust applications of alternative methodologies globally in evaluation projects, such as those funded by Heifer International.

There is a wealth of opportunity globally to learn about these methods and measures. Much benefit could come if funders would support direct comparison for the same impact studies of evaluations from the consistent and diverse perspectives. From the underlying good will and passion for better health, education, and welfare among evaluators of all persuasions may come a framework that better applies the cautions well known to advocates of science-based methods and that adopts as a global standard situationally appropriate methods and measures. Recent statements by science-based advocates of the need for and ways to achieve appropriate use of randomized control trials, recognition of the threats to their feasibility and execution, and evaluation research into other designs may offer bridges between consistency and diversity perspectives.

More descriptive research on what is happening and with what consequences for student learning, concurrent with more opportunities to bring evaluators together to work on common understanding of appropriateness, perhaps could move things along less stridently and more constructively. That and a passionate commitment to ensuring that the conditions known to limit appropriate use of any method or measure are reviewed, carried out, and monitored: doing what we say! Perhaps not entirely: I am not sure, for instance, about working through approximation to randomized control trials results as the criterion for the value of other methods, although perhaps if the criterion was approximation to appropriately applied and interpreted results, the discussions could progress.

Some would argue that it has to be one or the other. I do not. In my view, hopefully, advocates of science-based approaches will put energy into ensuring their well-stated methodological cautions get into practice and advocates of alternative models will present better documented evidence of their applicability and results at scales needed for impact evaluations. Both should have their proud and rightful places in global evaluations of student learning—no less, but very definitely no more, than they deserve.

References

Abma, T. (Ed.). (1999). *Telling tales: On evaluation and narrative. Advances in program evaluation.* Stamford, CT: JAI Press.

Ambles, W. (2001). *The education of Cyrus.* Ithaca: Cornell University Press.

Bamberger, M. (Ed.). (2000). *Integrating quantitative and qualitative research in development projects. Directions in Development Series.* Washington, DC: The World Bank.

Barron, D. (2007, June 19). *A new prescription for poverty. PRI's The World.* Retrieved June 21, 2007, from http://www.theworld.org/?q=node/10887.

Boruch, R. (1997). *Randomized experiments for planning and evaluation: A practical guide.* Thousand Oaks, CA: Sage.

Boruch, R. (2007). Encouraging the flight of error: Ethical standards, evidence standards, and randomized trials. In G. Julnes & D. J. Rog (Eds.), *Informing federal policies on evaluation methodology: Building the evidence base for method choice in government sponsored evaluation. New Directions for Evaluation* (pp. 55–74). San Francisco, CA: Jossey-Bass.

Chambers, B., Ambrami, P., Tucker, B., Salvin, R. E., Madden, N. A., Cheung, A., & Gifford, R. (2008). Computer-assisted tutoring for Success for All: Reading outcomes. *Journal of Research on Educational Effectiveness, 1*(2), 120–137.

Cook, T. D. (1985). Postpositivist critical multiplism. In R. Shotland & M. M. Mark (Eds.), *Social science and social policy* (pp. 21–62). Thousand Oaks, CA: Sage.

Costas, M. A. (2007). Reshaping the methodological identity of educational research: Early signs of the impact of federal policy. *Evaluation Review*, *31*(4), 391–400.

Cousins, J. B., & Earl, L. (Eds.). (1995). *Participatory evaluation in education: Studies of evaluation use and organizational learning*. Bristol, PA: Falmer Press.

Cundiff, D. K. (2007). Evidence-based medicine and the Cochrane Collaborative. *Medscape General Medicine. 9*(2), 56–59.

Datta, L. (2007). Why active control groups make a difference and what to do about it. *Journal of Multidisciplinary Evaluation, 4*(7), 1–12.

Donaldson, S. I., & Christie, A. (2005). The 2004 Claremont debate: Lipsey versus Scriven—Determining causality in program evaluation and applied research: Should experimental evidence be the gold standard? *Journal of Multidisciplinary Evaluation, 2*(3), 60–70.

Duflo, E. (2005, Winter). *Helping the poor. Spectrum: Massachusetts Institute of Technology*. Retrieved August 3, 2007, from http://web.mit.edu/giving/spectrum/winter05/helping_the_poor.html.

Elliott, C. (1999). *Locating the energy for change: An introduction to appreciative inquiry*. Winnipeg, Manitoba: International Institute for Sustainable Development.

Fetterman, D. M. (2005). *Empowerment evaluation principles in practice*. New York: Guilford.

Freire, P. (1972). *The pedagogy of the oppressed*. Harmondsworth, UK: Penguin.

Furubo, J. E., Rist, R. C., & Sandahl, R. (Eds.). (2002). *International atlas of evaluation*. New Brunswick, NJ: Transaction Publishers.

Garaway, G. (2003). Evaluating educational programs and projects in the third world. In T. Kellaghan & D. Stufflebeam (Eds.), *International handbook of educational evaluation* (pp. 701–720). Dordrecht: Kluwer Academic Publishers.

Grasso, P. G., Wasty, S. S., & Waeving, R. V. (Eds.). (2003). *World Bank operations evaluation department: The first 30 years*. Washington, DC: The World Bank.

Henry, G. T., Gordon, C. C., & Rickman, D. K. (2006). Early education policy alternatives: The quality and outcomes of Head Start and state prekindergarten. *Educational Evaluation and Policy Analysis, 28*, 77–99.

International Initiative for Impact Evaluation. (2008). Retrieved July 31, 2008, from http://www.3ieimpact.org.

International Program for Development Evaluation Training. (2008). Retrieved July 31, 2009, from http://www.ipdet.org.

Jansen, J. A. (2002). *Globalization, curriculum, and the Third World state: In dialogue with Michael Apple. Current issues in comparative education.* Retrieved January 23, 2007, from http:www.tc.columbia.edu/cice.

Jansen, J. A., & Christie, P. (Eds.). (1999). *Changing curriculum: Studies of outcomes based education in South Africa.* Cape Town: Juta Academic Publishers.

Jones, L. V. (2003). National assessment in the United States: The Evolution of the nation's report card. In T. Kellaghan & D. Stufflebeam (Eds.), *International handbook of educational evaluation* (pp. 883–904). Dordrecht: Kluwer Academic Publishers.

Karimov, A., Borovykh, A., Kuzmin, A., Abdykadyrova, A., Efendiece, D., Konovalova, E., Frants, I., Palivoda, L., Usifli, S., & Balakirev, V. (2007). Program evaluation development in the newly independent states (Azerbaijan, Russia, Kyrgyzstan, Kazakhstan, and Ukraine). *Journal of Multidisciplinary Evaluation, 4*(7), 84–91.

Kellaghan, T. (2003). Introduction to Section 10, Local, national, and international levels of system evaluation. In T. Kellaghan & D. Stufflebeam (Eds.), *International handbook of educational evaluation* (pp. 873–883). Boston: Kluwer Academic Publishers.

Kusek, J. Z., & Rist, R. C. (2001). Building a performance-based monitoring and evaluation system. *Evaluation Journal of Australasia, 1*(2), 14–23.

Lawrenz, F., & Huffman, D. (2006). Methodological pluralism: The gold standard of STEM evaluation. In D. Huffman & F. Lawrenz (Eds.), Critical issues in STEM evaluation. *New Directions for Evaluation* (pp. 19–34). San Francisco, CA: Jossey-Bass.

Lee, J. (2006). *Tracking achievement gaps and assessing the impact of No Child Left Behind on the gap: An in-depth look at national and state reading and math outcomes*. Cambridge, MA: The Civil Rights Project at Harvard University.

Lillard, A., & Else-Quest, N. (2006).The early years: Evaluating Montessori education. *Science, 313*(5795), 1893–1894.

Lindenfors, P., Mackinnon, P., Lillard, E., & Else-Quest, N. (2007). Studying students in Montessori schools. *Science, 315*(5812), 596.

Lipsey, M. W. (2007).Theory as method: Small theories of treatments. In D. Mathison (Ed.), Enduring issues in evaluation: The 20th anniversary of the collaboration between NDE and AEA. *New Directions for Evaluation, 114,* 27–62.

Mark, M. M., Henry, G. T., & Julnes, G. (2000). *Evaluation: An integrated framework for understanding, guiding, and improving public and nonprofit policies and programs.* San Francisco, CA: Jossey-Bass.

Ministry of Education, New Zealand (2003). *Thinking outside the square: Three case study evaluations (Innovation Funding Pool; Nga Huarahi Arataki; and Numeracy Development Project).* Available at www.minedu.govt.nz

Murray, C. (2006, July 25). Acid tests. *Wall Street Journal,* p. 4.

National Academy of Education. (2007). *Race-conscious policies for assigning students to schools: Social science research and the Supreme Court cases.* Washington, DC: Author.

Network of Networks on Impact Evaluation. (2007) *Guidance on impact evaluation.* Retrieved August 1, 2008, from http://www.oecd.org/dataoecd/10/30/40077051.pfd.

Nichols, S. L., & Berliner, D. C. (2007). *Collateral damage: How high-stakes testing corrupts America's schools.* Cambridge, MA: Harvard Education Press.

Ofir, Z. (2007). *Seeking impact evaluation case studies.* Retrieved July 26, 2007, from Evaltalk, http://bama.ua.edu/archives/evaltalk.html

O'Hara, J., McNamara, G., Boyle, R., & Sullivan, C. (2007). Contexts and constraints: An analysis of the evolution of evaluation in Ireland with particular reference to the education system. *Journal of Multidisciplinary Evaluation, 4*(7) 75–83.

Owen, J. M., & Rogers, P. J. (1999). *Program evaluation: Forms and approaches* (2nd ed.). St. Leonards, Australia: Allen & Unwin.

Patton, M. Q. (1997). *Utilization focused evaluation: The new century text.* Thousand Oaks, CA: Sage.

Patton, M. Q. (2007a). *Site visit reviews.* Retrieved February 27, 2007, from Evaltalk, http://bama.ua.edu/archives/evaltalk.html

Patton, M. Q. (2007b). *The PRI report on the MIT Poverty Action Lab.* Retrieved June 21, 2007, from Evaltalk, http://bama.ua.edu/archives/evaltalk.html

Pawson, R., & Tilley, N. (1997). *Realistic evaluation.* London: Sage.

Piaget, J. (1928). *The child's conception of the world.* London: Routledge and Kegan Paul.

Picciotto, R. (2005). The value of evaluation standards: A comparative assessment. *Journal of Multidisciplinary Evaluation, 2,* 31–51.

Plomp, T., Howie, S., & McGaw, B. (2003). International studies of educational achievement. In T. Kellaghan & D. Stufflebeam (Eds.), *International handbook of educational evaluation* (pp. 951–978). Dordrecht: Kluwer Academic Publishers.

Preskill, H., & Catsambas, T. T. (2006). *Reforming evaluation through appreciative inquiry.* Thousand Oaks, CA: Sage.

Rizvi, F. (2005). Rethinking brain drain in the era of globalization. *Asia-Pacific Journal of Education, 25*(2), 175–193.

Rizvi, F., & Lingard, B. (2006). Globalization and the changing nature of Organisation for Economic Co-operation and Development's educational work. In H. Lauder, P. Brown, J. Dillabough, & A. H. Halsey (Eds.), *Education, globalization, and social change* (pp. 247–260). Oxford: Oxford University Press.

Sarama, J., Clements, D. H., Starkey, P., Klein, A., & Wakeley, A. (2008). Scaling up the implementation of a pre-kindergarten mathematics curriculum: Teaching for understanding with trajectories and technologies. *Journal of Research on Educational Effectiveness, 1*(2), 89–121.

Savedoff, W. D., Levine, R., & Birdsall, N. (2006). *When will we ever learn? Improving lives through impact evaluation.* Available at http://www.cgdev.org/content/publications.detail/7973.

Segone, M., & Ocampo, A. (Eds.). (2007). *Creating and developing evaluation organizations: Lessons learned from Africa, Americas, Asia, Australasia, and Europe.* Retrieved March 22, 2007, from http://www.ioce.net/resources/case_studies.shtml

Sehon, S. R., & Stanley, D. E. (2003). A philosophical analysis of the evidenced-based medicine debate. *BMC Health Services Research, 3*(14).

Shadish, W. R. (2007). Methods for evidence-based practice: Quantitative synthesis of single-subject designs. In G. Julnes & D. J. Rog (Eds.), *Informing federal policies on evaluation methodology: Building the evidence base for method choice in government sponsored evaluation* (pp. 95–110). San Francisco, CA: Jossey-Bass.

Shadish, W. R., Cook, T. D., & Campbell, D. T. (2002). *Experimental and quasi-experimental designs for generalized causal inference.* Boston: Houghton Mifflin.

Smith, L. (1999). *Decolonizing methodologies: Research and indigenous people.* New York and London: Zed Books.

Stufflebeam, D. L., & Shinkfield, A. (2007). *Evaluation theory, methods, and practice.* San Francisco, CA: Jossey-Bass.

Tilley, N. (2004). Applying theory-driven evaluation to the British Crime Reduction Programme. *Criminal Justice, 4*(3), 255–276.

United Nations. (2000). *Millennium goals.* Retrieved October 17, 2007, from http:www.un.org/millennium goals.

United Nations Educational, Scientific and Cultural Organization. (1990). *Declaration of the World Conference on Education for All.* Retrieved October 17, 2007, from http://www.unesco.ru/files/doc/edu/wdefa.pfd.

Vulliamy, G. (2004). The impact of globalization on qualitative research in comparative and international education. *Monographs in International Education, 34*(3), 261–284.

Weiss, C. H., Murphy-Graham, E., & Birkeland, S. (2005). An alternative route to policy influence: How evaluations affect D.A.R.E. *American Journal of Evaluation, 26,* 12–30.

Williams, B., & Iman, I. (Eds.). (2006). *Systems concepts in evaluation: An expert anthology.* Point Reyes, CA: Edge Press.

World Bank. (2007). *Poverty impact evaluations database.* Retrieved August 31, 2007, from www1.worldbnk.org/pem/poverty/ie/evaluationdb.htm.

Yin, R. K., & Moore, G. B. (1988). Lessons on utilization of research from nine case experiences in the natural hazards field. *Knowledge, Technology and Policy, 1*(3), 25–44.

Zajda, J., Freeman, K., Geo-Jaja, M., Majhanovic, S., Rust, V., & Zajda, R. (2005). *International handbook on globalization, education, and policy research.* New York: Springer.

PART III

Educational Evaluation, Capacity Building, and Monitoring

This genre, *educational evaluation, capacity building, and monitoring*, comprises educational evaluation theories and practices that implicate performance measurement and organizational, policy, and performance improvement through enhanced evidence-based decision making. These approaches align with contemporary public service management accountability theories and frameworks. On the one hand, this section includes new public management audit mechanisms that make individuals and organizations accountable through auditable performance standards. On the other hand, evaluation capacity building involves utilization of evaluation in the context of organizational development and learning.

In a *theory* chapter devoted to performance measurement, evaluation, and accountability in education, Ryan and Feller (Chapter 10) identify an immediate problem that globalization creates for evaluation as "it [globalization] creates the surface appearance of common problems that are susceptible to common solutions." They argue that this is especially problematic for implementing educational accountability and performance measurements systems where educational requirements differ within and across national and international contexts. Moreover, in their analysis, Ryan and Feller conclude that the current emphasis on performance measurement as the meaning and method of accountability has had an impact on evaluation and the role of the evaluator. Levin-Rozalis, Rosenstein, and Cousins (Chapter 11) focus on evaluation capacity building. After summarizing contemporary discourse in the area, the authors consider globalizing influences for the precarious balance between evaluation that is relevant to local needs and evaluation that is acceptable in the wider evaluation community. They conclude with thoughts about implications for educational evaluation and capacity building. In their *methods* chapter examining international assessments and performance indicators, Tamassia and Adams (Chapter 12) provide a sketch of the methods and technical characteristics that serve as the foundation for warranting this kind of evidence. While noting the constraints of these kinds of data and the potential for misinterpretation, they show how these kinds of comparative data are used in policy development and decision making.

The three *case study* chapters in Part III exemplify how global audit-oriented educational evaluation practices are instantiated and then transformed in local contexts—sometimes confidently and often with unforeseen consequences. In their case study, Cisneros-Cohernour and Grayson (Chapter 13) illustrate some of the issues raised in earlier chapters about the appearance of common problems (how to improve achievement) and the difficulties that arise with the use of "common solutions" (implement performance-based accountability). The authors identify specific cross-cultural issues (human and fiscal resources) and consequences (increasing inequities for indigenous students) that arise when outcomes-based evaluation systems from one country (e.g., United States) are imported to another country (e.g., Mexico). In their case study, Rallis and Militello (Chapter 14) propose a specific antidote—collaborative inquiry—to help schools and educational actors in addressing hierarchical external educational accountability mandates such as No Child Left Behind (2002) in the United States. Although their promising study findings implementing this method with U.S. superintendents were not scaleable, the authors make the case that student learning and educational outcomes are improved with the collaborative inquiry cycle—an evaluative framework where solutions are tested and reexamined. The "Irish" case study by McNamara and O'Hara (Chapter 15) takes a decidedly different turn when the authors show that in Ireland the "glocal" (local control and circumstances in a global context) has significantly limited the influences of public service management accountability on educational evaluation. In their school self-evaluation study, McNamara and O'Hara illustrate school self-evaluation (internal evaluation) and inspection (external evaluation) (SSE/I) complexities. Their findings reveal that, although educator actors' perceptions were positive, the nature and quality of the SSE/I evaluative processes (e.g., stakeholder role, external evaluation information) were questionable. In the *critical appraisal* chapter for Part III, Nevo (Chapter 16) investigates the notion that the relations between external educational evaluation and internal evaluation are usefully distinguished as a simple dichotomy. Challenging the notion that external evaluation and accountability have no merit, he also calls on the advocates of audit-based educational evaluation practices to fund parallel school capacity building to improve internal evaluation.

CHAPTER 10

Evaluation, Accountability, and Performance Measurement in National Education Systems

Trends, Methods, and Issues

Katherine E. Ryan and Irwin Feller

Introduction

Across nations, recent policy initiatives and proposals relating to the governance, missions, revenue sources, and performance standards of both K-12 and higher education systems are suffused with the precepts and language of accountability and performance measurement. Influenced by a cluster of propositions about knowledge economies loosely packaged together under the term *globalization*, these trends include increased emphasis on education at all levels as a critical determinant of national economic competitiveness; intensified demands on educational institutions, as with many other public sector entities, that they document their accountability to larger publics for the quantity and quality of the services they provide; increasing

formal requirements that this performance be documented by standardized assessment means; and an increasing reliance of market forces, such as competition among providers and fee-based provision of services to determine the size and apportionment of educational services.

Generically, these trends have been and continue to be scrutinized (and critiqued) from a number of diverse analytical perspectives, including political science, economics, public policy, and the like (Burbules, 2002; Moynihan, 2008). Of special relevance to the evaluation community, this ferment is increasingly accompanied by calls or requirements that policy decisions concerning proposed changes be "evidence-based," implying a need for systematic studies of the effectiveness or impact of selective interventions.

In this chapter, we draw from several research traditions such as exegesis on the political and legal implications of accountability arrangements for research and education (Guston, 2000; Rhode, 2006); the often disputatious literature on the benefits, costs, and impacts of performance measurement systems and the new public management (Dahler-Larsen, 2007; Feller, 2002; Kettl, 1997; Perrin, 1998; Radin, 2006); and analysis of the accountability and performance measurement movements in education (Burke, 2005; Dill, 2000; Gormley & Weimer, 1999; Nichols & Berliner, 2007; Zumeta, 2001) to examine how these trends affect the evaluation of national education systems and, in turn, the role of evaluators participating in such undertakings. Our approach is both multilevel, encompassing both K-12 and higher education, and comparative, involving vignettes from many countries. We sketch the multiple, complex, and variegated denotations and connotations of the concepts of accountability and performance measurement, singly and interactively, as they engender changes in the educational evaluation arena, subjecting these concepts to the same type of analytical scrutiny that their use imposes on organizations, policies, and programs.

These analytical brushes produce a pointillist landscape that highlights the complex, diverse, and, at times, contradictory policy and program implications of implementing initiatives directed at fostering accountability and performance measurement in national education systems. This highlighting also makes more visible the importance of context, both within and across national borders, in designing and conducting policy- and program-specific evaluations. This perspective also leads to the identification of several looming and latent challenges for evaluators of educational programs that extend beyond standard methodological strictures or debates about evaluation's various modes, methods, or functions. As analyzed next, *performance assessment* and *measurement* are not synonymous terms and activities with *program evaluation*, considered in the

specific sense as a means for determining the worth, value, or impact of an intervention (Mark, Henry, & Julnes, 2000).

The concept of globalization with its sub-themes as sketched previously also presents an immediate problem for program evaluation as it creates the surface appearance of common problems that are thus susceptible to common solutions. National education systems differ in many ways, however. These differences include constitutional and legislative provisions for public sector regulation and financing of education across levels of support of education; the relative importance of public and private institutions, especially in higher education; external and internal governance; size; historic and current levels of absolute and relative performance; and so forth. These contextual differences confound, or so we argue, attempts to generalize the applicability of the precepts subsumed under globalization or the findings from evaluations of seemingly kindred policy interventions from one setting to another.

The chapter begins with a general overview of international trends toward new, more formal requirements for accountability and performance measurement. These trends are manifestly visible among Organisation for Economic Co-operation and Development (OECD) countries, but also are evident across several Latin American and Asian countries (Altbach & Balan, 2007; Cozzens & Turpin, 2000; Organisation for Economic Co-operation and Development, 2005). This overview emphasizes dominant "global" requirements on public sector organizations to demonstrate accountability and document performance (Power, 1997) and examines new precepts termed the *new public management* (NPM) that guide how public sector activities are to be managed, monitored, and measured. Next, the chapter examines how these trends and programs play out in the context of "local" national systems of education, citing specific national and international events to illustrate particular analytical themes. K-12 and higher education are initially treated separately in this chapter, with a summary assessment of the impacts of the accountability and performance measurements between levels deferred to the next-to-last section. The chapter then concludes by discussing the implications of this analysis for the design and conduct of evaluations and by posing additional policy and research questions.

The Landscape of Accountability and Performance Measurement

Accountability is a political and legal concept. It denotes the responsibility of an organization or individual (i.e., an agent) to perform within the specified boundaries set by some higher political authority (i.e., a principal) and to report to and justify one's actions to this authority. Accountability is a basic tenet of democratic political systems. As noted by Smith and Lipsky (1993), "Democratic governance requires that government adequately hold accountable for all agencies that implement public policy, whether they are government bureaus, businesses, or nonprofit contractors" (p. 13).

As Behn (2001) has highlighted, however, accountability has different meanings depending on the context in which it is used. It can mean proper use of appropriated funds; appropriate behavior by an agency in terms of prescribed rules, regulations, or prevailing norms of equity and fairness; production of the goods and services, or outcomes, expected of it; as well as various combinations of these items. For the most part, our concern is with accountability as defined and measured in terms of performance.

Performance measurement, by way of contrast, is an amalgam of organizational and economic concepts that relate to the means and measures by which an organization demonstrates that its activities have produced the outputs, outcomes, and impacts for which it was established and provided resources. More broadly, performance measurement is a compound product of the objectives for which an organization was established, the criteria used to

measure attainment of these objectives, and the measures used to operationalize the criteria.

Logically separate, accountability and performance measurement have become intertwined concepts. Accountability increasingly has come to include explicit requirements for documented (improved) performance; performance measurement is the increasingly preferred or mandated means by which agencies are expected to provide evidence to authorities and stakeholders that they are fulfilling their required or expected performance objectives.

This intertwining takes on true force when decision makers use evidence of an organization's past or current performance to make decisions that affect its future. These decisions can relate to the organization's continued existence, size, scope, mission, resources, structure, leadership, personnel, and more (Cronbach et al., 1980).

What makes accountability and performance measurement fertile and important subjects of interest for the evaluation community is that they are closely linked to other principal components of the NPM paradigm. Generally associated with a portfolio of government reforms in New Zealand beginning in the late 1980s (Nagel, 1997), the paradigm has diffused widely across other countries. As noted by the OECD in 1995, "A new paradigm for public management has emerged, aimed at fostering a performance-oriented culture in a less centralized public sector" (Organisation for Economic Co-operation and Development, 1995, p. 8). Among the paradigm's central features are decentralized decision making and control of resources "so that authority corresponds with accountability"; "operational specification of goals through substantial investment in performance measurement"; and "accountability for performance through reliance on competition (among both public and private service providers), explicit contracts, and material incentives" (Nagel, 1997, p. 350). Decentralization is designed to increase the flexibility and adaptability of organizations closer to end users than national or state ministries to customize programs that meet the needs of diverse audiences and to more quickly, effectively, and efficiently respond to new or changing needs or opportunities. Competition among public sector providers—and especially between public and private sector providers—is seen as compelling the former to meet customer needs lest those customers vote with their feet, reducing political support or otherwise causing organizational revenues to fall. Competition also serves as a means of establishing real-world benchmarks that can be used to identify differential performance and thus prod average and below-average performers to attain the performance levels of best practice performers.

National Education Systems

General Trends

National systems of K-12 and higher education have not escaped scrutiny or coverage from these trends. Initiatives relating to accountability, performance measurement, and the new public management permeate contemporary proposals for reforming K-12 and higher education in many countries. These proposals originate both from political and economic sectors external to the organizations that compose a nation's K-12 and higher education systems, as well as from within these organizations or systems, where they serve as internal management tools, often associated with quality improvement initiatives.

International Competitiveness. In the context of a knowledge economy worldview, a national goal of being (or becoming) the home of globally competitive research universities moves from being a solipsistic parlor game played by academics in their ivory towers to strategic assets that are to be developed and deployed as part of larger national policies. Likewise, for K-12 education, performance of elementary school students on international standardized achievement tests moves from being a reputational symbol of limited policy interest to a closely watched indicator of a nation's current and prospective

international economic competitiveness (Miller, Sen, & Malley, 2007). A related consequence of this internationally shared perspective, as Gardner (2004) has noted, is that, although distinctions clearly remain, "there is surprising convergence in what is considered a precollegiate education in Tokyo or Tel Aviv, in Budapest or Boston" (p. 238).

Databases and Data Mining. Another development abetting the spread of performance measurement systems is that of large-scale, readily accessible databases tied to new analytical and data-mining techniques that make it possible to construct comparative performance measures for academic units (e.g., departments, colleges, and research centers) and universities. International policy units such as the OECD, International Education Association (IEA), and National Center for Educational Statistics (NCES) have targeted policy initiatives supporting the organization and development of these databases. For example, cross-national K-12 comparisons on international assessments such as the *Third International Mathematics Science and Math Study* (TIMSS) and *Programme for International Student Assessment* (PISA) are directly connected to the proposition that educational quality is critical for educational development within a global economy (Kellaghan & Greaney, 2001; Stronach, 1999). National assessment systems likewise are being implemented worldwide—for example, in Chile, Argentina, and Uruguay in Latin America (Bienveniste, 2002) and in Uganda and Zambia in Africa (Kellaghan & Greaney, 2003). In the United States, the NCLB (2002) created a new institutional environment in which students, teachers, schools, and districts are held accountable through auditable performance standards and assessments.

Similar developments in data collection, especially relating to publication and citation counts, patents, licenses, and number of spin-off firms, have become increasingly popular means—both for good and bad—for evaluating department and institutional outputs, impact, or productivity

(Feller, 2002). Bibliometric-based or reputational rankings, such as the Times Higher Education Supplement rankings of the world's top 200 universities, have become influential measures by which academic administrators and national and regional policymakers evaluate the performance of colleges and departments, even in the face of considerable criticism by specialists in the field (Goldstein & Spiegelhalter, 1996; van Leeuwen, 2004; Weingart, 2005).

Yet another influence is the ability of individuals or organizations, but especially the media, to call attention to what they deem to be the underperformance of educational institutions. Notable examples of the press playing this role have surfaced in various countries. In Brazil, for example, a local newspaper spurred attention to the performance of Sao Paulo University by calling attention to the number of scholars with zero publications (Pereira, Pires, Duarte, Paes, & Okana, 1996). In the United States and Canada, the respective rankings produced by *U.S. News and World Report* and *Maclean's* command enough attention from various publics that university administrators at times either laud their standings, especially upward moves, or feel obligated to account, usually on methodological grounds, for downward moves.

Educational Accountability

Accountability, notes Burke (2005), "raises several deceptively simple but devilishly difficult questions," such as "*Who* is accountable to *whom*, for *what* purposes, for *whose* benefit, by *which* means, and with *what* consequences" (p. 2). Answers to each of these questions can differ across levels of education and countries. In the following section, we outline some of these differences.

K-12 Educational Accountability

The rationale for educational accountability includes improving both educational quality and educational equity (Bienveniste, 2002; Linn,

2000). Although the conceptualization and implementation of educational accountability differs to some extent across nations, the trend has been for the locus of responsibility for performance to shift from the government to schools (decentralization). It is the latter that are now accountable for both educational program quality *and* improving educational achievement. Further, through legislation (e.g., NCLB) or other forms of regulation, the state prescribes the means and provisions of holding schools accountable. Included with varying degrees of formal authority and informal influence are national, regional, and local governmental units, as well as parents, students, teachers, schools, and other educational units.

In some cases, the role of parents, communities, and the public (i.e., ordinary citizens interested in or affected by concerns and representing multiple viewpoints) at the local level has changed substantially with this rearrangement. The function and character of educational evaluation also shifts with the introduction of the accountability relationship between the state and schools. Although educational evaluation has often played a part in external control of education, introducing managerial and supervisory accountability affects the evaluator's role and practices.

The "what" facet of accountability also has undergone change. In K-12, educational actors are increasingly held accountable for ensuring that students have the essential skills and knowledge to ensure that their respective countries can remain competitive in the global economy. The consequences of accountability also vary. In the market-based approach of the United States, students are allowed to change schools if their school does not meet performance standards. There is in some sense "competition" among schools because parents as consumers can register dissatisfaction by moving to a different school with more desirable services signaled by higher test scores. In contrast, in England, when a school is determined to be failing based on a site visit inspection, the school is required to implement a school improvement plan, which is subsequently monitored by additional governmental site visits. Kenya has historically used a more indirect approach. Teachers and schools are held accountable by publicizing how students in particular schools performed on public examinations (Kellaghan & Greaney, 2003). It is assumed that by introducing this form of competition, called *incentive information*, teachers will be motivated to improve instruction.

The institutional structures—including management, government, administration, professions, policymakers, and discourses enabling the machinery of educational accountability requirements—also vary across nations. Two generic approaches to implementing accountability dominate, albeit with considerable local variation: (a) outcomes-based educational accountability, and (b) school self-evaluation. The educational evaluator's role and relationship to this machinery can differ in important ways.

Outcomes-Based Educational Accountability. Outcomes-based educational accountability involves some mandated form of systematic assessment of student achievement based on educational standards (e.g., content). Other indicators may be incorporated (e.g., teacher quality, school completion rates) for making judgments about whether educational standards are being met. Performance on these standardized assessments and indicators is a proxy that essentially defines educational quality. Within this institutional arrangement, the educational evaluator's role is designated as a "measurement technician" assisting with the assessment, analysis, and interpretation of reporting requirements (Benjamin, 2008).

High-stakes outcomes-based educational accountability provisions, reflecting decentralization and NPM, employ market- and incentive-based strategies as the key means for improving student achievement. The U.S. federal educational accountability system exemplifies high-stakes educational accountability in a decentralized, market-based environment. With NCLB, a historically unparalleled degree of federal government regulatory involvement was introduced into the workings of schools

(Manna, 2007). Reflecting the complexities of decentralization, schools, instead of districts or the state (central authority), are now held accountable for achieving specific educational standards (performance standards). At the same time, schools have autonomy and responsibility for improving student learning in order to meet performance standards measured with outcomes-based assessments.

"High stakes" (sanctions) are introduced when graduated school-level sanctions are implemented when schools repeatedly fail to make annual yearly progress (AYP) toward meeting those standards. These sanctions range from school choice (students can legally enroll in another school) to school closing. Within this set of institutional arrangements based on notions of competition and markets, schools unable to compete successfully are removed from the "school market" when they are closed. Further, in the United States, some states (e.g., Tennessee) have implemented reward and/or sanction-oriented compensation systems, where teacher salary increases are tied to improved achievement.

Latin American countries such as Argentina and Chile also have implemented top-down, high-stakes educational accountability systems that are substantively linked to deregulation and market competition environments (Bienveniste, 2002). In Chile, rewards include honoraria to professional staff for schools identified as effective based on educational indicators (e.g., standardized test scores), signaling teacher responsibility for student achievement. Similarly, high-performing schools in Argentina have received additional monies or in-kind awards (Bienveniste, 2002). At the same time, there are differences in the extent to which countries provide additional resources to schools that are not effective. For example, Chile provides low-performing schools with supplementary resources, whereas the United States does not.

Introducing the notions of markets and competition designates parents and students as consumers in high-stakes outcomes-based educational accountability. This rearrangement is expected to provide significant options (e.g., school choice) when their neighborhood schools are not adequate (Biesta, 2004; Ryan, 2007). As part of the market-oriented milieu, parents and students exercise consumer choice to change schools instead of advocating for local school improvement. Although the consumer role is intended to empower parents and students by offering school choice when their home schools are not adequate, opportunities for parents, other citizens, and communities to improve local schools then become more limited. Changing schools is the solution, instead of marshalling resources (e.g., local, state) to improve local schools.

The weakening of accountability linkages between families and schools has led to concerns about whether the interests of educational actors (e.g., teachers), schools, and families were included in the development and implementation of high-stakes educational accountability systems (Linn, 2008; McDonnell, 2008). An additional issue that has received heightened attention in the United States relates to whether recently introduced NCLB accountability actually improves equity and achievement or provides sufficient information to help schools (e.g., Fuller, Wright, Gesicki, & Kang, 2007). These questions, in turn, have led to renewed interest in policy alternatives based on "low-stakes" outcomes-based educational accountability systems and school self-evaluations (Linn, 2008; McDonnell, 2008; Ryan, 2005).

Low-stakes outcomes-based educational accountability provides descriptive information about student achievement levels and school performance. The underlying notion here is that information will motivate teachers, principals, communities, and other stakeholders to improve school performance, either individually or collectively (McDonnell, 2008). For example, Uruguay has implemented a large-scale standardized assessment program where results are used to describe student achievement. Developed with community collaboration, the public receives descriptive information about *national* student performance similar to the United States "Nation's Report Card," based on the *National Assessment of Educational Progress*. In Uruguay,

reflecting the "low-stakes notion," school-level information is reported only within the educational community and is not made available to the public.

Using test results for descriptive accountability (a low stakes technique) is receiving substantial attention in the United States as an alternative to high-stakes outcomes-based accountability (Linn, 2008). Although low-stakes approaches have several attractive features (e.g., including collaboration with parent, community, and public interests), moving from a high-stakes outcomes-based model may be difficult to accomplish in a market and deregulation milieu. However, school self-evaluation (SSE), another approach, is being implemented with some success in other regions and countries (e.g., England) that are committed to deregulation and market-based competition.

SSE. SSE or school-based evaluation is aimed at improving teaching and learning with some forms oriented toward external accountability requirements (e.g., MacBeath, 1999; McNamara & O' Hara, Chapter 15, this volume; Nevo, 1995; Ryan, 2005). SSE involves examining and monitoring the extent to which schools' goals are met by educational staff members or interested parents (Ritchie, 2007). Numerous protocols have been developed and implemented, particularly in Europe and Hong Kong (see MacBeath, Jacobsen, Meuret, & Schratz, 2000, for a study comparing school self-evaluation across 18 countries; Pang, 2003). Many countries (e.g., England, Iceland, The Netherlands) mandate SSE involving some kind of inspection by a national or regional educational authority (Nevo, 1995). In England, for example, school visitations have involved an accountability dimension since 2000 (Ritchie, 2007). Schools are visited (inspected) for several days every 3 years by a team of examiners from the Office for Standards in Education (1999). The SSE form, completed by the school prior to the visit, serves as the visit agenda.

SSE with an external accountability component integrates features from school effectiveness and school improvement theories. School effectiveness theory focuses on student outcomes and identifies characteristics that contribute to successful schools, whereas school improvement approaches are aimed at improving student learning by improving teaching and learning. In England, the goal of the inspection is to make a judgment about school quality with particular emphasis on leadership and capacity for school improvement. In addition to on-site observations, various forms of evidence are examined by inspectors in making judgments about schools, including performance data and teacher, parent, and student feedback. Examiners can judge a school as failing, recommending plans for improvement (Ritchie, 2007). The inspection report is an accountability provision that (a) goes beyond test scores to include a broader perspective about school performance, and (b) makes recommendations about how to increase capacity to improve (McDonnell, 2008; Ritchie, 2007).

This approach is receiving some attention in the United States. In the face of known tensions within SSE (e.g., organizational culture issues, lack of time; Alvik, 1995; Rallis & MacMullen, 2000; Ritchie, 2007; Ryan, Chandler, & Samuels, 2007), New York and Connecticut are experimenting with SSE in schools that are at risk of closing because they have not met AYP over consecutive years (Archer, 2006). Incorporating a school improvement component directly by providing feedback to schools about what to do and how to do it complements school report cards or league table information about school performance. Moreover, within this model, educational actors, parents, students, and community interests are served when, as part of the process, they provide feedback and advocate for local school improvement.

Within these kinds of institutional arrangements and value commitments, including improvement and effectiveness, the educational evaluator role expands substantially to "capacity builder" (Benjamin, 2008). The educational evaluator can serve the public good as an educational evaluation consultant helping educational institutions to increase their capacity to improve, as a meta-evaluator, and in other ways.

Higher Education Accountability

Accountability, in the case of national higher education systems, is viewed here in terms of two different but overlapping variables: (a) governance and administrative structures, and (b) sources of funding.

The tripartite governance and administrative structure framework formulated by Clark (1983) and widely used in comparative studies of higher education systems provides a baseline for describing recent developments. In this framework, national governance systems are described as being organized about one of three core models or ideal types: (a) bureaucratic control, as exercised by state ministries (e.g., France, Germany, Italy); (b) oligarchic, or collegial, control, as exercised by professionals operating on the basis of shared values and traditions (e.g., United Kingdom); and (c) market control, as expressed via competition for resources and standing (e.g., United States) (Dill, 1992).

The models reflect the relative degrees of control exercised respectively by governmental authorities and college and university personnel over decisions relating to higher education's core production processes. These decisions include both macrolevel ones (e.g., criteria for admitting students, curricula content, graduation criteria, selection of university administrative officers and faculty, revenue structures) and microlevel policies and actions (e.g., purchasing arrangements and per diem travel expenses). The finance variable relates to the share of the revenues provided to a nation's higher education institutions by, respectively, the public sector, including both national and subnational governments, and the private sector, including tuition, endowments, nongovernmental contributors, and others. National systems vary considerably here. For OECD nations in 2003, for example, public funding on average composed 76% of the revenues of institutions of tertiary education, but the range extended from Korea's low of 23% to Greece's high of 98% (Organisation for Economic Co-operation and Development, 2006).

A connection between a government's contribution to, and control over, university revenues and its ability to require financial and performance accountability is to be expected. National systems in which the government supplies almost all or the larger share of university revenues can be expected to control more aspects of a university's behavior than those in which the share is smaller.

A more complex setting, however, arises in national higher education systems characterized by a mix of public and private institutions. Here, one observes differential degrees of control exercised by political authorities over different facets of public and private university operations, with these differences in turn affecting the competitive position of one set relative to the other. Thus, public universities may find one or more legislative constraints on tuition rates, salary structures, intellectual property policies, and the like, at the same time that they compete in national- or state-level markets for students, faculty, and external resources with less regulated private universities.

Holding aside this complexity and diversity, the general trend in accountability arrangements for higher education is a shift away from direct, detailed control of inputs historically characteristic of the bureaucratic model toward what has been termed *governance by instruments*. As described by Dill (2003), "The new policy strategy can be seen as a 'stepping back' by governments from detailed centralized control through encouraging higher education institutions to be more autonomous, self-regulating and market oriented in their operations, albeit within an overall framework of government priorities" (p. 4).

An underlying driver of these changes is the workings of what Behn (2001) has termed the *accountability dilemma*, which arises because "the accountability rules for finance and fairness can hinder performance. Indeed, the rules may actually thwart performance" (p. 10). Adding to the acuteness of this dilemma is another international trend—namely, that public sector funding has failed to keep up with the rising costs of higher education (Institute for Higher Education Policy, 2007). Thus, several governments are

currently seeking to improve the overall research and educational performance of their higher education systems at the same time that competing pressures on the size and apportionment of government budgets constrain the share of these budgets that they are willing or able to devote to building globally competitive universities.

The widely pursued way out of this situation has been the adoption of policies that explicitly or implicitly constitute moves to a market model. Universities are being freed from the micromanagement controls formerly exercised by government ministries, but expected to generate a larger percentage of their operating budgets. In effect, a new social compact is being entered into between government and higher education in which institutions continue to receive the larger—if relatively smaller—share of their revenues from government, but are expected to generate relatively larger portions of their revenues in the form of fees (tuition) or from partnerships with the private sector (Krull, 2004). A further part of the bargain is that universities gain increased discretion about how to allocate these resources in exchange for more explicit and quantifiable commitments to attain agreed-on education, research, and third-mission objectives.

For example, Japan's national universities, although still funded primarily by the government, have been converted into independent administrative agencies, thus gaining more autonomy and flexibility (Kahaner, 2007). They are now permitted—indeed encouraged—to seek funding from industry. France's new president, Nicolas Sarkozy, has proposed that French universities, now mainly subject to a national ministry of education and nearly cost-free, be granted increased autonomy to select students and to charge tuition. Germany has begun a process of differentiating the missions of its universities; with a view toward establishing a select number of globally competitive research universities, it has opened up a competition for supplemental funds that would permit establishment of graduate schools, excellence clusters, and strategic institutions. In Canada, in 2005, the province of Ontario committed itself to major investments in postsecondary education, but required in turn that universities commit themselves to multiyear performance agreements centered mainly around targets related to student enrollments, access, retention, and instructional quality.

The impact of new commitments to accountability and performance measurement on governance structures do not, however, lead only in one direction. As described next, in nations currently characterized by collegial control or market models, such as the UK and the United States, increasing linkages of accountability and performance measurement have provided a rationale for increased governmental control over the educational or research performance of institutions of higher education. Within the UK, for example, the changed situation with respect to government funding of academic research has been described as shifting the locus of decision making from a group of academics acting as a quasi-ministry for higher education to the prime minister and his cabinet, each taking a closer interest in higher education. This interest, however, is not dictated by a full understanding of the issues involved in running universities. Rather, as argued by Shattock (2007), it is shaped by externally driven reforms needed to modernize all public services, such as top-down performance management, market incentives, and related new public management.

The changing institutional arrangements in higher education involving decentralization and market models not surprisingly expand the educational evaluator role considerably. Program reviews now involve the educational evaluator as a "performance auditor," who constructs and interprets broad-ranging performance metrics involving student performance, enrollments, access, retention, instructional quality, faculty performance, performance budgeting, and so on.

Educational Accountability Contradictions

In both the K-12 and higher education sectors, educational accountability is presented as a policy strategy designed to improve educational quality.

Decentralization and market competition, in turn, are tactics adopted to implement this strategy. Tensions, at times outright contradictions, however, can and do exist between strategy and tactics. With K-12 and higher education sectors, the state is maintaining authority while transferring responsibility over educational processes and outcomes (Bienveniste, 2002).

Within the K-12 sector, there are significant tensions in shifting the relationships among the state, schools, teachers, and other stakeholders. Paradoxically, the market-based consumer role diminishes the power and recourse of local communities, citizens, and groups to address specific local school issues such as the need for adequate financial resources. There is no direct accountability between schools and its public constituencies (i.e., communities, parents, and students; Biesta, 2004). By contrast, educational entities such as schools and districts (or other subunits) are accountable to the state for making progress toward performance standards, but not necessarily to parents, citizens, or the community.

Tensions also exist within higher education about the effects of thrusts toward increased accountability and performance measurement on governance and financing arrangements between governments and institutions. A notable example here is the United States, where the U.S. Department of Education's efforts to expand its regulatory authorities in order to foster a robust culture of measurement, accountability, and transparency along the lines recommended by the Commission on the Future of Higher Education (sometimes referred to as the "Spellings Commission," in reference to the U.S. Department of Education Secretary Margaret Spellings) have been opposed by many universities, especially private universities, as an unwarranted and dysfunctional intrusion on their historic autonomy.

Educational Performance Measurement

Performance measurement presents analytical complexities and contradictory perspectives, both in general and with specific reference to education. Performance measurement is obviously not a new concept in education; students have long had their performance evaluated by exam scores, decisions on faculty promotion tenure traditionally have involved some consideration of publication counts and survey responses about teaching effectiveness, and institutional eligibility for specific government programs with federal or state regulations have long been based on quantitative evidence of performance (or compliance).

What is new is that more aspects of the performance of K-12 and higher education institutions are being subjected to performance measurement requirements. Educational performance measurement is endorsed and promoted based on the assumption that (a) this kind of numerical information represents progress toward objectives, and (b) increases in the indices can be interpreted as reliable and valid indicators of higher quality education. However, Wholey's (1994) theory involving performance measurement identifies important precursors that are essential for quality performance measurement. A program's definition must be elaborated, and the program logic must be adequately developed before indicators can be selected (Wholey, 1994).

Current educational performance measurement practices are not always well aligned with Wholey's performance measurement theory. In education, the indicators are emphasized as opposed to the complex educational constructs that the indicators represent—an important deviation from "best practice recommendations" (Wholey, 1994). This problem is closely related to construct validity issues—namely, whether the measures chosen to assess performance of the several sectors of a nation's educational system accurately capture the values, outcomes, or impact sought by the larger system (Kane, 2006). Sizeable literatures exist about the strengths and weaknesses and the uses and misuses of each of the several measures—student test scores, bibliometrics, patent statistics—that currently form the portfolio of techniques used to assess the performance of the K-12 and higher education sectors,

and of individual organizations within these sectors. In the following, we draw on performance measurement and validity theory to identify a sampling of issues to illustrate educational performance measurement contradictions and complexities in K-12 and higher education.

K-12 Performance Measurement

A variety of literatures tie educational outcomes to the knowledge-based economy, international competitiveness, and so on. Educational outcomes (e.g., tests), however, may be specified without full understanding of how these educational outcomes are connected to the objectives subsumed in the knowledge economy worldview. Also unspecified is the manner in which findings from outcome measurements connect to performance improvement. Overall, the role that educational performance measurement is intended to play in ensuring efficient use of resources to achieve public ends is becoming conflated with what the ends *are*.

Low test scores in reading or school completion rates within a school, district, group (females, low income), or country do indicate a problem. This is critical information for identifying inequities and improving educational quality. Nevertheless, holding educational actors *accountable* on the basis of test scores instead of using these scores to *describe* achievement is much more complex. Evaluating (attempting to make judgments about) school quality, in particular ranking schools, from test score information alone has been criticized on technical grounds and concerns about fairness (Linn, 2008). For example, NCLB educational accountability is based on the *current status* approach to educational accountability, which attempts to compare all students to the same standard. That is, to meet AYP, the percentage of students for the school as a whole and for each of several subgroups must meet or exceed the annual performance targets in both reading/English language arts and mathematics. Because prior achievement is not taken into account according to the way AYP is currently measured, low-income schools are identified as failing to meet this performance standard more frequently in comparison with other schools due to a combination of low achievement and sampling error (e.g., small sample sizes; Linn, 2008; Raudenbush, 2004). Moreover, these indices are primarily based on multiple-choice assessments that do not adequately represent the content and performance standards that serve as educational targets.

Incorporating multiple measures can address two important K-12 performance measurement issues: failure to measure important learning outcomes and indicator corruption (Koretz & Hamilton, 2006). Noncognitive performance measurement information (e.g., test scores, truancy rates, school completion rates) are one source of multiple measures. There are also a wide variety of ways for students to show what they know that can serve as indicators of achievement and performance: performance assessment, portfolios, and assessment task types such as constructed response, where students prepare a response instead of selecting it (e.g., as is the case with multiple choice). There are multiple forms of assessment information (e.g., standards-based, norm-referenced, classroom assessments; Baker, 2003). More important, performance indicators of student performance are insufficient for identifying what to do and how to improve student achievement. There are school quality concerns that are likely to be related to curriculum, instruction, and systemic issues (e.g., inequities in the financial and human distribution of resources in schools often related to social class). These kinds of school quality issues are only indirectly measured with performance indicators of student achievement. Conceptualizing school quality in a broader framework that includes the measurement of resources, instruction, and organizational characteristics sets the stage for providing more formative information. Although the relationships among resources, instruction, and organizational characteristics are not well understood, assessments of these characteristics are critical to a more complete and accurate assessment of school quality and student achievement (Abernathy, 2007; Ryan, 2008).

Higher Education Performance Measurement

There is rising interest in higher education achievement outcomes. Here again, the United States illustrates both the nature of these trends and the debates over governance, methodology, and metrics associated with them. Underlying the U.S. Department of Education's proposals to link federal government approval of the accreditation procedures of various regional accreditation bodies—such accreditation being an eligibility requirement for a panoply of federal support programs—was the judgment that existing systems for accrediting colleges and universities, which relied heavily on institutional self-assessments and external, peer-reviewed-based assessments, were unduly subjective. Instead, according to the Commission, what were needed were more explicit statements of minimum levels of acceptance performance on student learning outcomes, accompanied by increased use of data that would permit interested parties to determine whether institutions were meeting these standards. According to its proponents, this combination would facilitate more precise comparisons of the performance of different institutions than is feasible under reputational surveys or peer reviews. In effect, the proposals constituted a shift from self-monitoring and policing by the institutions and professionals responsible for managing national higher education systems toward quantifiable performance objectives and measures set and monitored by government agencies or government-sanctioned regulatory bodies.

Fierce opposition to these proposals, especially those related to assessments of student performance, from several sectors of the higher education community led to specific prohibitions against them in the U.S. Higher Education Act in 2008, which reauthorized a cluster of federal higher education programs. Significantly, however, highlighting the continuing force of the accountability performance measurement movement, many universities, especially public institutions, both singly and collectively, have announced plans to voluntarily supply many of the datasets that would have been required under the Department's proposals (Ruben, Lewis, & Sandmeyer, 2008).

Higher education also is contending with performance funding systems. In higher education, the effects of performance-based systems on public sector budgets are visible in as widely geographically separated countries as Australia, which uses measures of university research output as part of the formula to determine allocation of institutional block awards for research, and Denmark and Finland, where institutional grants from research council awards are based in part on external research income (Geuna & Martin, 2003). Within the United States, several states, most notably Tennessee, Missouri, South Carolina, and Washington, have imposed performance funding systems (Zumeta, 2001). The most dramatic example of this approach was the state of South Carolina's enactment in 1996 of legislation that required the use of 37 performance indicators for allocating appropriations to the state's 33 public higher education institutions (Heller, 2004), with the further requirement that 100% of the state's appropriation be based on these measures by 1999. In this case, the state essentially manages educational institutions with performance indicators (House, 2004).

Performance Measurement Contradictions

By reducing complexity about educational performance to simple quantitative terms, the prior examples pose at least three broad sets of issues for the evaluation community. Two of these are staples; the third lies at the fuzzy boundaries between evaluation and policy analysis, but is interesting (and important) in its own stead. The first is the setting of the criteria by which performance is to be gauged. As noted earlier, to establish performance criteria requires (or implies) agreement about the purposes of education. The risk here is that technique and data preempt educational objectives: Selection of

measures may implicitly determine educational values or priorities, rather than the reverse. Relatedly, use of specific measures because of their availability, manipulability, or correlation with proxies for ultimate outcomes may mask or mislead consideration of fundamental educational objectives and associated societal values.

As the stakes associated with the use of these measures increases, so too must the attention paid to these construct validity critiques. The reasons here extend beyond methodological niceties about reliability and validity, although these obviously are important. The further consideration is a growing recognition of "situations where more measurement of quality may lead to everything else but better quality" (Dahler-Larsen, 2007, p. 19; see also McPherson & Schapiro, 2007; Perrin, 1998). Gaming the measures, or opportunistic behavior, has quickly (and predictably) accompanied the introduction of several performance measurement systems. For example, in studying the effects of the Australian system of tying government support of university research to faculty publications on the publication performance of Australian universities, Butler (2004) found:

> With no attempt made to differentiate between the quality, visibility or impact of the different journals when funding is allocated, there is little incentive to strive for publication in a prestigious journal. Whether a publication reports ground breaking research or is a more pedestrian piece; whether it appears in a highly visible journal such as *Nature* or a lower impact outlet, the rewards are identical. (p. 394)

In K-12 education, unintended negative consequences such as "teaching to the test" have been documented globally (e.g., United States, The Netherlands; de Wolfe & Janssens, 2007).

The third issue is why—at least to date—with few exceptions, the linkages between performance measurement systems and budgets appear to remain relatively loose and limited, even in those countries or states that have adopted such systems. The recent international and national surveys cited previously indicate that despite the considerable attention they have received, and even when formal requirements exist for their use, the rewards and penalties attached to mandated performance measurement systems appear to be implemented infrequently and then typically only in modest ways. This pattern suggests that the opposing forces represented, on the one hand, by adherents of the NPM and, on the other hand, by those speaking on behalf of the autonomy of educational institutions, especially for higher education, have arrived at a "low level" equilibrium involving the introduction of relatively modest reporting requirements with relatively modest prizes and penalties associated with meeting/not meeting performance goals. Again, whether this equilibrium is a stable one, and in which direction change might occur, is uncertain.

Conclusions

This cross-country scan highlights the extent to which the consequences of implementing accountability and performance measurement requirements can mean different things in different national contexts, as well as between K-12 and higher education systems within nations. Some of these outcomes can be positive and in accord with desired end results; at other times or in other places, introduction of these requirements may fail to produce their intended outcomes or, indeed, produce undesirable—if at times predictably dysfunctional—outcomes. This statement means more than "one size doesn't fit all"; it means that the wrong styles may be chosen.

Impacts Across K-12 and Higher Education

We are especially cautious about "one-size-fits-all" concerns across the K-12 and higher education sectors. At first blush, it seems there are important lessons from the K-12 sector experience that have

implications for the higher education sector. At the most surface level, as this chapter highlights, there are lessons from the K-12 sector about the potential consequences (e.g., narrowing of curriculum) of implementing large-scale assessments of student outcomes for higher education. More important, however, the extent to which policy levers such as educational standard setting, data systems to gauge progress, and performance-based accountability is effective in the K-12 sector is open to question; therefore, drawing lessons learned is complicated and difficult.

Furthermore, we advise against transferring K-12 sector issues directly to the higher education context. In the United States, there are "profound organizational, political, and cultural chasms" (Kirst, 2007, p. 203) between K-12 and higher education. These two sectors operate at distinct social locations that are based on the historic differences between the purposes of lower and higher education. High schools were designed for many and sometimes conflicting purposes, one of which is college preparation. As a consequence, the educational policies guiding these sectors are often unique to each sector, as illustrated in this chapter. Although these differences may be diminishing in attempts to shift to a vertically integrated K-16 system, policy instruments such as funding streams, accountability, assessments, and governance systems are still notably distinct between the two sectors (Callahan, Venezia, Finney, Kirst, & Usdan, 2005).

Educational Evaluation and Performance Measurement Relations

There is agreement that educational accountability does serve the public interests in regard to such matters as efficient and appropriate use of resources and educational equity issues. The divergence about educational accountability is in the fine points. In contemporary society, a technical-managerial notion of accountability is in ascendancy with domains that are distinct in nature and scope (e.g., education, environmental programs, health) being subject to performance management systems incorporating performance measurement and performance audit.

As a practice that is variously used to appraise, (de)certify, or improve governmental institutions (House, 1993), evaluation is in the thick of these matters. Although there is perhaps a new accountability countenance, the who, why, and what of accountability and evaluation are old dilemmas (Cronbach et al., 1980). Nevertheless, as illustrated in this chapter, in the educational domain, there are new tensions and contradictions in the meanings of and relations between performance measurement and auditing and evaluation that challenge the roles and character of the evaluator and evaluation.

For example, we identified at least three distinct roles for the educational evaluator. The current notions of educational accountability and educational performance practices are influencing the functional roles of the educational evaluator, as well as educational evaluator dispositions. In the following, we illustrate these distinctions: measurement technician, capacity builder, and performance auditor.

Evaluator as Measurement Technician. K-12 outcomes-based accountability is built on large-scale assessments and other indicators that are organized as performance monitoring or audit evaluation systems (Leeuw & Furobo, 2008). These kinds of evaluation systems are located within administrative structures with the educational evaluator located and aligned with administration. As a consequence, the educational evaluator role is more likely to resemble that of a "measurement technician" (Benjamin, 2008), assisting with the administration of educational affairs, including interpreting the information from this educational evaluation system. The evaluation information produced is "single-loop" learning—identifying problems within the educational performance standards framework. As a consequence, this kind of affiliation can create difficulties for the educational evaluator to serve the public good.

Evaluator as Capacity Builder. With an emphasis on improvement *and* performance measurement

accountability, there is more flexibility for the role of the educational evaluator, with opportunities for educational evaluators to serve the public interest in a variety of ways in the K-12 school self-evaluation and inspection approach. Evaluators can take on an "outsider" or "insider" role. As outsiders, evaluators can continue with their traditional roles as external evaluators or meta-evaluators. Alternatively, within these institutional arrangements, the evaluator can be located as an insider. As a capacity builder (Benjamin, 2008), the educational evaluator can help design and build SSE that encourages educational development and action taking oriented toward improved student learning. Further, the educational evaluator can work with educational actors, parents, students, and the community building local educational practices and policies that do not rely as much on global practices such as standardized tests and other educational indicators to represent educational quality.

Evaluator as Performance Auditor. With this increasing emphasis on outcomes in the higher education sector, the role of the evaluator falls squarely into the "measurement technician" category. At the same, there are new skills that are required of the evaluator within this kind of performance management system. Although cost-benefit analyses are part and parcel of educational evaluators' analytic frameworks, the higher educational performance budgeting requirements may require new skills and knowledge. Less common in the educational context, performance budgeting is linked to performance audit or value for money found in supranational organizations and the public sector (Leeuw & Furubo, 2008). Audit evaluations are oriented toward making administrative affairs more effective and efficient. As Leeuw and Furubo (2008) suggest, "It is not . . . the programme as such that is the focus of this kind of evaluation work . . . it is the way somebody or the organization has acted" (p. 162), which signals an important change in the character and role of the educational evaluator.

Outlooks on Evaluation and Performance Measurement/Management

The influences of accountability and performance management are not confined to unsettling and shifting the evaluator's role. There is some merging, blending, entangling, and the like across and between evaluation and performance measurement/management. The discourse on performance measurement and evaluation relations goes in several directions at the same time. For example, Nielsen and Ejler (2008) propose that the *complementarities* between performance management and evaluation need exploration while implicitly acknowledging that evaluation and performance management are two distinct professional practices. Citing disillusionment with evaluation as the reason for the increase in performance management, they propose "the boundaries between these practices may need to be redefined" (Nielsen & Ejler, 2008, p. 171; see also Mayne & Rist, 2006). Others suggest that evaluation and performance measurement already overlap or are entangled (House, 2004; Leeuw & Furubo, 2008). House (2004) characterizes performance measurement as "an important tool of evaluators" while expressing concerns about how it can "play an ugly role in people's lives" (p. 4). Taking a broader view, Leeuw and Furubo frame performance management as one of several evaluation systems (e.g., experimentalist, accreditation).

Critical analysis of these overlapping and entangled definitions and boundaries is an important direction for future work yielding critical theoretical and practical knowledge. From the performance management perspective, there are calls for a constructive dialogue between these professional practices, citing strengths that evaluation can bring to current performance measurement (e.g., improving data quality), as well as hints that evaluation is somewhat outdated (e.g., lacking timely information; Nielsen & Ejler, 2008). No doubt such a dialogue has the potential to be constructive. At the same time, we are cautious about engaging the relations between evaluation and performance

measurement. Such dialogue and engagement are likely to be a daunting challenge given performance management's powerful institutional location in contemporary society.

References

Abernathy, S. (2007). *No Child Left Behind and the public schools.* Ann Arbor, MI: University of Michigan Press.

Altbach, P., & Balan, J. (Eds.). (2007). *World class worldwide.* Baltimore: Johns Hopkins University Press.

Alvik, T. (1995). School-based evaluation: A close-up. *Studies in Educational Evaluation, 21,* 311–343.

Archer, J. (2006). *British inspectors bring instructional focus to NYC.* Retrieved November 3, 2008, from http://www.edweek.org/ew/articles/2006/05/17/37inspect.h25.html

Baker, E. L. (2003). Multiple measures: Toward tiered systems. *Educational Measurement: Issues and Practice, 22*(2), 13–17.

Behn, R. (2001). *Rethinking democratic accountability.* Washington, DC: Brookings Institution.

Benjamin, L. M. (2008). Evaluator's role in accountability relationships: Measurement technician, capacity builder, or risk manager. *Evaluation, 14*(3), 323–343.

Bienveniste, L. (2002). The political structuration of assessment: Negotiating state power and legitimacy. *Comparative Education Review, 46*(1), 89–118.

Biesta, G. J. (2004). Education, accountability, and the ethical demand: Can the democratic potential of accountability be regained? *Educational Theory, 54*(3), 233–250.

Burbules, N. C. (2002). The global context of educational research. In L. Bresler & A. Ardichvili (Eds.), *Research in international education: Experience, theory, and practice* (pp. 157–170). New York: Peter Lang.

Burke, J. (Ed.). (2005). *Achieving accountability in higher education.* San Francisco, CA: Jossey-Bass.

Butler, L. (2004). What happens when funding is linked to publication counts? In H. Moed, W. Glanzel, & U. Schmoch (Eds.), *Handbook of quantitative science and technology research* (pp. 389–405). Dordrecht, The Netherlands: Kluwer Academic Publishers.

Callahan, P. M., Venezia, A., Finney, J. E., Kirst, M. W., & Usdan, M. D. (2005). *Claiming common ground: Policymaking for improving college readiness and success*. San Jose, CA: National Center for Higher Education and Public Policy.

Clark, B. (1983). *The higher education system: Academic organization in cross-national perspective*. Berkeley: University of California Press.

Cozzens, S., & Turpin, T. (2000). Processes and mechanisms for evaluating and monitoring research outcomes from higher education: International comparisons. *Research Evaluation, 8*, 3–4.

Cronbach, L., Ambron, S., Dornbusch, S., Hess, R., Hornik, R., Phillips, D., et al. (1980). *Toward a reform of program evaluation: Aims, methods, and institutional arrangements*. San Francisco, CA: Jossey-Bass.

Dahler-Larsen, P. (2007). Constitutive effects of performance indicator systems. In S. Kushner & N. Norris (Eds.), *Dilemmas of engagement: Evaluation and the new public management* (pp. 17–35). Amsterdam: Elsevier.

de Wolfe, I. F., & Janssens, F. J. G. (2007). Effects and side effects of inspections and accountability in education: An overview of empirical studies. *Oxford Review of Education, 33*(3), 379–396.

Dill, D. (1992). Administration: Academic. In B. Clark & G. Neave (Eds.), *The encyclopedia of higher education* (Vol. 2, pp. 1318–1329). Oxford, UK: Pergamon Press.

Dill, D. (2000). Capacity building as an instrument of institutional reform: Improving the quality of higher education through academic audits in the UK, New Zealand, Sweden and Hong Kong. *Journal of Comparative Policy Analysis, Research and Practice, 2*, 211–234.

Dill, D. (2003, March). *The regulation of academic quality: An assessment of university assessment systems with emphasis on the United States*. Symposium on University Evaluation for the Future: International Trends in Higher Education Reform, Tokyo, Japan.

Feller, I. (2002). Performance measurement redux. *American Journal of Evaluation, 23*, 435–452.

Fuller, B., Wright, J., Gesicki, K., & Kang, E. (2007). Gauging growth: How to judge No Child Left Behind. *Educational Researcher, 36*(5), 268–278.

Gardner, H. (2004). How science changes: Considerations of history, science, and values. In M. Suarez-Orozco & D. M. Qin-Hillard (Eds.), *Globalization: Culture and education in the new*

millennium (pp. 235–258). Berkeley: University of California Press.

Geuna, A., & Martin, B. (2003). University research evaluation and funding: An international comparison. *Minerva, 41*, 277–304.

Goldstein, H., & Spiegelhalter, D. (1996). League tables and their limitations: Statistical issues in comparisons of institutional performance. *Journal of the Royal Statistical Society, Series A, 159*, 385–443.

Gormley, W., & Weimer, D. (1999). *Organizational report cards*. Cambridge, MA: Harvard University Press.

Guston, D. (2000). *Between politics and science*. Cambridge, UK: Cambridge University Press.

Heller, D. (2004). State oversight of higher education. In R. Ehrenberg (Ed.), *Governing academia* (pp. 49–67). Ithaca, NY: Cornell University Press.

House, E. R. (1993). *Professional evaluation: Social impact and political consequences*. Thousand Oaks, CA: Sage Publications.

House, E. R. (2004). The role of the evaluator in a political world. *The Canadian Journal of Program Evaluation, 19*(2), 1–16.

Institute for Higher Education Policy. (2007). *The global state of higher education and of the rise of private finance*. Washington, DC: Author.

Kahaner, D. (2007). Japanese technology policy: Evolution and current initiatives. In C. Wessner (Ed.), *Innovation policies for the 21st century* (pp. 121–128). Washington, DC: National Academies Press.

Kane, M. (2006). Validation. In R. L. Brennan (Ed.), *Educational measurement* (4th ed.). New York: American Council on Education and Praeger.

Kellaghan, T., & Greaney, V. (2001). The globalization of assessment in the 20th century. *Assessment in Education, 8*(1), 87–102.

Kellaghan, T., & Greaney, V. (2003, December). *Monitoring performance: Assessments and examinations in Africa*. Paper presented at the annual meeting of the Association for the Development of Education in Africa, Grand Baie, Mauritius.

Kettl, D. (1997). The global revolution in public management: Driving themes, missing links. *Journal of Policy Analysis and Management, 16*, 446–462.

Kirst, M. W. (2007). Separation of K-12 and postsecondary education policymaking: Evolution, impact, research needs. In S. H. Furman, D. K. Cohen, & F. Mosher (Eds.), *The state of educational policy research* (pp. 202–223). Mahwah, NJ: Lawrence Erlbaum Associates.

Koretz, D., & Hamilton, L. S. (2006). Testing for accountability in K-12. In R. L. Brennan (Ed.), *Educational measurement* (4th ed., pp. 579–622). New York: American Council on Education and Praeger.

Krull, W. (2004). Towards a research policy for the new Europe: Changes and challenges for public and private funders. *Minerva, 42*, 29–39.

Leeuw, F. L., & Furubo, J. (2008). Evaluation systems: What are they and why study them? *Evaluation, 14*(2), 157–170.

Linn, R. L. (2000). Assessments and accountability. *Educational Researcher, 29*(2), 4–14.

Linn, R. L. (2008). Educational accountability systems. In K. E. Ryan & L. A. Shepard (Eds.), *The future of test-based accountability* (pp. 3–24). Mahwah, NJ: Lawrence Erlbaum Associates.

MacBeath, J. (1999). *Schools must speak for themselves: The case for school self-evaluation.* London: Routledge Falmer.

MacBeath, J., Jacobsen, L., Meuret, L., & Schratz, M. (2000). *Self-evaluation in European schools: A story of change.* London: Routledge.

Manna, P. (2007). *School's in.* Washington, DC: Georgetown University Press.

Mark, M. M., Henry, G. T., & Julnes, G. (2000). *Evaluation: An integrated framework for understanding, guiding, and improving public and nonprofit policies and programs.* San Francisco, CA: Jossey-Bass.

Mayne, J., & Rist, R. C. (2006). Studies are not enough: The necessary transformation of evaluation. *Canadian Journal of Program Evaluation, 21*(3), 93–120.

McDonnell, L. A. (2008). The politics of educational accountability: Can the clock be turned back? In K. E. Ryan & L. A. Shepard (Eds.), *The future of test-based accountability* (pp. 25–46). Mahwah, NJ: Lawrence Erlbaum Associates.

McPherson, M., & Schapiro, M. (2007). Moral reasoning and higher education policy. *The Chronicle of Higher Education, 54*(2), B10ff.

Miller, D., Sen, A., & Malley, L. (2007). *Comparative indicators of education in the United States and other G-8 countries: 2006* (NCES Publication No. 2007-006). Washington, DC: U.S. Government Printing Office.

Moynihan, D. P. (2008). *The dynamics of performance management: Constructing information and reform.* Washington, DC: Georgetown University Press.

Nagel, J. (1997). Editor's introduction. *Journal of Policy Analysis and Management, 16*, 349–356.

Nevo, D. (1995). *School-based evaluation: A dialogue for school improvement.* Kidlington, Oxford: Pergamon.

Nichols, S., & Berliner, D. (2007). *Collateral damage.* Cambridge, MA: Harvard University Press.

Nielsen, S. B., & Ejler, N. (2008). Improving performance? Exploring complementarities between evaluation and performance. *Evaluation, 14*(2), 171–192.

No Child Left Behind Act of 2001. (2002). Pub. L. No. 107th Cong., 110 Cong. Rec. 1425. 115 Stat.

Office for Standards in Education. (1999). *Inspecting schools: The framework.* London: Author.

Organisation for Economic Co-operation and Development. (1995). *Governance in transition: Public management reforms in OECD countries.* Paris: Author.

Organisation for Economic Co-operation and Development. (2005). *Modernising government.* Paris: Author.

Organisation for Economic Co-operation and Development. (2006). *Education at a glance-2006.* Paris: Author.

Pang, S.-K. N. (2003). Initiating organizational change through school self-evaluation. *International Journal of Knowledge, Culture and Change Management, 3*, 245–256.

Pereira, J., Pires, M., Duarte, P., Paes, A., & Okana, V. (1996). Introducing a method of research evaluation into a university: Medical research at the University of Sao Paulo, Brazil. *Research Evaluation, 6*, 37–42.

Perrin, B. (1998). Effective use and misuse of performance evaluation. *American Journal of Evaluation, 19*, 367–379.

Power, M. (1997). *The audit society.* New York: Oxford University Press.

Radin, B. (2006). *Challenging the performance movement.* Washington, DC: Georgetown University Press.

Rallis, S. F., & MacMullen, M. M. (2000). Inquiry-minded schools: Opening doors for accountability. *Phi Delta Kappan, 78*(9), 766–773.

Raudenbush, S. W. (2004). What are value-added models estimating and what does this imply for statistical practice? *Journal of Educational and Behavioral Statistics, 1*(29), 121–129.

Rhode, D. (2006). *In pursuit of knowledge.* Stanford, CA: Stanford University Press.

Ritchie, R. (2007). School self-evaluation. In S. Kushner (Ed.), *Dilemmas of engagement: Evaluation development under new public management and the new politics* (pp. 85–102). Chevy Chase, MD: Elsevier.

Ruben, B., Lewis, L., & Sandmeyer, L. (2008). *Assessing the impact of the Spellings Commission.* Washington, DC: National Association of College and University Business Offices.

Ryan, K. E. (2005). Making educational accountability more democratic. *American Journal of Evaluation, 26*(4), 443–460.

Ryan, K. E. (2007). Changing contexts and changing relationships. In S. Kushner (Ed.), *Dilemmas of engagement: Evaluation development under new public management and the new politics* (pp. 103–116). Chevy Chase, MD: Elsevier.

Ryan, K. E. (2008). Fairness issues and test-based accountability. In K. E. Ryan & L. A. Shepard (Eds.), *The future of test-based accountability* (pp. 191–208). Mahwah, NJ: Lawrence Erlbaum Associates.

Ryan, K. E., Chandler, M., & Samuels, M. (2007). What should school-based evaluation look like? *Studies in Educational Evaluation, 33*(3–4), 197–212.

Shattock, M. (2007). From private to public governance of British higher education: The state, the market and competing perceptions of the national interest, 1980–2006. In *The crisis of the publics: Proceedings of a symposium organized by the Center for Studies in Higher Education* (pp. 187–200). Berkeley: University of California.

Smith, S., & Lipsky, M. (1993). *Nonprofits for hire.* Cambridge, MA: Harvard University Press.

Stronach, I. (1999). Shouting theatre in a crowded fire: Educational effectiveness as cultural performance. *Evaluation, 5*(2), 173–193.

van Leeuwen, T. (2004). Descriptive versus evaluative bibliometrics. In H. Moed, W. Glanzel, & U. Schmoch (Eds.), *Handbook of quantitative science and technology research* (pp. 373–388). Dordrecht, The Netherlands: Kluwer Academic Publishers.

Weingart, P. (2005). Impact of bibliometrics upon the science system: Inadvertent consequences? *Scientometrics, 62*(1), 117–131.

Wholey, J. S. (1994). Assessing the feasibility and likely usefulness of evaluation. In J. Wholey, H. Hatry, & K. Newcomer (Eds.), *Handbook of practical program evaluation* (pp. 15–39). San Francisco, CA: Jossey-Bass.

Zumeta, W. (2001). Public policy and accountability in higher education: Lessons from the past and present for the new millennium. In D. Heller (Ed.), *The states and public higher education policy: Affordability, access, and accountability* (pp. 155–197). Baltimore, MD: Johns Hopkins University.

CHAPTER 11

A Precarious Balance

*Educational Evaluation Capacity Building
in a Globalized Society*

Miri Levin-Rozalis, Barbara Rosenstein, and J. Bradley Cousins

Introduction

The integration of evaluation into organizational management culture is a topic of increasing interest in evaluation as general domain of inquiry (Cousins, Goh, Clark, & Lee, 2004; Sanders, 2003). Theoretically, to the extent that organizations embrace evaluative inquiry—systematic inquiry designed to support judgments about the merit, worth, and significance of programs and policies and to support ongoing decision making—as a management and learning system, they will be able to meet accountability demands better in addition to fostering individual, group, and collective learning about what does and does not work. Research-based knowledge on organizational learning, evaluation capacity building, and evaluation consequences (use, influence) provides growing support for this assertion (Cousins et al., 2004).

Related interests have been evident in research and theory about educational evaluation for quite some time. Beginning almost

15 years ago, Nevo (1994, 2002) inquired into processes, consequences, and virtues of school-based evaluation—school-level inquiry that combines internal and external evaluation. Similar interests in school-based evaluative inquiry have been evident in the United Kingdom (MacBeath, 2002), as well as Canada (Cousins & Earl, 1995; Cousins, Goh, & Clark, 2005) and the United States (Sutherland, 2004). In this chapter, our primary focus is the concept of educational evaluation capacity and how to bring that about—namely, evaluation capacity building (ECB).

The contemporary management of educational programs and policies is in some ways similar to other domains of practice in that, significantly, it has been predicated on a range of assumptions associated with a neoliberalism as a political ideology and new public management (NPM). In the name of good governance, NPM carries with it such characteristics and attributes as decentralized decision making; transparency; efficiency; a focus on results and outcomes as opposed to activities and outputs; and, most important, a strong emphasis on accountability. The implications of NPM for evaluation are many and varied, but in education they have naturally gravitated toward demonstrable improvement of student learning.

Pervasive in public sector governance, NPM has taken center stage within the context of intensifying globalizing influences and forces. An amorphous, complex, and contentious psychosocial phenomenon, *globalization*, is often characterized by the acceleration and perhaps concentration of worldwide relations, expansionism, and the compression of time and space. Osterhammel and Petersson (2005) argue that the world is a smaller place as a consequence of innovation in technology and communications, yet at the same time it is becoming larger because of broadening horizons. Increases in the quantity and availability of information have been fueled by the rapid and sudden appearance of new technologies (Adams & Carfagna, 2006). For others, globalization has meant an increasing scale, rate, variety, and extent of cross-border economic, military, political, social, and cultural interaction (Krieger, 2006); the decline of the nation-state; and the deterritorialization or liberalization of markets. Such influences have had remarkable impact on education and, concomitantly, educational evaluation.

Several authors in this volume framed educational evaluation's response to globalization in terms of technical-rationalist approaches, including those associated with performance measurement (Ryan & Feller, Chapter 10; Schwandt, Chapter 2), and scientific evaluation, such as the use of randomized control trial (RCT) designs (Henry & Rickman, Chapter 7; Mark, Chapter 4; Steiner, Wroblewski, & Cook, Chapter 5). In addition, globalization has contributed to evaluation trends such as international comparisons (see, e.g., Tamassia & Adams, Chapter 12). Accountability, consumer-, and performance-oriented approaches (Ryan & Feller, Chapter 10) align well with NPM.

Yet many contributors comment on the inadequacies of a technical-rationalist or structuralist

perspective and provide a critique based on moral-political grounds and what is in the public interest (e.g., Kushner, Chapter 23; Mathison, Chapter 30; Schwandt, Chapter 2). As Rizvi (Chapter 1) suggests, the proper role for evaluation is to raise contradictions and involve the public in determining what is educationally right and good (see also Mathison, Chapter 30). Evaluation approaches associated with principles of inclusion, citizen engagement, human agency, and democracy are cast as modes of inquiry guided by moral-political purpose.

In this chapter, our goal is to explore the implications for ECB in educational organizations and systems and beyond within the context of contemporary trends in educational governance in a global society. We first share some of our basic assumptions about education and educational evaluation, and then we quickly move to an overview of contemporary discourse on ECB, including the evolution of thinking about the capacity to *do* evaluation and the capacity to *use* evaluation. We then return to considerations of globalization and its implications for educational evaluation. Specifically, we examine the *precarious balance* between dual evaluation perspectives of structural and human agency and the tensions associated with this duality. We argue that challenges in balancing these tensions are exacerbated in an increasingly globalized society. Finally, we identify evaluation approaches that hold promise for maintaining a precarious balance and their implications for ECB.

Assumptions

We wish to explicate four main assumptions relative to our discussion of education and educational evaluation in a globalized society and its implications for evaluation capacity building.

First, we are guided by the idea that a worthy education is context-bound, where context includes social structures, values, cultures, emotions, and intuitions.

Second, as do many others, we consider evaluation to be essentially a political act (Simons,

2006; Weiss, 1973, 1991, 1999). Evaluation derives from and expresses policy (Stake, 2007) over and beyond the politics of being involved in the act of evaluation (Wholey, 1983, 1994). That the most powerful funding and regulating bodies in the world—the World Bank, the United Nations (UN) and its different agencies, the European Union (EU), and others—invest considerable sums of money and energy into the promotion of evaluation serves to underscore its political importance. We cannot ignore the fact that interests, ideologies, power struggles, and conflicts that stem from varying ontological and epistemological approaches are involved.

A third assumption underlying our thinking is that the way in which evaluation is conducted influences the evaluee's (or evaluand's) performance. In other words, evaluation has consequential validity. Evaluation does not occur in a vacuum, and the act can sometimes have subtle yet far-reaching influence. The potential influence of evaluation on the behavior of teachers, pupils, schools, and educational systems is considerable and, unfortunately, not always for the best (witness the phenomenon of "teaching to the test"; see, e.g., Torrance, Chapter 27, this volume). As Patton (1997) has observed, "What gets measured, gets done." Who, then, decides what gets measured, and with what consequences?

Finally, and perhaps most centrally for our purposes here, we assume that evaluation is perceived differently by different individuals and that, at a gross level, these differences may be understood from two fundamental and opposing epistemological perspectives: structure and human agency. An early grounding in the technical-rationalist perspective as a dominant paradigm in evaluation has encountered significant confrontations associated with the needs and interests of less powerful stakeholders, and the significance of context and culture. The responsive evaluation approach of Stake (1983, 1991, 2004) has been instrumental in elevating the role of context in understanding program meaning. On many levels, this approach has been consistent with and potentially instrumental in facilitating the development of alternative

approaches and concepts such as empowerment evaluation (Fetterman, 1994; Mertens, 1997), transformative evaluation (Mertens, 2001), and multicultural validity (Kirkhart, 1995). Yet despite these alternative directions, the demand for "rigorous" methods as well as experimental, quasi-experimental, and predominantly quantitative approaches has remained strong.

Thus, the pendulum swings between two main ontological approaches: structure versus human agency (Schwandt, 2001). The central question is: Who is in charge? The structure and external forces that determine human actions or the individuals who consciously monitor their actions? The structural approach, with its roots in the natural sciences, seeks to explain (Howe, 2005). It embraces replication and generalization as standards and aims to discover relations between dependent and independent variables generating a causal explanation for the purpose of prediction and control. The human agency approach, in contrast, is rooted in phenomenology, intentionalism, hermeneutics, or authenticity, and it seeks to understand (*verstehen*) human experiences and achieve intentional explanation and hermeneutic understanding (Alexander, 2006). As we know, the distinction between the two approaches is often put under the umbrella of positivism versus constructivism (Guba & Lincoln, 1981, 1989).

We present these contradicting ontological approaches and the tensions stemming from them in Table 11.1. We can see in the table how each of these overarching approaches is differentiated by a number of criteria ranging from function to benefit to methodology. For instance, in the area of function, the structural approach uses control and supervision as its main source of operation, whereas the human agency approach has learning as its main interest. According to the structural approach, the goal of the evaluation is standardization, whereas in the human agency approach, the purpose is to examine variance, difference, diversity, and so on. Clearly, the perceptions of each approach are quite different, and the duality we speak of is evident. With these

Table 11.1   Tensions Between Two Perspectives on Evaluation

Criteria	Structure	Human Agency
Function	Control, supervision, accountability	Learning, understanding
Goal	Standardization	Looking into variance, differences, and diversity
Frame	Structural	Diagnostic (distinguishing variation among pupil, teacher, or school)
Focus	Products	Processes
Benefit	Sorting	Strengthening
Outcomes (educational)	Knowledge	Skills
Methodology	Scientific, quantitative (e.g., RCT)	Responsive, diversified
Inquiry	Analytic	Holistic or naturalistic or systemic
Locus	External	Internal

assumptions in mind, we turn to our survey of contemporary discourse on evaluation capacity building. Later we return to the notion of dual perspectives and the implications of and for maintaining a precarious balance between the two in the interest of educational evaluation and ECB in a globalized society.

Contemporary Discourse on Evaluation Capacity Building

The traditional definition of *capacity* meaning "able to hold" remains the first of about eight different definitions listed in most contemporary dictionaries. Williams (2001) and McDonald, Rogers, and Kefford (2003) distinguish between *capacity* and capability, stating that capacity is what one holds, whereas capability is the ability to use and apply it. This distinction is most relevant when we discuss two sides of evaluation capacity. McDonald et al. use a fishing metaphor to describe both sides of the evaluation capacity coin: Starting from the position that one is better off teaching a hungry person to fish than just giving him or her a plate of fish, they explain,

one needs the proper paraphernalia for fishing, on the one hand, and a market in which to sell (or otherwise move) the catch, on the other hand. The core issue here is that ECB is about developing the capacity to *do* evaluation, as well as the capacity to *use* it. Let us examine this distinction a little more closely.

Conceptually Situating ECB

In North America, *evaluation capacity building* is the current terminology, whereas the World Bank, and consequently much of the world beyond North America, tends to use the term *evaluation capacity development* (ECD). According to MacKay (2002), ECD "encompasses a broad range of evaluative tools and approaches that include but go beyond program evaluation" (p. 82). For example, MacKay goes on to say, "governance priorities provide the context for the [World] Bank's ECD work" (p. 82) and the Bank's approach to ECD is not "to build M&E capacities per se: capacity building is simply one step along a 'results chain' " (p. 83). A similar definition is provided by Stockdill, Baizerman, and Compton (2002):

A context-dependent intentional action system of guided processes and practices for bringing about and sustaining a state of affairs in which quality program evaluation and its *appropriate uses* are ordinary and ongoing practices within and/or between one or more organizations/programs/sites. (p. 8; italics added)

Another important ECB element here is *intentionality*. Compton, Baizerman, and Stockdill (2002) distinguish between the "program evaluation practitioner" and the "ECB practitioner." They suggest that "ECB is the *intentional* work to continuously create and sustain overall *organizational* processes that make quality evaluation and its uses *routine*" (italics added). Three points are remarkable about this assertion. First, the Compton et al. definition is limited to what might be termed *direct* ECB: the intentional act of training nonevaluator stakeholders (e.g., decision makers, administrative staff, teachers, students, and interested parties) in evaluation logic and skill development. No mention is made of the more *indirect* approach to ECB that might arise from practical experience in doing evaluation. An obvious platform for *indirect* ECB would be participatory or some form of collaborative evaluation, where nonevaluator stakeholders work hand in hand with evaluators to do evaluation. Indeed, there is a trend to link ECB to participatory forms of evaluation and a strong recommendation to conduct "joint evaluations" using both external and local evaluators. We return to these themes later in the chapter. The UN standards Number 29, for example, calls for:

Qualified, competent and experienced professional firms or individuals from concerned countries should be involved, whenever possible, in the conduct of evaluations, in order, *inter alia*, to ensure that national/local knowledge and information is adequately taken into account in evaluations and to support evaluation capacity building in developing countries. The conduct of evaluations may also be out-sourced to national private sector and civil society organizations. Joint evaluations with governments or other stakeholders should equally be encouraged. (United Nations Evaluation Group, 2005, p. 15)

Second, Compton et al. (2002) delineate an organizational context in which the benefits of ECB would be likely to play out: The problem of integrating evaluation into the organizational culture is front and center in this perspective. Finally, the definition stipulates that good evaluation conduct and uses of evaluation are the proper objectives of ECB. A conceptual framework developed by Cousins et al. (2004) helps to bring these concepts into focus. We present this framework in Figure 11.1.

Cousins et al. (2004) conducted a review of the empirical literature associated with the problem of integrating evaluation into the organizational culture. Ultimately, they reviewed 36 studies from three distinct yet somewhat overlapping domains of inquiry: organizational learning, evaluation use and influence, and ECB. We can see in Figure 11.1 that organizational processes and consequences are dependent on a host of support structures, one of them being evaluative inquiry. In addition, we note that evaluation capacity depends either directly or indirectly on evaluative inquiry. Direct ECB might take the form of intentional formal or informal training opportunities, such as university credit programs and courses, short courses, and workshops. Indirect ECB, in contrast, would occur as a benefit of evaluation use and influence. Conceptual (learning), instrumental (support for discrete decisions), and symbolic (political, persuasive) uses of evaluation findings would qualify as such benefits. But so, too, would *process use*, or individual, group, or organizational development contingent on participation in evaluation or proximity to it (Cousins, 2007; Patton, 1997). In other words, organization members might develop conceptual understanding of evaluation logic, acquire new skills and abilities, question basic assumptions, and/or cultivate a sense of inquiry mindedness on the basis of proximity or exposure to evaluation.

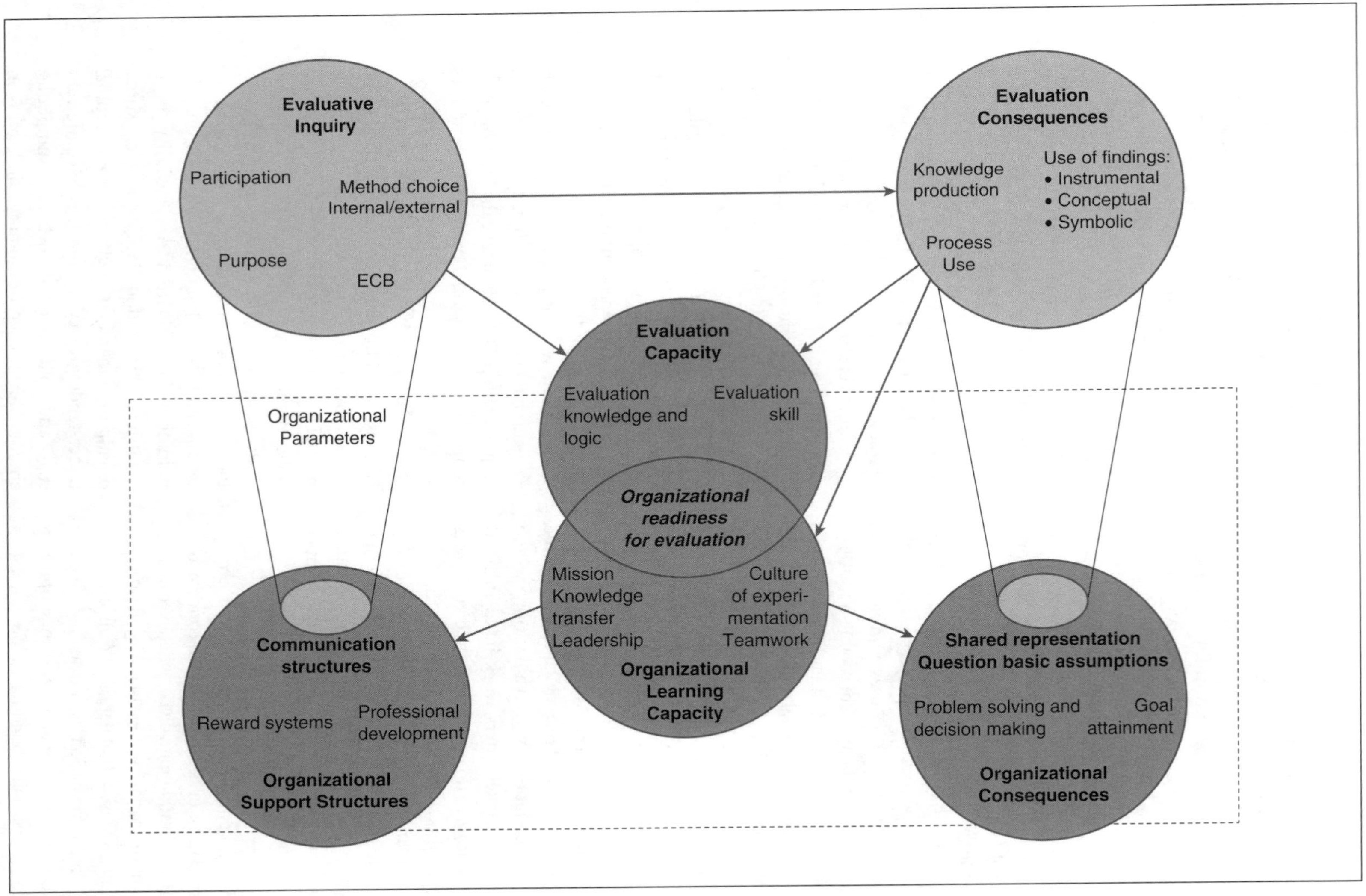

Figure 11.1 Conceptual Framework of Evaluative Inquiry as an Organizational Learning System

SOURCE: Reprinted with permission from Cousins et al. (2004)

An important point to be made is that direct ECB is always intentional. Yet intentionality is not always easy to focus. Many times unintended side effects occur alongside intended ones. Sometimes such effects are positive, but sometimes they are negative. For example, Lennie (2005) found that negative, even disempowering unintentional effects were present in an information technology intervention with an ECB component. Sometimes intentional and nonintentional ECB processes can be seen to comingle, as shown by Valery and Shakir (2005). The authors suggest the following components to improve ECB in humanitarian organizations: (a) employ a mix of participative and utilization-focused approach; (b) organize participative workshops and on-the-job training, with the continuity of collaborators ensured; and (c) use a myriad of dissemination/advocacy activities for a varied public. The same would be true for educational ECB involving relevant school stakeholders in the process (Cousins, Goh, & Clark, 2005; King, 2002; Sutherland, 2004). We now turn to a cursory examination of resource and training options available for direct ECB.

Building Capacity to "Do" Evaluation

Cousins and Aubry (2006) surveyed evaluation training programs and university centers of excellence globally in English-speaking countries and found the vast majority to be located in North America. In addition to university-level training, however, many noncredit programs and workshops have developed in North America and beyond. Development evaluation training opportunities are not yet widely available in developing and industrialized countries, but some programs are emerging. For example, the International Institute for Rural Reconstruction (Yen Centre, Philippines) offers a variety of workshops and training options on participatory monitoring and evaluation and related international development topics. Other training opportunities are being made available through the African Evaluation Association (AfrEA) in the form of short courses and ongoing professional development opportunities in South Africa and elsewhere (e.g., Kenya, Ethiopia). Other opportunities include postgraduate diploma programs at universities in South Africa and free online courses in monitoring and evaluation offered by the Inter-American Development Bank.

Materials for such training activities are abundant. Preskill and Russ-Eft (2005) have provided 72 activities to promote building evaluation capacity. Although thoughtful and stimulating, these activities were developed mostly within a North American context, with perhaps only limited attempts to adapt them to other contexts and cultures. But beyond this obvious and laudable example, various evaluation associations, societies, and organizations have provided a wealth of ECB information, tools, practical guides, and advice. A cursory look at the plethora of available evaluation websites can give an indication of the extent to which ECB information, tools, sourcebooks, and the like are available and accessible to the extent that the Web is accessible. A partial list of such sites appears in the appendix to this chapter.

Underlying many planned educational and training programs for direct ECB are either implicit or explicit understandings of evaluator competencies. A variety of lists of evaluator competencies have developed over the years, but, as observed by Stevahn, King, Ghere, and Minnema (2005) "none of the proposed frameworks appeared to be systematically derived or empirically validated through consensus building among diverse professionals across the field" (p. 103). In North America, the turn of the century brought two important projects that address this shortcoming. King, Stevahn, and associates (King, Stevahn, Ghere, & Minnema, 2001; Stevahn et al., 2005) developed and empirically validated a set of Essential Competencies for Program Evaluators (ECPE). In Canada, the Core Body of Knowledge (CBK) project was commissioned by the Canadian Evaluation Society (CES) in support of its evaluation advocacy agenda (Zorzi, Perrin, McGuire, Long, & Lee, 2002). Recently, on the basis of considerable consultation, CES decided to work toward the development of professional designations for evaluators (see www.evaluationcanada.ca), and a cross-walk of existing evaluator competency taxonomies was identified as an integral component of that project. The result of this cross-walk activity—which drew from seven existing taxonomies, including ECPE—is a framework of competencies with five separate domains of practice:[1]

- Reflective practice (e.g., professional standards, ethics, public welfare, respect)
- Technical practice (e.g., program theory, evaluation logic and methods)
- Situational practice (e.g., context sensitivity, identification of stakeholder interests)
- Management practice (e.g., feasibility assessment, coordination, process leadership)
- Interpersonal practice (e.g., communication, group facilitation, sensitive to diversity)

The extent to which evaluator competencies inform the development and implementation of direct ECB is not well understood. However, it is safe to say that significant progress in understanding the basic competencies for evaluators is being made and that many of these competencies include soft skills that would only be developed through practical experience, apprenticeship, and the like, as opposed to classroom-based training.

Building Capacity to Use Evaluation

Although interest is growing in determining evaluator core competencies and the development and management of educational and practical evaluation learning and development experiences, much less has been written about building capacity for evaluation use. According to Cousins et al. (2004), "the integration of evaluation into the culture of organizations . . . has

as much to do with the consequences of evaluation as it does with the development of skills and knowledge of evaluation logic and methods." McDonald et al. (2003, p. 10) have contributed to this conversation as well:

> Supply and demand are two broad aspects of evaluation capability. Many efforts at building evaluation capability have focused primarily or even exclusively on supply—on documenting and developing the skills, tools and resources that are available to produce evaluations. . . . In a similar way, Russon and Patel's (2002) review of evaluation capacity in Africa assessed capacity solely in terms of the technical expertise of existing external research and evaluation agencies. The danger in this is the risk of ending up "all dressed up with nowhere to go" (Williams, 2001)—capable of producing evaluations but unable to use them, or even worse, producing evaluations that are treated as irrelevant. In fact, Mackay, working in evaluation capacity development in the World Bank, has argued that "supply is not as crucial as demand." (World Bank, 1994)

The capacity to use evaluation is discussed in the literature linking organizational learning and evaluation (Cousins et al., 2004; Levin-Rozalis & Rosenstein, 2005; Preskill & Torres, 1999). Consideration is given to the role of the evaluator as a facilitator of organizational learning working toward the incorporation and internalization of evaluation findings and thinking into the organizational mindset. Much of this discourse focuses on stakeholder-oriented approaches to evaluation, where relationship building over time between evaluators and organizational decision makers and policy agents is essential (e.g., Dabelstein, 2003; Patton, 1997). Some forms of participatory and collaborative evaluation carry an implicit ECB element, in that participants are expected to carry on evaluating once initial participatory evaluation work has been completed (e.g., Fetterman & Wandersman, 2005). However, although participatory evaluation has been observed to further ECB it is not a panacea.

A candid case study of a United Nations Educational, Scientific and Cultural Organization (UNESCO) program by Forss, Kruse, Taut, and Tenden (2006) revealed that participating in an evaluation is not enough to develop evaluation capacity. Taut (2007) addressed the issue of evaluation use in conjunction with ECB at length in her frank examination of ECB in a large development organization. Both studies point to difficulties of time and commitment as sources of failure to accomplish sustainable ECB. Taut concludes that strong leadership support is needed to carry out the goals of ECB, a sentiment that has been echoed elsewhere (e.g., Cousins et al., 2004, 2005; Dabelstein, 2003; King, 2002). Inherent resistance to evaluation on the part of units within the organization, as well as a sense of "overburdenedness" on the part of staff members, are other challenges facing ECB initiatives, according to Taut (2007).

Based on their research in schools, Cousins et al. (2005) conclude that "data use leads to data valuing," an assertion that has important implications for developing the capacity to use evaluation. The essential idea here links to the educational change maxim that "belief follows practice." It is insufficient to merely market educational innovation or otherwise invest in strategies to motivate educators to adopt and institutionalize innovation. Rather, it is essential to use a mixture of pressure and support to stimulate educators into using the innovation and thereby directly experience its benefits, presumably defined mostly in terms of benefits to improved student learning. "Data valuing leads to data use" implies that the uptake of educational evaluation will be more likely if educators experience firsthand its benefits and uses. Leadership is an essential force in bringing this about through a mixture of pressure, support, and modeling evaluative inquiry. It seems likely, then, that indirect EBC is a more powerful force in the development of the capacity to use evaluation than it would be in a direct ECB context. Others such as King (2002) and MacKay (2002) concur. They stress the fact that ECB is "not a

quick fix," but takes time, persistence, and patience. "Awareness and demand have to be cultivated, and this is where a powerful and influential champion has a pivotal role to play" (MacKay, 2002, p. 93).

King (2002) proposed a four-sided system for educational ECB that divides contributing elements into four groups: teachers, students, curriculum, and context. The teachers in King's framework are the teachers of evaluation, administrators, and opinion leaders who show a commitment to evaluation and its use—who exercise the "clout factor." King stresses the importance of context in allowing the development of ECB. If the context is not conducive to such development, it is an uphill climb at best, and sustainability is extremely difficult. Similar conclusions about context were reached by Boyle and Lemaire (1999) in their work on governmental ECD in developing countries. They identify four key issues that affect approaches to ECD and evaluation practice: the presence of sound data systems, the presence of a history of social science, the presence of a cadre of trained analysts/evaluators, and the level of political and economical areas. Infrastructure development is high on their list of requirements for sustainable ECD.

Locus of ECB

Related to considerations about integration of evaluation into the organizational context are issues associated with the locus of evaluation logic and understanding and, indeed, of ECB. The Compton et al. (2002) distinction between program evaluation practitioners and the ECB practitioners is interesting and relevant. Both roles can be internal or external, but an essential difference is that the program evaluation practitioner is seen as addressing the "task on hand"— a sort of "putting-out-fires" role, rather than the ECB practitioner who is "mindful of how today's work will contribute to the sustainability of the unit in the longer term" (Compton et al., 2002). Beere (2002) has made the case that ECB should be the task of internal evaluators. She argues that internal evaluators have a stake in the program and organizational outcomes, as well as a commitment to professional standards of practice. Moreover, internal evaluators are well placed to undertake ECB and have an organizational responsibility in their organizations to do so. An internal locus of ECB is in keeping with conceptions of school-based evaluation described by Nevo (1994), MacBeath (2002), and others (see, e.g., MacNamara & O'Hara, Chapter 15, this volume).

Summary

ECB takes the form of direct approaches involving educational and training opportunities that are at least implicitly supported by systematically developed lists of evaluator competencies. ECB can also be indirect, a by-product of sustained collaborative and participatory work. Program and organizational decision makers, managers, and the like learn and internalize evaluation logic and skill by virtue of their participation in, or proximity to, evaluation. Such is a fundamental tenet of process use of evaluation. Although considerable attention has been devoted to the supply side of evaluation, in terms of capacity development, comparatively less has been written about the demand side, although several authors have underscored the essential need to include such considerations in any viable ECB initiative.

Much of the current work on ECB has been conducted in a North American context, although a good deal of interest has been shown in more international contexts, particularly in the context of development evaluation. Furthermore, ECB has been explicitly conceptualized predominantly in terms of organizational capacity at either the program or institutional level. But what are the implications for educational evaluation in a globalized society? Is current thinking about ECB adequate to meet the challenges that globalization brings? We now turn our focus to these issues and consider the challenges that may lie ahead and their implications

for ECB. We begin by returning to a reexamination of the dual perspectives on the role of evaluation and how this may be evolving in the context of a global society.

Relevant Globalizing Influences on Evaluation

The tensions caused by the duality of perceptions discussed earlier are even more pronounced within the context of globalization. Globalization is responsible for two opposite tendencies. On the one hand, it has made the world a relatively small place, where almost everything and everyone is within reach. On the other hand, it has exposed countless cultures to each other. Thus, although the process has shrunk distances, bringing everyone closer together, it juxtapositioned unknown and diverse traditions and customs. The encounters between so many civilizations result in different reactions, ranging from enthusiasm and acceptance, at one end, to resentment and mistrust, at the other end. In some parts of the world, there is a propensity to adopt Western civilization or, at least, part of it, whereas others reject it and feel pressured by Western domination. Modernization through industrialization and postindustrialization, as defined by Western values, has been adopted by many political regimes as a means of promoting economic progress. Consequently, we have witnessed a rise in the importance and level of education, as well as changes in gender roles all over the world (Ingelhart & Baker, 2000). Nevertheless, these wide-reaching changes and trends have not created a monolithic society, neither culturally nor economically (Ingelhart & Baker, 2000; Watson, 1998). On the contrary, it seems that they have exposed us to greater diversity than ever.

Educational evaluation is a field where this development is revealed clearly. Since 1995, as reported by Love and Russon (2000), the number of evaluation associations and evaluation networks has increased dramatically. Evaluators are building an international evaluation community (e.g., International Organization for Evaluation Cooperation and International Development Evaluation Association), bringing together evaluators from a variety of contexts to share their knowledge and experiences (see also Smith, Chapter 3, this volume). Their expertise can contribute tremendously to evaluators' professional development and to the development of the field of evaluation. However, such a gathering can result in tension and conflict, particularly if images of appropriate approaches to evaluation clash.

Ever since the 1960s, reformers have suggested caution in applying evaluative approaches grounded in the U.S. experience to other countries (Cronbach, 1983; Cronbach & Associates, 1980), and contemporary writers continue to echo these sentiments (e.g., Hood, 2004). The idea that North American thinking about program evaluation may have its limitations when applied without amendment in non-Western countries became more relevant as the movement toward building an international evaluation community arose. The refusal of the African Evaluation Networks and associations, in the late 1990s, to adopt U.S. standards of professional evaluation practice is only one example of resistance to Western ethnocentrism (Hopson, 2001). Eventually, the 1999 AfrEA conference modified a version of an article by Russon and Patel (1998) and proposed certain changes to the North American program evaluation standards (Joint Committee, 1994). Yet this adaptation was recently challenged at the Niger AfrEA conference (2007), where it was decided that the standards would be rewritten specifically for Africa. Love and Russon (2000) believe that this situation calls for a creation of new standards and ethical guidelines that will allow for building an international evaluation community.

Thus, we can see that multiculturalism has become a pressing issue in the last decades for evaluators and social researchers. Challenges facing cross-cultural researchers have been discussed, providing a rich understanding of the complexities of conducting such work (e.g.,

Barton 1998; Berk & Adams, 1970). Evaluators aspire to reach competent, responsive, and sensitive evaluation (Hood, 2004; Hopson, 2001; Letiecq & Bailey 2004) regardless of the populations they evaluate. Nevertheless, there seems to be insufficient guidance on how to execute such evaluation, as has been noted by Letiecq and Bailey (2004) in their account of evaluation in a Native American community. One of the problems to which they point is the implementation of outcome measures that have only been validated and normed using White middle-class samples. Another difficulty arises from the tendency to ignore the variability and diversity within cultural groups when evaluators focus on between-group differences instead of within-group variation (McLoyd & Randolph, 1985).

We must consider the basic questions, "Does traditional evaluation methodology have the adequate means to serve the information needs of other cultures, and if so, how can such metholodology be applied?" Here we refer to culture broadly, including shared representations of socioeconomic status, literacy levels, language(s), local political climate, and different group cultures. A second basic question that needs consideration concerns whether traditional evaluation methodologies and tools provide the adequate means to conduct and use evaluation in other cultures and, if so, how. In structural approaches to evaluation, a fuzzy concept in most global contexts, different groups are most often classified into different categories and clusters according to shared patterns—such as origin, race, ethnicity, language, gender, and other prominent characteristics—on the assumption that those characteristics represent specific behavior and beliefs. The viability of such assumptions is questionable, and the mere fact that a person can belong to more than one culture can lead to crucial mistakes in the interpretation of evaluation findings and the development of conclusions. It can even put into question the relevance, accuracy, and meaning of data in the first instance.

The answers to both of these basic questions have ramifications for the way evaluators are trained and qualified and the ways in which they are guided in the use of evaluation. We therefore see ECB as an essential component of any discussion of globalization and evaluation.

ECB and the Globalization Challenge

Globalization brings important challenges to the prospect of ECB. First of all, the field or scope in which evaluation takes place changes dramatically in an era of globalization. We propose that it may be prudent to rethink the idea that "organizations" constitute the main locus of evaluation, as is often the case in contemporary discourse on ECB, noted earlier. We have to enlarge the scope to include groups, communities, networks, and cultures (of which organizations are only one example). In modern Western culture, organizations with their nonpersonal standards represent the most important

characteristic of the social order. International bureaucracy diminishes other features and qualities of societies that have to obey its rules and regulations. But this is not the case in vast areas of the world, such as Africa, Asia, or the Middle East. In many premodern and traditional cultures, organizations do not exist,[2] or they are tolerable obstacles with which to be dealt. This expansion of the field or scope of evaluation is one of the big challenges facing evaluation if evaluation is to be conducted outside Western groups and societies.

Second, we return to the structural versus human agency duality presented earlier or the precarious balance between being relevant in the context where the evaluation occurs and being acceptable in a wider evaluation community. In Table 11.2, we present the duality as it pertains to evaluation in the global arena. The same conflicting practices that we illustrated in Table 11.1 in educational evaluation appear again. Once more, we can see tensions stemming from different

Table 11.2 Inherent Tensions in Evaluation in an Era of Globalization

Criteria	Structure	Human Agency
Function	Control, supervision, accountability	Learning, understanding
Goal	Standardizational/**Universality**	Looking into variance, differences, and diversity/**Particularity**
Frame	Structural/Macro perspective	Diagnostic (distinguishing variation among pupil, teacher, or school)/**Micro perspective**
Focus	Products/Conceptual definitions (etic)	Processes/Local meanings (emic)
Benefit	Sorting/Accountability	Strengthening/**Autonomy**
Outcomes (educational)	Knowledge/Professionalism	Skills/Politics and tensions between different stakeholders and interests
Methodology	Scientific, quantitative (e.g., RCT)	Responsive, diversified
Inquiry	Analytic	Holistic or naturalistic or systemic
Locus[a]	**External**	**Internal**

a. External or internal in almost any aspect: forces, knowledge, evaluators, interveners, culture, needs, and so on.

perceptions of the same reality. Although the same duality we showed earlier in this work exists here as well, and the tensions seem similar, we want to stress that, in an era of globalization, their intensity is much higher, creating new evaluation and ECB challenges. An evaluator must have the knowledge and skills to first identify these challenges and, second, to deal with them. It is an essential part of his or her training, role, and qualification. In essence, the evaluator is now moving with the pendulum. The challenge is indeed to be able to work within specific cultures with all their characteristics, social representations, values, and norms and still be able to meet universal accountability demands and standards. The latter are essential in the light of the pervasiveness of NPM as a governance framework and continual demands for broad communicability of evaluation findings; comparisons of findings across jurisdictions, nations, or other cultural borders; and expanding repositories of evidence as a basis to policy and decision making.

Let us consider an example by way of illustrating the point. An evaluator working with a group of illiterate Bedouin mothers committed to improvement of the kindergarten services in their poor town should be able to help them set priorities and do so in a culture where data collection, even through an interview, is difficult. The "contract" between interviewer and interviewee and the rules of the game in general are unfamiliar. She needs to do all this in ways that are acceptable and feasible in that society and then to be able to say something valid and worthy that will satisfy the National Authority for Measurement and Evaluation. In other words, the evaluator has to be able to collect data in a format compatible with the culture of the project level stakeholders and transform it into understandable formats for the commisionner of the evaluation.

Financing agencies and funds—whether the World Bank, the EU, the U.S. Agency for International Development (USAID), or other donor agencies and foundations—want the evaluation to provide them with data that meet accountability demands; they want to know what their investment has accomplished. It is the role of the evaluator to give reliable and helpful answers. For the answers to have reliability, we must work within the culture and the group because the culture and the group own knowledge that evaluators need, but are often unable to attain because their tools are inadequate. Furthermore, the evaluator's ear may be deaf to the local language (especially the subtexts), and his or her eye may be blind to the situation in the right light. Experience in Israel with Ethiopian immigrants has taught us that, despite speaking the same language—Hebrew— we do not mean the same while using the same words (Levin-Rozalis, 2000). Israeli immigrants of Ethiopian origin are perhaps one of only a few examples in which an entire tribal community migrates to a highly industrial Western country. Here, interviews, not to mention questionnaires, are in many cases worthless, especially if conducted by strangers (Weil, 1995).

The prior examples lead us to believe that the movement of the pendulum is no longer an adequate metaphor. The movements are now going in all directions, at a rapidly and perhaps random pace, a pace that is sometimes frantic. Range, direction, and pace are unpredictable. At this time of globalization, the evaluator has to know how to navigate in stormy water. She needs to be attentive to different kinds of evaluees, to be able to work within unfamiliar cultures, and to give the evaluees leeway for doing things in their own ways, despite the apparent similarity in appearance and even language. Evaluees need freedom to build on their ability to do things their way and to learn from what they are doing (simply because in many cases this is the only way to gain the information needed or otherwise get the job done). At the same time, the evaluator needs to be able to process these data in ways that can be reliable for and understandable to decision makers with privilege and access to power, resources, or both.

Implications for Evaluation

Despite the penchant of educational policy-makers and decision makers to favor quantitative evidence and their preference for scientific designs in the interest of enhancing confidence in the knowledge base, we would argue that, in an era of globalizing forces, shaping education and educational evaluation acceptance of more diversified approaches is essential to maintain a precarious balance. Evaluation as a field needs to think critically about the use of alternative approaches that are grounded in the policy or program implementation context and that carry with them the potential for satisfying local as well as more universal information needs. Several alternative approaches show much promise in this respect.

The concept of utilization-focused evaluation (UFE; Patton, 1997, 2008) was initially proposed in the late 1970s and has evolved considerably over time. This pragmatic approach to developing evaluation knowledge is centered on the notion of fostering the use and influence of evaluation and has, as a defining feature, relationship building between the evaluator and members of the program and policy community over time. Recent developments have included the integration of the concept of process use (benefits to the program community that extend beyond the use of findings; Patton, 1997) and sensitivty to cultural diversity (Patton, 2008). Both of these elements are essential to the problem of meeting diverse information needs.

Related would be forms of collaborative evaluation that have practical problem solving as their intent. Whereas UFE does not necessarily directly involve nonevaluator stakeholders in the evaluation knowledge-production process, Cousins' (2003; Cousins & Whitmore, 1998) notion of practical participatory evaluation (P-PE) has this as a defining feature. Evaluators work collaboratively with nonevaluator stakeholders on technical evaluation methods and practices to produce evaluative findings. The potential for process use, in addition to use of findings, is enhanced as evaluators bring evaluation logic knowledge and skill and standards of professional practice to the table, whereas nonevaluator stakeholders bring their knowledge of the evaluand and the context within which it is to be implemented. Evaluation questions and methods are jointly decided in this context. While being most appropriate in contexts where learning about the program with an eye to improvement is of central interest, under the right circumstances, we would argue that evaluative knowledge arising from P-PE serves to meet accountability demands and to support educational policy and program decision making.

Another relevant class of alternative approaches that favors the human agency perspective would be dialogic approaches that are centered on capacity-building interests. Democratic, deliberative evaluation (House & Howe, 2000), empowerment evaluation (Fetterman & Wandersman, 2005), transformative evaluation (Mertens, 2001), responsive evaluation (Abma, 1997; see Niessen et al., Chapter 21, this volume), culturally responsive evaluation (Hood, 2004, Chapter 25, this volume; Hopson, 2001, Chapter 24, this volume) and other forms of tranformative participatory evaluation (T-PE; Cousins & Whitmore, 1998) would fall into this family of approaches. Such approaches fit well with Rizvi's (Chapter 1, this volume) assertion that the proper role for evaluation is to raise contradictions and involve the public in determining what is educationally right and good. They carry with them the potential to foster self-determination and the amelioration of social injustice through the development of evaluation knowledge and skill. Although it might be argued that these approaches favor heavily the human agency perspective and would have limited potential to meet information needs more broadly defined (e.g., those of the program and policy elite) several proponents would contend that meeting these latter demands is the central purpose of evaluation. We would offer that in the broader scheme such dialogic approaches could be used in conjunction with other approaches to maintain a precarious balance.

A final alternative approach seems particularly relevant to maintaining a precarious balance between universal and local information needs. We propose combining principles of Pierce's abductive research logic (Levin-Rozalis, 2000; Rescher, 1978; Rosental, 1993) with cybernetic principles (Galison, 1994; Heylighen & Joslyn, 2001; Ray, 2005; VonFoerster, 1974) as a means of conducting educational evaluation in an era of globalization. A cybernetic evaluation system of interdependent feedback is a cyclic or spiral process of the mutual influences of evaluators and evaluees (or nonevaluator stakeholders) by means of gathering and processing information. Feedback is driven by the hierarchy existing between the knowledge resources of all parties. As in P-PE, the evaluation team possesses knowledge that the evaluees do not have, whereas the evaluee possesses bodies of knowledge that the evaluation team lacks. Each of the parties needs the knowledge

of the others, and the knowledge gap enforces knowledge exchange, and thus a feedback process is created (Clemson, 1984; Levin-Rozalis & Rosenstein, 2005). Evaluators must also create the procedures that enable the process. Figure 11.2 shows the cybernetic relationship. The process assumes equal partners with equal status and operates on the basis of a chain of dyads, each consisting of at least two persons (one evaluee and one evaluator).

Using iterative abduction research logic, the process involves drawing explanations and conclusions; turning conclusions into hypotheses; rechecking hypotheses against more data; and, most important, conceptualizing findings to a level that they can be communicable to other people outside the confined context. Jointly, participants are required to conceptualize the broader context for use, as well as the findings, because findings, conceptualized in the abstract,

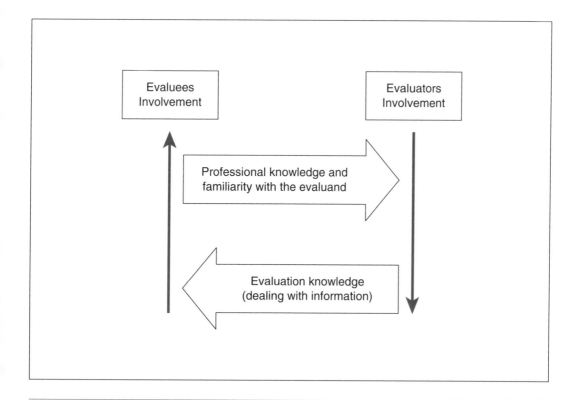

Figure 11.2 Cybernetic Relationship Between the Evaluator and the Evaluee

only have meaning within that specific context. The precarious balance between what can be seen as conflicting needs—the needs of the locals, the needs of evaluators, and the needs of global agencies or funders—is maintained. Although it is beyond the scope of the present chapter to provide more detail, we can see how such a cybernetic system tackles head on the problem of maintaining a precarious balance.

Implications for ECB

We have argued that educational evaluation in an era of globalization must be more intensely mindful of the dual perspectives of structural and human agency approaches to evaluation, and it must embrace the problem of maintaining a precarious balance between the information needs of these two perspectives. We identified several alternative approaches to educational evaluation that have the potential to address this problem. What then are the implications for ECB arising from these assertions? Here we provide a list of possible considerations:

1. *Beyond Organization*: In the first instance, we return to our contention that it is nessary to broaden the scope or unit of analysis in considering ECB, from the organization to social networks more widely defined. Such networks might include communities and cultures. There is little doubt that educational organizations such as schools, school districts, and state-level educational systems will continue to represent crucial structures within which we need to think about the capacity to do and use evaluation. Yet globalization brings with it border and boundary crossing and the comingling of diverse cultures and contexts in previously unknown and unexperienced ways.

2. *The Virtues of Indirect ECB*: Next, we would offer that ECB in a globalized society will continue to be well served by direct

initiatives focused on knowledge and skill building, but that powerful means of developing the capacity to do and use evaluation to maintain the aforementioned precarious balance is most likely to be served by intensive indirect ECB. Learning by doing is a central principle underlying indirect ECB and by virtue of involving nonevaluator stakeholders in the process— as is the case at some level in each of the alternative methods that we described earlier—we can expect to see considerably more opportunity for developing the capacity to use evaluation, as opposed to developing the capacity to do it. Although the assertion "data use leads to data valuing" requires considerably more evidence to justify confidence, we would argue that succesful experiencing of the benefits of evaluation will ultimately serve as a powerful source in developing an "evaluative habit of mind" (Katz, Sutherland, & Earl, 2002).

3. *ECB as a Professional Duty*: We suggest that it is the evaluator's professional duty to help evaluees understand the logic and power of evaluation. As professionals, evaluators should have the means (soft skills, abilities, understandings) to introduce and engage nonevaluator stakeholders in thinking about and developing evaluation logic and skill.

4. *Trust in Local Wisdom*: Much has been said about the evaluator's need to gain the trust of the evaluee, yet relatively infrequently do we consider the trust that we—as evaluators (and as interveners)— must have in the cultural wisdom of our evaluees, in their ways of doing things, in their understanding and interpretations of their own world. Evaluators have to acknowledge that their ways of thinking about and doing things are not always the best, and that there are alternatives that might be more appropriate in different

cultural situations. They must be more modest and less ethnocentric, and they must listen carefully. They will learn, their work will benefit, and they will be able to foster sensemaking evaluation capacity for nonevaluator stakeholders.

5. *Garnering Trust (A)*: In her lecture at the 2007 meeting of AfrEA, Mertens (2007) asserted that "being firmly rooted in a human rights agenda, ethical implications for evaluation are derived from the conscious inclusion of a broad range of people who are generally excluded from the mainstream in society" (p. 2). This is one important way of looking at the issue of inclusiveness: as an affirmative act. But if we continue the idea of trust and modesty, it is not only the need to include the least privileged groups (if they are wise and generous enough to do so) that is important, but evaluees need to include evaluators— to accept them into their ways of life, to share with them their ways of thinking, and to let them have a glimpse into local customs. We see as a central role for evaluators, gaining such trust through relationship building and continuous positive engagement over time.

6. *Garnering Trust (B):* Another dimension of the trust issue centers on the evaluator's credibility in the eyes of the broader community, since evaluation is necessarily a political activity, and competing interests and stakes are always at play. In the context of ongoing support and funding, it is fair to assume that the potential influence of self-serving interests on behalf of nonevaluator stakeholders is enhanced. To maintain a precarious balance, evaluators need to communicate beyond the program community in ways that are credible and trustworthy. Explicit adherence to professional standards will continue to provide one basis from which such credibility can be established and/or maintained.

We have identified a few implications for ECB in a global society, and in doing so we have been mindful of the need to maintain a precarious balance between the local and the universal. No doubt such considerations will have implications for how we think about and use evaluator competencies. As a general recommendation, we would assert that the development of any evaluator competency system should be mindful of this broader picture. To what extent are the soft skills required to meet the challenges outlined earlier integrated within contemporary competency systems? How can such systems be improved on the basis of such considerations?

Summary and Conclusions

Our challenge has been to consider ECB in the context of educational evaluation within a globalized society. We began by affirming our assumptions that educational policies and programs will necessarily be sensitive to context, that evaluation is a political activity, and that there exists a precarious balance between structural and human agency evaluation perspectives. To some degree, each of these assumptions is shaped by globalizing forces at play.

Drawing from contemporary discourse in the area, we began to address our challenge with a review and integration of what is known about evaluation capacity and ECB. Consideration was given to conceptualizations of ECB, including direct versus indirect approaches. We then delineated developments concerning building capacity to do evaluation and building the capacity to use it and the locus for practicing ECB. The chapter then laid out what we see as relevant globalizing influences as a foundation for considering implications for ECB. In looking at ECB and globalization, we first considered implications of the latter for the dual evaluation perspectives—structure and human agency. To maintain a precarious balance between these perspectives, we considered and identified a suite of alternative approaches that have some relevance. This provided a basis for the implications for ECB that we developed in the final section.

A significant part of the challenge of thinking about ECB in an era of globalization is that we need to consider what evaluation will look like in response to globalizing forces. Of course, in general terms, this question provides a foundation for the entire *Handbook*, and the task of providing reasoned answers to it is daunting. Yet we believe that the duality of evaluation perspectives that we laid out provides a reasonable framework from which to operate, and that ongoing ECB initiatives, be they direct or indirect, focused on doing evaluation or its use and influence, should be mindful of this juxtaposition of perspectives and how associated tensions have been exacerbated by globalizing forces.

Notes

1. This is a work in progress and has not yet been formally adopted by CES. Yet, inasmuch as the activity took into account several extant evaluator competency frameworks, we conclude that the resulting framework is comprehensive.

2. As is the case for people of Ethiopian origin in Israel. Understanding the notion of bureaucracy is still one of the most frustrating experiences for both the newcomers and the host society (Levin-Rozalis, 2000).

References

Abma, T. A. (1997). Playing with/in plurality: Revitalizing realities and relationships in Rotterdam, *Evaluation, 3*(1).

Adams, J. M., & Carfagna, A. (2006). *Coming of age in a globalized world: The next generation.* Bloomfield, CT: Kumarian.

Alexander, H. A. (2006). A view from somewhere: Explaining the paradigms of educational research. *Journal of Philosophy of Education, 40*(2), 205–217.

Barton, W. H. (1998). Culturally competent research protocols. In R. R. Greene & M. Watkins (Eds.), *Serving diverse constituencies: Applying the ecological perspective* (pp. 285–303) Hawthorne, NY: Aldine de Gruyter.

Beere, D. (2002). Evaluation capacity-building: A tale of value-adding. *Evaluation Journal of Australasia, 5*(2), 41–47.

Berk, R. A., & Adams, J. M. (1970). Establishing rapport with deviant groups. *Social Problems, 18*(1), 102–117.

Boyle, R., & Lemaire, D. (Eds.). (1999). *Building effective evaluation capacity: Lessons from practice.* New Brunswick, NJ: Transaction Publishers.

Clemson, B. (1984). *Cybernetics: A new management tool.* Kent: Abacus Press.

Compton, D., Baizerman, M., & Stockdill, S. H. (2002). Toward a definition of the ECB Process: A conversation with the ECB literature. In D. W. Compton, M. Baizerman, & S. H. Stockdill (Eds.), The art, craft and science of evaluation capacity building. *New Directions for Evaluation 93* (pp. 47–61). San Francisco, CA: Jossey-Bass.

Cousins, J. B. (2003). Utilization effects of participatory evaluation. In T. Kellaghan, D. L. Stufflebeam, & L. A. Wingate (Eds.), *International handbook of educational evaluation* (pp. 245–265). Boston: Kluwer.

Cousins, J. B. (Ed.). (2007). Process use in theory, research and practice. *New Directions for Evaluation 116.* San Francisco, CA: Jossey-Bass.

Cousins, J. B., & Aubry, T. (2006, April). *Roles for government in evaluation quality assurance: Discussion paper.* Ottawa: Treasury Board of Canada, Secretariat and University of Ottawa. Available at http://www.tbs-sct.gc.ca/eval/

Cousins, J. B., & Earl, L. (Eds.). (1995). *Participatory evaluation in education: Studies in evaluation use and organizational learning.* London: Falmer.

Cousins, J. B., Goh, S., & Clark, S. (2005). Data use leads to data valuing: Evaluative inquiry for school decision making. *Leadership and Policy in Schools, 4,* 155–176.

Cousins, J. B., Goh, S., Clark, S., & Lee, L. (2004). Integrating evaluative inquiry into the organizational culture: A review and synthesis of the knowledge base. *Canadian Journal of Program Evaluation, 19*(2), 99–141.

Cousins, J. B., & Whitmore, E. (1998). Framing participatory evaluation. In E. Whitmore (Ed.), Understanding and practicing participatory evaluation. *New Directions for Evaluation 80* (pp. 3–23). San Francisco, CA: Jossey-Bass.

Cronbach, L. J. (1983). *Designing evaluation of educational and social programs.* San Francisco, CA: Jossey-Bass.

Cronbach, L. J., & Associates. (1980). *Toward reform of program evaluation*. San Francisco, CA: Jossey-Bass.

Dabelstein, N. (2003). Evaluation capacity development: Lessons learned. *Evaluation, The International Journal of Theory, Research and Practice, 9*(3), 365–369.

Fetterman, D. M. (1994). Empowerment evaluation. *Evaluation Practice, 15*(1), 1–15.

Fetterman, D., & Wandersman, A. (Eds.). (2005). *Empowerment evaluation principles in practice*. New York: Guilford.

Forss, K., Kruse, S., Taut, S., & Tenden, E. (2006). Chasing a ghost? An essay on participatory evaluation and capacity development. *Evaluation, 12*(1), 128–144.

Galison, P. (1994). The ontology of the enemy: Norbert Wiener and the cybernetic vision. *Critical Inquiry, 21*, 228–266.

Guba, E. G., & Lincoln, Y. S. (1981). *Effective evaluation*. San Francisco, CA: Jossey-Bass.

Guba, E. G., & Lincoln, Y. S. (1989). *Fourth generation evaluation*. London: Sage.

Heylighen, F., & Joslyn, C. (2001). Cybernetics and second order cybernetics. In R. Meyers (Ed.), *Encyclopedia of physical science and technology* (Vol. 4, 3rd ed., pp. 155–170). New York: Academic Press.

Hood, S. (2004). A journey to understand the role of culture in program evaluation: Snapshots and personal reflections of one African American evaluator. *New Directions for Evaluation 102*. San Francisco, CA: Jossey-Bass.

Hopson, R. (2001). Global and local conversations on culture, diversity, and social justice in evaluation: Issues to consider in a 9/11 era. *The American Journal of Evaluation, 22*(3), 375–380.

House, E., & Howe, K. R. (2000). Deliberative democratic evaluation. In K. E. Ryan & L. DeStefano (Eds.), Evaluation as a democratic process: Promoting inclusion, dialogue, and deliberation. *New Directions for Evaluation 85*. San Francisco, CA: Jossey-Bass.

Howe, K. R. (2005). The question of educational science: Experimentism vs. experimentalism. *Educational Theory, 55*(3), 307–321.

Ingelhart, R., & Baker, W. E. (2000). Modernization, cultural change, and the persistence of traditional values. *American Sociological Review, 65*, 19–51.

Joint Committee on Standards for Educational Evaluation. (1994). *The program evaluation standards* (2nd ed.). Newbury Park, CA: Sage.

Katz, S., Sutherland, S., & Earl, L. (2002). Developing an evaluation habit of mind. *The Canadian Journal of Program Evaluation, 17*(2), 103–119.

King, J. (2002). Building the evaluation capacity of a school district. In D. W. Compton, M. Baizerman, & S. H. Stockdill (Eds.), The art, craft and science of evaluation capacity building. *New Directions for Evaluation 93* (pp. 63–80). San Francisco, CA: Jossey-Bass.

King, J. A., Stevahn, L., Ghere, G., & Minnema, J. (2001). Toward a taxonomy of essential evaluation competencies. *American Journal of Evaluation, 22*, 229–247.

Kirkhart, K. (1995). Seeking multicultural validity: A postcard from the road. *Evaluation Practice, 16*, 1–12.

Krieger, J. (Ed.). (2006). *Globalization and state power: A reader*. New York: Pearson.

Lennie, J. (2005). An evaluation capacity-building process for sustainable community IT initiatives: Empowering and disempowering impacts. *Evaluation, 11*, 390–414.

Letiecq, B. L., & Bailey, S. J. (2004). Evaluating from the outside: Conducting cross-cultural evaluation research on an American Indian reservation. *Evaluation Review, 28*, 342–357.

Levin-Rozalis, M. (2000). Social representations as emerging from social structure: The case of the Ethiopian immigrants to Israel. *Papers on Social Representations, 9*, 1–22.

Levin-Rozalis, M., & Rosenstein, B. (2005). The changing role of the evaluator in the process of organizational learning. *The Canadian Journal of Program Evaluation, 20*(1), 81–104.

Love, A. J., & Russon, C. (2000). Building a worldwide evaluation community: Past, present, and future. *Evaluation and Program Planning, 23*(9), 449–459.

MacBeath, J. (2002). Scotland: Schools speaking for themselves. In D. Nevo (Ed.), *School-based evaluation: An international perspective* (Vol. 8, pp. 243–259). Amsterdam: Elsevier.

MacKay, K. (2002). The World Bank's ECB experience. In D. W. Compton, M. Baizerman, & S. H. Stockdill (Eds.), The art, craft, and science of evaluation capacity building. *New Directions for Evaluation 93* (pp. 81–100). San Francisco, CA: Jossey-Bass.

McDonald, B., Rogers, P., & Kefford, B. (2003). Teaching people to fish? Building the evaluation capability of public sector organizations. *Evaluation, 9*, 9–29.

McLoyd, V., & Randolph, S. (1985). Secular trends in the study of Afro-American children: A review of child development. In A. B. Smuts & J. W. Hagen (Eds.), History and research in child development. *Monographs of the Society for Research in Child Development, 50,* 4–5.

Mertens, D. M. (1997). *Research methods in education and psychology: Integrating diversity with quantitative and qualitative approaches.* Thousand Oaks, CA: Sage.

Mertens, M. D. (2001). Inclusivity and transformation: Evaluation in 2010. *American Journal of Evaluation, 22,* 367–374.

Mertens, M. D. (2007, January 18). *Making evaluation our own: Strengthening the foundations for Africa-rooted and Africa-led monitoring and evaluation. The African mosaic and global interactions: The multiple roles of, and approaches to monitoring and evaluation.* Paper presented at the AfrEA conference, Niamey, Niger, Africa.

Nevo, D. (1994). Combining internal and external evaluation: A case for school-based evaluation. *Studies in Educational Evaluation, 20,* 87–98.

Nevo, D. (Ed.). (2002). *School-based evaluation: An international perspective* (Vol. 8). Amsterdam: Elsevier.

Osterhammel, J., & Petersson, N. P. (2005). *Globalization: A short history.* Princeton: Princeton University Press.

Patton, M. Q. (1997). *Utilization-focused evaluation: A new century text* (3rd ed.). Thousand Oaks, CA: Sage.

Patton, M. Q. (2008). *Utilization-focused evaluation* (4th ed.). Thousand Oaks, CA: Sage.

Preskill, H., & Russ-Eft, D. (2005). *Building evaluation capacity: 72 activities for teaching and training.* Thousand Oaks, CA: Sage.

Preskill, H., & Torres, R.T. (1999). *Evaluation inquiry for learning in organizations.* Thousand Oaks, CA: Sage.

Ray, W. (2005). On being cybernetic. *Kibernetics, 34*(3), 360–364.

Rescher, N. (1978). *Peirce's philosophy of science.* South Bend, IN: University of Notre Dame Press.

Rosental, S. B. (1993). Peirce's ultimate logical interpretant and dynamical object: A pragmatic perspective. *Transactions of the Charles S. Peirce Society, 29,* 195–210.

Russon, C., & Patel, M. (1998). Evaluation capacity in eastern and southern Africa. *Evaluation News and Comments, 8*(1), 14–15.

Russon, C., & Patel, M. (2002). The African evaluation guidelines: 2002. A checklist to assist in planning evaluations, negotiating clear contracts, reviewing progress and ensuring adequate completion of an evaluation. *Evaluation and Program Planning, 25*(4), 481–492.

Sanders, J. (Ed.). (2003). Mainstreaming evaluation. *New Directions for Evaluation 99.* San Francisco, CA: Jossey-Bass.

Schwandt, T. (2001). Understanding dialogue as practice. *Evaluation, 7*(2), 228–237.

Simons, H. (2006). Ethics in evaluation. In I. Shaw, J. C. Greene, & M. Mark (Eds.), *The international handbook of evaluation* (pp. 243–265). London: Sage.

Stake, R. (1983). Program evaluation, particularly responsive evaluation. In G. F. Madaus, M. Scriven, & D. L. Stufflebeam (Eds.), *Evaluation models: Viewpoints on educational and human services evaluation* (pp. 287–310). Norwell, MA: Kluwer Nijhoff Publishing.

Stake, R. E. (1991). Retrospective on "The countenance of educational evaluation." In M. W. McLaughlin & D. C. Phillips (Eds.), *Evaluation and education: At quarter century, 19th yearbook of the National Society for the Study of Education* (pp. 67–88). Chicago: University of Chicago Press.

Stake, R. E. (2004). *Standards-based and responsive evaluation.* Thousand Oaks, CA: Sage Publications.

Stake, R. E. (2007). NAEP, report cards and education: A review essay. *Education Review, 10*(1), 1–23.

Stevahn, L., King, J. A., Ghere, G., & Minnema, J. (2005). Evaluator competencies in university-based training programs. *Canadian Journal of Program Evaluation, 20*(2), 101–123.

Stockdill, S. H., Baizerman, M., & Compton, D. (2002). Toward a definition of the ECB process: A conversation with the ECB literature. In D. Compton, M. Baizerman, & S. H. Stockdill (Eds.), The art, craft and science of evaluation capacity building. *New Directions in Evaluation 93* (pp. 7–25). San Francisco, CA: Jossey-Bass.

Sutherland, S. (2004). Creating a culture of data use for continuous improvement: A case study of an Edison Project School. *American Journal of Evaluation, 25,* 277–293.

Taut, S. (2007). Studying self-evaluation capacity building in a large international development organization. *American Journal of Evaluation, 28,* 45–59.

United Nations Evaluation Group. (2005). *Standards for evaluation in the UN System.* New York: Author. Available at http://www.uneval.org/

Valery, R., & Shakir, S. (2005). Evaluation capacity building and humanitarian organizations. *Journal of Multidisciplinary Evaluation, 3,* 78–112.

VonFoerster, H. (1974). *Cybernetics of cybernetics.* Urbana, IL: University of Illinois Press.

Watson, J. (Ed.). (1998). *Golden arches east: McDonald's in East Asia.* Stanford, CA: Stanford University Press.

Weil, S. (1995). It is futile to trust in man: Methodological difficulties in studying non-mainstream populations with reference to Ethiopian Jews in Israel. *Human Organization, 54*(1), 1–9.

Weiss, C. H. (1973). Where politics and evaluation research meet. *Evaluation, 1*(3), 37–45.

Weiss, C. H. (1991). Evaluation research in the political context: Sixteen years and four administrations later. In M. W. McLaughlin & D. C. Phillips (Eds.), *Evaluation and education: At quarter century* (pp. 211–231). Chicago, IL: University of Chicago Press.

Weiss, C. H. (1999). The interface between evaluation and public policy. *Evaluation, 5*(4), 468–486.

Wholey, J. S. (1983). *Evaluation and effective public management.* Boston: Little, Brown.

Wholey, J. S. (1994). Assessing the feasibility and likely usefulness of evaluation. In J. S. Wholey, H. P. Hatry, & K. E. Newcomer (Eds.), *Handbook of practical program evaluation* (pp. 15–39). San Francisco, CA: Jossey-Bass.

Williams, D. (2001). Issues and practices related to mainstreaming evaluation: Where do we flow from here? In J. Sanders (Ed.), Mainstreaming evaluation. *New Directions for Evaluation 99* (pp. 63–83). San Francisco, CA: Jossey-Bass.

World Bank. (1994). *Evaluation capacity development. Report of the task force* (mimeo). Washington, DC: Author.

Zorzi, R., Perrin, B., McGuire, M., Long, B., & Lee, L. (2002). Defining the benefits, outputs, and knowledge elements of program evaluation. *Canadian Journal of Program Evaluation, 17*(3), 143–150.

Appendix: ECB Resources (a Modest Collection)

National Evaluation Association and Society Websites

CES Canadian Evaluation Society—source-book of methods http://www.evaluationcanada.ca/

AEA American Evaluation Association has 66 items listed in ECB. http://www.eval.org/

UKES United Kingdom Evaluation Society http://www.evaluation.org.uk/Pub_library/Good_Practice.htm

AES Australasian Evaluation Society http://www.aes.asn.au/

AfrEA African Evaluation Association http://www.afrea.org/

Note: Many of the National and Regional websites cross reference other resources and websites mentioned here.

International Evaluation Organizations

IOCE International Organization for Cooperation in Evaluation http://ioce.net/

IDEAS International Development Evaluation Association http://www.ideas-int.org/

Development Organizations

Organization of Economic Co-operation and Development http://www.oecd.org/

DEReC is an online resource center managed by the DAC Network on Development Evaluation. Launched in November 2005, DEReC contains development evaluation reports and guidelines published by the Network and its 30 bilateral and multilateral members. DEReC is designed as a one-stop shop for use by Network members, NGOs, civil society and other development organizations, researchers, academics, and the wider evaluation community to find and access key evaluation publications and reports. Note that although the majority of reports are in English, some reports can be found in other languages (including French, Arabic, Spanish, and German) when they have been made available by the members concerned.

Kellogg Evaluation Handbook available free on the website http://www.wkkf.org/Pubs/Tools/Evaluation/Pub770.pdf

The World Bank Independent Evaluation Group has its own website devoted solely to

Evaluation Capacity Development http://www.worldbank.org/ieg/ecd/

UNESCO guidelines for Educational Evaluation revised in 2003 http://portal.unesco.org/education/en/file_download.php/ac8df4c6da9c7424b034909d733dfeb0A.+Evaluation+Guidelines.pdf

World Health Organization—Workshops in Evaluation in the Health professions since 1998 http://www.euro.who.int/ENHPS/evaluation/20020605_1

Inter-American Development Bank. The IDB is actively exploring and applying distance-education technologies in order to facilitate each phase of its project cycle (from project identification and preparation to project management, implementation, and evaluation) http://www.iadb.org/int/rtc/ecourses/index.htm

United Nations Development Programme http://www.undp.org/eo/about-eo.htm

USAID evaluation website http://evalweb.usaid.gov/

Government and University Websites

Centers for Disease Control and Prevention, Evaluative Working Group http://www.cdc.gov/eval/

The University of North Carolina at Greensboro http://www.serve.org/Evaluation/Capacity/EvalFramework/cape01.php

CAPE is a suite of resources, tools, and professional development activities designed to assist program and project leaders in collecting and analyzing data they can use in making decisions about the implementation of their projects. CAPE is grounded in the belief that if school systems and individual schools have the capacity to plan and implement good evaluations, they will get the most out of their projects—to the ultimate benefit of students.

The WWW Virtual Library: Evaluation is an online database of high-quality Internet resources related to social policy evaluation (for further information, see brief online introduction to evaluation). At present, the database points to hundreds of websites, and each one has been selected and described. The catalogue is browsable or searchable by subject area.

Evaluation Institutes

University of Glamorgan http://www.glam.ac.uk/hassschool/Evaluation/index.php

Empowerment Evaluation Institute–Stanford http://www.stanford.edu/~davidf/institute.html

Evaluation, Assessment, and Policy Connections (EvAP) is a unit within the School of Education at the University of North Carolina at Chapel Hill. EvAP's mission is to build evaluation capacity and effectiveness of public, nonprofit, and private organizations to meet the challenges of developing and sustaining successful programs http://www.unc.edu/depts/ed/evap/about.html

Michigan State University http://www.carrs.msu.edu/summereval/

Supreme Education Council in Qatar http://www.english.education.gov.qa/section/sec/evaluation_institute/

CeDRE Malaysia is the leading evaluation development and research center in Malaysia. Originally established in 1996, it was restructured and incorporated as CeDRE Malaysia in 2004 http://www.cedre.org.my/

IPDET International Program for Development Evaluation Training. Operated by the World Bank and Carleton University, Ottawa, Canada http://www.ipdet.ca

United Nations Evaluation Group (UNEG): Standards for Evaluation in the UN System, April 29, 2005 http://www.fao.org/pbe/pbee/common/ecg/234/en/ACF61D4.doc

CHAPTER 12

International Assessments and Indicators

How Will Assessments and Performance Indicators Improve Educational Policies and Practices in a Globalized Society?

Claudia V. Tamassia and Raymond J. Adams

The prominent use of comparative data in educational decision making around the globe can be viewed as both reassuring and alarming—reassuring because technological and methodological advances have made it possible to use previously unobtainable comparative data to support decision making, yet alarming because of the often narrow focus of comparative data and the consequential risk of misinterpretation. Comparative data are now used to support debate and reform in education, and linkages are made to the fields of economy, finance, and labor markets at a level never before seen.

Today's fast-growing economies and technologically challenging labor markets require ever-increasing levels of basic communication and critical thinking skills (Sum, Kirsch, & Taggart, 2002). Cross-national programs provide comparative data that allow countries to assess the

extent to which they and others are meeting these challenges. The result is a frame of reference that assists countries in identifying their strengths and weaknesses, provides them with an opportunity for a better understanding of their own system, and offers ideas for further research and policy development. Perhaps most important, participation in international programs also increases awareness of the methods, strategies, and policies employed by other countries and education systems.

A priority of much of current education policy is the improvement of educational outcomes for all through higher investments and better professional development. Such policies often include requirements to monitor student performance using assessment programs that are sensitive enough to detect improvements over time (Ross et al., 2006). International programs serve as one class of tool for countries to verify whether these targets are being met.

There have been considerable developments in international programs and international comparative data use since the early 1990s. Both the number and range of participating countries have increased tremendously, along with the sophistication of the methodologies (Owen, Stephens, Moskowitz, & Gil, 2004). These programs are now mostly implemented in cooperation with national governments that identify priorities and inform policy debates, and their results are used extensively in examining and evaluating the effectiveness of, and debating the conditions of, education.

Chapter Overview

This chapter focuses on two types of cross-national data that are used for international benchmarking—indicators and assessments. Education indicators are comparable statistics about a particular aspect of the education system that rely on existing national databases. Under such programs, data are gathered from existing national sources and are then mapped onto internationally agreed and comparable reporting frameworks. In contrast, international assessments are data-collection activities undertaken to develop indicators that cannot be sourced from existing national databases, such as outcomes of education. They usually involve the collection of student achievement data according to agreed-on international protocols.

These two data types overlap in many aspects, as the current focus of international assessments is on the production of educational indicators of performance outcomes of education, which are later related to indicators from other areas. However, due to the unique methodologies surrounding these assessments, they are separately addressed. This chapter uses the terms *international programs* to refer to the data-collection programs and *international comparative data* when referring to the use of the outcomes from international programs or the

use of existing data. It also illustrates the context in which developments in this field have occurred and how the developments have been impacted by globalization.

The next section of this chapter outlines the importance of benchmarks in the new globalized society, where characteristics of human capital are now compared cross-nationally. In the following, the chapter presents indicators and assessment programs, including their methodological and technical aspects that impact the quality and usefulness in their data for policy and accountability. The chapter's final section focuses on the importance of comparative data to policy development and decision making, and how increased participation of governments has resulted in higher levels of acceptability and understanding of international results.

The Importance of International Benchmarks in a Globalized Society

The world has changed dramatically over the past few decades. Demographic and technological changes have had a widespread impact on developed societies (Kirsch, Braun, Yamamoto, & Sum, 2007; Organisation for Economic Co-operation and Development, 2001; Organisation for Economic Co-operation and Development and Statistics Canada 2000; Sum, Kirsch, & Taggart, 2002). Labor market research has linked lack of skills with higher levels of unemployment, which forces societies to prioritize higher quality educational standards and outcomes (Organisation for Economic Co-operation and Development and Statistics Canada, 2000). As a consequence, it has become widely recognized that education systems need to emphasize new, more complex skills to meet the demands of technological labor markets and compete globally. Human capital sharpened through education and training has been considered an important resource for economic and social development for both individuals and countries (Murray, 2004; Organisation for

Economic Co-operation and Development, 2001, 2002; Sum et al., 2002). A further consequence is an increased interest in international comparisons—countries are seeking comparative data because they believe that an economy's health is, in part, determined by the capacity of its citizens to compete in a global environment by virtue of their educational attainment level (Owen et al., 2004).

Globalization, when seen as an integration of economies and societal characteristics from around the world, exposes locally trained and educated workers to competition from foreign-skilled immigrants or foreign-trained and educated citizens. It reduces the distinction between foreign and national issues such as education.

Countries and education systems are more frequently looking outside for input on appropriate education content specifications, standards, and implementation policies. These international comparisons lead "to the development of much more ambitious and appropriate standards for student learning" (Rowan, 2002, p. 324). Without a doubt, our societies face internationalization of learning, with international activities playing integral parts in this shift.

International assessment and indicator programs offer a variety of attractive benefits for participating countries. First, these programs help countries to assess how well their own education systems perform in comparison to others and, as such, are increasingly being built into national educational policy reform as an accountability component. Second, participation in international studies increases global awareness about education and motivates researchers to examine national issues from alternative perspectives. Third, international studies offer opportunities to examine the impact on educational outcomes of system-level characteristics that cannot often be examined within a national context (because they do not vary), such as starting age, instructional hours, grade-retention practices, ability grouping, and school tracking structures—uniform variables within systems (Owen et al., 2004). Fourth, international assessments are being used to

provide a natural complement to in-depth, system-level analyses by systematically examining educational outcomes, practices, and relationships across educational settings (Adams, 2003). Finally, international programs support capacity building that will consequently improve the quantity and quality of national research.

The understanding about education in a country can be enriched when national results are interpreted within a larger and international context and countries can identify strengths and weaknesses of an education system. This is known as *benchmarking*. Hence, it is clear that international programs for benchmarking are challenging activities that require sophisticated and appropriate methodologies to ensure valid and accurate outcomes because the development of high-quality indicators is dependent on the nature of the data that are being collected. Data from existing national databases, for example, can rarely be used cross-nationally because of differences in the content specifications, assessment methodologies, and performance expectations. Recognizing these deficiencies and developing methodologies that are comparable across countries and valid in the research community requires a concerted effort.

Globalization has also changed the way international data are collected and analyzed. More important, the growing recognition of the importance of international indicators has led to key international organizations playing a leading role in managing international data collections. The International Association for the Evaluation of Educational Achievement (IEA), the Organisation for Economic Co-operation and Development (OECD), and the United Nations Educational, Scientific, and Cultural Organization (UNESCO) have each harnessed the expertise of companies and individuals worldwide to cooperatively develop and implement state-of-the-art methodologies that enhance the comparability and validity of the collected data.

When the international study paradigm was first introduced by IEA, the methodology was clearly research-oriented, with countries participating through independent research centers or universities. More recently, however, the involvement of intergovernmental organizations such as OECD and UNESCO has shifted this paradigm so that the focus of the studies is on gathering data for accountability purposes and to support educational policy development. Although some may bemoan this change in paradigm, the involvement of national governments has had clear benefits for these studies. Most important, the quality of international studies has been enhanced because the involvement of intergovernmental agencies has ensured continuity of implementation and adequacy of funding. Although improvements are still possible, Porter and Gamoran (2002) have positively reviewed recent assessment surveys such as PISA and TIMSS (which are overseen by the IEA and OECD, respectively). These have exhibited high levels of methodological quality, allowing for higher confidence in their results. They have also improved assessment frameworks, offered greater breadth of coverage and common scales, improved country reviews of item pools, and implemented better translation procedures. Together, these characteristics "justify confidence in statistical inferences."

International Indicators

Indicators have been narrowly viewed as "any statistic that casts light on the conditions and performance of schools" (Lashway, 2001). However, in their broadest sense, indicators are in fact "derived measures, often combining multiple data sources and several 'statistics' that are uniformly developed across nations, are repeated regularly over time, and have come to be accepted as summarizing the condition of an underlying complex process" (Smith & Baker, 2001, p.141). Not all statistics are indicators, and according to Shavelson, McDonnell, and Oakes (1991), statistics only qualify as indicators when "they serve as yardsticks." Further, according to Kanaev and Tuijnman (2001), the development and eventual use of indicators is "oriented towards informing

and facilitating the decision-making process on the basis of benchmarks and performance criteria for the education system" (p. 3).

Indicator systems go beyond a collection of information on specific discrete components; these systems provide a more comprehensive picture of how the parts are interrelated (Shavelson et al., 1991) and "allow governments to give concrete results to a sometimes skeptical public" (Plank & Hodgkinson, 2004, p. 121). Thus, indicators represent an integral part of accountability systems as they offer "unambiguous, timely and above all policy-sensitive information on the functioning of education systems" (Bottani & Tuijnman, 1994, p. 22). These systems are attractive to statisticians and academics, as well as to policymakers and the public in general. Indicator systems are likely to provide a wide range of information, raise awareness and commitment, and support school improvement, particularly when accompanied by incentives. Therefore, although quantitative in nature, indicators should be accompanied by qualitative, added value, and policy aspects; consequently, they should always be reported as part of a broader indicator system so as to link individual parts into a meaningful context (Kanaev & Tuijnman, 2001).

Similar to indicators in economics, environment, and health, education indicators are now integral components of accountability systems, education politics, and strategic mobilization. These many possible uses call for a cautionary note: Indicators can be misused in a number of ways. For example, their dissemination as raw numbers without appropriate contextualization can easily lead to overinterpretation or naive interpretation. Further, there is a danger of collecting and reporting data indiscriminately; this costs effort and money, and it swamps decision makers with a sea of numbers, making it difficult to distinguish the significant from the trivial (Lashway, 2001). Indicators alone cannot set goals and priorities for the education system or evaluate education programs (Shavelson et al., 1991). Furthermore, the development of high-quality indicators is dependent on the nature of the data that are being collected.

Perhaps the biggest concern is that indicators alone do not convey the message that education is embedded within particular historical, social, cultural, and economic contexts. Prioritizing and relating indicators to current programs of work and ensuring that the interpretation of any set of indicators needs to take this contextual embedding into account are essential. The selection of indicators should be based on their purpose and their relationship with the education goals; their presentation and interpretation should recognize context to ensure that the numbers are meaningfully interpreted.

The OECD's annual series of Education at a Glance (EAG), first published in 1992, is now considered a central reference for comparative education indicators and has contributed to the methodological development and dissemination of data for OECD countries. In its beginning, EAG often published information from other data sources (i.e., IEA), but presented them "within a policy context and used an indicator approach to present the results"—an approach that extended accessibility of indicators beyond researchers to a wider and more diverse audience (Owen et al., 2004, p. 9).

Of equal importance, the UNESCO Institute for Statistics (UIS), working jointly with the OECD, has expanded this work to non-OECD countries through its World Education Indicator (WEI) Project. This program focuses on aspects such as governance, teachers, and financial investments in education, counting on the participation of 19 countries and financial support from the World Bank.[1] The World Bank also compiles education data, compares them with data collected by UIS and the OECD, and offers them in various formats including the country profiles that are called Country at a Glance.[2]

Data for contextual indicators (contrasted with indicators of outcome) are mostly collected by national systems, following preestablished criteria for quality and comparability, which are then forwarded to the organizations responsible for coordinating them. The development methodology is widely discussed and well documented in each publication. An embedded limitation of this type of indicator system is that the institution coordinating this work cannot guarantee the primary data collection—although they do oversee and coordinate the process of creating the indicators. However, the intensive cooperation that these institutions have developed with participating countries and their national staff has important side benefits (such as national capacity building and cross-fertilization of approaches) that is likely to improve the quality of national data collections.

In contrast, data for international surveys follow different procedures, with a higher control through the data collection. The approach taken to develop outcome indicators through international surveys is discussed in the next section.

International Surveys of Educational Achievement

Cross-national programs of educational achievement complement indicator systems that use existing national collections by providing data (usually outcome data) collected through highly controlled procedures. Such programs started with the IEA's First International Mathematics Study (FIMS) in the 1960s, which involved a single data collection, had a research orientation, and was sufficiently successful to represent a new paradigm of international assessments that produced outcome data permitting useful cross-national comparisons.

Methodological and technical challenges are embedded in every aspect of the design and implementation of international surveys, particularly when their results carry a strong political and accountability emphasis. This section provides a design overview related to the content and scope of the instrumentation, the target population, and the analysis methodologies of these surveys.

Content and Scope: What to Assess

What to assess has been a key factor in international surveys. Characteristics such as content domain, type of skills, and scope are the main areas of concern. The need to assess new and more complex skills has created wider networks within the research community to continuously improve conceptual frameworks and develop innovative methodologies (Owen et al., 2004). An example of such an attempt is the Definition and Selection of Competencies (DeSeCo) Project,[3] which aimed to improve the theoretical basis of key competencies that individuals need for successful participation in society. In its definition, a *competency* involves "the ability to meet complex demands, by drawing on and mobilizing psychosocial resources (including skills and attitudes) in a particular context" (Organisation for Economic Co-operation and Development and Definition and Selection of Competencies, 2005, p. 4).

Although the assessment of traditional domains predominates, more recent programs have also examined civics and citizenship, information and communication technology (ICT), written composition, and problem solving.[4] The process of achieving consensus about the specifics of what to assess remains perhaps the most contentious component of international programs.

A second issue is to identify and specify the range of content (or specific skills) that are to be assessed. One approach is to examine school subjects through a survey of the curriculum content intentions of all participating countries and then build an assessment that covers the key elements of the participants' curricula, an approach typically taken in IEA programs such as TIMSS. In this case it is possible to examine the "intersection" of national curricula or the "union" of the national curricula, a more comprehensive approach (Linn, 2002; Porter & Gamoran, 2002; Rowan, 2002). Linn actually states that most of the current surveys examine aspects of both approaches. Independent of the chosen direction, this issue may still lead to further speculation about fairness within what is referred to as an opportunity-to-learn perspective. Linn (2002) stated that "for individual countries the fairness of the assessment necessarily varies as a function of the degree of correspondence between each country's curriculum and the

content boundaries and the relative emphasis given to covered topics of the assessment" (p. 30) and later specifies that the TIMSS curriculum programs "revealed considerable between-country variation in topic coverage and relative emphasis" (p. 39). Independent of the selected approach, the chosen path may still be used by some as a justification for low performance.

An alternative approach involves using expert panels and consultations with participating countries to identify key knowledge and skill requirements that are necessary for individuals to successfully negotiate their daily lives. In the PISA context, this is referred to as a literacy perspective (Organisation for Economic Co-operation and Development, 2002). Rather than ensuring coverage of an agreed interesting curriculum, the focus is on the extent to which students can use the knowledge and skills they have learned and practiced at school when confronted with situations and challenges for which that knowledge may be relevant.

Population: Whom to Assess

The population of interest is determined by the purpose of the survey and the expected level of policy decisions. When school-age populations are targeted, one of two approaches is usually taken to ensure alignment of the populations across the participants.

The first approach—grade-based populations—aligns the target populations by matching (or attempting to match) grade levels across school systems and countries. That is, the target population in each country is given as grade x, where x varies across countries and is chosen so that the average number of years of schooling for students in each country's target grade (x) is approximately equal. When grade-based population definitions are used, it is also common to use classrooms as the primary sampling unit—that is, all students in an intact classroom are sampled and tested from schools that have in turn been randomly selected. Grade-based populations (particularly when implemented with classroom bases as primary sampling units) have advantages when there is a particular interest in examining the influence of classroom characteristics, teacher characteristics, and instructional practices. One consequence of this approach is a potentially large variability across countries in the average of the sampled students. This variation occurs because of differences in the starting school age, retention policies, and, in some cases, the legal age for leaving school.

The second approach—age-based populations—aligns the target populations in terms of the age of the assessed students at the time of the test. That is, the target population in each country is all students (in school) of age x, where x is typically a 12-month interval. When age-based population definitions are used, it is not usually possible to sample intact classes because the students in the target population will be spread across a number of grades, and/or any single class will likely include students who do not satisfy the population definition. Because they sample from a number of classes and perhaps grade levels, age-based populations are not appropriate for examining issues such as the influence of classroom characteristics, teacher characteristics, and instructional practices. Age-based samples are optimized in terms of age comparability. They are suitable for comparisons of educational systems in terms of yield of educational experiences (i.e., the cumulative effect) and in evaluating "the 'pay-off' of educational systems" (Murat & Rocher, 2004, p. 192).

Both grade- and age-based samplings have been widely used. IEA studies have typically been grade-based. For example, the PIRLS target population is children enrolled in the upper of the two adjacent grades, with the largest proportion of 9-year-olds at the time of testing. The TIMSS target populations are students in their fourth and eighth years of schooling.[5] PISA, in contrast, uses an age-based population definition—namely, 15-year-old students attending educational institutions irrespective of the grade attended; this definition was later refined to include 15-year-old students in Grade 7 or above (Organisation for Economic Co-operation and Development, 2005a).

In the case of non-school-based programs, the population definition is far broader. The International Adult Literacy Study (IALS), the Adult Literacy and Lifeskills (Study) (ALL), and the new OECD Programme for the International Assessment of Adult Competencies (PIAAC) have target populations of household adults between ages 16 and 65 and provide a profile of literacy skills (Murray, 2004).

Cross-Sectional Versus Longitudinal Programs

To date, international assessment programs have typically been cross-sectional (i.e., they have involved a single data collection based on a sample from the target population). It is generally recognized that a longitudinal approach will be more powerful if the focus of the study is on determining instructional and pedagogical correlates of student outcomes, such as influence of educational environment on student performance (Ross et al., 2006). A cross-sectional study offers only a snapshot of current instructional and pedagogical variables to correlate with outcome variables that are the result of student's full school career.

One longitudinal study was the Second International Mathematics Study (SIMS; Robitaille & Garden, 1989), which included a longitudinal component designed to investigate causal relationships between the output and input measures of mathematics education.[6] Although, somewhat disappointingly, truly longitudinal programs have not yet been implemented, both TIMSS and PISA have been able to conduct a series of programs that are cross-sectional programs yet repeat the same target population. Such programs permit the analysis of trends in outcomes and relationship with contextual variables over time. For example, to examine the transition between educational training and work, Canada is implementing the Youth in Transition Survey with a cohort of 15-year-olds from PISA 2000 to gather information on their school experiences, achievements, aspirations and expectations, and initial employment experiences. Australia implements a similar survey linked to PISA 2003, referred to as the Longitudinal Survey of Australian Youth.[7]

Methodologies: How to Assess

How to assess represents an area surrounded by methodological challenges, but also one where many recent developments have occurred. The complex design and implementation procedures of international programs often lead researchers to misunderstand or underestimate their complexities. This is due in part to the need to account for the social and cultural characteristics of participating countries, the functioning of their educational system, and their levels of physical and human resources.

A combination of the content to be assessed and budgetary constraints determines how instruments will be delivered. Paper-and-pencil instruments using traditional item types have dominated existing programs for both cognitive and contextual instruments, but demands of authenticity and validity have forced more recent programs to examine new item types and modes of administration that involve computers. This shift has added complexities to test development, scoring, and scaling procedures, and it has resulted in a need for cross-national verification of the marking outcomes (Adams, Wu, & Macaskill, 1997; Martin, Mullis, & Chrostowski, 2004; Organisation for Economic Co-operation and Development, 2005b).

The potential advantages of the use of computer-based testing in international programs are both operational and conceptual. Operationally, the use of computers brings cost savings in test production (printing and distribution), data entry, and scoring (at least for many common item types), and it increases the efficiency of the measurement. Conceptually, the use of computers increases the range of item types. Lennon, Kirsch, Davier, Wagner, and Yamamoto (2003) argue that changes in information and communication technologies represent important reasons for adding computers in general assessments. The

"nature and value of knowledge and information" has changed. This is the primary motivation behind the Electronic Reading Assessment (ERA) in PISA 2009 and problem solving in technology-rich environments in PIAAC in 2011.

International assessments are designed to focus on population modeling rather than individual inferences. Item response theory (IRT) improved the measurement capabilities of these programs by allowing sophisticated matrix sampling procedures to optimize their coverage of domains while minimizing the response burden at the student level (Childs & Jaciw, 2003). In this method, booklets are organized using common sets of items that serve as a linking device between booklets and allow results to be reported on a single scale, even when students answered to a different set of items.

Finally, in addition to changes to the cognitive instruments, contextual questionnaires now complement the assessments to meet the demands of researchers and policymakers. These questionnaires represent tools that collect information about the socioeconomic backgrounds of students; teacher qualification, teaching styles, experiences, and pedagogy of teachers; learning environments; and human and financial resources of schools. Contextual information permits the examination of cross-country differences in the relationship between achievement and student- or school-level factors. These variables are also useful for describing the population of students participating in the survey, evaluating potential bias associated with nonparticipation, examining opportunity-to-learn issues, and examining the distribution of educational and physical resources among different groups of students and how these impact individual-level variables (Floden, 2002; Harvey-Beavis, 2002; Mullis, 2002). Countries' interests differ, and assessment programs have allowed for a variety of innovations classified under international or national options. For example, PISA has provided countries with options such as self-regulated learning, problem solving, or computer familiarity that are comparable at the international level. National options are allowed, on previous agreement, and are targeted to address national interests. For example, Australia added an extra booklet in PISA 2000 to compare the results of PISA with those of TIMSS (Lokan, Greenwood, & Cresswell, 2001); both Australia and Canada (as mentioned earlier) have added longitudinal components to PISA; Germany has regularly supplemented PISA with assessments of problem solving and expanded samples to allow within regions comparisons; and a number of countries assess additional samples at higher levels to examine growth between cohorts of students.

Issues of Comparability, Fairness, and Bias

Among other challenges, survey designs strive to control errors—both random and systemic (i.e., bias)—to permit valid and accurate comparisons across education systems (Chromy, 2002). A major source of both random error and bias rests in sampling. Good sampling techniques result in final samples that accurately represent the population from which they were drawn and, consequently, generate results that permit valid inferences. Much development has occurred in sampling procedures: detailed sampling information and manuals to guide countries through the many steps of this process; standards that ensure quality in issues of coverage, response rates of students, and participation of the school; and the dissemination of sampling results and outcomes in the main reports as validity evidence.

In addition to sampling errors introduced through variations in the programs' implementation, another key source of potential bias and error is the item development and selection processes, including translation and national adaptations. An assumption is that "translation of an item does not change its nature" (Murat & Rocher, 2004, p. 193). But it is clear that some characteristics can facilitate understanding—such as word repetition, use of synonyms, or length of translated texts—and need to be carefully controlled.

International surveys by their nature deal with enormous historical, cultural, linguistic, and economic diversity. Building tests that are seen to fairly and equivalently assess educational outcomes that are valued by all participants is particularly challenging. This challenge is growing with the increasing popularity of international programs. In 1964, the first IEA study involved 12 countries, with a need to adapt instruments for use in eight languages. More recently, PISA 2006 and TIMSS 2007 involved approximately 60 countries and about 40 different languages. In such an enterprise, the need to ensure comparability of the test material across all test administrations is no small matter. The term *test translation* embraces "all activities from deciding whether or not a test could measure the same construct in a different language and culture, to selecting translators, to deciding on appropriate accommodations to be made in preparing a test for use in a second language, to adapting the test and checking its equivalence in the adapted form" (Hambleton Merenda, & Spielberger, 2005, p. 4).

Test adaptation deals with broader issues such as the impact of differences in text length among languages, item formats, directions, and verb tenses. Consequently, this definition encompasses both changes in the instrument because of regional differences (as in the case of instrument differences between the various English-speaking countries) as well as differences between languages. International surveys must ensure equivalent constructs across languages—the competence and difficulty of the item should remain the same whatever the language. Poor adaptation may lead to errors that may change the difficulty of the test, change the meaning of the results, or invalidate the results.

The methodology for translation and adaptation of instruments has evolved substantially over the decades, but the overall purpose of obtaining instruments that are equivalent in multiple languages remains (Hambleton, 2002). The traditional method of back translation for linguistic equivalence has been replaced by newer models that include the involvement of well-trained multiple translators, multiple source languages, international verification of the national versions, and better statistical methods. The first step of achieving cross-national equivalence lies in ensuring that the test materials are appropriate for use across such culturally diverse settings, and that the different versions used in those different settings are equivalent.

Bias plays a role in surveys and assessment, whether from external factors or unwanted sources of variation that does not equally exist across countries (Hambleton et al., 2005). That is, bias is caused by the presence of any characteristic that puts one group at a disadvantage as a result of irrelevant cultural differences (Murat & Rocher, 2004). This characteristic is often associated with the application of the instrument to a certain population of examinees, rather than a characteristic of the instrument. The awareness of bias and the implementation of procedures that identify and control it represent important improvements in survey development. These procedures are now continuously integrated into the test development process and include national judgments, cultural reviews, focus groups, think-aloud protocols, field testing, stricter translation guidelines, and detailed item analyses that take account of differential item functioning (DIF). Even with these procedures in place, the responsibility for test developers lies in distinguishing differences in performance that are due to cultural differences, or bias, from true differences in the domain being assessed.

Nevertheless, public attention still focuses on specific characteristics of single items to conclude that one country or one group of examinees is at a disadvantage. This is an inappropriate approach as programs have invested resources into the elimination of bias at the test level, rather than at the item level, hoping to keep students more interested and motivated by embedding topics of their interest into the items. As a result, although one item may be easier to a first group of examinees, such as females, another item may be easier to a second group, such as males.

The combination of stricter adaptation procedures and studies of equivalence are still fundamental to test development and data interpretation. These represent prerequisites for valid and interpretable results that allow results to meet the needs of decision makers. When these processes are not properly addressed and transparent, they will incorrectly become common justification for low performance.

Despite developments and progress, international assessment programs are not without their limitations and dangers. First, a key concern is that their instruments can only measure a narrow subset of what is valued by educational systems; as such, they can become narrowing devices that value that which can be validly and economically assessed. Second, on many occasions, more attention has been given to league tables or ranking charts of achievement than they deserve, and such tables can be easily misinterpreted by the public and may underestimate the true value of these surveys in terms of their capacity to provide contextual information and offer a complete picture of the overall condition of education. Finally, the complex results and relationships that underlie the data gathered in such programs are often reduced to isolated cause-and-effect statements, resulting in potentially misleading interpretations that do not reflect the true complexities of the relationships that exist. Therefore, meaningful inferences need to consider important social, cultural, and economical differences among participants.

The Role of Comparative Data in Policy Development and Decision Making

The movement toward education indicators and assessments started several decades ago, but only became hot items on political and policy development agendas when organizations incorporated national governments and experts into their design and development processes (Smith & Baker, 2001). International organizations draw on the skills of experts to improve data collections, increase validity, and produce results that are more accurate and more representative of the national situation.

The growing involvement of international experts in international programs has given policymakers confidence in the dependability of their outcomes; policymakers are relying on, and accepting, the outcomes of international programs more so than they do national data. In essence, international data are often seen as more authoritative than national data (Porter & Gamoran, 2002). This high acceptance is due, in part, to higher quality resulting from the involvement of governmental organizations and international experts that enforce strict quality-assurance procedures through the most sound and modern methodologies.

Countries now feel that isolated data no longer meet all of their requirements for accountability in the globalized society. Consequently, more recent programs include multiple data collections that allow countries to monitor their systems through continuous cycles. This requires long-term commitments—a difficult task with constantly changing governments—with loss of benefits when this commitment is discontinued. Additionally, recent surveys have implemented procedures that allow countries to withdraw data only for technical reasons and before the results are known. This technique avoids national judgments on whether the results are worth disseminating or whether they meet the political agenda during the dissemination period.

As a consequence, governments are also assuming a stronger role in disseminating international data. Countries participating in PISA, for example, participated in the development of the dissemination strategy of results and were also part of the dissemination process. Governments of participating countries were constantly informed of the content materials to be published and had opportunities to express concerns or disagreements with language or technical aspects. Many countries released national reports in the local language at the same time as the international release, either with translated sections from the international report or with specific nationally relevant analyses. These materials emphasize the national results, but also contextualize the international

results within national educational agendas. Finally, workshops for data analysis and interpretation ensure that national data are accurately analyzed and comparable with the international analyses while offering capacity building for national experts.

The increased participation of countries in developing and disseminating results has also impacted the level of awareness given to these results in both extremes. At one extreme, PISA 2000 results created a media frenzy in some countries that continues with each new set of results. For example, the PISA 2000 results showed German students performing below the OECD average in all domains, a larger proportion of low-performing students, the strongest impact of socioeconomic background on education performances among OECD countries, and a large gap in performance between native and non-native students (Fertig, 2003; Organisation for Economic Co-operation and Development, 2001; Sroka, 2006). These German results, what researchers and the media referred to as the "PISA Shock," resulted in policy recommendations to include early childhood education, greater autonomy, longer school days, and more support for schools, teachers, and students (Bulmahn, 2002; Sroka, 2006).

At the other extreme, countries that achieved superior results, such as Finland, are constantly questioned about their current practices and recipe to success. A trend in educational tourism has emerged, where educators from other countries visit them and their schools, hoping to identify strengths and successful practices that could be replicated in other countries. As a result, the Finnish Board of Education website even includes a page called "Background for Finnish PISA Success,"[8] which highlights possible explanations for its success.

Countries have expanded the role of international programs to examine intracountry comparisons and develop indicators at lower levels, such as states or provinces. Without these, national data are useful, but limited for policy development. Canada, Australia, and Germany have implemented this in PISA through oversampling at the unit level (i.e., provinces, states, and territories), which generated information at lower levels. This allowed researchers to compare their national data with one another, as well as with other countries. In these cases, in addition to examining the international results, their reports included a strong national component, making it more appealing to policymakers as well as to other local target groups.[9]

The dissemination of international results is now a major event in the media worldwide. A constant problem is that the media tend to simplify complex relationships by focusing on ranking order, thus ignoring any level of uncertainty that exists around the measures of central tendency, most commonly the mean. The academic reporting language that until recently dominated the style of dissemination products has now been modified to more appealing and friendly styles. It is inevitable that these reports will mention failures and limitations for low-performing countries. But whenever possible, they should also mention improvements, reforms, and other forms of national achievements that consider the economic and social situation of these countries—a balance of positive and negative findings. Therefore, reporting should be done in a sensitive and friendly way because any result will have a strong political impact within countries (Ross et al., 2006).

International programs have resulted in regional partnerships across the globe in two different ways. First, the WEI represents an example where methodologies that were initially developed for OECD member countries were later expanded and adapted to developing countries. The UIS has also cooperated with the OECD in releasing results from PISA 2000 for non-OECD countries (in the publication *Literacy Skills for the World of Tomorrow: Further Results from PISA 2000* [Organisation for Economic Co-operation and Development and United Nations Educational, Scientific and Cultural Organization–Institute for Statistics, 2003]), as well as funding regional activities for data analysis (i.e., data analysis workshops in

Latin American countries). Second, regional partnerships have also resulted in new programs, focusing on capacity building and cooperation among countries, as in the cases of the Southern Africa Consortium for Monitoring Education Quality (SACMEQ) and the Second International Comparative Study (SERCE).

SACMEQ is a voluntary and collaborative network of 15 Ministries of Education from Eastern and Southern Africa, launched in 1995, with assistance from the UNESCO International Institute of Educational Planning (IIEP).[10] It is intended to improve the quality of education through collaborative work in policy analysis and specialized training programs. Unlike the OECD and IEA, which have a central implementation center for their programs, SACMEQ's unique characteristics include capacity building and training in the field of educational assessment and consensus building among participating ministries. Consequently, programs are implemented using the approach learning-by-doing, where participating countries exercise more control over the implementation of the assessment activities.

The First and the Second International Comparative Studies in Latin America represent further examples of regional partnerships. These studies were implemented by the Latin American Laboratory for Assessment of the Quality of Education (LLECE) and are coordinated by the UNESCO Regional Office of Education in Chile. They emphasize assessment of the quality and equity of education systems, as well as examination of the associated factors that influence performance.

Participation in international programs involves strong commitments in terms of human, material, and financial resources. The benefits from such programs should justify the investments by targeting the appropriate audience in terms of the questions asked and results produced. Target audiences have traditionally included personnel within ministries of education and academia (universities and colleges, research and educational organizations). However, ministers of education have considered this to be a narrow focus and have recommended the involvement of the groups that also play a role in accepting and implementing policy reforms. This wider involvement should include "people from the media, religious organizations, the private sector, non-governmental organizations, parliaments, teachers' unions, parent groups, and schools" (Ross et al., 2006, p. 303). It is worth recognizing that recent programs have emphasized communication to a wider audience by producing various types of reports (some more technical and others more policy oriented), as well as involving representatives from these groups in their technical meetings and symposiums. A known fact is that complex methodologies still remain a barrier in making these results known by and accessible to all.

Concluding Remarks

International data can impact educational policy and research and are vital in political agendas of countries. According to Plank and Hodgkinson (2004), the benefits of international cooperation include "system monitoring, assessment anchoring, international placement of system effectiveness, international agreement on competence standards and on benchmarking, assessment measurement expansion into more complex domains and encouragement of its scientific community for measurement-driven research in education" (p. 115).

International assessments and indicators are not designed to provide decisive answers to complex questions. Nevertheless, they are used generally to identify issues for discussion about the desirable future directions of policies and further research, particularly at the national level. Relationships that are found between variables at the international level do not always hold at the national level and vice versa. It is also possible to identify trends within a particular group of countries with similar cultural, social, and economic characteristics.

Rather than producing clear-cut answers to complex questions, international data provide

policymakers, researchers, educational communities, and the general public with a broader understanding of how educational input, process, and outcome variables are interrelated. Plank and Hodgkinson (2004) further state that "the value of indicators lies not only in the data and in their direct use in the policy context, but in their role as a source of information about possible approaches to education, as a stimulus to begin questioning and as an opportunity to look at one's own education system with fresh eyes" (p. 121).

Therefore, indicators allow users to better appreciate the strengths and scope for improvement in their own systems, connect the international results with information collected at the regional and national levels, and, eventually, identify areas for further research. These accomplishments require the continuous involvement of actors at all levels of the system—from pupils and teachers to researchers and policymakers—emphasizing the need for constant communication among actors at different levels.

The reliance on international indicators has become commonplace in educational politics and in benchmarking. Countries can identify themselves through economic or regional partnerships. An example of the former approach is the publication *Comparative Indicators of Education in the United States and Other G-8 Countries: 2006* by the U.S. Department of Education (Miller, Sen, & Malloy, 2007) that focuses on five areas. An example of the second approach includes the Regional Education Indicators Project (Spanish acronym of PRIE), an education program to develop comparable social indicators in the Americas implemented in cooperation with the UNESCO Institute for Statistics. Participation in international programs has increased dramatically. The OECD EAG 2004 includes educational indicators for 45 countries. The UNESCO Global Education Digest 2006 includes indicators for more than 200 countries. Participation in international assessment has increased from 12 countries in the IEA First Mathematics Study in 1964 to around 60 countries in each of PISA 2006 and TIMSS 2007.

It is clear that international indicators will continue to play a role in political agendas in part due to developments in validity, reliability, and comparability. The future of these programs is not without challenges. They must evolve with society to include innovative ways to assess traditional domains, identify skills for future relevant age groups, and (most important) address the impact of ICT. This latter topic impacts indicators in two directions: as an innovative content that can be assessed independently or across domains (see Lennon et al., 2003), as well as a process when it refers to the use of technology in the delivery of assessments.

Adaptive testing is yet another broad concept that could become relevant in the future. At the individual level, it would bring benefits in terms of time and efficiency of measurement, as students would most likely answer items around their own levels of ability. At the country (or groups of countries) level, adaptive testing would better target the average ability of countries by improving differentiation between the low and the high performers within countries because "if a very easy test is put to a very able group of people, all the individuals will succeed and they will be all seen as very capable" (Murat & Rocher, 2004, p. 204). This concept is being incorporated in an international assessment by OECD PIAAC in 2011. Hopefully, these new methodologies will add to the effectiveness of programs, the comparability of outcomes, and the identification of better ways to address bias and cultural differences within a wider range of participating countries.

Consequently, participation has expanded from policy-related decisions based on the purpose of the survey (i.e., what to assess and whom to assess) to a decision also based on who the other participants are—a question related to globalization and its impact on labor market and economic characteristics. The involvement of more countries increases variability—from levels of national resources to the structure of their education systems—thus impacting the content, purpose, and methodologies of the programs. Decisions about the type of instruments, from paper-and-pencil to computerized, and

from cognitive instruments to contextual questionnaires (i.e., students as well as teachers, administrators, and parents) impact the content of the survey, the level of inference, and also budgets. As a second step, these previous decisions will consequently influence the types of questions asked—from objective (i.e., multiple-choice types) to subjective (i.e., open-constructed response types) questions, with the latter impacting costs because of the need for stricter procedures to ensure comparability across countries. Finally, the breadth versus depth of the content impacts the design of the instruments, implementation procedures, methodology of analysis, and type of inferences.

The benefits of international assessments and indicators programs are clear, but such programs require a high level of human, material, and financial investment, particularly in developing countries. Policymakers are now required to weigh the costs and benefits of each program by understanding their characteristics, design, and potential outcomes. The large number of existing or planned programs organized by different organizations is forcing policymakers to evaluate the general characteristics of potential programs in terms of scope, methodology, cost, and interpretability of results. Additionally, recent programs require an active contribution to all phases of the program—a task that for some countries is demanding due to a lack of expertise and resources. The profile of decision makers varies, with some coming from a field other than education and unfamiliar with educational surveys or their methodological complexities. From the countries' points of view, organizations should increase transparency through accessible documentation, particularly concerning overall purposes, goals, methodologies, clear expectations, and detailed timelines. Therefore, these programs, through the organizations that implement them, should increase communication among themselves, as well as with countries and complement each other. This would lead to higher levels of coherence and greater benefits for participating countries. As the characteristics of high skills have changed with globalization, this would also allow countries to visualize themselves in this newly integrated society that is impacting our human capital, education systems, and labor markets.

Notes

1. According to the OECD and UIS, "the objectives of the WEI program are to: explore education indicator methodologies; reach consensus on a set of common policy concerns amenable to cross-national comparison and agree upon a set of key indicators that reflect these concerns; review methods and data collection instruments needed to develop these measures; and set the direction for further developmental work and analysis beyond this initial set of indicators" (United Nations Educational, Scientific and Cultural Organization–Institute for Statistics and Organisation for Economic Co-operation and Development 2005, p. 5).

2. This can be assessed electronically through the website http://web.worldbank.org/WBSITE/EXTER NAL/DATASTATISTICS/0,,contentMDK:20485916~ menuPK:1297819~pagePK:64133150~piPK:64133175~ theSitePK:239419,00.html.

3. This project was implemented by the OECD, the Swiss Federal Statistical Office, and the U.S. Department of Education through the National Center for Education Statistics.

4. For more information about these programs, see www.iea.nl for the Civic Education Study, the Second Information and Communication Technology Study, the Written Composition Study, and www.pisa.oecd.org for information about the PISA.

5. TIMSS 1995 also examined performance of students in the final year of secondary school.

6. The TIMSS study was also originally planned to be longitudinal, but this component was eventually dropped due to the associated costs and methodological difficulties. Similarly, an additional longitudinal component for PISA was proposed in 2001, but as with the TIMSS case, it was not implemented due largely to cost issues.

7. More information about YITS can be found at http://www.pisa.gc.ca/yits.shtml; for LSAY, see http://www.acer.edu.au/lsay/study.html.

8. http://www.oph.fi/english/SubPage.asp?path= 447;65535;77331.

9. Links to national reports and other publications and resources can be found at the following web addresses for PISA: http://mypisa.acer.edu.au; http://www.pisa.oecd.org/document/3/0,2340,en_32 252351_32236159_33680899_1_1_1_1,00.html; and http://www.pisa.oecd.org/document/62/0,2340,en_3 2252351_32236159_34575550_1_1_1_1,00.html.

10. See www.sacmeq.org for further information.

References

Adams, R. J. (2003). Response to "cautions of OECD's recent educational survey (PISA)." *Oxford Review of Education, 29*(3), 377–389.

Adams, R. J., Wu, M. L., & Macaskill, G. (1997). Scaling methodology and procedures for the mathematics and science scales. In M. O. Martin & D. L. Kelly (Eds.), *TIMSS technical report: Vol. II. Implementation and analysis* (pp. 111–145). Chestnut Hill, MA: Boston College Press.

Bottani, N., & Tuijnman, A. (1994). International education indicators: Framework, development and interpretation. In A. Tuijnman (Ed.), *Making education count: Developing and using international indicators* (pp. 21–35). Paris: Organisation for Economic Co-operation and Development.

Bulmahn, E. (2002). PISA: The consequences for Germany. *OECD Observer,* pp. 231–232.

Childs, R. A., & Jaciw, A. P. (2003). Matrix sampling of items in large-scale assessments. *Practical Assessment, Research & Evaluation, 8*(16). Retrieved February 18, 2009, from http://PAREonline.net/getvn.asp?v=8&n=16.

Chromy, J. R. (2002). Sampling issues in design, conduct, and interpretation of international comparative studies of school achievement. In A. C. Porter & A. Gamoran (Eds.), *Methodological advances in cross-national surveys of educational achievement* (pp. 80–114). Washington, DC: National Academy Press.

Fertig, M. (2003). *Who's to blame? The determinants of German students' achievement in the PISA 2000 study* (Discussion Paper Series IZA DP No. 739). Bonn, Germany: Institute for the Study of Labor.

Floden, R. E. (2002). The measurement of opportunity to learn. In A. C. Porter & A. Gamoran (Eds.), *Methodological advances in cross-national surveys of educational achievement* (pp. 231–266). Washington, DC: National Academy Press.

Hambleton, R. K. (2002). Adapting achievement tests into multiple languages for international assessments. In A. C. Porter & A. Gamoran (Eds.),

Methodological advances in cross-national surveys of educational achievement (pp. 58–79). Washington, DC: National Academy Press.

Hambleton, R. K., Merenda, P. F., & Spielberger, C. D. (Eds.). (2005). *Adapting educational and psychological tests for cross-cultural assessment.* Mahwah, NJ: Lawrence Erlbaum Associates.

Harvey-Beavis, A. (2002). Student and school questionnaire development. In R. J. Adams & M. Wu (Eds.), *PISA 2000 technical report* (pp. 33–56). Paris: OECD Publications.

Kanaev, A., & Tuijnman, A. (2001). *Prospects for selecting and using indicators for benchmarking Swedish higher education.* Stockholm: Institute of International Education, Stockholm University.

Kirsch, I., Braun, H., Yamamoto, K., & Sum, A. (2007). *America's perfect storm: Three forces changing our nation's future.* Princeton, NJ: Educational Testing Service.

Lashway, L. (2001). Educational indicators. In *Eric Digest* (Vol. 150). Eugene, OR: University of Oregon Press. Retrieved February 18, 2009, from http://eric.uoregon.edu/publications/digests/digest150.html.

Lennon, M., Kirsch, I., Davier, M. V., Wagner, M., & Yamamoto, K. (2003). *Feasibility study for the PISA ICT literacy assessment: Report to Network A.* Retrieved January 17, 2007, from http://www.pisa.oecd.org/dataoecd/35/13/33699866.pdf.

Linn, R. L. (2002). The measurement of student achievement in international studies. In A. C. Porter & A. Gamoran (Eds.), *Methodological advances in cross-national surveys of educational achievement* (pp. 27–57). Washington, DC: National Academy Press.

Lokan, J., Greenwood, L., & Cresswell, J. (2001). *15-up and counting, reading, writing, reasoning: How literate are Australian students? The PISA 2000 survey of students' reading, mathematical and scientific literacy skills.* Melbourne: Australian Council for Educational Research.

Martin, M. O., Mullis, I. V. S., & Chrostowski, S. J. (2004). *TIMSS 2002 technical report.* Chestnut Hill, MA: TIMSS & PIRLS International Study Center, Lynch School of Education, Boston College Press.

Miller, D. C., Sen, A., & Malley, L. B. (2007). *Comparative indicators of education in the United States and other G-8 countries: 2006* (NCES 2007-006). Washington, DC: National Center for Education Statistics, Institute of Education Sciences, U.S. Department of Education.

Mullis, I. V. S. (2002, January). *Background questions in TIMSS and PIRLS: An overview.* Paper commissioned by the National Assessment Governing Board. Available at http://www.nagb.org/publications/Mullis.doc.

Murat, F., & Rocher, T. (2004). The methods used for international assessments of educational competences (J. Tarsch, Trans.). In J. H. Moskowitz & M. Stephens (Eds.), *Comparing learning outcomes: International assessment and education policy* (pp. 190–214). New York: Routledge Falmer.

Murray, T. S. (2004). The assessment of adult literacy: History and prospects. In J. H. Moskowitz & M. Stephens (Eds.), *Comparing learning outcomes: International assessment and education policy* (pp. 46–58). New York: Routledge Falmer.

Organisation for Economic Co-operation and Development. (2001). *The well-being of nations: The role of human and social capital.* Paris: OECD Publications.

Organisation for Economic Co-operation and Development. (2002). *Education policy analysis.* Paris: OECD Publications.

Organisation for Economic Co-operation and Development. (2005a). *PISA 2003 data analysis manual: SPSS manual.* Paris: OECD Publications.

Organisation for Economic Co-operation and Development. (2005b). *PISA 2003 technical report.* Paris: OECD Publications.

Organisation for Economic Co-operation and Development and Definition and Selection of Competencies. (2005). *The definition and selection of key competencies: Executive summary.* Retrieved September 10, 2007, from http://www.oecd.org/dataoecd/47/61/35070367.pdf.

Organisation for Economic Co-operation and Development and Statistics Canada. (2000). *Literacy in the information age: Final report of the international adult literacy survey.* Paris: OECD Publications.

Organisation for Economic Co-operation and Development and United Nations Educational, Scientific and Cultural Organization—Institute for Statistics. (2003). *Literacy skills for the world of tomorrow: Further results from PISA 2000.* Paris: OECD Publications.

Owen, E., Stephens, M., Moskowitz, J., & Gil, G. (2004). Toward education improvement: The future of international assessment. In J. H. Moskowitz & M. Stephens (Eds.), *Comparing learning outcomes:*

International assessment and education policy (pp. 3–23). New York: Routledge Falmer.

Plank, F., & Hodgkinson, D. (2004). Reflections on the use of indicators in policy and practice. In J. H. Moskowitz & M. Stephens (Eds.), *Comparing learning outcomes: International assessment and education policy* (pp. 108–122). New York: Routledge Falmer.

Porter, A. C., & Gamoran, A. (2002). Progress and challenges for large-scale studies. In A. C. Porter & A. Gamoran (Eds.), *Methodological advances in cross-national surveys of educational achievement* (pp. 3–23). Washington, DC: National Academy Press.

Robitaille, D. F., & Garden, R. A. (1989). *The IEA study of mathematics II: Contexts and outcomes of school mathematics.* Oxford: Pergamon Press.

Ross, K. N., Donner-Reichle, C., Jung, I., Wiegelmann, U., Genevois, L. J., & Paviot, L. (2006). The "main messages" arising from the policy forum. In K. Ross & I. J. Genevois (Eds.), *Cross-national studies of the quality of education* (pp. 279–311). Paris: International Institute for Educational Planning.

Rowan, B. (2002). Large-scale, cross-national surveys of educational achievement: Promises, pitfalls, and possibilities. In A. C. Porter & A. Gamoran (Eds.), *Methodological advances in cross-national surveys of educational achievement* (pp. 321–349). Washington, DC: National Academy Press.

Shavelson, R. J., McDonnell, L. M., & Oakes, J. (1991). What are educational indicators and indicator systems? *Practical Assessment, Research & Evaluation, 2*(11). Retrieved February 18, 2009, from http://PAREonline.net/getvn.asp?v=2&n=12.

Smith, T. M., & Baker, D. P. (2001). Worldwide growth and institutionalization of statistical indicators for education policy-making. *Peabody Journal of Education, 76*(3&4), 141–152.

Sroka, W. (2006). *Educational monitoring and assessment: Policy strategies and challenges in Germany.* Paper presented at the Education Evaluation conference, Frascati, Italy.

Sum, A., Kirsch, I., & Taggart, R. (2002). *The twin challenges of mediocrity and inequality: Literacy in the U.S. from an international perspective.* Princeton, NJ: Educational Testing Service.

United Nations Educational, Scientific and Cultural Organization—Institute for Statistics and Organisation for Economic Co-operation and Development. (2005). *Education trends in perspective—Analysis of the world education indicators.* Montreal and Paris: UIS and OECD.

CHAPTER 13

Exemplary Case

Implementing Large-Scale Assessment of Education in Mexico

Edith J. Cisneros-Cohernour and Thomas E. Grayson

Introduction

Globalization's[1] effects on economic markets are often the subject of discussion for scholars around the world, but too little attention has been given to understanding its effects on education. As stated in the United Nations Educational, Scientific and Cultural Organization's (UNESCO's) position paper titled *Higher Education in a Globalized Society*, "globalization affects each country in a different way due to the individual history, traditions, cultures, resources, and priorities" (United Nations Educational, Scientific and Cultural Organization, 2003, p. 4). These differing effects are particularly apparent in the case of developing nations such as Mexico, given its limited resources and its ethnically and culturally diverse populations.

Certainly, national and international large-scale assessment of student achievement in education is a worldwide trend that is commonly

being used to define what students should know and are able to do (Linn & Herman, 1997). In Mexico, as in other developed countries, school districts are similarly using standardized assessments to judge the quality of schools, improve teaching and student learning, and make educational policy decisions (Association of American Publishers, 2006). This chapter presents the Mexican case for implementing large-scale assessment in education and delves into the implications of using such large-scale assessments for such purposes.

In Mexico, with the widespread publication of international and national assessment results, educators, scholars, and some political leaders are asking questions about the meaning of a quality education and the need for improving conditions of schooling in both rural and urban communities (Guevara, 2005). There is also concern about substantive differences among social classes and access to education for students from low socioeconomic background, particularly in the rural areas (Cisneros-Cohernour, 2007; Fernández & Blanco, 2004; Martínez-Rizo, 2006, 2007). Other scholars such as Treviño (2006) are raising questions about low academic performance on standardized tests of students of indigenous ancestry. Zorrilla and Fernandez (2003) are examining relationships between assessment results and certain variables, such as the mother's educational level and school location (rural vs. urban), school schedule, and student gender (Carvallo, Caso, & Contreras, 2007). Further, Backhoff and Solano (2003) have raised concerns about adopting instruments and tests from one country without paying attention to the problematic nature of translating and revising the instrument.

This chapter focuses on how globalization has influenced educational and assessment reforms in Mexico, and it identifies and examines some of the major issues resulting from the implementation of large-scale standardized assessment practices in Mexico. Messick's (1989, 1995) validity framework is used to analyze these reform consequences, as well as to suggest implications for serving the educational needs of students of low socioeconomic status (SES) and of ethnically and culturally diverse backgrounds. Ethical and fairness issues in the use of assessment results for making high-stakes decisions affecting students' lives and their access to education are also discussed.

Further, this chapter has implications for educational evaluation practice and policy especially when evaluation is conducted in a cross-cultural context. Issues of generalizing educational evaluation practice that is results-focused with a purpose of accountability from one country to another country are addressed. The literature on standardized assessment practice in Latin America, particularly in Mexico, is detailed and should prove to be particularly valuable for future instructional and program evaluation practitioners employed by educational policymakers interested in improving the quality of education in Mexico.

The chapter is divided into sections. First, characteristics of the Mexican case are presented, followed by an examination of globalization effects on Mexico's economy and education and the push for standards in Mexico. Next, there is the application of Messick's framework to the Mexican case to better understand validity issues inherent in implementing large-scale assessment practices. Finally, an analysis of implications and consequences of adopting standardized assessment practices is presented.

The Mexican Case

As a case, Mexico presents special characteristics related to decentralized government structure but centralized control, ethnic and cultural diversity, differing conditions of rural and urban communities, and unequal distribution of wealth.

Decentralized Government Structure, But Centralized Control

Mexico is a federal republic that, according to policy documents, is decentralized. However, government control remains strong for companies engaged in mining, fishing, transportation, and exploitation of forests (International Education Media, 2008). In addition, although in recent years the federal government has expressed an interest in decentralizing the educational system and other social services, educational and social services remain heavily centralized.

In the educational arena, centralization[2] is evident in the curriculum for teacher preparation. Teachers are usually prepared at the Mexican Normal Schools, which are decentralized, but the curriculum is designed at the central level. In a study conducted in secondary schools in southeastern Mexico, Cisneros-Cohernour (2007) found that teachers at these schools identified problems with curriculum content sufficiency and sequence, and they had reported this situation to their school academic groups as well as to officials at their local Department of Education. Despite the persistent problems identified and reported by teachers and teachers' requests that the curriculum be modified to include relevant missing content required for student learning, the Mexican Department of Education in Mexico City did not at that time approve changes.

As Tapia (2005) noted, both Latin American and European nations have initiated decentralization[3] efforts in schools over the last three decades. Although some decentralization has taken place, in some countries, control has grown at the national level. In Mexico, educational decentralization is reflected in greater state and local level accountability for student outcomes and use of resources. However, reform conceptualization and decisions about curriculum content remain highly centralized (Cisneros-Cohernour, 2007).

Ethnic and Cultural Diversity

Mexico is the world's largest and most populated Spanish-speaking country, with 104 million inhabitants and an economically active (working) population estimated at 36,580,000 (International Labour Organization, 2005). It is a nation in which mingling of races has taken place. As noted by the Organisation for Economic Co-operation and Development (2003a) in its report on Adult Learning, "the Mexican society is characterized by a vast economic, social and cultural diversity" (p. 4).

During colonial times, seven main ethnic groups comprised Mexico's population: Españoles (Whites of Spanish descent born in Spain), Criollos (Whites of Spanish ancestry born in Mexico),[4] Mestizos (people of both Indian and Spanish ancestry), Mulattos (people of both Spanish and Black ancestry), Negros (Blacks), Zambos (people of both Black and Indian ancestry), and Indians[5] (originally 270 groups, now only 87). Over the years, new immigrants from China, Korea, Lebanon, France, Italy, Germany, and Spain began to settle in various parts of the country. These immigrants and the refugees of Central America contributed to the cultural and ethnic mosaic that constitutes the Mexican people of today, of whom 30% are Indians, 10% are Whites, and 60% are of mixed ancestry. The ethnic diversity of Mexico is further evidenced by the fact that more than 62 indigenous groups speak 80 distinct native languages in addition to Spanish (Andrade, 2002).

Despite the Mexican government's recognition of the indigenous culture, Indians are segregated in rural areas and isolated from mainstream Mexican society. The marginalization of the Indian people is reflected in the small number of students of indigenous ancestry in middle and high school and, particularly, in higher education (Blat-Gimeno, 1983; Cisneros-Cohernour, 2007; Prawda, 1989). Although recently elected government officials have created new policies for multicultural education, these policies have not resulted in real changes in the schools, nor have they led to teacher preparation programs at the Normal Schools and universities that better address multicultural and diversity issues. The need for better bilingual and bicultural teacher preparation programs remains (Gómez & Bocanegra, 2000). As Cerda (2007) stresses, for multicultural education to work, it is necessary to implement changes that improve the quality of education that go beyond the official discourse of politics. More effort needs to be directed toward moving from the existence of a small number of schools teaching indigenous students in their particular languages to the development of a multicultural educational system for all Mexican students that recognizes, values, and promotes indigenous languages and cultures.

Rural Versus Urban Communities

Significant differences can be observed in the conditions of rural and urban communities in Mexico. Seventy-three percent of Mexico's population lives in urban centers, where most of the hospitals, schools, banks, and social services are concentrated. In the capitals of the states, European (particularly Spanish and French) and

North American influences are evident (International Education Media, 2008).

Rural areas, in contrast, are isolated and lack essential services and work opportunities. They are populated mainly by Native American peoples, who are mostly farmers and laborers living in great poverty. Illiteracy within the adult population is higher in rural communities than in urban settings. Although the government has made efforts to improve the situation in these rural areas, more needs to be done to better living and working conditions in these regions.

Schools located in rural communities are characterized by low levels of existing resources, less well-trained instructors, minimal school supervision, larger numbers of students of indigenous ancestry, higher student dropout rates, and less access to additional resources than schools in urban settings. In a study conducted in the southeast of Mexico, Cisneros-Cohernour and Merchant (2005) confirmed several differences between rural and urban high schools. As a principal working in one of the poorest schools in the zone interviewed said when referring to school resources:

> You just can't accomplish the same quality of learning when you work in a rural school with no resources, not enough space and no electricity.

Another high school principal working in a rural school added:

> Our school has a very limited budget. We ask some parents, who can afford it, to pay $100.00 (less than nine U.S. dollars) every year. We use this money for school necessities and for paying the transportation of our poorest students. Most of them live in nearby communities, but their families can't afford paying for transportation.

Another study conducted by Cisneros-Cohernour in 2007 in federally funded middle schools found conditions similar to those described earlier. She reported that in some rural schools, teachers do not teach the whole week. Many of the teachers live in the capital of the state and travel to the rural communities to work, but they tend to miss 1 or 2 days of work every week. Zorrilla and Fernandez (2003), Carvallo et al. (2007) and Cisneros-Cohernour (2007) also found that the performance of students attending rural schools was lower than the performance of students attending schools in urban settings. The findings are suggestive that the conditions of the schools and communities, particularly in rural areas, may account for low student performance on assessments.

Unequal Distribution of Wealth

In addition to centralized control, ethnic differences, and limited resource allocation in rural areas, Mexico has an unequal distribution of wealth. Although a small number of Mexicans have privileged positions, the vast majority of Mexican people live in poverty. This is especially true for people living in inner-city neighborhoods and rural communities. According to the Consejo Nacional de Evaluación de la Política de Desarrollo Social (2007),[6] only 4.3 million Mexicans can be said not to live under extreme poverty.

The high level of poverty of those living in rural areas has been reported by several studies. According to the World Bank, in 1992, 14.2 million Mexican people were living in rural communities under the poverty level. This means that 55% of the Mexican population lived in these areas. During 1992, the rural population in Mexico increased from 37.1% to 40.8% (Boltvinik, 1999).

According to the Organisation for Economic Co-operation and Development (2002), despite Mexico's structural reforms and improved economic performance, the level of poverty for most Mexicans is still high. Data from the latest census indicate that half of the population experiences various degrees of poverty. According to the latest reports from Consejo Nacional de Evaluación de la Política de Desarrollo Social (2007) and from the World Bank (2007), 49 million Mexicans still live in poverty. In some regions, particularly those with high indigenous populations, the percentage of people under the poverty level is higher than 60%. This is the case in some areas of Chiapas, where the percentage of people living under the poverty level is as high as 84%. Rates of access to electricity, water, and sanitation are 90% for those living in poverty and 80% for those living in extreme poverty. The situation worsens in rural areas, where 42% of the population cannot satisfy their basic food needs. Further, according to census data, 80% of the Indian population lives in poverty, and 60% of women who live in urban settings are living under the poverty level. These findings are consistent with the work of Fernandez and Blanco (2004) and Martínez-Rizo (2007), who also stressed the link between poverty and low performance in standardized tests.

Globalization and Mexico's Economy

Globalization of economic systems has brought about several changes in Mexican society. From 1990 to 2007, the number of transnational companies locating in Mexico, mainly from the United States, has significantly increased. According to Castellanos (1999), due to the North America Free Trade Agreement (NAFTA), foreign companies' participation in Mexico's economy grew from 1.9% in 1994 to 2.5% in 1998. Since then, the number of transnational companies has increased, mostly in the automobile industry, manufacturing, food, and technology sectors (Carrillo, 2004).

Coupled with the increasing number of transnational companies in Mexico is a growing rate of immigration of Mexican families to the United States and Canada. Since 1995, in addition to people from the rural areas of Mexico, working-class citizens and professionals from urban settings are migrating abroad. In some cases, return migration is also taking place (i.e., immigrants go back and forth between Mexico and the United States or Canada).

This increase in migration has become a matter of concern for Mexico and other Latin American countries because "for these countries, international migration is resulting in brain drain" (Adams, 2003, p. 13). Research about the extent of the brain drain in Mexico is limited. However, a study conducted by Carrington and Detragiache (1999) reports that "Mexico is by far the largest sending country (2.7 million), with the large majority of its migrants (2.0 million) having a secondary education and some 13 percent having a tertiary education" (p. 3) This latter percentage constitutes, in absolute numbers, 351,000 migrating professionals, which in turn represents around 2% of the higher educated Mexican population. For a developing country, this is a significant loss of a long-term and expensive investment. According to Vitela (2002), although 12% of Mexico's workers live in the United States, 30% of Mexicans with PhDs live in that country, and 79% of the science students whom Mexico funds to study abroad never return to work in Mexico.

In addition to the number of professionals who actually leave the country, a large group of professionals remaining in Mexico are underemployed. According to the International Labor Organization (OIT, 2005), in 2004, there were 7,492,102 Mexican professionals, of whom 271,700 were unemployed. The situation is similar in other developing countries, as Williams (2000) states: "just as international mobility of skills may deplete a nation's productive capacity, so may the malfunctioning of internal labor markets and weaknesses in personnel management at the level of employing organizations lead to ineffective deployment of human capacities within countries" (p. 2).

Globalization and Mexican Education

In the educational arena, globalization has led to increased interest among political leaders and government officials for quantitative indicators of student outcomes in mathematics and science. As Castro, Carnoy, and Wolf (2000) state: "the growing interdependency between the markets and the increasing intellectual content of production are demanding a labor force with solid competencies in mathematics, language and communications, as well as students with high flexibility, creativity and the capacity for working with others" (p. 1). As a result of these demands, multilateral organizations and international agencies such as the World Bank, UNESCO, and the U.S. Agency for International Development began promoting the systemic measurement of student performance in math and science around the world (Kellaghan & Greaney, 2001; Martínez-Rizo, 2007; Organisation for Economic Co-operation and Development, 2003). Since the 1990s, support from these institutions greatly aided the development of national assessment systems in all Latin America, as well as the increased participation of Latin American countries in international comparisons of student assessment results (Benveniste, 2002)

Student Achievement Data

According to international comparisons, Mexican student achievement in basic education has been poor. In the Third International Mathematics and Science Study (TIMSS) of 1993, Mexican students from elementary and secondary schools obtained low achievement results in math and sciences compared with their peers from 40 developing countries. On average, Mexican students were 100 points below the world mean. Among all groups, Mexican secondary school students obtained the lowest achievement scores (Backhoff & Solano, 2003; Wang, 2003).

TIMSS's results indicate that approximately half of the Mexican elementary school students who took the test did not accomplish the objectives of the educational levels in which they were placed. Further, in secondary education, low levels of achievement of student learning outcome

goals persisted despite efforts made by the Mexican Department of Education to change the school curriculum (Cisneros-Cohernour, 2007; Domínguez & Guillermo, 2007).

Similar findings have been reported in other measurements of student learning achievement. The Programs for International Student Assessment (PISA)[7] assessed students during 2000 and found low achievement of Mexican students on international assessments (Organisation for Economic Co-operation and Development, 2003). Results showed that Mexican students obtained an average of 387 points in mathematics, far below the OECD average of 500, ranking Mexico in 35th place out of 40 countries. Assessment results obtained for Mexican students on nearly all scales of PISA 2000 were among the lowest recorded.

TIMSS and PISA results were consistent with other studies conducted by the Laboratorio Latinoamericano de Evaluación de la Calidad Educativa (2001) in 1998 and 2000.[8] This laboratory is part of UNESCO's Regional Office for Latin America and the Caribbean. It is responsible for conducting standardized assessment in the region to measure the achievement level of third- and sixth-grade students in reading, mathematics, and writing. The studies conducted by Latinoamericano de Evaluación de la Calidad Educativa (LLECE) provide additional evidence of the relatively lower academic achievement of Mexican and other Latin American students in mathematics and sciences.

Educational Reforms

Findings from LLECE studies, along with findings from TIMSS and PISA studies, generated strong interest in pushing for educational reforms in Mexico. In March 1993, educational reform was implemented, stressing innovation and pushing for the greater development of children's academic skills, support for increased student retention, and creation of national standards (Secretaría de Educación Pública, 2002). Further, new policies were designed to decentralize education, increase the participation of the community in the schools, reassign financial responsibilities to the states, modernize education, and reorganize educational functions to encourage a better collaboration between schools and families. The LLECE reports also proposed increasing the national investment in education and making education responsive to the needs of the indigenous population (Secretaría de Educación Pública, 2002).

Due to reform efforts, teacher preparation was extended, as was the minimum educational requirement for Mexican children. All Mexican children became required to complete 1 year of kindergarten, 6 years of elementary school, and 3 years of secondary education. A fellowship program for teachers was also created, contributing to improved teacher income.

While K-9 curriculum reform was being implemented, other changes were taking place in higher education. Emphasis was being placed on the diversification of education and on closer coordination with business leaders. Curriculum evaluation, institutional assessment, and an increased role of research were also being emphasized (ANUIES, 2000).

The Push for Assessment Standards in Mexico

With the publication of results from TIMSS and PISA studies came pressure for the Mexican government to adopt a standardized assessment policy incorporating quantitative indicators of educational quality, testing of all students, and accountability of schools. This new direction is reflected in various policy documents, including, for example, the Mexican Plan for Educational Development (2001–2006), which proposed policies stressing the need for regular assessments of students, teachers, and overall school performance.

Evidence of Mexico's growing interest in standardized assessment was also reflected in the movement for education reform. In 1994, just 1 year after the implementation of curriculum reform, standardized assessment reform policy was adopted by the Mexican government, following in the footsteps of international trends. This reform resulted in the creation of entrance examinations for universities and the development of minimum competencies for various disciplines and professions (ANUIES, 2000). To implement these changes, the Centro Nacional para la Evaluación de la Educación Superior (CENEVAL), a new evaluation center, was created.

The number of standardized student assessments conducted by CENEVAL grew over the years. From 1994 to 2000, the number of students tested rose to more than 4 million. The associated costs were:

- $12 for students exiting ninth grade,
- $4.60 for those who completed high school and aspired to earning a bachelor's degree at a technological institute or university,
- $79 for those completing undergraduate education, and
- $93 for those entering graduate education.

In 2000, after international comparisons continued to show discouraging educational achievement results for the country (Vidal & Díaz, 2004), the Mexican government established another evaluation center known as the National Institute of Educational Evaluation (INEE). The INEE was created for the purposes of developing quality indicators for assessing the basic education system, test development, and evaluating schools. This newly formed institute began using standardized assessments for determining the level of achievement of elementary and junior high school students. INEE developed a new standardized assessment system known as EXCALE to measure school quality based on student academic achievement.

Studies conducted by the INEE have identified differences between and within Mexican states regarding student achievement. For example, the Institute found that schools located in municipal areas outside the city proper, primarily in rural communities with a high percentage of indigenous students, were among those with lower student achievement and higher dropout rates. These findings were consistent with the results of international testing where the data was disaggregated by region.

Further, policy documents, such as the Programa Nacional de Educación (2001–2006) and local policy documents and plans, began stressing accountability, assessment, and accreditation for all educational processes, schools, personnel, and results. Moreover, the Mexican Department of Education began to implement a new standardized assessment test known as ENLACE. This test was designed to identify schools with lower student performance in each district, and the findings are published to inform the public about assessment results and school rankings.

The creation of national assessment institutes such as the INEE and CENEVAL fostered a trend toward comparing assessment results and using those results as a basis for setting student admission requirements for high schools and higher education.

Despite improvements that resulted from curriculum and standardized assessment reforms, Mexican student performance remains among the lowest in international comparisons. In the 2003 PISA Plus international study, results for Mexican students were lower than those of PISA 2000. Mexican students' mean score went from 387 to 385 in the PISA Plus, placing Mexico 37th out of 40 countries. Results in the sciences were no better, with 2003 student assessment results again placing Mexico in the 37th position. This ranking puts Mexico among the countries with a notably lower assessment performance among the Organisation for Economic Co-operation and Development (OECD) countries surveyed in mathematics and science (Vidal & Díaz, 2004).

Recently, the Mexican government initiated another secondary educational reform aimed at improving student outcomes. This reform is expected to provide continuity of progression among educational levels and improve educational opportunities for students. This new

reform was implemented in the 2006–2007 academic year. As was the case with earlier reform efforts in Mexico, the new policy follows the global trend of stressing the development of professional competencies for students, and it was developed at the central level.

What are the issues in adopting this kind of standardized assessment system for judging educational quality? To better understand the implications of adopting standardized assessment practices in Mexico, Messick's (1989, 1995) validity framework was used to test hypotheses about test score significance and the relationship of test scores to actual student learning in the classroom. In the following section, we briefly define validity and the Messick validity framework, as well as present a critical analysis of validity issues in the Mexican case.

Application of Messick's Framework to the Mexican Case

Messick's Construct Validity Framework

In the late 1980s and early 1990s, Samuel Messick (1989, 1995) provided new insights to understanding the complex nature of validity with his well-known theoretical framework on various aspects of construct validity. According to Messick, validity is not a property of a test, but "an overall judgment of the extent to which empirical evidence and theory support the adequacy and appropriateness of the interpretations based on the assessment" (Messick, 1995, p. 741). Moreover, validity refers not only to meanings and interpretations of test scores, but also to the inferences and social consequences that result from the assessment. Indeed, meaning and consequence are essential to validity (Messick, 1989, 1995). In Messick's (1989, 1995) model, six aspects of construct validity are important and useful for identifying sources of invalidity in educational and psychological assessment practices: construct, substantive, structural, external, generalizability, and consequential. These aspects along with sources of evidence are listed next (Messick, 1994, pp. 11–12).

- **Content aspects:** Includes evidence of content relevance, representation, and technical quality (Lennon, 1956; Messick, 1989).
- **Substantive aspects:** Refers to theoretical rationales for the observed consistencies in test responses, including process models of task performance (Embreston, 1983), and addresses empirical evidence that the theoretical processes are actually engaged by respondents in the assessment tasks.
- **Structural aspects:** Appraises the fidelity of the scoring structure to the structure of the construct domain at issue (Loevinger, 1957).
- **External aspects:** Includes convergent and discriminant evidence from multitrait-method comparisons (Campbell & Fiske, 1959), as well as evidence of criterion relevance and applied utility (Cronbach & Gleser, 1965)
- **Generalizability aspects:** Examines the extent to which score properties and interpretations generalize to and across population groups and tasks (Cook & Campbell, 1979; Shulman, 1970), and looks at validity generalization of test-criterion relationships (Hunter, Schmidt, & Jackson, 1982).
- **Consequential aspects:** Appraises the value implications of score interpretation as a basis for action, as well as the actual potential consequences of test use, especially with regard to sources of invalidity related to issues of bias, fairness, and distributive justice (Messick, 1980, 1989).

Examples illustrating particular kinds of validity issues in the Mexico case are presented next. The examples relate to the special characteristics of the Mexican case described earlier: decentralized government structure but centralized control, ethnic and cultural diversity, rural versus urban communities, and Mexico's

unequal distribution of wealth. This is followed by discussion of implications and consequences of implementing standardized assessment practices in Mexican schools.

Decentralized Government Structure by Centralized Control: Content Aspects of Validity

One of the most important considerations of construct validity is the capacity of the assessment to reflect the content of the construct that is intended to be measured. Two main sources of invalidity can be associated with content aspects: construct underrepresentation and construct-irrelevant variance. Construct underrepresentation takes place when the assessment too narrowly represents the construct being measured. Construct-irrelevant variance takes place when the assessment includes elements that are irrelevant to the construct being measured.

In the case of Mexico, the decentralized government structure coexisting with a highly centralized control of education raises questions related to content validity, particularly in terms of content representation and relevance. Because standardized assessment in Mexico is not a direct measure of student learning, there is a need for more research examining the relevance of assessment to what students are learning in the schools. In addition, it is important to examine whether all important aspects of student learning are being assessed and whether any elements included in the assessment are irrelevant to the construct *student learning*.

Decentralization reforms in Mexico have not significantly reduced centralized control of curriculum content, financial support, and school governance. As a result, important elements within the teaching and learning context tend not to be taken into consideration in assessment. Some content may be included according to central officers' perception of needs, whereas more relevant elements, such as curriculum, school conditions, and student needs, may be excluded.

The recent curriculum and assessment reforms influenced the use of assessment outcomes for making academic decisions, with resultant changes in both curriculum content and pedagogy. Following the Department of Education's publication of school rankings based on student assessment tests such as ENLACE, and also in recognition of the growing use of assessment results for admissions purposes, schools began to dedicate more time to covering test content.

Research conducted in the southeast of Mexico from 2002 to 2007 (Cisneros-Cohernour, 2007) found that both curriculum and assessment reforms influenced the expansion of subject-matter coverage in mathematics, physics, chemistry, and biology. Because curriculum design took place at the central level, teacher authority and decision making were limited. Curriculum expansion also contributed to content fragmentation. These findings are consistent with those of research studies conducted in the United States, which identify certain negative consequences of standardized assessment, such as narrowing the curricula to subjects, topics, and skills readily tested by the tests and increasing public embarrassment for those schools ranked low due to poor performance by students on assessment tests (Backoff & Contreras, 2007; Segall, 2003; Vogler, 2003).

In the Cisneros-Cohernour, López Ávila, Canto Herrera, and Alonzo Blanqueto (2003) study conducted in secondary schools in the southeast of Mexico, teachers at a rural middle school encountered obstacles trying to implement a constructivist teaching project in mathematics because the school principal was concerned about how this student-centered teaching approach might affect student performance on standardized assessment. These math instructors were concerned with developing higher cognitive skills for middle-school students while reducing memorization. They utilized activities that could help students connect math in a meaningful way with the world outside the school. Their approach reduced the cost of educational materials for low socioeconomic

students and increased student enthusiasm for this subject. As one of the teachers commented:

> Children were so engaged in the course, Math became their favorite subject. The kind of teaching and learning promoted in the school contrasted with more traditional approaches for teaching Math in other schools. It was a success!

Unfortunately, after one semester, the project was cancelled because school administrators were under pressure from curriculum supervisors at the State Department of Education to use traditional testing, even if traditional testing might not be appropriate for the kind of teaching and learning being promoted by the math instructors. Students who participated in the project showed no significant difference in assessment scores from other students, so the principal decided to cancel support for the project. Unfortunately, however, traditional assessment failed to include all the cognitive learning that took place in the classroom. Further, officials completely disregarded two important outcomes of the project: (a) the project helped to reduce the cost of educational materials for children whose families could not afford the calculators used in the traditional math courses, and (b) participating children's enthusiasm for learning math increased.

Other examples of schools implementing innovative projects in science learning were found in the rural areas. In some cases, the projects continued due to the political skills of the principal, but in most cases they were cancelled because of external pressures for conforming to the norm.

Ethnic and Cultural Diversity: Substantive, Structural, and External Aspects of Validity

Mexico's ethnic and cultural diversity raises issues related to three main aspects of Messick's framework: substantive, structural, and external validity. Cultural context may promote the development of different learning styles, cultural understandings, meanings, and conceptions, all of which can affect student understanding of test questions, thus influencing their responses. There has been no research conducted in Mexico about the structural and external validity of the assessment process.

The appropriateness of assessment for various groups of students, especially those of different cultures, has been recognized as an important issue in the United States. As Medina and Neill (1990) stressed in the National Center for Fair and Open Testing (FairTest) Report on standardized assessment:

One of the problems with standardized assessment is that test scores do not necessarily reflect real differences among people, and they often do not adequately eliminate underlying biased cultural assumptions built into the test as a whole. Standardized tests are not really fair and helpful tools because they reward the ability to answer superficial questions quickly and do not measure the ability to think or create in any field. They assume that test takers have been exposed to a white, middle-class background.

Examining the substantive aspects of construct validity is important because "the response consistencies or performance regularities are reflective of the domain processes" (Messick, 1994, p. 13). Evidence regarding substantive aspects of validity can be obtained "from 'think aloud protocols' or eye-movement records during task performance, from correlation patterns among part scores, from consistencies in response times for task performance, or from mathematical or computer modeling of task processes" (Messick, 1989, pp. 53–55).

Research studies conducted in the southeast of Mexico (Cisneros-Cohernour, 2007) provide valuable information about cultural and ethnic differences between subgroups within the Mexican society, as well as differences between Mexican cultural values and behaviors and those embraced by the United States.

Cultural differences may be reflected in student understanding or lack of understanding of test items. Because these differences can influence understandings as well as response patterns, they raise questions about the appropriateness of the assessment for different student subgroups. Ignoring those questions could result in unfairness and discrimination, as well as in the diminution of educational quality if, in fact, the tests are inappropriately assessing learning and punishing nontraditional teaching and learning.

Although some studies have been conducted by specialists from INEE, more research is needed on the substantive validity of the assessment, particularly as it relates to students of indigenous ancestry. Because of the persistent underperformance of these students in relation to their peers, it is necessary to examine what may account for score differences. For example, we need to understand how students use rating scales to respond (i.e., we need to know whether there is a fit between the intended meaning of the scale and the meaning of the scale as seen by students). In addition, it is important to determine whether all students follow similar processes when responding to the tests or whether some subgroups of students respond differently than others. In summary, more research is needed to ascertain whether the assessment is appropriate for different groups of students of diverse ethnic and cultural backgrounds.

Issues regarding structural validity must be taken into consideration because there has been insufficient research into the structural aspects of the assessment. The "Estándares de Calidad Para Instrumentos de Evaluación Educativa," developed by the Centro Nacional de Evaluación para la Educación Superior (2000), include important points regarding the design of assessment instruments and provide valuable recommendations for improving the quality of educational testing in Mexico. But, given the importance of examining the structure of assessment tasks as well as scoring criteria and rubrics, and given that standards or criteria that are preordinate may not be responsive to all assessment validity issues, more research is needed on this aspect of construct validity. Moreover, more careful examination of the external aspect of validity is needed, including analysis of the relationship of the assessment to other variables external to the tests, in order to provide validity evidence.

Urban Versus Rural Communities and Unequal Distribution of Wealth: Generalizability and Consequential Aspects of Validity

The differing conditions between urban and rural communities, along with the unequal distribution of wealth, raise important questions related to generalizability and consequential aspects of validity. Research studies conducted by Cisneros et al. from 2002 to 2007 identified differences between urban and rural schools that apparently are not considered by the assessment. Rural schools were characterized by having a high number of students of indigenous ancestry, many of whom worked full time while attending school. Teachers at these schools were not always sensitive to student cultural values and, in some cases, misinterpreted student behavior. During the focus group interviews conducted with principals in one of the rural schools, one principal of the Cisneros-Cohernour, Moreno, and Cisneros (2000) study stated:

> Some teachers do not understand the cultural differences and punish students because they attribute their behavior to a negative attitude towards learning. Other teachers are more sensitive to students' culture; they know collaborative learning works better with them than other kinds of activities that promote competition. (p. 8)

Another principal of Cisneros-Cohernour and Merchant (2005) raised other issues regarding differences between students of low socioeconomic background living in the city and those of similar socioeconomic background living in rural areas:

> Before I became the principal in this rural school, I worked in an urban high school located in a poor neighborhood in the city. When you work in poor schools in the city you have to deal with issues of safety, low resources, and serious discipline problems. Sometimes, you have to deal with theft or even with drug problems.
>
> In the rural areas, the school is a very important part of the community. There is more poverty but crime is not an issue. Families here are very shy, so are the children, but they help you whenever you need help. For example, they came to help us paint the school when we didn't have resources to pay for someone to do it.
>
> At the same time that you have less discipline problems in the rural areas, you have to provide more background knowledge for students to learn.
>
> Students in the rural areas are also less exposed to so many things. You can teach about dinosaurs in the city and the kids know what you are talking about. In the rural areas, kids don't get the same exposure to things. Their parents may have a TV or not but they don't have the same access to libraries, movies, and information than those who are living in the city. In rural areas you deal with different problems and conditions that influence the way you teach and the way you work with students. (p. 32)

Although all schools can use their assigned resources and can sometimes obtain additional financial support, funding decisions (e.g., about how much support is to be provided, in what areas schools can be improved, and how the resources are to be applied) are made at the central level. As a result, although schools have become accountable for the results, they do not generally have authority for control over class content, teaching strategies, and use of resources (Astiz, Wiseman, & Baker, 2002; Cisneros-Cohernour et al., 2003).

The centralized approach for making decisions affecting the implementation of curriculum reform could worsen conditions in schools with already limited support, particularly in rural areas where schools serve a high percentage of culturally diverse students. This problem is illustrated in the following excerpt from interview data with a principal participating in the Cisneros-Cohernour et al. (2003) study:

> The Department of Education wants all schools to use computers. So, they sent us a computer but we can't use it because the electric capacity of the school doesn't allow for it. We also lack teachers who know how to use it. I asked if we could get books instead of buying the computer because they can be more useful for our students, but the people at the Department of Education said that we can't do that. (p. 31)

As illustrated earlier, standardization of reform can result in decisions that are not in the best interest of all schools and in waste of already scarce resources for school improvement.

Issues identified by teachers and administrators in the studies conducted in southeastern Mexico were not identical across all schools. It is important to realize that there is not homogeneity among all Mexican students and in all school contexts.

It is clear that more research is needed to address the generalizability aspects of construct validity. Generalizing to other contexts, settings, times, or subjects involves more than translating assessment instruments to another language. Assessment instruments need to be appropriate to the culture of the subjects taking the test. In addition, it is important to study the *consequential aspects of validity* of the assessment, examining the value implications of score interpretations as a basis for action and the consequences of test use.

Implications and Consequences of Standardized Assessment Practices

As a result of the implementation of standardized assessment in Mexico, high-stakes decisions have been made that limit the educational opportunities of students of low SES. Compared with schools in urban communities, poor schools in rural communities are in a weaker condition and consequently have less potential for accomplishing the expected student outcomes.

Data from research conducted in southeastern Mexico from 2002 to 2007 (Cisneros-Cohernour, 2007) identified some important consequences of the implementation of standardized student assessment. In the contexts of teaching and learning, financial support, and school governance in basic education, these consequences relate specifically to (a) the tension between focusing on student- versus on teacher-centered pedagogy, and (b) equity issues for low SES and culturally and ethnically diverse students living in rural communities.

First, with respect to student- versus teacher-centered pedagogy, despite declarations made in policy documents such as the National Education Program (2001–2006) regarding the need for the educational system to promote a holistic education for basic education students, the Cisneros-Cohernour et al. (2003) study found that the consistent use of test results for making decisions about student admissions for college and high school shifted the focus from holistic education to a more test-driven student preparation. In addition, the emphasis on testing outcomes resulted in a changed concept of student achievement, which became synonymous with student assessment scores.

As a consequence of the growing emphasis on improving assessment scores, the Mexican government promoted reforms that resulted in an expansion of subject matter, particularly in math, science, and Spanish, at the secondary school level. This reform also resulted in altered teacher pedagogy, which began to emphasize teaching and memorizing certain assessment content and facts. Studies conducted from 2002 to 2007 in the southeast of Mexico by Cisneros-Cohernour et al. (2003) indicate that the expansion of curriculum content increased pressure on teachers to cover all course content during the limited time allocated for particular subjects.

As a result, teachers became less interested in introducing innovations in the classroom, even when they may have been more relevant to the context of the schools, because innovation would reduce the already limited time available to teach the required curriculum.

Second, with respect to equity issues, one of the most critical consequences of assessment reform in Mexico has to do with equity and social justice, primarily in the case of students of indigenous ancestry, low SES, living in rural settings. Mexico is still a centralized country, with most schools and resources located in the capitals of the states. Rural communities lack most of the facilities and opportunities available in the capitals, and their populations also lack access to education at all levels. These rural schools are precisely the schools attended by most students of indigenous ancestry. Although the Mexican government has made an effort to open more schools and universities in rural areas, the invested resources have been insufficient to satisfy student demands.

Cisneros-Cohernour et al. (2003; Cisneros-Cohernour, 2007) found that secondary schools with high numbers of students of indigenous ancestry faced the challenge of educating students who worked full time while attending school. Most student families were under the poverty level and spoke a language or dialect different from Spanish, with different levels of illiteracy in Spanish. Teachers at these schools faced additional problems when educating these children. As one of the teachers of the Cisneros-Cohenour and Merchant (2005) study commented:

> The reform stresses a kind of teaching that encourages children to be actively involved in their own learning; they are expected to question established notions of knowledge, to discuss alternative views. But, most students come from indigenous families. Their parents encourage different values at home, for them to be obedient, quiet and not assertive is something good. The curriculum is asking students to do the opposite of what these kids learn at home. It

expects them to question authority, to be assertive and to take initiative in their work. I see this as a conflict for us, if we encourage students to change, this will get them in trouble at home. (p. 21)

The principal at another rural high school from the same study added:

> Some of us feel that it is important for the students to change, to learn other ways of doing things because this will help them to better their lives. Others feel conflicted because they feel that we are destroying their culture, but if you preserve it, they won't get anywhere. The system values are different, almost opposite from the values of the students and their families. (p. 18)

Because Mexico is centralized, students from rural areas are also less exposed to content knowledge than students from the capitals of the states. Most schools in rural communities have more limited resources than those in the cities. Of the rural population 15 years and older, 53.1% do not finish middle school, but indigenous students occupy a unique position in the Mexican educational landscape (Instituto Nacional de Estadística Geografía e Informática, 2004). The following statistics describe the situation of indigenous students in basic education in Mexico:

- The national dropout rate is 1.3%; among indigenous students, it is 3.05%.
- The national average of failure is 5%; among indigenous students, it is 9.81%.
- In Mexico, the rate of completion of elementary school is 89%; among indigenous students, it is only 81.44%. (Secretaría de Educación Pública, 2005)

Indigenous student performance on standardized tests has been significantly lower than the performance of nonindigenous students (Treviño, 2006). Studies in Mexico have reported similarly low performance results for these students when compared with performance results of indigenous populations in Peru. In some studies, researchers found that indigenous students performed at a level 15% lower than nonindigenous students on standardized assessment tests for elementary school students (Winkler, 2004).

This situation is not surprising when we consider the conditions in which indigenous students are taught and the fact that, after elementary school, these students receive no education in their own languages nor do they have mathematics and science textbooks available in their native languages. There is growing concern about the appropriateness of the national assessment because it has not been culturally validated and because some studies have found evidence that there may be cognitive differences among indigenous students that can influence the way in which they understand and answer test questions (Magaña, 2003, 2006; Ostrosky-Solis, Ramírez, Lozano, Picasso, & Velez, 2004).

The same kinds of differences found between indigenous and nonindigenous student performance on standardized tests have been found when examining differences between performances of immigrant and nonimmigrant students in The Netherlands (Helms-Lorenz, Van de Vijver, & Poortinga, 2003). This fact points to the need to examine more carefully issues of substantive validity and generalizability of standardized tests when administered to students from different countries and cultures. As Hambleton and Patsula (2000) state, ignoring these issues could lead to three main sources of error when adapting the tests to other cultures: cultural and linguistic differences, adaptation techniques, and results interpretation.

The decision to use standardized assessment as a prerequisite for admission to secondary school after completing ninth grade has limited even more opportunities for low-income students to access higher levels of education, a result that is particularly true for those students who are of indigenous ancestry. Given the over-representation of indigenous students among those living in poverty in Mexico, many of the families of these students cannot afford the cost of the assessment. For families whose income is equivalent to one or two minimum wages (from $4.3 to $9.2 per day), paying for these tests is not possible unless they receive additional financial support. Because indigenous students attend mostly rural schools lacking the financial and personnel resources of the city schools, the possibility that they will accomplish the expected educational outcomes and enter higher education is almost nonexistent.

Some important consequences are beginning to emerge from the decision to use assessment results for accountability purposes. For example, as Backoff and Contreras (2007) state, some assessment tests, such as ENLACE, have been in controversy over their validity, as well as over the possible misuse of assessment results when making high-stakes decisions about low-performance schools.

Although there has been a large increase in Mexican government expenditure on education, the increase has not been enough to satisfy funding needs for improving schools, raising teacher salaries, and supporting reform efforts aimed at improving the quality of educational outcomes. From 1995 to 2003, Mexican government spending for basic education increased by 49%. However, OECD's (2006) *Education at a Glance* Report states that Mexico's investment in education remains insufficient because it "is approximately one quarter of the OECD average of $US 6,500" (p. 1). Teacher salaries also remain low when compared with OECD's standards.

In the study conducted by Cisneros-Cohernour et al. (2003), secondary school teachers and school principals indicated that the emphasis on quantitative indicators of school effectiveness resulted in pressures for schools to reduce the percentage of student dropouts in low-performance schools. As one of the principals interviewed stated: "There is an unwritten policy of not failing more than five students for each group."

Moreover, the decentralized focus of Mexican educational reforms shifted the responsibility for student performance and outcomes from the Mexican State to school communities. It also promoted a business and managerial approach to education that makes principals and school teachers accountable for student results.

Issues of bias and unfairness in relation to standardized assessment need more attention (Kohn, 2000; Parker, 2000; Stake, 2000). Finally, the damaging effects of test abuse, concerns about the psychometric integrity of tests, and dependence on tests as the sole primary source of data for making decisions that affect the educational opportunities of students—particularly those students who are culturally diverse, of low SES, and living in rural communities—warrant further study.

Conclusions

According to Ferrer and Arregui (2003), globalization trends are characterized by a set of premises that involve establishing stronger links among education, productivity, and the labor market to improve national economies. Consequently, the emphasis in education internationally has shifted from increasing educational access to introducing changes in educational systems that ultimately will serve to increase a nation's competitiveness in the international market.

For Mexico, a positive result of globalized assessment reform and its influence on the creation of national assessment systems is that Mexican society generally has become more aware of unsatisfactory levels of student achievement. Assessment, however, has thus far not been useful in identifying the reasons behind low student performance.

Importing educational assessment reform from another country and culture can have serious negative consequences when the new practices are not sensitive to the needs and cultural understandings peculiar to the society in which they will be implemented. Although Mexico and the United States are geographically close, significant variation exists between these two countries' educational systems. In addition, there are noteworthy differences in the availability of resources in the two countries.

In the United States there is constant review of educational practice that results in change, whereas Mexico is a nation where educational change is not always supported by scientific research, but may be implemented in response to political concerns (Cisneros-Cohernour et al., 2003). In addition, because of the weight of tradition within the Mexican society, once standardized assessment becomes institutionalized, it has little possibility of being eliminated or even modified. The appearance of objectivity, along with a lack of awareness of the philosophical and epistemological assumptions of standardized assessment and the lack of understanding of the validity of assessment results, can be especially dangerous. Using assessment scores to deny funding or educational opportunity to children or to prevent teachers and schools from implementing meaningful approaches to learning, can worsen the condition of education in Mexico.

The cost of implementing standardized assessment has serious implications for indigenous and working-class students. Paying for standardized testing becomes an additional obstacle for students of indigenous ancestry who are already underrepresented in higher education. For working-class students also, assessment costs can become a serious economic burden that can diminish their educational opportunities.

In some instances, assessment centers in Mexico are not held accountable, and their work is not subjected to the sort of review that takes place in developed nations. The lack of legal protection for students, together with the lack of accountability for the assessment centers, pose serious concerns because of the important role that these centers can play in the denial of educational opportunities for students. As Díaz-Barriga (2005) suggests, no one assesses the evaluators.

Research on the validity of assessment practices when transferred from one country to another country and culture is scarce. We have just scratched the surface in this Mexican case. However, we have learned that educational situations and conditions in rural and urban communities in Mexico offer a plausible explanation for differences in assessment results of ethnically and culturally diverse students. This case illustrates how the push for standardization of large-scale assessment is moving Mexican educators away from meaningful, innovative teaching strategies that may be more consistent with student learning styles and conditions. Further, it illustrates how the pressure for raising student test scores is moving educational practice away from a holistic approach for educating children to a test-driven instructional approach.

The push by the Mexican government to institutionalize standardized assessment seems to reinforce the political belief that results-focused evaluation is the only way to achieve accountability and satisfy the government's need to know how educational funds are being used. However, good teaching balances instruction between the need for common learning and the need for recognition of learner uniqueness. This is especially critical in a highly diverse country such as Mexico. It seems apparent that large-scale standardized assessment would not and does not lend itself to capturing the uniqueness and quality of individual learning nor the quality of educational practice in Mexico's schools.

Regarding standardized assessment in education, Stake (1987) has pointed out that what constitutes an education is not established by objectives all students must master or by tests all students must pass. If the Mexican government wants to improve its schools and foster good teaching practice that results in a balance of common learning and individual uniqueness, then it must also include learning-focused evaluation methods. Standardized tests do not typically tell what and how teachers have taught or what the students have learned. Learning-focused evaluation means exploring participatory and responsive evaluation methods for better understanding and learning about what teachers do and what students learn, without overlooking the need for accountability.

It is essential for professional evaluators to be trained on both results- and learning-oriented evaluation methods to improve the quality of education in Mexico's schools. Evaluation practice must take into consideration the cultural and ethnical diversity of Mexico when introducing future innovations for school improvement and for making decisions about school quality. In addition, we recommend a responsive approach for assessing student learning that takes into consideration student learning conditions and circumstances and that provides a holistic understanding of student cognitive growth.

Access to higher education in both Mexico and the United States constitutes an individual's opportunity for a better life, as well as a way for the country to educate those who can make a meaningful contribution to society. There is reason for concern when globalized assessment reform is adopted without empirical support for considerations of appropriateness and validity in the adopting country and culture. Issues of inequity may arise, educational quality may be diminished, and meaningful innovation in the schools may be impeded when these considerations are not adequately addressed.

Notes

1. In this chapter, globalization is understood as a historical phenomenon with contemporary implications. It is a phenomenon that mainly has economical and political characteristics, and it is associated with the development of communication, information, and transport media with increasingly broad world coverage. Globalization has deep effects in the sphere of nation-states and on the people and cultures under its influence. Because globalization is understood as a historical phenomenon, we assume its current and future configuration will be, necessarily, modified by the interaction among diverse economic, political, and cultural forces acting in global, national, and local contexts.

2. As Brennen (2008) states: "centralization refers to the condition whereby the administrative authority for education is vested, not in the local community, but in a central body" (p. 1). In Mexico's case, this is the Mexican Department of Education in Mexico City.

3. As Brennen (2008) states, "decentralization refers to the extent to which authority has been passed down to the individual school" (p. 1).

4. Over the years, the word *mestizo* has changed its meaning. Now it is used to refer to people of mixed ancestry, not necessarily of White and Indian background.

5. Native people of the Americas.

6. National Council for the Assessment of Social Development Policies. It focuses on social program outcome assessment and accountability (Consejo Nacional de Evaluación de la Política de Desarrollo Social, 2008).

7. PISA conducts assessments of 15-year-old students on how far along they are in compulsory education programs, which are geared toward helping students acquire the knowledge and skills essential for full participation in society.

8. The LLECE is the network of quality assessment systems for education in Latin America. It is coordinated by UNESCO's Regional Bureau for Education in Latin America and the Caribbean. Its objectives are to (a) produce information about students' learning achievements and analyze associated factors that explain this progress; (b) support and advise the measurement and assessment units of the different countries; and (c) serve as a forum for reflection, debate, and exchange of new approaches with a focus on educational evaluation.

References

Adams, R. K. (2003). *International migration, remittances, and the brain drain: A study of 24 labor exporting countries* (World Bank Policy Research Paper WPS3069). Available at http://www-wds .worldbank.org/servlet/WDSContentServer/WDSP/IB/2003/07/08/000094946 _03062104301450/ Rendered/PDF/multi0page.pdf

Andrade, P. G. (2002, September–October). Pedagogy. *Diversidad. Paedagogium* (Mexico), *13*, 34–37.

ANUIES. (2000). *Higher education statistics, 2000 school population in graduate school.* Available at www.anuies.mx

Association of American Publishers. (2006). *Standardized assessment: A primer* (rev. ed.). Available at http://www.publishers.org/School Div/issues/issues_08_Testing/issues_08_Teting_ PDFs/TestingPrimerRevised2.pdf

Astiz, M. F., Wiseman, A. W., & Baker, D. P. (2002). Slouching towards decentralization: Consequences of globalization for curricular control in national education systems. *Comparative Education Review, 41*, 435–459.

Backoff, E., & Contreras, L. A. (2007). Evaluación del aprendizaje y rankings escolares. *Educación 2001, 142*, 7–10.

Backhoff, E., & Solano, J. (2003, December). *Tercer Estudio Internacional de Matemáticas y Ciencias (TIMSS): Resultados de México en 1995 y 2000.* Instituto Nacional para la Evaluación de la Educación (INEE), México.

Benveniste, L. (2002). The political structuration of assessment: Negotiating state power and legitimacy. *Comparative Education Review, 46*(1), 89–118.

Blat-Gimeno, J. (1983). *Education in Latin America and the Caribbean: Trends and prospects, 1970–2000.* United Kingdom: United Nations Educational, Scientific and Cultural Organization (UNESCO).

Boltvinik J. (1999). El conocimiento de la pobreza en México. In J. Boltvinik & E. Hernández Laos (Eds.), *Pobreza y distribución del ingreso en México.* México, D.F.: Siglo XXI.

Brennen, A. M. (2008). *Centralization versus decentralization. Articles and resources in educational administration and supervision by Annick M. Brennen, MA.* Available at http://www.soencour agement.org/centralizationvsdecentralization.htm

Campbell, D. T., & Fiske, D. W. (1959). Convergent and discriminant validation by the multitrait matrix. *Psychological Bulletin, 56*, 81–105.

Carrillo, J. (2004). *Transnational strategies and regional development: The case of GM and Delphi in MEXICO. Industry and innovation.* Available at http://findarticles.com/p/articles/mi_qa3913/ is_200403/ai_n9404349

Carrington, W. J., & Detragiache, E. (1999). How extensive is the brain drain? *Finance and Development, 36*(2). Available at http://www.imf .org/external/pubs/ft/fandd/1999/06/carringt.htm

Carvallo, P. M., Caso, J., & Contreras, L. A. (2007). Estimating the effects of contextual variables in the academic achievement of students in Baja California. *Revista Electrónica de Investigación Educativa, 9*, 2. Available at http://redie.uabc.mx/ vol9no2/contenido-carvallo.html

Castellanos, C. (1999). *Foreign interest.* Bridge News' Mexico Bureau. Available at http://www.mexcon nect.com/mex_/travel/bzm/bzmtop50-99.html

Castro, C., Carnoy, M., & Wolf, L. (2000). *Secondary schools and the transition to work in Latin*

America and the Caribbean: Sustainable development (Department Technical Papers Series). Publications, Education Unit, Inter-American Development Bank. (No. de servicio de reproducción de documentos ERIC ED474307).

Cerda, A. (2007). Multiculturalism and intercultural education: Between neo-Indigenismo or authonomy. *Andamios: Revista De Investigacion Social* (Mexico), *3*(6), 97–135.

Cisneros-Cohernour, E. J. (2007). *The teaching of science in secondary schools of Yucatan: Critical issues, challenges and possible solutions.* Consejo Mexicano de Ciencia y Tecnología-Universidad Autónoma de Yucatán.

Cisneros-Cohernour, E. J., López Ávila, M. T., Canto Herrera, P. J., & Alonzo Blanqueto, C. G. (2003). *The teaching of science in Yucatan: Critical issues for improving teaching and learning* (Final report). College of Education, Universidad Autónoma de Yucatán.

Cisneros-Cohernour, E. J., & Merchant, B. (2005). *The Mexican high school principal: Impact of the national and local culture in the principalship* (Research report). Urbana-Champaign, IL: University of Illinois Press.

Cisneros-Cohernour, E. J., Moreno, R. P., & Cisneros, A. A. (2000). *Curriculum reform in Mexico: Kindergarten teachers' challenges and dilemmas.* U.S. Government, Educational Resource Information Clearinghouse (ERIC ED470886).

Consejo Nacional de Evaluación de la Política de Desarrollo Social. (2007). *Los mapas de pobreza en México.* Available at http://www.coneval.gob.mx/coneval/mapas/presentacion.pdf

Consejo Nacional de Evaluación de la Política de Desarrollo Social. (2008). *Assessing social policy promotes the achievement of results and accountability.* Available at http://www.coneval.gob.mx/coneval/

Cook, T. D., & Campbell, D. T. (1979). *Quasi-experimentation: Design and analysis for field settings.* Chicago: Rand McNally.

Cronbach, L. J., & Gleser, G. C. (1965). *Psychological and personnel decisions* (2nd ed.). Urbana, IL: University of Illinois Press.

Díaz-Barriga, A. (2005, June). *Riesgos de los Sistemas de Evaluación y Acreditación de la Educación Superior.* Paper presented at the Seminario Regional: Las nuevas tendencias de la evaluación y acreditación en América Latina y el Caribe.

Comisión Nacional de Evaluación y Acreditación Universitaria (CONEAU) y el Instituto Internacional para la Educación Superior en América Latina y el Caribe (IESALC-UNESCO), Buenos Aires, Argentina.

Domínguez, G., & Guillermo, C. (2007, February). *Evaluación de las estrategias de enseñanza de los profesores de Matemáticas de primer año de preparatoria en Mérida.* Paper presented at the International Conference, Pedagogía, La Habana, Cuba.

Embreston, W. S. (1983). Construct validity: Construct representation versus nomothetic span. *Psychological Bulletin, 93,* 179–197.

Fernández, T., & Blanco, E. (2004). How important is schooling? The case of Mexico within the context of Latin America. *REICE—Revista Electrónica Iberoamericana sobre Calidad, Eficacia y Cambio en Educación.* Available at http://www.ice.deusto.es/rinace/reice/vol2n1/FernandezyBlanco.pdf

Ferrer, G., & Arregui, P. (2003). *Las pruebas internacionales en América Latina y su impacto en la calidad de la educación: Criterios para guiar futuras aplicaciones* (Documento de trabajo N° 26). Santiago: PREAL.

Gómez, S., & Bocanegra, N. (2000). Ser maestro: Experiencias binacionales (Protocolo de Investigación). *Semillero de Ideas* (Mexico), *8*(29), 23–30.

Guevara, G. (2005). Una política educativa para la democracia y la equidad. In R. C. Campos (Ed.), *Política Social de México.* Available at http://www.rolandocordera.org.mx/textos/politica.pdf

Hambleton, R., & Patsula, L. (2000). *Adapting tests for use in multiple languages and cultures* (Laboratory of Psychometric and Evaluation Research Report). Amherst, MA: Massachusetts University Press.

Helms-Lorenz, M., Van de Vijver, F., & Poortinga, Y. (2003). Cross-cultural differences in cognitive performance and Spearman's hypothesis: g or c? *Intelligence, 31,* 9–29.

Hunter, J. E., Schmidt, F. L., & Jackson, C. B. (1982). *Advanced meta-analysis: Quantitative methods of cumulating research findings across studies.* San Francisco, CA: Sage.

INEGI. (2004). *El rezago educativo en la población mexicana.* Aguascalientes, México: Instituto Nacional de Estadística Geografía e Informática. Available at http://www.inegi.gob.mx/prod_

serv/contenidos/espanol/biblioteca/default.asp?
accion=yupc=702825497538&seccionB=bd

International Education Media. (2008). *Mexico education.* Available at http://www.internationaleducationmedia.com/mexico/index.htm

International Labour Organization. (2005). *Unemployment by level of education.* Mexico: International Labour Organization. Available at http://laborsta.ilo.org/cgi-bin/brokerv8.exe

Kellaghan, T., & Greaney, V. (2001). *Using assessment to improve the quality of education.* Fundamentals of Educational Planning, UNESCO.

Kohn, A. (2000). *The case against standardized testing: Raising scores, ruining the schools.* Portsmouth, NH: Heinemann Publishers.

Lennon, R. T. (1956). Assumptions underlying the use of content validity. *Educational and Psychological Measurement, 16,* 294–304.

Linn, R. L., & Herman, J. A. (1997). *Policymaker's guide to standards-led assessment.* Denver, CO: ECS Distribution Center.

LLECE. (2001). *Technical report: First international study comparing language, mathematics and factors related to third and fourth grade elementary school students.* UNESCO, Laboratorio Latinoamericano de Evaluación de la Calidad de la Educación.

Loevinger, J. (1957). Objective tests as instruments of psychological theory (Monograph). *Psychological Reports, 3,* 635–694.

Magaña, F. (2003, October). *The quadratic root in Mayan arithmetic.* Memorias del Congreso Calcolo Matematico Precolombiano. Instituto Italo latinoamericano di Cultura, Roma, Italy, pp. 322–339.

Magaña, F. (2006, March). *Mayan mathematics: The fascinating, fast and fun mathematics of the Maya.* Actas del Seminario de Problemas Científicos y Filosóficos de la UNAM.

Martin, C. J. (1998). The conflictive relations within the schools in the context of educational reform. *Revista Mexicana de Investigación Educativa, 3*(6), 273–279.

Martínez-Rizo, F. (2006). PISA in Latin America: Lessons of the Mexican experience from 2000–2006. *Revista de Educación, Extraordinario,* pp. 153–167.

Martínez-Rizo, F. (2007, October 25–26). Large scale assessment in basic education: Recent progress and future challenges. *Memorias del Simposium Internacional Evaluación: Lecciones aprendidas y perspectivas futuras.* Dirección General de Evaluación Educativa, UNAM.

Medina, N., & Neill, D. M. (1990). *Fallout from the testing explosion: How 100 million standardized exams undermine equity and excellence in America's public schools* (3rd ed.). Cambridge, MA: FairTest.

Messick, S. (1980). Test validity and the ethics of assessment. *American Psychologist, 35,* 1012–1027.

Messick, S. (1989). *Validity.* In R. L. Linn (Ed.), *Educational measurement* (3rd ed.). New York: Macmillan.

Messick, S. (1994, October). *Alternative modes of assessment: Uniform standards of validity.* Paper presented at a conference on Evaluating Alternatives to Traditional Testing for Selection, Bowling Green, OH.

Messick, S. (1995).Validity of psychological assessment: Validation of inferences from person's responses and performances as scientific inquiry into score meaning. *American Psychologist, 50*(9), 741–749.

National Institute of Educational Evaluation. (2004). *Resultados de las pruebas PISA 2000 y 2003 en México: Habilidades para la vida en estudiantes de 15 años.* México, D.F.: Instituto Nacional de Evaluación de la Educación.

Organisation for Economic Co-operation and Development. (2002). *Programme for international student assessment.* Paris, France: Author.

Organisation for Economic Co-operation and Development. (2003a). *Learning for tomorrow's world: First results from PISA 2003.* Available at http://www.pisa.oecd.org/dataoecd/1/60/34002216.pdf

Organisation for Economic Co-operation and Development. (2003b). *Beyond rhetoric: Adult learning policies and practices.* Paris: Author.

Organisation for Economic Co-operation and Development. (2006). *Education at a glance 2004.* Paris, France: Author.

Ostrosky-Solis, F., Ramírez, M., Lozano, A., Picasso, H., & Velez, A. (2004). Culture or education? Neuropsychological test performance of a Maya indigenous population. *International Journal of Psychology, 39*(1), 36–46.

Parker, L. (2000, January). *The social "deconstruction" of race to build African American education: A critical race theory to instruction, curriculum assessment and evaluation in schools.* Paper presented at the RACE conference, Tempe, AZ.

Prawda, J. (1989). *Logros, inequidades y retos del futuro sistema educativo Mexicano.* Colección Pedagógica, Grijalbo.

Secretaría de Educación Pública. (2002). *National agreement on the modernization of basic education* (document signed and presented on May 18, 1992). Mexico City: Author.

Secretaría de Educación Pública. (2005). *Lay general de education*. Mexico City: Author. Available at http://www.cddhcu.gob.mx/leyinfo/pdf/137.pdf

Segall, A. (2003). Teachers' perceptions of the impact of state mandated standardized testing: The Michigan Educational Assessment Program (MEAP) as a case study of consequences. *Theory and Research in Social Education, 31*(3), 287–325.

Shulman, L. S. (1970). Reconstruction of educational research. *Review of Educational Research, 40,* 371–390.

Stake, R. (1987). Confusing standardization with standards: An expert on testing and evaluation questions our reliance on centrally-mandated standards. *The Networker, 2*(3), 29 (published newsletter of the Evaluation Network).

Stake, R. (2000, January). *Evaluation and assessment: Discriminatory against minorities.* Paper presented at the RACE conference, Tempe, AZ.

Tapia, G. (2005). La autonomía de las escuelas de educación básica: Nuevas perspectivas y exigencias para la supervisión escolar. *DIDAC* (Mexico), *45,* 4–9.

Treviño, E. (2006). Evaluación del aprendizaje de los estudiantes indígenas en América Latina: Desafíos de medición e interpretación en contextos de diversidad cultural y desigualdad social. *Revista Mexicana de Investigación Educativa, 11*(28), 225–258.

United Nations Educational, Scientific and Cultural Organization. (2003). *Higher education in a globalized society.* Private Linkages, Public Trust.

Vidal, R., & Díaz, M. A. (2004). *Results of PISA 2000 and 2003 in Mexico. Life skills for fifteen year old students.* Mexico City: INEE.

Vitela, N. (2002). *Brain drain, cited by Hector Carreón, The Great Mexico Brain Drain: The other face of Mexican immigration.* Available at http://www.aztlan.net/mexico_brain_drain.htm

Vogler, K. E. (2003). An integrated curriculum using state standards in a high-stakes environment. *Middle School Journal, 34*(4), 10.

Wang, J. (2003, April). *An analysis of item score difference between 3rd and 4th grades using the TIMSS database.* Paper presented at the annual meeting of the American Educational Research Association, Chicago, IL.

Williams, P. (2000). *Brain drain. Federation for American immigration reform.* Washington, DC: Author. Available at http://www.fairus.org/site/PageServer?pagename=iic_immigrationissuecenterse514

Winkler, D. (2004). Investigaciones sobre etnicidad, raza, género y educación en las Américas. In D. Winkler & S. Cueto (Eds.), *Etnicidad, raza, género y educación en América Latina.* Santiago, Chile: PREAL.

World Bank. (2007). *Poverty in Mexico—Fact sheet.* Available at http://go.worldbank.org/MDXERW23U0

Zorrilla, M. M., & Fernandez, M. T. (2003). Levels of educational achievement in Spanish and Mathematics of students attending public secondary schools, Aguascalientes, México. *Revista Electrónica Iberoamericana sobre Calidad, Eficacia y Cambio en Educación, 1*(1), 1–11.

CHAPTER 14

Inquiry-Minded District Leaders

Evaluation as Inquiry, Inquiry as Practice

Sharon F. Rallis and Matthew Militello

Introduction

The term *accountability* dominates the vocabulary of educators: Schools are accountable to demonstrate annual yearly progress, leaders are accountable to hire and retain qualified teachers and to provide instructional leadership; and teachers are accountable to ensure that all students meet standards. Yet whether all stakeholders share common understandings of what it means to be accountable is doubtful. This narrow focus on outcomes over instruction has created normative bureaucratic frameworks and directive stand-and-deliver professional development that prevents meaningful and real accountability (O'Day, 2002). Accountability does not have to imply coercion or imposition of external standards or measures. To be accountable means to be obligated to explain one's actions and to demonstrate effectiveness—and to accept responsibility for reaching a desired outcome (see Newmann, King, &

Rigdon, 1997; O'Day, 2002; Rallis & MacMullen, 2000). Accountability relies on inquiry with feedback that links performance with results, inquiry that looks inside the school and classroom where instruction occurs and questions the practices, their origins, their supports, and their impact on student learning. Internalizing accountability as a professional responsibility turns processes and outcomes into ones the professionals can control. To be accountable, educators must engage in ongoing iterative evaluation. They must be inquiry-minded.

The dominance of accountability crosses national borders. Accountability is a global phenomenon both because it is everywhere and because the forces of globalization are changing schools. Scarce resources; issues of migration, immigration, and refugees; along with a globalized market economy are influencing national policy and local practices. Students throughout the world come to school bringing greater diversity and greater needs than ever before, and more and greater demands are put on them. Reactions to these challenges have been legislative in nature and focused on outcomes. For example, the Dakar Framework for Action in 2000 emphasized the improvement of "all aspects of the quality of education and ensuring excellence of all so that recognized and measurable learning outcomes are achieved by all, especially in literacy, numeracy and essential life skills" (United Nations Educational Scientific and Cultural Organization, 2000, p. 8).

In the United States, federal mandates via No Child Left Behind (NCLB) have directed educators away from an evaluation process that considers inputs and inquiry toward a narrow emphasis on student achievement outcome measures. This accountability package, in part a response to global forces, raises the stakes for student performance (Darling-Hammond, 2004). The policy, however, ignores the multiple and varying local contexts. The result is a rush to disjointed and ambiguous implementation activities (e.g., overuse of waivers in urban settings to meet the "highly qualified teacher in every subject" mandate). On an international level, a similar phenomenon is occurring; for example, the rush to implement policies that increase access for all students has led to overcrowded classrooms with unqualified instructors (Association for the Development of Education in Africa, 2003; Independent Evaluation Group, 2006; United Nations Educational, Scientific and Cultural Organization, 2005). As a consequence of this external pressure, educational organizations throughout the world respond with command-oriented implementation (to say/show that it is being done) (Rowan, 1990), and leaders engage in command-directive behavior (this is what you have to do) (Spillane, 2000). The approach is additive (i.e., solutions are layered on), *not* evaluative (i.e., solutions are continually reexamined and modified).

An alternative approach for improvement stipulates that student outcomes are improved through collaborative inquiry-based processes around teaching and learning; leaders facilitate these processes. But how the theory plays out in real schools and classrooms is less clear and simple; what actions do leaders take to alter teaching and learning? The ability to translate accountability efforts into new behaviors and structures in schools has proved difficult (Elmore, 2003, 2004; Massell & Goertz, 2002; O'Day, 2002). Use of an inquiry cycle, which begins and ends with questions of evaluation, is crucial to this approach, which is the antithesis of the layering solutions often prescribed in schools.

We suggest that asking schools to evaluate (over *being accountable*) is foundational to successful teaching and learning because the process entails explicating what actions are taken, why, and to what effect—and then learning *from* and acting *on* that knowledge. We define *evaluation* as a planned, purposeful, and systematic process for collecting information, decision making, and taking action as a means of contributing to improvement of policy and programming for the well-being of all within an organization or a community (see Weiss, 1998). Evaluation employs an inquiry cycle that iteratively frames and examines problems of practice, chooses actions to address the problems, assesses effects of these actions, and then reframes the original problems of practice. The inquiry framework combines elements of people and action beyond an individual school leader. Elements include individual attributes or capacity (e.g., mindsets, vision, self-recognition) as well as activities (e.g., engaging in dialogical conversations, professional learning communities). For us, evaluation is a dispositional quality that, much like social justice and collaboration, is an essential process embedded within and throughout any efforts to improve learning. When evaluation is inquiry, then inquiry becomes practice. Only practice can strike at the accountability demands of improving student achievement.

From our perspective, rather than demand that schools be held accountable for externally defined results, schools should be accountable for evaluating their processes, progress, and outcomes (i.e., they would engage in a cycle of questioning and informing action). In such a scenario, school leaders would ask the evaluation questions of: What do we want our students to learn and why? What are we doing to meet these goals? Specifically, what instruction do we offer to facilitate this learning? What happens as a result of our efforts? What do students do and learn? What successes do we experience and what challenges do we encounter? What counts as evidence of success or failure? How do we support, modify, or change our practices to better meet our purposes? Because most would agree that the purpose of schools is student learning, what happens *inside* the school and classroom—instruction—is key. An inquiry-minded school is constantly engaged in learning-based tasks that are naturally evaluated and measured. We note that these questions about internal choices have become more insistent and complex in the increasingly globalized and politicized world where external environments permeate the school boundaries.

In U.S. schools, the burden of buffering and bridging the school boundaries and facilitating meaningful evaluation falls to the district leader. However large the forces influencing their worlds, superintendents realize they must act as instructional leaders in their districts. Their actions can shape building leaders' actions that in turn shape what teachers do in the classroom with students. How to turn each school into such a learning organization is the superintendent's challenge. Our experience working with superintendents who do engage in the evaluation inquiry cycle reveals that their efforts have moved the standards for success and the criteria for meeting them toward their local schools and in turn increased their districts' capacities for improvement. We call these superintendents *inquiry-minded leaders,* and we offer the Connecticut Superintendents Network as a case of these leaders in practice.

This narrative case describes the Connecticut Superintendents Network as a community of practice for instructional improvement. The case explores what these inquiry-minded leaders do and how their actions change policies and practices in their schools. The case raises questions of the effectiveness of the process: Whose capacity is built for what? How are student learning and achievement affected? Is organizational

learning culture strengthened? What supports or hinders the process? Equally important are the questions of the leaders' own growth and development. The case considers the challenges of defining and meeting standards in a world deeply shaped by external forces. The details of this case are informed by Rallis' role as documenter/evaluator of the network's activities.[1]

Collaborative Inquiry: Change Through Communities of Practice

The case of the Superintendents Network is grounded in the belief that successful leaders who engage in inquiry for improvement cannot operate in isolation. Given the distributed perspective of leadership as a construct of relationships rather than roles (Firestone, 1996; Halverson, 2003; Spillane, Halverson, & Diamond, 2001, 2004), inquiry-minded leaders collaborate in their search for organizational coherence, clarity, and reform (Elmore, 2003). Communities of practice that collect data on what people do in schools offer one structure for meaningful collaboration. Such communities explore "the activities engaged in by leaders, in interaction with others in particular contexts around specific tasks" (Spillane et al., 2004, p. 5) with a goal of supporting the members' work toward instructional reform. Such groups focus on their practice.

Wenger (1999) explains that a "practice is the source of coherence of a community," and this coherence is manifested in a community as three basic characteristics: joint enterprise, mutual engagement, and a shared repertoire. Wenger defines *joint enterprise* as the meaning or understanding that the members of a community have negotiated regarding what they will mutually accomplish. *Mutual engagement* requires that members of the community of practice interact with one another regularly to develop new skills, refine old ones, and incorporate new ways of understanding (Wenger, 1999). In a community of practice, *shared repertoire* is the "communal resources that members have developed over time through their mutual engagement" (Wenger, 1999). This shared repertoire may consist of artifacts, documents, language, vocabulary, routines, technology, and so on.

Still, the ultimate influence of the community on practice remains unknown (Rallis, Tedder, Lachman, & Elmore, 2006). A community of practice that is not rooted in elements of inquiry-based practice may only provide a superficial belief system without impact on practice and student achievement. Consequently, we posit that a community of practice must work within a *cycle of inquiry*. Rallis and MacMullen (2000) developed a set of activities that make up an inquiry cycle for inquiry-minded schools:

- Establish outcomes for which we accept responsibility,
- Identify important questions concerning student learning,
- Collect and manage data derived from the assessment of performance,
- Conduct mindful analyses of the data in light of the desired outcomes and interpret information in light of the school's purposes,
- Take action based on knowledge, and
- Assess the effects of action.

Such an inquiry-minded school, born into the belief system of a community of practice and rooted in a cycle of inquiry, should spawn organizational learning focused on improved teaching and learning. As an organization learns, coherence is established and individual capacity is built. Under such circumstances, forces of reciprocal accountability (Resnick & Glennan, 2002) or comparative advantage (Elmore, 2000) will highlight school improvement efforts, rather than a set of abstract, ambiguous external efforts to promulgate improvements. Under these circumstances, internal professional accountability can be built to consider and leverage external accountability efforts in the local context.

This internal professional accountability is facilitated by inquiry-minded leaders who know how to transform data into meaningful information that becomes useful knowledge for practice (see Petrides & Guiney, 2002). These leaders recognize that their practices and problems are not theirs alone. Thus, they join informal and formal communities of practice that harness the power of collective knowledge (see Brown & Duguid, 2000). This collective knowledge goes beyond local and national boundaries to achieve more than the ends for which immediate reforms press. The following case illustrates such a community of inquiry-minded leaders. Although this case is based in the U.S. context, it strikes at a global theme—advancing student learning.

A Community of Practice in Practice

The Superintendents Network, in its sixth year of operation, consists of a dozen public school superintendents who wrestle with establishing high-level, demanding curriculum and instruction in classrooms throughout their districts, which are geographically and demographically diverse, serve more than 57,000 students, and range from postindustrial cities to affluent suburbs to less wealthy small towns. The Network is sponsored by the Connecticut Center for School Change (hereafter called the Center), a local school reform organization, and has met monthly for 6 years with the goal of forming a community of practice to explore the improvement of teaching and learning. Nonsuperintendent members of the group are present as facilitators: the executive director and the program officer of the Center and two university professors whose expertise is leadership and school reform. Another member is the documenter, a university professor of leadership and school reform whose specialization is evaluation.

This blended network of practitioners, academics, and change agents espouses a model of professional development that differs from more traditional single-event, decontextualized, sit-and-listen practices prevalent in education settings. The model recognizes that learning is both social and situated—that professional adults learn not through workshops, but through multiple opportunities to examine closely real problems of practice with peers (Lave & Wenger, 1991). They are committed to a process where members go into classrooms to observe teaching and learning directly and then support each other in problem solving around what they have seen in practice. For 2 months, they focus on a problem related to student learning in a particular school identified by a superintendent. Specifically, the host superintendent articulates his or her theory of action (a causal *if, then* statement). The group visits that school, conducting 20-minute observations in several classrooms and collecting data. After the observations, they meet with the school leaders to debrief. The following month, they meet for a reflection session, during which they analyze the instructional issues raised in the observations, consider potential solutions and implications for practice, and make sense of what has been learned. In the sixth year, the network added a consultation follow-up to occur after the second site-based superintendent's visit. The consultation follow-up consists of two superintendents returning to the district to serve as critical friends (see Rallis & Rossman, 2000).

The Superintendents Network Theory of Action

Central to the social nature of learning is the concept of *community of practice* for the purpose of learning and capacity building. Members work "together to test out ideas, critique one another's work, offer alternative conceptualizations, and provide both emotional and intellectual support" (Rossman & Rallis, 2003, p. xvi). Discourse within the community becomes dialogic, new ideas emerge, individuals develop deeper knowledge about their work, and these new conceptualizations prompt and guide improved practice. Specifically, the Network's goals are to:

- Develop superintendents' knowledge and skill to lead large-scale instructional improvement;

- Assist superintendents in developing *distributed leadership* (Gronn, 2002; Spillane et al., 2001, 2004) throughout their districts (i.e., building a cadre of knowledgeable and skilled leaders who assume responsibility for developing their own practice around improvement); and

- Enable superintendents to build an infrastructure that supports improvement work—evaluation, professional growth, networks, and opportunities for collaboration.

The Network has explicitly stated its axiomatic theory of action:

If we collectively participate in a community of practice grounded in on-site classroom observation and focused on large-scale instructional improvement, *then* participating superintendents will become more effective instructional leaders as demonstrated by changes in their practice (as a result of their use of leverage points to affect classroom teaching) and ultimately improvements in student achievement.

The Network emphasizes that their focus is on instruction, their talk must be grounded in data over opinion, the activities are collaborative and context-specific (site-based), and goals are focused on impacts on practice. Figure 14.1 illustrates that the Network is situated in an inquiry cycle.

We examine the Network's theory of action through discourse analysis (Gee, 2005) from transcripts of the visit debrief sessions and the subsequent reflection sessions.

Evidence of Network Practices: What Really Happened?

The group began working in October 2001. Initially, the university facilitator assumed leadership by proposing topics, but he emphasized that members of a community of practice accept collective responsibility for how it should engage

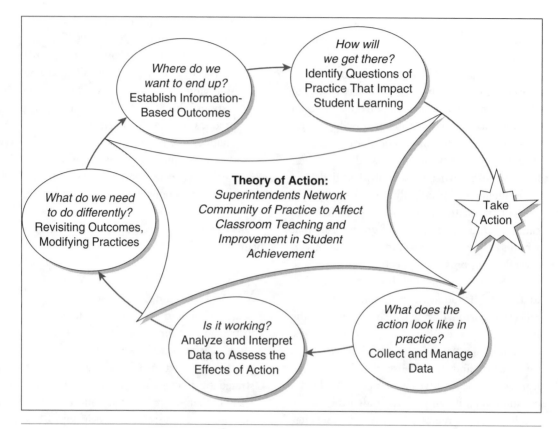

Figure 14.1 Community of Practice Within the Inquiry Cycle

in the work. The expectations were explicit: Everyone in the Network had to do the work, everyone had to model the practice of sustained focus on an issue, *and* everyone had to base their discussions on the details of teaching and learning. To provide a concrete focus, the facilitator posited as a leadership strategy the notion of *leverage points* (key components of the system around which people agree to work to realize large-scale systemic improvement): resources, knowledge/skill/expertise, accountability, assessment, curriculum, capacity building and professional development, and structure.

A crucial move toward the Network functioning effectively was the establishment of group operating norms. These norms included agreements on: *attendance* (Everyone attends every meeting), *involvement* (Everyone puts work out for discussion), *respect for confidentiality* (All agree not to discuss sensitive matters beyond the group), *candor and humility* (All

commit to be candid and willing to acknowledge what they don't know), and *attentiveness* (Every member invests in listening).

However, disconnect remained between the ideal of community practice and the actuality of the Network's performance. Talk was not concrete and dialogic, but rather abstract and univocal (e.g., "In my district, we are always striving to increase achievement for all students"). To put actual practice at the center, the facilitator and the Center staff recommended that the group move to the next activity of the inquiry cycle (i.e., data collection) and visit classrooms together. A site visit would be driven by practice-oriented questions about instruction, and direct observation would provide members with a shared experience. Follow-up conversations would be data-based, tolerating only minimal "degrees of separation"[2] from instruction. Defined protocols would guide both the visit and the reporting out of the observations.

The superintendents were initially reluctant but agreed to give the observation process a try. The first site visit occurred in April 2002 at an elementary school in a small suburban district. Just prior to the observations, the facilitator reminded the Network to focus "on what we actually see going on in classrooms, not judgments we make about what we see." Just before the debrief, he reminded members to "try to stick to the discipline of responding to the question: 'What did you see?' " Yet by the end of the debrief, it was clear to all present that the superintendents were not *seeing* classrooms as thoroughly as the facilitator. The facilitator's notes were precise—clinical in the sense of medical grand rounds (e.g., numbers of students doing particular tasks, verbatim teacher remarks, and detailed summaries of student work on desks). Other reports on the same classes were more generalized, subjective, and judgmental (e.g., "Teacher used evaluative language" and "A marvelous lesson"). Early transcripts reveal that network members avoided specifics and were hesitant to be critical. The following remark, made during a visit debrief, is representative: "Let's spend some time validating the positive things happening in that school." Others followed with warm generalizations about the culture and feel of the school. Later, the group came to call this stance as operating in the "land of nice."

As a result of the visit, all the Network members agreed on the value of informing selected instructional problems through data gathered directly in classrooms. One participant spoke for the group by affirming that the "site visit experience brought us to a different level of discussion."

The development of the community of practice emerged as the superintendents' candor increased, and they overcame the tension they had originally felt in giving critical and descriptive feedback. Compare the comments after the first site visit with the following conversation that occurred 4 months later:[3]

Bea: I did not see what I would call effective instruction in either 3rd grade. Children were just rotating in groups through the same activities. There were no less than eight groups. The teacher was running from group to group. [He had] no time to give more than 5-8 seconds of attention to any child.

Don: I was struck that two students were sitting off by themselves and never had any interaction with any adult.

Ellie: Every group was doing essentially the same worksheet. Not clear how the groups were determined. Differentiated instruction is not just dividing kids into groups.

This exchange illustrates members' growing willingness to critique and question what they had observed and to use observational data to uncover the reality of the setting. Over time, comments became increasingly detailed and focused. Descriptions of what members saw in class became richer and finer grained, and judgments were increasingly grounded in specific observed data.

By the end of Year 2, feedback was grounded in evidence, not mere opinion. Members asked: "Did you see what I saw?" For example, the following conversation is drawn from the debrief following the last school visit of Year 3:

Alan: [The teacher] was having them write a story. She did not give them the elements. They wrote it, and then she went around and critiqued—why didn't she go over what we want in a good story? Some of the pieces were lacking, but I did not see how the children would have known.

Mario: We saw that part, how they would know—it was the "diamond" [a figure on the board that came from the writing program].

Don: I saw writing in almost every classroom, but nobody was addressing things like audience. Basically prompt writing. That is what [they think] good writing is—the "diamond."

Ellie: That was not my observation—she was not following a script.

Fran: She had kids working. I saw her give them a lot of signals and cues about what would make their writing distinctive. She asked: "What am I looking for?" They gave her a bunch of well-rehearsed answers.

Discourse grew from this fine-grained description to interpretations grounded in the observed data. The interpretations became increasingly analytical and dialogic. An example is the discussion during a reflection session about the relationship between behavior and beliefs; note the development of insight:

Fran: Our [state test] scores came in, but they did not want the scores to be the focus. They wanted the focus to be on beliefs and what we need to do with kids.

Tom: Do you have a theory about change?

Fran: Yes. The only way they can change is by themselves—get their mental models out on the table and then look at the data and reflect on their beliefs.

Tom: What about behavior?

Fran: I think behavior is tied to beliefs.

Tom: I sort of surprised myself by coming down on the other side—that behavior comes first, especially around how students learn. Teachers seem to change their values and beliefs in response to what they have seen students do in response to their [teacher] behaviors—rather than change behavior based on beliefs.

Fran: Teachers see that the practice creates a positive change in kids' behaviors, so they are willing to examine their beliefs. Now they are able to put their beliefs on the table and change their own ways of thinking.

Pete: This suggests to me that teachers might learn to behave into a way of thinking differently.

Although discourse became increasingly dialogic during Year 2, at least one person's responses remained unconnected, and a few members contributed only marginally. The Center's staff recognized the issue and intervened, reiterating the norms that superintendents speak first and that all members have a chance to comment before anyone offered a second observation. At that time, the group had not assumed direct and collective responsibility for the nature and process of the discourse. However, as evidenced in the transcripts by the end of Year 3, discourse was predominantly dialogic; all members contributed at each meeting, and seldom was discourse dominated by only a few. Frequently, members commented on the value of talking and learning specifically about instructional practice together with respected colleagues.

By the sixth year, the group talked directly about their community of practice, questioning and critiquing themselves. The following comments are from a reflection session in January 2007:

Gary: Yes, I believe we are a community of practice. We've made decisions about norms and the processes. I don't know if we've made any decision about our learning and what as a group we do about our learning.

Mario: I suspect that each of us could share the impact of our conversations over time in what we are doing in our districts, but I don't think we've ever done that in a systematic way—only anecdotes. But if the intent has been to expand our own knowledge-base in the way we do things in our districts and to share that—that's not something we have done.

Mara: Maybe that's what we're starting to get to with this revisit—we are revisiting relatively soon the problem and what we've done—holding our feet to the fire in terms of what went on. I agree that we're pretty good at dialogue, but I think we've avoided making group decisions and thinking about and sharing with the group the actions we've taken.

In summary, they agree they have learned through their participation in this professional learning community; they also recognize that their practice back home in their districts may not yet be sufficient to affect teaching and learning in their schools.

Analysis of Superintendents' Learning

Evidence demonstrates that the superintendents were engaged in an inquiry-based community of practice. This did not happen through the mere organization of a formalized network. Rather, the development came, like most processes, with frustration and difficulties. In the end, the superintendents were no longer using a series of independent comments to talk about instruction; they were creating new learning through threads of linked comments. Rather than carry on parallel conversations, their ideas intersected and interacted. The fledgling community of practice had taken hold. The new community was defined by elements of practice; instructionally based, problem-focused work; agreed-on protocols for evidence gathering; strategies of instructional improvement; strong group norms and periodic reflection; devoted use of evidence; and peer-to-peer collegiality. As a result, the Network discourse developed in the following ways:

- Less expressing positive generalizations ("land of nice") to more rigorous questioning, critiquing, and "truth telling";
- Avoidance of storytelling (fewer "In my school we. . . .");
- Rules, norms, and common language of engagement established over time;

- Consistent, site-based meetings rooted in cases of *actual* practice;
- Movement from mostly univocal opinion-based discourse (one speaker, one idea) to evidence-based, analytical, and dialogic interpretations of what was happening; and
- Transactively generating new understandings.

We posit that this community of practice developed by the convergence of two forces: experience and specific attention to an inquiry-focused purpose. To begin, the group engaged in difficult activities (e.g., debriefs) that resulted in establishing new norms of practice. Second, over time, Network practice incorporated elements of the inquiry cycle. Both the norms and the cycle were critical for the evolution from a group of superintendents toward a community of practice. These two forces combined and paved the way for *learning in action*. That is, participants set the norms and then used and reflected on them. This process proves to be an important step toward a culture of inquiry-minded practice. While we see evidence of the development of a community of practice within the Network, how this inquiry-minded community did or did not impact practices in the schools and in the classroom warrants additional analysis. This is the focus of the next section.

Learning in Action

Use of the inquiry cycle shaped the practice of the Network—that is, *learning in action*. This phrase captures the iterative process whereby the superintendents were learning from action and acting on their learning. Prior to a visit, the host superintendent shared his or her theory of action and posed a related problem of practice. The identified problem served as a focus for classroom observations and data collection. During the visit, teams of four observed for 20 minutes in five classrooms collecting data using a common protocol that asked observers to note what the teacher was doing and saying, what the students were doing and saying, and what arti-facts were present in the room. Often an obser-vation of a teacher team or administrative work meeting was included.

After a morning of observation, the teams reunited for lunch and a debrief in which the principal participated. During this time, net-work members were encouraged to state simply what they had observed—for example, "In the third grade class four of the students not work-ing with the teacher were looking out the win-dow, three were completing the worksheet, and one was kicking the chair in front of her." Commentary moved away from offering opin-ions and toward reporting data-based observa-tions and then drawing interpretations from them. What follows are two examples illustrat-ing the Network's practice from problem fram-ing to considering changes in the schools.

Example 1: Raising Expectations and Increasing Energy

A fall 2003 Network visit to a high school reveals leadership focus on how teachers addressed student achievement. The superinten-dent (Lin) framed her problem in these words: "As the leader of a district where community expectations for students in many areas are either very low or non-existent, I struggle with the change that must take place if all students are to achieve at high levels." The superintendent moved to the high school one of her effective elementary school principals and charged him to lead this change. In turn, the principal chal-lenged each of the high school teachers to ensure that every child learned to an appropriately high level each day. The superintendent asked Network members to focus their observations of the high school classrooms on two questions: (a) What are teachers doing instructionally? (b) Are high expectations for student achievement evident in classroom instruction? A section of the debrief reveals the superintendents' critique of instruction and expectations:

Tom: The civics teacher had kids doing noth-ing at all. They were polite, nice kids, but they were not on-task. Some were just sitting there. The teacher kept saying to us [the observers] how hard it was to have kids with different skills in the class.

Al: In what we saw, he did all the work. He handed out a page and read it all.

Pete: A student in the class told me: "this is what we do every day. He comes and he talks and then he hands us an assign-ment. We read the book, answer the questions, and hand it in."

Mara: I could see into their notebooks—what he was teaching them on the board was already in some of their notebooks.

Dick: Another pattern—constant repetition.

Jill: The repetition struck me—I asked one girl how long they had been on this one unit. She said a week and half. Roughly half was new instruction and half preparation for the exam. And it was not a mid-term. Just a lesson to test out the unit.

Carl: He had all this stuff on minerals. I asked him why this? He said, "Oh, I did this when I was in college and liked it. The guy down the hall does gems. He likes them." No alignment; they do their own thing.

Dialogue during the reflection session sum-marized the observed patterns of practice: failure to use available instructional time; low energy levels; low performance expectations, no cur-riculum alignment. One observer commented:

I was angry—that [teacher] in civics was too ignorant to be embarrassed. The staff is so comfortable because they have not been asked to do anything for 30 years. This principal can get by for one year, but he needs to set some goals by spring. He needs to evaluate teachers—say to them, "You're negligent in your teaching." Putting people on notice that change is coming. I'd take some of the best teachers and put them in the lower-level classes so that those teachers cannot say that these kids cannot learn.

Network members acknowledged the superintendent's bravery in exposing her problems so openly with her colleagues and recognized both challenges and opportunities for change. For example, one superintendent commented:

I have been thinking about [the principal] as opportunity. He is new. But he is also an elementary-trained educator. He has two channels he can go. He can see the outside perspective. The risk for him is enormous but positive. Or he can take the other path—live in that barbed-wire atmosphere and pretty soon he ceases to be the outsider. How do you take someone in that leadership position and give him the psychological fortitude to take this crew the first anguishing step to teach differently? A very exciting challenge but how can you transfer what you know about leadership into practice that works? If we came back in three years, what would we see?

The reflection ended with the superintendent asking what she could do to support the principal in his efforts and the Network members generating ideas. Suggestions (such as modeling language and practices and arranging teacher visits to other schools) focused on the need for teachers to see new instructional behaviors and to hear positive ways for talking about and with students.

The September 2006 visit returned to this same high school. At this time, the superintendent's theory of action had become explicit: *If we use student data to inform instruction, then student achievement will increase.* The concern was still student achievement, but the superintendent asked for two foci for observation, the

classroom and team meetings: (a) Can we see evidence in the *classroom* of improvement in the problems of practice identified during the first visit (i.e., teacher misuse of available instructional time, low student energy levels, and low performance expectations)? (b) Can we see evidence in the *team meetings* of a shared-results orientation across the leadership and faculty (i.e., shared vision, collaborative work, commitment to improvement, data-driven decision making)? In reference to the first question, the debrief transcript indicates that the energy and expectations remain low and that teachers' use of time does not challenge students to achieve:

Gary: The teacher used the microphone and sat on a rolling chair in front of the computer. Said we are not learning anything new. There was a boy on the front row who never even opened his notebook but at 9:15 he got up and sharpened his pencil. A girl was doing her other homework.

Tom: The teacher was using the PowerPoint as the main lesson. He read the slides. Gave students chance to respond to one example. Who got it and who did not? Not what you would call teaching. Mostly just a PowerPoint review.

Gary: The PowerPoint was by McGraw Hill. It came with the book.

Pete: We saw the same behavior [during our visit]. The formulas were up on the board, and the teacher asked students if they understood. Students were compliant. Passive non-engagement. After they read—or re-read them, teacher asked them to calculate, but the only way to do it was to go to a table in the book. As the kids were working, the teacher sat in the chair and from time to time asked the individual students: "Joe, did you get that yet? OK, keep working. You know how to use the chart." Finally he asked the kids if they had an answer; only two were correct. Not much discussion about how they got the answer or how they got it wrong. He assumed they saw the process and understood.

Other segments report similar classroom interactions, whereas others explore the question about results orientation. As after the earlier visit, Network members again applauded the superintendent for her bravery in opening her doors, revealing that the problem continued. Yet they found no evidence that her theory of action (teachers used data to inform their instruction) was operational.

Next, the debrief turned to analyzing the team meeting. The Network focused on how the high school principal modeled leadership with his team. One Network member observed that he did not hear the principal clearly articulate how mission, expectations, curriculum, and instruction were to be connected. Others noted that they heard a lot of "if" statements that were not connected to a "then" statement and wondered how faculty would know what the principal wanted. Another noted that the principal had not explicitly prioritized the expectations for the faculty and asked: "Are they all equally important?" Others heard that the principal was trying to do too many things at once with the danger that "you don't do any well." In summary, Network members observed that the principal appeared to assume actions more than model them.

A Network facilitator asked, "But how would the principal know what to model?" The superintendent felt she was trying to model with her administrative team: "We're always looking at data, informing our instruction, reading." However, she wondered why her theory of action was working with some principals but not with the high school principal. Another Network member asked, "How do you develop that capacity in the entire administrative team?" This led Lin to consider that the high school principal might not have the skills to lead the instructional improvement. The question becomes less a search for answers and more an inquiry into specific aspects of the problem.

At this point, the group discourse reveals their recognition that a problem of practice needs to be more targeted before solutions can be explored. Within the context of this example, they looked at the impact of their own work on helping each other:

Bea: This is just a back and forth. Our talk takes place, and Lin [superintendent] listens and responds.

Pete: One problem is that we set it up that way.

Gary: I say to the entire group: I think we need to be cognizant that Lin *is* asking for some advice. And therefore we should respect her direction to us, that this is how our debrief should go. I think we should proceed and then end with questions for Lin. Do you think the question is lack of the principal's skill? Or that he does possess the skill, but that it's that there's no accountability?

Mario: I'm wondering if part of the challenge is to find answers to those questions. I think in a way we're all on a rescue mission; we can say to each other "hey, I need help!" I would ask us to frame a theory of action relative to the work Lin does. *If* Lin does the following things—and we don't know what they are—*then* the principal would be more successful. Part of it is *if* Lin can find out the principal's need is a lack of skill, *then* it might point you to how to improve his skill set. *If* it's an inability for him to take skills and operate with them, *then* the question is how do you help him use the skills?

Rather than supply ready-made solutions, the debrief session broke down the original questions into a set of more meaningful questions. They resisted becoming a garbage can that simply matches the unexamined problem with the first solution that appears (see Cohen, March, & Olsen, 1972; March, 1999). The discourse moved from how can Lin help the principal to what really is the principal's problem? What began as a set of questions into a problem of practice from Lin has developed into an inquiry process about what the problem really is and how she will deal with it. The Network's observations and reflections contribute to building Lin's capacity to have an impact on the system. The Network helped Lin reframe her inquiry.

Example 2: Can We See the Strategies in the Classroom?

Another visit in February 2003 to an elementary school illustrates a superintendent's focus on a specific instructional problem. A group of students consistently scored at *Basic* or *Below Basic* levels on the state test even though the school's average Connecticut Mastery Test (CMT) scores were above the state goal. The superintendent theorized that achievement for all students would increase were the norm for daily planning and classroom practice to be differentiating instruction, consistent checking for understanding, and modifying instruction based on that feedback. To that end, he and the principal built professional development efforts around differentiated instruction, creating, they hoped, an environment where teachers knew the needs of each student and provided instruction accordingly. The question for the Network was: How did differentiated instruction look in the classroom?

The superintendent and principal asked the network members to address these specific questions in their observations of Grades 1 and 3 (teachers were aware of the protocol):

- What is the teacher doing? What are the aides doing?
- What modes of instruction are you seeing? What kinds of questions are being asked?
- What activities/questions does the teacher use to assess student understanding?
- What adjustments do teachers make (e.g., accelerate instruction, regroup students,

remediate, reteach, and vary pace) based on observations of student work or responses?

During the debrief, detailed descriptions of what network members saw paint a picture that reveals inconsistencies among teaching practices including the misuse or misunderstanding of differentiated instruction as a teaching strategy (e.g., "I saw a 1st grade where there was no differentiated instruction. There was whole class math instruction with choral reading. All were filling out worksheets and responding to simple prompts").

When the Network met the next month for the reflection session, the superintendent reported the principal's insights from the visit debrief:

> I asked her: "What did you learn?" She answered, "Well, it made me aware that I could see a class and observe something that may not be real." This *Aha* is really important for instructional leaders not to just make decisions from observation, but to connect with teachers. To approach the teacher to say, "Here is what I saw; tell me about it." We need to make sure that the talk is always about the instruction.

Dialogue during the reflection session casts doubt on the effect of district efforts at implementing differentiated instruction to improve student learning (e.g., "Differentiated instruction should be evident in every lesson. They are not there yet as a routine. Or they are confused. If there were collective understanding, we would have seen patterns; we did not"). The group questions whether the principal's leadership and the accompanying professional development had changed instructional practices as the superintendent and principal had hoped.

By 2006–2007, the Network was revisiting schools to gauge improvement, so in February the Network returned to this school. The principal described her efforts to support teachers' use of formative assessments to modify instruction accordingly. She reported that she was trying to get into classrooms often to collect data as a basis for conversing with teachers, but she also indicated that the teachers want more of her drop-in, nonformal visits. Network members were asked to look for evidence that teachers were using formative assessments and differentiating instruction. Network observations revealed some progress in use of differentiated instruction, but also raised questions of how much principal leadership practices and teacher instructional practices had changed. Later, one of the superintendents summarized his impressions:

I was so disappointed last week. Nothing had changed in the classrooms at the school; the principal admitted that she still seldom got into classrooms. Is it the size of the districts that make the difference? Is it that superintendents assume that principals understand broad concepts in the same way they do?

Evaluation in Action: Using the Full Inquiry Cycle?

The Network has engaged in the first activities of an inquiry cycle: They frame and accept the problem of practice; and they collect, analyze, and make sense of data related to the problem. Still, if the cycle is to result in action and that action is to initiate a renewed cycle, we ask what actions emerge from the Superintendents Network community of practice and how they evaluate their actions so as to shape the inquiry anew? Do their deliberations and dialogue actually change their practices back in their districts? If so, do their changed practices influence instruction and in turn improve teaching and learning? Transcripts during Years 2 and 3 provide evidence of insights and activities to improve instruction that superintendents are taking back to their districts.

- Many report their own efforts to visit schools and get into classrooms more often: "The work of the superintendent is far more intimately connected to the classroom than I had thought."
- Many are replicating this process with their management teams: "We are having classroom visits modeled after the Network school visits."
- Another has scheduled visits for principals with another district: "I have them take a day off and visit another school."
- Another talked about understanding how systems/organizations work: "Principals teach teachers; I teach the principals. Replicating is the next step."
- Still, superintendents identified obstacles to replication in their districts.
  o "You have to make sure [inquiry] does not become a 'project.' You make it a way of being and operating—integral to the other [items on the agenda]. People in the district must make it a part of the way they do things."
  o "People think the critique is saying something 'about me.' People are afraid, so they want you to stay out of your schools."
  o "Part of the problem in replicating is us. We are seen as the ones who have the answers. Now we are saying to forget that I am the boss; I do not have the answers."
  o "Time . . . principals would say the visit and reflection is the most important thing, but we do not have time for it."

None of these comments indicate direct changes in teacher behavior or student outcomes attributable to the superintendent's actions. They do, however, clearly express awareness of their struggle in facilitating change.

More recently, the questions about action and results have surfaced in the group discourse during reflection sessions. The following dialogue occurred in the January 2007 reflection session in response to this question: Are we a community of practice that includes action as part of our inquiry cycle?

Jim: Certainly the esprit de corps is real, but I am very anxious about the next level of work [refers to action steps taken back in districts]. If we have concluded that we know what we know—then okay, now what?

Bea: For me, we are successful if I grow in my role and we collectively grow stronger and function better with one another. Any one of us might take individually what we heard here today, but I don't see these pieces as influential for the group. That may be what we should pursue—engage more together in looking at how this experience reflects back on our work in our districts. I don't necessarily do that, and if others do, we don't hear that.

Kit: I agree. The group has helped keep me grounded. I return with more energy and passion to my district. The next level—I'm not sure what that is. Are we at the point where we can talk about this? I wish we could share more of what's going on [back in our districts] even if we don't have a visitation.

Mario: I think we spend enough time on how we interact with one another, and we get better at it. It's so different than it was three years ago. We are all about instruction, and our talk is grounded in data. But I don't think I would define action as essential to community of practice.

Dick: There is a certain value of a community with consequences. We could say: "I think we've learned something from this visit—I'm going out and try X. I'd like some support from other members of the network, and I'd like to come back and say what I did and the consequences." That requires a higher level of consequences than we have. That's one way in which a community of practice becomes tighter. We do that, sort of. When we put a superintendent on the spot after the visit, but we don't do it when we're not in the bucket. That's the

next level of work—specific ways we can support each other in our work in addition to doing the routine?

Lin: Really what I asked this group to do—be a community of practice—to come in and to really push me, help me make decisions, make me accountable. So that's really what I was looking for. I think there was hesitance because we don't own, we're all separated, independent, rather than owning our accomplishments. We were relatively gentle around the table concerning me, when we were debriefing after the visit. It was difficult for me to say "Look at what I'm doing—help me change." Very difficult. I think collectively we need to talk about whether this is where we want to go?

Tom: One of the things that is hard to measure is the extent we choose to do this work. By default this Network has kept me on this work. All of us use this Network to help us stay in the work. We make conscious choices to stay in the work. Many of our colleagues who don't belong to the Network don't have the reinforcement and can't stay in the work.

Dick: There is an accountability in that. If you're not involved in the work you're a spectator—no collegial accountability. We have an effect on each other's standards of what the work is—being in school. When we're in somebody's school we're going through a [lateral accountability] process. Those social expectations are part of being in a network—putting yourself in the way of that influence.

This interchange revisits the Network's theory of action. Together members fulfill the first part of the statement, the *If we collectively participate in a community of practice grounded in on-site classroom observation and focused on large-scale instructional improvement*. The *then* is more challenging. Dialogue indicates that participating superintendents have become more effective instructional leaders because their interactions revitalize them and keep them in the work, but not as demonstrated by changes in their practice, as a result of their use of leverage points to affect classroom teaching and ultimately improvements in student achievement. They see their work together as meaningful, but they may not be connected once they are apart. The experience helps them "stay in the work," but they are not sure exactly how the work affects teaching and learning in their districts. Evidence shows beliefs and interactions among themselves to be changing, but is this enough to improve teaching and learning? What occurs between Network meetings and visits and teaching and learning in classrooms remains a black box.

Conclusion

Accountability via national mandates using standardized measures has proved difficult to operationalize for improving classroom instruction and learning. Rather than be held accountable solely by external forces, school districts can take charge of accountability through internal mechanisms of ongoing evaluation, defining terms, and demonstrating outcomes. Action in an inquiry cycle such as described in this chapter provides a more powerful accountability: professional accountability. Engagement in dialogue with other professionals about *real* problems of practice in contextualized settings allows educators to make choices and take responsibility for their actions; they become accountable *through* their actions.

We framed evaluation as an inquiry cycle that raises problems of practice, explores behaviors, and generates changes that iteratively raise new problems of practice. We also posited that leadership for change develops through interaction *and* action. We set out to explore how school leaders who participate collaboratively in a community of practice that uses the inquiry cycle for school improvement can make changes in their

practice, their principals, and in classroom instruction. What the case reveals is that the real changes occurred within the community of practice. For example, these brave superintendents took risks by opening their schools and their practices to collegial critique. Moreover, they were willing to give and receive this critique. The Network exemplifies the elements identified as essential for effective and meaningful professional development: centered on instruction, collaborative, ongoing and iterative, and context-embedded (Ball & Cohen, 1999; Hawley & Valli, 1999).

But the case also reveals that major improvements have not yet been realized to scale within the classrooms back in the superintendents' district schools. Without inquiry as practice at the school level, the danger of teachers' misuse or misunderstanding of new instructional practices is highly likely (see D. K. Cohen, 1990), as revealed in our example of differentiated instruction. In summary, while there was a culture shift for this network of superintendents, their ability to have substantive influence within their schools is less visible.

Figure 14.2 illustrates the gap between the *theory-of-action* and what Argyris and Schon (1974) call *theory-in-use*. The theory-of-action (in the grey area in the center circle) stipulates changes in practice to establish leverage points. The good news is that the use of the inquiry cycle established a true professional learning community among the superintendents. The process begins with an openness to expose theories-of-action versus theories-in-use (Argyris & Schon, 1974) or the "gap between the ideal and the actual" (Wiggins, 1996, p. 6)—and to confronting the stark reality of the gap and the difficulty in narrowing it.

However, comparing theories offers a counternarrative. What began as single-loop learning (Argyris & Schon, 1974) was turning into double-loop learning as the inquiry cycle became part of their practice. The superintendents began by examining their beliefs about instruction, and their real work became embedded in concrete, on-site practice (e.g., what is actually

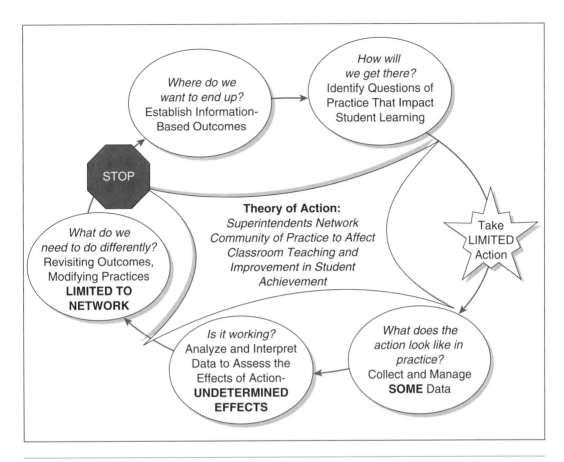

Figure 14.2   The Theory-in-Use: Incomplete Inquiry Cycle

happening in their classrooms). Iteratively, action had deep impact on their belief systems, but they have miles to go in regard to making an impact at the building level (teaching and improved student achievement). Specifically, we do not have clear evidence that network superintendents' work affected teaching and student achievement in district schools. Instead, we see limited action, undetermined impact of actions, and the constraint of collecting, managing, analyzing, and interpreting a partial set of data. A fully implemented inquiry cycle promises to be the tool to narrow the gap between theories-of-action and theories-in-use.

The next challenge for these superintendents is to bring the inquiry cycle to those closest to student achievement—the teachers. The model suggests that a similar process embedded at the school level may pave the way for teaching and

learning improvements. We see emerging evidence that continuing action and collaboration at the school and classroom levels may yet yield the impact anticipated from the theory-of-action: If teaching and learning are to be effects, the roots will be grounded in the development and replication of evaluation as inquiry and inquiry as practice. But the theory needs to be revisited and constantly revised; the axiomatic implementation of policies based on theories has not proved wholly rational or scientific (M. D. Cohen et al., 1972). Without a meaningful, effective, and iterative internal accountability cycle, educators will continue to react in institutional ways to the external mandates and sanctions that are employed in the absence of achievement results.

We believe superintendents can lead use of inquiry cycles in schools through the persistent attention to the genesis, support, and resourcing of collaborative work in each building. Such leadership demands new norms of collegiality to be sure. Most important, action must be a vital component of the work. Activity can generate new learning and additional distribution of leadership. As our analysis indicates, belief may follow action. Elmore (2002) stipulates, "Only a change in practice produces a genuine change in norms and values. Or, to put it more crudely, grab people by their practice and their hearts and minds will follow" (p. 3).

At the end of the day, every school around the world is accountable for its core technology: learning and instruction. Global forces have defined accountability outside of the school, but

> accountability systems will foster improvements to the extent that they generate and focus attention on information relevant to teaching and learning, motivate individuals and schools to use that information and expend effort to improve practice, build the knowledge base necessary for interpreting and applying the new information to improve practice, and allocate resources for all of the above. (O'Day, 2002, p. 294)

Whether the classroom is located in the United States, Japan, or Malawi, district leaders recognize instruction and inquiry centered on instruction as the means for the accountability ends. Authentic and professional accountability uses evaluation by integrating the external accountability demands with the internal goals and challenges. Moreover, such accountability is feasible because it draws on existing resources and capacities.

In recent decades, accountability has driven educational research to track output on national- or state-level assessments. Well-conducted international comparisons of student achievement (e.g., TIMSS and PISA in science and mathematics) provide data on education outcomes in many countries. Yet critics have noted that much remains to be learned from these outcomes, "especially when they are examined in fine detail and considered alongside other relevant findings, e.g., those relating to school improvement and effectiveness" (Jenkins, 2002, p. 157). Moreover, we suggest that differences in achievement across states and nations are less important than understanding what lies behind them. Discovering reasons for differences is complex and requires profound sensitivity to the social, cultural, and historical contexts of education systems. Until we understand both theories-of-action and theories-in-use of world education systems, policies for improvement will be simply policies, not practices that bring change. Meanwhile, little research has been directed toward evaluating the utility and effectiveness of local efforts to improve schooling. The framework in this chapter provides such a lens for local inquiry, as well as for future research on professional accountability efforts.

Improving practice is a never-ending process that requires collaboration, dialogue, and communication. The superintendents in the Network sought to become—and did become—self-learners. They used an evaluation process as inquiry, and inquiry became their practice. They became collaborative learners in a professional learning community—the Network. As such, each has become the district chief learning officer. Their work allowed a leadership flow embedded in an inquiry cycle that was reflexive, not static—proactive, not reactive. Now their challenge is to lead inquiry-minded practices within their schools so that principals and teachers also engage in the evaluative practice that is the inquiry cycle—and thus improve instruction and student learning. In short, inquiry as practice requires inquiry-minded leaders.

Notes

1. Having been the documenter of the Network for 5 years now, I (Rallis) have come to feel as a member of the group. Thus, I recognize that I write this case narrative with a more personal perspective than commonly attributed to such studies. I do not feel that my closeness to the events and activities is a detriment to my portrayal of the case On the

contrary, I believe that my relationships and longevity with the members facilitates insights and offers ample opportunity to test these ideas. Still, I cannot imagine that I have captured the depth and nuance of the Network operation. My analyses only scratch the surface of the dialogic processes. I can only hope to honor the intellect and practices of the Network superintendents (Kathy Binkowski, Mary Conway, Sal Corda, Chris Clouet, Betty Feser, Doris Kurtz, Mike McKee, Pat Proctor, John Ramos, Diane Ullman, and Bob Villanova) and the facilitators (Dick Elmore, Andrew Lachman, Jane Tedder, Lee Teitel, and Steve Wlodarczyk).

2. This is a term used by Elmore to emphasize that the focus of the discourse must be tightly tied to instruction.

3. All names used in the dialogues throughout the chapter are pseudonyms.

References

Argyris, C., & Schon, D. (1974). *Theory in practice: Increasing professional effectiveness.* San Francisco, CA: Jossey-Bass.

Association for the Development of Education in Africa. (2003). *The challenge of learning: Improving the quality of basic education in sub-Saharan Africa.* ADEA Biennale on Education in Africa 2003, Libreville, Gabon.

Ball, D., & Cohen, D. (1999). Developing practice, developing practitioners: Toward a practice-based theory of professional education. In L. Darling-Hammond & G. Sykes (Eds.), *Teaching as the learning profession* (pp. 3–32). San Francisco, CA: Jossey-Bass.

Brown, J. S., & Duguid, P. (2000). *The social life of information.* Boston: Harvard Business School Press.

Cohen, D. K. (1990). A revolution in one classroom: The case of Mrs. Oublier. *Educational Evaluation and Policy Analysis, 12*(5), 311–329.

Cohen, M. D., March, J. G., & Olsen, J. P. (1972). A garbage can model of organizational choice. *Administrative Science Quarterly, 17*(1), 1–25.

Darling-Hammond, L. (2004). Standards, accountability, and school reform. *Teachers College Record, 106*(6), 1047–1085.

Elmore, R. (2000). *Building a new structure for school leadership.* Washington, DC: Albert Shanker Institute.

Elmore, R. (2002). *The limits of "change."* Retrieved February 2002 from http://www.edletter.org/past/issues/2002-jf/limitsofchange.shtml

Elmore, R. (2003). Accountability and capacity. In M. Carnoy, R. Elmore, & L. S. Siskin (Eds.), *The new accountability: High schools and high-stakes testing* (pp. 195–209). New York: Routledge Falmer.

Elmore, R. (2004). The problem of stakes in performance-based accountability systems. In S. H. Fuhrman & R. Elmore (Eds.), *Redesigning accountability systems for education* (pp. 274–296). New York: Teacher's College Press.

Firestone, W. (1996). Leadership roles or functions? In K. Leithwood, D. Chapman, P. Corson, P. Hallinger, & A. Hart (Eds.), *International handbook of educational leadership and administration* (pp. 395–418). Boston: Kluwer Academic Publishers.

Gee, J. P. (2005). *An introduction to discourse analysis: Theory and methods* (2nd ed.). New York: Routledge.

Gronn, P. (2002). Distributed leadership. In K. Leithwood & P. Hallinger (Eds.), *Second international handbook of educational leadership and administration* (pp. 653–696). Dordrecht, The Netherlands: Kluwer Academic Publishers.

Halverson, R. (2003). Systems of practice: How leaders use artifacts to create professional community in schools. *Educational Policy Analysis Archives, 11*(37), 1–35.

Hawley, W., & Valli, L. (1999). The essentials of effective professional development: A new consensus. In L. Darling-Hammond & G. Sykes (Eds.), *Teaching as the learning profession: Handbook of policy and practice* (pp. 151–180). San Francisco, CA: Jossey-Bass.

Independent Evaluation Group. (2006). *From schooling access to learning outcomes: An unfinished agenda. An evaluation of World Bank support to primary education.* Washington, DC: World Bank.

Jenkins, E. W. (2002). Making use of international comparisons of student achievement in science and mathematics. In D. Sharrocks-Taylor & E. W. Jenkins (Eds.), *Learning from others: International comparisons in education* (pp. 137–157). Dordrecht, The Netherlands: Klüwer.

Lave, J., & Wenger, E. (1991). *Situated learning: Legitimate peripheral participation.* Cambridge, MA: Cambridge University Press.

March, J. G. (1999). Exploration and exploitation in organizational learning. In J. G. March (Ed.), *The pursuit of organizational intelligence* (pp. 114–136). Malden, MA: Blackwell.

Massell, D., & Goertz, M. E. (2002). District strategies for building instructional capacity. In A. M. Hightower, M. S. Knapp, J. A. Marsh, & M. W. McLaughlin (Eds.), *School districts and instructional renewal* (pp. 43–60). New York: Teacher's College Press.

Newmann, F., King, M. B., & Rigdon, M. (1997). Accountability and school performance: Implications from restructured schools. *Harvard Educational Review, 67*(1), 41–74.

O'Day, J. (2002). Complexity, accountability and school improvement. *Harvard Educational Review, 72*(3), 293–329.

Petrides, L. A., & Guiney, S. Z. (2002). Knowledge management for school leaders: An ecological framework for thinking schools. *Teachers College Record, 104*(8), 1702–1717.

Rallis, S., & MacMullen, M. M. (2000). Inquiry minded schools: Opening doors for accountability. *Phi Delta Kappan, 81*(10), 766–773.

Rallis, S., & Rossman, G. B. (2000). Dialogue for learning: Evaluator as critical friend. *New Directions for Evaluation, 86*, 81–92.

Rallis, S., Tedder, J., Lachman, A., & Elmore, R. (2006). Superintendents in classrooms: From collegial conversations to collaborative action. *Phi Delta Kappan, 87*(7), 537–545.

Resnick, L. B., & Glennan, T. K. (2002). Leadership for learning: A theory of action for urban school districts. In A. Hightower, M. S. Knapp, J. A. Marsh, & M. W. McLaughlin (Eds.), *School districts and instructional renewal* (pp. 160–172). New York: Teacher's College Press.

Rossman, G. B., & Rallis, S. (2003). *Learning in the field: An introduction to qualitative research* (2nd ed.). Thousand Oaks, CA: Sage.

Rowan, B. (1990). Commitment and control: Alternative strategies for the organizational design of schools. In C. B. Cazden (Ed.), *Review of research in education* (Vol. 16, pp. 353–389). Washington, DC: American Educational Research Association.

Spillane, J. (2000). Cognition and policy implementation: District policymakers and the reform of mathematics education. *Cognition and Instruction, 18*(2), 141–179.

Spillane, J., Halverson, R., & Diamond, J. B. (2001). Investigating school leadership practice: A distributed perspective. *Educational Researcher, 30*(3), 23–28.

Spillane, J., Halverson, R., & Diamond, J. B. (2004). Toward a theory of leadership practice: A distributed perspective. *Journal of Curriculum Studies, 36*(1), 3–34.

United Nations Educational, Scientific and Cultural, Organization. (2000). *The Dakar framework for action: Education for all—Meeting our collective commitments.* World Education Forum, Dakar, Senegal.

United Nations Educational, Scientific and Cultural, Organization. (2005). *Education for all global monitoring report 2005: The quality imperative.* Paris: UNESCO.

Weiss, C. (1998). *Evaluation* (2nd ed.). Upper Saddle River, NJ: Prentice-Hall.

Wenger, E. (1999). Communities of practice and social learning systems. *Organization, 7*(2), 225–246.

Wiggins, G. (1996). Embracing accountability. *New Schools, New Communities, 12*(2), 4–10.

CHAPTER 15

Where Global Meets Local

*Contexts, Constraints, and Consensus in
School Evaluation in Ireland*

Gerry McNamara and Joe O'Hara

I n recent years, Irish civil and public services have undergone a reform agenda in which evaluation, accountability, and quality assurance have become central themes. At first glance, this agenda seems to resemble similar developments in other Anglophone and certain European Union (EU) countries and to be part of the process of globalization (Bottery, 2004; Martin, 2005; Olssen, Codd, & O'Neill, 2004; Spring, 2004). The new public management or managerialism, which has characterized the reform agenda of many governments—and is enthusiastically endorsed by key international bodies such as the EU and the Organisation for Economic Co-operation and Development (OECD)—appears also to have found favor in Ireland (Callanan, 2007). The strategic management initiative in the civil service sector, whole school evaluation (WSE) in the education system, and quality review in higher education are just three of many examples that seem to stem directly from the influence of neoliberal

policies and values such as efficiency, entrepreneurship, the application of market principles to public services, and performance management and accountability (Boyle, 2002, 2005; Furubo & Sandahl, 2002; Ruane, 2004).

However, it is argued in this chapter that appearances can be deceptive and that, in fact, much of what has happened in Irish educational evaluation has been significantly tempered by local constraints and circumstances (Murray, 2001; Pollitt & Bouckaert, 2000). The present authors suggest that neoliberal ideology actually has found little political support in Ireland. This, coupled with a corporatist approach to economic management in the form of partnerships between the state and "social partners" such as trade unions, has undoubtedly limited the extent to which managerialist notions such as performance-based pay or intrusive inspection and appraisal of work quality can be employed.

Paradoxically, then, although many neoliberal concepts and processes appear in various national agreements that have formed the cornerstone of economic and social policy for nearly two decades, their implementation is highly constrained by the partnership context and niceties (Lenihan, Hart, & Roper, 2005; McNamara & Kenny, 2006). Litton (2006), for example, made the case that social partnership in Ireland has emerged to encourage a less adversarial approach toward deliberation on policy matters. As Boyle (1997, 2005) argued, the Irish reform program might better be conceptualized as akin to that pursued in other small European countries, such as The Netherlands and Denmark. As in these countries, a corporatist political tradition predominates, and *accommodation, compromise,* and *consensus* are key words in the political lexicon. The evaluation of schools is a case in point. This chapter discusses the positives and negatives of an evaluation system heavily influenced by an overriding need for consensus and partnership.

The new system, known as WSE, was constructed as the result of an extensive pilot project influenced by emerging school evaluation policies and practices in other countries with similar educational traditions. Particularly influential were developments in Scotland, where the "schools must speak for themselves" philosophy of the leading theorist in the field, John MacBeath (1999), seemed to offer an approach to school evaluation potentially compatible with contextual constraints within Ireland. These constraints include the negotiated partnership agreements on which economic and social policies rest and the continued strength of teacher unions. Also influential in Irish education policy has been the advocacy by Michael Fullan (2005, 2006, 2007) of the concept of *capacity building,* defined as "any strategy that increases the collective effectiveness of a group to raise the bar and close the gap of student learning" (Levin & Fullan, 2008, p. 295). Capacity building has become an underpinning theory in a range of school reform efforts, including WSE and the School Development Planning Initiative. The final structures and methods of WSE were agreed on only after

prolonged discussions with various stakeholders, particularly teacher unions. School evaluations under the new system began in 2004.

As a result of the context outlined earlier, the emerging school evaluation system in Ireland is characterized by negotiation, cooperation, collaboration, and school self-evaluation with "light touch" supportive external monitoring by the inspectorate. In line with the theories of MacBeath (1999) and Fullan (2005, 2006, 2007), school autonomy through capacity building is encouraged, and professional and organizational development is prioritized ahead of accountability. The naming and shaming of individual teachers or schools and comparisons among them are strictly forbidden (McNamara & O'Hara, 2004). Although this is the theoretical position expressed in the policy documents underpinning WSE, how close is the reality to the rhetoric? The remainder of this chapter tries to answer that question by analyzing the implementation of WSE in the Irish school system.

The Spectrum of School Evaluation

Internationally, school evaluation is complex and ambiguous. This contextual complexity has led to some confusion when attempting to define what is meant by *educational evaluation* and *school evaluation.* Arguably, one of the clearest definitions of these terms was offered by Scheerens (2002), who defined *educational evaluation* as "judging the value of educational objects on the basis of systematic information gathering in order to support decision making and learning" (pp. 37–39). In defining school evaluation, Scheerens simply replaced "educational objects" with "schools." In the same passage, he continued that external school and teacher evaluation occurs when "evaluators are external to the unit that is being evaluated." In contrast, he defined *school self-evaluation* as

the type of evaluation where the professionals that carry out the programme or core service of the organisation carry out the evaluation in their own organisation (this definition also applies where internal evaluators voluntarily make use of external advisors to provide them with support, advice, data gathering and so on). (Scheerens, 2002, pp. 37–39)

In the rest of this section, we examine the major trends that have led to the emergence of this type of definition of school evaluation.

In much of the English-speaking world, school evaluation has become focused on student attainment and teacher accountability, with a strong emphasis on external monitoring and control (Elmore & Fuhrman, 2001; Johannesson, Lindblad, & Simola, 2002; Whitty, Power, & Halpin, 1998). In contrast, as the work of Nevo (2002, 2006) shows, there remains, in most of Europe, a significant emphasis on school and teacher autonomy and on capacity building and self-evaluation as the best way forward. There are a number of reasons for this seemingly paradoxical situation.

First, the rhetoric of positivism in social science research and the neoliberal agenda of mistrusting public services and servants—although strong in much of the English-speaking world (perhaps excluding Ireland and Scotland) and in the higher levels of the OECD and EU—has little purchase in many European countries, where context and tradition are still influential in educational policy and where teaching and teachers are still highly regarded (Sugrue, 2006).

Second, even where vigorous external forms of school evaluation have developed, as in England, or where school evaluation is closely linked to student testing, as in much of the United States, there is some evidence that the limitations and side effects (particularly in relation to teacher morale and retention) is resulting in a rethink. Research by Hargreaves (cited in Wolf & Craig, 2004) demonstrates serious morale issues among teachers in North America, and a range of recent research in England confirms the prevalence of similar problems in that country (Cunningham & Raymont, 2008; Galton & MacBeath, 2002;

Hoyle & Wallace, 2005; Plowright, 2007; Shaw, Newton, Aitken, & Darnell, 2003).

Third, and perhaps most important, additional complexity and ambiguity is added to school evaluation by the range of objectives that governments hope to achieve by undertaking it. These certainly include improved standards, accountability, and transparency, but they also include increased local decision making, the development of an evidence base for practice and as a platform for capacity building, teacher professional development, and school improvement. In an ideal world, school evaluation might be able to deliver on all of these goals simultaneously. In practice, however, what seems to be becoming clear is that these objectives are more competing than complementary. The greater emphasis an evaluation system places on teacher appraisal and accountability, the less useful that system is likely to be for school improvement and professional development (Nevo, 2006). This may be because, despite rhetoric to the contrary, teachers will probably fear such a system and resist, subvert, or sullenly acquiesce to the system's demands.

For these and other reasons, in particular the high cost of external inspection, the direction of school evaluation in many education systems is undoubtedly moving toward capacity building for school-based self-evaluation. In recent work on school evaluation, MacBeath (2003) stated that "self-evaluation is now seen as a matter of priority in most economically advanced countries of the world" (p. 2). MacBeath's statement has been echoed by commentators from all sides of the school evaluation debate. The European Parliament and Council of the European Union (2001) called on member states of the EU to "encourage school self-evaluation as a method of creating learning and improving schools" (p. 1). This analysis was echoed in the recent highly influential Organisation for Economic Co-operation and Development (2005) report on the future of the teaching profession, *Teachers Matter*, which sees the development of self-evaluation capacity within the education system as being a critical component of the drive to improve educational provision in OECD member states. Meurat and Morlaix (2003) suggested that "school self-evaluation is on the agenda in all European countries" (p. 53), and in Belgium, Devos and Verhoeven (2003) reported that the inspectorate is strongly supporting a self-evaluation culture.

Recent developments in both England and Ireland exemplify the emergence of the concept of capacity building for self-evaluation as a key component of school evaluation. In England, there has been a gradual dilution of the objective external evaluation approach historically synonymous with the Office for Standards in Education (OFSTED). Plowright (2007) suggested that, "at the heart of the new school inspection framework introduced in 2005 is the concept of self-evaluation" (p. 374). Indeed, the British government minister with responsibility for the area at the time, David Milliband (2004), publicly celebrated the emergence of a new "simplified school improvement focus, where every school uses robust self-evaluation to drive improvement" (p. 3).

Official Office for Standards in Education (2004) documents state that "intelligent accountability should be founded on the school's own views of how well it is serving its pupils and its priorities for improvement. This is what is meant by school self-evaluation" (p. 7). OFSTED, together with most Local Education Authorities in England, has developed substantial research materials for schools to use in self-evaluation, most notably the online Self-Evaluation Form (Office for Standards in Education, 2005). Other agencies, such as the Centre for Curriculum Evaluation and Management (CEM) at the University of Durham, which collect data to support school-based evaluation, are thriving (Tymms, 1999). A good example of the rise of consensus-driven evaluation and self-evaluation is provided by Ireland. The remainder of the chapter explores this development.

School Evaluation—Irish Style

The Education Act (Government of Ireland, 1998) describes the task of school inspection

and WSE as being "to monitor and assess the quality, economy, efficiency and effectiveness of the education system" (Section 7[2][b]). This terminology is closely aligned with neoliberal philosophy and EU/OECD policy, but what has emerged in practice is considerably diluted. Flynn (2006) captured this dichotomy well when describing WSE in Ireland as answering the challenges of accountability in an Irish way rather than an EU way.

Schools and teachers in Ireland have a long history of being evaluated by a centralized inspectorate, a division of the Department of Education and Science (DES). However, by the early 1990s, this system had broken down significantly. The inspection of primary schools had become sporadic and rather idiosyncratic; in secondary schools, inspection had nearly ceased entirely. The largest teacher union supported its members in refusing to teach in front of an inspector (Chevalier, Dolton, & Levacic, 2004; Egan, 2007; Sugrue, 1999).

The reasons for this decline are varied, but what is significant is that the impetus for a new approach to inspection and school evaluation in the mid-1990s came from external sources rather than from any pressing domestic demand. This is made clear in the evaluation report prepared by the Department of Education and Science, Ireland (1999) after the first WSE pilot project from 1996 to 1999. For example, the introduction justifies the development of the WSE pilot scheme by noting that "across the European Union a wide range of approaches is evident to the assessment and evaluation of schools" (Department of Education and Science, Ireland, 1999, p. 8); it later states that "there is now a growing tendency across Europe to see external and internal school evaluation processes as being inextricably linked" and suggests that "there is an increasing effort in many countries to encourage schools to review their own progress in a formal way ... to engage in their own development planning" (p. 9).

Based on a 3-year pilot project, and after extensive negotiations with the teacher unions, the DES in Ireland issued a framework for school evaluation and self-evaluation in 2003. This framework, titled *Looking at our Schools* (*LAOS*), contains five areas of evaluation: (a) quality of learning and teaching in subjects, (b) quality of support for students, (c) quality of school management, (d) quality of school planning, and (e) quality of curriculum provision (Department of Education and Science, Ireland, 2003a, 2003b). Schools are required in theory to gather evidence and then make judgments about their own performance on a four-part rating scale in respect to each area. This process of self-evaluation then informs the work of a visiting team of inspectors that carries out WSEs at unspecified intervals, usually not more than once every 5 years.

In the *LAOS* documents, an elaborate system of evaluation is outlined as the basis on which school management and staff can make "professional judgments regarding the operation of the school" (Department of Education and Science, Ireland, 2003a, p. ix). Each of the five evaluation

areas is divided into aspects, and the aspects are divided into components. Each component is then teased out into several themes that guide the self-evaluation process (see Table 15.1 for an example of an evaluation area and its multiple levels). It is noteworthy that terms such as *area*, *aspect*, and *component* replace terms such as *evaluation criteria*, which were used in the WSE project. This highlights the immense sensitivity to anything smacking of evaluation in any form in the Irish education system.

The document suggests that themes (the smallest units of evaluation) "can be used by the school as a guide in judging or measuring its own performance" (Department of Education and Science, Ireland, 2003a, p. x). The methodology suggested for using the themes is described as follows:

A school may decide to focus on an area, an aspect or a component. The school will gather information in relation to the theme

Table 15.1   Sample *LAOS* Area for Evaluation

Area: Quality of Learning and Teaching in Subjects

Aspect: Planning and Preparation

Component: Planning of Work

Themes for Self-Evaluation

1. Long-term planning for the teaching of the subject and its consistency with the school plan

2. The extent to which planning documents describe the work to be completed within the subject

3. The degree to which planning is in line with syllabus requirements and guidelines

4. The degree to which planning provides for differential approaches to curriculum coverage in accordance with the spectrum of student ability, needs, and interests

5. The extent to which provision for corrective action for learning problems or difficulties is an integral part of the planning of work in the subject

6. Evidence of cross-curriculum planning and integration

7. The provision for monitoring, review, and evaluation of the planning of work in the subject.

or themes under evaluation. Having engaged in a process of collecting and analysing this information and evidence, the school will be in a position to make a statement or statements indicating its own performance in the relevant component, aspect or area. (Department of Education and Science, Ireland, 2003a, p. x)

Schools are invited to make statements regarding each area, aspect, or component evaluated based on "a continuum consisting of a number of reference points representing stages of development in the improvement process" (Department of Education and Science, Ireland, 2003a, p. x). The continuum encompasses four situations: (a) significant strengths (uniformly strong), (b) strengths outweigh weaknesses (more strengths than weaknesses), (c) weaknesses outweigh strengths (more weaknesses than strengths), and (d) significant major weaknesses (uniformly weak).

LAOS places great emphasis on school self-evaluation and downplays evaluation by external inspectors. In the fraught field of student attainment, great caution prevails. In primary education, there is no national standardized testing and, therefore, no accepted benchmarks against which to compare student achievement and teacher performance. At the secondary level, inspectors review data on the outcomes of national examinations before evaluating a school. However, teachers are not individually held accountable for results, and the use of examination results to compare schools or teachers is prohibited by law. It is clear that the acceptability of the evaluation process to schools and teachers was a central concern of the DES.

Overall, LAOS produces a template for schools undertaking self-evaluation; the role of external inspection is significantly downplayed. The model that emerges is remarkably similar to the ideas of MacBeath (1999), who suggested that the role of external inspection should be merely to ensure that internal systems of evaluation and

self-review are implemented effectively, and who supported "a model in which external evaluation focuses primarily on the school's own approach to self-evaluation" (p. 152). The LAOS framework was designed with an emphasis on cooperation and partnership, rather than monitoring and accountability. It was agreed that it was the work of schools as a whole that would be examined and that individual teachers would not be identified or punished for poor performance. The scheme of evaluation was agreed on only after long and difficult negotiations with stakeholders; views of the teacher unions were highly influential (O'Dalaigh, 2000).

The WSE system was first implemented in 2004. Since then, two studies of the implementation of WSE have been completed. The first was conducted by the present authors and involved interviews in 24 schools that had recently undergone WSE. In total, 28 school leaders, including principals and deputy principals, and 20 teachers were interviewed. Six interviews with inspectors were also held. The interviews were conducted during 2005 and 2006 and concentrated on the perceptions of the respondents concerning the advantages and challenges of WSE. This research is reported in more detail in McNamara and O'Hara (2008) and forms the basis of the following section. The second piece of research was conducted by the company MORI Ireland for the DES on schools' responses to WSE (Department of Education and Science, Ireland, 2005). This work, referred to hereafter as the Customer Survey, involved a questionnaire sent to approximately 150 schools that had undergone WSE.

WSE: Research Findings

Given the scope of the research, it is impossible to provide more than a brief overview of the main findings. The research outcomes are divided into two themes: The Inspection Experience and The Implementation of Policy.

The Inspection Experience—Positive Perceptions

The initial phase of the inspection involves preparatory meetings between the inspection team and school management. The next phase involves the team of inspectors conducting the evaluation over a 3- or 4-day period. The inspection breaks down into two almost separate processes: whole school inspection and department/subject inspection. The latter consists of meetings with subject teachers, examination of plans, classroom observation, and appraising pupil work. In primary schools, all or most teachers received classroom visits from inspectors, whereas in postprimary schools, between two and four subjects were evaluated. With regard to WSE, the process involves meetings with management, staff, special duties teachers, parents' representatives, and pupils. The meetings are described as opportunities for the school to produce and explain required policy documents in relation to planning, guidance, discipline, bullying, and similar activities. The final phase of the process involves discussion between the leading inspector and the principal about the content of the final report, a draft of which is given to the school for comment before issue of the final version.

Almost without exception, the respondents in the study indicated that the inspection teams managed this potentially fraught process in such a way that the schools, although relieved to have it over, regarded it as a positive and worthwhile experience. This interpretation is confirmed by the *Customer Survey* (Department of Education and Science, Ireland, 2005), which reported overwhelmingly positive responses from both teachers and principals, such as, "inspectors adopted a professional approach in their interactions with me" and "inspectors were courteous and respectful of my professionalism" (p. 12). One principal interviewed in the present authors' study, attempting to summarize the feelings of his staff, noted:

We were all a little surprised at how well the process went. I think we were maybe working on the model of inspection that we knew from our teacher training days and in some cases, from our primary school days. This was nothing like those experiences. It was courteous, professional, and ultimately affirming. Indeed, it brought us together in a way that I have seldom seen before.

A significant number of respondents stated that the WSE process brought staff together during the preparation phase and gave them a new sense of focus and collegiality. In many cases, the evaluation process required teachers to cooperate, as well as learn about each others' professional practices for the first time. As mentioned previously, in the majority of secondary schools, only two to four subject areas were chosen for individual observation. In a number of cases, principals remarked that the rest of the staff rallied around those who "drew the short straw." Interestingly, one principal claimed that the subject inspections were perceived as so positive, affirming, and helpful that, by the end of the process, those not chosen for evaluation wished they had been included. Similarly, with regard to the whole school aspects of the evaluation, school leaders were grateful and indeed a little surprised that the staff assisted a great deal in preparing the significant amount of documentation demanded by the inspectorate.

The majority of schools also felt that the framework, by covering such a wide set of themes for self-evaluation, was able to obtain a comprehensive picture of all the schools' activities and not just academic outcomes—a point endorsed, with some caveats, by the three teacher unions (for example, see Association of Secondary Teachers in Ireland, 2006, 2007). This point was particularly stressed by respondents from the schools designated as disadvantaged, who felt strongly that the affirmation of good practice provided by the inspectors was of critical importance to teachers who rarely feel valued or supported. These schools suggested that the final reports did manage to describe the often problematic context in which they operate. This finding was again confirmed by the *Customer Survey* (Department of Education and Science, Ireland, 2005), which reported that close to 90% of teachers supported or strongly supported the view that "inspectors took account of school/class context factors during the evaluation process" (p. 14). Likewise, it was felt by many respondents that the extensive framework could be used as scaffolding for improvement strategies. One principal interviewed by the present authors suggested that WSE creates "a template under so many headings of where we are trying to go" and is "an excellent start, heading in the right direction."

Overall, the consensus was that the *LAOS* framework as implemented by the inspectors was worth doing, had affirmed teachers and schools, dispelled fear of evaluation, and convinced school staffs that this way of conducting evaluations worked. At times, the endorsement was rather lukewarm, but fulsome compliments were more common. Most school communities agreed that the process helped them reexamine how they did things for the first time in many years. Many felt this had been achieved by taking a light approach and by downplaying inspection and emphasizing school self-evaluation. Therefore, given the care and caution of its construction and execution, *LAOS* appears initially to have been positively received as an accepted addition to school life. This is a considerable achievement in an educational community deeply suspicious of evaluation and inspection.

The Inspection Experience— Negative Perceptions

However, the inspection experience also generated some negative perceptions. Both teachers and school leaders tended to be skeptical about the long-term impact of WSE, although instances of short-term positive change were

mentioned. One principal captured this widely held view when she remarked, "All is quiet, the water closes over it, we will hear no more for five years at least!"

A second negative finding related to poor feedback, which was a common theme in the interviews with principals, deputy principals, and teachers. Principals tended to be particularly annoyed by things not said in the final reports. By far the most common complaint from school leaders referred to the process for dealing with poor teaching and underperforming teachers. This topic, it was alleged by many principals, is studiously avoided because there is still no mechanism to deal with a weak teacher, despite the apparently impressive accountability structure established. One principal, speaking for many, said, "They [the inspectors] did not want to get involved in tackling weak teachers, it is just as well, there is no follow up and it would cause huge resentment with no solution."

This issue points to one of the more significant challenges to any system of evaluation within Irish education: the power of teacher unions and representative bodies. As a result of this, there is a discernable feeling among the school principals interviewed, that WSE is actually turning into a management evaluation. Although it is acknowledged that WSE pays lip service to the whole school nature of evaluation, some feel that it is really only interested in publicly identifying management shortcomings. As one principal remarked, "If this system is about accountability at all, it is about management accountability, certainly not teacher accountability."

This frustration carried over into principals' comments about the value of the final written reports produced by the inspection team. Although they generally welcomed the positive and affirming nature of the reports, interviewees expressed a clear sense of doubt and skepticism that the evaluations would ever be critical, regardless of the reality of the situation, given a perceived cultural inability to accept constructive criticism. Again, the lack of transparent structures for dealing with critical issues such as underperforming teachers led many to believe that the final reports would deliberately fudge such topics. Even if these or other important issues were raised, it was felt that there was no method established to allow schools to address identified problems because this type of structure would require support and funding that was simply not available. As part of this study, the present researchers conducted an analysis of the reports pertaining to the participating schools. It was hard to disagree with the principal who remarked that the reports seemed to range "from effusive to merely positive."

It is interesting to note that in recent months, however, the tenor of some reports has begun to change. In a sea of supportive affirmations, nuggets of critical advice emerged in a small number of the reports studied. For example, in one school, a particular subject department was told that "some students get good feedback and correction." In another school, the level of absenteeism was commented on unfavorably, whereas other schools and departments were gently chided on lack of planning, limited use of varied methodologies, lack of student work displayed on the walls, and similar issues (Department of Education and Science, Ireland, 2008). Overall, however, it seems that, despite the publication of inspection reports, clear definitive judgments are lacking, and the outing of weak teachers is doomed to disappointment.

With regard to feedback, a somewhat similar view can be traced in the interviews with teachers. They indicated a high level of dissatisfaction with the level and quality of postobservation feedback. In the interviews, teachers reported feeling demeaned, upset, and amazed at the haphazard nature of the feedback process. There was a perception that there was no structure established to provide teachers with an analysis of what had been observed. This was seen as hugely problematic by more experienced teachers, many of whom had not been observed teaching since their college days and virtually all of whom were nervous at the prospect. One reported that "we got a few minutes in the corridor afterwards—very unprofessional."

A regret expressed regularly by teachers was that no reference was made by inspectors to good practice or ideas from elsewhere. There was a sense that an opportunity to disseminate best practices had been missed in many cases. Many teachers were hoping to be enlightened or challenged, but few felt they were anything other than watched. The teachers indicated that, although the process is stressful and it is unlikely that other professionals would accept such an imposition, it might still be regarded as valuable if the quality of feedback was higher. In summary, the teacher feedback about WSE highlighted a need for more discussion time with inspectors and a need for more specific recommendations, regardless of whether criticisms were offered.

A second substantial area of interest that emerged from the research was conceptualized as the implementation of policy. According to the *LAOS* document on which WSE is based, a key element of the process is the concept of self-evaluation and the development of the capacity of schools to collect evidence and analyze practice. A second theoretical underpinning is the importance of parents and students to have an adequate role in WSE. The research shed some light on the implementation of both of these imperatives.

The Implementation of Policy— Self-Evaluation as an Ongoing Process

A striking theme in the present authors' research was the extent to which the respondents alluded to *LAOS* as a one-time event to prepare for and then forget. The central idea of the *LAOS* framework—namely, that self-evaluation would be an ongoing process between inspections—had failed to take hold. Questions about plans to continue the process of self-evaluation after *LAOS* were met with puzzlement. It became clear that, although endless meetings were held and a great deal of documentation was prepared for both subject and WSEs, this consisted almost entirely of gathering and updating existing planning and policy documents (e.g., class plans, homework policies, school plans, discipline codes, admittance procedures). Although some additional materials were produced, they were viewed as final products, rather than as artifacts generated by an ongoing process. That, for example, the discipline code might be evaluated as a success or failure through some process of data collection and analysis was a completely alien concept in most cases.

Further probing in this area resulted in some interesting new thinking. School principals indicated on a number of occasions that they sensed a particular attitude toward evidence or data was implicit in the structure of the WSE process. Many thought that impressionistic conclusions were favored over analytic evaluations by the inspectorate. Despite a general view that Irish schools are not data-rich, there are significant sources of information available, including absentee lists, late lists, in-class assessments, and so on. What is noteworthy is that, at least in the early stages of the WSE rollout, there is little indication that the inspectors chose to examine these information sources. As a result, the idea that this was an evaluation system that was somewhat evidence-free was suggested in more than one school. One principal summarized the views of most, saying, "When you think about it, I suppose it is very impressionistic, not really evaluation at all."

This view was echoed by school leaders who were attempting to engage in more systematic forms of self-evaluation and evidence collection. These respondents were critical of the WSE process and inspection teams, alleging that not only were schools not encouraged to rigorously self-evaluate, but when they had done so, no interest was shown in the evidence produced. In these settings, the inspectorate was perceived as afraid to examine the locally generated data, preferring to concentrate on structures, rather than implementation and outcomes. It is noteworthy that not one school reported being asked to use the four-point rating scale in the *LAOS* handbook to make a judgment on any aspect of performance. This is somewhat ironic considering that in the interviews with inspectors, schools having any organized data were perceived as a rarity.

Several teachers expressed a similar viewpoint. They argued that a perceived lack of interest in developing a genuinely self-evaluating culture among school staffs was at least partly a result of the failure of the inspectorate to take into account data generated by teachers. This was particularly galling to practitioner-researchers who had engaged in postgraduate studies in recent years and who are committed to engaging in evidence-informed practice. Some teachers stated quite specifically that the absence of any questions from the inspectors regarding the evidential base of classroom practice caused them to question the value of the entire process. For example, one teacher said, "We have evidence that the literacy scheme we are using with weak pupils is not working, but there was no interest—once we had a scheme and regular meetings, they were happy. It is all about processes, not outcomes."

Another issue that arose when examining the role of self-generated school data was the perception that most school communities were not in a position to analyze or interpret this material. In general, it was felt that, although it might be useful and desirable to examine a range of data, schools were not equipped (and staff were not trained) to do it. One principal said, "We have lots of data here, but it would be a huge job to organize it and we have neither the training nor the time." Implicit in this comment is a desire for the evaluation process to take on a capacity-building role. In this view, school leaders, teachers, and perhaps other stakeholders would be provided with the training and support necessary to enable them to become genuine data-generating, self-evaluating professionals.

Finally, it is important to note that a minority view appeared in the research that was negative about any idea that evaluation needed to be based on more systematic research. Teaching was seen as something that was not really measurable in the classic sense. Rather, it was felt that the role of the teacher was developmental and centered on encouraging and nurturing young people. In this view, the attempt to measure and codify was wrongheaded and potentially dangerous.

Notwithstanding the frustration expressed by some teachers about the lack of inspectors' interest in real evaluation, some inspectors were highly critical of the lack of systematic self-evaluation going on in schools. Several remarked that, due to a lack of regular testing in both primary and secondary education in Ireland, the "hard data" on which to base "real" judgments are not available. Representative comments by inspectors included, "Access is required to better organized in-school data on pupil performance" and "the WSE process should involve the collection of hard data." In the view of some of the inspectorate, key data that schools should possess, such as dropout rates and levels of absenteeism, were not available in a usable, accessible format. Likewise, individual teachers or subject departments had little in the way of collected or collated information on pupil results, aptitudes, or attitudes. From this perspective, no process that could remotely be regarded as systematic, evidence-based self-evaluation was occurring in schools. Because self-evaluation and the presentation of evidence to support judgments was in theory a cornerstone of WSE, this represents a major problem for the emerging system. The lack of usable data, whether provided by the schools and teachers or by some other mechanism, emerged as a key weakness of WSE that needs to be addressed.

This criticism of the original WSE pilot project was flagged clearly in the evaluation report of that project (Department of Education and Science, Ireland, 1999). The final section of the report suggested that key points had been taken seriously by the Department. Under the heading "Moving Forward," the report discussed the need for better quantitative information:

Both individual schools and the inspectors carrying out whole school evaluation would derive considerable benefit from having access to a range of quantitative information, including statistical and other information, on patterns of early school leaving and pupil participation and on the catchment area from which the school draws its pupils. Information of this kind would greatly enrich the WSE process for the school and should form part of the preparation for the future whole school evaluation. (Department of Education and Science, Ireland, 1999, pp. 47–48)

Smyth (1999) suggested that "schools could monitor their own attendance and dropout rates, etc.," but that "information collected at the school level is likely to be of limited utility without comparable information on the National context . . . providing value added analysis to schools would be worthwhile" (p. 226). Such an approach would require information on pupil ability at the point of entry and additional information (e.g., through surveys) on pupil background. This information could be used by the school in setting targets for improvement and in monitoring the introduction of new programs or teaching methods. There is also evidence from other sources that supports the notion that a lack of school-based research is a major issue at the heart of school planning and evaluation.

The Department of Education and Science, Ireland (2006a) recently published *An Evaluation of Planning in Thirty Primary Schools* and noted that only 20% of these schools could be considered "good" in the area of using evidence to track improved school attainment. The few schools that showed good practice in this area are described as having "a comprehensive policy on assessment, measuring attainment systematically, devising formats for plotting progress and monitoring improvements in pupils' behaviour and attendance" (Department of Education and Science, Ireland, 2006a, p. 73). A second report of the same year makes similar criticisms: "They did not engage in formal evaluation of impact . . . there needs to be a greater focus on setting targets and evaluating how well they have been achieved. There was little evidence of this mindset" (Department of Education and Science, Ireland, 2006b, p. 7).

What is important here is twofold. First, the research of the present authors shows that when schools and teachers had gathered evidence, little interest was shown by the inspectors. Moreover, schools and teachers were not aware that such evidence gathering was required, expected, or even welcomed. Second, it also appears that the DES wants schools to gather systematic data and evidence, but it has done nothing to support, encourage, or train schools and teachers to do so. Although 20% of schools were identified as doing a good job of self-evaluation, our research indicates that this is a rare phenomenon. It seems clear that the empowerment of schools and teachers to self-evaluate will have to come from sources other than the DES (McNamara & O'Hara, 2006, 2008).

The Implementation of Policy—The Role of Parents and Students

A final area of importance that only emerges fleetingly in this research is the role of parents and students in the evaluation process. The final report of the WSE pilot project (Department of Education and Science, Ireland, 1999) suggested that more account would have to be taken of the rights of key stakeholders, such as parents and pupils, to provide input into school evaluation. However, there was little reference to these stakeholders in the LAOS document; in fact, the emphasis was greater than ever on management and staff. However, none of the interviewees in the present research reported any issues raised by parents or students, and on a national level, neither parent nor student representative bodies have made critical statements in relation to LAOS. In the research interviews conducted, it was reported that the evaluating inspectors did speak to parents (usually the representatives on the Board of Management) and students on an ad hoc basis. No structured research to ascertain the views of the broad body of parents or students appears to have occurred. One can only conclude that protests about the voices of parents and students being left out are, at this stage, largely rhetorical.

Pointing to the Future— Building Capacity for Self-Evaluation

Internationally, there is evidence of a shift from confrontational forms of school evaluation primarily concerned with accountability toward systems more focused on capacity building for self-evaluation and professional development (MacBeath, 2006; McNamara & O'Hara, 2005; Nevo, 2006). For example, a recently completed research project on school evaluation in 11 European countries, titled SYNEVA, showed a striking convergence toward models emphasizing self-evaluation (Patscheider, Turra Rebuzzi, & McGinn, 2006). The case of Ireland as described in this chapter exemplifies this trend.

These models of school evaluation, and again Ireland is a good example, display several discernable common characteristics—emphasizing self-evaluation with light touch external inspection, stressing that many forms and sources of knowledge and not just quantified student attainment data should inform improvement, and prioritizing organizational and professional capacity building over monitoring and control (McNamara & O'Hara, 2008). However, although educational evaluation, which focuses on professional autonomy, professional development, and capacity building, is beneficial to the status of teaching and the promotion of genuinely educational values, it also raises certain questions. Two in particular need to be considered. First, if—as the present authors would argue—this is in fact the correct policy direction, what are the implications for accountability? Second, how can self-evaluation be effectively encouraged in practice?

These issues are not confined to Ireland. It becomes clear from a study of the documentation of the SYNEVA project that they are, rather, characteristic of school evaluation systems with a major emphasis on self-evaluation. This seems to be due to a common tendency to assume that schools can and will implement policies regardless of their perceived credibility or the resources offered to support them. Meurat and Morlaix (2003) comment on this in relation to France:

> School self-evaluation is not very popular among school staff . . . they were a little more inclined to appreciate self-evaluation as opposed to external evaluation, but only a third declared that it was liked by most staff (and these schools were chosen for supposedly having positive attitudes to evaluation!). (p. 54)

Speaking of Iceland, Lisi and Davidsdottir (2005) reported that, although schools have been mandated to conduct self-evaluation since 1996, few do so because "all such ideas are met with distrust in the beginning, particularly as Icelanders are used to their independence and find it insulting that anyone would tinker with their freedom to do as they wish as teachers" (p. 3). Our research indicates that similar problems exist in Ireland and are inextricably linked to the relationship between self-evaluation and accountability.

Implications for Accountability

MacBeath (2006), the apostle of self-evaluation, is at pains to deny that it is an easy option or that it excludes an accountability component:

> Inside the velvet glove of support and critical friendship is the fist of accountability, intolerant not only of low standards but also of self-delusion. Self-evaluation must be owned by a school staff and is manifestly not a soft option. Schools have to prove their ability to know themselves with appeal to authoritative and verifiable evidence. (p. 2)

Other influential theorists, however, suggest that concerns over accountability are fundamentally misplaced and that teacher autonomy and development is the key to educational improvement. For example, Elliott (2004) argued that because "human life is accompanied by a high degree of unpredictability as a condition . . . limiting the predictive power of social science generalization . . . trusting teachers in their capacities to exercise wisdom and judgment . . . is the wise policy" (p. 170).

Similarly, in describing her approach to educational evaluation, the influential action research theorist McNiff (2002) advocated an unashamedly teacher-centered approach. She contended that, in the interests of enhancing the status of teaching and teachers, what counts as evaluation needs to be urgently addressed in educational debates; she proceeded to outline a perspective that is different from the dominant positivistic paradigm now in vogue: "I regard evaluation as a process of self-study in which people make claims, supported by evidence, to have improved the quality of their work in terms of their educative influence in the lives of others" (p. 2).

McNiff (2002) asserted that evaluation should be conducted participatively. Its epistemological base would be self-study, and its methodology would be action research. In the school, teachers and principals would undertake their action research enquiry into their practice and produce accounts to show how they felt they were justified in claiming that they have improved the quality of educational experience for themselves and for the children in their schools. In espousing this view of evaluation, she rejects external monitoring and control of teachers, saying, "My own view is that people are capable of thinking, learning and acting for themselves" (McNiff, 2002, p. 4).

Research on teacher autonomy seems to confirm this view. Pearson and Moomaw (2005) suggested that the evidence demonstrates that as "general teacher autonomy increased, so did empowerment and professionalism"—they also argued that "empowering teachers is an appropriate place to begin in solving the problems of today's schools," and they define the teacher empowerment process by saying, "like other professionals, teachers must have the freedom to prescribe the best treatment for their students, as doctors and lawyers do for their patients and clients" (p. 45).

In light of this, and notwithstanding MacBeath's (2006) position, it may well be that the policy direction toward emphasizing self-evaluation will require the modification or even abandonment of neoliberal concepts of professional accountability as being concerned with meeting externally devised and monitored standards and criteria. This is perhaps not yet fully realized by policymakers, but will emerge as it becomes clear that self-evaluation properly understood must be primarily about professional empowerment and development.

Encouraging Self-Evaluation in Practice

Whether self-evaluation, understood as earlier, will work any better than external inspection as a method of enabling improvement and empowering teachers remains to be seen. Its implementation on a system-wide basis is really only commencing in most countries. Evidence from particular projects and programs where genuine practitioner-led evaluation—with some support from external agencies—has taken place is positive. Simons (2002), who has facilitated several such self-evaluations, concluded:

When the motivation is intrinsic, schools respond . . . schools, teachers and administrators become their own best critics if they have control over the evaluation process, over the choice of issues to be evaluated, the methods and procedures to be employed and the audience to whom the results will be disseminated. (p. 33)

Simons goes on to summarize the case for self-evaluation for teachers and schools: (a) teachers are in the best position to evaluate curriculum change; (b) the quality of education can best be improved by supporting the professional

autonomy of teachers and schools; and (c) this is best done by creating a collaborative, nonthreatening, professional culture in which work can be publicly discussed and evaluated.

Fitz-Gibbon (1999), founder of the CEM at Durham University and a strong supporter of school self-evaluation based on solid evidence, suggested that if schools have good self-evaluation systems, external evaluation should only need to be "light touch," saying, "U.K. schools currently lead the world in self-evaluation, demonstrating that teachers are quite willing to be accountable if the methods of assessment of their work are clear and believable" (p. 18).

However, as our research indicates, WSE in Ireland is a long way from meeting these criteria. The key question, perhaps, is whether, within the WSE framework as currently constituted, there exists enough room for maneuver to solve some of these shortcomings. In the case of the most significant negative outcomes—low levels of school capacity for research and self-evaluation, poor feedback to schools and teachers, and the limited role accorded to parents and students—it seems that significant improvements could be made to WSE without impairing its widespread acceptance. In fact, it is evident from this research that greater clarity and support in these areas would in fact be welcomed by schools and teachers.

Recent research in Ireland by the present authors shows that teachers and schools quickly come to see the value of research-led practice, provided it is in a context of professional development devoid of threatening elements (McNamara & O'Hara, 2008). Similarly, research in the United States indicates that evaluation capacity building can play a significant role in school improvement (Hamilton et al., 2007; Nelson & Eddy, 2008). However, it is also clear that, as in many other countries, self-evaluation will not happen simply because it is mentioned in documents. Instead, "building evaluative capacity in any staff is a long–term process" (Nelson & Eddy, 2008, p. 43). There must be a concerted effort to inculcate the values and methodologies of self-evaluation through specific, targeted training programs during initial teacher education and continuing professional development.

Of course, self-evaluation in schools requires more than training. It also requires schools and teachers to buy into its rationale. Because, as this chapter demonstrates, many school principals and teachers are skeptical, or at least not fully convinced of, the benefits of WSE, overcoming these feelings will be a crucial and necessary first step to the future reform process. As Leithwood, Aitken, and Janizi (2001) explained:

> The chance of any reform improving student learning is remote unless . . . school-teachers agree with its purpose and appreciate what is required to make it work. Local leaders must, for example, be able to help their colleagues understand how the externally initiated reform might be integrated into local improvement efforts, provide the necessary support for those whose practices must change, and must win the cooperation and support of parents and others in the local community. (p. 4)

Meeting this challenge should be the immediate priority of policymakers if WSE is to become a viable and effective mode of school evaluation.

References

Association of Secondary Teachers in Ireland. (2007, November 17). *Teachers will not support ill-judged, superficial or inadequately resourced education reform.* Retrieved April 2, 2008, from http://www.asti.ie/pr2007/prnov07.htm#educonf

Association of Secondary Teachers in Ireland, Irish National Teachers Organisation, & Teachers Union of Ireland. (2006). *Benchmarking submission: Joint submission by ASTI-INTO-TUI.* Retrieved July 6, 2008, from http://www.into.ie/ROI/WhatsNew/Issues/Benchmarking/filedownload,3280,en.pdf

Bottery, M. (2004). *The challenges of educational leadership.* London: Paul Chapman Publishing.

Boyle, R. (1997, January–March). Civil service reform in the Republic of Ireland. *Public Money and Management*, pp. 49–53.

Boyle, R. (2002). Two-tiered approach: Evaluation practice in the Republic of Ireland. In J. E. Furubo, R. C. Rist, & R. Sandahl (Eds.), *International atlas of evaluation* (pp. 261–272). New Brunswick, NJ: Transaction Publishers.

Boyle, R. (2005). Evaluation capacity development in the Republic of Ireland. *Evaluation capacity development working paper* (Series 14). Washington, DC: The World Bank.

Callanan, M. (2007). Retrospective on critical junctures and drivers of change. In M. Callanan (Ed.), *Ireland 2022: Towards one hundred years of self-government* (pp. 16–41). Dublin: Institute of Public Administration.

Chevalier, A., Dolton, P., & Levacic, R. (2004). School equality and effectiveness. *Department of Economics Working Paper, 04*(10). Dublin: University College Dublin.

Cunninghan, P., & Raymont, P. (2008). Quality assurance in English primary education. *Primary Review Research, 4*(3). Retrieved August 10, 2008, from http://www.primaryreview.org.uk/Downloads/Int_Reps/7.Governance-finance-reform/RS_4-3_briefing_Quality_assurance_080229.pdf

Department of Education and Science, Ireland. (1999). *Whole school evaluation.* Dublin: Author.

Department of Education and Science, Ireland. (2003a). *Looking at our schools: An aid to self-evaluation in primary schools.* Dublin: Author.

Department of Education and Science, Ireland. (2003b). *Looking at our schools: An aid to self-evaluation in second level schools.* Dublin: Author.

Department of Education and Science, Ireland. (2005). *Customer survey.* Dublin: Author.

Department of Education and Science, Ireland. (2006a). *An evaluation of planning in thirty primary schools.* Dublin: Author.

Department of Education and Science, Ireland. (2006b). *Cooperative school evaluation project: Final report.* Dublin: Author.

Department of Education and Science, Ireland. (2008). *School inspection reports.* Retrieved April 2, 2008, from http://www.education.ie/insreports/school_inspection_report_listing.htm

Devos, G., & Verhoeven, J. (2003). School self-evaluation—Conditions and caveats: The case of secondary schools. *Educational Management Administration & Leadership, 31*, 403–420.

Egan, E. (2007). The evaluation of teachers and teaching in primary and post primary schools by the inspectorate of the Department of Education and Science. In R. Dolan & J. Gleeson (Eds.), *The competences approach to teacher professional development: Current practice and future prospects* (pp. 37–49). Armagh, Ireland: The Centre for Cross Border Studies.

Elliott, J. (2004). Making evidence-based practice educational. In G. Thomas & R. Pring (Eds.), *Evidence-based practice in education* (pp. 164–186). Maidenhead: Open University Press.

Elmore, R. F., & Fuhrman, S. H. (2001). Research finds the false assumption of accountability. *Educational Digest, 67*(4), 9–14.

European Parliament and Council of the European Union. (2001). *Recommendation of the European Parliament and of the Council of 12 February 2001 on European cooperation in quality evaluation in school education.* Retrieved February 20, 2008, from http://www-ilo-mirror.cornell.edu/public/english/employment/skills/recomm/instr/eu_10.htm

Fitz-Gibbon, C. T. (1999). OFSTED is inaccurate and damaging: How did we let it happen? *Forum, 41*(1), 14–18.

Flynn, C. (2006, October). *The attractiveness of the school leaders' role.* Paper presented at the Leadership Development for Schools Consultative Seminar, Dublin, Ireland.

Fullan, M. (2005). *Leadership and sustainability.* Thousand Oaks, CA: Corwin.

Fullan, M. (2006). *Turnaround leadership.* San Francisco, CA: Jossey-Bass.

Fullan, M. (2007). *The new meaning of educational change* (4th ed.). New York: Teacher's College Press.

Furubo, J. E., & Sandahl, R. (2002). Introduction. In J. E. Furubo, R. C. Rist, & R. Sandahl (Eds.), *International atlas of evaluation* (pp. 1–23). New Brunswick, NJ: Transaction Publishers.

Galton, M., & MacBeath, J. (2002). *A life in teaching? The impact of change on primary teachers' working lives.* Cambridge: Cambridge University.

Government of Ireland. (1998). *Education act.* Dublin: Stationery Office.

Hamilton, L. S., Stecher, B. M., Marsh, J. A., McCombs, J. S., Robyn, A., Russell, J. L., Naftel, S., & Barney, B. (2007). *Standards-based accountability under No Child Left Behind.* Santa Monica, CA: Rand Education.

Hoyle, E., & Wallace, M. (2005). *Educational leadership: Ambiguity, professionals and managerialism.* London: Sage.

Johannesson, I. S., Lindblad, S., & Simola, H. (2002). An inevitable progress? Educational restructuring in Finland, Iceland and Sweden at the turn of the millennium. *Scandinavian Journal of Educational Research, 46*(3), 325–338.

Leithwood, K., Aitken, R., & Janizi, D. (2001). *Making schools smarter: A system for monitoring school and district progress.* Thousand Oaks, CA: Corwin.

Lenihan, H., Hart, M., & Roper, S. (2005, Summer). Developing an evaluative framework for industrial policy in Ireland: Fulfilling the audit trail, or an aid to policy development. *Economic and Social Research Institute Quarterly Economic Commentary,* pp. 69–85.

Levin, B., & Fullan, M. (2008). Learning about system renewal. *Educational Management Administration and Leadership, 36*(2), 289–303.

Lisi, P., & Davidsdottir, S. (2005, December). *Empowerment and deliberative democracy in educational evaluations.* Paper presented at the Interlearn Conference and Life as Learning Research Conference, Helsinki, Finland.

Litton, F. (2006). The civil service and a new design for democracy. In F. Litton, T. Farmar, & F. Scott-Lennon (Eds.), *Ideas at work: Essays in honour of Geoffrey MacKechnie.* Dublin: A. & A. Farmar.

MacBeath, J. (1999). *Schools must speak for themselves: The case for school self-evaluation.* London: Routledge Falmer.

MacBeath, J. (2003). *The self-evaluation file.* Glasgow: Learning Files Scotland.

MacBeath, J. (2006). New relationships for old: Inspection and self-evaluation in England and Hong Kong. *International Studies in Educational Administration, 34*(2), 2–18.

Martin, S. (2005). Evaluation, inspection and the improvement agenda: Contrasting fortunes in an era of evidence-based policy making. *Evaluation, 11*(4), 496–504.

McNamara, G., & Kenny, A. (2006, October). *Quality evaluation: Policy, theory and practice in the education sector.* Paper presented at the Joint International Conference of the European Evaluation Society and the U.K. Evaluation Society, London.

McNamara, G., & O'Hara, J. (2004). Trusting the teacher: Evaluating educational innovation. *Evaluation, 10*(4), 463–474.

McNamara, G., & O'Hara, J. (2005). Internal review and self-evaluation: The chosen route to school improvement in Ireland. *Studies in Educational Evaluation, 31,* 267–282.

McNamara, G., & O'Hara, J. (2006). Workable compromise or pointless exercise? School–based evaluation in the Irish context. *Educational Management Administration and Leadership, 34*(4), 134–147.

McNamara, G., & O'Hara, J. (2008). *Trusting schools and teachers: Developing educational professionalism through self-evaluation.* New York: Peter Lang.

McNiff, J. (2002, April). *Evaluating information and communications technology: New ways of evaluating new ways of knowing.* Paper presented to the Special Interest Group, Research on Evaluation, at the American Educational Research Association annual meeting, New Orleans, LA. Retrieved October 23, 2007, from http://www.jeanmcniff.com/evaluationgrev.html

Meuret, D., & Morlaix, S. (2003). Conditions of success of a school's self-evaluation: Some lessons of the European experience. *School Effectiveness and School Improvement, 14*(1), 53–71.

Milliband, D. (2004, January). *Personalised learning: Building a new relationship with schools.* Speech delivered to the North of England Education Conference, Belfast. Retrieved March 30, 2008, from http://publications.teachernet.gov.uk/eOrdering Download/personalised-learning.pdf

Murray, J. (2001). *Reflections on the SMI: Policy Institute working paper.* Dublin: Policy Institute, Trinity College Dublin.

Nelson, M., & Eddy, R. M. (2008). Evaluative thinking and action in the classroom. *New Directions for Evaluation, 117,* 37–46.

Nevo, D. (2002). *School-based evaluation: An international perspective.* Oxford: Elsevier Science.

Nevo, D. (2006). Evaluation in education. In I. Shaw, J. Greene, & M. Mark (Eds.), *The SAGE handbook of evaluation* (pp. 441–460). London: Sage.

O'Dalaigh, C. (2000). School development planning: A Department of Education and Science perspective. In C. Furlong & L. Monaghan (Eds.), *School culture and ethos: Cracking the code* (pp. 141–151). Dublin: Marino Institute of Education.

Office for Standards in Education. (2004). *A new relationship with schools.* Retrieved April 2, 2008, from http:// www.ofsted.gov.uk/publications/index.cfm?fuseaction=pubs.summary&id=3666

Office for Standards in Education. (2005). Self-evaluation and the Self-Evaluation Form. *OFSTED Direct Issue.* Retrieved April 2, 2008, from http://www.ofsted.gov.uk/ofsteddirect/index.cfm?fuseaction=displayarticle &type=4&articleid=28& issueno=2

Olssen, M., Codd, C., & O' Neill, A. (2004). *Education policy, globalisation, citizenship and democracy.* London: Sage.

Organisation for Economic Co-operation and Development. (2005). *Teachers matter: Attracting, developing and retaining effective teachers.* Paris: Author.

Patscheider, F., Turra Rebuzzi, L., & McGinn, M. (Eds.). (2006). *Examples of interesting practice of internal and external evaluation of schools.* Brussels: Socrates Research Programme.

Pearson, L. C., & Moomaw, W. (2005). The relationship between teacher autonomy and stress, work satisfaction, empowerment, and professionalism. *Educational Research Quarterly, 29*(1), 37–53.

Plowright, D. (2007). Self-evaluation and OFSTED inspection: Developing an integrated model of school improvement. *Educational Management Administration and Leadership, 35*(3), 373–394.

Pollitt, C., & Bouckaert, G. (2000). *Public management reform: A comparative analysis.* Oxford: Oxford University Press.

Ruane, F. (2004, September). *Creating a culture of evaluation: Getting from rhetoric to possibility.* Paper presented at the Irish Evaluation Network, Inaugural Conference, Dublin City University.

Scheerens, J. (2002). School self-evaluation: Origins, definition, approaches, methods and implementation. In D. Nevo (Ed.), *School-based evaluation: An international perspective* (pp. 35–73). Oxford: Elsevier Science.

Shaw, I., Newton, D. P., Aitken, M., & Darnell, R. (2003). Do OFSTED inspections of secondary schools make a difference to GCSE results? *British Educational Research Journal, 29*(1), 63–75.

Simons, H. (2002). School self-evaluation in a democracy. In D. Nevo (Ed.), *School-based evaluation: An international perspective* (pp. 17–34). Oxford: Elsevier Science.

Smyth, E. (1999). *Do schools differ?* Dublin: Economic and Social Research Institute.

Spring, J. (2004). *How educational ideologies are shaping global society.* Mahwah, NJ: Lawrence Erlbaum Associates.

Sugrue, C. (1999). Primary principals' perspectives on whole-school evaluation. *Irish Journal of Education, 10*(2), 15–31.

Sugrue, C. (2006, October). *School leadership and OECD policy.* Paper presented at the Leadership Development for Schools Consultative Seminar, Dublin.

Tymms, P. (1999). *Baseline assessment and monitoring in primary schools.* London: David Fulton.

Whitty, G., Power, S., & Halpin, D. (1998). *Devolution and choice in education.* Buckingham: Open University Press.

Wolf, L., & Craig, D. (2004). Tiptoe through the plateaus: Personal reflections on interviews with Andy Hargreaves and Molly Quinn. *Journal of Curriculum and Pedagogy, 1*(1), 131–153.

CHAPTER 16

Accountability and Capacity Building

Can They Live Together?

David Nevo

At the heart of the debate among accountability versus professional development, bureaucratization versus professionalization, audit-oriented evaluation versus capacity building is the distinction between external evaluation and internal evaluation, self-evaluation, and evaluation by others. On the one hand, there is external evaluation aiming to control and motivate action for improvement; on the other hand, there is capacity building for self-evaluation and self-improvement. This might also be the distinction between internal and external accountability (Carnoy, Elmore, & Siskin, 2003), which accepts the legitimacy of accountability, but questions its effectiveness when imposed by means of external audit-oriented evaluation. But before we go further into the distinction between internal and external evaluation, here are some clarifications of the concept of evaluation and the essence of educational evaluation.

Relating to accountability and capacity building, the focus of this chapter is on the concept of accountability. It points out the strengths and limitations of internal and external evaluation, discussing the possible synergy between both as a potential contribution to the improvement of evaluation and thus the improvement of education. The chapter comprises four sections. In the first section, *the essence of evaluation* is discussed, pointing to its *raison d'etre* as a means for distinction between internal and external evaluation and their use for self-improvement and improvement. The discussion is based on a review of major perceptions of student assessment and program evaluation, mainly during the second half of the 20th century. The second section clarifies *the distinction between internal and external evaluation*, pointing out their strengths and weaknesses. Moreover, it discusses the use of evaluation for improvement through accountability and external monitoring, by means of external evaluation, and through self-improvement and professional development, by means of capacity building for internal evaluation. In the third section, *the synergy of internal and external evaluation* is discussed from three perspectives: (a) the roles of evaluation in education and the extent to which the two types of evaluation can serve such roles, (b) the perception of evaluation in a pluralistic postmodern society, and (c) the need to increase the usefulness and utilization of evaluation as a major justification for its existence. The chapter concludes by suggesting that both internal evaluation and external evaluation are needed and delineating terms for their fruitful co-existence. The *terms of co-existence* are discussed at three levels: the conceptual level (the need for new perceptions of educational evaluation), the methodological level (the need to combine educational practice with evaluation expertise), and the communicational level (the need to change ways of communication between evaluators and their audiences).

The Essence of Educational Evaluation

Current perceptions of educational evaluation have gone a long way since its initiation by Ralph Tyler (1950) more than half a century ago. It actually started with the evaluation of students' achievements, as it has been practiced in classes and schools around the world for thousands of years. Initially part of the learning and teaching process, educational evaluation as an academic discipline came to be used for curriculum development and evaluation, but mainly, to begin with, in conjunction with schools and classes. Only in the mid-1960s and early 1970s, with the increased demand for educational program and project evaluation coming from governmental organizations and other agencies, did educational evaluation expand beyond the classroom and into the entire educational system.

Most of these early developments in program evaluation took place in the United States and were "exported" to other parts of the world only

10 or 20 years later (Alkin, 2004; Norris, 1990). This might be of special significance in the context of globalization. *Globalization* can be defined in more than one way reflecting multiple perspectives on its meaning (Scholte, 2005). It can be perceived as *internationalization*, reflecting growth of transactions and interdependence between countries. It can be perceived as *liberalization*, removing constraints on movements of resources and people between countries. It sometimes is perceived as *universalization*, described as a process of dispersing ideas and experiences to people around the world. The concept of globalization can also be defined as *Westernization* and modernization. Globalization perceived in this way is often interpreted as Americanization, colonization, and imperialism (Gowan, 1999; Petras & Veltmeyer, 2001).

Thus, on the one hand, evaluation is being "globalized" as its theories and practices travel across national and cultural boarders from its American origin with the notion of internationalization and universalization. On the other hand, like globalization, it might also be perceived as Westernization and Americanization and criticized for its lack of sensitivity to local stakeholders and their special needs.

In Europe, for instance, the major concern was—and in some countries still is—testing and student assessment (Harlen, 2007), although with time, tests and other achievement measures began to be used not only for this purpose. Gradually, they also became outcome measures for other evaluation objects such as programs, schools, teachers, and educational systems—sometimes together with other information regarding the goals and processes of implementation of such evaluation objects. Evaluations now can be found around the world and come in many shapes and sizes reflecting multiple perspectives on its nature, relevance, and utilization (Bhola, 2003).

Educational evaluation has many faces, and different people mean different things when they use the word *evaluation*.[1] Some people perceive it as judgment of quality. Others think of it as a systematic way of looking into important matters. Still others perceive it as a daily activity that we perform (hopefully) whenever we make a decision. In education, it is sometimes associated with testing and narrowly limited to student achievement. In government, it might be seen as reassessment of major policies or courses of action. Sometimes evaluation is viewed as a constructive tool for improvement and innovation. Sometimes it is seen as a destructive activity that threatens spontaneity and paralyzes creativity. Occasionally administrators think that evaluation is no more than a way to make things look good when they really are not.

What then is educational evaluation? What does it mean? Is it a complex concept or a simple one, in essence, that gets complicated by evaluation experts? Many attempts have been made in recent years to explain the meaning of evaluation and clarify the distinction between evaluation and other related concepts, such as measurement or research. The literature contains many approaches to the conceptualization of evaluation and the determination of its countenance in education. Many of those approaches have been unduly referred to as "models" (e.g., the CIPP Model, the Discrepancy Model, the Responsive Model, or the Goal-Free Model), although none of them reaches a sufficient degree of complexity or completeness to justify the term *model.* Stake (1981) rightly suggested that they be referred to as "persuasions" rather than "models."

Evaluation in education has acquired a variety of definitions over the years. Some of them have been in use for almost a half a century and became the "cornerstones" of modern evaluation in education. Ralph Tyler's (1950) well-known definition perceived evaluation as "The process of determining to what extent educational objectives are actually being realized" (p. 69). Another widely accepted definition of evaluation, suggested by leading evaluators such as Cronbach (1963), Alkin (1969), and Stufflebeam et al. (1971), was providing information for decision making. In recent years, there has been considerable consensus among evaluators that evaluation is basically the assessment of merit or worth (Joint Committee, 1994: Scriven, 1993) or an activity comprising both description and judgment.

Following Stake (1967) and Guba and Lincoln (1981), Nevo (1995) defined *educational evaluation* as an "act of collecting systematic information regarding the nature and quality of educational objects" (p. 11). This definition combines description and judgment, but distinguishes between them because of their different nature. Description can be based on systematic data collection and thus results in highly objective information. Judgment is based on criteria that, in most cases, are determined by values, social norms, and personal or professional preferences of stakeholders associated with the evaluation. Judgment may thus be subjective in nature. Description and judgment, although coexisting in most evaluations, in education as well as in other fields, are used in different proportions for different purposes. Although both are needed, judgment seems to be inevitable in summative evaluation, whereas informative descriptions seem to be crucial for formative evaluation.

It is also important to notice that educational evaluation, although having much in common with other types of evaluation in areas such as social work, health services, criminal justice, and so on, has some unique features. First, the source of evaluation in education is, as we have seen, in program evaluation, which started in the United States around the mid-1960s, as well as in student testing and assessment, which has been conducted in schools around the world for centuries. Second, public involvement in its practice and usage is especially apparent because education is a general social service relevant to most members of a society, far beyond social work, health, and criminal justice. Third, the role of teachers and their experience as evaluators (although, traditionally, mainly student evaluators) cannot be ignored when applications of general evaluation theories or methods are suggested to them. Teachers are involved in modern evaluation as evaluators, evaluation objects, or evaluation stakeholders. Promising innovative evaluation approaches are often rejected by teachers and other educators because their proponents are not sensitive enough to one or more of the unique characteristics of evaluation in education.

In general, the perception of evaluation, including description and judgment, which can never be totally objective, comes from a single perspective (e.g., external evaluation) together with the unique nature of educational evaluation. This perception leads us to suggest that a perspective for educational evaluation is necessary and it can be developed by combining internal and external evaluation. But first, we provide more about the distinction between the two.

Internal and External Evaluation

Internal and external evaluation have long been under discussion in the evaluation literature (Love, 1991; Mathison, 1991; Scriven, 1967, 1991; Sonnichsen, 2000; Stufflebeam et al., 1971). Scriven (1991) gave the following definitions for internal and external evaluation in the context of program evaluation:

> Internal evaluators (or evaluations) are those done by project staff, even if they are special evaluation staff—that is, even if they are external to the production/writing/service part of the project. (p. 197)

> An external evaluator is someone who is at least not on the project or program's staff, or someone—in the case of personnel evaluation—other than the individual being evaluated, or their family or staff. . . . It is best to regard externality as a continuum along which one tries to score as high as possible. (p. 159)

At the school level, internal evaluation can be performed by a teacher or a group of teachers, by other members of the school's professional personnel, by the principal or other school administrators, or by a special staff member designated by the school to serve as a *school evaluator*. An external evaluation of the school can be performed by the school district, the state department of education, or a ministry of education

using professional evaluators, regional inspectors, or a district/state/national evaluation department. An external evaluation of the school could also be conducted by an independent evaluation consultant or evaluation firm commissioned by the school or its governing board.

For many years and in many countries, school evaluation was tantamount to external evaluation. In some countries, it was done mainly by inspectors (e.g., Her Majesty's Inspectors in the UK), whereas in other countries, it was done by means of state assessment programs (e.g., in the United States). Many educational systems combined both student assessment programs and overall school reviews, some of them conducted in a systematic way by central units in the educational system (e.g., Office for Standards in Education [OFSTED] in the UK). The idea of *accountability*, apparently initiated in the United States (Lessinger, 1970), which has been around for almost 40 years, and relatively newer ideas of setting *standards* and *benchmarks* as major means for school improvement (Wilson, 1996), can all be traced back to this long tradition of controlling schools by means of external audit-oriented evaluation.

But even before the term *accountability* came into use, there was a clear demand by politicians, bureaucrats, parents, and the public at large that schools be evaluated externally to find out whether they were fulfilling their duties. There was also a hope that such external evaluations would motivate teachers and school principals to work harder to improve their schools. This was true for democratic and non-democratic societies and for centralized and decentralized educational systems alike. The demand never ceased even when external evaluation was highly criticized by innovative educators and when internal evaluation was encouraged by way of an alternative.

Parallel to the almost universal phenomenon of external school evaluation, many countries have more recently tended to apply newly developed evaluation methods at the school level in the form of internal evaluation or self-evaluation. *School-Based Evaluation* (Nevo, 1995, 2002; Ryan, 2004), *Participatory Evaluation* (Cousins &

Whitmore, 1998), and *Empowerment Evaluation* (Fetterman, 2005; Fetterman, Kaftarian, & Wandersman, 1996) are some attempts made to apply internal evaluation methods at the school level. These seem to be in line with other prevailing ideas, such as *reflection* (Schon, 1983) and *professionalization* of teachers (Darling-Hammond, 1992) and educational administrators. Reflection is, in a way, one kind of self-evaluation, although its proponents do not sufficiently stress the important role of systematic data collection as a basis for reflection. A professional perception of teaching regards teaching as a complex undertaking, suggesting that teachers should identify needs, analyze goals, choose instructional strategies, and plan and monitor their work. No longer narrowly limited to evaluating student achievements, evaluation becomes an integral part of the teaching profession, relevant to various aspects of teachers' responsibilities.

Internal evaluation is also an important component of schools in decentralized or decentralizing educational systems, which are following models of school-based management or autonomous schools (Nevo, 1997). Autonomous schools are urged to define their own educational aims, be in charge of the educational process, and evaluate their actions. With the expansion of school authority, schools are also expected to take greater responsibility and be accountable for their deeds. These demands have emphasized the importance of internal self-evaluation to support improvement, as well as to respond to the school accountability requirement.

Internal evaluation becomes a major *tool for school management*, serving decision making at various administrative levels. The improvement of decision-making processes is especially important within the broader context of ongoing decentralization and school empowerment mentioned earlier. Schools are granted significant authority and are, in return, expected to make decisions autonomously. Internal self-evaluation is highly salient in such situations: It can provide schools with means to improve decision-making processes and make them more effective. An internal evaluator is usually better acquainted with the local context of the evaluation and less threatening to those being evaluated. She or he knows the local problems, communicates better with the local people, and remains on-site to facilitate the implementation of the evaluation recommendations. Developing an internal evaluation mechanism in a school is also an investment in an enduring resource for serving the information needs of the school.

Internal evaluation is, moreover, an expression of school *empowerment* and transfer of authority from the center to the periphery, from central government to local community. Participation in the evaluation process may contribute to the empowerment of an organization as a whole because the latter acquires the ability to monitor itself in a more systematic way and gains greater confidence in its educational direction. Participation in the evaluation process can furthermore empower individuals in the organization by providing them with evaluation skills, which they can later apply in various contexts. The principals and teachers participating in evaluation activities can apply the newly acquired evaluation skills and knowledge in other areas of their work. For example, teachers can use their knowledge of research methodology to teach pupils to perform investigative tasks as part of their school work. This would be in line with the concept of process use (Patton, 1997) and the distinction between evaluation use and evaluation influence (Alkin & Taut, 2003; Cousins & Shulha, 2006; Kirkhart, 2000).

Teachers might also benefit from their participation in evaluation activities, increasing their involvement in decision-making processes outside the classroom, fostering collegiality and collaboration among teachers, and promoting reflection. All these are central to the development of teacher professionalization (Darling-Hammond, 1992).

Why Do We Need Both?

But pointing out the importance of internal evaluation or self-evaluation and its relevancy to professional teachers and autonomous schools should not lead us to ignore external evaluation. Demands for accountability, even when their effectiveness in improving education is dubious, and the right of the public to know in democratic societies also have to be kept in mind. Although internal evaluation, by providing information to parents and the community at large, can also enhance accountability, the credibility of its findings might be limited without external evaluation. Evaluation has to serve many functions and fulfill many roles. Can they all be served by one kind of evaluation, internal or external? In our diverse and pluralistic societies, can we trust one kind of evaluation, internal or external, to represent the truths of human life? Can evaluation be useful when we do it in a subjective way or in a way that might be a threat to our well-being?

The need for both, internal and external evaluation, and their significance to education can be discussed from three perspectives: (a) the roles of evaluation in education and the extent to which both kinds of evaluation can better serve such roles, (b) the perception of evaluation in a pluralistic postmodern society, and (c) the need to increase the usefulness of evaluation as a major justification for its existence.

The Roles of Evaluation

Scriven (1967) was the first to suggest the distinction between formative evaluation and summative evaluation, referring to two major roles or functions of evaluation. The formative function of evaluation is used for improvement and the development of ongoing activities (or programs, persons, products, etc.). In its summative function, evaluation may be used for selection, certification, or to demonstrate transparency or accountability.

A third role of evaluation is what we might call its psychological or sociopolitical role. It is often apparent that a specific evaluation does not serve any formative purpose nor is it used for selection, accreditation, or other summative purposes. Its main use seems to be to increase awareness to

specific activities or for public relations serving "the right of the public to know" in democratic societies. This category also includes the function of motivating desired behavior by means of testing and assessment, as expressed by programs of high-stakes accountability, such as No Child Left Behind (NCLB) in the United States.[2]

Another, somewhat unpopular, function of evaluation is its use for the exercise of authority or control. In formal organizations, it is the privilege of the superiors to evaluate their subordinates. Often the person in a management position does so to demonstrate his or her authority and also to fulfill his or her responsibility to control others' performance. This function may be referred to as the administrative role of evaluation. Some teachers think it is legitimate to use tests and grades "to make sure that students do what they are expected to do," and school principals use evaluation to exercise their authority over teachers (Glasman & Nevo, 1988).

Although many evaluators have, for the obvious reasons, felt more naturally sympathetic to the formative aspect of evaluation, the formative function of evaluation, the general perception nevertheless seems to be that there are no "right" or "wrong" roles of evaluation, at least regarding the formative and summative roles of evaluation, with the general notion that the overall purpose of educational evaluation is to improve education. A single evaluation can deliberately serve more than one function, and various functions can be served in more than one way and by more than one kind of evaluation. But on the whole, it seems clear that the formative role of evaluation is better served by internal evaluation, whereas accountability, control, motivation, and other administrative and sociopolitical functions of evaluation tend to be better—and sometimes only—served by external evaluation.

Evaluation in a Pluralistic Society

In a pluralistic democratic society with a multicultural population and diverse values, priorities, and needs and in an era of internationalization and globalization, it seems to be almost impossible to reach consensus on one set of standards that could be used as a common yardstick to assess students and serve as a basis for the evaluation of schools. This is difficult when we talk about states and countries and even more so when we talk about the "Global Village." There is a need to maintain a balance between what is common to the whole society and what is unique to its components. Evaluation has to be sensitive to the needs and values of the whole society, but it also has to listen to the voices of communities and individual stakeholders. It has to focus on both the general and the unique. It has to reflect the common as well as the diverse.

Educational sociologists are concerned with the relations between center and periphery. Educational administrators are moving from centralization to decentralization and seem to be realizing that neither one of the two can live without the other, and many educational systems (e.g., the UK, New Zealand, and sometimes the United States) think the "right answer" might be a combination of both.

Postmodernists suggest that there is more than "one truth," and their representatives in evaluation (Mabry, 1997) doubt whether evaluation can make any objective judgments at all. Participatory evaluation and empowerment evaluation gained a lot of recognition by the evaluation profession and can be seen as another inclination toward self-evaluation and internal evaluation and an attempt to increase the participation of stakeholders in the evaluation process.

We seem to live in a world in which one external-professional-objective evaluation that "knows it all" and holds the whole truths has become unfeasible. It is impossible to leave all those empowered components of society or the educational system disconnected without looking for any common denominator. National goals have to live with local needs. School administrators must respect the professional perceptions of teachers. National majorities must respect the needs and values of minority groups. Minority groups, from their side, must accept some common values and goals of the society to which they belong. Ministries of education must also trust schools and teachers when they draw conclusions from the results of national assessment programs. A combination of internal and external evaluation seems to be the required solution.

Evaluation Utilization

Over the years, the evaluation profession has been concerned with the question of evaluation use and utilization. This was based on the assumption that usefulness is the *raison d'etre* of evaluation and the major justification for its existence. Conceptual and empirical studies have tried to understand the meaning of evaluation use, assess the extent to which evaluation studies are actually used, and identify the variables that might affect utilization and increase the use of evaluation findings.

In an attempt to define evaluation use, the evaluation utilization literature has suggested a distinction among three kinds of evaluation use: *instrumental use*—for decision making and action; *conceptual use*—for understanding; and *symbolic use*—for compliance (Rich, 1977). Instrumental use is demonstrated when the evaluation findings are used for decision making (e.g., the recommendations of an evaluation study are accepted by decision makers and actually implemented). By conceptual use of evaluation, we refer to the utilization of evaluation to get a better understanding of the major problems of an evaluation object (e.g., school, program, teacher, student, etc.) on the basis of its strengths and weaknesses. We talk about symbolic use of evaluation when it is carried out to comply with an evaluation requirement, or it is used by individuals or organizations to create an image of innovation, planning, or thoughtfulness.

Research findings and our own professional experiences as evaluators regarding the extent to which evaluation is being used are not encouraging. Evaluation is not always used, and when it actually is—it is mainly in the conceptual and symbolic senses.

An extensive synthesis of 65 empirical evaluation utilization studies (Cousins & Leithwood, 1986) suggested two groups of variables that might affect evaluation utilization. The first group of variables relates to evaluation implementation and includes methodological quality, credibility of the evaluator, relevance of findings, communication quality, findings, and timeliness. The second group of variables relates to the decision setting where the evaluation has to be used and includes: information needs, decision characteristics, political climate, competing information, personal characteristics, and commitment to evaluation.

Eleven years later, an update of this synthesis was published (Cousins & Shulha, 2006; Shulha & Cousins, 1997), including a similar set of predictors of evaluation utilization. They were relevance, credibility, user involvement, communication effectiveness, potential for information processing, need of information, anticipated change, quality of the evaluation, and context/decision setting.

In my view, the evaluation utilization literature can be summarized as suggesting three major predictors of evaluation utilization: *evaluation quality* (accuracy and relevancy), *stakeholders' involvement*, and *evaluation culture*.

Experience in working with schools that are developing their internal and external evaluation capabilities (Nevo, 1995, 2002) suggests that combining internal and external evaluation and maintaining a dialogue between them will promote those three predictive variables. This way, (a) external evaluation (which is usually professional evaluation) will enhance *accuracy and objectivity*, (b) internal evaluation will increase *relevancy* by ensuring that the unique nature of the school is reflected in the evaluation, and (c) the dialogue will increase *stakeholders' involvement* and create an *evaluation culture* in the school receptive to evaluation and its utilization.

Thus, if indeed we want evaluation to be useful and to be used, we need both internal and external evaluation, and we need a dialogue between them. The question is not anymore: Which one is better, internal or external evaluation? What is more important, accountability or capacity building? The question is, rather, how can they live together? I conclude this chapter by suggesting how such a thing can happen by creating terms of existence for a dialogue between internal and external evaluation.

Dialogue Evaluation

Of course, we all love the concept of *dialogue* in various contexts, and not many people would dare to argue against it. But dialogue does not come free of charge and cannot flourish on all grounds and in all climates. Some terms of existence have to be provided to create an appropriate habitat for constructive dialogue. These terms of existence are not self-evident and sometimes quite difficult—although not impossible—to achieve. They were derived from work with schools in several countries in developing school-based evaluation (Nevo, 1995, 2002), but can be applied to other evaluation objects, such as programs, projects, personnel, or students (Nevo, 2006). They relate to three aspects of evaluation practice: *conception, methodology,* and *communication.*

The Conceptual Level

Evaluation has to be perceived as a means for *understanding rather than judgment.* There is no meaningful way to judge the overall quality of a school by one single criterion or a justified combination (Stake et al., 1997), nor is there any real need to do so. Evaluation is concerned with quality and thus should provide judgmental statements based on multiple criteria related to the various aspects of schools and schooling. It should refrain from an overall assessment of students, programs, or schools. Thus, evaluators should provide *quality profiles,* rather than *composite scores,* which require justification of weights for the various components that would comprise the composite score. Such profiles could enhance understanding to be used sensibly for improvement, selection, certification, or accountability in a specific context and under given constraints. Composite scores provided by assessors tend to be perceived as being "objective," and they are frequently misused or abused for social and political purposes and high-stakes accountability. Actually, such overall judgments are unnecessary. If the aim is formative evaluation, they are too general to provide constructive guidance for improvement. For summative evaluation, making an overall assessment is actually like making the decision, and that is the responsibility of the decision maker not the evaluator.

Evaluation (internal and external) has to be modest, acknowledging its limitations, as they are dictated by the state of the art of the profession. Some evaluators tend to promise their clients objective descriptions and unbiased assessments, which they hope to obtain by virtue of their powerful evaluation methodology and instrumentation. Such promises are far beyond the capabilities of current evaluation methods and are usually an expression of exaggerated professional pride, bordering on arrogance and deceit.

Although I suggest that evaluators—external and internal—refrain from overall judgments, *providing recommendations* should be part of the responsibility of evaluation. The evaluation literature does not universally accept recommendations as part of the responsibility of the evaluator. Scriven (1995) perceives recommendations as being beyond the scope of the evaluator's knowledge and expertise. In contrast, Patton (1997), who is strongly oriented toward evaluation utilization, suggests that "well-written, carefully derived recommendations and conclusions can be the magnet that pools all the other elements of an evaluation together into a meaningful whole" (p. 324).

Thus, providing sound, specific, and practical recommendations should be an integral part of evaluation and, as we see later, a first step in sharing the responsibility for coping with the consequences of an evaluation.

The Methodological Level

Evaluation should be practiced as a *process* and not as a one-shot activity. Evaluation is a complex process trying to understand complex issues, unless you want to deal with trivia. Sometimes we use figures to understand things. Sometimes we create thick descriptions and portrayals to grasp complex realities. It is a process of presenting findings, analyzing them, discussing them with pertinent audiences, comparing them with other findings, collecting additional information, getting more findings, and coping with added complexities.

The interaction between internal and external evaluators should be based on a *two-way flow of information* in a process of mutual learning. The parties involved in the dialogue are not necessarily equal in their authority, but there is symmetry in the assumption that each has something to learn from the other and something to teach the other. To start with, nobody knows everything, but each party knows something: Through the dialogue, they learn more and more. Each party can take advantage of its unique sources for data gathering, but for a two-way flow of information, both parties (the school and the external evaluator) have to be engaged in some kind of *systematic data-collection* activity. Hence, a school needs an internal evaluation team, or some other evaluation mechanism, to be trained in using available methods and instruments for systematic data collection and analysis guided by either a quantitative or a qualitative research paradigm. Qualitative research may seem more attractive to teachers, but at a later stage the data are often found to be too complicated to handle and untrustworthy in the eyes of parents and administrators. However, quantitative research methods tend sometimes to be used simplistically by "crunching numbers" with trivial data. Thus, school people should be acquainted with qualitative as well as quantitative methods, understanding both strengths and weaknesses of those research paradigms.

Evaluation should focus on *relevant issues and pertinent data*. A dialogue, any dialogue, is a demanding undertaking, requiring openness, self-confidence, and a great deal of energy from its participants. People tend to avoid dialogue if it is not related to issues that are really important to them. If an external evaluation deals mainly with trivial issues or is preoccupied with methodological sophistications, rather than with issues of substance and important information, school people might lose interest and stop participating in any dialogue. Delineating major issues and relevant information should be an important component of school evaluation, as well as any other evaluation.

The Communication Level

There must be *mutual respect and trust* between the parties. Both have to believe that each has a genuine interest in understanding what is at stake and can make a significant contribution to such an understanding. An educational system that follows a bureaucratic conception of teaching, defining the role of its teachers as implementers of a curriculum prescribed to them by administrators and experts, does not trust teachers to understand teaching or have the ability to assess its quality. Such a system will probably seek an accountability program based on external evaluation or employ national supervisors, whose job it is to evaluate and supervise teachers' work rather than improve it. An educational system with a more professional conception of teaching will expect its teachers to plan, design, conduct, and evaluate their work; strive to achieve identified goals; and meet defined standards of excellence. Such a system will perceive teachers as professionals who are interested in understanding the problems of their profession, maintaining its standards, and ensuring its quality. In such an educational system, teacher evaluation can be based on a dialogue between external evaluation and internal self-evaluation of teachers.

Professional evaluators tend to be arrogant, something they rationalize by means of an ideology of isolation, which urges that to preserve their objectivity and avoid bias and cooptation they have to detach themselves as much as possible from clients and evaluatees. Such evaluators think they (should) know everything. For them, a

dialogue with amateur—nonprofessional—nonobjective school evaluators would compromise their objectivity and be a waste of time. For a dialogue, professional external evaluators must be modest and respectful to teachers who serve on internal school evaluation teams. Teachers should be respected as professionals and equal partners even though they are not professional evaluators.

Evaluation has to be fair in several ways to both parties [involved] in the dialogue. First of all, propriety standards have to be observed, ensuring that evaluation is conducted legally, ethically, and with due regard to the welfare of those associated with the evaluation and those who may be affected by its consequences. Teachers who believe they are being unfairly evaluated by the principal or the parents cannot be expected to participate in a sincere dialogue regarding such evaluation.

It must also be clear to both sides what the purpose of evaluation is, what its expected benefits are, what its price will be, and who will have to shoulder the costs. An evaluator commissioned by a school to assess its mathematics program for the designated purpose of improvement and innovation, and who later discovers that he has been trapped into a power struggle between the principal and some of the teachers, although there is no intention on the part of the school to improve its math program, cannot be expected to be a willing partner for a dialogue.

It is also unrealistic to expect a school to maintain a dialogue with an external evaluation, even one that the school has joined voluntarily, if at a certain point the school feels it is being exploited for purposes that clash with its needs. This can happen when a school believes that the evaluation mainly serves the research interests of the evaluator/researcher or the information needs of the educational system.

Both parties should take some responsibility for handling the consequences of the evaluation. If a dialogue is to be developed between external and internal evaluation, there must be a sense of joint responsibility for the consequences. If a national or regional authority conducts the external evaluation of a school, and we want to move into a dialogue between the school and that authority regarding the quality of the school, the school cannot be left alone to bear the consequences of such evaluation. The external evaluation agency must commit itself to some kind of partnership in developing solutions to the problems that will be revealed by the evaluation even when the authority, and expertise it has to solve such problems, is limited. Professional evaluators serving in or for national or regional evaluation authorities might not be qualified to solve the problems that they uncover. Even so, they should see it as their responsibility to provide useful and practical recommendations and help the school at least to find the way to those who have the necessary skills and resources. However, some external evaluators, such as school inspectors in many European countries, have a clear definition of authority and responsibility to evaluate their schools as well as facilitate their overall functioning. They should definitely commit themselves to fully share the responsibility to bear the consequences of the evaluation. There is little motivation for a school to move into a serious dialogue for school improvement if the burden of improvement lies only with the school. Leaving the school alone to struggle with the problems revealed by the evaluation decreases the chances to find appropriate solutions and implies that the school is to be blamed for those problems. Accusations usually arouse defensiveness and counteraccusations, rather than stimulating problem solving and constructive action. Unfortunately, demands for accountability, and the use of parental choice as a remedy for school problems, are examples of the tendency of educational systems *not* to share with their schools the responsibility for bearing the consequences of school evaluation and providing appropriate resources for their improvement.

Conclusion

In many educational systems, *everybody seems to hate external evaluation while nobody trusts*

internal evaluation. I have contended in this chapter that both types of evaluation are needed because both have important roles in the life of schools, teachers, programs, and educational systems. I have also suggested some conditions that have to be met to establish a constructive dialogue between internal and external evaluation as a basis for their co-existence.

I would like to conclude by suggesting that those of us, in every country and around the world, who are proponents of external audit evaluation should invest in capacity building to empower schools and teachers to participate as equal partners in the evaluation process and make use of it. Those of us who believe in capacity building for internal evaluation as a means for school autonomy, self-improvement, and teacher professionalization must admit the legitimacy of accountability requirements and the right of the public to know. They, in their turn, should seek external evaluation as a partner for dialogue, rather than an object for criticism and rejection.

Notes

1. Throughout this chapter, I use the term *evaluation* as it is used mainly in the American literature, referring to program evaluation, student evaluation, teacher evaluation, and so on. Occasionally, I also use the British synonyms of *student assessment* for student evaluation, *teacher appraisal* for teacher evaluation, and *school review* for school evaluation. I do so to draw attention to the common elements of the various evaluation activities and their conceptualizations. I would also like to avoid, as much as possible, the confusion between the British use of *student assessment* (rather than student evaluation) and the U.S. usage of student *assessment* to make the distinctions between "student testing" and "student assessment," referring to performance assessment and authentic assessment, as opposed to traditional/objective testing.

2. I would like to make a distinction between *accountability* and *high-stakes accountability*, as suggested by Carnoy et al. (2003). Accountability can be perceived as a synonym to responsibility and transparency, whose legitimacy and justification cannot be

denied, especially in democratic societies. However, high-stakes accountability refers to the use of testing and assessment, usually associated with positive or negative rewards, as a means to improve education. This use of evaluation has been challenged in many studies (e.g., Carnoy et al., 2003; Darling-Hammond, 2004; Linn, 2000; Ryan, 2005; Stake, 2004), and it was found not quite effective and having many harmful side effects.

References

Alkin, M. C. (1969). Evaluation theory development. *Evaluation Comment, 2,* 2–7.

Alkin, M. C. (2004). *Evaluation roots: Tracing theorists' views and influences.* Thousand Oaks, CA: Sage.

Alkin, M. C., & Taut, S. (2003). Unbundling evaluation use. *Studies in Educational Evaluation, 29,* 1–12.

Bhola, H. S. (2003). Social and cultural contexts of educational evaluation: A global perspective. In T. Kellaghan & D. L. Stufflebeam (Eds.), *International handbook of educational evaluation.* Dordrecht: Kluwer.

Carnoy, M., Elmore, R., & Siskin, L. S. (Eds.). (2003). *The new accountability.* New York: Routledge Falmer.

Cousins, J. B., & Leithwood, K. A. (1986). Current empirical research on evaluation utilization. *Review of Educational Research, 56*(3), 331–364.

Cousins, J. B., & Shulha, L. M. (2006). A comparative analysis of evaluation utilization and its cognate fields. In I. Shaw, J. Greene, & M. Mark (Eds.), *Handbook of evaluation: Program, policy and practice* (pp. 266–291). Thousand Oaks, CA: Sage.

Cousins, J. B., & Whitmore, E. (1998). Framing participatory evaluation. In E. Whitmore (Ed.), Understanding and practicing participatory evaluation. *New Directions in Evaluation 80* (pp. 3–23). San Francisco, CA: Jossey-Bass.

Cronbach, L. J. (1963). Course improvement through evaluation. *Teachers College Record, 64,* 672–683.

Darling-Hammond, L. (1992). Teacher professionalism. In M. C. Alkin (Ed.), *Encyclopedia of educational research* (6th ed., pp. 1359–1366). New York: Macmillan.

Darling-Hammond, L. (2004). From "Separate but Equal" to "No Child Left Behind": The collision of new standards and old inequalities. In D. Meier & G. Wood (Eds.), *Many children left behind* (pp. 3–32). Boston: Beacon Press.

Fetterman, D. (2005). *Empowerment evaluation principles in practice.* New York: Guilford.

Fetterman, D., Kaftarian, S. J., & Wandersman, A. (Eds.). (1996). *Empowerment evaluation.* Thousand Oaks, CA: Sage.

Glasman, N. S., & Nevo, D. (1988). *Evaluation in decision making: The case of school administration.* Boston: Kluwer.

Gowan, P. (1999). *The global gamble: Washington's Faustian bid for world dominance.* London: Verso.

Guba, E. G., & Lincoln, Y. S. (1981). *Effective evaluation.* San Francisco, CA: Jossey-Bass.

Harlen, W. (2007). *Assessment of learning.* London: Sage.

Joint Committee on Standards for Educational Evaluation. (1994). *The program evaluation standards* (2nd ed.). Thousand Oaks, CA: Sage.

Kirkhart, K. (2000). Reconceptualizing evaluation use: An integrated theory of influence. In V. Caracelli (Ed.), The expanding scope of evaluation use. *New Directions in Evaluation.* San Francisco, CA: Jossey-Bass.

Lessinger, L. (1970). *Every kid a winner: Accountability in education.* Palo Alto, CA: Science Research Associates.

Linn, R. (2000). Assessment and accountability. *Educational Researcher, 23*(9), 4–14.

Love, A. J. (1991). *Internal evaluation: Building organizations from within.* Newbury Park, CA: Sage.

Mabry, L. (Ed.). (1997). *Evaluation and the postmodern dilemma.* Greenwich, CT: JAI.

Mathison, S. (1991).What do we know about internal evaluation? *Evaluation and Program Planning, 14,* 159–165.

Nevo, D. (1995). *School-based evaluation: A dialogue for school improvement.* Oxford: Pergamon.

Nevo, D. (1997). The function of evaluation in school autonomy. In R. Shapira & P. W. Cookson (Eds.), *Autonomy and choice in context: International perspectives.* Oxford: Pergamon.

Nevo, D. (Ed.). (2002). *School-based evaluation: An international perspective.* Amsterdam: JAI.

Nevo, D. (2006). Evaluation in education. In I. Shaw, J. Greene, & M. Mark (Eds.), *Handbook of evaluation: Program, policy and practice* (pp. 441–460). Thousand Oaks, CA: Sage.

Norris, N. (1990). *Understanding educational evaluation.* London: Kogan Page.

Patton, M. Q. (1997). *Utilization focused evaluation* (3rd ed.). Thousand Oaks, CA: Sage.

Petras, J., & Veltmeyer, H. (2001). *Globalization unmasked: Imperialism in the 21st century.* London: Zed.

Rich, R. F. (1977). Use of social science information by federal bureaucrats: Knowledge for action and knowledge for understanding. In C. H. Weiss (Ed.), *Using social research in public policy making.* Lexington, MA: Lexington Books.

Ryan, K. E. (2004). Serving the public interest in educational accountability. *American Journal for Evaluation, 25,* 443–460.

Ryan, K. E. (2005). Making educational accountability more democratic. *American Journal of Evaluation, 26*(4), 532–543.

Scriven, M. (1967). The methodology of evaluation. In R. E. Stake (Ed.), *AERA Monograph Series on Curriculum Evaluation No. 1.* Chicago: Rand McNally.

Scriven, M. (1991). *Evaluation thesaurus* (4th ed.). Newbury Park, CA: Sage.

Scriven, M. (1993). Hard-won lessons in program evaluation. *New Directions for Evaluation 58.* San Francisco, CA: Jossey-Bass.

Scriven, M. (1995).The logic of evaluation and evaluation practice. In D. M. Founier (Ed.), *Reasoning in evaluation: Inferential links and leaps. New Directions for Program Evaluation 68.* San Francisco, CA: Jossey-Bass.

Scholte, J. A. (2005). *Globalization: A critical introduction* (2nd ed.). New York: Palgrave Macmillan.

Schon, D. A. (1983). *The reflective practitioner: How professionals think in action.* New York: Basic Books.

Shulha, L. M., & Cousins, J. B. (1997). Evaluation use: Theory, research and practice since 1986. *Evaluation Practice, 18*(3), 195–208.

Sonnichsen, R. C. (2000). *High impact internal evaluation.* Thousand Oaks, CA: Sage.

Stake, R. E. (1967). The countenance of educational evaluation. *Teachers College Record, 68,* 523–540.

Stake, R. E. (1981). Setting standards for educational evaluators. *Evaluation News, 2*(2), 148–152.

Stake, R. E. (2004). *Standards-based and responsive evaluation.* Thousand Oaks, CA: Sage.

Stake, R. E., Migotsky, D., Davis, R., Cisneros, E., DePaul, G., Dunbar, C., et al. (1997). The evolving synthesis of program value. *Evaluation Practice, 18*(2), 89–103.

Stufflebeam, D. L., Foley, W. J., Gephart, W. J., Guba, E. G., Hammond, R. L., Merriman, H.O., & Provus, M. M. (1971). *Educational evaluation and decision making.* Itasca, IL: Peacock.

Tyler, R. W. (1950). *Basic principles of curriculum and instruction.* Chicago: University of Chicago Press.

Wilson, T. A. (1996). *Reaching for better standards.* New York: Teacher's College Press.

PART IV

Educational Evaluation as Learning and Discovery

*E*ducational evaluation as learning and discovery reflects educational evaluation theories and practices that emphasize the learning and discovery function of evaluation and find their grounding in contextual notions of
localism, stakeholder engagement, and values pluralism. A broad array of evaluation theories are represented in this educational evaluation family, including practical participatory and postmodern evaluation approaches. The power of
evaluation to deepen the understanding of complex psychosocial phenomena, such
as interventions aimed at enhancing student learning, characterizes the rationale for
learning-oriented approaches. These evaluation theories are further distinguished by
preferences for case study methodology and for mixed or qualitative methods.

After elaborating how globalization processes speed up and intensify the social
practices surrounding learning, Dahler-Larsen (Chapter 17) presents an in-depth
analysis of various learning-oriented educational evaluation approaches in his *theory* chapter. Acknowledging that learning-oriented evaluation can be successful in
current circumstances, he argues that this evaluation approach can logically be
extended to serve dual functions: learning and accountability. Further, he challenges learning-oriented evaluators to move from the local to engagement with
accountability demands within contemporary society. In a pair of *methods* chapters, Greene (Chapter 18) and Mabry (Chapter 19) elaborate how mixing methods
and case study are essential for attending to program contexts, representing stakeholders' views and their involvement, and values pluralism. After presenting a
"mixed methods way of thinking," Greene argues that mixing methods is especially
important in a contemporary society that values outcomes-based educational
accountability. To engage the sociopolitical differences reflected in different values
and interests in evaluation, she illustrates how to "mix" different evaluation purposes and stakeholders with examples in the international development context. In
showing how case study can work in educational evaluation, Mabry argues persuasively

that case study has a significant role in educational policy development and refinement. After elaborating how knowledge is warranted in case study through explicit description of epistemology, methods, and so forth, she shows how narratives can present the complexities found in contemporary society when seeking to understand educational issues across national borders and boundaries, sociocultural contexts, and at sites with language variation.

In their *case exemplar* chapter, Christie and Klein (Chapter 20) tell the story of how a college transition/ bridge program was transformed to a learning community over an 8-year period. After elaborating the role of the participatory evaluation team, they present a variety of evidence demonstrating the key role that the evaluation findings played in this transformation. They argue that their findings have implications for national and international contexts engaging with equity issues and higher education in a knowledge-based society. As a partial antidote to standardized performance indicators, Niessen, Abma, Widdershoven, and van der Vleuten (Chapter 21) present a compelling case study of problem-based learning in higher education. In their case, these scholars illustrate their retheorized responsive evaluation approach framed within an "enactivist" perspective defining stakeholders as coresearchers. Arguing for complex, nonlinear learning "within and from evaluation," situated within the dialogical turn, the narratives they present are persuasive evidence of this evaluation learning. In the *critical appraisal chapter*, Elliott (Chapter 22) begins by contending that globalization processes are constituted by "multiple culturally attuned capitalisms," a globalization perspective more aligned with educational evaluation theories sensitized to context. As part of his critical appraisal, he gives due diligence to analyzing both: "evaluation as learning" and "evaluation as measurement science." After concluding that both fall short in considering how to improve learning within contemporary society, he argues for developing educational evaluation theories and practice that incorporate how the global and local intersect in particular local arenas as essential next steps.

CHAPTER 17

Learning-Oriented Educational Evaluation in Contemporary Society

Peter Dahler-Larsen

Introduction: The Ambiguities of Learning

Learning is obviously a good idea. It is difficult to find reasonable persons arguing convincingly against learning. However, the general popularity of the idea of learning has been bought at a high price. As the concept of learning has lent itself to an increasing number of theoretical and practical applications across sociohistorical contexts, it runs the risk of becoming a buzzword without a specific meaning.

Learning usually denotes some sort of transformative process, but there is not much consensus about the nature of this process. Learning is also the outcome of that process, but that outcome may be specified in a variety of ways.

Although some describe learning as a process marred by hard work, if not turmoil and anxiety, others promise easy ways to instant learning through courses, training programs, smart consultancy, or "distant learning."

Some view the learner as creative and constructive. Consequently, the learning process is seen as relatively unpredictable. Some view the learner as autonomous, which means that learning cannot take place, which is not in line with the constitution and free will of the learner. Some put an emphasis on the individual learner, whereas others see learning as part of a collective social process. No society has left socialization totally up to the free will of the new learners; any society, by definition, imposes its norms and values on its new members. Especially in modern society, both the process and outcome of learning have been codified and institutionalized, sometimes strictly. In the contemporary version of modern society, by some called "reflexive modernity," if not "the learning society," learning has never been more important.

Globalization intensifies this development. Globalization expands in time and place the social arenas in which learning can take place. By spreading information about how things are done in different social contexts, globalization helps expand opportunities for action. At the same time, globalization also creates new arenas for competition, such as markets for e-learning or the common European space for education. Digital connectedness offers access to unforeseen amounts of information, but it also poses a threat of social marginalization to those who are not optimally connected to ever-changing streams of information, money, technology, and power. The effects of globalization reach all the way to the selves of each of us as we experience the undermining of tradition, the opening of opportunities, the variability of social life, and the threatening forces of competition and new global risks (Beck, Giddens & Lash 1994; Giddens, 1990).

Constant and intensified "learning" presents itself as the chic way to handle these ambivalences of globalization. The wear and tear on the concept of learning has perhaps never been bigger.

How learning is viewed in society provides a context for, but is not the same as, the kind of learning that may result from evaluation. Evaluation is a relatively distinct activity with relatively distinct purposes. In that context, "learning" may take on more specific meanings.

For some, a variation of learning, including development and improvement of program activities, constitutes the general and most important purpose for evaluation. For others, this purpose is only one among several noble ambitions for evaluation, the others being enhancing accountability, developing knowledge, and informing the public (Chelimsky, 2006). Evaluators hold different views about the extent to which any of these are generally more worthwhile than others, or the different purposes are all respectable, but should be served by different types of evaluations.

Over the years, however, a number of educational evaluation practices have occurred that claim to be especially fit for enhancing learning. These learning-oriented approaches include school-based evaluation, variants of self-evaluation, and practical participatory evaluation. In recent years, these approaches and other initiatives in

evaluation have led to an increased interest in evaluation capacity building (Compton, Baizerman, & Stockdill, 2002). Although the cultural and structural preconditions for evaluation cannot be ignored, and are sometimes of interest in and of themselves, I refer the reader to a later section on these issues. Here, I focus on approaches that explicitly seek learning as an outcome of evaluation.

For in-depth literature on these approaches, see Cousins and Earl (1992), Cousins (2003), Nevo (2006), and Preskill and Torres (1999). There is an affinity between the literatures on evaluation for learning and what might broadly be called evaluation for responsiveness, understanding, and discovery. I have in mind, for example, Stake (2004), Greene and Abma (2001) on responsive evaluation, and Schwandt (2002) on evaluation as a sort of interpretive undertaking called practical hermeneutics. All these approaches are interested in the local context, in some degree of stakeholder involvement, and they value a dialogue that implies an exchange among multiple views. However, the term *learning* does not appear in the index of Stake's (2004) book, and most of the literature on responsiveness and understanding is less optimistic, or more modest if you will, compared with the visions of progression and improvement that undergird much belief in learning-oriented approaches.

However, no evaluation approach can guarantee a particular outcome. If evaluation processes are collective, contextual, relational, organizational, and political endeavors, and if they are embedded in complex social systems, the purpose of an evaluation does not predict its outcome precisely. In fact, the influences of evaluation are sometimes capricious, sometimes complex, and sometimes overrated by evaluators who cling normatively to their own preferred evaluation approaches (Mark & Henry, 2000).

Although evaluators over time have learned to recognize the importance of the social context in which evaluation takes place, evaluators often do not see it as their job to theorize more generally about the social constitution of these contexts and changes therein. So can some characteristics of contemporary society be identified, which makes it possible to discuss how appropriately learning-oriented approaches to educational evaluation respond to the challenges posed by contemporary society?

To unpack this question, I first put the concept of learning into a societal context and a contemporary context, that of "reflexive modernity." Next, I outline what I take to be central features of learning-oriented forms of educational evaluation and look at some of the practical experiences with these approaches. Then I attend to the relation between learning-oriented approaches to evaluation and the need for accountability. Finally, I raise a couple of problematic issues for the future.

Before I do that, however, an important note on terminology is appropriate. Central issues in educational evaluation are becoming increasingly global. Global competition, international comparisons of student achievement, and techniques for cross-national performance measurement set a global agenda. Although the "ideascapes" and "datascapes" (Appadurai, 1996) thus created are increasingly loosened from tight connections to time and space, there is no consensus on the cultural meanings of central terms in educational evaluation. An *International Handbook of Educational Evaluation* (2003) hosts the following view:

> The normative component of the American professional culture of educational evaluation, as codified, is Western in tone and content. This normative content is almost fully acceptable to evaluators abroad because the evaluation discourse is indeed conducted in Western terms, and most frequently in the English language. (Bhola, 2003, p. 403)

Furthermore, it is said that "America today both leads and represents the West" (p. 400), and that "the non-Western world [graciously referred to as "The Rest" (Bhola, 2003, p. 399)] would have taken decades to invent all this knowledge" (of evaluation theory and practice).

Instead, my view is that we will only know of the different cultural meanings attached to central evaluation terms if we attend to them. In fact, terms in the English language such as *performance* and *achievement* have no equivalents in several other languages. The same is true for *participatory*, *empowerment*, and *equity*. This is often because the values, norms, and ideas providing meaning to these terms also do not exist or do not exist in the same version, in the cultural contexts of these other languages. In a similar vein, terms that are central to understanding the preconditions for educational evaluation in some national contexts do not always translate into English. As a corollary, *learning* does not have a totally univocal meaning across cultural contexts, and many languages do not have an abstract and disembedded term for who learns equivalent to *the learner* in English. A (too) smooth use of key terms in this chapter may thus (partly) misrepresent a culturally multifaceted and sometimes contested reality. Evaluation terminology is a contribution to, but has no monopoly on, the understanding of and definition of this reality. Having asked the reader to keep this in mind, I have no choice but to proceed in a version of English.

Learning and Society

To illustrate and hopefully not overstate the point, let us begin our brief sociological account of how learning takes its meaning from society with the term *Bildung*. The rough equivalent to this German term is *dannelse* in Scandinavian languages, but no direct English translation exists. Bildung denotes the transformation of one's personal character, which flows from good education. Bildung denotes the acquisition of knowledge, as well as a road to autonomy that presupposes the values of civilization, democracy, ethics, and knowledge in combination. Bildung thus offers an interpretation of learning tightly knit into a normative framework of civilization and modernity. Bildung is a coin with two sides: one personal and the other collective.

The ambivalence of the modern project of Bildung is illustrated by the fact that a number of regulatory institutions have been designed to educate and normalize citizens in its image. In modernity, emancipation and regulation have never been far apart (Bauman, 1992).

In line with the functional differentiation so characteristic of modern society, educational institutions were specially designed to facilitate nation-building, person-building, and learning at the same time. However, as a response to continuous pressures for change in late modernity, learning can no longer be confined within the narrow boundaries of educational institutions. Characteristically, lifelong learning is to take place in a broad variety of social arenas, including workplaces. Workplaces today are supposed to organize themselves in such a way that they become learning organizations.

Not only professionally, but also personally, the idea of learning and development constitutes an overarching theme in the contemporary social order. Learning as a socially embedded idea is no longer a monopoly of educational institutions, but now increasingly a phenomenon without boundaries (Edwards & Usher, 2001, p. 276). To capture both the diffusion and centrality of learning to contemporary social life, some have coined the term *learning society*. According to Edwards (1997), this term carries at least three different connotations. To conventional modernists, it means roughly an "educated society," in which personal and social development still remains well connected. To others, the learning society is more like a learning market, where the consumer has replaced the citizen as the central subject. In the learning market, the customer is king, but social relations are fragmented, and there is no higher meaning connected to learning than its market value suggests. Finally, the learning society to some means a complex constellation of networks and arenas in which learning takes place. Although these are everywhere, they are also heterogeneous and ephemeral, signifying the general sense of change and flexibility in contemporary society.

At least two broad sociological interpretations of this situation are possible. According to a postmodernist view, the meaning of appropriate or worthwhile knowledge breaks down as learning becomes an all-encompassing code word for *performativity* (a term for how smoothly someone turns an input into an outcome devoid of any content or moral meaning; Edwards, 1997; Lyotard, 1982). Knowledge becomes "up for grabs" (Edwards & Usher, 2001, p. 279), and learning becomes disconnected from its earlier connotations, such as rationality, progress, and science-based knowledge. The general move from qualifications to competencies illustrates this point.

Furthermore, the learner is decentered. Because learning demands flexibility, learning subjects must make themselves endlessly flexible. What was earlier regarded as sociological "havens," such as family life and personal character, now becomes subsumed under the regimes of flexibility and fluidity (Bauman, 2000; Sennett, 2002).

Another sociological diagnosis, and indeed a rich one, is that of "reflexive modernization" proposed by Beck (Beck, 1992; Beck, Giddens, & Lash, 1994). According to his central thesis, modernity is not over, and neither are all hopes for rationality and democracy, but modernity has indeed entered a new phase in which critical and investigative tools of modernity have now turned against modern institutions. Advocates of reflexive modernization disagree with postmodernists because the former insist that modernity is not giving up, but marred by doubt, side effects, contingency, and reflexivity. For a reflexive modernist, no postmodern view of a "hyper-reality" is accepted. Instead, modern society really constitutes itself, although of course reflexive modernization installs new complexities.

Side effects are constantly produced by complex organizations and technology. Reflexive modernity attends to side effects and is therefore constantly seeking ways to investigate them, measure them, handle their risks, and turn this awareness into institutional renewal. Contingency means an ongoing social awareness that practically everything could be different. The social order knows that it is not solidly constructed. Technology, globalization, and widespread social doubt lead to a sense of instability. Reflexivity implies an ongoing application of techniques of monitoring, inquiry, discussion, and doubt. It also means reacting to disturbances that are at least partly self-inflicted by society.

In this light, learning refers to several types of social and individual adjustments to changing circumstances. However, in reflexive modernization, learning is difficult to standardize as the feedback loops of reflexivity take place in many forms, on many levels in the social system, and under constantly unstable circumstances.

Needless to say, evaluation can be understood as a child of reflexive modernization. Doubt, contingency, and reflexivity enhance the need for evaluation, but they are also enhanced by it. There are several streams of evaluative knowledge (Rist & Stame, 2006) that manifest themselves as adequate or appropriate under the social conditions of reflexive modernization.

One such stream is international comparisons. Large expert systems working across time and space (Giddens, 1990) disembed local and national facts from their specific social contexts and integrate data in larger, comparative, and statistical systems. Expert systems such as PISA tests and international educational indicators create new interoperational arenas for social and political maneuvering. Such expert systems increase the feeling of contingency in local contexts, as local units must compare themselves to international benchmarks, standards, and averages. When expert knowledge is reembedded, it tends to soften the social fabric. The social order becomes "fragile" as a result of the application of systematic knowledge (Stehr, 2001).

Another stream has to do with how institutions such as schools report back to society. Because societal institutions lose their "obvious" and "natural" character to become more contingent, there is a need from a variety of positions in society (politicians, journalists, users, clients, and other stakeholders) to receive data about how well institutions manage their contingent situation. A reference to, for example, "school tradition" no longer suffices. Instead, solutions are sought in, for example, accountability-oriented, objectives-based, performance-oriented, and customer-oriented forms of evaluation.

Institutions also seek to find their own feet and manage their own way forward under contingent situations. As instruments for the necessary reflexivity, they often turn to participatory and learning-oriented approaches to evaluation.

In other words, the broad societal sweeps of globalization and reflexive modernization make multiple streams of evaluative information relevant, some of which are specifically oriented toward some form of learning. This broad and general sociological perspective in no way suggests that these streams of information form a harmonious whole. Instead, they are often contested and applied reflexively, partly in response to or conflict with each other. They are also sometimes connected, for example, when a school seeks to engage teachers, parents, and pupils in local learning processes as a response to poor results with performance indicators or when managers seek to use outstanding local results as a "benchmark" in a comprehensive management information system.

The social and political game involving various forms of evaluation is not only about which values and criteria would constitute a proper starting point for educational evaluation. It is also sometimes about taking or displacing responsibility, displacing risk between different layers of the political and administrative regime (Rothstein, Huber, & Gaskell, 2006), and seeking to avoid blame (Hood, 2002).

Each form of evaluation is under potential scrutiny from reflexive criticism. Under reflexive modernization, several forms of evaluation are thus promoted, and the underlying agendas are multiple. No particular form of evaluation, however learning-oriented, can claim a monopoly on evaluation or a monopoly on learning.

With this in mind, we now move into the field of evaluation to take a closer look at specifically learning-oriented forms of evaluation.

Experiences With Learning-Oriented Approaches to Evaluation

There is no easy way to identify a particular set of evaluation practices. There is no general consensus about how to label and categorize evaluation models. Furthermore, the same evaluation model or approach would probably work differently depending on the political, strategic, cultural, and organizational conditions under which it is applied, and evaluators would be intelligent if they kept their evaluation practices flexible and adaptive to varying contexts. Therefore, it is unknown how much of actual evaluation practices are captured by reference to any specific model. What evaluators cling to may be persuasions rather than specific models (Stake, 1981).

Furthermore, advocates of particular convictions often make problematic assumptions. For example, an approach to evaluation may be defined by its purpose, which in turn is assumed to be practically equivalent to a certain outcome. In other words, the success of an evaluation approach is sometimes built into its self-representation. Under these circumstances, it would be conceptually misleading to analytically define an evaluation model in the same way.

There are advocates of some approaches to evaluation, including learning-oriented ones, who are more keen on promoting their conviction than on maintaining an analytic view on their own practice. Some take positive standpoints on learning-oriented approaches that are motivated largely out of dissatisfaction with testing, with performance indicators, with existing educational policies, or flatly out of solidarity with teachers and schools.

Nevertheless, a cluster of evaluation practices can be relatively rigorously identified as learning-oriented evaluation and analyzed as such. The term *-oriented* is deliberately chosen to show that no automatic success of these approaches is assumed; instead, experienced advocates of these and similar approaches honestly report that there are tensions in their approaches (Greene,

1997) and that the success of their approaches is highly context-dependent (Cousins & Earl, 1995a). Some even express serious doubt about the process and the motivations of teachers to participate herein (Monsen, 2003).

Learning-oriented evaluation approaches share all or most of the following characteristics:

1. a belief that learning is the most important purpose of evaluation;

2. for learning to happen, the evaluation should be seen as relevant in the eyes of practitioners;

3. to enhance relevance, ownership or deep involvement on the side of practitioners in the evaluation process is necessary; and

4. because this approach requires personal contact and some degree of trust, the appropriate social arena for this type of involvement is more often than not a local group, community, or institution.

Examples of more specific evaluation approaches in this broad category would be Weaver and Cousins' (2004) practical participatory evaluation, school-based evaluation (Nevo, 2002), and other variants of self-evaluation where "people look critically at something for which they themselves are responsible" (Ålvik, 1996, p. 3).

Weaver and Cousins (2004) offered five conceptual dimensions to characterize various evaluation approaches: (a) depth of participation, (b) technical control of evaluation process, (c) diversity among stakeholders, (d) power relations, and (e) manageability of the evaluation process.

Learning-oriented approaches to evaluation all imply deep or relatively deep participation from stakeholders. I here regard a school organizing its own evaluation ("self-evaluation") as an extreme case of deep participation. Learning-oriented approaches may vary with respect to the technical control of the evaluation process, from a balanced, shared responsibility between a researcher and practitioners (practical participatory evaluation) to a total control on the side of practitioners (school self-evaluation).

Finally, stakeholder selection may vary, but learning-oriented evaluation tends to tilt toward primary users involving a wider range of legitimate groups only to the extent that it would enhance learning among primary users of the evaluation. Although a matter of degree rather than of dichotomy, this factor distinguishes practical and learning-oriented approaches to evaluation from transformative participatory evaluation. The latter seeks participation from a broader set of stakeholders because this is seen as democratically worthwhile in itself or because it promotes a larger social and political agenda. Thus, stakeholder diversity and power differences are likely to increase, and the predictability and manageability of the process may decrease.

Instead, pragmatic, practical, and learning-oriented approaches keep the main focus on those who are in position to change the activity under evaluation (Cousins, 2003). If this is a group or a collective of teachers, so be it, but the focus is constantly on practical change, rather than wider social transformation. Given that difference in focus, transformative and practical participatory evaluation often overlap in secondary functions (Cousins, 2003), and in practice neither of them can afford to ignore what the other keeps in focus.

What are the experiences with learning-oriented approaches? The general picture is moderately positive, with some contextual modifications (Nevo, 2002). Referring to both a survey and multiple case studies, Cousins (2003) and Preskill and Torres (1999) have found that participatory evaluation actually produced results that were used both instrumentally and conceptually.

An important aspect of learning-oriented evaluation is also positive implications of evaluation not directly related to findings—sometimes referred to as "process use" (Forss, Rebien, & Carlsson, 2002; Patton, 1998). Process use includes gaining self-confidence for the future, understanding the program and its context better, being more attentive to the views of others, and being more prepared to engage in a dialogue with external stakeholders. Process use also leads to an increased preparedness to use data when

reflecting about practices, thus sometimes paving the way for systematic empirical inquiry and/or increased evaluation capacity. Preskill and Torres (1999) add outcomes such as increased responsibility, better sharing of work, better work climate, and quicker adaptation to change.

Dahler-Larsen, Andersen, Hansen, and Strømbæk (2003) found that evaluation helped question or clarify assumptions underlying the activities of schools and helped reorganize data otherwise collected so that more aspects of school life would be in alignment with the overall mission of the school. Evaluation also led to deep discussions about the nature of schools in their capacity of being commercial entities, pedagogical milieus, political institutions, and deep-seated cultural communities. Especially in the latter capacity, evaluation came into tension with how some perceived the identity of the school (Schwandt & Dahler-Larsen, 2006). Yet more often than not, participants found that the evaluation was largely a positive endeavor.

Evaluators experienced in learning-oriented evaluation have also identified a number of problems with the approach or, more specifically, a number of situational factors that may threaten the success of the approach unless they are dealt with carefully.

An overall problem is that the participation of practitioners often takes place under what is perceived as intense time pressure (Cousins, 2003; Ryan, Chandler, & Samuels, 2007). Practitioners have other things to do and often do not see evaluation, or at least not large-scale evaluation, as part of their main mission. This finding may be understood in the light of the sociology of knowledge. Every practice is guided by a particular socially available stock of knowledge, which is, in turn, guided by a particular relevance structure (Berger & Luckmann, 1966). Teachers may not be inclined to see systematic and large-scale documentation of their practice as a relevant part of that practice.

Even under otherwise favorable circumstances, this factor works against the motivation of practitioners to participate in learning-oriented evaluation. To compensate for the time spent by practitioners in evaluation through extraordinary allocation of specific hours, money or other resources is not always a good solution. It may be misperceived as pressure; once the extra resources are spent, evaluation activities may not be sustainable (Monsen, 2003).

With limited time and resources, the technical and methodological quality of the evaluation may be in jeopardy. Cousins (2003) identifies a trade-off between technical quality and responsiveness. Cousins and Earl (1995a) suggest that if technical quality is not to be sacrificed, a careful division of labor should be established between the participating practitioners and an external evaluator. Although practitioner participation may be deep, certain technical and methodological decisions are better left in the hands of the researcher. Without intensive training of practitioners or the involvement of methodological assistance, the technical quality of evaluation may be in jeopardy. However, if practitioners are both producers and consumers of the evaluation, they may not discover this problem. On this specific point, school self-evaluation is extremely vulnerable and much more so than participatory evaluation. This observation is relevant because in some regimes of school government across the world, school self-evaluation is a mandatory component, and it is often not supported by technical and methodological mobilization.

Another general problem is the balance between evaluation and learning in learning-oriented approaches to evaluation. An overall focus on learning and development may lead to a sacrifice of the integrity of the evaluation part of the process. If valuing is seen as normatively threatening and evaluation methodologically demanding, the evaluation phase may be dealt with too quickly, and learning-oriented evaluation may easily degenerate into a normal and perhaps unambitious process of dialogue and professional development among practitioners (Ålvik, 1996). However, if practitioners keep their definition of *learning from evaluation* loose enough, they will be satisfied with the process anyway. If process use becomes the main criteria of success, it is almost always possible to identify some positive side of what was called an evaluation process. In the extreme and perhaps caricatured situation, there will be more internal satisfaction with the evaluation process the less productive it is.

Finally, advocates of learning-oriented approaches to evaluation recognize that the political and organizational context around evaluation makes a great difference. Factors in the national debate, such as changing educational policy and negative press on schools and teachers, influence the overall mood and motivation of teachers to engage in evaluation (Monsen, 2003). Learning-oriented evaluators, however, tend to focus more on immediate factors in the nearby organizational environment because they may be influenced to enhance conditions favorable to learning-oriented evaluation. Dahler-Larsen (2003) found that two important factors were management attention to evaluation and the organizational location of the one holding the initiative for evaluation (not peripheral or management, but centrally located). In addition, the development of evaluation skills within the organization is important.

None of these factors, however, is without tension. Managerial interest in evaluation may be motivated by an agenda of internal control and accountability as much as by an interest in learning. The development or acquisition of evaluation skills within the organization may signify rather than ameliorate a conflict between friends and foes of evaluation within the organization.

Apart from these specific tensions around evaluation, learning-oriented evaluators and others have generally found the following factors to be conducive to organizational learning:

- open flows of information and communication in the organization (Preskill & Torres, 1999);
- an organizational language that allows problems and possible solutions to be described (Dahler-Larsen, 2006);
- the absence of a hierarchical structure that prevents problems from being reported upward and downward (Morgan, 1986);

- a climate in which errors are tolerated and dealt with, but not ignored, concealed, or defensively explained away (Argyris & Schon, 1978);
- an organizational culture open to multiple perspectives (Preskill & Torres, 1999); and
- a low or moderate level of political conflict (Cousins, 2003).

Learning-oriented evaluators have not hesitated to seek to incorporate an attention to these and similar factors into their interventions in organizations. On this point, there is a direct line from learning-oriented evaluation to an interest in building evaluation capacity (Compton, Baizerman, & Stockdill, 2002; Cousins, Rosenstein & Levin-Rozalis 2007), evaluation culture (Mortimore, David-Evans, Laukkanen, & Valijarvi, 1994), and organizational evaluation systems (Preskill & Torres, 1999), although, of course, this interest can also be spurred in a number of other ways as well.

To add complexity to their findings, evaluators interested in organizational learning have found that organizations learn at different levels. In single-loop learning, organizations improve their performance within a given frame consisting of particular values, understandings, and tools. In double-loop learning, however, organizations find out how to improve their performance through critical reflections on that frame. They learn to learn (Morgan, 1986). The tragic paradox is that as organizations improve their single-loop learning, they end up in competence traps that make it more difficult to engage in double-loop learning. Whether ever more double-loop learning is a universally recommendable medicine is discussed in the final part of the chapter.

The Relation Between Learning and Accountability

Suppose we conclude that learning-oriented evaluation is, under at least some circumstances, relatively successful. How does the learning function of evaluation thus unfold together with or in contradiction to other important functions of evaluation, such as the accountability function? Evaluators (and stakeholders) tend to advance at least three fundamentally different arguments on whether the two functions are genuinely functional alternatives or supplements.

According to the first argument, any single evaluation has to be committed to either learning or accountability, either a formative or a summative use. The summative/formative distinction has to do with types of evaluation. This is because the cultural and psychological preconditions for successful learning, such as trust, openness, and willingness to admit errors, are spoiled if an external threat is present. That is why formative and summative evaluations should be kept separate and why testing, exams, and external monitoring should touch on nothing more than the end results of schooling, but not interfere with the daily practices of teachers and pupils. In other words, for any particular evaluation, learning and accountability should be understood as functional alternatives. The external view precludes learning. An illustration of the argument is drawn from theaters, where actors do all sorts of exercises among themselves during their training and rehearsal. External reviewers are invited from the premiere onward only. However, counterexamples exist. Some modern restaurants have an open kitchen so that guests can watch the cooks preparing the food. Some like the atmosphere created by cooks working, and by the sight and smell of food, and there is little reason to believe that an external eye on the production process should be detrimental to kitchen hygiene or the quality of the cooking. The cook's formative tasting of the soup is not undercut by the presence of guests. It is unknown whether cooks like to work in open kitchens, but, in and of itself, an external eye does not spoil cooking or the formative evaluation of it.

A second argument says that the same evaluation can, in fact, be used in several ways. The formative/summative distinction is now pertaining to the use of the evaluation (Scriven, 1991) and not to how it is conducted or the climate in which it takes place. For that reason, the same evaluation has the potential to be used both formatively and summatively. The classical explanation of the summative/formative distinction ("When the cook tastes the soup, it's formative evaluation, when the guest tastes it, it's summative"; Scriven, 1991) is thus imprecise. If the cook decides to add spices after tasting the soup, it's formative evaluation. If he decides to throw away the soup, it's summative, or, more precisely, it is a summative use of the evaluation. Here the evaluator is the same, and the evaluative action, tasting, is the same. Only in the actual moment of use is the use of the evaluation in fact decided. Therefore, several simultaneous uses are logically possible. A teacher may decide to skip a particular method in teaching after using an evaluation summatively (on the level of singular practices), while the same evaluation is used formatively (on the level of the teacher's overall professional development). On different levels of a school system, including management, a number of different simultaneous uses are similarly possible.

A third argument connects to a holistic view of a democractic society. In this perspective, learning and accountability are absolutely not functional alternatives. Both are necessary. Choosing one, say learning as the main purpose in one evaluation, does not reduce the need for the other function. The argument holds whether it is formulated on normative or empirical levels. Normatively, it is impossible to imagine a representative democracy without some form of control, feedback, and accountability (Vedung, 1997). Democratic accounts do form a constitutive part of the normative framework of democracy (March & Olsen, 1995). As Nevo (2002) quite straightforwardly argues with teachers: "If you won't respect the authority and responsibility of the Ministry of Education and the right of parents to know about the schools their children go to, don't expect them to respect your right for autonomy and reflection and trust your judgment as a professional teacher" (p. 15). In other words, the accountability function of evaluation cannot be suspended just because there is a need

for the learning function, too. The two are supplementary if not in one evaluation, then in society.

Empirically, the demands for external accountability of educational institutions have not withered away in recent years. Due to the extreme importance of education in globalized economies, and due to the popularity of performance-oriented regimes in policymaking and management, the pressure to meet accountability demands has only intensified. That being said, performance-oriented and quantitative indicator systems have been criticized for being reductionist, for unintended consequences (van Thiel & Leeuw, 2002) and for being unfair to schools (Rowe, 2000).

For this reason, accountability is bedevilled by ambivalence for educational institutions. Some of the present forms of accountability regimes often make it difficult to respect the idea of democratic accountability as such. However, again, none of this makes the demand for accountability disappear. Under reflexive modernization, the use of data and evaluation as a means of handling contingency is an appropriate way forward and more adequate than appeals to, say, authoritarianism or tradition or appeals to endless "trust." Some people in the educational world have thus made a mistake when they recommended purely internal, learning-oriented evaluation as the best and only response to increasing demands for external accountability under the assumption that the former could functionally replace the latter.

For this reason and others, some advocates of learning-oriented evaluation seek new forms of cooperation with accountability-oriented, external evaluation. Although some insist that internal evaluation should come first in time (Ålvik, 1996), the important point is the new and explicit search for cooperation between the two. Nevo suggests a number of ways in which the two can support each other. External evaluation can stimulate internal evaluation, expand its scope, and supports its validity. In turn, internal evaluation can expand the scope of external evaluation, improve the interpretation of findings, and enhance utilization (Nevo, 2002). Internal evaluation can also be used to present the core values and beliefs of a school vis-à-vis external stakeholders. The Internet provides new opportunities for combining such evaluation with external promotion.

In other words, although the distinction between formative and summative evaluation has usually been taken to be congruent with the internal/external distinction (Nevo, 2006), the lack of logical necessity in this conceptual pairing becomes increasingly visible.

In a similar vein, Dahler-Larsen (2003) suggests a more flexible use of the terms *internal* and *external* evaluation than the conventional dichotomy allows. Suppose that an evaluation process is broken down to its elements, such as initiative agenda setting, evaluation questions, research design, data collection, analysis, drawing conclusions, and utilization, the following scheme suggests a rich set of internal/external permutations.

In each phase, the emphasis may be mostly internal, mostly external, or some negotiated balance between the two (see Figure 17.1). Although not all permutations are equally likely to be realistic and productive, a number of them are.

Lines to the extreme right and extreme left (Lines 1 and 2, respectively) signify the conventional dichotomous forms of internal and external evaluation, just for illustration. Lines 3 and 4 show two variants of so-called "self-evaluation," which is in Europe the typical word for what is called internal evaluation on the other side of the Atlantic (Love, 1998). The two forms both seek to promote external as well as internal uses, but they have different emphases in the agenda-setting phase, suggesting two different sets of political histories and overtones.

I have also illustrated what I take to be an approximation of a form of practical participatory evaluation oriented to both internal and external uses (Line 5). The reader is invited to consider fruitful combinations other than those presented for illustration.

Although unconventional forms of cooperation between internal and external aspects of evaluation can thus be found, controversy is not likely to disappear.

In a survey, school teachers and professionals were asked to rate their ability to do a number of aspects of evaluation. Although they reported that many aspects of evaluation were integral parts of their daily practice, the lowest scoring items were doing evaluation in a methodological competent way and using evaluation toward external partners (Dahler-Larsen, 2006). This suggests some of the difficulties with an increased external focus.

Internal and external perspectives may typically embody different views on how broad a spectrum of evaluation criteria should be included. Politicians, bureaucrats, and journalists tend to believe that school quality can be captured in measures of pupils' achievements and that schools will work harder to improve their quality if they are measured along these lines (Nevo, 2006). Teachers (and with them many educational researchers) tend to believe in a more multidimensional depiction of school quality, including the mission of the school, its educational philosophy, the characteristics of its students, the variety of its programs, its physical and economic resources, its social climate, and sometimes the quality of its teachers (Nevo, 2006).

There is also likely to be a discrepancy concerning the extent to which pedagogical practice should be evidence-based and codified (Biesta, 2007). From an external perspective, some would see good teaching as merely an implementation of theoretical, abstract, and/or evidence-based knowledge. Others regard teaching as a complex, self-reflexive practice, which is contextual, relational, and artistic, and thus cannot be reduced to any codifications. Although the codification/noncodification issue is not completely coterminous with the external/internal distinction, it is often made relevant.

There is also likely to continue to be controversy over who should hold control over which parts of data (Monsen, 2003), which data should be made public (Rowe, 2000), and, if yes, within which interpretive frames (Andersen & Dahler-Larsen, 2008).

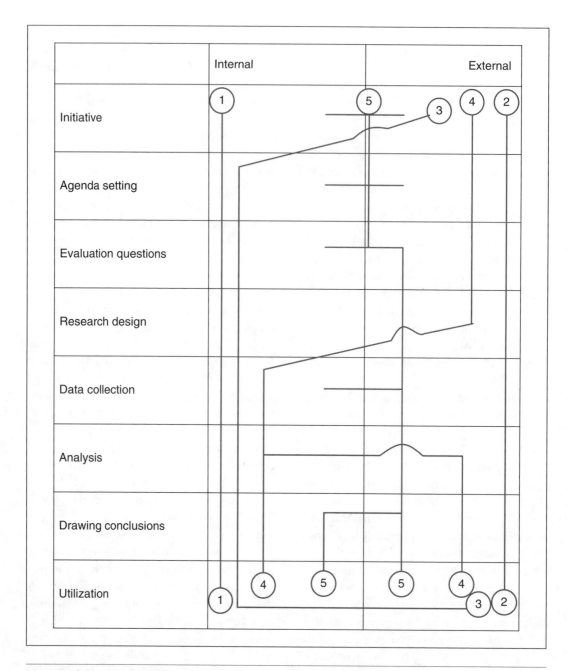

Figure 17.1   Combinations of Internal and External Aspects of Evaluation

Further Challenges: Learning In and Away From Society

In the final section, I discuss three further challenges to learning-oriented evaluation approaches in the order of increasing criticality. They all have to do with the role of learning-oriented evaluation in a societal perspective.

If the increasing need to confront the demand for accountability is acknowledged, learning-oriented evaluators cannot remain confined to working personally with people in small local arenas only. They must be ready to engage in a dialogue with those representing demands for accountability. If a division of labor develops where accountability-oriented, performance-measuring regimes dominate the larger social arena, and learning-oriented evaluation is relegated to local arenas only, a biased starting point for a democratic debate is established. Longstanding and sworn advocates of school-based evaluation have revised their views after realizing the immense social influence of PISA surveys and other quantitative measurements in the public arena. To counterbalance the dominance of such quantitative regimes, learning-oriented evaluators would be wise to bring their knowledge, experience, perspective, and sometimes critical voices more clearly into the larger social arena. One of the ways in which they may contribute specifically is with reports about the actual effects of increased monitoring on the practices in schools in local contexts. More generally, they should contribute to the societal dialogue between societal and institutional views. This would require that some of the learning-oriented evaluators revise their ideology saying that they can work and exert influence in local arenas only.

Next, learning-oriented evaluators might also take a closer look at their engagement in the construction of organizational regimes for evaluation capacity, evaluation culture, and evaluation systems. Truly, for evaluation to be sustainable, its organizational conditions should be addressed. Truly, the interest in organizational matters is, at least partly, a logical consequence of practical experiences of learning-oriented evaluators. But the alliance between learning and organization is not without costs. If organizations define the use of evaluation, more attention may be given to management issues than to deeper looks at policy assumptions or professional practices. If evaluation is integrated in organizational routines, evaluation may be institutionalized and become obligatory also in situations where a careful evaluability

assessment would indicate that resources would be better spent otherwise. The integration of evaluation in the mainstream of organizational life may lead to self-sustaining need for evaluation between organizations (Lindeberg, 2007). Critical research on contemporary auditing, accreditation, and evaluation suggests that, to reduce complexity, those who evaluate other organizations often focus not on what organizations do, but on the systems organizations have to monitor, audit, and evaluate what they do (Power, 2005). Reports on systems designed to enhance learning take the place of learning. The classical idea of goal displacement in large organizations may not be far away.

Finally, perhaps the most critical view on the idea of continuous learning is based on an observation of how well it serves a dominant mentality of our time that cherishes constant change and development. Advocates of learning have argued that single-loop learning is not enough. Double-loop learning should be encouraged. But also more and more of it? Are there no limits to reflection and change, logically, culturally, or morally?

Double-loop or second-order learning is relative to single-loop or first-order learning. But why not third- or fourth-order learning (Bateson, 1972)? Does it make sense to ask for more of something that is truly relational unless flexibility and change have become social mantras?

Furthermore, if a sense of moral integrity is to be maintained, not all aspects of life can be made the flexible object of any given learning process. The ever-increasing demand for flexibility in workplaces leads, according to a leading sociologist, to the "corrosion of character" (Sennett, 2002). We should also listen to the critical voices of researchers who study "development," a phenomenon close enough to "learning" in its socio-historical typicality. Feminist researchers (Klouzal, Shayne, & Foran, 2003) maintain that "development" in the abstract only loosely describes the actual destinies of specific human subjects who are sometimes "caught" under specific circumstances in time and place, always bound to personal histories, and to specific personal relations. In each situation, "development" manifests itself as a sometimes ambivalent, painful, and never smooth process. There is no such thing as a free development. The same is true for learning. A general, smooth, and overly optimistic use of the term learning is, thus, misleading.

Summary and Conclusion

Learning-oriented evaluation approaches share all or most of the following characteristics:

1. a belief that learning is the most important purpose of evaluation;

2. for learning to happen, the evaluation should be seen as relevant in the eyes of practitioners;

3. to enhance relevance and a sense of ownership to the evaluation, deep involvement of practitioners in the evaluation process is necessary; and

4. because this approach requires personal contact and some degree of trust, the appropriate social arena for this type of involvement is more often than not a local group, community, or institution.

We have looked at a number of reports on the success of such approaches. They are moderately positive, indicating that learning-oriented evaluation can be used both instrumentally and conceptually. In addition, a number of positive forms of "process use," such as increased insights, reflection, self-confidence, and energy for the future among practitioners, have been reported.

Still, an experienced observer of the field of evaluation is probably correct in noticing that the evidence base under learning-oriented evaluation is still weak (Mark & Henry, 2000). It is likely to remain so to the extent that learning-oriented evaluation is no fixed procedure, but instead a flexible set of ideas that are always applied in close interaction with contextual

specifics. The jury is still out concerning the specific decision about how unfavorable contexts one can live with and still recommend learning-oriented evaluation, and about how the exact balance of pros and cons of learning-oriented evaluation comes out in particular situations.

Issues that deserve special attention are the time pressure on participants, the technical quality of evaluation, and the political configuration of the context in which learning-oriented evaluation takes place.

In recent years, it has been clear that even good learning-oriented evaluation does not make the societal demand for accountability-oriented evaluation disappear. Some have therefore sought new forms of cooperation between the two functions of evaluation, and the internal/external dichotomy has been made much more nuanced and flexible.

Further challenges for learning-oriented evaluation have been identified. These relate to the role that learning-oriented evaluators may play in the larger social arena, how they may critically reflect on the pros and cons of an integration of evaluation into organizational systems, and finally how they might critically reflect on the constant demand for change, development, and flexibility in our contemporary society. Learning-oriented evaluators should think about how they not only mirror this tendency, but also contribute to it. In other words, there are many ways in which learning-oriented evaluators need to reflect on and improve their practice.

At the same time, at another front, the massive social forces enhancing standardization, quantification, and bureaucratization of evaluation seem to leave less, not more, space for learning-oriented approaches. The future of learning-oriented evaluation will depend on how this double squeeze is handled.

References

Andersen, V. N., & Dahler-Larsen, P. (2008). The framing of public evaluation data: Transparency and openness in Danish schools. In R. Boyle,

J. D. Bruel, & P. Dahler-Larsen (Eds.), *Open to the public* (pp. 99–116). New Brunswick, NJ: Transaction Publishers.

Appadurai, A. (1996). *Modernity at large. Cultural dimensions of globalization.* Minneapolis: University of Minnesota Press.

Argyris, C., & Schon, D. (1978). *Organizational learning. A theory of action perspective.* Reading, MA: Addison-Wesley.

Ålvik, T. (1996). *Self-evaluation: What, why, how, by whom, for whom.* Dundee: CIDREE.

Bateson, G. (1972). *Steps to an ecology of mind.* New York: Ballantine Books

Bauman, Z. (1992). Legislators and interpreters: Culture as the ideology of intellectuals. In Z. Bauman (Ed.), *Intimations of postmodernity* (pp. 1–25). London, New York: Routledge.

Bauman, Z. (2000). *Liquid modernity.* Cambridge, MA: Polity Press.

Beck, U. (1992). *Risk society—Towards a new modernity.* London: Sage.

Beck, U., Giddens, A., & Lash, S. (1994). *Reflexive modernization.* Stanford, CA: Stanford University Press.

Berger, P. L., & Luckmann, T. (1966). *The social construction of reality.* New York: Doubleday.

Bhola, H. S. (2003). Social and cultural contexts of educational evaluation: A global perspective. In T. Kellaghan, D. L. Stufflebeam, & L. A. Wingate (Eds.), *International handbook of educational evaluation: Part I. Perspectives* (pp. 397–416). Dordrecht: Kluwer Academic Publishers.

Biesta, G. (2007). Why "What Works" won't work: Evidence-based practice and the democratic deficit in educational research. *Educational Theory, 57*(1), 1–22.

Chelimsky, E. (2006). The purposes of evaluation in a democratic society. In I. Shaw, J. C. Greene, & M. M. Mark (Eds.), *The Sage handbook of evaluation* (pp. 35–55). London: Sage.

Compton, D. W., Baizerman, M., & Stockdill, S. H. (2002). Editors' notes. *New Directions for Evaluation, 93*, 1–6.

Cousins, J. B. (2003). Utilization effects of participatory evaluation. In D. Kellaghan, L. Stufflebeam, & L. A. Wingate (Eds.), *International handbook of educational evaluation* (pp. 245–265). Boston: Kluwer Academic Publishers.

Cousins, J. B., & Earl, L. M. (1992). The case for participatory evaluation. *Educational Evaluation and Policy Analysis, 14*(4), 397–418.

Cousins, J. B., & Earl, L. M. (1995a). The case for participatory evaluation: Theory, research. In B. J. Cousins & L. M. Earl (Eds.), *Participatory evaluation in education: Studies in evaluation use and organizational learning* (pp. 397–418). London: Routledge Falmer.

Cousins, J. B., & Earl, L. M. (Eds.). (1995b). *Participatory evaluation in education: Studies in evaluation use and organizational learning.* London: Routledge Falmer.

Cousins, J. B., Rosenstein, B., & Levin-Rozalis, M. (2007, November). *Precarious balance: Educational evaluation capacity building in the era of globalization.* Paper presented at the American Evaluation Association conference, Baltimore, MD.

Dahler-Larsen, P. (2003). Hvad er selvevaluering? In P. Dahler-Larsen, V. N. Andersen, K. M. Hansen, & C. S. Pedersen (Eds.), *Selvevalueringens Hvide Sejl* (pp. 29–40). Odense: Syddansk Universitetsforlag.

Dahler-Larsen, P. (2006). *Evalueringskultur* [*Evaluation culture*]. Odense: Syddansk Universitetsforlag.

Dahler-Larsen, P., Andersen, V. N., Hansen, K. M., & Strømbæk, C. (2003). *Selvevalueringens Hvide Sejl* [*The white sails of self-evaluation*]. Odense: Syddansk Universitet.

Edwards, R. (1997). *Changing places? Flexibility, lifelong learning and a learning society.* London: Routledge Falmer.

Edwards, R., & Usher, R. (2001). Lifelong learning: A postmodern condition of education. *Adult Education Quarterly, 51*(4), 273–287.

Forss, K., Rebien, C. C., & Carlsson, J. (2002). Process use of evaluations. *Evaluation, 8*(1), 29–45.

Giddens, A. (1990). *The consequences of modernity.* Cambridge: Polity Press.

Greene, J. C. (1997). *Participatory evaluation.* In L. Mabry (Ed.), *Evaluation and the postmodern dilemma* (pp. 171–189). London: JAI Press.

Greene, J. C., & Abma, T. (Eds.). (2001). Responsive evaluation. *New Directions for Evaluation 92.*

Hood, C. (2002). The risk game and the blame game. *Government and Opposition, 37*(1), 15–37.

Klouzal, L., Shayne, J. D., & Foran, J. (2003). Visions 4. In K.-K. Bhavnani, J. Foran, & A. P. Kurian (Eds.), *Feminist futures: Re-imagining woman, culture and development* (pp. 256–275). London, New York: Zed Books.

Lindeberg, T. (2007). *Evaluative technologies: Quality and the multiplicity of performance.* København: Copenhagen Business School.

Love, A. J. (1998). Internal evaluation: Integrating evaluation and social work practice. *Scandinavian Journal of Social Welfare, 7*, 145–151.

Lyotard, J. F. (1982). *Viden og det Postmoderne Samfund.* Århus: Sjakalen. ("La Condition Postmoderne" 1979.)

March, J., & Olsen, J. P. (1995). *Democratic governance.* New York: The Free Press.

Mark, M. M., & Henry, G. T. (2000). The mechanisms and outcomes of evaluation influence. *Evaluation, 10*(1), 35–57.

Monsen, L. (2003). School-based evaluation in Norway: Why is it so difficult to convince teachers of its usefulness? In D. Nevo (Ed.), *School-based evaluation: An international perspective* (pp. 73–88). Oxford: Elsevier Science.

Morgan, G. (1986). *Images of organization.* Thousand Oaks, CA: Sage.

Mortimore, P., David-Evans, M., Laukkanen, R., & Valijarvi, J. (1994). *Pilot review of the quality and equity of schooling outcomes in Denmark. Examiner's report.* Paris, France: Organisation for Economic Co-operation and Development.

Nevo, D. (2002). Dialogue evaluation: Combining internal and external evaluation. In D. Nevo (Ed.), *School-based evaluation: An international perspective* (pp. 3–16). Oxford: Elsevier Science.

Nevo, D. (2006). Evaluation in education. In I. F. Shaw, J. C. Greene, & M. M. Mark (Eds.), *Handbook of evaluation* (pp. 441–460). Thousand Oaks, CA: Sage.

Patton, M. Q. (1998). Discovering process use. *Evaluation, 4*, 225–233.

Power, M. (2005). The theory of the audit explosion. In E. Ferlie, L. E. Lynn, & C. Pollitt (Eds.), *The Oxford handbook of public management* (pp. 327–344). New York: Oxford University Press.

Preskill, H., & Torres, R. T. (1999). *Evaluative inquiry for learning in organizations.* Thousand Oaks, CA: Sage.

Rist, R. C., & Stame, N. (2006). *From studies to streams.* New Brunswick, NJ: Transaction Publishers.

Rothstein, H., Huber, M., & Gaskell, G. (2006, February). A theory of risk colonization: The spiralling regulatory logics of societal and institutional risk. *Economy and Society, 35*(1), 91–112.

Rowe, K. J. (2000). Assessment, league tables and school effectiveness: Consider the issues and "Let's Get Real." *Journal of Educational Inquiry, 1*(1), 73–98.

Ryan, K. E., Chandler, M., & Samuels, M. (2007). What should school-based evaluation look like? *Studies in Educational Evaluation, 33*, 197–212.

Schwandt, T. A. (2002). *Evaluation practice reconsidered.* New York: Peter Lang.

Schwandt, T. A., & Dahler-Larsen, P. (2006). When evaluation meets the "Rough Ground" in communities. *Evaluation, 12*(4), 496–505.

Scriven, M. (1991). Beyond formative and summative evaluation. In M. W. McLaughlin & D. C. Phillips (Eds.), *Evaluation and education: At quarter century* (pp. 18–64). Chicago: University of Chicago Press.

Sennett, R. (2002). *The corrosion of character. The personal consequences of work in the new capitalism.* New York: W.W. Norton.

Stake, R. E. (1981). Setting standards for educational evaluators. *Evaluation News, 2*(2), 148–152.

Stake, R. E. (2004). *Standards-based and responsive evaluation.* Thousand Oaks, CA: Sage.

Stehr, N. (2001). *The fragility of modern societies—Knowledge and risk in the Information Age.* London: Sage.

van Thiel, S., & Leeuw, F. L. (2002). The performance paradox in the public sector. *Public Performance and Management Review, 25*(3), 267–281.

Vedung, E. (1997). *Public policy and program evaluation.* New Brunswick, NJ: Transaction Publishers.

Weaver, L., & Cousins, B. (2004). Unpacking the participatory process. *Journal of MultiDisciplinary Evaluation, 1*, 19–40.

CHAPTER 18

Meaningfully Engaging With Difference Through Mixed Methods Educational Evaluation

Jennifer C. Greene

Along the jet way in a major international airport frequented by thousands of travelers every day, there are the following images, or images like them. Each image is a picture about 2 feet by 3 feet, and the pictures are hung side by side along the walls of the jet way. First, the traveler passes a picture of an old and very worn work boot. The boot is the color of dirt, heavily scuffed, with a visible tear along its top and a bit of red lining sticking out. There is a deep gash along the inner heel of the boot, and the threads of the laces are unraveling. The boot is perched on a pitted wooden timber, which is lying on the ground amid nails, wood shavings, pieces of insulation, and other detritus of a construction site. The caption underneath the picture reads "trash." The next picture in the row offers the traveler a mélange of bright primary colors, painted on a black canvass, arrayed in a rough fan shape over a barely discernible triangular base, also painted black. The base is askew, tilted at an angle that is off line with the colorful bouquet. If the base is a vase, the flowers are not in it, but rather hovering above it. If not a vase and flowers, maybe a kaleidoscope of hot air balloons? Or a flock of tropical birds? Or a colorful expression of passion? In the top right corner, there is also a faint smudge of blue—sky, perhaps? Or sadness? The label under this image is "art." The next image is again the old work boot. Only this time, the label under the image is "art." Next, under a repeat of the painting of bright colors on black is the label "trash." A bit further along the jet way are pairings of pictures of a chipped ceramic coffee mug and a plastic pink flamingo lawn decoration, each labeled both "trash" and "art."

One person's trash is another person's treasure is the idea of this display, at least as I interpret it. More profoundly, this simple display evokes intricate reflections on the role of life experience, culture, commitments, and ideology in the interpretive process. Sensemaking and interpretation, that is, are always embedded within the particular lenses of the viewer, lenses that are molded and shaped over a lifetime. How do people who have worn and loved work boots make sense of the jet way images? Or people with a deep background in modern and post-modern painting? Or people for whom the color black signifies death and destruction? Or people who have lost a loved one in a construction accident? Or people with an environmental conscience who believe that everything should be recycled and so nothing is "trash"?

These differences in interpretive stance matter in our everyday life. They are what make our interactions and relationships with one another interesting and ever lively. Further, they offer important opportunities for learning (e.g., learning to openly consider the possibility that a picture of an old work boot *and* a picture of a few splotches of bright color on a black background are each artistic and expressive). Interpretive differences, that is, can be framed as important occasions for learning, rather than contests to be won or lost. To frame difference as an opportunity for learning, rather than a contest or a battle, requires fundamental respect for and acceptance of the perspectives and viewpoints that are other than one's own. To frame difference as an opportunity for learning requires a legitimization of each standpoint and set of commitments. To frame difference as an opportunity for learning requires a valuing of difference and an active willingness and desire to engage with it.

All domains of human endeavor present ongoing opportunities for differences in interpretation and understanding because human activity is exceptionally complex, dynamic, and contextual. This, of course, includes social inquiry, particularly the social practice of educational evaluation. The field of evaluation is rich with difference and has been for some decades. Multiple approaches to evaluation are available to the practitioner, as are multiple methodologies and multiple tools for data collection, analysis,

and interpretation. This handbook is organized around four families of different approaches to evaluation—the scientific family, the management and capacity-building family, the learning family, and the political or ideological family. This structure legitimizes each family, encourages acceptance of all, and kindles the possibility of dialogues among them.

This chapter presents a mixed methods approach to educational evaluation and is located within the learning family, although it could also be considered a member of the political family or perhaps a cousin of all families. A mixed methods approach by definition includes facets or components drawn from different evaluative traditions and methodologies. A mixed methods approach, therefore, offers important opportunities for meaningfully engaging with difference in the service of better understanding and learning. Like a walk along the jet way, learning from mixed methods evaluation can be about the methodological differences. More important, because each methodology is directed toward understanding something about an evaluand, like an educational program, it is enhanced learning about the evaluand that is the most important contribution of a mixed methods approach to evaluation.

In the remainder of this chapter, I first present a more elaborated statement about and justification for a "mixed methods way of thinking" (Greene, 2007) and the importance of meaningfully engaging with difference in mixed methods studies. This justification will be linked to the contemporary phenomenon of globalization and to selected critical contemporary issues challenging educational evaluation practice around the globe—specifically, the radical simplification of educational phenomena by commercialized demands for outcome accountability and the continuing inequities in the distribution of education most everywhere. Then, I discuss in more detail just what can be mixed in a mixed methods evaluation study to include possible mixes from four defining domains of social science methodology. This conceptual discussion about mixing methods will be interspersed with brief examples that focus on the critical global issues of educational accountability and equity and will then be followed by a more extended illustration of these conceptual ideas from the domain of international development evaluation of educational programs and practices. The chapter concludes with a brief final word.

A Mixed Methods Way of Thinking

A mixed methods way of thinking is a stance or an orientation toward social research and evaluation that actively engages in respectful dialogue—one with the other—multiple ways of seeing and hearing, multiple ways of making sense of the social world, and multiple standpoints on what is important and to be valued and cherished. A mixed methods way of thinking rests on the assumption that there are multiple legitimate approaches to social inquiry and that any given approach is inevitably partial. Any single approach necessarily offers but one window on human phenomena positioned from but one vantage point. So, multiple approaches—each legitimized, each valued, and each positioned at a different angle—can offer a more complete and fuller understanding of the human endeavors being studied (Greene, 2007).

Mixing Methods to Address the Complexities of Human Phenomena

This is important because human phenomena are extraordinarily complex (Greene, 2009). Few are more complex than teaching and learning despite contemporary policy pressures for simple measures of both. The esteemed American educational researcher David Berliner (2002) recently observed that educational phenomena are ever so much more complex than most natural phenomena in domains such as physics and astronomy. These complexities, argued Berliner, include the extraordinary particularity of context, the ubiquity of interactions, and the temporality or short half-life of many of our findings.

The argument of this chapter is that better understanding of the complex and multifaceted character of human, specifically educational phenomena, can be obtained from the use of multiple approaches and ways of knowing. For example, in counterpoint to pressures for simple measures of simplified outcomes, a mixed methods educational evaluation study could include multiple measures of the central outcome of student learning, each crafted from a different perspective on the particular meanings of learning in that context. Congruence in results from the different assessments would increase the warrant for evaluative conclusions about the effectiveness of the program; incongruence would offer an "empirical puzzle" (Cook, 1985) requiring further analysis and likely generating greater insight.

Mixing Methods to Engage With Difference

A mixed methods way of thinking *also* offers opportunities for meaningfully engaging with difference—methodological, substantive, and sociopolitical. In fact, a mixed methods way of thinking situates social inquiry as a safe space for meaningful and respectful conversations across differences toward new learning and insights not possible from one vantage point alone.

In mixed methods evaluation, the mixing can extend beyond method and methodology to include different evaluation theories and approaches, each engaging the interests and concerns of different stakeholders. Imagine, for example, an evaluation of the character and equitable distribution of educational access in a selected region of the world that joins a consumer-oriented evaluation approach (Scriven, 1993) with a policy-oriented evaluation approach (Cook, 2002). In such an evaluation, the interests and values of *both* educational consumers and educational policy makers would be respectfully engaged. The fierce desire of a parent to send her daughter to school, to give her daughter the opportunity to escape the limited life options in their rural village, would be legitimized and engaged *in tandem with* the policymaker's near-impossible challenge of deciding how best to distribute meager resources for rural families in her jurisdiction and how best to choose among families' competing needs for sustainable food supplies, health care, communications infrastructure, and education. In a mixed methods evaluation, each of these distinct stakeholder standpoints would be legitimized and respected toward a more complete portrait of the possibilities and challenges of equitable educational access in the context at hand.

Engaging With Difference in Evaluation, Globally

An evaluation approach that proactively respects and engages with difference offers one valuable alternative for educational evaluation in today's increasingly globalized world. The concept of globalization often signals the transnational movement—and concomitant cross-cultural blending, even homogenization—of markets and products, music and art, cultures and traditions, ideas and inspirations, governance and human rights, and so forth. The idea of transnational communication, collaboration, and even competition also signals increasing exposure to and contact with differences of many kinds for many people around the globe.

An evaluation approach that proactively respects and engages with difference can offer opportunities for (a) learning and understanding across borders, (b) adopting and adapting ideas from elsewhere while also honoring local beliefs and values, (c) preserving the richness of difference, and (d) honoring the full spectrum of human endeavor amid the homogenizing power of globalization. An evaluation approach that proactively respects and engages with difference values both inside and outside perspectives, both tradition and innovation, both the local and the global, and thus rejects the hegemony of one or the other. In these ways, an evaluation approach that proactively respects and

engages with difference can contribute to inclusive and open discourse about important issues, both local and global, and to a basic respect for the human rights of all individuals and peoples (Greene, 2005). This stance is not intended to exaggerate the power of evaluation to save the world (Stake, 2004a), but rather much more modestly to position evaluation as a social practice that advances values of respect, tolerance, affirmation, and dialogue.

Global Challenges in Contemporary Educational Evaluation

The field of educational evaluation faces a number of challenges in today's globalized world. As noted, the present discussion is concentrating on the contemporary challenges of oversimplified outcome measures and continuing inequities in educational access and opportunity.

Educational Outcomes, Simplified

The contemporary emphasis on a delimited set of educational outcomes has been significantly wrought by the recent emergence of the global new public management (NPM) movement (Power, 1997). This approach to government operations is designed, in part, to restore citizen trust in government, enhance governmental efficiency, and anchor policy and management decisions in trustworthy evidence about the quality of public initiatives and programs. The NPM is centrally oriented around the concept of outcomes accountability, such that an NPM government is transparently accountable to its citizens through the visible and regular publication of data on indicators of successful or unsuccessful performance for programs and policies in all public sectors. Up and down the line, public employees are accountable for enabling and supporting the successful attainment of the performance indicators relevant to their sphere of operations.

In education, this accountability era is most clearly manifest in the emergence of large and powerful systems of high-stakes achievement tests and institutional performance measurement in many countries, in both the north and south. In the United States, for example, the stakes involved in educational testing for K-12 schooling include possible job loss for teachers and administrators, loss of local control over a neighborhood school to the state or to an outside private corporation, and even the survival of a school. In the UK higher educational system, major university research funding is allocated according to the number of points accrued by each institution within the nation's higher education performance measurement system. In Malawi, centrally administered standardized achievement tests serve as gatekeepers at Grades 8, 10, and 12. Only students who pass the test at each of these grades are eligible to continue their education, even as there is space for only a fraction of those eligible. Despite the high personal stakes involved in this testing program, the program is plagued with problems of security, cheating, insufficient resources, psychometric instability, and vulnerability to public and policy pressures (Chakwera, Khembo, & Sireci, 2004).

The NPM management movement also has contributed to a privileging of educational outcomes over educational processes and experiences. Achievement tests and performance management systems alike only assess outputs (short-term results), outcomes (realization of policy aims), or impacts (long-term sustainable changes) in some combination. The character and quality of the learning experience for students, the excitement and enthusiasm generated by excellent teaching, and the disillusionment and discouragement that result from pedagogy and content disconnected from learners' lives are not featured—and therefore not valued—in the vast global landscape of contemporary educational accountability.

These NPM accountability policies have further contributed to a radical simplification of the commonly understood character of meaningful learning. The old American adage of "what gets measured is what counts" is no more true than in today's times. What gets measured in our new public management accountability systems for education are limited samples of relatively simplistic knowledge and skills largely because measures of more complex and sophisticated learning outcomes, or measures of the quality of the educational experience, are not feasible within the assessment systems as currently designed. With such a large stick as high-stakes achievement testing, public educational systems worldwide are conducting wholesale reorientations of their curricula and instruction around largely instrumental activities that enable students to pass the test.

Educational Evaluation, Constrained

The character of educational evaluation today is importantly influenced by this global infatuation with educational outcomes (over processes and experiences) and with performance indicator, high-stakes systems of assessing student learning. In particular, there has been an increased demand for outcomes-oriented and impact evaluation, *along with* the methodologies assumed to best assess outcomes and their causal links to the intervention being studied. These privileged methodologies are anchored in an objectivist social science framework, which eschews values as outside the domain of science and which focuses on method as the safeguard against bias.

The promotion of this objectivist framework for educational evaluation has catalyzed another go-round of contestations about methodology in evaluation (and social inquiry more broadly), recalling the fractious methodological debates of the 1970s and 1980s. Once again, on the one side are aligned proponents of "rigorous" quantitative methodologies that can yield accurate, unbiased estimates of program outcomes, represented as performance indicator targets or longer term program impacts. These methodologies include experimental designs (Airasian,

1983; Cook, 2002) and econometric impact studies (e.g., Duncan & Magnuson, 2002). On the other sides are the advocates for other kinds of methodologies, including qualitative (Patton, 2002) participatory (Whitmore, 1998), and democratic (House and Howe, 1999) methodological traditions. These other methodologies privilege experiential dimensions of education and the complexities and contextualities of teaching and learning, rather than outcomes alone. Moreover, the outcomes engaged by these other methodologies go well beyond performance indicator thinking to embrace some of the grand aims of education—personal development, cultivation of civic sensibilities and responsibilities, and, on a societal level, democratization in the form of equalization of educational access and opportunity.

Educational Equity, Forgotten?

Clearly, methodology here is a proxy for deeper contestations about philosophical and ideological stances relevant to the role of evaluation amid controversial political and policy issues. Most critical to the present discussion is the contested place of normative values and ideals in evaluation methodology. In an objectivist orientation, values are the province of priests and policymakers, but not science. So, in an objectivist evaluation practice, there is no sanctioned place to engage with the values of the policies and programs at hand as represented, most important, in stated policy goals or program outcomes because such engagement is not what evaluators legitimately do. In such an evaluation, values issues, which include localized priorities for meaningful learning *alongside* globalized human rights arguments for equity of educational access and outcome, are displaced by the emphasis on "rigorous evidence" and the importance of "scientifically" assessing program outcomes and impacts. In turn, proponents of the other evaluation methodologies argue that absent meaningful engagement with the values

embedded in particular educational goals, educational evaluation today risks becoming but an instrumental practice that contributes to an instrumental and singularly barren view of the role of education in a knowledge-oriented global economy. It is only by directly engaging with the normative dimensions of educational policies and practices, argue these evaluators, that educational evaluation can fulfill its potential to meaningfully enlighten policy and program conversations about how best to attain educational quality, effectiveness, and equity in the context at hand and thereby enable education to fulfill its grand contribution to democratization and the cultivation of informed and active citizenries worldwide.

Educational Evaluation, Reclaimed

Within this contested global milieu, it is critical to the integrity of educational evaluation that it *not* be used as an additional lever in the ongoing political battle. The stakes are too high. The critical issues involved in these important debates are too readily masked by methodological rhetoric. Instead, evaluation should provide a safe and open forum within which contemporary controversies can be openly and respectfully engaged. One way to engage these contemporary debates about globalization, performativity, democratization, and the role of education therein—without taking sides—is to use a mixed methods approach to educational evaluation. A mixed methods approach fully acknowledges the values implicit in our theories and methods, but inclusively rests on a fundamental (even radical) acceptance of the legitimacy of these different stances, assumptions, value commitments, and, yes, methodologies. A mixed methods approach thus offers the possibility of genuinely engaging with difference, of dialogue and reciprocal learning, and thereby of advancement anchored in a collective sense of what has been defensibly *and* meaningfully learned about the quality of a given educational intervention.[1]

The discussion now turns to the various kinds of differences that can be engaged through a mixed methods approach to educational evaluation. To say it another way, just what differences can be productively and generatively mixed in a mixed methods approach to educational evaluation within the contemporary context of globalization?

Domains of Inquiry and Domains of Mixing: Engaging With Different Kinds of Difference

A framework for social inquiry encompasses four overlapping domains: philosophical assumptions and stances, inquiry logics, guidelines for practice, and sociopolitical commitments related to the role of social science in society (Greene, 2006). Collectively, the domains present a justificatory framework and a set of practical guidelines for a given approach to social inquiry. In this section of this chapter, these domains provide a general framework for discussing various possibilities for mixing and thereby for engaging with difference in a mixed methods approach to educational evaluation in a global context. Domains 2 and 3 are discussed jointly because there is little of specific relevance in the practical domain (Domain 3) for this discussion. In conjunction with Domain 4, selected issues from evaluation theory are also discussed. These issues extend well beyond methodology, even as they are entangled with it, and include the consequential dimensions of evaluation purpose and audience, evaluator role, and evaluation utilization.

Philosophical Assumptions and Stances

From the Western perspective that constitutes my education, the domain of the philosophy of science includes assumptions and stances related to the nature of the social world, the nature of the knowledge we can attain about that world, the relationship of the knower to what is known, priorities for what is important to know, and other related concerns. These ideas are often clustered under the label of *paradigm* from Thomas Kuhn's (1962) revolutionary work. The challenges and controversies related to mixing at this philosophical level continue to bedevil mixed methods scholars (Greene, 2007; Greene, Benjamin, & Goodyear, 2001; Howe, 2003; Maxwell, 2004; Phillips, 2005). These challenges include issues related to the possible incommensurability of the assumptions of different paradigms, to the contested relationship between paradigm and practice (Howe, 1985, 1988), and to the desirability of an alternative paradigm—most popularly, American pragmatism—for mixed methods inquiry (Johnson & Onwuegbuzie, 2004; Morgan, 2007). These challenges notwithstanding, the questions for the present discussion are: What are the possibilities for mixing in this philosophical domain? What differences could be meaningfully engaged?

One major idea is that, instead of engaging these abstract and rarefied philosophical assumptions, a mixed methods evaluation can respectfully engage differences in their associative inquiry features. Such features include, for example, distance and closeness, outside and inside perspectives, generality and particularity, recurring regularities and contextualized narratives, the unusual and the representative, prediction and consequentiality, and social norms and social critique (Bryman, 1988; Greene & Caracelli, 1997). It makes common sense, as an evaluator, to gather data related to external perspectives on fidelity of program implementation, as well as to internal perspectives on participants' program experiences. It makes sense to ask about dimensions of the program experience that may occur across contexts, as well as dimensions that may be context-specific. The latter invokes this question: What is it about this context that matters for the program experiences observed, leading in turn to both narrative depth and possible contextual generalization?

Take, for example, an evaluation of the introduction of a computer laboratory, including Internet access, to a school serving young students in rural Bolivia. This is an evaluation context with manifest equity dimensions because a significant "digital divide" still remains between those with and without access to the incomparable information resources of the Internet. "School-day stories" gathered from students in this Bolivian school, along with records of their computer use, may afford insights into the specific, contextual learning experiences of these children, as well as may inform other educational technology initiatives regarding the range and distribution of children's sensemakings of the vast landscape of the Internet as they first encounter it. This idea of respecting difference in underlying philosophical stances by focusing on the practical features of these stances in evaluation—in this case, the particular and the general—is ripe for experimentation and field trials.

A second idea regarding mixing at the assumptive level is that, with a mixed methods way of thinking, educational evaluators in today's globalized world can strive to meaningfully engage with different stances and orientations that are linked to different cultures—east and west, north and south—and thereby demonstrate respect for and affirmation of such cultures. Local cultural traditions and beliefs are vulnerable amid the contemporary homogenizing currents of globalization. Ideas and perspectives, material products and trends, and aspirations and ideals all flow easily across borders and boundaries because electronic and Internet channels are not guarded by passport checkpoints, customs inspections, or high fences and heat-sensing remote cameras. Cross-national and cross-cultural influences are readily apparent in our contemporary daily lives, especially in music and the arts, fashion, politics and media, and even language. Some degree of global melding of culture is inevitable given global currents of communication. Such melding can be enriching and beneficial to the diverse citizenries of the world because it generates new imaginings and new horizons, and it also provides opportunities to learn about and from one another. Yet it is all too easy for dominant cultures (notably in the west) to overpower traditions and beliefs of less dominant cultures (notably in the south), demonstrating disregard, disrespect, and likely continued ignorance of the commitments and beliefs of such cultures (unintentionally or not). Indeed, these are among the greatest risks of globalization. Educational evaluators should be especially mindful of these risks and seek not to impose the beliefs and assumptions associated with a particular worldview, but rather to openly and proactively invite multiple worldviews to engage in dialogue with one another en route to reciprocal learning, insight, and mutual benefit.

This idea of respecting cultural traditions in mixed methods educational evaluation is not intended to romanticize such traditions or encourage their uncritical acceptance. Take, for example, the longstanding tradition in many cultures to promote educational opportunities first and foremost for boys and only if resources permit for girls. From gender equity and feminist perspectives, such customs are viewed as radical violations of the basic human rights of girls. In such perspectives, and in Western views, education is considered a powerful route to both individual self-actualization and societal democratization via an informed citizenry. Yet to impose such views is to disregard and disrespect local cultural beliefs and worldviews, which clearly have their own history and rationality. Moreover, an educational evaluation misguided by external cultural beliefs may well misjudge the quality and effectiveness of an educational program. The argument being presented herein would encourage the educational evaluator in this context to seek internal alongside external criteria of quality and local alongside global (Western) views of education as a potentially democratizing institution, and thereby to provide spaces for dialoguing across such differences.

Inquiry Logics and Guidelines for Practice

A second domain intrinsic to a given approach to social science is what is commonly called "methodology." This domain "identifies appropriate inquiry purposes and questions, broad inquiry strategies and designs, sampling preferences and logic, criteria of quality for both methodology and inference, and defensible forms of writing and reporting. The role and location of the inquirer in the study is also delineated in this domain" (Greene, 2006, p. 93), as are appropriate logics of justification for each of these methodological components. A third domain is comprised of the specific practical procedures of inquiry.

> Domain three is the "how to" of social science inquiry . . . [and] includes, for example, alternative inquiry designs, sampling strategies, and analysis techniques that meet the broad parameters specified in domain two. In domain three are also located the specific methods of data gathering, analysis, interpretation, and reporting. (Greene, 2006, p. 94)

To make this more concrete, Domain 2 includes designs such as quasi-experimentation, and Domain 3 specifies various options for quasi-experimental designs (e.g., pre-post comparison group, regression discontinuity). Also, Domain 2 identifies purposeful sampling as appropriate for a given design, and Domain 3 then lists a number of different types of purposeful sampling (e.g., of the typical or the unusual case, or for maximum variation).

Mixing at the methodological and procedural levels of social inquiry is the signature characteristic of mixed methods inquiry in general. By definition, then, mixed methods social inquiry includes a diversity of methodological traditions, inquiry designs, methods for data gathering and analysis, criteria of warrant, and forms of interpretation and reporting.

So, what dimensions of difference can be productively, meaningfully, and generatively engaged by mixing at the levels of overall methodology and specific method or technique? In practice, evaluators routinely mix methods at the procedural or technical level (Domain 3), gathering data in qualitative, quantitative, and symbolic form; sampling both representatively and purposefully; representing specific features of a context as well as cross-context regularities; and reporting in both textual and tabular form. The differences engaged by mixing at this technical level are primarily related to different features or characteristics of the educational program or policy being evaluated (e.g., the specific contextual and cultural relevance of curricular materials *and* the character of student engagement with these materials).

Mixing at the broader level of methodology (Domain 2) also primarily engages different features or characteristics of the educational program or policy being evaluated. A mixed design that includes a quasi-experiment and selected mini-case studies can generate insights into the comparative advantage of the evaluand as well as its experiential meaningfulness in selected sites. A mix of a large-scale survey measuring key program variables pre and post with a historical assessment of educational policy history in relevant sites can provide some localized explanatory power for the pre-post differences observed or not. These kinds of methodological mixes, although not as common as technical mixes, are consonant with early advice from some of our wisest thinkers. Cronbach and Associates (1980) discouraged evaluators from signing on to just one methodological framework and instead encouraged us to conduct "fleets of studies," each capturing a distinct perspective on the evaluand. Toward better understanding of evaluands, Cook's (1985) postpositivist critical multiplism encouraged evaluators to make many features of our studies multiple, including, at the technical level, (a) measures of important constructs, (b) methods of data gathering, (c) approaches to data analysis, (d) theories and rival hypotheses being tested, and, at the methodological level, (e) stakeholder perspectives on key evaluation questions, and (f) value frameworks for interpreting evaluation results.

Take as an example an evaluation of a newly installed problem-oriented science curriculum for high school students in a major East Asian city. This curriculum was adapted from problem-based learning ideas in the United States. Its intention is to foster mastery of scientific knowledge, as well as critical thinking skills and expert proficiency with scientific equipment among the city's students. Anticipating the next wave of technology development, the city is endeavoring to prepare its students for high-level science research and development jobs in the near future. Under an accountability mindset, an evaluation of this science curriculum would likely focus on standardized, internationally recognized assessments of intended outcomes, including scientific knowledge and critical thinking, but not technological proficiency due to its performance and cost demands. Although valuable, such an assessment offers a small window into the educational meaningfulness and effectiveness of this curriculum intervention. A mixed methods evaluation, in contrast, could assess both the character and quality of the learning experience *and* a range of student learning outcomes. At the technical level (Domain 3), structured classroom observations could be mixed with open-ended interviews of students and teachers as ways to capture the quality of the learning experience; and pre-post follow-up measures of student learning could be mixed with reviews of samples of student work as ways to measure the extent and character of student learning. These mixes of methods are able to capture and represent more comprehensively the new curriculum as implemented and experienced. At the design level, the evaluation could creatively mix a repeated measures design with a set of mini-case studies, investigating *both* the cultural meaningfulness of this imported and adapted curriculum *and* its effectiveness as a citywide innovation.

Mixing at the levels of methodology and technique in order to engage multiple diverse features of the evaluand is also consonant with contemporary understandings of the use of program theory in evaluation. Program theory is an explanatory account of how program resources and activities are expected to generate or lead to intended outcomes. Some evaluation theorists today champion an overall program theory approach to evaluation (e.g., Donaldson, 2007; Pawson & Tilly, 1997; Rogers, Hacsi, Petrosino, & Huebner, 2000; Weiss, 1998). Others perceive the inclusion of program theory as a useful enhancement of their own evaluation approach and practice. In the context at hand, program theory could provide a useful framework for engaging with *different* conceptualizations and experiential understandings of the program or policy being evaluated. Specifically, gathering the multiple program theories of multiple, diverse stakeholders could provide the input for lively dialogues of substance and consequence in particular evaluation contexts.

In short, by using a mixed methods approach, possibly in combination with a program theory orientation, educational evaluators can productively engage multiple and diverse facets or characteristics of the program or policy being evaluated, including again culture-specific characteristics. In this way, a mixed methods approach generates broader, deeper, and better understanding than a single method or methodology alone. In this way, a mixed methods approach also inclusively engages and respects multiple, diverse value stances and commitments as elaborated in the next section.

Sociopolitical Commitments

In the fourth general domain of a social science framework, the location of the inquiry in society is articulated and defended. What purposes and whose interests does social inquiry in this tradition serve? What values are advanced by this approach to social inquiry? Clearly, although these Domain 4 questions are not independent from the other domains, the role of social science in society is a distinctive issue. Moreover, because questions of purpose, audience, and values distinguish among evaluation theories or approaches (Greene, 1997), Domain 4 is of special importance to this exploration of a (globally mindful) mixed methods approach to educational evaluation.

So, what sociopolitical differences can be meaningfully and generatively engaged in a mixed method approach to educational evaluation? In the vision being advanced in this chapter, a mixed methods approach to educational evaluation expressly engages the sociopolitical issues of greatest contestation in the contexts at hand even if or perhaps *especially if* such issues remain implicit instead of explicitly named. Further, by intentionally engaging with differences of values and interests, educational evaluation becomes situated as an open forum for dialogue and deliberation about the critical issues at hand.[2] Rather than being used as a political lever or an argument for one side or another, and rather than masking the underlying issues of values with debates about method, evaluation becomes the common meeting ground for dialogue, learning, and understanding.

One of the most direct ways to enact this idea of evaluation as a site for engaging with different interests and values is to explicitly mix *different evaluative purposes and audiences* precisely because different stakeholders characteristically have different interests in an evaluation study, as well as different value commitments and stances. Table 18.1 presents one categorization of evaluative purposes and audiences, along with their characteristic (although not essential) links to evaluation questions, philosophical frameworks, methodologies, and evaluation theories. This table is intended to be illustrative not exhaustive of all possible evaluation purposes and audiences.

So, in contexts where more than one methodology, approach, or framework is possible, just imagine the (metaphorical) conversations that

could be catalyzed by data on how well the evaluand addresses important needs of consumers/users alongside data on the contributions of the evaluand to organizational learning and productivity. Or imagine a conversation between impact and effectiveness data, on the one hand, and data on the contributions of the evaluand to equity and social justice, on the other hand. These are the kinds of mixed methods evaluation conversations that could meaningfully engage with differences in underlying interests, beliefs, and values. Thus, these are the kinds of mixed methods conversations that position evaluation as a forum for learning, a safe space for dialogue, and a social practice that advances values of respect, acceptance, affirmation, and wise moral judgment.

In the next section, these ideas are illustrated in the domain of international development evaluation, with a focus on education.

Mixing Methods in International Development Evaluation of Educational Programs

The world of international development evaluation is currently embroiled in a highly significant controversy. On the surface, the controversy is about evaluation methodology, but in actual substance, it is about assumptions, commitments, beliefs, and values—much like the qualitative-quantitative debate of 30 years ago. This controversy is thus fertile ground for a mixed methods engagement with difference.

The Controversy

The controversy has been provoked by strong calls for *impact evaluations* of international development projects and programs, sounded by a new foundation-funded organization called the Center for Global Development (CGD) (http://www.cgdev.org/). Under the provocative

Table 18.1 One Portrayal of Evaluation Approaches Differentiated by Purpose and Audience

Evaluation Purpose (and Intended Use)	Usual Audience	Typical Evaluation Questions	Usual Philosophical Orientation (Domain 1)	Characteristic Methodology (Domain 2)	Relevant Evaluation Theories
Inform policy and program decision making	High-level policymakers and decision makers	Did the program obtain desired outcomes? How cost-effective is the program?	Post-positivism	Experimental Econometric	Policy-oriented, social experimentation (Campbell, 1971; Cook & Sinha, 2005)
Provide accountability	Legislature General public	How well were performance targets met?	Post-positivism	Survey, quantitative	Managerialism, results-based practice (Hatry & Wholey, 1999)
Improve the program, enhance organizational learning	Program or organizational managers	What improvements are needed in the program? How can the program support organizational goals?	Depends on the stances of evaluator	Eclectic, selected to fit demands of the context	Utilization, organizational development (Owen & Alkin, 2007; Patton, 1997; Torres, Preskill, & Piontek, 2004)
Contribute to conceptual or practical knowledge	Program staff, program developers	What has been learned about the efficacy of the program? What has been learned about wise professional practice?	Interpretivism Constructivism Hermeneutics	Case study, qualitative	Responsive, theory-oriented, practical wisdom (Rogers, 2008; Schwandt, 2002; Stake, 2004)
Advance democratization or social change	Program participants, their families, and their communities	In what ways does the program advance equity and social justice for those with least access to resources?	Critical theory Transformation	Participatory, dialogic, deliberative	Democratic, participatory (House & Howe, 1999; Whitmore, 1998) Culturally responsive (Hood, Hopson, & Frierson, 2005)

title of "When Will We Ever Learn? Closing the Evaluation Gap" (http://www.cgdev.org/section/initiatives/_active/evalgap), a working group representing the CGD has advanced a strong argument that now is the time for "rigorous" impact evaluations of international development projects.

> To achieve real improvements in health, education, and welfare in the developing world, social programs have to work. For decades, development agencies have disbursed billions of dollars for programs aimed at improving living conditions and reducing poverty; developing countries themselves have spent hundreds of billions more. Yet the shocking fact is that we have relatively little knowledge about the net impact of most of these programs. In the absence of good evidence about what works, political influences dominate, and decisions about the level and type of spending are hard to challenge. Without question, the results are suboptimal. But if evidence about what works were systematically developed and made public, that information could be used for better public policymaking and thus for more effective international aid and domestic spending. (Savedoff & Levine, 2006, p. 1)

The argument continues:

> The missing puzzle piece in learning about what kinds of social interventions can succeed is impact evaluations, studies that document whether particular programs are actually responsible for improvements in social outcomes relative to what would have happened without them. An "evaluation gap" has emerged because governments, official donors, and other funders do not demand or produce enough impact evaluations and because those that are conducted are often methodologically flawed. (Savedoff, Levine, & Birdsall, 2006, p. 2)

The CGD argument is that critical decisions on promising development interventions cannot be made from research knowledge or from monitoring or accountability data alone (Savedoff et al., 2006, p. 11). Also needed is strong evidence from evaluations that utilize sophisticated, experimental methodologies that can "rigorously" include a designed counterfactual and thereby assess without bias, and with validity, the extent to which *intended program outcomes* are attained by the intervention being studied.

Challenges to this argument have been sounded by evaluation specialists in a number of quarters. Some of these challenges echo past methodological discussions about the real-world limitations of experimentation. These include the significant practical and ethical challenges of (a) randomization, (b) fidelity of treatment implementation both within and across sites, (c) substantial contextual variation, (d) modeling a complex program intervention with a simple linear model, and (e) privileging of outcome information over information on how such outcomes were obtained (the "black box" challenge to experimental evaluations). These are legitimate concerns, which proponents of impact studies characteristically counter by highlighting the value of advances in technical sophistication (such as hierarchical linear modeling) and by arguing the vital importance of providing unbiased accounts of what difference an intervention makes, a unique contribution of impact studies.[3] Other challenges to the push for impact evaluation underscore its exclusion of assessments of other important dimensions of the program (e.g., the quality of implementation, the contextual meaningfulness of the program's curriculum and pedagogy, and student responses that fall outside the focus on quantitative assessments of intended outcomes). Impact evaluations can capture only a simplified version of program outcomes. Other challenges also document ways other than randomized experimentation to legitimately evaluate program impacts (Network of Networks on Impact Evaluation, 2008).

But this is the technical debate, bounded by the parameters and discourse of methodology. That is, this is a debate bounded by the concepts and practices of Domains 2 and 3 of social science—the domains of methodology and procedure or technique. The limited emphasis on narrowly defined educational impacts, to the exclusion of all other dimensions of teaching and learning, echoes the general challenges facing educational evaluation around the globe today. Important as this methodological debate is, it too readily masks and obscures critical underlying matters of values, commitments, and priorities, as well as political control, power, and agency. Excluded from the debate, that is, are the assumptive stances and values of Domain 1 and the sociopolitical commitments of Domain 4. These other dimensions of educational evaluation must also be part of the conversation, lest our craft be relegated to one of technical proficiency in unquestioned service of contemporary accountability and marketplace knowledge exchange. One way to bring in these other dimensions of educational evaluation is via a mixed methods way of thinking.

Reframing the Controversy With a Mixed Methods Way of Thinking

The issue at hand is that, after decades of investment in international development, the basic needs of too many people in the "developing world," including basic needs for education, remain radically under-met. This state of affairs is not debated. The debate featured in the present discussion rather focuses on how the field of evaluation should respond to this state of affairs. One side argues that good data on program impacts will rescue development decision making from "political influences" by providing rigorous and credible evidence about what does and does not work. The other side challenges the feasibility of large-scale experimentation in development contexts and the narrow and limited evaluative focus on selected impacts or outcomes.

Underlying these opposing stances are different assumptions and values regarding the character of educational evaluation as a social practice (from Domain 1) and different ideological commitments regarding the role of evaluation in society (from Domain 4). For example, many proponents of impact evaluation likely subscribe to an objectivist epistemology and to a consultant role for evaluation, positioned in service to elected decision makers. Opponents of impact evaluation in this may well subscribe to an interpretivist or critical epistemology and to an activist, engaged role of evaluation, positioned in service to comprehensive understanding or ideals of justice or equity, respectively. Under a mixed methods umbrella, these different assumptions, stances, and commitments are *all* considered to be legitimate and worthy of respect. Under a mixed methods umbrella, these different assumptions, stances, and commitments would be surfaced, explicitly named, and generously invited for conversation and dialogue. In this manner, the conversation includes assumptions, stances, and commitments, and not just methodological disputes. In this manner, the conversation shifts from a technical debate about method to a more expansive and inclusive dialogue across difference. In this manner, educational evaluation becomes an active player on the global stage, offering insights that are neither narrowly focused on measurable outcomes nor trapped in economically driven considerations of what matters and what counts.

The kinds of issues, beyond method, that could be included in this more expansive conversation include the following:

- What and whose conceptualization of the "problem" is represented in the educational project being evaluated? Problems can be understood as deficits or limitations of individuals, as in lack of student motivation to pursue learning; gaps in public services, as in inadequate teacher preparation in science and mathematics; inequities in the structure and distribution of services, as in fewer resources allocated to rural schools; or some combination thereof.

- What and whose understandings and assumptions are reflected in the design of the project intended to address the problem identified? Educational innovations can be developed by external experts using theory and research from elsewhere, by local experts and practitioners using practical wisdom and experience, or by some combination thereof.

- How were the educational outcomes of highest priority identified and by whom? What and whose values do they embody—values of efficiency, economic competitiveness, and modernization; values of agency and empowerment; values of active citizenship and social justice; values of democratization; or some combination thereof?

- What provisions does the project have for sustainability beyond current funding, and how will decisions about sustainability be made? Importing an innovative curriculum, supported by intensive teacher professional development, may well boost student learning, but who will pay the continued costs of such an educational intervention?

A mixed methods approach to international development educational evaluation would intentionally seek to engage the multiple legitimate perspectives that exist on these kinds of critical issues. It is precisely because different methodological traditions privilege certain perspectives and carry with them certain value commitments that a mixed methods evaluation can provide spaces for respectful conversations and dialogues among different perspectives and commitments.

Final Word

Amid the often fierce eddies and currents of globalization, educational evaluation today faces particular challenges from the accountability (NPM) movement, alongside the economically driven

negotiations of the knowledge economy. These contemporary movements threaten the field of educational evaluation with challenges to cherished meanings of teaching and learning and to the widely prized role of education as a force for individual self-actualization and societal democratization, even as they punctuate conversations about education with rhythms of reality. In this chapter, a mixed methods way of thinking and a mixed methods approach to educational evaluation have been advanced as a way of engaging contemporary rhythms with the counterpoint of long-established ideals and aspirations. A mixed methods approach to educational evaluation provides places and spaces for diverse stances, values, beliefs, and commitments, and in the ideal a venue for dialogue, conversation, and learning.

Notes

1. It is also important to point out that other evaluators are exploring other evaluative responses to these contemporary controversies and challenges of globalization, including an interactive dual-level—local and national—approach (Allen & Black, 2006), a responsive approach (Van der Knaap, 2006), and a collaborative action inquiry approach (Cook, 2006).

2. The idea of a deliberative, dialogic evaluation is credited to House and Howe (1999). In their democratic evaluation ideal, diverse stakeholders actually dialogue and deliberate with each other as a route to democratization. In the mixed methods approach being advocated herein, dialogue and deliberation more modestly happen through the methodological mixes so that evaluation becomes a metaphorical forum rather than an actual one, although direct dialogue among stakeholders remains an ideal.

3. The CGD argument also fully recognizes that impact studies are not appropriate for all development contexts, but must be an essential part of the evaluation repertoire.

References

Airasian, P. W. (1983). Societal experimentation. In G. F. Madaus, M. Scriven, & D. L. Stufflebeam (Eds.), *Evaluation models* (pp. 163–175). Boston: Kluwer-Nijhoff.

Allen, M., & Black, M. (2006). Dual level evaluation and complex community initiatives: The local evaluation of Sure Start. *Evaluation, 12*(2), 237–249.

Berliner, D. C. (2002). Educational research: The hardest science of all. *Educational Researcher, 31*(8), 18–20.

Bryman, A. (1988). *Quantity and quality in social research.* London: Unwin Hyman.

Campbell, D. T. (1971). Reforms as experiments. *Urban Affairs Review, 7*(2), 133–171.

Chakwera, E., Khembo, D., & Sireci, S. G. (2004). High-stakes testing in the warm heart of Africa: The challenges and successes of the Malawi National Examinations Board. *Educational Policy Analysis Archives, 12*(29).

Cook, T. D. (1985). Postpositivist critical multiplism. In R. L. Shotland & M. M. Mark (Eds.), *Social science and social policy* (pp. 21–62). Thousand Oaks, CA: Sage.

Cook, T. D. (2002). Randomized experiments in educational policy research: A critical examination of the reasons the educational evaluation community has offered for not doing them. *Educational Evaluation and Policy Analysis, 24*(3), 175–199.

Cook, T. D. (2006). Collaborative action research within developmental evaluation: Learning to see or the road to myopia? *Evaluation, 12*(4), 418–436.

Cook, T. D., & Sinha, V. (2005). Randomized experiments in educational research. In G. Camilli, P. Green, & P. B. Belmore (Eds.), *Complementary methods in educational research.* Washington, DC: American Educational Research Association.

Cronbach, L. J., & Associates. (1980). *Toward reform of program evaluation.* San Francisco, CA: Jossey-Bass.

Donaldson, S. I. (2007). *Program theory-driven evaluation science: Strategies and applications.* Mahwah, NJ: Lawrence Erlbaum Associates.

Duncan, G. J., & Magnuson, K. A. (2002). *Economics and parenting.* Unpublished manuscript, Northwestern University, Evanston IL. Retrieved August 24, 2008, from http://www.northwestern.edu/ipr/publications/papers/2004/duncan/econandparenting.pdf.

Greene, J. C. (1997). Evaluation as advocacy. *Evaluation Practice, 18*, 25–35.

Greene, J. C. (2005). Evaluators as stewards of the public good. In S. Hood, R. K. Hopson, & H. T. Frierson (Eds.), *The role of culture and cultural context: A mandate for inclusion, truth, and understanding in evaluation theory and practice. Evaluation and Society Series* (pp. 7–20). Greenwich, CT: InfoAge.

Greene, J. C. (2006). Toward a methodology of mixed methods social inquiry. In R. B. Johnson (Ed.), *Research in the schools: Special issue. New directions in mixed methods research* (pp. 93–99). San Francisco, CA: Jossey-Bass.

Greene, J. C. (2007). *Mixed methods in social inquiry.* San Francisco, CA: Jossey-Bass.

Greene, J. C. (2009). Evidence as "proof" and evidence as "inkling." In S. I. Donaldson, C. A. Christie, & M. M. Mark (Eds.), *What counts as credible evidence in applied research and evaluation practice?* (pp. 153–167). Thousand Oaks CA: Sage.

Greene, J. C., Benjamin, L., & Goodyear, L. (2001). The merits of mixing methods in evaluation. *Evaluation, 7*(1), 25–44.

Greene, J. C., & Caracelli, V. J. (1997). Defining and describing the paradigm issue in mixed-method evaluation. In J. C. Greene & V. J. Caracelli (Eds.), Advances in mixed-method evaluation: The challenges and benefits of integrating diverse paradigms. *New Directions for Evaluation 74* (pp. 5–17). San Francisco, CA: Jossey-Bass.

Hatry, H. P., & Wholey, J. S. (1999). *Performance measurement: Getting results.* Washington, DC: Urban Institute Press.

Hood, S., Hopson, R., & Frierson, H. (Eds.). (2005). *The role of culture and cultural context: A mandate for inclusion, the discovery of truth, and understanding in evaluative theory and practice.* Greenwich, CT: InfoAge.

House, E. R., & Howe, K. R. (1999). *Values in evaluation and social research.* Thousand Oaks, CA: Sage.

Howe, K. R. (1985). Two dogmas of educational research. *Educational Researcher, 14*(8), 10–18.

Howe, K. R. (1988). Against the quantitative-qualitative incompatibility thesis (or dogmas die hard). *Educational Researcher, 17*(8), 10–16.

Howe, K. R. (2003). *Closing methodological divides.* Boston: Kluwer Academic Publishing.

Johnson, R. B., & Onwuegbuzie, A. J. (2004). Mixed methods research: A research paradigm whose time has come. *Educational Researcher, 33*(7), 14–26.

Kuhn, T. (1962). *The structure of scientific revolutions.* Chicago: University of Chicago Press.

Maxwell, J. A. (2004, April). *Realism as a stance for mixed methods research.* Paper presented at the annual meeting of the American Educational Research Association, Chicago, IL.

Morgan, D. L. (2007). Paradigms lost and pragmatism regained: Methodological implications of combining qualitative and quantitative methods. *Journal of Mixed Methods Research, 1*(1), 48–76.

Network of Networks on Impact Evaluation. (2008, January). *Impact evaluation guidance.* Subgroup 2 Draft Report.

Owen, J., & Alkin, M. C. (2007). *Program evaluation: Forms and approaches* (3rd ed.). New York: Guilford Press.

Patton, M.Q. (1997). *Utilization-focused evaluation: The new century text* (3rd ed.). Thousand Oaks, CA: Sage.

Patton, M. Q. (2002). *Qualitative research and evaluation methods* (3rd ed.). Thousand Oaks, CA: Sage.

Pawson, R., & Tilly, N. (1997). *Realistic evaluation.* London: Sage.

Phillips, D. C. (2005). *A guide for the perplexed: Scientific educational research, methodolatry, and the gold versus platinum standards.* Invited lecture at the University of Illinois at Urbana, Champaign, IL.

Power, M. (1997). *The audit society. Rituals of verification.* Oxford: Oxford University Press.

Rogers, P. J. (2008). Using programme theory to evaluate complicated and complex aspects of interventions. *Evaluation, 14*(1), 29–48.

Rogers, P. J., Hacsi, T. A., Petrosino, A., & Huebner, T. A. (Eds.). (2000). Program theory in evaluation: Challenges and opportunities. *New Directions for Evaluation 87.* San Francisco, CA: Jossey-Bass.

Savedoff, W. D., & Levine, R. (2006, May). *Learning from development: The case for an international council to catalyze independent impact evaluations of social sector interventions* (Policy Brief). Washington, DC: Center for Global Development.

Savedoff, W. D., Levine, R., & Birdsall, N. (2006, May). *When will we ever learn? Improving lives through impact evaluation* (Report of the Evaluation Gap Working Group). Washington, DC: Center for Global Development.

Schwandt, T. A. (2002). *Evaluation practice reconsidered.* New York: Peter Lang.

Scriven, M. (1993). Hard-won lessons in program evaluation. *New Directions for Evaluation 58.* San Francisco, CA: Jossey-Bass.

Stake, R. E. (2004a). How far dare an evaluator go toward saving the world? *American Journal of Evaluation, 25*(1), 103–107.

Stake, R. E. (2004b). *Standards-based and responsive evaluation.* Thousand Oaks, CA: Sage.

Torres, R. T., Preskill, H., & Piontek, M. E. (2004). *Evaluation strategies for communicating and reporting: Enhancing learning in organizations.* Thousand Oaks, CA: Sage.

Van der Knaap, P. (2006). Responsive evaluation and performance management: Overcoming the downsides of policy objectives and performance indicators. *Evaluation, 12*(3), 278–293.

Weiss, C. H. (1998). *Evaluation* (2nd ed.). Upper Saddle River, NJ: Prentice-Hall.

Whitmore, E. (Ed.). (1998). Understanding and practicing participatory evaluation. *New Directions for Evaluation 80.* San Francisco, CA: Jossey-Bass.

CHAPTER 19

Case Study Methods in Educational Evaluation

Linda Mabry

In 1989, Phi Delta Kappa (PDK) commissioned a national study (Frymier & Gansneder, 1989) to identify and evaluate the relative significance of factors correlating with student academic failure. At each of 100 sites, researchers collected and analyzed quantitative data of about a dozen types and conducted a case study of one at-risk student at an assigned grade level. PDK planned to use the quantitative data to categorize risk factors, prioritize them according to the seriousness of their impact on student achievement and persistence in school, and report which combination of factors put students "at risk." The effort promised to support education policy designed to spur academic success. However, the qualitative case studies convinced PDK that each student and his or her conditions and contexts were unique and inaggregable into a predictive model. Instead of policy recommendations, a selection of the case studies was published as a book (Strother, 1991), a demonstration of the power of case studies for developing the understanding preliminary to the improvement of public policy.

As evaluation responds to the demands of globalization, a consequent trans- and international scope may similarly benefit from detailed studies of particular cases and their contexts. There may be even greater need for case study as researchers and evaluators cross national borders and encounter increased variation in language, historical, political, religious, and sociocultural contexts. Multiple settings embedded in even more numerous contexts expand the array of influences on a program and the details that need to be understood if a program is to be evaluated well.

Mirroring the gradual recognition and use of evaluation to improve national and international policy, the credibility of case study as an approach to educational evaluation has waxed and waned over time, its acceptability rising and falling as understandings of evaluation methods generally have also evolved. Case study's methods and rationale have become better known, as has recognition of its limits and those of alternative approaches. Like good public policy, good evaluation requires strategic adaptation, and successful use of case studies as evaluations and as components of a variety of different types of evaluation designs suggests its flexibility. In discussing the role of case studies as evaluations and as components of evaluations, this chapter explores the benefits and challenges to case studies in evaluation for the purpose of policy development and refinement, including current controversy among evaluators and policymakers about its utility. Discussion includes the uses of case study in educational evaluation and this approach's epistemology, focus, methods, and issues.

What Works in Education: How Case Study Works in Educational Evaluation

From the initiatives of the 1960s, which spawned the professionalization of evaluation in education in the United States, to the *What Works Clearinghouse* of today (http://ies.ed.gov/ncee/wwc), evaluators have undertaken studies of the effectiveness of initiatives large and small intended to improve the policies, outcomes, processes, and conditions regarding public schooling. Some of these evaluations have been—or have involved—case studies that provided details about specific programs, about contexts and circumstances at different implementation sites which shape procedures and effects, and about competing interests and values which impact whether programs are considered effective or successful. Case study as an approach to inquiry is uniquely capable of providing such information for studies at many levels from small, single-site programs to large, multinational ones.

In a sense, every evaluation can be considered a case study in which the evaluand is the case (Mabry, 1998). *Bounding the Case* (Smith, 1978) delineates the scope of the case study, the focal points, the figure and ground, establishing the entry points that will lead to understandings of whether a program (or a site of program implementation or a policy) should be understood as

successful given its opportunity for success and the possibilities supported or obstructed by an interconnected complex of local players, infrastructure, expectations, and ideologies. The mission of the case study researcher or evaluator is to understand and portray the case so that readers and stakeholders can also understand it.

Contributions of Case Study to the Field of Evaluation

Failure to appreciate the contributions that case studies offer is to deny certain kinds of information and understanding to stakeholders and policymakers. Because different methodologies provide different advantages, the rejection of one or another represents a loss of opportunity to understand fully (American Evaluation Association, 2004). Yet today, as in the past, the particularity of the scope of case studies for policymaking and evaluation is at issue: Can enough be learned to justify study of individual cases, or should funding be reserved for studies designed to provide case-to-population generalizations (American Evaluation Association, 2004; U.S. Department of Education, 2005)? Case studies typically yield *petite generalizations* (Erickson, 1986) that hold within the case and empower readers to perform case-to-case generalizations or analytic generalizations (Firestone, 1993) in which:

> The aim is to draw large conclusions from small, but very densely textured facts; to support broad assertions about the role of culture in the construction of collective life by engaging them exactly with complex specifics. (Geertz, 1973, p. 28)

Case studies function well as stand-alone evaluations of either single or multiple sites. For example, as components of evaluation, they have focused on how identified program aspects are implemented at different sites and how outcomes are affected by local contingencies. The scope implies different levels of opportunity for generalizing. Recent efforts have demonstrated the capacity of case study for the development of expansive generalizations (Yin & Davis, 2007). More often, case studies contribute to such grand generalizations. They can illustrate outcomes common across cases and sites as well as outliers and the reasons that they are unusual, providing information for policy refinement by making patterns of the so-called "noise" unexplained in other approaches to inquiry.

Moreover, because human beings learn from experience, may even learn best from experience, the experientiality of most case study reports provides a distinct advantage for the generalizations that may be made by evaluation audiences as they improve their efforts, including policymaking efforts.

Epistemology of Case Study: Pluralism, Indeterminacy, and Flexibility

If the [evaluator] were to read more widely in history, ethnology, and the centuries of humanistic writings on man and society, he would be better prepared. (Cronbach, 1975, p. 125)

With his increasing interest in the methods of history, ethnography, and journalism, Cronbach highlighted the importance of particularistic inquiry into complex social phenomena (see also Shadish, Cook, & Leviton, 1991). To understand his meaning is to grasp that a program's quality is not sufficiently indicated by its goals, procedures, budgets, or countable outcomes; to recognize that a program does not meaningfully exist outside the experiences of stakeholders and the meanings they give to their experiences. Stakeholder behaviors are manifestations of those meanings and result in program adjustments, contributing to the dynamic nature of programs and a view of programs as ongoing co-creations of stakeholders. Case studies in

educational evaluation are founded on an epistemology that embraces the ambiguities and complexities of social phenomena, rather than attempting to reduce variation and confusions. Still, useful efforts to clarify ambiguities and complexities, rather than preserving them as black boxes within which inappropriate behaviors can lurk, serve an important educative function for policymakers and other stakeholders.

Tacit Knowledge and Deep Understanding

The history of science demonstrates the malleability of knowledge, the shifts in human understanding of even the most tangible aspects of the world. The knowledge possessed by the oracle at Delphi gave way to that possessed by Copernicus, which gave way to Newton, which gave way to Einstein, with no end in sight. However comforting certainty and bottom lines may be, indeterminacy may better describe reality—the fallibility of our collective understanding of reality compounded by the idiosyncrasies of personal perspectives.

Since before the Inquisition threatened to burn Galileo at the stake for knowledge that disconfirmed the Church's view of the world, mankind has lived with dueling ontologies and epistemologies, contrasting views of reality and truth in which each step forward represented—to some—a step backward. Aristotle's advance beyond mythology to empirical science served as a foundation for Déscartes and the Enlightenment, a foundation built on quicksand, postmodernists might say. Controversy rages today in physicists' disagreements as to whether string theory is science or philosophy and in contemporary evaluators' arguments about whether natural or hard or quantitative science is *incommensurable* (Lincoln & Guba, 1985) with social or soft or qualitative science.

Case study methodology corresponds to a theory of knowledge, *constructivism*, which holds that human beings construct their own individual knowledge bases from their perceptions and experiences (Piaget, 1955), including their social interactions (Vygotsky, 1978). Case study also corresponds to theories that human action is based less on received knowledge and more on personal *experience* (Dewey, 1916), less on formal *explanation* and more on personal *understanding* (von Wright, 1971), and less on *propositional* or articulable knowledge and more on *tacit* or inarticulable knowledge (Polanyi, 1958). Accordingly, people develop and respond to their own personal, often subconscious, understandings as they participate in programs and as they read evaluation reports. Case studies offer contextualized details and vicarious experiences that contribute to tacit personal understanding.

Phenomenology and Postmodernism

The place of personal understanding in philosophy is less challenged than it is in science, including the applied social science of evaluation. Philosophy is less threatened than science by claims that truth is plastic and individualistic. With only conceptual turf at stake, philosophers can disagree about which (if any) conceptions of the world are real or delusional (Hegel, 1807/ 1977) or are language games (Wittgenstein, 1953), whether there is a crisis of legitimation (Habermas, 1975) in which knowledge fails to rise above speculation (Lyotard, 1984), whether signs constitute reality (Saussure, ca. 1913/ 2006), whether mass reproduction has eclipsed reality (Baudrillard, 1983), or whether knowledge is a means of all-too-real social subjugation (Foucault, 1980).

What price knowledge! It took six centuries of human history, until the Greek Animaxander's deductive reasoning from axioms, for science to begin to prick the balloon of mythology. It took two more for Aristotelian empiricism and causality, distant causes of the imprisonment of Galileo fifteen centuries later. And for what? Aristotle's teacher, Plato, considered knowledge an interaction between perceiver and perceived, whereas Aristotle's

contemporary, Pyrrho, considered doubt itself central. In the sixth century, Boethius (524/1999) was still questioning "whether things actually exist or are found only in the mind," somewhat less famously than René Déscartes' (1644/1984–1991) later pronouncement, "Cogito ergo sum."

A positivist sociology developed from Compte's (1851–1854) "positive method" of analyzing the connections among observable facts and, as promoted by the Vienna Circle of the nineteenth century, verifying them. Nietzsche (1879/1996) was unconvinced: "Truth, like morality, is a relative affair. There are no facts, only interpretations." If that's true, what's the point? Poststructuralists and postmodernists, seeing that science could be manipulated for political gain, figured the point was power. Where reality, truth, facts, and even the meanings of words are indeterminate, it is hard to know whether it is all about the facts, as the empiricists, rationalists, and positivists claim; all about language and sign systems, as the structuralists and semiologists claim; or all about the exploitation of knowledge for power, as the critical theorists or radicals, poststructuralists, and postmodernists claim.

These claims and counterclaims echo in evaluation from proponents of stakeholder-oriented, objectives-oriented, and ideological approaches and from quantitative and qualitative practitioners, including phenomenologists as most case study practitioners are. From Kant's (1781/1996) distinction between *phenomena* or appearance and *nuomena* or reality, phenomenology evolved from a descriptive philosophy of experience into a sociology focused on the perceptions and meanings of the people directly involved in the experience (Dilthey, 1883/1976). Case study researchers seek insiders' perceptions, experiences, and meanings as essential to understanding cases.

Of course, as constructivists, case study researchers realize that each insider's perceptions, experiences, and meanings are unique, but also that patterns of commonality will emerge from the layers of detail in a dataset. The variations and uncertainties about meaning in the complex mass will promote a sense of disequilibrium

(Piaget, 1955), which will spur efforts to dig deeply, to watch carefully, to listen keenly—to understand.

Narratives to Convey Complexity

The understanding achieved by a case study practitioner is usually documented and transmitted narratively. From ancient sagas to current events—from Homerian epics to the rise of the Islamic republic in the Iran that has replaced Troy, from Pocahontas to Native Americans' fight for treaty rights, from Cuchulainn to the Troubles in Northern Ireland, from *Uncle Tom's Cabin* to affirmative action—narratives have conveyed deep, complex meanings to people. Narrative reporting in case studies builds on this time-tested manner of conveying meaning.

The capacity of narratives to convey complex interpretations along with the details that warrant them has been argued (Carter, 1993) and demonstrated. Narrative has been described as a way of thinking (Lyotard, 1984), suggesting the analytic process of both creating and comprehending a well-crafted text that

> locat[es] cultural interpretations in many sorts of reciprocal contexts and . . . oblig[es] writers to find diverse ways of rendering negotiated realities as multisubjective, power-laden, and incongruent. (Clifford, 1986, p. 15)

As many dots are connected, the reader's understanding and the capacity to use narratives to improve programs grow. One peril remains: If storytellers' knowledge is individually constructed, their truth a matter of perspective, attempting accurate and comprehensive representations is a daunting challenge.

The difficulty is magnified by understanding that meaning is negotiated between author and reader. Readers sometimes read between the lines and form their own conclusions, not always grasping authors' intended messages. Readers may also reject authors' meanings in favor of their own. They may deconstruct the text to discover and perhaps reject the authors' agenda or values (Derrida, 1976), as they would be well advised to do with evaluation reports that heap unearned accolades on programs, as in pseudoevaluations (House, 1993), but not with valid reports that merely fail to confirm their own cherished beliefs. Because validity and credibility do not always go hand in hand, representations of and findings about programs may be either inappropriately believed or disbelieved.

Inevitably, even when some stakeholders feel their experiences have been validated, others will feel misrepresented. Yet attempts at negotiated representations that preserve unresolved ambiguity can confuse and irritate those desirous of clear external judgments and specific recommendations (e.g., Abma, 1997). Moreover, because case study narratives are outsiders' portrayals of insiders' perspectives, textually constructing and conveying the reality of others can invite challenges to the evaluator's authority or to the report as a meta-narrative power tool (Derrida, 1976; Foucault, 1979; Lyotard, 1984). Not limited to evaluative case studies, these difficulties are faced by every author.

Focus in Case Study: The Eyes/Is Have It

The success of a narrative representation depends, in part, on the focus of a case study. After an initial focus is determined during the commissioning of an evaluative case study, the focus should continuously be refined during its conduct (Cronbach, 1982). What is seen by the evaluator, and what is seen by stakeholders and reported to the evaluator, is filtered for the reader's eyes—and by the reader's eyes—by background knowledge, values, and personal experience.

Multiple Perspectives in the Understanding of Complex Phenomena

In phenomenological case study, a program, project, or policy implementation is not considered to exist meaningfully outside the experiences of the stakeholders who shape it. Their many perspectives ensure that the meaning of program success will vary. Although educational program officers, for example, may consider success to depend on higher test scores or increased enrollment in advanced classes, teachers may reckon success on the basis of sufficiency of resources and parents on their children's enthusiasm for school. Case studies attempt to capture the variety and analyze the distinctiveness of stakeholders' multiple perspectives, whose different views of what constitutes good education naturally result in different criteria for judging the success of outcomes.

Understanding multiple perspectives calls for analysis of the content of what stakeholders say, write, and do—data that are often fuzzy and messy, rarely countable. Persistence and tolerance of ambiguity are needed, as is capacity to form preliminary interpretations while suspending final judgments. The goal is holistic understanding, not the effects of isolated factors—there are too many to identify, and they are too interdependent to meaningfully isolate.

Local Contexts in the Global Landscape

Contextualized accounts of complex phenomena that offer vicarious experience can enhance understanding and enrich the background knowledge that shapes each reader's capacity to make the personalized generalizations that ultimately matter: those that inform current and future policy and practice

(Cronbach, 1982; Firestone, 1993). Contexts are complex, interwoven, dynamic. From an ecological perspective (Bronfenbrenner, 1979), at the macrosystem level, policy aims may congrue or conflict with local values; at the exosystem level, procedural requirements may confirm or clash with local traditions; at the mesosystem level, relationships among those involved with program implementation may be trusting or antagonistic— all of which may affect stakeholder experiences at the microsystem level. Case study methods recognize the shaping effects of many types of contexts—political, sociocultural, organizational, and ideational—and direct attention to understanding their interdependency and effects on programs and outcomes.

Case studies illustrate program contexts and effects, but the differences among potential contexts deny generalizability as traditionally construed (see Campbell & Stanley, 1963). Attention to context promotes understanding of why things work as they do but problematizes the context-free generalizations often demanded by policymakers in a global society. In education, demands for case-to-population generalizations correlate with policies increasingly dedicated to large-scale systematization and standardization. Still, the gradual development of young minds remains a delicate, unique, and individual enterprise more like—and better revealed by—case study. That case study is also well suited to capture the nuances of policy effects on educational practice may be illustrated with a vignette from a case study of the implementation and impact of the 2002 No Child Left Behind federal education policy in the United States (Mabry & Margolis, 2006):

March 21, 2005: A third-grade classroom in the U.S. After lunch, the students sat in a circle on the floor around the teacher who passed a token about the size of a flattened softball to the first child who volunteered to show-and-tell. The boy told of a family building project: "Well, my barn should be done, um, April first or, if it isn't, my mom isn't going to hire him for any more jobs, and he won't get as much money." The teacher took this opportunity to explain why it was important to learn to turn in schoolwork on time.

She passed the token to another boy who told of an infraction on the playground and its consequences: "I jumped off the swing, and the monitor spotted me, so I'm off of it for a month. And I'm writing a story about it called 'The Worst Recess in the History of Me.' And I'm never, ever, ever, ever, ever going to jump off the swing again," he said, increasingly stressing the word *ever*.

"Why not?" the teacher followed up.

"'Cuz you could hurt yourself and have to go to the hospital," he said, unabashed. "And it was kind of stupid of me."

The teacher smiled, "I like that honesty about you."

The next child announced, "I'm going to be really sad not to be here in April because I'm still going to have to take the [state test]." Actually, the test would not be administered to him until he was in the fourth grade, the following year.

His reference to the state test animated a classmate. "Oh!" she interrupted excitedly. "It's a really, big, big, big test! Last year, at my other school, people even had to take it in third grade." A small hubbub of chatter erupted. "It's like the biggest test of the year!" she went on emphatically.

"Big meaning *important* or big meaning *long*?" the teacher asked.

"It's important *and* it's long!" she reported. "It takes like two weeks or three weeks to finish it—I don't remember how long, but it takes more than one week." She paused, dropping her hands in her lap as if she were seeking a way to explain the magnitude and gravity of the test. "I mean, *everybody* in my class was scared of the test! And everybody didn't want to move up to the next grade where they'd have to take it!"

"My brother had to take it a bunch of times," a boy said. "His brain is rotted." The teacher seemed doubtful that the state test had caused cognitive malfunction.

"My sister had to take it three or four times already," another said in a somber tone.

"And did she survive?" the teacher asked hopefully. The boy nodded, shrugging and looking at his feet.

This vignette, along with others, reveals the microlevel effects (Bronfenbrenner, 1979) of state and federal educational policy by presenting data from classrooms. In response, policymakers might discontinue initiatives that have the effect of frightening and demoralizing young children, or they might deem such effects unfortunate but acceptable. That is, the detailed on-the-ground information provided by qualitative case study may enable policymakers to understand and improve their mandates.

But experiential detail may not satisfy policymakers. Many programs are intended as models to be replicated, if successful, in other contexts.

Such pilot programs' outcomes may suffer if personnel work harder toward replicability in potential future contexts than toward adaptation to their actual contexts (DeStefano, 1992). Evaluative case studies, too, may be undermined by attempts to develop context-independent findings. Still, the transferability of a program or its aspects, modified for different circumstances, may sometimes be intuitively obvious. *Analytic generalizations* (Firestone, 1993) by evaluators may find their way into reports, and intuitive generalizations by readers may support educational improvements beyond the immediate program.

Methods of Case Study: Not Just What Works But Why

From its modern emergence in the 1960s, educational evaluation has been focused on the effectiveness of policies, programs, and practices for helping children and adults learn. From their initial dependence on indicators, evaluators became aware of needs to understand how well indicators actually indicated educational quality and how outcomes were affected by a variety of circumstances (Cronbach, 1982; Madaus, Scriven, & Stufflebeam, 1987). Educational programs do not exist in descriptions or flowcharts, nor are their outcomes fully captured by such indicators as test scores and retention and graduation rates. Firsthand observation and verification of what is achieved and how are needed. This awareness moved educational evaluation toward qualitative case study but not without recurring controversy.

Discovery of Things Hidden in Plain Sight: Emergent and Heuristic Approaches

Why should national or international managers hire outsiders to tell them about programs they themselves know intimately? Personal knowledge of a program (or other type of evaluand) both focuses and screens attention, helpful in some ways and obstructive in others. Often understanding may be gained by *making the familiar strange* (Clifford, 1986; Erickson, 1986), strange enough to bring overlooked aspects to attention. Outsiders can contribute their fresh eyes and their lack of investment in a program, negotiating a place for both internally and externally identified issues.

Understanding the actual complexity of social and educational programs requires *in situ* investigation. Time on-site helps evaluators recognize the importance not only of policymakers' issues but also other program aspects and the perspectives and experiences of nonmanagerial stakeholders. Contact with program personnel

and beneficiaries gives entrée to the experiences and perceptions of those who co-create it and to their criteria for and judgments of its quality. To apprehend multiple perspectives, evaluative case studies more commonly employ qualitative or mixed methods studies than quantitative methods alone.

Ethnographers insist on sustained engagement and the development of *thick description* (Geertz, 1973), often a reflexive cultural analysis of perspectives and events (Clifford, 1986). However, except for internal evaluations and self-studies, few evaluations luxuriate in resources sufficient for such long-term fieldwork. The ethnographer's gradual development of themes and cultural categories from extensive observational and interview data becomes, for qualitative evaluators, compressed by the contract period. Consequently, special care is needed in the selection of occasions for observation and in the selection of interviewees, complemented by alertness to unanticipated opportunities to learn.

Evidence and Analysis in Qualitative and Mixed Methods

An evaluation case study need not (or not exclusively) be qualitative in approach, but many case studies employ the hallmark methods of qualitative data collection—observation, interview, and documents analysis. In mixed methods designs, these methods are often combined with survey instruments, pre- and posttests, and reference to such preexisting quantitative data as, in education, enrollment and attendance figures, retention and dropout rates, grades and standardized test scores, numbers of students eligible for special services or free and reduced-cost meals, educational attainment of teachers, per-pupil expenditures, and other budgetary information. In the *constant comparative* manner described by Glaser and Strauss (1967; see also Strauss & Corbin, 1990, 1994), data yield preliminary interpretations, which, in turn, focus further data collection.

Each source and data-collection technique offers opportunity to confirm and disconfirm data, helping to ensure the accuracy of the dataset through *triangulation*. Qualitative data such as observation narratives and interview transcriptions may be presented to selected stakeholders (Lincoln & Guba, 1985) or to each respective stakeholder (Mabry, 2003) for *validation*. Findings also may be validated by stakeholders as preliminary interpretations (Stronach & Maclure, 1996) or drafts of reports, and they may be subjected to the scrutiny of internal review by evaluation team members and external review by peers or advisory boards. The rigor of these levels of validation and review helps ensure accuracy and comprehensiveness and helps minimize bias.

Holistic analysis, interpretive and situational, avoids decomposition of the program into aspects not separable in practice. Data organized around the questions and issues guiding inquiry are studied for themes, which are refined in repeated, and increasingly detailed, searches for trends and relationships in the dataset. Consistencies and inconsistencies, patterns and correlations, are thus grounded in data. Findings in a case report are supported by accompanying data, such as vignettes of observed events and excerpts from interviews, offering a nuanced representation of a program from multiple lines of sight. As with any conclusions, interpretive findings in case studies are based not only on data but also on the judgment of the investigator, underscoring the importance of triangulation and validation.

Challenges, Tensions, and Issues

About three additional challenges to evaluative case studies, more should be said: (a) the difficulty of generalizing case study findings beyond the case; (b) methodological preferences, especially those among education policymakers in the United States at present, against qualitative case

study; and (c) the problem of truth and credibility in a postmodern global society marked by extreme differences in experiences and perspectives.

Generalizing From Cases

The context of a case limits the degree to which findings can be readily generalized to all cases of the same type. Case studies reveal what works where, when, why, and according to whom for the sites studied. Whether and how findings from a site or set of sites are useful in other instances, other places, and other times are debatable and debated. The challenge is exacerbated in a global society, where contexts vary dramatically in kind and degree. How well an elementary science instructional program can succeed in the United States may depend on whether the local community favors evolution or theistic "intelligent design" as an explanation for genetic variety. On a global scale, the success of such a program also may depend on the availability of teaching materials and facilities, on whether girls can be spared from the domestic economies of impoverished families, on the distance between schools and students. The difficulty of generalizing whether the science program would be beneficial in such a variety of settings shows the constraints on all generalizations when the scale is global.

Most case study evaluators are careful to state findings in a situation-specific manner—to say what they have learned about a particular case without explicitly implying broader applicability, to make *petite generalizations* (Erickson, 1986), and to avoid grand or case-to-population generalizations. But often what they learn about a case seems readily applicable or adaptable for understanding other cases, or for expanding programs for wider implementation, on an "if this, try that" basis. This type of *analytic generalization* may be offered by evaluators or made as *case-to-case generalizations* by readers (Maxwell, 1992).

Recent developments show that case studies may be planned for the purpose of generalization

(Yin & Davis, 2007). Other adaptations also move in the direction of growing generalizability. For example, the *success case study method* involves identifying a small number of exemplary elements within an evaluand (e.g., implementation sites, personnel units, training strategies) and studying them as "success cases" that might be emulated for greater success overall (Brinkerhoff, 2003). In the *most significant change technique*, designated groups of stakeholders discuss what they consider significant program, project, or policy outcomes, and then they deliberate next steps (Dart & Davies, 2003), which might include scaling up.

Methodological Preferences

Positive and positivistic attempts to harness science for policy purposes have recurred across the globe, in the West moving from Aristotle, a Greek, in the third century BCE; to Auguste Compte, a Frenchman, a century and a half ago; to current federal education policymakers in the United States. Meanwhile, most of science, most of research, most of evaluation—even among those whose professional commitments tend toward experimental design (e.g., Lipsey, 2007)—have developed more expansive views of methodology. Especially qualitative social scientists and educational evaluators have developed better appreciation of nonisolable and nonmeasureable factors and their sometimes subtle, sometimes formidable, and often deeply embedded effects on the dynamic and interwoven parts of programs. But greater appreciation of qualitative, interpretivist, or ethnographic methods, always uneven, has proved unstable as well. Issues from the so-called *paradigm wars* in educational research and evaluation (Julnes & Rog, 2007; Rossi, 1994), repeatedly declared over or moot (e.g., Howe, 1992), have sparked new skirmishes in national and global policies.

Policymakers and other clients often hold limited or outdated views of the array of approaches developed in social science, unaware of limitations of relatively familiar methods or of the possibilities offered by unfamiliar and mixed methods. Their views may be lay echoes of the derision of case studies, famously described in the 1960s as having "such a total absence of control as to be of almost no scientific value" (Campbell & Stanley, 1963, p. 6). In such situations, "client education" may be needed for evaluators to meet professional expectations regarding accuracy and comprehensiveness (American Evaluation Association, 2004; Joint Committee, 1994).

The difficulty and its attendant dangers are illustrated by an example. Educational evaluations commissioned by the World Bank have traditionally focused on countable indicators and preferred experimental and quasi-experimental designs involving experimental groups (i.e., program beneficiaries) and control groups (i.e., persons similar to them but not receiving benefits; Jones, 1992; Psacharopoulos & Woodhall, 1991). Defining, isolating, measuring, and aggregating indicators—such as per-pupil costs or numbers of stakeholders served—commonly leads to the neglect of the context-bound interdependence of program aspects:

> Focus on quantitative growth can overshadow improvements in educational quality and . . . student learning outcomes. . . . More, better, and more contextualized analytic work is needed. (World Bank Independent Evaluation Group, 2006, p. 26)

Unfortunate policy outcomes have resulted, including, in education, increased "subsidization of private schools" at the expense of public education (Jones, 1992). Nevertheless, funding preference for quantitative designs has become U.S. government policy for education research funding (U.S. Department of Education, 2002) and for educational evaluation funding (U.S. Department of Education, 2005). Protests by many researchers (e.g., Maxwell, 2004) and evaluators (American Evaluation Association, 2004) argued the usefulness of qualitative approaches such as case study, for example:

Unless considerable proportions of a research budget, even in a large-scale formal experiment, are devoted to documenting the treatment as delivered on the ground, the causal inferences drawn from inspection of outcome data will remain unwarranted, and they are likely to be partially misleading half truths. (Erickson & Gutierrez, 2002, p. 21)

Incomplete or distorted evaluation results can undermine policy decisions. Further, when policymakers are unwilling to be educated by professionals, the evaluation profession may suffer from methodological setbacks or stagnation (Mabry, 2008b).

Truth and Credibility in a Postmodern Global Society

Although arguably no greater a challenge in qualitative than in quantitative methods, the obviousness of the role of human judgment in qualitative case study makes clear the possibilities for subjective error. Although subjectivity can never be totally eliminated, case study practitioners strive for

a delicate balance of subjectivity and objectivity . . . [in which] personal experiences, especially those of participation and empathy, are recognized as central to the research process, but they are firmly restrained by the impersonal standards of observation and "objective" distance. (Clifford, 1986, p. 13)

Qualitative methodology is founded on the presumption that subjectivity is ubiquitous and can be productively disciplined (Peshkin, 1988). Each person's—and each case study practitioner's—subjective mind is formed within a highly deterministic cultural context (Vygotsky, 1978) that profoundly affects what that person wonders, notices, accepts as evidence, and concludes.

Trans- and cross-cultural investigators not only *study* but also *bring* a widened array of perceptual and interpretive lenses, each offering a particular take on truth. The more different the cultures from which these takes arise, the more extreme the differences in what investigators will see and interpret.

Subjectivity

The potential for error in any type of human understanding may be compounded by the phenomenological turn in case study. The effort to understand the perceptions and experiences of insiders presses toward the evaluation equivalent of "going native" for ethnographers. Evaluators at close quarters with program participants are sure to find themselves more interested in some folks than others, more in agreement with some than others, more likely to focus on some than others, and more careful to represent their interests. Those who most resemble the evaluator culturally have a natural advantage as their interests and opportunities are represented and interpreted in evaluation reports. In addition to implications for ethics, imbalances of attention presage inaccuracies and invalidities.

Maintaining balance is aided by triangulation—deliberate attempts to confirm, elaborate, and disconfirm facts and interpretations by reference to a variety of data sources. Accuracy can also be enhanced by the perceptions of different evaluators, by sustained engagement over time, and by analysis of data from different theoretical perspectives (see, e.g., Denzin, 1989). These strategies of triangulation are not limited to either qualitative inquiry or case study but are among its important safeguards against undue subjectivity.

Validation is another way to protect the *trustworthiness* of data and findings. Member checking as a validation process involves review of data by representatives of the relevant categories of stakeholders (Lincoln & Guba, 1985), each perspective helping to balance the others and all helping to balance that of the evaluator. A more comprehensive validation process involves providing each interviewee the opportunity to review his or her data before analysis and then a similar review of findings prior to reporting (Mabry, 1998, 2008a).

These safeguards, along with review by evaluation peers and advisory boards, protect validity but cannot guarantee it. Fed by awareness of the subjectivity of data sources and data collectors practicing subjective interpretation, concerns about potential error based on judgment-intense case studies persist. Policymakers find it easier to dismiss qualitative data as emanating from a misguided point of view than to deny quantitative "hard data." With globalization, they may also find it easy to dismiss case studies by outsiders as insensitive, straining but failing to reach accuracy regarding cultural subtleties, missing the difference between "our truth" and "your truth."

Validity

Triangulation and validation of data address issues of *descriptive validity*, whereas validation of findings addresses *interpretive* and *evaluative validity* (Maxwell, 1992). Validity is not absolute, and it cannot be absolutely known; rather, arguments that something is more or less valid can be made (Messick, 1989). It has been argued that truth—including the truth about a policy and its effects—can also not be absolutely known, but that arguments about the quality and value of what has been achieved are needed (Cronbach, 1982).

The convergence of constructivist theorists' position that people create individual knowledge bases, with phenomenologists' focus on the perceptions and experiences of individuals, with philosophers' doubts about the existence or verifiability of an objective reality, and with the history of scientific revolutions and paradigm shifts (Kuhn, 1962), all suggest the malleability, the idiosyncrasy of truth. Truth may be more struggle than achievement. Nevertheless, because clients do not hire evaluators to debate the nature of truth, most evaluators follow the advice of Pascal (1670/1995)—substituting *truth* or *objective reality* for *God*:

We are then incapable of knowing either what [God] is or if He is . . . [so] you must wager. . . . [I]n wagering that God is. . . . [i]f you gain, you gain all; if you lose, you lose nothing. Wager then without hesitation that He is.

Practitioners of interpretivist evaluation approaches, such as qualitative case study, are thus advised to bet their professional efforts that the truth about the quality and outcomes of a program or policy can be known—at least known well enough that findings can make a contribution to future policymaking. Placing this modernist bet, in effect, by conducting an evaluative case study is an effort to work within epistemological constraints to achieve as much validity as possible, rather than a postmodern denial of the subjectivity of truth.

Many truths, a number increasing exponentially with globalization and all of them contestable, might be told to represent a given policy context. What can be known is "situated *between* powerful systems of meaning" (Clifford, 1986, p. 2; italics original) as well as within them, rendering such "truths . . . inherently *partial*" (p. 7; italics original). Still, for the needy who might benefit from judicious policy decisions, mere speculation about the nature of truth and reality is superfluous, even irresponsible. An effort to discover as much truth as possible is needed.

Credibility

Acknowledgment of subjectivity and the elusiveness of validity and generalizability may be reasonable within the evaluation community but disastrous with clients. For evaluation findings to support policymaking, evaluators must strive not only for validity but also for *catalytic validity* (Lather, 1993). For the evaluation to catalyze change, policymakers must be persuaded of their validity—they must take the findings as credible. Although validity and credibility are associated and are pursued in similar ways methodologically, they are distinct. Just as minorities may be right but outvoted, substantially valid findings may be unpersuasive to clients. In contrast, case studies that misrepresent cases may be readily accepted, especially those with unjustifiably positive findings. In multinational situations, culturally appealing reports—reports that offer culturally appropriate language and tone, reports that are historically and ideologically situated or respectful—may similarly gain acceptance even over more accurate but tone-deaf ones.

Although no data and no findings can be beyond challenge, warranting findings with a thorough evidentiary base offers support. Comprehensive, detailed, and microanalyzed data are a specialty of case study with its commitment to multiple views of reality. The phenomenological disposition to try to understand the lived experiences and perspectives of those connected to a program pushes case study toward understanding and documenting multiple realities of events and other social phenomena. Layers of warranting, drawn from different ways of seeing things, help improve understanding of what works in education, for whom, and why.

More than simple judgments of program merit or recommendations, case studies provide rich datasets, fulsome backdrops for informed decision making. The complexities of such datasets and of different cultural contexts and perspectives complicate, rather than ease, understanding and decision making. Although evaluation clients, like everyone, prefer unambiguous findings and directions, the need to think through complex realities provides better opportunities to dovetail policy with situational specifics. In the thinking through, as in the conduct of the evaluation, contrasting interpretations and plans are an inevitable consequence of diverse ways of knowing. Dissensus, not consensus, is to be expected, and ways of reaching working agreement are needed if programs and policies are to be refined. What constitutes sufficient working agreement to move forward—and how best to attempt to reach such agreement—will vary by cultural or multicultural context.

Whether findings can be accepted as credible is complicated by the extreme differences among far-flung stakeholders and their diverse contexts and experiences. The narrative style traditionally used for reporting qualitative studies can prove helpful in such circumstances. Stories, early and continuing to the present, are found in all cultures, and many tales are appreciated across cultures. It is a small leap from the recognition of human capacity to intuit knowledge from stories to an awareness of the analytic density of narratives (Carter, 1993). The vicarious experiences of readers of case studies, experiences based on vignettes of human activities, and excerpts from interview transcripts encourage deep understanding (Spiro, Vispoel, Schmitz, Samarapungavan, & Boerger, 1987). Widespread understanding supports both credibility and enlightened policymaking.

Conclusion

Case studies provide views from constituent elements—from implementation sites, from program aspects and personnel, from stakeholders. These views are often occluded in other types of evaluations, especially those concentrating on managerial issues, measurement of isolated factors, and standardized indicators. By attending to the experiences and perceptions of many, a democratic impulse is served by case studies and an understanding of the case is promoted—an understanding that supports policymaking. Thus, case studies promote access to ground-level policy processes and outcomes for policymakers *and* access to the policymaking process (at least vicariously) for stakeholders. As the democratic impulse expands in fits and starts globally, general comprehensibility of policies and their evaluations can deepen understanding, broaden participation, and improve the policymaking process and its results.

Every approach to evaluation has limitations and special merits. For example, the potential for the case study practitioner's subjectivity to threaten validity and credibility can be counteracted by triangulation and validation. Also, although case studies do not offer ready case-to-population transfer, they can be adapted for this purpose, and they can reveal the circumstances in which a policy succeeds or fails in attaining its objective, showing the way to strategic improvement.

Although no methodology can ensure enlightened policy, among evaluation approaches, case study is well positioned epistemologically and methodologically to contribute to policy development in a diverse global society. Practitioners of case study appreciate pluralism, contextuality, and indeterminacy, and they respond with flexibility and attention to polyvocality, detail, and nuance. In a global postmodern world of multifaceted truths and competing needs, detailed portrayal of what works, how, for whom, and under what conditions can greatly assist policy development. This is precisely the special benefit of case study—documentation of situation-specific details from the many perspectives of many stakeholders, layers of perceived realities that contribute to a holistic understanding of the experienced effects of programs and policies. As programs and policies expand to an international scale, case studies can help avoid heavy-handed insensitivities that obstruct success—real or perceived—in improving education.

References

Abma, T. (1997). Sharing power, facing ambiguity. In L. Mabry (Ed.), *Evaluation and the postmodern dilemma* (pp. 105–119). Greenwich, CT: JAI Press.

American Evaluation Association. (2004). *Guiding principles for evaluators*. Fairhaven, MA: Author. Retrieved July 5, 2006, from http://www.eval .org/Publications/GuidingPrinciples.asp.

American Evaluation Association. (2004, November 4). Response to U.S. Department of Education notice of proposed priority, "Scientifically Based Evaluation Methods" (*Federal Register* RIN 1890-ZA00). Available at http://www.eval.org/doepage.htm.

Baudrillard, J. (1983). *Simulations* (P. Foss, P. Patton, & J. Johnston, Trans). New York: Semiotest(e).

Boethius, A. M. S. (524/1999). *Consolatio philosophiae* [*Consolation of philosophy*] (V. Watts, Trans.). London: Penguin.

Brinkerhoff, R. O. (2003). *The success case method: Find out quickly what's working and what's not.* San Francisco, CA: Berrett-Koehler.

Bronfenbrenner, U. (1979). *The ecology of human development.* Cambridge, MA: Harvard University Press.

Campbell, D. T., & Stanley, J. C. (1963). *Experimental and quasi-experimental designs for research.* Boston: Houghton Mifflin.

Carter, K. (1993). The place of story in the study of teaching and teacher education. *Educational Researcher, 22*(1), 5–12, 18.

Clifford, J. (1986). Partial truths. In J. Clifford & G. E. Marcus (Eds.), *Writing culture: The poetics and politics of ethnography* (pp. 1–26). Berkeley, CA: University of California Press.

Compte, I. A. M. F. X. (1851–1854, ed. 1898/2002). *Système de politique positive* [*System of positive polity*] (J. H. Bridges, F. Harrison, E. S. Beesley, et al., Trans.). Paris: Thoemmes Continuum.

Cronbach, L. J. (1975). Beyond the two disciplines of scientific psychology. *American Psychologist,* pp. 116–127.

Cronbach, L. J. (1982). *Designing evaluations of educational and social programs.* San Francisco, CA: Jossey-Bass.

Dart, J., & Davies, R. (2003). A dialogical, story-based evaluation tool: The most significant change technique. *American Journal of Evaluation, 24*(2), 137–155.

Denzin, N. K. (1989). *The research act: A theoretical introduction to sociological methods* (3rd ed.). Englewood Cliffs, NJ: Prentice-Hall.

Derrida, J. (1976). *On grammatology* (G. Spivak, Trans.). Baltimore, MD: Johns Hopkins University Press.

Déscartes, R. (1644/1984-91). *Principia philosophiae* [*Principles of philosophy*]. In J. Cottingham, R. Stoothoff, D. Murdoch, & A. Kenny (Eds. and Trans.), *The philosophical writings of Déscartes* (Vol. 1). Cambridge: Cambridge University Press.

DeStefano, L. (1992). Evaluating effectiveness: A comparison of federal expectations and local capabilities for evaluation among federally funded model demonstration programs. *Educational Evaluation and Policy Analysis, 14*(2), 157–168.

Dewey, J. (1916). *Democracy and education: An introduction to the philosophy of education*. New York: Macmillan.

Dilthey, W. (1883/1976). *Einleitung in die Geisteswissenschaften* [*Introduction to the human sciences*]. In H. P. Richman (Ed.), *W. Dilthey: Selected writings* (pp. 157–263). London: Cambridge University Press.

Erickson, F. (1986). Qualitative methods in research on teaching. In M. C. Wittrock (Ed.), *Handbook of research on teaching* (3rd ed., pp. 119–161). New York: Macmillan.

Erickson, F., & Gutierrez, K. (2002). Culture, rigor, and science in educational research. *Educational Researcher, 31*(8), 21–24.

Firestone, W. A. (1993). Alternative arguments for generalizing from data as applied to qualitative research. *Educational Researcher, 22*(4), 16–23.

Foucault, M. (1977). What is an author? (D. F. Bouchard & S. Simon, Trans.). In D. F. Bouchard (Ed.), *Michel Foucault: Language, countermemory, practice: Selected essays and interviews* (pp. 113–138). Ithaca, NY: Cornell University Press.

Foucault, M. (1979, Spring). What is an author? *Screen, 20*(1), 13–34.

Foucault, M. (1980). *Power/knowledge*. Cambridge, MA: Harvard University Press.

Frymier, J., & Gansneder, B. (1989). The Phi Delta Kappa study of students at risk. *Phi Delta Kappan, 71*(2), 142–146.

Geertz, C. (1973). *The interpretation of cultures: Selected essays*. New York: Basic Books.

Glaser, B. G., & Strauss, A. I. (1967). *The discovery of grounded theory*. Chicago, IL: Aldine.

Habermas, J. (1975). *Legitimation crisis* (T. McCarthy, Trans.). Boston: Beacon Press.

Hegel, G. W. F. (1807/1977). *Phenomenology of spirit* (A. V. Miller, Trans.). Oxford: Oxford University Press.

House, E. R. (1993). *Professional evaluation: Social impact and political consequences*. Newbury Park, CA: Sage.

Howe, K. (1992). Getting over the quantitative-qualitative debate. *American Journal of Education, 100*(2), 236–256.

Joint Committee on Standards for Educational Evaluation. (1994). *The program evaluation standards: How to assess evaluations of educational programs* (2nd ed.). Thousand Oaks, CA: Sage.

Jones, P. W. (1992). *World Bank financing of education: Lending, learning and development*. London: Routledge.

Julnes, G., & Rog, D. (2007). Current federal policies and controversies over methodology in evaluation. In G. Julnes & D. Rog (Eds.), Informing federal policies on evaluation methodology: Building the evidence base for method choice in government sponsored evaluation. *New Directions for Evaluation, 113*, 1–12. San Francisco, CA: Jossey-Bass.

Kant, I. (1781/1996). *The critique of pure reason* (W. S. Pluhar & P. Kitcher, Trans.). Indianapolis, IN: Hackett.

Kuhn, T. (1962). *The structure of scientific revolutions*. Princeton, NJ: Princeton University Press.

Lather, P. (1993). Fertile obsession: Validity after poststructuralism. *Sociological Quarterly, 34*(4), 673–693.

Lincoln, Y. S., & Guba, E. G. (1985). *Naturalistic inquiry*. Newbury Park, CA: Sage.

Lipsey, M. (2007). Method choice for government evaluation: The beam in our own eye [commentary]. In G. Julnes & D. Rog (Eds.), Informing federal policies on evaluation methodology: Building the evidence base for method choice in government sponsored evaluation. *New Directions for Evaluation, 113*, 113–123. San Francisco, CA: Jossey-Bass.

Lyotard, J.-F. (1984). *The postmodern condition: A report on knowledge* (G. Bennington & B. Massumi, Trans.). Minneapolis: University of Minnesota Press. (Original work published 1979)

Mabry, L. (1998). Case study methods. In H. J. Walberg & A. J. Reynolds (Eds.), *Advances in educational productivity: Vol. 7. Evaluation research for educational productivity* (pp. 155–170). Greenwich, CT: JAI Press.

Mabry, L. (2003). In living color: Qualitative methods in educational evaluation. In T. Kellaghan & D. L. Stufflebeam (Eds.), *International handbook of educational evaluation* (pp. 167–185). Boston: Kluwer-Nijhoff.

Mabry, L. (2008a). Case study in social research. In P. Alasuutari, L. Bickman, & J. Brannen (Eds.), *Handbook of social research methods* (pp. 214–227). London: Sage.

Mabry, L. (2008b). Consequences of NCLB on evaluation purpose, design, and practice. In T. Berry & R. Eddy (Eds.), Consequences on NCLB on educational evaluation. *New Directions for Evaluation, 119,* 21–36. San Francisco, CA: Jossey-Bass.

Mabry, L., & Margolis, J. (2006). NCLB: Local implementation and impact in southwest Washington State. *Education Policy Analysis Archives, 14*(23).

Madaus, G. F., Scriven, M. S., & Stufflebeam, D. L. (Eds.). (1987). *Evaluation models: Viewpoints on educational and human services evaluation.* Boston: Kluwer-Nijhoff.

Maxwell, J. A. (1992). Understanding and validity in qualitative research. *Harvard Educational Review, 62*(3), 279–300.

Maxwell, J. A. (2004). Causal explanation, qualitative research, and scientific inquiry in education. *Educational Researcher, 33*(2), 3–11.

Messick, S. (1989). Validity. In R. L. Linn (Ed.), *Educational measurement* (3rd ed., pp. 13–103). New York: American Council on Education, Macmillan.

Nietzsche, F. (1879/1996). *Human, all too human* (R. J. Hollingdale, Trans.). Cambridge, MA: Cambridge University Press.

No Child Left Behind Act. (2002). Public Law No. 107-110. 107th Congress, 110 Congressional Record 1425, 115 Stat.

Pascal, B. (1670/1995). *Pensées* (A. J. Krailsheimer, Trans.). London: Penguin Classics.

Peshkin, A. (1988). In search of subjectivity–one's own. *Educational Researcher, 17*(7), 17–22.

Piaget, J. (1955). *The language and thought of the child.* New York: World.

Polanyi, M. (1958). *Personal knowledge: Towards a post-critical philosophy.* Chicago, IL: University of Chicago Press.

Psacharopoulos, G., & Woodhall, M. (1991). *Education for development: An analysis of investment choices.* New York: Oxford University Press.

Rossi, P. H. (1994). The war between the equals and the quants: Is a lasting peace possible? In C. S. Reichardt & S. F. Rallis (Eds.), The qualitative-quantitative debate: New perspectives. *New Directions for Program Evaluation, 61,* 23–36. San Francisco, CA: Jossey-Bass.

Saussure, F. (ca. 1913/2006). *Écrits de linguistique générale* [*Writings in general linguistics*] (S. Bouquet, R. Engler, C. Sanders, & M. Pires, Eds.). Oxford: Oxford University Press.

Shadish, W. R., Jr., Cook, T. D., & Leviton, L. C. (1991). *Foundations of program evaluation: Theories of practice.* Newbury Park, CA: Sage.

Smith, L. (1978). An evolving logic of participant observation, educational ethnography and other case studies. In L. Schulman (Ed.), *Review of research in education* (Vol. 6, pp. 316–377). Itasca, IL: Peacock.

Spiro, R. J., Vispoel, W. P., Schmitz, J. G., Samarapungavan, A., & Boerger, A. E. (1987). Knowledge acquisition for application: Cognitive flexibility and transfer in complex content domains. In B. C. Britton (Ed.), *Executive control processes* (pp. 177–199). Hillsdale, NJ: Lawrence Erlbaum Associates.

Strauss, A., & Corbin, J. (1990). *Basics of qualitative research: Grounded theory procedures and techniques.* Newbury Park, CA: Sage.

Strauss, A., & Corbin, J. (1994). Grounded theory methodology: An overview. In N. K. Denzin & Y. S. Lincoln (Eds.), *Handbook of qualitative research* (pp. 273–285). Thousand Oaks, CA: Sage.

Stronach, I., & Maclure, M. (1996). Mobilizing meaning, demobilizing critique? Dilemmas in the deconstruction of educational discourse. *Cultural Studies, 1,* 259–276.

Strother, D. B. (Ed.). (1991). *Learning to fail: Case studies of students at-risk.* Bloomington, IN: Phi Delta Kappa.

U.S. Department of Education. (2002, November 18). Report on scientifically based research supported by U.S. Department of Education [press release]. Retrieved March 14, 2008, from http://www.ed.gov/news/pressreleases/2002/11/1118 2002b.html.

U.S. Department of Education. (2005, January 25). Scientifically based evaluation methods (RIN 1890-ZA00). *Federal Register, 70*(15), 3586–3589.

von Wright, G. H. (1971). *Explanation and understanding.* London: Routledge & Kegan Paul.

Vygotsky, L. S. (1978). *Mind in society: The development of higher mental process.* Cambridge, MA: Harvard University Press.

Wittgenstein, L. (1953). *Philosophical investigations* (3rd ed.) (G. E. M. Anscombe, Trans.). Oxford: Blackwell.

World Bank Independent Evaluation Group. (2006). *From schooling access to learning outcomes: An unfinished agenda; evaluation of World Bank support to primary education.* Washington, DC: Author.

Yin, R. K., & Davis, D. (2007). Adding new dimensions to case study evaluations: The case of evaluating comprehensive reforms. In G. Julnes & D. Rog (Eds.), Informing federal policies on evaluation methodology: Building the evidence base for method choice in government sponsored evaluation. *New Directions for Evaluation, 113,* 75–93. San Francisco, CA: Jossey-Bass.

CHAPTER 20

Developing a Community of Practice

Learning and Transformation Through Evaluation

Christina A. Christie and Brock M. Klein

In July 2002, Pasadena City College's (PCC) Teaching and Learning Center (TLC) launched .XL, its new summer bridge/first-year experience program. One afternoon, a week before the start of the program, 60 recent graduates from local Pasadena, California, high schools wandered apprehensively into the center for the prebridge orientation. Many arrived late; the vast majority of them came without their invited parents. Generally, the clothes were extra baggy for the boys and extra tight for the girls. Few had ever set foot on a college campus. After 12 years of schooling, all had placed into the lowest levels of precollege-level math and English.

Into the evening, the .XL program director, counselors, instructors, and instructional aides worked to help students register for classes; fill out long, complicated financial aid forms; and get their student ID cards. Along the way, they tried to solve problems: Who doesn't know their social security number? Who doesn't have a social security number? Who forgot to bring a pencil? Who can't attend the first day of class because they have to look after younger siblings? Who will have to leave early because of work?

After the .XL program orientation, a member of the TLC external evaluation team from Claremont Graduate University (CGU) who had observed the event led a debriefing. The .XL faculty thought, what have we gotten ourselves into? Clearly, helping nontraditional college students make a smooth transition from high school to college and stay and succeed in school would be a challenge requiring a flexible, creative, and well-informed process.

Guided by evaluative inquiry, the TLC team embarked on a path of learning and transformation. Along the way, the team would learn about young, urban, minority students, how they define academic success, and how easily so many accept failure. The team would also discover how inadequately prepared many community college faculty members are to teach underprepared students and how difficult it is for faculty to transform their attitudes and practices as they relate to teaching and learning. With experience, expertise, and systematic inquiry, the TLC has created a cohesive set of successful learning community programs, including .XL, to address the needs of low-income, traditionally underrepresented students who come to PCC profoundly underprepared for college.

The goal of this chapter is to offer a case exemplar of evaluation for learning and discovery in response to a transforming U.S. urban educational environment. We hope to illustrate an approach to evaluation in a culturally diverse context with marginalized student populations that has implications for an increasingly globalized society. We describe our experiences as a participatory evaluation team and how evaluation has been used to guide, shift, and direct program refinement, improvement, and development. When our collaboration began almost 8 years ago, we did not anticipate that the program would evolve into an expanded yet more focused learning community initiative, guided in large part by information yielded from the evaluation. The program and its evaluation that we describe in this chapter serve not only as an example for the state of California but also for other regions (both national and international) that are grappling with issues of equity and access to higher education and the preparation of marginalized groups for active participation in a knowledge-based society.

There are several ways in which we could share our story of the development of PCC's TLC program. We have chosen to first describe the theories underlying our work and the alignment of them as a way to understand what drives our process. We then describe four points during the program's development and evaluation process, which we believe have been critical to advancing the TLC's work. These points help describe our participatory process and the impact it has had on our learning and transformation.

Introduction

California's community college is, by design, the gateway for transfer to the state's 4-year college/university system, as well as the primary source for career and technical education for California's low-income, immigrant, and ethnically and racially diverse population. Located in northeast Los Angeles County, PCC serves the multiethnic, urban community of the Pasadena Area Community College District, which has a population of approximately 390,000. It is the third largest single-campus community college in the United States, with a full-time enrollment of more than 16,500. Nearly 80% of PCC students are minorities, 52% receive financial aid, and 47% are the first in their families to attend college. Of all first-time students, 82% are under the age of 20.

Over the past decade, PCC, like the other 108 community colleges in California, has witnessed a steady influx of low-income, first-generation students of color who enter the college lacking the skills they need to succeed academically. During the 2005–2006 academic year, for example, more than 68% of PCC's entering students placed below college-level composition and 89% below college-level math. Approximately 40% of students enrolled in precollege (sometimes referred to as "basic skills" and is equivalent to preteen coursework) math and English courses earned a D or an F or withdrew. First-time students under the age of 20 are the least likely to succeed in precollege courses, and success rates within this age group are dramatically lower for African-American and Latino students. As the world's seventh largest economy, such low persistence and success rates are alarmingly troublesome and potentially disruptive to California's social harmony, economic stability, and workforce readiness, and to developing and maintaining a leading role in the growing knowledge-based economy in the United States and beyond.

PCC's Teaching and Learning Communities Program

Faced with the challenge of educating the growing number of students entering PCC at the basic skills level, the overrepresentation in this group of minorities, and the depressingly low rates of retention (remaining enrolled in a course), success (receiving a grade of C or better in a course), and persistence (remaining enrolled in school) for this group, the college sought external funds to develop innovative strategies to address the serious issues faced by precollege students. In 2000, PCC was awarded a 5-year, Hispanic-Serving-Institutions Title V grant from the U.S. Department of Education,[1] which included funds for a TLC to house a computer lab and staff and counseling offices, new student and faculty development programs, and internal and external evaluation.

The primary focus of the Title V grant was the establishment of learning communities: student-centered environments that emphasize collaboration and interdisciplinary and theme-based instruction. Learning communities have gained popularity among postsecondary educators during the last two decades for their ability to engage students and faculty in the learning process and because of their promising results among at-risk, underrepresented college students (MacGregor, Tinto, & Holland Lindblad, 2000). To begin, TLC staff, composed of a program director, an administrative assistant, and a counselor, developed and piloted simple learning communities (e.g., paired courses) in the first year of the grant. Guided by careful study and evaluative inquiry, the TLC program has been refocused[2] and has grown to include two versions of an intensive summer bridge program (including .XL) and a much less intensive 3-day college orientation; career-focused "pathway programs" for the health professions, art/design, and business; a transfer program for traditionally underrepresented students in science, technology, engineering, and math; and a faculty development program. The TLC staff now includes three program directors, one full-time and one part-time counselor, a lab assistant, an outreach and recruitment coordinator, and four student interns. TLC activities are currently supported by the U.S. Department of Education, the National Science Foundation (NSF), and two separate private partnerships, one with the Hewlett Foundation and the other with the Irvine Foundation. Total funding for the TLC is now approximately $3.5 million.

Theoretical Underpinnings of the TLC Program and Evaluation

TLC staff attempt to understand the issues surrounding learning communities by drawing on the work of Wenger (1998), Lave (1996), Rogoff (1994), and others, who view learning as a process of social participation. Participation refers to engagement in certain activities with certain people, as well as a more encompassing process of being active participants in the "practices of social communities and constructing identities in relation to these communities" (Wenger, 1998, p. 4). Wenger defines three dimensions of community as they pertain to learning through practice: learning occurs as individuals engage in activities whose meanings are negotiated within the community (mutual engagement); practice is the result of a collective process, defined by members involved in the process (joint enterprise); and practice develops resources, including routines, stories, symbols, and concepts for negotiating meaning (shared repertoire).

In applying these theoretical notions to practice, a challenge for the TLC program and evaluation team has been the traditional and individualistic view of knowledge and learning that continues to be supported by Western institutions of higher education. Lave (1996) argues that such traditional beliefs about learning reinforce the sociocultural categories that divide teachers from learners in schools and run counter to the "crucial ways in which learning is fundamental to all participation and all participants in social practice" (p. 157). Few U.S. community college faculty members have been trained to teach, and few expect, once hired, to transform their teaching practices by collaborating with their colleagues and students. Therefore, as the TLC program evolved, it became increasingly important for program directors and staff to develop opportunities for themselves and faculty to negotiate an understanding of their projects and students. Likewise, it became evident to the evaluation team that we too would have to form a community and collaborate to align our practices with those of the communities of teachers and students we were evaluating. During this process of learning and discovery, new ideas and projects would emerge.

Allowing program and evaluation activities to emerge in response to the needs of the context is a core principle of the TLC learning community model. A helpful theory for gaining an understanding of emergent design and its relationship to process is Gray's (1989) notion of *negotiated order*, which refers to a social context in which relationships are negotiated and renegotiated and where social order is shaped through the social interactions of participants. Negotiated order theorists, according to Gray, emphasize process, but also the "temporary and emergent character" of collaboration, as well as interdependence, joint ownership, an understanding of differences, and shared responsibility. From the outset, TLC program managers have worked to help all participants understand that collaboration is a process: Goals and tasks transform; understanding and perceptions of a project evolve; and members undergo changes within and outside of the group, causing interactions and outcomes to emerge. From a sociocultural perspective, this process is essential to the formation of knowledge and learning (Brown & Renshaw, 2000).

Programs that are intentionally designed to emerge or develop over time require evaluation that is flexible and responds to the evaluand as it develops. In the context of the TLC work, a developing program prompted the need for an evaluation that is participatory (Cousins & Whitmore, 1998) and emergent in nature. Our evaluation is designed to foster learning and change, which in turn initiates the development of new program and evaluation activities. The constant influences that the evolving program and evaluation have on one another are intended to create a dynamic, iterative process. The emergent participatory evaluation framework used to

guide our evaluation process is most similar to what Smith and Hauer (1990) refer to as investigative, emergent design process evaluation. Here, the emergent design is one in which an understanding of the evaluand and its context continues to develop as the study progresses, and the study design continues to transform as a result of these changing understandings.

Negotiated order theorists suggest that the structure of a program depends, in large part, on how the participants view process and their roles within it. Grant proposals contain specific objectives, budgets, and deadlines, all of which encourage a linear, step-by-step approach to program implementation. Yet some program managers—as in the case of the TLC program—assume that, as time passes, projects will evolve, participants will change, and funds will have to be adjusted to support those changes. This evolving nature of emergent programs often requires continual renegotiation of program processes and participants' roles, which influence and change the scope of the evaluation, the measurement of evaluation questions, the standards to measure data against, and the information that is reported.

Because it can be difficult for evaluators to understand and adjust to subtle (and sometimes obvious) program changes, stakeholder participation is a critical part of a successful emergent evaluation design. The notion of participation, and the identities that are revealed and transformed in the process, is central to the theories of communities of practice and the work of Lave and Wenger (1991). Through numerous levels of participation, Lave and Wenger believe that the identities of learners form trajectories that can be inbound, leading to full participation—developing an identity as a member of a community and becoming knowledgeably skillful; peripheral, leading to limited participation; or outbound, leading to nonparticipation. "[T]he term trajectory suggests not a path that can be foreseen or charted but a continuous motion—one that has a momentum of its own in addition to a field of influences" (Wenger, 1998, p.154).

Participation among students, teachers, grant managers, and evaluators has been an important feature of all TLC projects and is essential to the measurement of learning. In a participatory evaluation, the roles and interactions of those involved are defined, but participation in evaluation processes as a whole is not prescribed. Fully active participants are referred to as pacers (Wenger, 1998), and their attitudes and behavior are noted by program staff and evaluators, who look to them to set standards, innovate, and transform programs and projects. Increased participation offers team members an opportunity to develop and shift roles during the evaluation process, allowing for new leaders to emerge while previous leaders transition to advisory or consultative "teaching" roles.

The TLC program and the evaluation team's work offer many examples of this kind of learning and transformation. As an example of a student pacer, a former .XL student who transferred to a 4-year college continued to participate in the program by serving as a summer bridge tutor/mentor for 2 years and now, after graduating with a BA, oversees the TLC student follow-up data-collection activities. As an example of a faculty pacer, an English professor who taught in the TLC program for a year became coordinator of the .XL program and is now principal investigator for a large federal grant, where she oversees all grant evaluation activities. Although these two team members are obvious pacers, it is important to note that neither one of them would have ever identified themselves as an "evaluator" prior to participation in our work. Indeed, this highlights the power of the learning and discovery that can result from an emergent, collaborative, and participatory program development and inquiry processes.

The Evaluation Team

The Title V grant, which created and supported the TLC program and Center, included funding for both internal and external evaluation activities. Internal evaluation activities were to be carried out by the college's Institutional Planning and Research Office (IPRO). However, like many other community colleges, PCC's IPRO was unaccustomed to providing internal programs with evaluative information. Rather, IPRO staff members were primarily responsible for providing descriptive data to college administrators for planning purposes. With this in mind, the external evaluator from CGU served as the lead on TLC program evaluation activities.

During this early stage of the evaluation, the TLC evaluation team's primary members included two IPRO research analysts, the external evaluator from CGU, and the TLC program director. As expected (and desired) in a participatory emergent evaluation, the team has evolved over the past 7 years—new members have joined the original team, some have evolved into leaders and others peripheral participants, and others have left. For example, the English professor exemplified previously as a TLC pacer (i.e., a fully active faculty participant) is now a highly active evaluation participant. A CGU graduate student research assistant joined the team soon after the start of the Title V grant and over time emerged as a lead evaluator. One of the original research analysts from IPRO left her position at PCC but has continued to work as a consultant to the evaluation, shifting from a core to a peripheral team member. The lead external evaluator and TLC program director (and authors of this chapter) have continued to serve as the team's core participants.

From the outset, we have convened regular evaluation team meetings that both core and peripheral members attend. Our first team meeting agenda included a general discussion of grant evaluation requirements for the TLC's Title V award. It was at this early point in the process, prompted by the external evaluator, that team members began to negotiate a shared understanding of the evaluation, the context in which it was taking place, the roles each could and should play in the process, and areas of individual and shared interests and expertise (Fitzpatrick, Christie, & Mark, 2008).

Our regularly scheduled evaluation meetings have been critical to the practice of the community and have provided opportunities for multigenerational encounters: Experienced, competent members guide and help integrate new members into the community through the social process of shared learning. Because each team member brings different strengths to the evaluation, it is critical that each feel comfortable enough with the others to ask for suggestions or clarification when necessary and to offer the same in return. Beyond opportunities for support, these meetings allow for discussions about evaluation practice. During these meetings, the evaluation team members assign and accept individual and shared tasks; report their progress; collaborate on writing and disseminating reports; reveal new insights; form new ideas; and transform their roles, identities, and participation within the team. The meetings foster a learning community among the evaluation team members. They guide the evaluation practice and allow team members to come to new understandings about evaluation and the program.

Obviously, team members participate in evaluation-related activities beyond the team meetings. Our evaluation team has embraced Cronbach's (1963) reasoning for the implementation of small studies that can be linked together to understand the overall program. Cronbach argues that, rather than conduct one large evaluation study, evaluators should "conduct several small studies that are programmatically linked, most being rapid efforts with only modest yields but that contribute to better questions and more refined designs in later studies" (cited in Shadish, Cook, & Leviton, 1991, p. 338). In the context of the TLC evaluation, most often the evaluation questions that guide each of our smaller studies are generated by the core team members, but are designed and carried out by a subgroup of the evaluation team. Consensus must be reached around each study focus and design. Then different team members take responsibility for leading the implementation of each study; responsibilities include identifying and developing instruments for data collection and reporting findings, all of which are overseen by the lead external evaluator.

The team also collectively presents evaluation findings, in both written and verbal modes. For example, findings are periodically reported to PCC's Board of Trustees, Executive Committee (College President and Vice Presidents), Academic Senate, program sponsors, and other audiences. A process has emerged in which external evaluators write long, in-depth evaluation reports, with executive summaries, which the project director shortens (retaining the integrity of information in the longer report) for dissemination to different stakeholder audiences, including the College Executive Committee, grantors, and other community college learning community program participants. These activities, along with the day-to-day evaluation work, have provided team members with an opportunity to be involved in the evaluation in many different capacities.

A final important feature of our evaluation learning community is the open and honest environment we have strived to cultivate. When discussing program shortcomings and strengths, no individual personalizes an event, nor does the team attribute a success or failure to any one member. The team shares responsibility for its successes and failures in a receptive and candid fashion. Open communication allows TLC team members to question, prod, and challenge one another, all of which have led to increased learning and transformation.

Critical Events in Program and Evaluation Development Process

There are many points during the program and evaluation development process that we can identify as important learning opportunities and experiences. On reflection, four events stand out as critical to advancing the TLC's programs and evaluation. We have chosen to discuss them as a way to illustrate our participatory process and the impact of this process on learning and transformation. These four events are: (a) the development of the .XL summer bridge/first-year experience program, (b) an evaluation study focusing on various levels of program participation in relationship to program outcomes, (c) a logic modeling/program theory development process, and (d) the planning for a randomized control trial.

Critical Event 1: .XL Program Development

Prompted by less than promising preliminary data on the impact of paired courses on student learning outcomes and attendance at the 2001 Annual Learning Communities Institute, a group of TLC staff and faculty created its most complex learning community model, .XL, a 6-week summer bridge and two-semester first-year experience program targeting Latino students recently graduated from local feeder high schools. The team's decision to take this ambitious step reflected their desire to respond to the needs of the growing number of young, underprepared students entering the college and the team's belief in the power of learning communities to engage students and faculty in the learning process. The decision to create .XL was also evidence of the team's growing competence in the areas of program design, management, and evaluation.

Although common at 4-year institutions, summer bridges and first-year experience programs have only begun to appear at community colleges in the past decade as a means of addressing the serious issues that underprepared students face. Briefly, summer bridges provide opportunities for college orientation, community building, networking, and academics. Generally, first-year experience programs (also referred to as freshman interest groups) are learning communities that link two or more courses required of first-year students. The TLC's model has evolved into an intensive math and study skills program in the summer; math, English, and counseling in the fall; and math and English in the spring. At the time of this writing, the .XL program was launching its seventh cohort.

Since its inception, .XL program implementation has presented challenges for the staff in

several areas, including high school outreach and recruitment, program and curriculum design, scheduling and room assignment, and faculty development. The process of overcoming these challenges has led to powerful learning opportunities and has transformed the .XL program. For example, new learning outcomes for specific courses have been developed, the number of essential course concepts has been reduced, and the revised math curriculum is application-based. A transformation of .XL has led to three summer bridge variations and a 5-year program funded by the NSF.

.XL students dominate the TLC; for many, it is their home away from home. Their strong level of comfort, intimacy, and participation in the center's student support and extracurricular programs have helped us study and better understand their behaviors and attitudes in ways not possible in a typical college classroom setting. We began to learn about .XL students' high school experience (through a survey administered on the first day of program participation), their teachers' low standards and expectations, their inability to identify academic challenges, their notion of success as retention (e.g., I didn't drop out of my math class) rather than achievement (e.g., I earned a B in my math class), and their financial struggles. We also have grappled with barriers to success that stretch beyond the program's design, such as homelessness and gang violence.

The intensity that is often a product of small, longer term cohort programs such as .XL has affected instructors, who often face a class of 30 eighteen-year-olds who are more than willing to disclose personal challenges and issues in the classroom. As a result, .XL instructors have slowly begun to integrate life and study skills into coursework. Their individual "ah-ha" experiences are shared at regularly scheduled .XL staff meetings and have led to their participation in an organized faculty inquiry process designed to help them and their colleagues address the issues raised as a result of working with .XL students. .XL has provoked conversations within and outside of the TLC program about the scholarship of basic skills teaching and learning.

Critical Event 2: Descriptive Quantitative Studies of Program Impact

Throughout the process of creating and piloting new programs and the learning communities within them, TLC staff relied on regular reports from the college's IPRO on retention, success, and persistence—data available only through this office. These data were required for grant reporting purposes, but the TLC team also wanted to know how the students in their various programs were doing. Most important, were they passing their courses and staying in school? The TLC team recognized that the manner in which IPRO data were being analyzed and presented was limited and, in some instances, misleading. For example, descriptive semester snapshots of student outcomes indicated that .XL retention rates were consistently higher than those of comparison groups, but success rates were inconsistent. These data raised questions such as: Do the data tell us about the program impact or simply about the grading habits of individual instructors? How legitimate are our comparison groups? In an effort to use IPRO's data in a way that would allow TLC staff to better understand and reshape program activities, the lead external evaluator initiated a study using IPRO data and more advanced statistical techniques to examine student academic outcomes longitudinally. We modeled the data using latent class analysis techniques and, for the first time, had an informative quantitative study.

From this analysis, we learned that students enrolled in Future Nurses, the TLC's career-focused pathway program for nursing majors, fared better in terms of success, retention, and persistence than students enrolled in nonpathway courses. The analysis also revealed that success, retention, and persistence rates were higher for .XL students than for their non-.XL counterparts. Although the evidence was statistically significant for both, it was less impressive for .XL students than for Future Nurses. However, this information was viewed in the context of issues related to sample size, statistical power,

and comparison groups. One issue of concern was that we examined only one cohort of nursing pathway students, compared with three cohorts of .XL students. This raised questions about whether we had identified a finding specific to this first cohort of Future Nurses and whether we would see similar results in subsequent Future Nurses cohorts. Another important finding that caused TLC staff to pause, but not change the overall TLC program design, was that paired and "stand-alone" (unpaired) TLC courses that did not include cohorts of students who remained together for more than one semester had no significant impact on student success or persistence.

In the fall of 2006, just 2 years after the initial larger scale quantitative study, the TLC evaluation team asked a former IPRO senior research analyst to provide data about new students at the college who place into basic skills math and/or English, as well as data about TLC students enrolled in a variety of programs. The findings from this analysis confirmed those of the previous quantitative study: The more intense and sustained the intervention, the more likely it is that students will stay in school and succeed. This analysis highlighted the importance of enrolling first-time, underprepared students in precollege math and English courses as soon as possible and, in particular, the benefits derived from enrollment in year-long learning communities, such as the .XL program. .XL students persisted in college at a significantly higher rate than their non-.XL counterparts. When looking at students after successful completion of their initial math course, it was found that .XL students were four times more likely to succeed at the next higher level than their non-.XL counterparts.

Findings from this second study were not as strong for the pathway program, Future Nurses, as they had been in the initial study. Although the program was still found to increase success, retention, and persistence rates, the data for the .XL program showed a much stronger relationship between program participation and overall student success. In addition, the study once again found that "stand-alone" TLC courses had no effect on student success. At this point, the evaluation team encouraged the TLC staff to consider focusing solely on summer bridge, first-year experience, and pathway programs. With little resistance, TLC staff members reduced stand-alone course offerings significantly and have contemplated eliminating them all together. There is concern, however, for the potential resistance from faculty, academic deans, and administrators on campus who may perceive such a program change as "scaling down," rather than refining and focusing the program.

These quantitative studies helped the TLC team redefine how we determine success within the TLC programs. Specifically, we now consider how well students do after a particular course, rather than how well they do in the course. In addition, data provided evidence for reshaping TLC programs and redirecting resources to expand summer bridge and first-year experience programs.

Critical Event 3: Developing an Overall Program Theory and Logic Model

In 2004, as the TLC staff neared the end of their initial 5-year Title V grant, they sought and received funds over a period of 2 years from two new federal sources: Title V Cooperative (a collaboration with another postsecondary institution) and the NSF, and two private sources: the Hewlett and Irvine Foundations. These grants have kept the TLC program financially secure for several years and provided the staff with opportunities to continue to develop the career pathways in nursing, teaching, art/design, and business; target different types of students (e.g., science, technology, engineering, and math majors); and make use of external resources, such as statewide consortia of educators and advocates of precollege students at community colleges. In addition, the transition from one funding source to several was accompanied by a reorganization within the college that placed the TLC programs under the direction of the

college's Office of Academic Support. These changes were observed and monitored by the evaluation team. What impact were these new grant projects having on the TLC's short- and long-term goals? How would the administrative reorganization affect the TLCs' efforts to reach more students and transform departmental and institutional practices?

Recognizing the TLC's growth in size, scope, and vision, the lead CGU evaluator initiated a program theory and logic model development process that included two TLC program directors, the TLC counselor, a CGU graduate student research assistant, and, from time to time, PCC's Assistant Dean of Academic Support. The group's goals were to summarize each grant's objectives and identify overlap among them so to develop a new, cohesive set of short- and long-term outcomes for the TLC, consolidate resources to strengthen and expand those TLC programs and services that evaluation data had identified as positively impacting student success, and develop a "road map" that the college could use to transition from grant-funded "boutique" programs to enduring institutions that are deeply woven into the fabric of educational policy and practice. In addition, evaluation findings had taught the team that just as PCC students are underprepared, so too are many PCC faculty. For that reason, sustained, cohesive, and intensive faculty development would be integrated into the program theory and logic model.

During the college's winter intersession, the group met weekly in a small classroom; each session ended with a whiteboard filled with multicolored bubbles, lists, arrows, and lines. The lead evaluator, her graduate assistant, and the two program directors questioned one another about past experiences, lessons learned, program changes, and future goals, all of which demonstrated their individual and collective learning. Their responses shaped decisions and would determine the direction the program and the college would take for several years. Relying on the findings of the two quantitative studies, as well as years of CGU evaluation reports on the psychological, social, and behavioral impacts of TLC programs, the members collaboratively developed a vision of the TLC program that included an array of summer bridges (of varying intensities, including .XL), first-year blocks of classes, and second-year career pathways leading to certificates or transfer. This process and the resulting product(s) continue to serve as a reference for discussion about TLC programs and the evolving vision of how the TLC can better address the needs of underprepared community college students.

Critical Event 4: Designing a Randomized Controlled Trial to Test Summer Bridge Program Impact

The TLC currently has two substantive summer bridge programs, .XL and Math Jam. .XL is a 6-week program in which students attend school from 9:00 a.m. to 3:00 p.m. 4 days a week. They attend an intensive remedial math course linked to a math study skills course and engage in counseling activities designed to provide an orientation to the campus as well as college life more generally. Every Friday, students participate in community-building activities, including field trips.

Questions about the cost-effectiveness of the .XL program have emerged over the years, including whether the college should commit institutional funds to support such a program after grant funding ends (institutionalization, as it is called). Prompted by evaluation data that have identified the three-level, precollege math course sequence as the primary "gatekeeper" courses for TLC students (and remedial students more generally), TLC program staff pursued funding from the Irvine Foundation to develop a cheaper, shorter, math-focused summer bridge experience, Math Jam, the second substantive summer bridge program. Math Jam is an intensive, no-credit, 2-week program that integrates innovative, application-based math activities with tutoring, college orientation, and community building.

TLC staff also developed a 3-day campus orientation (including financial aid advisement and education planning), supported by the NSF, for new students who are enrolled in TLC fall programs but have not participated in or qualified for either of the two summer bridge programs. The college does not offer new students an orientation beyond its large, campus-wide Welcome Day, so the 3-day orientation is indeed an intervention beyond what new students would receive when entering the college, albeit not comparable to and qualitatively distinct from the TLC's .XL and Math Jam programs.

A question we have yet to answer is the extent to which the .XL program, with its additional courses and extended session, actually increases the likelihood of student success beyond what Math Jam offers students or what students might achieve with a limited 3-day summer orientation, or with no intervention at all. A well-designed randomized controlled trial (Campbell, 1969) is one way to answer this question.

Implementation of a randomized controlled trial will require TLC program staff to first employ new strategies for recruiting students into TLC programs. Previously, students have been recruited for specific programs based on interest. To conduct this study, students will be recruited to participate in "a TLC program," rather than a particular program based on interest, and they will be randomly assigned to one of the four conditions: .XL, Math Jam, the 3-day college orientation, or no summer intervention. An extensive precondition instrument will be administered to all study participants at the time of recruitment to ensure that differences in outcomes can be explained by program participation rather than something else. After participation in the assigned summer program, students will be offered the same first-year course schedule, although students will be enrolled in different classes with different faculty. We examine differences in success, retention, and persistence rates among the groups to identify differences (if any) in the impact among the three summer bridge programs, taking into account the effects of the nested nature of the educational context.

Designing and implementing a study in which students are randomly assigned to a program is outside what PCC administrators and faculty (including some TLC staff and faculty) consider "good" educational practice. By and large, members of the college community believe that educational programs are designed to meet the specific needs of specific students, who are carefully identified and selected for participation. Thus, it has taken careful presentation and thoughtful discussion on the part of the evaluation team to gain the buy-in necessary for us to conduct such a study. It is our belief that the composition of our participatory team, which includes respected faculty, was critical to our gaining permission to conduct a study stipulating random assignment. A lesson from our experience may be that participatory evaluation approaches, which are not traditionally associated with the conduct of experiments, may offer the internal credibility and legitimacy necessary to conduct experiments more smoothly in educational contexts.

Of course, this critical event is distinct from the others previously described because it has yet to happen. Thus, we cannot discuss our learning and discovery processes. We can only suggest that, given the current understanding of the program and the current program context and culture, an experimental approach offers an understanding of program impact that is important and timely.

Reflections on Learning and Transformation: Process Use as an Outcome of an Emergent Participatory Evaluation

We have observed that creating a learning community by way of a participatory evaluation team has had significant impact on process use. By process use, we are referring to "individual changes in thinking and behavior, and program and organizational changes in procedures and culture that occur among those involved in evaluation as a result of the learning that occurs during the evaluation process" (Patton, 2008,

p. 90). We believe that an emergent, collaborative, participatory approach was necessary because it was consistent with the theory and practices negotiated (and continually renegotiated) by the community of teachers and learners with whom we were collaborating and the TLC staff members who have grown to assume that, as the evaluation process continues, new ideas will emerge and practice will transform.

The theoretical underpinnings of the TLC program include the notions of identity and participation. According to Wenger (1998), "our identities form trajectories, both within and across communities of practice" (p. 154). Within a community, all members have the opportunity to transform their identities and acquire competence as practitioners. The process of negotiation within a community and the resultant trajectory that sets an individual on a path toward or away from full participation are at the core of transformation and learning. We briefly describe several examples of transformation that we believe have occurred as a result of the evaluation process—for the institution as well as for members of the various communities of practice within the TLC program (evaluators, faculty, and students). These examples of process use serve to describe what may result from a participatory, collaborative process of learning and transformation that is guided by systematic inquiry (Patton, 2008).

Institutional Transformation

PCC's collective perception of evaluation could be summarized as being a laborious and time-consuming process yielding minimal results. Individuals at all levels of the institution complain about long surveys and reports, which they pile up in great leaning towers in the corners of their offices, hide in drawers and soon forget about, or toss into trash bins. More important, the majority of people at the college are skeptical about evaluation findings and recommendations ever leading to positive transformation of policies or practices at the institutional, departmental, or individual classroom levels.

During the past 7 years, the TLC program has become an on-campus example of an externally funded program that takes evaluation seriously and uses evaluation for improvement by holding itself accountable and engaging program participants in the evaluation process. We do not want to suggest that the college has dramatically transformed institutional planning or research or the way members of the broad campus community view evaluation. However, we do believe that TLC evaluation has begun to modify the practices of individuals within the college's IPRO and the negative and cynical attitudes of a few key administrators and faculty. Through the actions of the TLC team, evaluation is now viewed by some on campus as a worthwhile activity. TLC evaluation practices, for example, have led to revision of the college's annual Fall Survey, college participation in a nationwide student engagement survey, the use of action research among faculty to develop and evaluate student learning outcomes, and data sharing about precollege teaching and learning with other community colleges in California.

Evaluation Team Member Transformation

An important example of process use we have observed has been the impact of the evaluation process on evaluation team members. From Wenger's (1998) perspective, "membership in a community of practice translates into an identity as a form of competence" (p.153). The evaluation team collectively has enhanced their knowledge of evaluation (as a process as well as specific methodologies), the college, teaching and learning, faculty, students, and one another. Internal evaluation members have learned to conduct focus groups; they revised several of the college's surveys so that they better capture TLC's student experiences; and they have developed evaluation projects that are designed to inform program improvement.

As a powerful example of learning through evaluation, we point to the 1-year faculty inquiry process initiated and conducted by the TLC codirectors and two prealgebra instructors participating in the TLC's summer bridge and first-year experience program. Guided by an analyst from the college's IPRO, the team developed student learning outcomes and new curriculum and conducted action research. Their process and findings are documented on the Carnegie Foundation for the Advancement of Teaching website, and they subsequently presented their process and findings to audiences on and off campus. Most important, they have continued the faculty inquiry process at the two higher levels of precollege math with several of their colleagues, transformed their teaching practices, invigorated themselves professionally, and become change agents within the math department.

Currently, the core evaluation team leaders are a CGU faculty member, a CGU graduate student, an IPRO analyst, and two TLC program directors. The lead external evaluator (CGU faculty member) has transitioned from her original position as "teacher" and "expert" to that of "advisor" and "consultant." As other team members offer new ideas, this lead external evaluator still provides guidance and oversight but is no longer looked on to implement evaluation activities. The CGU graduate student recently left the team; she became involved through the lead external evaluator, and the team regarded her involvement as an opportunity to expand the evaluation effort, as it was. She initially assisted with data collection and analysis and evaluation reporting, and eventually she became the lead on several smaller evaluation studies. Another CGU graduate student, who previously had a more peripheral role, has emerged to take her place.

At the start of the evaluation, the TLC program director role was mostly that of liaison between the "official" evaluators (i.e., the TLC evaluation team) and "others" (e.g., college administrators). As he has become more comfortable and knowledgeable about evaluation practice, he has moved from being a more peripheral participant to becoming a full, active team member. For example, he now takes part in data analysis and interpretation. Additionally, evaluators now work directly with "others" and have engaged staff, faculty, and administrators campus-wide at various stages of the evaluation process.

The TLC's first counselor joined the evaluation team voluntarily. Her interest in evaluation and belief that the counselor's perspective should be heard led her to become an important member of the evaluation team. She participated in and contributed to the evaluation in numerous ways. For example, she assisted in the development of several pre-post survey instruments, worked with a consultant and the lead external evaluator to create a student database and tracking system, and worked with IPRO staff on data collection and analysis for end-of-the-semester evaluation summaries. Her successor has followed in her steps by attending and participating actively in TLC evaluation meetings. Finally, TLC faculty members who have transitioned into administrative positions have also moved from peripheral to full participation in evaluation activities. For example, the principal investigator for the TLC's NSF grant, an .XL math instructor, now attends evaluation meetings and has initiated several course and program-level evaluation projects.

Student Transformation

Ultimately, the members of the evaluation team look to TLC students to measure the success of TLC programs. In the past 7 years, we have witnessed many examples of student transformation, all of which have helped us learn more about the "TLC student" and have caused us to rethink our notions of their success and indeed our own. Pedro, an .XL student from the second cohort, stands out. Although he was an unusual .XL student because as a high school senior he had been accepted by California State University at Los Angeles (a 4-year bachelor's and master's degree-granting institution) for the fall term, he was similar to his summer bridge classmates in several crucial ways.

Pedro is the son of Mexican immigrants who entered the United States without proper documentation. His father, with only a junior high school education, struggles to support his family but has set a goal for his four children—they will all receive a university degree. In the summer of 2003, as Pedro was planning to begin his studies at Cal State LA, his older brother was preparing to transfer from PCC to the University of California at Davis. However, because of their father's immigration status, neither Pedro nor his brother had access to financial aid; unable to borrow money for school, both boys would have to rely solely on support from the family. Pedro's father asked him to postpone university; he could not afford to send two sons to university at the same time. In fact, he could not afford the expenses incurred by one. Pedro would have to attend PCC, and he would also have to work two jobs to help finance his brother's education.

Also like his .XL classmates, Pedro was in need of English and math remediation. Because he spoke Spanish at home and with his friends, writing and reading in English were difficult for him. In addition, Pedro's high school math education had not been the best. He never had homework, and the exams seemed pretty easy to him. He received respectable grades in math and actually enjoyed the subject, so he was quite surprised when he did not place into college-level algebra. Later, Pedro, like many of his .XL classmates, reported in a focus group interview that, on reflection, he realized his K-12 education had not prepared him adequately for college—not even for community college basic skills courses.

The .XL summer bridge/first-year experience allowed Pedro to flourish. Bright, determined, and mature, he kept his eyes on his goal to transfer despite the fact that working two jobs meant that he could only attend school part time and often did not have time to study or do homework once leaving campus. He quickly became a permanent TLC fixture, visiting the center between classes for tutoring, which helped him get through his challenging English and history courses. When the .XL director offered him a summer job tutoring and mentoring the third cohort of .XL summer bridge students, Pedro jumped at the opportunity. When a job tracking .XL students by telephone for the evaluation team came up, he grabbed that as well. Before long, Pedro was able to quit his off-campus jobs.

Four years after he entered PCC, Pedro is beta-testing the TLC's new student database, tutoring and mentoring .XL and Math Jam students, helping with high school recruitment, and preparing to copresent at a national first-year experience conference. No longer a business major, Pedro is studying psychology at University of California, Riverside, plans to get a master's degree in counseling, and intends to work at a community college. He is also participating in an evaluation study of multigenerational learning among peer tutors and mentors and students in the .XL program. Pedro serves as an appropriate example of how the TLC can offer students an opportunity to access resources and services that help to transform notions of learning and success in community college and beyond.

Considerations Beyond the Classroom

The TLC serves students whose parents are, by and large, immigrants of Latino descent, many of whom have less than an eighth-grade education. These parents have found their way to the United States, only some through legal processes, for increased access to education and economic opportunities for their children. Yet as we have learned, marginalized groups such as first-generation, underprepared college students face challenges both in and out of the classroom that distinguish them from their nonimmigrant peers. The information we have gained through our evaluation work has allowed TLC program staff to refine activities that transpire outside of the classroom to improve the likelihood that students will do well in school. For instance, the TLC program now offers students financial aid advisement, scholarship opportunities, book loans, TLC work opportunities, and, in some cases, lunch. Specifically, such support increases

students' social capital by offering them access to tools and opportunities that promote equity and thus increase the likelihood that they will remain in school and, after several years of program persistence, succeed academically and, later, professionally.

Here we discuss the findings of a study we conducted that point to a relationship between TLC program participation and students' adaptation to college, perceptions of the college environment, and levels of acculturative stress—factors outside of the classroom that impact persistence and success in school. We then describe a feature of the TLC program, the computer lab, which we believe plays an important role in supporting classroom activities and helps to promote learning communities on campus and beyond, yet its utilization is not required as part of the TLC program.

Connectedness to Campus, Adaptation to College, and Access to a Virtual World

Programs such as the TLC play a critical role in preparing multilingual students with dual cultural identities for intellectual, knowledge-based careers. Arguably, this process begins with summer bridges, such as the .XL program. Helping students feel connected to the campus and comfortable among their peers and professors is essential for reaching the TLC's mission of helping students set and achieve academic and career goals. Students' perceptions of the college environment, acculturative stress, and student adaptation to college have been consistently related to Latino student retention and academic achievement (Anaya & Cole, 2001). To better understand the complex interrelated components of what impacts students' attitudes and behaviors in and out of the classroom, the evaluation team conducted a study to assess how TLC students fared on these factors compared with non-TLC Latinos with similar academic profiles (this also serves as a good example of the kinds of "small studies" the team pursues). The goal of our study was to assess the impact of participation in the TLC program among Latino students on noncognitive factors, including: (a) perceptions of the college environment, (b) acculturative stress, and (c) student adaptation to college. In previous research, each of these factors has consistently demonstrated the ability to predict Latino student retention and academic achievement.

Data were collected from 132 Latino students; 70 students were participants in the TLC program and 62 were nonparticipants (non-TLC). Students completed the college environment scale, which assessed student comfort with the college, as based on several factors, including their perceptions of support from faculty and belief that minority students are valued on campus. They also received an acculturative stress inventory, which assessed the difficulties associated with adjustment to a new culture. Finally, they completed a student adaptation to college questionnaire. This assessed social adjustment, which is the extent to which students are able to manage the interpersonal/social demands of college, and academic adjustment, which is the extent to which students can handle the educational demands of college. It also assessed personal/emotional adjustment, which is a student's feeling of psychological well-being and commitment to staying in college.

Our results showed that TLC students demonstrated more positive perceptions of the college environment than their non-TLC peers. For example, they were more likely than non-TLC students to feel faculty were available outside of class and that PCC staff were warm and friendly. Students in the TLC program also demonstrated greater social adjustment to college than non-TLC students. For example, they experienced greater general social adjustment, such that they reported greater participation in and comfort with social activities on campus, and they reported greater adjustment to other people (i.e., they report feeling greater comfort interacting with students, faculty, and staff on campus). Although TLC students were more likely to be first-generation immigrants and thus less acculturated than non-TLC students, TLC and non-TLC students reported similar levels of acculturative stress. To summarize, our data suggest that TLC students demonstrated levels of college adaptation, perceptions of college environment, and levels of acculturative stress that tended to be equal to or better than non-TLC students.

There are other benefits to participating in the TLC program that students report as important factors that contribute to their ability to stay in school and help prepare them for participation in a globalized knowledge-based society. TLC students have access to a well-equipped, well-staffed, technologically advanced, and comfortable computer lab in the TLC center. This is in stark contrast to what TLC students report having in their homes: either no or limited access to late-model computers that accommodate high-speed Internet connections. Access to the TLC computer lab offers students an opportunity to participate in virtual (learning and other) communities with peers, as well as family and friends from their home countries, which we have learned decreases students' feelings of isolation and depression and offers them an opportunity to retain some of their cultural and national identities. It also allows students to complete assignments and conduct research over the Internet, which complements TLC classroom activities, where students are taught to critically evaluate the quality of information obtained from the Internet, a skill necessary for competitive participation in knowledge-based society.

Concluding Thoughts

Taken together, our evaluation data suggest that, without the TLC, it is likely that the students it serves would find themselves, rather haphazardly, out of school and in minimum-wage jobs. As we have learned through our evaluation work, it may take many TLC students several years to complete precollege course work. Nonetheless, they have the opportunity to enter pathway programs that focus on preparing future nurses, teachers, engineers, and scientists. Notably, with only an 18% rate of completion among Latino students intending to transfer into California's large public university system (the 10-campus University of California system and 23-campus California State University system), the TLC also helps to increase the completion rate at PCC, thereby addressing serious issues of access and equity in both higher education and the workforce for Latinos in the United States.

When we began our work, we aspired to develop a process by which the TLC program staff could use the information generated by our evaluation activities to improve program performance and outcomes. We cannot underestimate the power and importance of using evaluation, learning, and educational theories to guide our thinking, actions, and decisions about how to proceed. At the first TLC team retreat, program managers, staff, instructors, and counselors committed themselves to "working together to help one another learn." Our collaborative, participatory, and emergent evaluation approach has provided us with the opportunity to develop the program and the interests and competencies of current and new team members using a process whereby we learn about ourselves and others.

> As we build communities of practice . . . we work out our relations with each other and with the world, and we gain a lived sense of who we are. . . . We explore our ability to engage with one another, how we can participate in activities, what we can and cannot do. [A]ll this takes place in the doing. (Wenger, 1998, pp. 192–193)

The core members of the TLC evaluation team have worked together since the early implementation of the initial Title V grant more than 7 years ago, a relatively long relationship compared with other small-scale educational evaluation studies conducted in the United States. Our work continues with great momentum. We believe our energy, interest, and enthusiasm are due, in large part, to the community of practice we have created. It has led to (a) important discoveries about underprepared, first-generation college students and the faculty who are charged with teaching their courses; (b) appreciation for the power of evaluation as a process and a tool for decision making, learning, and transformation; and (c) respect and collegiality among the individuals within the community of evaluators. A TLC program staff member said in passing one day, "Evaluation feels like a natural part of my work. We make decisions with the lights on—not in the dark."

Only recently have we begun to understand that our work extends beyond our program context. This is evidenced by the attention and recognition that has been paid to our work through invitations to consult and mentor others with similar interests and concerns throughout the state of California, including the Carnegie Foundation, the Chancellor's Office for the Community Colleges of California, and the California State Legislature. With leadership from these groups, the TLC's approach and the principles used to promote learning and discovery in a localized urban Southern California context are now being translated to other environments that share similar challenges related to working with marginalized populations. It is our process of learning and discovery, rather than the specific program interventions or evaluation activities, that we believe has implications for and can be adopted by others globally. What we share with others across the globe is a desire to learn and transform. So long as we stay true to the process of learning through inquiry, the specific practices that emerge to promote transformation will be as diverse as the issues and populations that we each encounter. It is our respect for a collaborative, participatory emergent process that yields effective practices reflecting the values and norms of the community in which they were created.

Notes

1. Title V seeks to improve the retention, success, and transfer rates at 2- and 4-year institutions with student populations that are at least 25% Hispanic, 50% of whom are at or below a designated income level.

2. It is important to note that Title V allows grantees to modify program design and delivery as long as the program goals remain consistent with the initially proposed and funded program. This allowed TLC faculty to change the structure and focus of the learning community model implemented during the first year of the grant to a summer bridge program model.

References

Anaya, G., & Cole, D. G. (2001). Latina/o student achievement: Exploring the influence of student-faculty interactions on college grades. *Journal of College Student Development, 42*, 3–13.

Brown, R. A. J., & Renshaw, P. D. (2000). Collective argumentation: A sociocultural approach to reframing classroom teaching and learning. In H. Cowie & G. van der Aalsvoort (Eds.), *Social interaction in learning and instruction: The meaning of discourse for the construction of knowledge* (pp. 52–66). Oxford, UK: Pergamon Press.

Campbell, D. (1969). Reforms as experiments. *American Psychologist, 24*, 409–429.

Cousins, J. B., & Whitmore, E. (1998). Framing participatory evaluation. *New Directions for Evaluation, 80*, 5–23.

Cronbach, L. (1963). Course improvement through evaluation. *Teachers College Record, 64*(8), 672–692.

Fitzpatrick, J., Christie, C., & Mark, M. (2008). *Evaluation in action: Interviews with expert evaluators.* Thousand Oaks, CA: Sage.

Gray, B. (1989). *Collaborating: Finding common ground for multi-party problems.* San Francisco, CA: Jossey-Bass.

Lave, J. (1996). Teaching as learning, in practice. *Mind, Culture, and Activity, 3*(3), 149–164.

Lave, J., & Wenger, E. (1991). *Situated learning: Legitimate peripheral participation.* Cambridge: Cambridge University Press.

MacGregor, J., Tinto, V., & Holland Lindblad, J. (2000, June). *Assessment of innovative efforts: Lessons from the learning community movement.* Presented at the American Association of Higher Education Assessment Forum conference, Charlotte, NC.

Patton, M. Q. (2008). *Utilization-focused evaluation* (4th ed.). Newbury Park, CA: Sage.

Rogoff, B. (1994, April). *Developing understanding of the idea of communities of learners.* Scribner Award Address at the American Educational Research Association, New Orleans, LA.

Shadish, W. R., Cook, T. D., & Leviton, L. C. (1991). *Foundations of program evaluation: Theories of practice.* Newbury Park, CA: Sage.

Smith, N. L., & Hauer, D. M. (1990). The applicability of selected evaluation models to evolving investigative designs. *Studies in Educational Evaluation, 16*, 489–500.

Wenger, E. (1998). *Communities of practice: Learning, meaning, and identity.* Cambridge: Cambridge University Press.

CHAPTER 21

Learning-in-(Inter)Action

A Dialogical Turn to Evaluation and Learning

*Theo J. H. Niessen, Tineke A. Abma, Guy A. M. Widdershoven,
and Cees P. M. van der Vleuten*

Introduction

In this chapter, we explore a case in which a problem-based learning (PBL) course at Maastricht University is responsively evaluated. Within responsive evaluation, the value of an educational practice or educational regime is dependent on the multiple, sometimes conflicting, perspectives of stakeholders in the evaluation setting.

A common presumption about evaluation is that it contributes to the knowledge of program, participants, and other stakeholders and that they will learn from an evaluation. Yet what it means to learn from an evaluation and what we assume about learning, knowing, and resistance are underdeveloped concerns in evaluation practice (Schwandt, 2004). A traditional model of learning from evaluation assumes that learning occurs when evaluators transmit findings and conclusions to program participants and stakeholders and that they will then process and absorb that information. This transmissional and linear view on information "processing" understands learning as an a priori planned and individual cognitive act.

In this chapter, we argue that learning is far more; it is a complex, contextually sensitive, and dialogical process that situates itself within the interstices between people being attentive and mindful about what is said on the spot during the evaluative process. Learning is not a planned, linear, and individual cognitive process; rather, it is a dialogical accomplishment attuning oneself to what the other is bringing up. In this case, recognizing, acknowledging, and playing with this plurality was a rewarding process for all participants. We illustrate these narrative and collective processes of learning drawing on our evaluation of the course on PBL for newly appointed staff members at Maastricht University. PBL as used within Maastricht University is a didactical approach. Within PBL, students collaboratively within small groups engage in learning tasks to obtain the necessary knowledge and communication skills. For teachers, this also assumes other, more coaching-related skills. They should refrain from frontal instructions. New staff members coming to Maastricht University are often not or insufficiently acquainted with these principles of PBL. Within "The introductory course on PBL for new staff members," newly appointed teachers are trained in the basics of PBL. It is this course—as part of a PhD study on teacher learning that was finished in 2007 (Niessen, 2007)—that we have evaluated through means of responsive evaluation.

Responsive evaluation is an approach in which the value of a practice or program is established by focusing on the perspectives of and deliberative dialogues between stakeholders in the evaluation setting. *Evaluation* is thus defined as a dialogue or conversation with all stakeholders about the value and meaning of a particular program or practice as a vehicle for learning, understanding, and improvement (Abma, 2005; Abma & Widdershoven, 2005). Worldwide, governments, schools, and other organizations are under increasing pressure to deliver tangible results and to compete for the best performance (Greene, 1999; Stronach, 1999). These, however, are measured against standardized performance indicators often defined by one stakeholder group. Against the background of results-oriented management— assessing efficiency and effectiveness—one becomes aware of the paradoxical nature of performance indicators: On the one hand, they are "frozen ambitions," yet on the other hand, they must facilitate dialogue and learning (Noordegraaf & Abma, 2003; Van der Knaap, 2006). We would even state that these ambitions and indicators obtain their meaning within dialogue. Building on a responsive approach as a dynamic perspective on evaluation, we are able to question the validity of the policy objectives and performance indicators *without* compromising their value and significance altogether. The "dialogical turn" in evaluation helps us to raise the quality of dialogue, learning, and decision making among all stakeholders.

Within this chapter, the reader first gets acquainted with responsive evaluation and its development, core concepts, and worldview

premises. Then we present the case example. This is followed by a section on the issue of learning within and from evaluation. Finally, we deal with the issue of how local case knowledge provided within this chapter can be of global importance.

Responsive Evaluation

Guba and Lincoln (1989) have depicted the development of evaluative research into four historical generations or orientations, denoting them as the *measurement, description, judgment,* and *negotiation generation.* The *measurement* orientation is about the collection of data as, for example, the measurement of student outcomes as a denominator for educational success. *Description* entails pointing out the characteristics to an educational policy or program. In the case of an educational course, this means describing the activities taken by teachers, students, and the interactions within the classroom. This information may be supported by descriptive statistics. The generation phrased as *judgment* will pass a final ruling about the quality, for example, by comparing the factual effects of an educational program with the formed goals and standards. A fixed set of standards and criteria are used, determined by one stakeholder group (policymakers). The assessment is concentrated on the realized outcomes (and less or not on the process of implementation). This type of evaluation—whereas it may be called performance measurement or standard-based evaluation—is prevalent within contemporary society. It is policy-centered and stands in contrast to the pluralistic, interactive, and dialogical character of fourth-generation evaluation (negotiation generation). Within fourth-generation evaluation, the design emerges on the basis of a conversation with and among stakeholders and their issues of concern. The deliberative dialogues between stakeholders evoke a collective process of social learning and enhance the personal and mutual understandings. This stands in contrast to the idea of learning within a standards-based evaluation approach, where learning starts after the evaluation on the basis of the application of evaluation findings. Table 21.1 summarizes the main differences between responsive and standard-based evaluation.

Strands Within Responsive Evaluation

Before their seminal work in which Guba and Lincoln (1989) proclaimed the need for a more democratic and participative form of evaluation, Robert Stake articulated his dismay about the narrow selection of data being used for formal evaluation within his "countenance paper." Responsive evaluation, a vision and rationale for evaluation within education, can be traced back to Stake (1975; see also Stake & Abma, 2005), who developed it in the mid-1970s as an alternative to "preordinate evaluation." This he saw as the dominant approach emphasizing strong (preferably experimental and quantitative) measurement procedures and only legitimizing two

kinds of data: goals and outcomes. Stake wanted to make responsive evaluation meaningful to all the different stakeholders experiences (Abma & Stake, 2001). According to Stake, there was a need for contextualized data, which acknowledged the situated and cultural nature of instructional programs. To Stake, this entailed an approach that was responsive to the multiple perspectives and values that any program or practice incorporates. Being responsive meant for him that a researcher should take into account the multiple perspectives in a manner that was as truthful as possible to the intentions and values of each stakeholder. Providing emic tales and using thick descriptions, these cases were portrayed as holistic.

In line with Lincoln (2003), Abma and Widdershoven (2005; Abma 2000) elaborated the responsive approach extending the ideas of Stake and Lincoln within a social-critical frame. Within such a framework, evaluation should actively steer toward the inclusion of marginalized voices. A measurement orientation is biased because

Table 21.1   Differences Between Responsive and Standard-Based Evaluation

	Standards-Based Approach	Responsive Evaluation
Evaluation criteria and standards	• A priori set by one stakeholder group • Policy-centered • Effects and outcomes	• Emergent to deliberative dialogue between stakeholders • Pluralistic: the values and interests of all stakeholders • Effects and process of implementation
Evaluation process	• Fixed hypothetical-deductive design • Stakeholders are information-givers • Monological • Evaluator as expert	• Emergent design based on stakeholder issues • Stakeholders are partners in the process • Interactive and dialogical • Evaluator as facilitator
Learning	• Individual/cognitive phenomenon • Starts after the evaluation with the application of data • Enhanced knowledge "about" an evaluand	• Collective/social phenomenon • Begins during the evaluation process • Personal and mutual understanding

only the intentions from the management are used to judge the worth of a program or practice. Participants are solely taken serious for the information they are able to provide. They are approached instrumentally. This does not lead to acceptance and implementation of evaluation data and results. Within responsive evaluation, deliberative dialogue striving toward consensus is pertinent. In case of an education program, teachers, students, but also parents and directly linked other partners may enter a mutual dialogue about the value of an education practice.

Worldview Premises and Core Concepts

We have argued elsewhere (Niessen, Vermunt, Abma, Widdershoven, & Vleuten, 2004) that core theoretical concepts are grounded within more encompassing worldviews. A worldview might be denoted as a more or less coherent outlook on how we view reality (ontology), what can be known about it (epistemology), how to acquaint ourselves with it (methodology), and how we should deal with it all (axiology; Heron & Reason, 1997; Niessen et al., 2004). Placing responsive evaluation within this framework, we can elaborate the differences among Stake's, Guba and Lincoln's, and Abma and Widdershoven's interpretation of responsive evaluation more clearly. Although the differences regard various issues, we confine ourselves to the researcher's role and the implied worldview.

Stake (1986) characterizes the researcher's role within responsive evaluation as that of an anthropologist describing or portraying stakeholders' interests as accurately as possible. This could be done by means of using thick descriptions (Abma & Stake, 2001). Although Abma and Widdershoven (2005) agree on the assumption that the value of a program is not being established a priori, but rather accomplished in conversation by the different stakeholders, the role of the evaluator as well as the ontological postures differ. According to Abma and

Widdershoven, a responsive evaluator should be a sound anthropologist, as well as a caring researcher trying to actively attend marginalized voices. This is what Heron and Reason (1997) call the axiological dimension within research providing human flourishing through means of action research (action turn). This axiological dimension is missing from the constructivist perspective of Stake as well as Guba and Lincoln. Within Stake's view, but also that of Guba and Lincoln, the researcher responsible for responsive evaluation is framed as a distant interpreter, whereas within the account of Abma and Widdershoven, the responsive evaluator is more of a "passionate participant as facilitator of a multivoice reconstruction" (Guba & Lincoln 2005, p. 196), and the purpose is to attend to those who are in danger of being ignored.

A seemingly small difference between Guba and Lincoln's approach and that of Abma and Widdershoven resides in the term used to denote the exchange between the participants within responsive evaluation. Guba and Lincoln—in line with the fourth depicted developmental stage within evaluation—speak about *negotiation*. Abma and Widdershoven (2005) refer to it as *deliberative dialogue* evaluating the worth of a program:

Deliberation refers to the interaction and dialogue between participants. They do not just accept each other's beliefs and persuasions, but will explore these. Listening, probing and dialogue characterise this process, rather than confronting, attacking and defending. Central features of dialogue are openness, respect, inclusion and engagement.

For us, the term *negotiation* is placed within a more competitive interpretational framework in which formality, not inclusion, is paramount.

To provide more texture to these terms, we also could look at the basic philosophies that are informative to the research paradigm and scholars' worldviews. Abma and Widdershoven's

(2005) account of responsive evaluation is grounded within narrative psychology and dialogical ethics (Abma, 1999; Abma, Molewijk, & Widdershoven, 2007; Widdershoven & Sohl, 1999). Narrative psychology helps to understand how people make sense of and give meaning to their own identity and life context. Stories help to endow meaning to situations, weave events into a meaningful whole, and relate varied elements into a plotline (Josselson & Lieblich, 1999). A narrative is always context-bound; it positions a character in a specific time and place. A story describes a specific situation and enables the narrator to find guidelines for action and to influence others to adjust their actions. Stories have a performative character. Stories are appropriate to make sense of situations because they acknowledge particulars (Josselson & Lieblich, 1999; Lyons & LaBoskey, 2002).

In recent work, Niessen, Abma, Widdershoven, Akkerman, and van der Vleuten (2008) place responsive evaluation within an enactivist framework, thus changing and/or acknowledging stakeholder participation as an ontological necessity rather than an epistemological issue. Responsive evaluation is then placed in what Heron and Reason (1997) would refer to as the participatory research paradigm: "Co-researchers are initiated into the inquiry process by facilitator/researcher and learn through active engagement in the process; facilitator/researcher requires emotional competence, democratic personality and skills" (p. 290).

Enactivism and the participatory paradigm as exemplified by Heron and Reason (1997) share many characteristics. Within enactivism, the central point is that life in all its forms (e.g., education, nursing, etc.) is actively enacted as we engage in it. To enact means to bodily work on and experientially engage in a preexisting world that already has meaning. The world is conceived as dialogical (e.g., "who we are" emerges in our moment-to-moment coping with the contingencies of our existence). This continuous coping with our existence (bodily and experientially) requires a radical empirical turn, described by Heron and Reason (1997) as: "This form of radical empiricism is not to be confused with behaviourism, which has never been empirical enough, since it preconceives and delimits experience in terms of its positivist paradigm. On the contrary our empiricism is the radical sort long since commended by phenomenologists: a pristine acquaintance with phenomena unadulterated by preconceptions." Schwandt (2003) has called it an engagement with the "rough ground." He explains: "Rather than first thinking 'scientifically' and 'theoretically' about ourselves, others and our world, we begin with our being in the world and the ways we interweave our talk and action to develop and sustain ways of connecting with and relating to one another" (p. 355). What we infer from these segments and what is central within enactivism is that being is grounded, first and foremost, in a nonpropositional resonating "feeling" of interconnectedness.

Moreover, from this inherent relational ontology enactivism as well as the participatory research paradigm explicitly and naturally foreground the axiological dimension to research. The axiological question deals with the issue of what is intrinsically worthwhile. Within evaluative research, this "ethical" turn can be found in the work of Whitmore (1994) and Greene (1997). Whitmore (1994) is grounded in the empowerment tradition and focusing on the participation of unheard voices providing them a voice and control to shape their own destiny, whereas Greene (1997)—also wanting to provide stakeholders with a voice—departs more from a democratic tradition in which deliberation and dialogue are the means to accomplish this task. Cousins and Earl (1995) are most pragmatic (i.e., instrumental in their axiological quest), stating that participation within evaluative research will stimulate stakeholders to use the information that is gathered. There is no reference to an ethical commitment to involve stakeholders a priori. The participatory framework as we have appropriated it within our research has most commonalities with the work of Greene (1997). While denoting this resemblance, we acknowledge that at the final stretch what is intrinsically valuable in our eyes (our axiological aim) is human flourishing, meaning balancing autonomy, cooperation, and hierarchy in our culture in general and within research. This ideal of human flourishing and research initiatives to practice this ideal are visible in the work of Titchen and McCormack (2008).

Although not explicitly based on enactivism or the participatory paradigm, the work of Abma has evolved over time into this direction. The shared responsibility within her interpretation of responsive evaluation searching for a minimal shared experiential (practical) base using analytical and nonanalytical procedures is a reflection of this turn (Abma & Broerse, 2007).

Case Example: Responsive Evaluation of a PBL Course

Within Maastricht University, PBL has been the prime instructional method to introduce university students for the last 30 years. PBL as used within Maastricht University is a didactical approach. Within PBL, students collaboratively engage within small groups in learning tasks to obtain the necessary knowledge and communication skills. Teachers should refrain from frontal instructions and are expected to acquire other, more coaching-related skills. New staff members coming to Maastricht University are often not or insufficiently acquainted to these principles of PBL. Within "the introductory course on PBL for new staff members," newly appointed teachers are trained in the basics of PBL. It is this course we have evaluated through means of responsive evaluation.

At the time of the evaluation of the PBL course, a discussion took place at the university about the nature of PBL and its future. Several curriculum developers and academics noticed that the PBL curriculum at Maastricht

University had changed considerably over the last 30 years. In some instances, students study less. Their preparation time to the PBL sessions has dropped increasingly. PBL is structured along a stepwise frame. Students tend to skip certain steps. Staff members also altered the PBL model. Instead of facilitating the PBL process, they tend to revert in old frontal modes of teaching. Research demonstrated that these changes crept in coincidently or were sometimes implemented by faculty officials explicitly (Moust, Berkel, & Schmidt, 2005). Whether this was desirable was subject of debates among curriculum developers and theoreticians. We hoped that the evaluation of the PBL course would create a social learning platform to also include the voices of the teachers and teacher-trainers, and their voices and experiences with PBL.

In our context of the PBL case, we included new staff members (junior teachers), the course developers, and teacher-trainers in dialogues about their experiences with PBL. We did not include the students, although we understand them to be the real end users. The reason to not include the students could be contested certainly given the shared and distributed nature and meaning of PBL. We chose not to do so because the nature of the project focused on teacher learning. We did not evaluate the PBL curriculum, but a training course for (new) staff members (teachers) at Maastricht University. Students could well have made remarks about the PBL in general, but not about the PBL course because they did not attend the training. The new staff members, often junior teachers following the course, can be considered students in a way. They were trained by a group of teacher-trainers in the educational department of the university. The relation between the trainers and junior teachers was asymmetrical; the trainers were educational experts, whereas the teachers lacked formal educational expertise. Most of the new teachers were quite young and inexperienced. Although the teachers did not have to do an exam, they were assessed by the trainers.

Given this asymmetry, we paid deliberate attention to the stories of the teachers and amplified their voices.

Enhancing Personal Understandings Through Learning Histories

We have characterized responsive evaluation as a dialogical approach for evaluating programs or practices. A full-fledged responsive evaluation involves a cyclical sequence of individual and group interviews with and among different stakeholders. First, we started to identify stakeholder issues and concerns. To the introductory course on PBL, the relevant stakeholder groups were the former participants of the introductory course (new staff members at Maastricht University), the teacher-trainers (providing the course), and the course developers (which were in most cases also the teacher-trainers).

Stakeholder issues and concerns are not given, but are to be developed in conversation with the stakeholder groups. The design is emergent (as opposed to a preordinate design) to attend to the issues evolving in the process. To delineate stakeholder issues and underlying meanings, several methods can be used; in this case, we held open, conversational interviews. These are appropriate to gain an insight into the experiences of respondents from an insider's perspective and understand the meanings the respondents endow to their teaching experiences. Within conversational interviews, participants are invited to talk about the topic being evaluated—in this case, the PBL course, sharing experiences and stories. The interviews and focus groups were entirely transcribed by the researcher (Niessen). The individual interviews were held at a place most appropriate and comfortable to the respondent. In many cases, the conversations took place at the university, although we also organized one interview at a person's home and one in a quiet café. The focus groups were held at the university. Within our

evaluation study, we used the term *thick stories*—in line with Geertz's (1973) phrase *thick descriptions*—to denote the dense texture of these experiences. Roth, Lawless, and Tobin (2000) refer to these experiences and stories as the lived or enacted curriculum, as opposed to the theoretical curriculum.

During the first phase of our study, we completed 19 individual conversational interviews with participants from the relevant stakeholder groups: 10 teacher-trainers and 9 former participants to the introductory course (new staff members/teachers). The maximum variation sampling technique (Patton, 1990) was used to attain the participants. These differed with regards to faculty affiliation: Medicine (4), Law (4), Economics (3), Health Sciences (4), Arts & Culture (3), and University College (1). In all interviews, we had we started off with a general question ("What stood out for you having participated in the Introductory PBL course?"); through subsequent probing, the contextual, embodied, and personal nature became heightened.

Box 21.1 provides an example of the type of issues identified in the individual interviews. The example is drawn from an interview with Josie. She is a junior teacher-trainer at the Faculty of Economics and Business Administration. As a former student at Maastricht University, she has had experience with the PBL system. Working as a teacher-trainer helping new staff members to get acquainted with the PBL system is another topic altogether. As a trainer, Josie tries to "get the group excited about PBL." However, sometimes this appears to be difficult. Josie relates about their experiences with PBL in the context of a group of experienced students. It did not go very well in her opinion; with all the information coming from the group members, she had not been able to provide the students with a closure. This experience triggered her to rethink and reflect on her ideas about PBL and whether she had been a good teacher in that situation. Box 21.1 depicts Josie's story.

Box 21.1   Josie's Case

Josie:	In a training session last week, there was a group of student tutors, and this group was really very critical because they had attended other PBL courses. That was when I found myself trying to create more structure—that's where I felt inadequate because there were so many people with so much experience. In these instances, it's important to offer students guidelines and structure. You should be able to deviate from this structure—but only in those cases—when it's possible. Some teachers see this very clearly. Personally, I tend to create structure together with the group—on the spot. With some groups this works out just fine, and with other groups it would have been better if I had provided a clear structure from the start. We would have come further.
Researcher:	Students get restless?
Josie:	No, yes, well, there's too much input and too few conclusions. I think that's a major thing in PBL—it's a major issue that too often, maybe, no actual conclusion is reached. That's really what I think is probably my own shortcoming, something that as a student I thought was missing in the system. That structure—the framework in which you work.
Researcher:	What does this framework look like—what is it made of?
Josie:	A connecting thread.
Researcher:	You say that, on the one hand, you're trying to find this thread—and you want to connect it with the experiences of the participants—but that's difficult because their experiences are so diverse and a common theme is hard to discern.
Josie:	Well, maybe that's because there just isn't one single thread and because PBL is based on the assumption that the available knowledge is relative. So you cannot say there's one single solution to a particular problem. The important thing is that you are working toward a solution.

Josie's account illuminates that experiences with teaching and PBL are influenced by the context of the situation. PBL might work well in a small group of students with similar experiences, whereas it is much harder in a context of a diverse group, according to Josie. It also becomes clear in the interview with Josie that her evaluation of the situation is influenced by her own experiences as a student. Josie notices that she often missed a structure in the PBL courses, and she is afraid that her students will experience the same. Josie wants to prevent that pitfall, but has not yet found a manner to provide students with a "connecting thread" in situations where there is a diverse input from the group. Like Josie, we found that other teachers and teacher-trainers were also influenced by their own educational background and personal history. We therefore decided to analyze the interviews of the respondents in terms of "learning histories." The term *learning history* is used here to refer to our reconstruction of someone's educational learning path during childhood and adult life. It is composed of the experiences the participants told us about (Basten, 2000). The guiding framework to reconstruct these experiences into a learning history was developed partly parallel and partly after the responsive evaluation (Niessen, Abma, Widdershoven, Akkerman, & van der Vleuten, 2008).

Box 21.2 illustrates a learning history. The history is based on an interview with Robert. Robert is new at Maastricht University. He teaches contemporary history at University College Maastricht. In the interview, Robert talks extensively about his education in primary and secondary school and at university, which was characterized by conventional frontal, teacher-centered teaching. Robert's traditional educational background was reinforced by his father being a history teacher of the traditional school and proud to be so. This background fed Robert's initial misgivings about PBL. These misgivings were not based on deliberate reflection. Rather, they stemmed from Robert's upbringing in a family of traditional school teachers where good teaching was considered synonymous with imparting to students what you knew (i.e., being a proper teacher). His initial reservations about PBL were changed into a more neutral/positive attitude by his educational experiences at the Central College Study Abroad Program in Leiden. As a teacher, he learned firsthand that many hours of frontal classroom teaching can be exhausting. As a result, he gradually came to see teaching as a process in which students might take an increasingly active role in their own learning. Box 21.2 depicts Robert's story.

Box 21.2   Robert's Story

I've come to realize that my primary and secondary school were very traditional schools. Then I went to Leiden. That was in the early 1980s, where I read history, and there teaching was again mostly extremely traditional. The sad thing of course is that I really didn't have all that many ideas about PBL but just thought the term seemed outrageous, just one of those modernisms. Perhaps this had something to do with my father. He is also a teacher or was, until he took early retirement a year ago. He taught history too. He was a real storyteller, who told stories, and I think he would tell you that pupils enjoyed listening to his stories.

I don't remember when I first heard about the PBL system. It must have been years ago. In the meantime, I had been teaching and I had also thought things like. . . . Well, stimulated by those Americans, I noticed that I didn't like it myself, because at the college in Leiden we had to teach in long blocks of many hours, say 3 hours on the same subject every week. Then you discover that it is really boring to talk nonstop for 3 hours, and from the start I had thought well, they should do something with that, so you start with a sort of paper which you want to be really about what has been dealt with in class and not just some sort of add-on and that gradually expands into projects which students report in class and discussions.

Robert learned about PBL in the introductory course at Maastricht. After his early experiences at school and university and his gradual change of view induced by his teaching experiences, he immediately felt attracted to the interactive aspect of PBL. His concerns related to the introductory course, which he (paradoxically) experienced as too traditional and consisting of talks and training learning skills.

Our intention with these learning histories was to provide the participants with valuable learning experiences. Some participants did indicate that our learning histories or reenactments provided them with a sense of closure and a grasp of the past and helped them attain a sense of self or identity (Giddens, 1991). The enhancement of personal understanding was considered an indicator of the quality of our evaluation. Guba and Lincoln (1989) call this enhancement of personal understanding *ontological authenticity*[1]: the extent to which individual respondents' own constructions are improved, matured, expanded, and/or elaborated.

Communal Conversations and Developing Shared Understandings of PBL

The next phase of the responsive evaluation process aimed to engage stakeholder groups in deliberative dialogues about the issues generated in the first phase. To attain this goal, we provided the different stakeholder groups the chance to discuss their issues about PBL in general and about the PBL course specifically. We set up homogeneous groups so the stakeholders would not feel threatened; this provided the stakeholders the opportunity to voice and crystallize their thoughts among like-minded people. Although the teachers (former participants of the PBL course) did not seem

threatened at any point by the teacher-trainers, and although there is no hierarchical relationship between both groups, there is nevertheless a difference with regards to the knowledge both have about PBL. This might influence their relationship. This is the reason that we chose to have separate focus group interviews. Two focus groups were organized: The first group was composed of six former participants of the PBL course, and the second group consisted of five teacher-trainers. Case descriptions based on the concerns and issues generated in Phase 1 were used to start a dialogue within the groups. Box 21.3 presents an example of the emerging conversation in a focus group among teacher-trainers to illustrate the type of issues raised and the development of these issues in interpersonal interactions.

The citation starts with Marc, a teacher-trainer at the faculty of Health Sciences of Maastricht University. He enters the conversation at a point when the other teacher trainers are reaching consensus about a central issue in PBL (i.e., whether teachers should restrict their role to facilitating the group process or whether it is also acceptable for them to make content-related contributions). Among new staff members, there is a widespread unwritten persistent belief that in PBL teachers must rigorously refrain from formally instructing students in any way. We discovered that this makes new staff members feel guilty—think of Josie—when they talk too much during tutorials instead of adhering to their role of facilitator of the learning process, encouraging students to find the necessary information and insights for themselves. However, to Marc, this is not the core issue. His concern is how to raise the awareness of teachers about the learning processes among students. The participants in the discussion recognize his concern and relate about their own experiences of how to alert teachers to students' development.

Box 21.3   Group Discussion Among Teacher-Trainers

Marc: Can I make a suggestion about the group process? We should distinguish it from the learning process. Then there are not two, but three components you have to work with as a tutor.* Self-directed learning, let's call that the learning process. I have great difficulty explaining to my tutors how they can intervene in students' learning processes to help them become self-directed learners. This I find the hardest part of the role of the tutor. The content-related aspect is easy to deal with: take it with a bigger or smaller pinch of salt. It depends on the situation, what you feel comfortable with, et cetera. For the group process, we have quite a few instruments as well. Usually you can explain all sorts of things to people—use texts, use videotapes. But as for the learning process, that's very hard to get across in groups, at least in our tutor training sessions in the Faculty of Health Sciences. In our faculty, the tutors who attend the tutor training sessions are mostly graduate students or prospective graduate students. Well, this is a very special population. All these people say, well I've done PBL. Nearly all of them have been a tutor at some time in their student career. And then you find yourself facing a group in which it is really hard to come to grips with self-directed learning. That's my real problem.

Lucy: I think that you go too far for a group in an introductory course. In my experience, you should mention it, but it goes a bit too far to discuss this in detail in the tutor training. In my experience, this is a topic for advanced tutor training. Novice tutors are all very much focused on content. They're very pleased when they manage to master that. What I do find important, and that's something I'm very clear about in training the tutors, is that tutors should come to an understanding with the students about the rules for the group in the first meeting. About what the tutor expects of the students, how they see the role of the discussion leader, about the quality of the credits, about the quality of the presentation.

Dorothea: It's funny to see that we have three aspects that are very important in teacher training: that is the content, the group process, and the learning process. I agree with Marc; you cannot put the learning process at the very start of the course, but it does remain the hardest part; how to alert tutors and show them how learning processes work. How do you get an idea of what students are going through in a learning process?

Elisabeth: One of the things you can observe as a tutor is that certainties are being called into question. When that happens, you see symptoms which at first

(Continued)

(Continued)

> may mistakenly be seen as negative. Students start to display a violent hatred toward you or are troubled or think they're headed for chaos. I read an official term for it—and I thought that's a really good way of putting it—and that's disjunction. When you're learning something really new, it's never enjoyable from a to z. No way. Then you're going through a crisis. Often they say to you afterward. That means that as a tutor you have to prepare the students and that's something you don't learn. . . . Students are so keen to enjoy themselves. . . . They want to have a good time all of the time, and we give them that impression by talking about education in terms of consumers and products. Learning is not enjoyable all of the time.

Marc: One of the biggest problems is that the teachers don't know anything about didactics. A teacher in primary education has had 4 or 5 years of teacher training, and university teachers have had hardly any training in our situation. You are lucky when they show up on all 4 days. I know that the timing is not right, for these teachers have only just started their professional development, but well—you have only 4 days, so you try to put some pressure on them. What I try to do is to give them some didactic assignments to make them think about the question: What is teaching really all about?

---

* *A tutor*, as used here, means *a teacher within a PBL-related teaching environment. Tutor* is derived from the Latin word *tueri*, which means, according to the Merriam-Webster online dictionary, "a person charged with the instruction and guidance of another." According to the Oxford pocket dictionary, *tutor* signifies one who teaches a single student or a small group of students. It may be noted that in this chapter where *teacher* is used, we refer to the explanation mentioned here.

Notice that the ideas about how to raise teachers' awareness about learning processes develop in close interactions that are not without strife. Participants exchange experiences and, as a result of the conversation, come to a fuller, contextually embedded understanding of what it means to train teachers in PBL. Participants explore three components in which PBL trainers have to be trained: handling the content, the group dynamics, and the learning processes. Participants develop these ideas in a dialogue where each of them brings in various, sometimes conflicting ideas and experiences. As the conversation evolves, they start to acknowledge the things brought in by each of them. Slight changes in views can be observed. Marc, for example, remains convinced that teachers should be trained in didactics, yet at the end of the conversation, he also acknowledges Lucy's comment that the timing might not be right for those teachers who have just started their professional development. Moreover, he formulates his claim more modestly, saying that new staff members should become somewhat more aware. This suggests that Lucy has made him aware of an important issue. The enhanced mutual understanding is exactly what we would consider as the additional value of communal dialogues between and among stakeholders in a responsive evaluation.

Referring to Josie's fragment, but also the subsequent fragments taken from the learning history and dialogue during one of the group interviews, one might wonder whether the enactivist perspective is not overly naive or idealistic, assuming a too egalitarian and democratic portrayal of teaching. Within teaching, power inevitably plays a role, potentially disturbing the processes of mutual tuning and balancing. In case of the example of Josie, she might have been a person holding on rigidly to her epistemological notions. This would have been an obstacle to reaching mutual understanding. We think that learning can only take place when curiously and courageously opening up to the other within dialogue. Holding on mindlessly to one's own authority is a major obstacle, potentially harming any learning taking place within student-teacher encounters (Langer, 1989, 1997). We acknowledge that this happens all too often in our schools and universities. Yet we also notice that in many instances people are willing to listen to others, such as Josie. She does not just give up her beliefs (which would have made her incredible), but is willing to adjust them to the situation at hand. Of course, consensus is not always possible. Yet in many instances, people do reach a temporary, practical agreement that enables them to cooperate and collaborate. Such a consensus is fragmentary; differences and conflicts may occur over time and will yield a new process of searching and learning. The role of the evaluator/researcher within enactivist research in general, and the way it has been played out within Josie's case, is that of an open and careful listener. A bicolor reflects and mirrors what he is provided with through the stories that are told, not explicitly with the intention to change. Change or learning often occurs, as was also the case in this situation, when people speak out loud and are probed by the researcher to restory their experience. As researchers, we tried to act with fidelity, which means, according to Blumenfeld-Jones (1995),

> by being true to the situation of the teller by recognizing, constructing, and establishing linkages between events, small and large, immediate and distant, immediate and historical. An attempt at fidelity illuminates

the way the world is a web within which actions are performed and motivated and understandings are directed. (p. 28)

This calls for sensitivity and a mindful attitude at the side of the researcher.

In the third phase of the responsive evaluation process, the conversations were extended to dialogues among stakeholders in two heterogeneous focus groups. Within a heterogeneous focus group, the participants of all identified stakeholder groups are mixed to engage in deliberative dialogue (in our case, the former participants, the teacher-trainers, and the course developers). This last phase aimed to formulate an agenda for resolved and unresolved issues among the stakeholders. It is in this meeting that we engaged the group first in developing ground rules to which the participants would agree. Guba and Lincoln (1989) acknowledge this procedure as a way of creating an environment that can facilitate deliberative dialogue.[2] Within a deliberative dialogue, the participants are willing to participate, are open and willing to change, and are willing to distribute power. To share or distribute power in a setting such as this might mean that teacher-trainers would not be forcefully and strategically proclaiming their opinions on the staff members due to their information advantage. However, because information differences between both groups are realistic with regards to PBL, we used this procedure. Both parties agreed on the previously mentioned claims. Within responsive evaluation, there is not absolute need to reach consensus about the raised issues. Often the end outcome is an agenda for further dialogues. This was also the case within this third phase. Mutual understanding was heightened. Both parties found the conversations enriching. They made arrangements to continue the dialogues also after the research had finished. Besides this, both the teacher-trainers and the teachers having talked to each other identified concrete "nuggets of knowledge" (i.e., immediately applicable knowledge bits for their schooling; Scribner, 1999).

Reflections on the Responsive Process in the Case

We already mentioned that the responsive evaluation process of the PBL course enhanced the participants' personal understanding. The learning histories, such as that of Robert, appeared to be a fruitful tool for helping participants in restorying their experiences, finding new meanings in their experiences, and gaining a fuller sense of self. The process also helped to attain a richer, contextually embedded understanding of what it means to train PBL teachers and what it means to be a PBL teacher. Another value of the responsive process is found in the reestablishment of connections among stakeholder groups and participants within stakeholder groups. The teacher-trainers mentioned that they often miss contacts with fellow teacher-trainers. This supports the statement that teaching and training are still individualized professions in which it is not common to talk with each about the dos and don'ts of a course in general and their functioning within it in particular. Still another value to the teacher-trainers was their need of concrete information on which to change their course. Listening to and probing each others' experiences was a rewarding learning experience because they each could take out the issues relevant to their practice. One of the first actions within responsive evaluation is the identification of the key stakeholders to the program or practice being evaluated. When talking about educational practices, the inclusion of students is of eminent importance when evaluating pedagogical training programs that are central to students' educational experiences.

Within responsive evaluation, the evaluator takes on the role of a facilitator creating conditions for genuine dialogues. First, he or she should be a *conversationalist*: assisting participants in making explicit what is unfolding around them and inside them, continually renaming these changing nuances, and unlocking the persistent grasp of old categories and dichotomies. Second, the researcher becomes a *story developer*, helping to trace and meaningfully record the interactions of the actors and objects

in the expanding spaces. To do so, facilitators should ask for context, thickening the stories told and adding detail to experiences. We have done so in the interviews and in the representation of their stories in the form of personal learning histories. This enhances the participants' indexical sensitivity (Roth et al., 2000), meaning the capacity to feel and accurately denote small, but significant differences between contexts. Langer (1997) has called this the capacity of mindfulness (i.e., the ability to think beyond habitually formed demarcations, boundaries, and dichotomies). When all participants are being stimulated to think this way—helped by a facilitator—all parties are invited to think beyond the given into new creative directions. In the next section, we provide a more in-depth discussion of the social learning processes taking place during the responsive evaluation.

Learning Within Responsive Evaluation

Traditional cognitivist models of learning from evaluation assume that learning occurs when evaluators transmit findings and conclusions to program participants and stakeholders and that they will then process and absorb that information. This transmissional view on information processing understands learning as a cognitive act, something that occurs in the mind of an individual and separated from other activities. Conducting an evaluation, acquiring knowledge, and applying it are thought of as distinct steps.

Schwandt (2004) specified the underlying assumptions, which also can be found in both behaviourist and cognitive theories of learning: (a) basic psychological processes of learning and cognition are considered the starting point for what it means to know and learn; (b) knowledge is thought of in terms of generalized propositions (statements) and symbolic representations that one "possesses" or "has" as a kind of knowledge capital; and (c) learning is an "internal" operation—it takes place in the mind of individual knowers.

This conceptualization of learning has been criticized by a number of scholars who argue that this model is based on questionable assumptions (Brown & Duguid, 1996; Nicolini, Gherardi, & Yanow, 2003; Niessen et al., 2008; Schwandt, 2004). First of all, practitioners do not have a static relation to knowledge. Ideas and knowledge change over time and in relation to context. Second, this model does not acknowledge the fact that people will have to interpret knowledge and that interpretation and application of knowledge is normative and thus always influenced by interests and values. These criticisms suggest that a new way of studying what it means to learn from an evaluation is to attend carefully to the actual and unfolding learning process amid the people entering the dialogue. To provide an understanding to the concept of learning within evaluation, we look more closely to the information gathered during the responsive evaluation process. We outline and understand the learning taking place during evaluation using an enactivist account and drawing on complexity theories.

Individual Dialogical Learning

From an enactivist perspective, learning is not a "thing" or a characteristic found "over there" "in the individual" objectively. Josie, for example, talked about an occasion in which her usual teaching approach to create a common thread together with the participants did not work. Reflecting on it, she realized that it could not work in this particular situation because the group was too large, the participants had too much experience, and her trainings skills at that point had reached the level of an advanced beginner. The learning in this example consisted of the realization that the confrontation between her ideals and the specifics (other elements) of the teaching situation led to the situation as it did (i.e., her being unable to create a common thread). The learning that took place within this situation is not to be located solely within the individual, but within the interstices or the

cracks surfacing as a result of the collision of elements that make up each teaching situation.

Learning also can be regarded as an inner dialogical process among multiple voices or colliding I-positions (Hermans, 2002; Hermans, Kempen, & Van Loon, 1992). Robert, for example, talked enthusiastically about his childhood and his father being a classical teacher. From this position, it made sense to talk about teaching as telling students what they need to know. Talking about other experiences and subsequent schoolings, he felt more at ease being a teacher that was more facilitating and less telling students what to do. This was another more contemporary voice acquired during later schoolings. The struggles and resistances he met related to the question of which of these voices or I-positions should take precedence within what teaching situation. The difference between this story and that of Josie was that the latter was set at the interface level being in dialogue with students and other elements. The experiences from Robert showed that simultaneously on an inner level a dialogue took place between different I-positions.

Communal Dialogical Learning

In our responsive evaluation of the introductory course on PBL, we did not only engage in individual talks with participants. We also held homogeneous and heterogeneous focus group interviews trying to capture some of the issues and dynamics mentioned earlier *in situ*. We have shown that changes and learning within the dialogues as part of responsive evaluation came about by evolution, not revolution. People did change and alter their views within the dialogues' setting place. However, we also acknowledge that these changes might be overlooked by the participants or be ignored as insignificant because they are minor and taking place within short and quick timeframes.

Within one of our interviews, for example, a teacher-trainer, talking about training new staff members, specifically referred to the culture in his faculty and the specific population of participants within his introductory course. Highlighting these specifics and talking about them in conversation with others resulted in adding even more detail. The process of adding context and texture to general PBL-related issues and concerns within an open atmosphere resulted in more openness and susceptibility to detail. It also allowed participants to alter their views in small steps. This is important because people do not change their views radically overnight.

Given that the changes in perspective are often small, they might not be acknowledged as changes. Often the change in a participant's view rests in the acknowledgment of the other person's view, such as Marc acknowledging Lucy's remarks about the appropriateness of talking to novice teachers about didactics (see Box 21.3), thus changing the tone of the conversation minutely, yet significantly. Such changes, although minor, enable adaptation to local and situational contingencies. Potentially, such acknowledgments do provide the space for participants to fuse horizons. The verb *occasioning*, as used by Davis (2004), aptly represents the way in which minor perturbations (the contributions by different participants in a conversation) may influence dialogues in small but significant ways. In contrast to a linear approach, the term *occasioning* signifies unawareness of the direction in which perturbations and their effects are heading.

Conversations are meaningful because they contain various implicit values. References are made to values grounded in personal experiences and related to issues that are important to participants at a personal level. Perhaps the phrase *meaningful knowing* is a more appropriate description of the dialogic process. The aim is not necessarily to reach consensus about certain values. Rather, it may be to converse and learn about these values so as to achieve some clarification. As participants in a conversation reflect on and explicate their values to each other, a small distance or breach is created between the situation at hand and the values that are being enacted. This breach is a precondition for becoming attentive to one's own and other people's values.

Conclusion

Our responsive evaluation of the introductory course on PBL presupposes that teacher involvement within curriculum revision initiatives is of utmost importance. In line with enactivist theories, we propose a way of thinking that is dialogical in nature. This dialogical approach regards the learning process of the participants, as well as our own work as evaluators.

Responsive evaluation states that the need for revisions and the kind of alternations needed in the revision of an educational program are not primarily determined by the scientist-researcher-evaluator. Responsive evaluation stresses that realities are constructed within social-relational processes. This means that the changes one would like to make concerning a curriculum will depend on the position one has vis-à-vis the curriculum being evaluated. The teachers may want to change other features of the course or the curriculum than the teacher-trainers or course developers. Within the responsive evaluation process, the different stakeholders should engage in deliberative dialogues about the meaning of their practice and the modifications that are needed. Within such a conversation, one stakeholder group should not claim precedence over the other. As pointed out by Roth et al. (2000), educationalists and curriculum revisionists should differentiate between the theoretical and enacted curriculum. Both are necessary to make the program or curriculum work.

We think a responsive approach could be applied more systematically throughout the whole design or revision process of a curriculum, as is done within participatory design (Button & Dourich, 1996). Within this approach, the end users of the program or curriculum are legitimate partners throughout the design or revision activities. The common or general goal within participatory design is to democratize technologies and invite end users of a technology as legitimate partners in the design process because the daily praxis cannot be accounted for by the designers accurately (Button & Dourich, 1996).

The role of the end user and end product should and cannot be determined only by the goal the designer has in mind. The dialogue among participants in a gradually developing design process is constitutive of working programs (Anderson & Crocca, 1993).

Stressing egalitarian dialogue, and thus blurring the lines between educational developer and teacher, does not mean that the contribution by the educationalist should be minimized or dismissed. Rather, the value of a program is determined dialogically and anchored within the positions of the relevant stakeholders to the program being evaluated. This results in local contextually sensitive knowledge. Thick descriptions, such as the ones provided in this chapter, assist readers to translate locally developed knowledge to other contexts. Thick descriptions illuminate the complexity of a studied setting and provide readers with a vicarious experience. Local knowledge naturally fits with people's need for stories. According to Stake (1986), people change their views and ideas evolutionarily, relating vicarious experiences to their own experiences. In this respect, Stake calls for "naturalistic generalizations" (Abma & Stake, 2001). Over time, researchers can deduce petite generalizations from several case histories to build small (vs. grand) theories.

Within a society that values evidence, facts, general knowledge, and grand theories, contextually sensitive and empirically embedded knowledge sometimes meets hostility. Expert, scientific knowledge is claimed to be objective, general, and abstract, as well as to be superior to what is then called subjective, emotional knowledge. Local knowledge is underprivileged: It is associated with antimodern traditionalism with backward parochialism (Yanow, 2004). Yet at the same time, we notice that there remains a fundamental need among people as storied beings for the particular, tacit, everyday understandings. In an age of globalization, defined as a process of transformation of local phenomena into global ones, the capability of organizations and governments to deal with "local" problems has been further reduced (Stern, 2006).

Interdependences between actors increase, and in such a multistakeholder environment, "evaluators have to become consensus builders, conciliators and negotiators. . . . When the purposes of evaluation include empowerment then the need for these skills becomes even more vital" (Stern, 2006, p. 299). Responsive evaluation provides a model for engagement and dialogue and fosters interactive learning circles building on culturally sensitive, locally inspired, and contextual forms of knowing.

Notes

1. Guba and Lincoln (1989), moreover, identify catalytic authenticity, educative authenticity, tactical authenticity, and fairness.

2. "Deliberation refers to the interaction and dialogue between participants. They do not just accept each other's beliefs and persuasions, but will explore these. Listening, probing and dialogue characterise this process, rather than confronting, attacking and defending. Central feature of dialogue are openness, respect, inclusion and engagement" (Abma, 2005, p. 280).

References

Abma, T. A. (1999). Powerful stories about the role of stories in sustaining and transforming professional practice within a mental hospital. In R. Josselson (Eds.), *The narrative study of lives* (Vol. 6, pp. 169–196). Thousand Oaks, CA: Sage.

Abma, T. A. (2000). Dynamic inquiry relationships: Ways of creating, sustaining, and improving the inquiry process through the recognition and management of conflicts. *Qualitative Inquiry, 6*(1), 133–151.

Abma, T. A. (2005). Responsive evaluation: Its meaning and special contribution to health promotion. *Evaluation and Program Planning, 28,* 279–289.

Abma, T. A., & Broerse, J. E. W. (2007). *Agency in science: Patient participation in theory and practice.* Lemma: Den Haag.

Abma, T. A., Molewijk, B., & Widdershoven, G. A. M. (2007). Good care in ongoing dialogues. Improving the quality of care through moral deliberation and responsive evaluation. *Health*

Care Analysis. Retrieved January 13, 2009, from Springerlink.com.

Abma, T. A., & Stake, R. E. (2001). Stake's responsive evaluation: Core ideas and evolution. In J. Greene & T. Abma (Eds.), *New Directions for Evaluation* (pp. 7–21). San Francisco, CA: Jossey-Bass.

Abma, T. A., & Widdershoven, G. A. M. (2005). Sharing stories: Narrative and dialogue in responsive nursing evaluation. *Evaluation & the Health Professions, 28*(1), 90–109.

Anderson, W., & Crocca, W. (1993). Engineering practice and co-development of product and prototypes. *Communication of the ACM, 36*(4), 49–56.

Basten, F. (2000). *Metaforen en verhalen over organisatiewetenschap en onderwijsinnovatie. Een leergeschiedenis.* Venlo, Netherlands: Repro Press.

Blumenfeld-Jones, D. (1995). Fidelity as a criterion for participating and evaluating in narrative inquiry. *Qualitative Studies in Education, 8*(1), 25–35.

Brown, J., & Duguid, P. (1996). Organizational learning and communities-of-practice. In M. Cohen & L. Sproull (Eds.), *Organisational learning* (pp. 40–57). London: Sage.

Button, G., & Dourich, P. (1996). *Technomethodology: Paradoxes and possibilities.* Cambridge: Cambridge University Press.

Cousins, J. B., & Earl, L. (1995). *Participatory evaluation in education: Studies in evaluation use and organizational learning.* New York: Falmer Press.

Davis, B. (2004). *Inventions of teaching: A genealogy.* Mahwah, NJ: Lawrence Erlbaum Associates.

Geertz, C. (1973). Thick description: Toward an interpretive theory of culture. In C. Geertz (Ed.), *The interpretation of cultures: Selected essays* (pp. 3–30). New York: Basic Books.

Giddens, A. (1991). *Modernity and self-identity: Self and society in the late modern age.* Stanford, CA: Stanford University Press.

Greene, J. C. (1997). Participatory evaluation. In L. Mabry (Eds.), *Evaluation and the postmodern dilemma, Advances in program evaluation* (Vol. 3, pp. 171–190). Greenwich, CT: JAI Press.

Greene, J. C. (1999). The inequality of performance measurements. *Evaluation, 5*(2), 160–172.

Guba, E. G., & Lincoln, Y. S. (1989). *Fourth generation evaluation.* Beverly Hills, CA: Sage.

Guba, E. G., & Lincoln, Y. S. (2005). Paradigmatic controversies, contradictions, and emerging confluences. In N. Denzin & Y. Lincoln (Eds.), *Handbook of qualitative research* (pp. 191–215). Thousand Oaks, CA: Sage.

Hermans, H. J. (2002). Special issue on dialogical self. *Theory & Psychology, 12*(2), 147–280.

Hermans, H. J. M., Kempen, H., & Van Loon, R. J. P. (1992). The dialogical self beyond individualism and rationalism. *American Psychologist, 47*(1), 23–33.

Heron, J., & Reason, P. (1997). A participatory inquiry paradigm. *Qualitative Inquiry, 3*(3), 274–294.

Josselson, R., & Lieblich, A. (1999). *Making meaning of narratives: The narrative study of lives* (Vol. 6). Thousand Oaks, CA: Sage.

Lave, J., & Wenger, E. (1991). *Situated learning: Legitimate peripheral participation.* Cambridge: Cambridge University Press.

Langer, E. J. (1989). *Mindfulness.* New York: Addison Wesley.

Langer, E. J. (1997). *The power of mindful learning.* Reading, MA: Merloyd Lawrence Book, Perseus Books.

Lincoln, Y. (2003, January 27–28). *Tracks toward a postmodern politics of evaluation.* Earlier version of paper prepared for delivery at the fifth annual conference of the Southeast Evaluation Association, Tallahassee, FL.

Lincoln, Y. S., & Guba, E. G. (1985). *Naturalistic inquiry.* Beverly Hills: CA: Sage.

Lyons, N., & LaBoskey, V. K. (2002). *Narrative inquiry in practice: Advancing inquiry in practice.* New York: Teacher's College Press.

Moust, J. H. C., Berkel, H. J. M. V., & Schmidt, H. G. (2005). Signs of erosion: Reflections on three decades of problem-based learning at Maastricht University. *Higher Education, 50,* 665–683.

Nicolini, D., Gherardi, S., & Yanow, D. (2003). Introduction: Toward a practice-based view of knowing and learning in organizations. In D. Nicolini, S. Gherardi, & D. Yanow (Eds.), *Knowing in organizations: A practice-based approach.* Armonk, NY: M. E. Sharpe.

Niessen, T. J. H. (2007). *Emerging epistemologies: Making sense of teaching practice.* Unpublished doctoral dissertation, University of Maastricht, Maastricht.

Niessen, T. J. H., Abma, T. A., Widdershoven, G. A. M., Akkerman, S., & van der Vleuten, C. P. M. (2008). Contemporary epistemological research in education: Reconciliation and reconceptualisation of the Field. *Theory & Psychology, 18*(1), 27–45.

Niessen, T. J. H., Vermunt, J. D. H. M., Abma, T. A., Widdershoven, G. A. M., & Vleuten, C. P. M. (2004). On the nature and form of epistemologies: Revealing hidden assumptions through an analysis of instrument design. *European Journal of School Psychology, 2*(1), 39–64.

Noordegraaf, M., & Abma, T. A. (2003). Management by measurement. *Journal of Public Administration*, *81*(4), 853–872.

Patton, M. (1990). *Qualitative evaluation and research methods*. Newbury Park, CA: Sage.

Roth, G.-W., Lawless, D., & Tobin, K. (2000). Time to teach: Towards a praxeology of teaching. *Canadian Journal of Education*, *25*, 1–15.

Schwandt, T. A. (2003). Back to the rough ground! Beyond theory to practice in evaluation, *Evaluation*, *9*(3), 353–364.

Schwandt, T. A. (2004, October). *Some thoughts on learning in and from evaluation*. Stimulus paper presented at the panel "Learning Evaluation: The Relevance of Communities of Practice," European Evaluation Society sixth biennial conference, Berlin, Germany.

Scribner, J. P. (1999). Professional development: Untangling the influence of work context on teacher learning. *Educational Administration Quarterly*, *35*(2), 238–266.

Stake, R. E. (1975). *Evaluating the arts in education: A responsive approach*. Columbus, OH: Merrill.

Stake, R. E. (1986). An evolutionary view of program improvement. In E. House (Ed.), *New directions in educational evaluation* (pp. 89–102). Philadelphia: The Falmer Press.

Stake, R. E., & Abma, T. A. (2005). Responsive evaluation. In S. Mathison (Ed.), *Encyclopedia of evaluation* (pp. 376–379). Thousand Oaks, CA: Sage.

Stern, E. (2006). Contextual challenges for evaluation practice. In I. F. Shaw, J. C. Greene, & M. M. Mark (Eds.), *The Sage handbook of evaluation* (pp. 292–314). London: Sage.

Stronach, I. (1999). Shouting theatre in a crowded fire: "Educational effectiveness" as cultural performance. *Evaluation*, *5*(2), 173–193.

Titchen, A., & McCormack, B. (2008). A methodological walk in the forest: Critical creativity and human flourishing. In K. Manley, B. McCormack, & V. Wilson (Eds.), *International practice development in nursing and healthcare* (pp. 59–83). New York: Blackwell Publishing.

Van der Knaap, P. (2006). Responsive evaluation and performance measurement: Overcoming the downsides of policy objectives and performance indicators. *Evaluation*, *12*(3), 278–293.

Whitmore, E. (1994). To tell the truth: Working with oppressed groups in participatory approaches to inquiry. In P. Reason (Ed.), *Participation in human inquiry* (pp. 82–98). Newbury Park, CA: Sage.

Widdershoven, G. A. M., & Sohl, C. (1999). Interpretation, action and communication: Four stories about a supported employment program. In T. A. Abma (Ed.), *Telling tales. On narrative and evaluation, advances in program evaluation* (Vol. 6, pp. 109–130). Westport, CT: JAI Press.

Yanow, D. (2004). Translating local knowledge at organizational peripheries. *British Journal of Management*, *15*, 9–25.

CHAPTER 22

Educational Evaluation as Mediated Mutual Learning

John Elliott

Introduction

The purpose of this chapter is to outline a perspective on globalization that is quite different from the "convergence of cultures" perspective embedded in much contemporary educational policymaking. This different perspective depicts the globalization process as the production of "multiple culturally attuned capitalisms." It presents different challenges for education and therefore has different implications for policy and the evaluation of educational programs. The theory of globalization that drives contemporary educational policymaking shapes a genre of program evaluation that Nussbaum (1990) has depicted as the "science of measurement." The "multiplicity of cultures" perspective, in contrast, is commensurate with notions of program evaluation that are articulated and illustrated in this section of the handbook. These emphasize the importance of developing "situational understanding" through portrayals of the complexity of program contexts in all their particularity. Such portrayals strive to capture multiple perspectives on the program by engaging a range of stakeholder groups in their construction. They can be summed up in genre terms as *Evaluation as Learning.*

However, program evaluations within the Evaluation as Learning genre may neglect to systematically address the question of how to improve student learning in the context of globalization. In this respect, I would argue that this form of evaluation is paying insufficient attention to the global aspects of the program context. I attempt to demonstrate the significance and importance of the question from the multiplicity of cultures perspective. This chapter supports a critical appraisal of program evaluation construed as a science of measurement, as well as an Evaluation as Learning genre that claims sensitivity to particular contexts but fails to discern the interactions within those contexts between the global and the local. Globalization, I argue, permeates the contexts of educational program evaluation in a form that renders the question of how to improve student learning a major object of learning for evaluation. However, it conceives of this question in different terms to those employed in the globalization theory that underpins much contemporary educational policymaking.

In the course of this chapter, I hope to indicate a future direction for the development of the Evaluation as Learning genre at the levels of both theory and practice. At the level of theory, I argue that educational program evaluation needs to evolve an explicit democratic theory of rationality; and at the level of practice, it needs to be shaped in the form of more discursive designs.

Culture and Education in a Single-Commodity World

The view of educational evaluation developed in this chapter is informed by a particular theory about the relationship between the globalization of markets and particular cultures, which has implications for education. This theory states that international markets are shaped by the particular cultures in which they remain embedded. There are many versions of capitalism, and each has its own unique combination of benefits and costs (see Gray, 1998).

This theory of globalization differs from the one that appears to be currently driving education policymaking, particularly in the Anglo-Saxon world. It has been described as the *convergence of cultures* thesis (Beck, 2000; Gray, 1998), which rests on a utopian notion of a generic free market driven by multinational corporations that emancipate international markets from regulation by particular states and their institutions. I wish initially to outline this thesis in sufficient detail to draw out its quite different implications for education and educational program evaluation to the theory of globalization that underpins my argument in this chapter.

The theory contends that the creation of a global free market (see Gray, 1998) led to greater convergence in the use of cultural symbols and ways of life. Beck (2000) argues that the key word for this thesis is *McDonaldization*, with its implication that "as the last niches are integrated into the world market, what emerges is indeed *one world*" (pp. 42–43). On this thesis, the growth of a *single commodity world* has the effect of uprooting local identities and cultures. According to Beck, the thesis leaves no space for the recognition of "multiplicities or mutual openness where images of oneself and foreigners are pluralist and cosmopolitan" (pp. 42–43). Cultural boundaries are dissipated, and the function of nation-states is reduced to promoting economic growth through minimizing costs and maximizing profits. Globalization is viewed exclusively as an economic process in which diverse market economies are integrated into a single global free market freed from social and political constraints. In such a market, everything becomes commoditized—thinking processes, mindsets, and worldviews—beyond what might be considered to be the normal range of consumer goods (see Gray, 1998).

Gray (1998) contends that the deregulation of markets is not simply a *laissez-faire* refusal of governments to intervene in the economic sphere. It also involves strong state intervention to "wage war" on powerful intermediary institutions—the trade unions and professional associations—that have traditionally served as buffers between individuals and market forces. The emergence of a global market, what Gray regards as a decisive moment in the development of a late modern species of anarchic and disordered capitalism, demands that these institutions are weakened or destroyed. The use of market mechanisms—such as competitive tendering for public funds and performance-related and profit-related pay—have all been injected into the public services to this end. In engineering a global free market, Gray claims that states find themselves increasingly unable to predict and control its behavior. Job insecurity is a basic feature of late modern capitalism. Technological innovation combined with deregulated market competition leave decreasing space for stable career structures and vocations within the social organization of work. Increasingly, the latter is in a continuous state of flux.

According to Gray (1998), the United States, Britain, Australia, and New Zealand are the standard bearers of the new late modern species of capitalism. Indeed, he argues, it is a peculiarly American project that is shaped by Anglo-Saxon cultural values and beliefs about the relationships between the market, individuals, and social institutions. He is keen to point out that, although the main features of disordered capitalism are projected from the Anglo-Saxon world into nearly every country, their impact on economic and social life differs considerably. These "differences arise from historical divergences in cultures and economic institutions" (Gray, 1998, p. 74).

Globalization in the longer term may well consist of an increasing multiplicity of culturally attuned capitalisms, as opposed to the emergence of a generic free market and the subsequent creation of a single-commodity world. Hence, "each version of capitalism articulates the particular culture in which it remains embedded. This is true of the free market, which expresses local American values of individualism" (Gray, 1998, p. 191).

Education as Human Capital Production for the Global Free Market

From the utopian perspective of the *global free market*, educational systems become an integral part of the global economy, with the key function of producing the human capital that the nation needs to secure competitive advantage in the global market over other countries. Human capital consists of those human qualities that have high-commodity value in the labor market inasmuch as they are perceived to augment production possibilities in the country and thereby contribute to its economic growth. In the context of globalization, abilities to use new technologies for processing large amounts of complex information are privileged because they enable organizations to gain a competitive edge and will be in short supply. Such abilities are presumed to be generic context-free skills that do not depend on a lot of experience and discernment of the particularities of circumstance. They are the skills required of the flexible knowledge worker in the New Capitalism

depicted by Sennett (2006). For Sennett, they are embodied in the process work of consultants "moving from scene to scene, problem to problem, team to team" (pp. 121–122). The abilities privileged by process work will avoid probing for deeper situated meanings beneath the surface meanings of the information given. They are about getting things done quickly without a lot of time-intensive work. Sennett refers to the importance of the social skill of cooperating with others in the fast-changing organization where it cannot matter who the other is. The skill lies in cooperating regardless of circumstance. He contends that high-commodity value is placed on "hollowed-out" abilities whose operation:

> cuts reference to experience and the chains of circumstance, eschews sensate impressions, divides analysing from believing, ignores the glue of emotional attachment, penalizes digging deep—a state of living in pure process which the philosopher Zygmunt Bauman calls "liquid modernity." (Sennett, 2006, pp. 121–122)

If Sennett and Bauman accurately depict the notion of skills in late modern societies, then an education that focuses exclusively on human capital production will place a premium on the worker's performativity in a rapidly changing working environment. As a consequence, it will display little concern that in such an environment the qualities it produces will create a deficit of trust and loyalty and erode the value of accumulated experience (see Sennett, 2006).

The prospect of education augmenting the production of a single-commodity world implies increasing *curriculum convergence* across the education systems of nation-states as a direct effect of globalization. Mental processes become hollowed out for production purposes in the form of standardized and commoditized generic skills. Educational systems will display little variation in their valued knowledge and skill outcomes, allowing these systems and their curricula to be judged and compared against a uniform set of "world-class" measurable standards. This will explain the increasing attraction of international comparisons and benchmarking to politicians and civil servants, as well as their proliferation.

With the growth of new technologies, there will be, on the one hand, a need for educational institutions to equip students to perform relatively mechanical and routine tasks, whereas, on the other hand, they equip a new meritocracy of "knowledge workers" and "process managers" with generic thinking and social skills. However, as Sennett (2006) points out, employers will tend to increasingly seek people with high levels of generic knowledge and skill for routine low-paid work because they are able to handle situations that critically, if not frequently, arise when the routines break down or simply fail to apply. The labor market will tend to search for talent on the cheap.

Within a free market global economy, those curriculum experiences that are deemed to possess little commodity value, such as in the humanities and the fine arts, become marginalized "twilight subjects" that are allowed to "whither on the vine" through the device of *student choice.* Because in educational policy contexts priority currently tends to be given to the formation of students' identities as economic subjects, policymakers will presume that their *personal* curriculum choices will, in the main, be economically motivated. Rational preferences will be understood as those learning experiences that enhance the competitive advantage of individuals in the labor market.

When education is largely directed toward the production of human capital, its institutions become an integral part of the economic system. Such an aim, it is argued, is necessary for the economic growth of the country as well as for reducing income poverty. Evidence is frequently cited to demonstrate that the acquisition of human capital through education brings a high return to individuals in the form of private wealth. "Human capital theory" aspires to reconcile "economic growth" at the level of the nation-state with equality of opportunity to accumulate private wealth. What it glosses over is that supply is likely to exceed demand, and that the idea of a

new kind of skills-based meritocracy to replace the old one, shaped by hierarchicalized and stable career structures, is a fanciful one. Many students recognize this and opt out of lengthy periods of education and training as soon as they can leave school and earn some ready cash. Human capital theory fails to convincingly show how it will enable educational institutions to meet the requirements of justice. Despite claims that educational achievements are rising across the population, the achievement gap between the rich and the poor continues to widen (see Grossman & Golab, 2007). This is because, as Sennett (2006) argues, the educational system is now turning out large numbers of educated young people when the new skills economy may increasingly function perfectly well by "drawing on an ever-smaller elite" (p. 86). An educational system aimed exclusively at human capital production can never meet the requirements of justice because "the skills economy still leaves behind the majority." The relatively small number of the educated who possess talents that are actually required will, according to Sennett, tend to be drawn into "the cutting-edge realms of high finance, advanced technology, and sophisticated services." Perhaps the service provided by the educational evaluator might be included among the latter.

Educational Evaluation as the Science of Measurement

The idea of the global free market, and the subordination of educational institutions to the economic imperatives that stem from human capital theory, has resulted in a policy mindset that Nussbaum (1990) anticipated over a decade and a half ago with her characterization of "the science of measurement" as the picture of practical reasoning that dominates "public policy formation in our time." I would argue that the prevailing hegemony of the science of measurement in educational planning is the outcome of a global tendency of governments to abstract economic from social ends.

Nussbaum (1990) contends that this picture of reason embodies four claims:(a) the claim of metricity, which is the use of a single standard to weigh alternative choices; (b) the claim that the same standard applies in all situations (singularity); (c) the claim of consequentialism—that the chosen actions only have instrumental value as a means of producing good consequences; and (d) by combining each of these claims, we have the principle of maximization—"that there is some one value, that it is the point of rational choice, in every case, to maximize" (pp. 56–57).

The rationality of policymaking that is shaped by this picture of practical reason implies an objectivist and instrumental conception of rationality. Such a rationality, according to Dryzek (1990), depends on a capacity to "devise, select and effect good means to clarified ends" (pp. 3–4) and on a set of objective standards for measuring the achievement of such ends and which apply to all individuals. Technologies of educational evaluation have rapidly evolved on a global scale to guarantee and preserve a form of rationality that:

1. Excludes any consideration of learning as a convivial, spontaneous, and intrinsically meaningful process;

2. Serves the interests of an unequal distribution of power to define worthwhile learning and is to that extent antidemocratic;

3. Represses the individual as a learner by placing limits on his or her freedom to control his or her own learning;

4. Is incapable of grasping learning as a complex phenomenon; and

5. Fixes educational standards and fails to capture quality in learning in all its manifold aspects. (These five points are based on Dryzek's [1990] analysis of what counts against a reliance on instrumental reason.)

From the standpoint of the *global free market project* and the *convergence of culture* thesis, the expertise of the educational evaluator is primarily depicted as his or her command of a method for gathering and processing information that fits and can be justified in terms of *the science of measurement*. She or he is expected, in the course of conducting an evaluation of an educational program, to demonstrate a *mastery of techniques*, rather than her or his capabilities as a learner. The principles of practical reason employed ensure that:

1. There are no complexities to be grasped regarding the program, arising from multiple interpretations of its evaluative significance in the situation of choice;

2. Standards of judgment are given in advance of the process and do not need to be determined *in process* on the basis of situated and reflective understandings of the program in action; and

3. There is nothing to be learned about the merits of the program other than on the basis of evidence about the extent to which it maximizes intended outcomes.

The skill of the evaluator lies in his or her mastery of a battery of techniques for gathering and processing large amounts of quantitative data in accordance with the methodological principles of the science of measurement. Once mastery has been achieved, there is little learning to be done during the course of an evaluation. *Evaluation as learning* is *learning to evaluate*, and it applies to the apprenticeship phase only. Of course, the point of the evaluation is to learn whether the program is worth adopting. However, such learning is an outcome of the evaluation and not an intrinsic part of the process. There is little space for learning in an evaluation process shaped by the science of measurement. The more evaluation creates space for methodology, the less space there is for learning. It could be argued that this is no bad thing because the idea of evaluation as a methodology renders it a field of professional expertise.

I now wish to turn to the multiplicity of cultures perspective on globalization that I referred to at the start of this chapter and explore its implications for education and educational evaluation. I argue that, on this account, globalization challenges educational evaluation to take the form of a learning process that is *democratic, discursive,* and *developmentally oriented.* Another way of putting this is to claim that globalization can create conditions that free educational evaluation from the tyranny of experts and method. More of this later.

Globalization as the Spread of Indigenous Forms of Culturally Attuned Capitalism

As I indicated earlier, Gray (1998) contends that the global free market is a transient project that is already aborting, arguing that, although the spawning of new technologies is the basic mechanism driving the globalization of markets, their impact in many parts of the world is the reverse of what the free market experiment anticipated. Hence, in spreading to East Asia, new technologies do not serve as carriers of the economic cultures that produced them, such as that of the free market and the individualism that underpins it. Instead, the new technologies are interacting with indigenous cultures to generate new types of capitalism. Gray (1998) summarizes his general thesis as follows:

> The growth of a world economy does not inaugurate a universal civilization, as both Smith and Marx thought it must. Instead it allows the growth of indigenous kinds of capitalism, diverging from the ideal free market and from each other. It creates regimes that achieve modernity by renewing their own cultural traditions, not by imitating western countries. There are many modernities and many ways of failing to be modern. (p. 195)

On the view outlined previously, globalization is a process in which the economic activities of countries become locked into networks of relationships that transcend national boundaries.

In this sense, they become *delocalized.* However, rather than leading to a convergence of economic cultures, globalization depends on the diversity of such cultures. Economic activity through networks that cross national boundaries stimulates the renewal of indigenous cultures, rather than result in cultural uniformity. The relationship between economic activity and indigenous culture is an interactive one. On the one hand, it is embedded in the indigenous culture; on the other hand, it is stimulating its renewal in the process of protecting and conserving it. Globalization is a dialectical process in which the global and the local intersect in *transnational space.* This space is an intensification of mutual dependence across national boundaries, not a decontextualized space of appearance for a single commodity world. As the economic activities of different countries become increasingly interdependent, rather than uniform, the different cultures that shape them interpenetrate each other. Transnational space is where a world horizon appears in "the cross-cultural production of meaning and cultural symbols" (see Beck, 2000, p. 47). Each culture draws on elements in the others without collapsing into a single commodity world and losing its distinctiveness. Beck (2000) argues that, in transnational space, the distinctions between cultures are *inclusive* rather than *exclusive.* The borders between them delineate "mobile patterns that facilitate overlapping loyalties" rather than separate worlds. Hence, in the course of their lives, individuals can construct multiple and transcultural identities that cross geographical, ethnic, and cultural borders.

Both Gray (1998) and Beck (2000) point out that cultural convergence—the creation of a single commodity world—would stifle the globalization of markets. The latter depends on localization—the extent to which indigenous cultures are able to generate cultural symbols that can open up new commodity worlds at the global level.

Robertson (1992) has proposed that the term *glocalization* be used to replace that of *globalization,* arguing that the *local* and *global* are not best understood as exclusive categories (see

Beck, 2000). *Localization* must now be understood as an aspect of *globalization* and the latter as a bringing together of *clashing localities* in transnational space and in the process redefining and integrating them into a larger whole. The key terms of this new cultural perspective are, according to Beck (2000), those of "politics of culture, cultural capital, cultural difference, cultural homogeneity, ethnicity, race, and gender" (pp. 48–49).

From the standpoint of a cultural perspective on globalization, the major purpose of education is to prepare students for *glocal living* in transnational space. In such space, there is no appearance of a single and uniform commodity world and no stable set of occupational structures that can be linked to its production. What appears to the individual is a plural transcultural world and an unstable labor market in which opportunities for secure paid employment are in decline. The challenge to individuals is how to create an identity and a life for themselves out of the multiplicity of cultural resources that surrounds them and in circumstances where they cannot rely on external organizations to supply them with stable employment and careers.

Education for Global Living in Transnational Space

As Beck (2000) claims, "the meaning of learning changes within the transcultural nexus" (p. 138). The "dialectic of globalisation," he contends, replaces traditional didactic pedagogy with "dialogic attentiveness and the courage to disagree." In responding to the challenges of globalization, educational institutions will need to work with a different conception of learning to the instrumental conception that has increasingly come to frame their pedagogical practice. They will need to portray learning as a convivial, spontaneous, and intrinsically meaningful process of inquiry, in which the only constraints are conversational ones "provided by the remarks of our fellow inquirers" (Rorty, 1982, p. 165). When learning is conceived in these terms, the power to define what are to

count as worthwhile outcomes is evenly distributed through the community of inquirers. It leaves no space for standardizing and fixing learning outcomes in advance of the process.

Such an open-ended view of learning is necessary if educational institutions are to enable students to make themselves, to become centers for self-organizing and managing the construction of their identities and destinies in life. In the process, students will:

1. Take increasing responsibility for forging and developing their personal learning agendas. Such agendas will specify the objects of learning believed to be worth engaging with and the questions, issues, and topics believed to be worth addressing in relation to them.

2. Search out, select, and use information as a resource for their thinking and reflection, engaging with it dialogically and discussing its diverse meanings with others.

Traditionally, pedagogy has taken the form of instruction directed toward bringing about intended learning outcomes couched in the form of content objectives. As such, the teacher is *an authority* on what is worth learning, and the learner is expected to internalize the norms that govern the classification and framing of the content to be learned. Within a transformed pedagogy, the teacher will be *in authority* over a learning process that is directed toward giving students more control over their future lives, and thereby reducing the compliance of their thinking with externally imposed norms. In this context, learning will be assessed in terms of criteria that specify qualities of thought and action inherent in a process of self-directed (autonomous) learning, rather than in terms of outcome measures.

An education that prepares students for life in transnational and glocalized space will decreasingly be solely driven by notions of human capital production that are couched in terms of either occupationally specific productive knowledge and skills or hollowed-out generic skills. Instead, such an education will be concerned with the development of capabilities to exercise agency in a wide range of action contexts, including the world of work.

A culturally attuned perspective on globalization implies the construction of curriculum frameworks around the problems, issues, dilemmas, and opportunities that glocalization will pose for students in the course of their lives. These specific objects of learning will both differ and overlap from one country to another, because the impact of world markets will shape up in ways that are both similar and different across national/local contexts. Although their content will overlap, their curriculum content will not converge into a uniform global curriculum. Similarly, the range of functionings (see Sen, 1999), which students will have opportunities to achieve in their education, will be similar in some respects and different in others across national/local boundaries.

From "Human Capital" Theory to "Capability Theory" as a Basis for Educational Reform

The reorientation of education outlined earlier is entirely consistent with Sen's (1999) "capability theory" and his idea of "development as freedom." Sen links his definition of *capability* to the Aristotelian notion of *human functionings*. He states: "A person's capability refers to the alternative combinations of functionings that are feasible for her to achieve. Capability is thus a kind of freedom: to achieve various lifestyles" (Sen, 1999, p. 75).

Functionings are activities that are experienced as worth pursuing for their own sake. Specific capabilities are therefore capacities to enrich one's life by realizing in action the values inherent in particular functionings. They are capacities to do something well in accordance with standards that are internal to the activity. A person's general capability, in contrast, is the capacity to rationally choose a particular combination of functionings as a way of life. Sen's

(1999) concept of capability, therefore, embraces both capacities for realizing particular functionings, and the general capacity to reason about which functionings should make up one's chosen way of life. This distinction reflects Dewey's distinction between *valuing* and *evaluation*. *To value* refers to a direct appreciation of the quality of an experience, unmediated by the use of words and symbols, whereas *evaluation* refers to the passing of a reasoned judgment "upon the nature and amount of its value as compared with something else" (Sen, 1999, p. 238). Viewed in this light, capability refers to both capacities for appreciative realizations of value and a capability for evaluating the relative merits of different functions in choosing a way of life.

Dewey (1916) depicts the formation of evaluative judgment as a mode of reasoning that comes into play in a concrete practical situation, where an agent is faced with a choice of ends that are equally worth pursuing for their own sake but conflict with each other. Faced with a concrete situation of choice, the agent seeks a reason for preferring one course of action to another in the light of her understanding of what is needed in the situation. Finding a reason for judging the relative worth of different ends is a context-bound affair. "In the abstract, or at large," Dewey (1916) argues "there is no such thing as degrees or order of value" (p. 239). There are no context-free standards of evaluative reasoning (I also explore later the implications of this for educational evaluation). The situated form that evaluative reasoning takes implies that choosing a way of life will not be a one-off event. It will be a gradual and deliberative process that integrates and synthesizes specific evaluative judgments across a range and variety of concrete situations of choice into a coherent way of life. This situated form of reasoning also implies that choosing a way of life will be flexible and open to change in the light of further experience, rather than fixed and closed.

Dewey's distinction between valuing and evaluation also helps to illuminate a distinction that Sen (2002) draws between "the opportunity aspect" and the "process aspect" of freedom. The opportunity aspect is "concerned with our actual capability to achieve functionings that we value" (Sen, 2002, p. 506), whereas the process aspect relates to autonomous choice, "having the levers of control in one's own hands (no matter whether this enhances the actual opportunities of achieving our objectives or not)" (Sen, 2002, p. 506). Autonomous choice, for Sen, is a matter of opening up one's choices to a process of rational self-scrutiny, which bears marked resemblances to Dewey's notion of evaluative reasoning. It involves people being capable of rationally assessing their goal values or ends in view and the best means of pursuing them. The latter type of assessment will take the form of instrumental reasoning, weighing up the consequences of different alternatives, as well as involve a consideration of reasons for restricting choice of means on the grounds that some are more consistent than others with nongoal values (e.g., moral obligations toward others).

For Sen (2002), the development of society consists of expanding people's capabilities to do things *they value* and *have reason to value*, rather than simply increasing economic prosperity. This is because he views *development as freedom* and capabilities to be constitutive of freedom. Such freedom presupposes both negative and positive conditions (i.e., freedom from external constraints on opportunities to do things, and the development of capacities for doing them that are internal to the person; see Sen, 2002). Capabilities should not be confused with the hollowed-out generic skills that will tend to constitute human capital from the standpoint of global free market capitalism. They are bound to particular functional contexts and depend on the accumulation of appreciative experience in these contexts.

The linkage between the economic wealth of a nation and the overall capability of its citizens to live lives they have reason to value is a contingent and complex matter, according to Sen (2002), and can vary in strength from society to society and depend on other circumstances. Just as the expansion of people's capabilities or substantive freedoms may, at least in part, be a consequence of economic prosperity and general increases in income levels, it also may be the case that such expansion contributes indirectly to economic growth. In certain contexts, the development of capabilities does not have to be explicitly structured by economic ends as a condition of serving them. For example, Sen (2002) points out that China's success, compared with India, in making use of market mechanisms to promote economic growth depended on a well-educated and highly literate population that existed prior to efforts to move toward a more market-oriented economy.

Sen (2002) redefines *poverty* in broader terms than income deficit—as "capability deprivation." This has implications for the theory of social justice that underpins educational programs. An education for capability will meet the requirements of justice better than an education that is more narrowly focused on the production and distribution of human capital. From Sen's (2002) perspective, education serves the requirements of justice if it equally develops and extends individuals' capabilities (freedoms) to choose lives they have reason to value. Such requirements cannot be solely served by an educational system that only focuses on the equal distribution of human capital.

Sen (1999) argues that capability and human capital theory need not represent alternative perspectives on the role of educational institutions in the context of the development of society. Although the two perspectives are distinct, he claims that they are compatible because, while presenting a narrower view of development, human capital theory can nevertheless fit into "the more inclusive process of human capability" (Sen, 1999, p. 293).

For Sen (1999), the different perspectives are largely reflected in the "yardstick of assessment." The same content can be evaluated according to different standards of achievement. From the human capital perspective, human capabilities are appraised in terms of their commodity value within the processes of production, whereas from the capability perspective, they are appraised in terms of the expansion of people's freedom to lead lives they have reason to value and "to enhance the real choices they have" in this respect (Sen, 1999, p. 293). Sen (1999) writes:

> If education makes a person more efficient in commodity production, then this is clearly an enhancement of human capital. This can add to the value of production in the economy and also to the income of the person who has been educated. But even with the same level of income, many benefit from education—in reading, communicating, arguing, in being able to choose in a more informed way, in being taken more seriously by others and so on. The benefits of education, thus, exceed its role as human capital in commodity production. The broader capability perspective would note—and value—these additional roles as well. (p. 294)

National curriculum frameworks, which are informed by a culturally attuned understanding of globalization and focus attention on the development of capability as an educational aim, in both its opportunity and process aspects, will not thereby converge with respect to the *functional space* (see Sen, 2001) they open up. Although, in the context of glocalization, enlarging and internationalizing functional space in all curriculum frameworks will enhance capability, their contents will inevitably reflect a multiplicity of different cultural values. One can expect to find combinations of functions within each framework that are both similar and different in many respects.

The Evaluation of Educational Programs in Transnational Space

Programs of educational reform increasingly strive to be responsive to the impact of globalization on people's experience of living. In this chapter, I have tried to show that globalization is a contestable concept and different theories of globalization carry rather different implications for education and learning. Drawing on culturally

attuned theories of globalization developed by Gray, Beck, Sennett, Robertson, and others, I have argued that an appropriate educational response would take the form of an Education for Capability. Educational institutions need to be transformed in ways that enable them to enhance students' sense of agency in every sphere of life—social, cultural, political, and employment—through the development of their capabilities to do the things they value and have reason to value. Such a transformation, however, would require more than a fine-tuning of the current educational system. It involves radical change.

As Rue (2006) points out, enhancing students' sense of agency through education has proved difficult to achieve because so much unlearning and new learning has to take place in institutions that shaped up as "systems of production" for "educating the masses" in industrial societies. Rue argues that educational institutions have too many shock absorbers to having their functioning as transformers of human beings into labor market resources easily disrupted. He confirms the experience of those education program evaluators who found themselves producing "pathologies of innovation" rather than "narratives of change." The learning and unlearning that are required to change the educational system in ways that enable students to choose a way of life they value and have reason to value will be extremely difficult to accomplish.

Radical proposals for change along the lines I have proposed cannot simply be generated by policymakers, with a minimum of consultation, in the expectation that those who have responsibilities for educating children and young people will be able to straightforwardly implement them. Policymakers often assume their reforms will work if only teachers and others involved implement the program for change properly. They expect the evaluations they commission to take the form of implementation studies, rather than ask question about whether the program is based on an adequate understanding of the circumstances they are addressing. For example, in transnational *local space*, students will increasingly be drawn from different countries of origin, different linguistic communities, cultures, and ethnic groups. Learning to make a life for oneself in a glocal world, among often conflicting and sometimes clashing visions of the good life, is a complex business and a radical shift from the passive and authority-dependent process that still prevails in the system. Any decent evaluation will want to know whether the program is an appropriate response to the changes in the local environment of education that result from globalization and to the multilayered challenges these present (e.g., for pedagogy, curriculum, assessment, and organizational development). This kind of evaluation will involve a great deal of learning of a holistic kind.

If globalization presents challenges that require a radical, multilayered, although not uniform transformation of the educational system in many countries, this can only be achieved through the democratic participation of the key players—teachers, school managers, lay governors, parents, employers, and students—in an action research process of designing, testing, evaluating, and further developing the change program. Without a high level of democratic participation, it will be impossible to secure the kind of coordinated action necessary to secure change. Not all those with a stake in education will welcome the direction of change, which is why the ends in view, as well as the means of realizing them, need to become the focus for a high-quality evaluatory discourse among the key players that is disciplined by evidence. Conceived as a democratically constituted, holistic, discursive, and action-oriented process of mutual learning, educational evaluation should shape up in transnational glocalized space as an integral component of educational change. As such, it will mirror the conception of learning I outlined earlier as an appropriate educational response to the challenge of globalization. In doing so, Evaluation as Learning will be committed to realizing in action a particular conception of educationally worthwhile learning. The globalization context challenges evaluators to articulate their value biases and to stop pretending that they can portray educational

programs from the standpoint of an impartial spectator.

One cannot expect educational evaluation to shape up naturally as the dynamic core of a process of radical educational reform in an age of globalization. There is too much resistance to be overcome. Some form of strong mediation within an educational institution or within the system generally will be required. Drawing on Dryzek's (1990) notion of the discursive design as a form of mediation in disputes, I now argue that educational evaluation in the future needs to take the form of a discursive design for mutual learning, and that the role of the external evaluator should be the pedagogical one of establishing and sustaining this design for learning. Dryzek (1990) defines a *discursive design* as:

> A social institution around which the expectations of a number of actors converge. It therefore has a place in their conscious awareness as a sight for current communicative interaction among them. (p. 43)

He sets out a number of conditions governing the functioning of such an institution:

1. That the institution is oriented towards *holistic experimentation* i.e. "to the generation and coordination of actions situated within a particular problem context."

2. "The focus of deliberations should include, but not be limited to, the individual or collective needs and interests of the individuals involved."

3. The institution should create a public space, within which individual's associate, that is situated between the individual and the governing administration. Complicity in governance (e.g. the State) should be avoided.

4. Individuals should participate as concerned individuals ("citizens") in their own right, rather than as representatives of an organisation or group.

5. The discourse should be free of constraints that emanate from any source (e.g. formal hierarchical structures) other than the informal canons of free and open communication.

6. The institution should be socially inclusive (i.e. "No concerned individual should be excluded") and the institution should have an educative mechanism to "promote the competent participation of persons with a material interest in the issues at hand who might otherwise be left out." (Dryzek, 1990, p. 43)

If educational evaluation is cast in the form of a discursive design, a number of longstanding issues in evaluation theory get resolved. First, it shows how the idea of democratic evaluation in the form first proposed by MacDonald (1976) can be integrated into an action research approach to educational change (see Elliott, 1991, 2007a). Democratic evaluation is an attempt to create a public space that is free from both the methodological constraints inherent in academic disciplines like psychology and sociology and the political constraints imposed by the bureaucratic state. It is the task of evaluation to create conditions under which the views of concerned citizens who have a stake/interest in education can be authentically voiced and exchanged. This is done by the evaluators casting themselves in the role of impartial brokers in an exchange of information. The aim is to reduce hierarchical control over the flow of information around a program for change. Although democratic evaluators have achieved some success in achieving this aim, they are in the main unable to sustain a discourse community that can make good use of their evaluation reports. This is because the evaluation teams tend to exercise considerable control over the gathering and processing of data within the wider community of discourse. It is the evaluation teams that process "the voice data" and draw them together for deliberative

purposes. Yes, democratic evaluators create public space for discussing their reports with interested parties, but such forums are unstable, temporary, and overdependent on the evaluation experts. Then after the funding runs out and the evaluation ceases to exist, the discourse withers away, and subsequently little changes. Democratic evaluation fails to generate an institution that is capable of sustaining a process of holistic experimentation.

At the same time (the 1970s and 1980s), action research emerged in the form of the "teachers as researchers" movement (see Stenhouse, 1975). This movement integrated the evaluation of action to bring about change with the process of generating action to realize educational values. In doing so, it transferred a great deal of responsibility for data gathering and processing to teachers and cast academics in the pedagogical role of facilitators. In this role, they often collaborate with teachers to gather and process data in the light of shared educational values, hence teaching them how to do research by example. However, the aspiration underpinning the teachers as researcher's movement was to give teachers ultimate control over what counts as useful knowledge about their practice. Educational action research has assumed that teachers should be free to make change on the basis of their own professional knowledge. In doing so, it generated discourse communities of teachers within and across schools that were oriented toward the generation of shared professional knowledge as a basis for connected action. Unlike democratic evaluation, it has failed to acknowledge that educational change requires a discourse community that is open to all educationally concerned citizens. Hence, we have a situation in which (a) action research often succeeds in establishing relatively stable discourse communities that are too restricted in their membership to sustain a process of holistic experimentation in public space and (b) democratic evaluation fails to realize its vision of democratically constituted discourse communities in any relatively stable form.

Standards-Based Evaluation in Global Space: Some Concluding Remarks

The challenges globalization presents to educational institutions will shape up rather differently both between and within countries. Responses to these challenges will need to be sensitive to context and circumstance. The assumption that one can measure educational programs against a set of cross-cultural uniform standards, implicit in the notion of a world-class education, is carried over from the global free market project aimed at producing a single commodity world. The attempt to produce a universal set of performance indicators in the form of quantitative measures creates enormous distance between what Stake and Schwandt (2003) call *quality as experienced* and *quality as measured* (see also Stake, 2004). The former implies that the discernment of quality is a form of practically embodied knowledge—"at once both cognitive and emotional"—that is acquired in the course of immediate and direct experience of practical situations and events and manifest in the actions and language of participants. On this view, the evaluation of quality takes the form of "experience near understandings" that involve grasping the subjective and intersubjective meanings that the evaluand attaches to "events, personal encounters and places" and their "sensitivities to virtue and trauma." Under these conditions, *quality* is represented through narratives of personal experience (see Kushner, 2000). Such narratives are exemplified by case study-based evaluations of educational change programs carried out by professional evaluators based in the academy (see MacDonald & Kushner, 1982; Parlett & Hamilton, 1976; Simons, 1980, 1987; Stake, 1986, 1995) or in the context of practitioner-based action research (see Simons, 1987; Elliott, 2007a). They are accounts of what Dewey (1916) depicted as "appreciative experience."

For Stake and Schwandt (2003), *quality as measured* involves an evaluation stance that distances the evaluation from the concrete experiences of those who are engaged with the program in action. From this standpoint, discernments of quality involve "explicit comparison of the object in question with a set of standards for it." Stake and Schwandt point out that, from a *quality-as-measured* perspective, the meaning of quality "is structured—by a set of constructs" that tend to be derived not so much from the actions and language of the evaluand as from the communities of discourse to which the evaluator belongs. The need to develop such standards stems, they suggest, from confrontational situations where "few people are willing to accept personal perceptions of quality from opponents" (pp. 404–418). Such situations are recurrent in the context of government-initiated reforms that aim to modernize education as a public service by introducing market mechanisms and private sector notions of quality assurance and control. It is presumed that, by holding educational institutions and teachers to account for their performativity (getting the best equation between output and input measures) by maximizing measurable outputs at relatively low cost in terms of inputs, the country can successfully compete in an imagined global free market.

Stake and Schwandt (2003) point at the tendency in practice for the criterial thinking involved in determining *quality as measured* to "reduce the number of views of what quality is" in pursuit of a composite score with which all evaluators might agree. This is entirely consistent with the principles inherent in what Nussbaum (1990) calls the "science of measurement." The more judgments of quality are reduced to a single measure, Stake and Schwandt claim, the greater the distancing from *quality as experienced*. It may secure agreement in judgments among evaluators, but only do so at the expense of *quality as experienced*. Such agreement does not represent "the most valid meanings" of quality as a matter of common and universal experience. Stake and Schwandt (2003) conclude that criterial thinking needs to be rooted in narratives of experience. When it is so rooted, the number of quality criteria will tend to increase because *quality as experienced* is always "multifaceted, contested, and never fully representable" (pp. 404–418).

If globalization requires a radical response from educational institutions, that response should nevertheless shape up differently according to variable contexts and circumstances. Although there are no context-free general standards against which to measure the quality of a change program or intervention, there is a point in reflectively making explicit the kinds of things participants in the change process have come to experience at the emotional and intuitive levels as of value in the process. In this way, the dichotomy between *quality as experienced* and *quality as measured* can be transcended. If *quality as experienced* corresponds with Dewey's (1916) notion of appreciative valuing, then self-reflective criterial thinking that is grounded in such experience corresponds with his notion of evaluative reasoning. Evaluations of educational reform programs need to create a better balance between distance and intimacy than approaches that emphasize either *quality as measured* or *quality as experienced*. This is what Michael Fielding, I, and others (see Fielding et al., 2006; Elliott, 2007b) attempted in an evaluation of Bishops Park College in the UK. We engaged a number of concerned individuals who had a stake in the work of the college to participate in a discursive and self-reflective process of developing a quality framework that was rooted in the collective experience of members of the college and its community. This framework did indeed reflect the multifaceted, contestable, and not fully representable nature of *quality as experienced*. Because most of the indicators referred to qualitative rather than quantitative data, they formed a basis for the college to systematically assemble data for the purpose of public accountability in a form that was rooted in *quality as experienced* by those familiar with its work.

The challenges that *glocalization* presents to educational institutions in many parts of the world is such that attempts to meet them cannot and should not escape public scrutiny. There is

much to learn and unlearn in meeting these challenges. The core tasks for educational evaluation in an age of globalization are to learn how best to effect change in glocalized situations and to depict the lessons learned in some publicly accessible form. In this way, the dual functions of education evaluation—to contribute to the development of practice and to render the program publicly accountable—can be satisfied. However, these are not tasks for external evaluators with specialist expertise. They are appropriately tasks for democratically constituted discursive designs operating at different levels in the educational system. Such institutions may help to build the social capital that will make evaluations, when they are conceived as a mutual learning process, publicly credible. They will serve the restorative function of "creating the relational conditions under which trust, mutual understanding, and the forging of a rational consensus about educational values and purposes" can reemerge in the context of the increasingly diverse and pluralistic societies that are evolving in a glocalized world (Elliott & Kushner, 2007, p. 330). Indeed, the sixth Cambridge Conference in 2004 on educational program evaluation explicitly addressed the problem of creating space in the contemporary policy milieu for educational program evaluation to serve such a function. The outcome was reported by Elliott and Kushner (2007) in the form of a new manifesto to succeed the one generated at the first conference in 1972 (see MacDonald & Parlett, 1973). Like its predecessor, it is couched in the form of a set of principles to orientate and guide the practice of evaluation as a democratically constituted, discursive, and developmental process. In comparing the two manifestos, it becomes clear that the Evaluation as Learning genre is continuously evolving in response to social change.

I have argued in this chapter that one important aspect of contemporary social change is the way in which globalization now permeates the particular contexts of educational program evaluation in a form that renders the question of how to improve student learning a major object of learning for educational evaluation. As I stated in the introduction, the Evaluation as Learning genre has always claimed sensitivity to particular contexts. I hope to have demonstrated that it now needs to evolve to focus on the ways in which global and local factors interact in these contexts. Only by doing so can it yield useful insights into how educational programs can improve the quality of students' learning in educational settings.

References

Beck, U. (2000). *What is globalization?* Cambridge: Polity Press.

Dewey, J. (1916). *Democracy and education.* New York: Free Press, Macmillan (1944 ed.).

Dryzek, J. S. (1990). *Discursive democracy: Politics, policy, and political science.* Cambridge: Cambridge University Press.

Elliott, J. (1991). *Action research for educational change.* Buckingham: Open University Press.

Elliott, J. (2007a). *Reflecting where the action is?— The selected works of John Elliott.* Abingdon, Oxon, and New York: Routledge World Library of Educationalists.

Elliott, J. (2007b). Reinstating social hope through participatory action research. In *Action research and education in contexts of poverty: A tribute to the life and work of professor Orlando Fals Borda.* Bogota: Universidad De La Salle.

Elliott, J., & Kushner, S. (2007). The need for a manifesto for educational evaluation. *Cambridge Journal of Education, 37*(33), 321–336.

Fielding, M., Elliott, J., Burton, C., Robertson, C., & Samuels, J. (2006). *Less is more? The development of a schools-within-schools approach to education on a human scale.* London: University of London Institute of Education.

Gray, J. (1998). *False dawn: The delusions of global capitalism.* London: Granta Books.

Grossman, K., & Golab, A. (2007, November 1). Chicago students' achievement gap. *Chicago Sun-Times,* p. 10.

Kushner, S. (2000). *Personalizing evaluation.* London: Sage.

MacDonald, B. (1976). Evaluation and the control of education. In D. Tawney (Ed.), *Curriculum evaluation today* (pp. 125–136). London & Basingstoke: Macmillan Education.

MacDonald, B., & Kushner, S. (1982). *Bread and dreams: A case study of bilingual schooling in the USA* (CARE Occasional Publications No. 12). Norwich, UK: University of East Anglia.

MacDonald, B., & Parlett, M. (1973). Rethinking evaluation: Notes from the Cambridge Conference. *Cambridge Journal of Education, 2,* 74–81.

Nussbaum, M. (1990). An Aristotelian conception of rationality. In M. Nussbaum (Ed.), *Love's knowledge.* Oxford: Oxford University Press.

Parlett, M., & Hamilton, D. (1976). Evaluation as illumination: A new approach to the study of innovatory programmes. In D. Hamilton, D. Jenkins, C. King, B. MacDonald, & M. Parlett (Eds.), *Beyond the numbers game: A reader in educational evaluation.* London: Macmillan.

Robertson, R. (1992). *Globalization: Social theory and global culture.* London: London University Press.

Rorty, R. (1982). *Consequences of pragmatism.* Minneapolis: University of Minnesota Press.

Rue, J. (2006). Reconstructing teacher professionalism in the new modernity: An agenda for new action narratives. *Educational Action Research, 14*(1), 119–138.

Sen, A. (1999). *Development as freedom.* Oxford: Oxford University Press.

Sen, A. (2001). Interview with Madoka Saito. Cited in M. Saito (Ed.). (2003). Amartya Sen's capability approach to education: A critical exploration. *Journal of Philosophy of Education, 37*(1), 26.

Sen, A. (2002). *Rationality and freedom.* Cambridge, MA: Harvard University Press.

Sennett, R. (2006). *The culture of the new capitalism.* New Haven, CT, and London: Yale University Press.

Simons, H. (1980). *Towards a science of the singular: Essays about case study in educational research and evaluation.* Norwich: CARE Occasional Publications, University of East Anglia.

Simons, H. (1987). *Getting to know schools in a democracy.* London: Falmer Press.

Stake, R. E. (1986). *Quieting reform: Social science and social action in an urban youth reform.* Chicago: University of Illinois Press.

Stake, R. E. (1995). *The art of case study research.* London, Thousand Oaks, CA, and New Delhi: Sage.

Stake, R. E. (2004). *Standards-based and responsive evaluation.* London, Thousand Oaks, CA, and New Delhi: Sage.

Stake, R. E., & Schwandt, T. A. (2003). On discerning quality in evaluation. In I. Shaw, M. Mark, & J. Greene (Eds.), *International handbook of evaluation.* London, Thousand Oaks, CA, and New Delhi: Sage.

Stenhouse, L. (1975). *An introduction to curriculum research and development.* London: Heinemann.

PART V

Educational Evaluation in a Political World

The evaluation theories in Part V are distinguished by a commitment to a particular set of values or ideology. These values are diverse and include empowerment (empowerment evaluation, transformative participatory evaluation) as well as democratic principles such as justice and equality (democratic evaluations theories). Evaluation approaches that take a particular theoretical position toward society, such as critical theory-based approaches or action-oriented evaluation, are also part of this genre. Many of these theories explicitly acknowledge the political dimensions of educational evaluation. Approaches within this family presuppose that educational programs are best understood in relationship to the political currents that influence them.

Evaluation theories in this genre are often open to mixed methods, including both quantitative and qualitative methods. There are no methods chapters in this part because it is value commitments, rather than particular methods, that define the character of this educational evaluation genre.

Part V opens with two theory chapters that represent the range and diversity in the kinds of value commitments in this educational evaluation family. In one theory chapter, Kushner (Chapter 23) proposes that educational programs in contemporary society are facing a conundrum by being unique in their local contexts while also being considered comparable and accountable to national and international educational standards. Building on the foundations of democratic evaluation theory, Kushner considers whether "rights-based evaluation" based on international conventions and treaties could be a means for traversing the distances being the local and global in educational evaluation. Alternatively, Rodney Hopson (Chapter 24) defines and elaborates the foundations of culturally responsive evaluation (CRE)— a new and rapidly growing strand in evaluation theory— while distinguishing CRE from other evaluation approaches. Drawing on a diverse set of conceptual frameworks such as indigenous epistemologies, Hopson sets a large task for evaluation by arguing for "legitimizing the lived experiences of and building and implementing efforts at traditionally underrepresented underserved groups."

Hood's case study (Chapter 25) of the Navajo Nation school instantiates CRE in practice, showing how CRE evaluations can reflect the lived experiences of stakeholder groups. At the same time, he elaborates the challenges of practicing CRE when, for instance, he describes the intersections and meanings of clanship within and between cultures. Illustrating some of the difficulties in their deliberative democratic evaluation case, Karlsson Vestman and Segerholm (Chapter 26) present an exemplar of how and why educational programs are best understood in relationship to the political systems and currents that influence them. They write a compelling story about the complexities of exporting dialogue and deliberation during a professional development program evaluation in Russia—a country with different political and social contexts than Sweden, for example. Although instrumental evaluation (single-loop) learning was achieved, Karlsson Vestman and Segerholm contend that the Russian bureaucratic structure interfered with deeper levels of evaluation learning (i.e., double loop). In the critical appraisal chapter for Part V, Torrance (Chapter 27) analyzes how current political governance systems in contemporary society are creating strains on the construct of educational evaluation particularly at the local level. After offering a case for the return or even extension of deliberative evaluation in the educational arena, he presents specific snapshots about how this might be instituted (e.g., teachers' assessment of student work in the classroom).

CHAPTER 23

Own Goals

Democracy, Evaluation, and Rights in Millennium Projects

Saville Kushner

Introduction and Summary

I argue that international organizations are caught in the middle of a paradox as they seek to implement international goals in local contexts. Events and phenomena such as schools and educational ideas have what appear to be mutually exclusive properties—they are both unique to context and comparable with other contexts, and they have both a global and a local character. Schools, for example, are both comparable across countries and cultures and unique to their host communities. This is a paradox that afflicts UNICEF, as with other international agencies, as it struggles to resolve the tension between its global accountabilities and its roots in a local (in-country, often municipal) action base with obligations to children, families, and communities.

One of the implications of this paradox is that we have to think flexibly about what counts as a standard or goal, allowing them to be determined locally—to reflect the priorities and preferences of citizens and communities—and globally—to reflect international agreements and advances in internationally recognized moralities. With respect to evaluation, I show how thinking simultaneously of democracy and rights in evaluation—in fact, as determinants of evaluation design—allows for the mediation of the global and the local, especially with respect to Millennium Development Goals (MDGs). Although rights and democracy are frequently thought of by rights theorists as being in tension, program evaluation allows for their unification. I talk briefly about a rights-based approach to evaluation.

Democratic Evaluation and Good Governance

Evaluators have rehearsed proposals for democratic evaluation for many years. For some, the search for singular calculations of the productivity of a program was secondary to the need to ensure that programs were properly held to public account, but also that judgments to be made about programs were not the sole prerogative of a social or political or administrative elite. Indeed, democratic evaluators have argued that measures of program productivity may well, in themselves, be insufficient to meet the democratic obligations of the evaluator—taking into account the diversity of values in a program, the instability of output measures, program politics, and typical conflicts over program purposes.

What is argued for in democratic evaluation is: (a) open exchange of information across stakeholder groups, (b) evaluation as a space in which power inequalities can be (procedurally) neutralized (i.e., equal treatment for all, including mother, manager, minister), (c) independence and impartiality of the evaluator whose obligation is to address everyone's dilemmas, (d) free and open publication of evaluation reports, and (e) a recognition of collective responsibility for enhancing public information (MacDonald, 1976; Ryan & DeStefano, 2000; but see later for a more detailed account). Clearly, the key to any democratic evaluation process is participation as a form of direct representation.

Notwithstanding the weight of issues considered by its theorists, democratic evaluation as a methodology has been more popular than practiced. This may be due to the demands it makes for sophistication in action, together with the fact that it is often unattractive to sponsors who are wary of the loss of contractual control over the evaluation and its publication and jealous of the resource for which they see themselves as having paid. It also may be the case that where public evaluation is mostly practiced is in those advanced industrial countries where it is less compelling to make the link between democratic evaluation and good governance—a link that lies at the heart of the methodology.

Perhaps most significant of these factors has been the widespread failure of the link between democratic evaluation and governance. As originally conceived, the methodology both made up for a democratic deficit in social programs (e.g., enhancing the accountability of program managers and political sponsors to other program stakeholders) and offered to make the conditions of our democracies transparent by seeing a social program as a microcosm of society at large (i.e., each evaluation is a case study of political society). Democratic structures and assumptions are sufficiently strong in Europe and the United States to dilute the political imperative behind democratic evaluation.

The imperative behind this link is stronger in international development settings, where the absence of "good (i.e., democratic) governance" and the frequent absence of program accountability to stakeholders and citizens is prevalent. Here, democratic evaluation would seem to hold promise for those who advocate more open, accountable, and responsive forms of governance at program, municipal, and national levels. However, preoccupations over democracy and information rights have permeated only little into evaluation practices in international development (see, e.g., Cameron & Ojha, 2007; Segone, 2006). Program evaluation for development is mostly confined to impact assessment and, increasingly, audit and accountability. The search for the elusive unified calculation of quality or program productivity dominates international organizations that are under accountability pressures from their donors to see programs of intervention less as opportunities to engage citizens in deliberations over priorities and more as delivery systems for prespecified results. The link between democratic evaluation and democratic governance has not been sufficiently well forged.

But democratic evaluation has always been promoted within the context of national political cultures and does not easily transfer to global contexts. It is probably fair to say that democratic evaluation was implicitly modeled on civic democracy in a liberal, Western state, with expectations of social exchange, deliberation, and the building of social consensus. Indeed, deliberative democratic evaluation (House & Howe, 1999)—its most recent expression—emphasizes the kind of social exchange that is almost inconceivable beyond levels of local intimacy in political cultures. Democratic evaluation functions through social conversation, so it needs to talk in a national "language." The warrant of the democratic evaluator emanates from the democratic aspirations of the society that commissions it—it is an echo of political ambition.

At a level of global action, we cannot assume or achieve political singularity—there is no such clear echo. There is no civic context to a global world. Here, we struggle to find the source for that same democratic warrant. The signatories to MDGs, for example, are too diverse in their political hue, at too diverse stages on democratic journeys, to provide a stable base for evaluation mandates placing these goals under critical scrutiny. I take a detailed look at MDGs a little later because they stand as a global program and are the test case for looking at the constraints and possibilities of democratic evaluation in global contexts. The challenge for the democratic evaluator is to find a way of grounding a constructive critique of MDGs in what are often referred to as "beneficiary communities"—as a way of transferring ownership to them of the goals.

In this chapter, I explore a *rights-based approach to evaluation*, which draws for its warrant from international statements of authority—treaties and conventions. A rights-based approach to evaluation is not a substitute for democratic evaluation; rather, it is merely an adaptation that may be appropriate to global programs and international contexts—a means for bridging awesome distances between international elites and disadvantaged communities. It has the added advantage of a vocabulary that is familiar to development workers and organizations. All contemporary international development programs are required to be rights-based (Black, 2008; Jonsson, 2003).

I start the chapter, however, with a paradox that always faces the educational evaluator, but that is heightened in the case of global action. This is the paradox of what we might think of as "situated generalization"—that any educational event has Heisenberg-like properties that make it simultaneously idiosyncratic and law-like. How we resolve the paradox in action (e.g., in designing an evaluation) often has grave implications for how we distribute rights.

A Global Paradox

Wherever we travel in the world, we find classrooms recognizable—instructional arrangements, many small people facing one large person, authority structures and power asymmetries, repressed desires, scrutiny, revelations, learning, judgment, and confusions between play and work; we see and readily recognize them all. Under a Baobab tree in Central Africa, in an adobe shack in the Bolivian highlands, in the suburbs of an English city, in the shadow of a Buddhist temple in Thailand, and in a tent in a Middle-Eastern desert, teachers teach and pupils learn in ways that make it easy for us to hold educational conversation across cultural boundaries. Classrooms are familiar settings. Partly as a result, the language of pedagogy has become a global language. From all over the world, educators come to Europe to reflect on their practice, and our cultural and political differences apparently present no barrier to conversation. I have visited Malaysia only fleetingly, and yet through a series of doctoral supervisions, I seem to have come to know Malaysian schooling to the point where I am taken seriously in conversation by educators there. How can it be that we pretend to such cross-cultural knowledge while still cherishing the view that our cultural traditions confirm our uniqueness and make us exotic to each other?

Look again at classrooms. We enter a primary school in our own back yard as a parent or as a researcher, and we are acutely aware—especially as parents—that two classrooms next to each other on the same corridor are two different worlds. One, perhaps, has a middle-age, energetic teacher with a progressive approach to open education and holding an overriding educational principle that you have to love the children—and from that, all else flows; in the other class, a young, inexperienced teacher made nervous by overwhelming complexity and a fear of children is conservative and disciplinarian, focusing not on the children, but on the formal curriculum. The two teachers can as easily talk to each other as walk together to the canteen, but they may well find the distance between their respective value positions too great to overcome. Their classrooms are their invented countries, the gap between them is as wide and as deep as the gap between cultures, and it frustrates attempts at conversation. We know this well from the history of school-based innovation, which too often fails through the difficulties that innovative teachers have of negotiating their way with colleagues. On this side of the paradox, classrooms are unique and far from readily familiar, and the unpredictability of their cultural formation denies the possibility of universal description. Not only this, as pupil cohorts and teachers change from year to year, so the cultural formation of each classroom shifts and changes. The global classroom dissipates into unstable idiosyncrasy.

The same, of course, goes for schools—again, especially primary schools—where the head teacher, as head of a professional "family," sets the cultural tone in ways that are as distinctive as his or her own personality and biography. Schools, too, are both recognizable and different from one another. The social order of schooling is, in one sense, enduring—"frozen" as House (1974) put it—both stable and predictable across time. Schools are places for the reproduction of cultures; metaphorically speaking, they are genetically programmed for the continuity of a political strain, and that strain is increasingly international. A national curriculum in Malaysia and England teaches the same mathematics, the same grammar, the same science, and the same music since English schools started teaching world music. History may be different, but the historiography stays the same. There is no Asian state schooling approach to science or calculation. Whatever the hopes of development agencies for child-friendly schools,[1] the global order of schooling is as unfriendly to children but friendly to the economic and political elites as is portrayed in the impressive superstructure of the PISA and IAEA[2] studies: relentlessly focused on numeracy and literacy and on the production of an economic workforce. The PISA/IAEA studies compare reading ability in the UK and Thailand!

In the other sense, the order of schooling is local and variable—of course, knowledge varies with culture. Curriculum fits into a child's life and is accommodated and adapted there. All knowledge is personal, and schools are instruments of local meaning—it is not useful to talk of "all schools" because their effects and their products define them, and these are both unpredictable and variable. An adult literacy class in that adobe shack in the Bolivian highlands has indigenous men and women playing out the shifting village politics of gender and entertaining their personal dreams of empowerment.

This is the point of the paradox—that schools and classrooms are identical and different at one and the same time. The PISA studies are both valid and invalid according to the criterion of judgment you choose. Neither is deniable. Here is the central methodological challenge of educational evaluation—how to estimate the worth of an educational activity where we face these contradictions. Do we measure one classroom or school against others? Do we define universal standards against which to measure and compare performance based on the assumption that schools and classrooms are comparable—as in the global PISA and IAEA comparative studies? Do we have to reinvent measurement that is tailor made for each classroom? Do we define standards appropriate to each classroom and each school? Here, indeed, is a challenge for international development agencies whose liberalism insists on equal treatment for all—the global expression of rights.

The constant reinvention of measurement was, indeed, the view of Stenhouse (1967), who regarded a standard as a set of local agreements over what was worthwhile. By standard, he referred to "criteria which lie behind consistent patterns of judgement of the quality and value of the work" (p. 70)—that is, a standard was a procedural principle or a process, not a universal and fixed measure of performance. More important, the "consistency" of these criteria rested on interaction and communication—they were, in Stenhouse's terms, based on local judgments and values. Let us look at their implications for the measurement of quality. Stenhouse (1967) says:

> When we say that we regard the work of one class as better than that of another, we are not simply judging it to reach a "higher" standard. Such a conception implies a common measure against which both classes can appropriately be assessed, but in fact standards can be qualitatively different. When they are, a comparative assessment is not a matter of measurement but a matter of value-judgement. For example, we may opt for creativity or correctness. . . . Such choices are founded upon conviction rather than demonstration. The sources of standards in school work lie in the teacher's values. (p. 75)

We cannot deny the value that global measures of classrooms and schooling have created. For example, Gage (1996) reviews the successes of meta-analysis in the behavioral sciences and the concept of generalization across educational contexts. He analyzes empirical experience with educational generalization following Cronbach's (1975) critique that "generalizations decay" (i.e., over time and location).[3] Gage's (1996) issue is this:

> How often do ecologies studied in the behavioural sciences yield main effects . . . sufficiently substantial, consistent and enduring to support lasting generalisation? The important question concerns, not the magnitude of main effects and interaction effects, but their consistency. (pp. 10–11)

Consistency rests on the assumption of universal or global characteristics of classrooms and classroom interactions that allow for ecological, cross-context measurement. Gage (1996) points to a range of key educational generalizations that appear to be founded on such consistency. They take the form of relationships: socioeconomic status related to academic achievement, years of schooling related to amount of knowledge

gained, cooperative learning related to race relations, personalized instruction related to achievement levels, and behavioral instruction related to learning gains. Indeed, so successful have some of these been that they form part of a widely accepted folklore of education. Perhaps they do form a set of global (PISA-type) criteria against which we can successfully make measured comparisons of the performance of education systems globally. Perhaps there is hope for a global liberalism in education.

The implications of the paradox are far reaching and pose questions at the heart of contemporary school effectiveness movements, the new public management (NPM), and their global equivalents in education. This new context is based on low-trust accountability, performance management, and results-based programming (Norris & Kushner, 2007), and it embraces the global liberalism of international agencies that are all committed to it. NPM is only possible where we are able to control for context because cross-site comparisons and benchmarking are key to its legitimacy and functioning. In this sense, intercontextual comparison is designed for ensuring compliance with policy (i.e., control-for-consistency), not for arriving at broad generalizations of the kind suggested earlier. For NPM to operate effectively, we have to assume the comparability of classrooms and schools—that the few can be measured against the many. Let us take a critical look at the global approach to NPM that is represented by MDGs and their implication for global evaluation.

MDGs[4]

An international agreement was adopted by 189 nations and signed by 147 heads of state and governments during the UN Millennium Summit in September 2000. The agreement established eight universal goals that would drive all international development work and be realized by the year 2015 (although their baseline was taken as 1990).[5] Each MDG has subtargets to specify the action frame, and each target has a series of indicators against which progress can be measured toward its attainment—there are 18 quantifiable targets that are to be measured by 48 indicators. These are the goals:

Goal 1: Eradicate extreme poverty and hunger

Goal 2: Achieve universal primary education

Goal 3: Promote gender equality and empower women

Goal 4: Reduce child mortality

Goal 5: Improve maternal health

Goal 6: Combat HIV/AIDS, malaria, and other diseases

Goal 7: Ensure environmental sustainability

Goal 8: Develop a Global Partnership for Development

To give a single example, Goal 1 has one of two targets, which is to reduce by half the proportion of people who suffer from hunger; this target has one of two indicators that is stated as: *Prevalence of Underweight Children Under Five Years of Age.* So: Goal–Target–Indicators. The goal provides the moral/political aim, the target provides the strategic focus, and the indicators express the target in quantifiable terms ready for measurement of progress toward the goal. The hierarchy is like this:

Goal (× 8)

↓

Target (× 18)

↓

Indicator (× 48)

↓

Measurement

Agencies within the UN carry mandates for monitoring progress toward these goals, and there are many monitoring systems in place generating volumes of data. The scale of this program is gargantuan—all UN agencies design their programs around these goals; most nongovernmental organizations (NGOs) are doing so (not all; see Black, 2008), and increasing numbers of governments are signing up to drive their social legislation in relation to them. For an appropriate sense of proportion, we have to measure the MDG program against global movements, such as the spread of Islam and Catholicism, the Freudian diaspora, the internationalization of Flight Aviation Authority standards, and the spread of Napoleonic Law. Resourcing is vast—that is to say, the resources dedicated to organization and to interventions related specifically to the MDG program and its derivatives. Each MDG has an associated UN agency that carries a mandate for measuring progress in each country toward each of the goals.

MDGs and Accountability

As an accountability system, this is, again, a program of massive proportion. Almost anywhere in the world (certainly in the developing world), the efforts of large numbers of people are being measured in the same way, against the same indicators—often against the same database. Governments are setting up MDG monitoring units; national and regional statistical agencies and UN agencies are working on the ever-present dilemmas of data quality, harmonization of MDG indicators, and data availability; all international agencies are subject to intensifying results monitoring; and one measure many adopt is to import MDG performance targets as an off-the-shelf solution. The quality of many international development interventions is measured in terms of their claimed success at stimulating progress toward meeting MDGs—no matter how appropriate or otherwise that may be to the nature and mission of a particular organization—or, indeed, to the field being developed. In terms of our global paradox, MDGs promote the homogeneous, universal comparative view. Let us then enter into this side of the paradox to review its strengths and weaknesses. Later, we come back to the other side of the paradox to remind ourselves of the inevitability of localism.

Global Educational Evaluation

The accountability aspect of MDGs is supported by a subprogram within the MDGs—results-based management (RBM).[6] This evaluation approach, familiar to many in the public sectors of advanced industrial countries, requires the prespecification of goals as program objectives and the subsequent comparative analysis with outcomes. The principles of evaluation through comparison of program outputs with its goals are the centerpiece of the NPM and its reliance on performance management. They are designed to import efficiency into programming by enhancing predictability and control, as well as to define accountability in terms of efficiency and compliance. High value is given to logic modeling as an approach to the design of programs in line with management by results because logic modeling encourages the belief in a unifying program rationale and a causal mechanism for improving the predictability of outputs. It is assumed to build in the evaluability of the program. In a global context, it is taken to ensure that programs in different parts of the world can be evaluated in identical and comparable ways so as to compare results. Hence, for example, in UNICEF, there is a great deal of interest in comparing the performance of child-friendly schooling across the world's regions. Much evaluation in development settings is designed to emphasize the universalist side of our paradox.

The MDG + RBM approach has its advocates and its critics. One prominent argument in favor has it that prespecifying results allows for joined-up action leading to synergies across otherwise fragmented agency resources—something we

know to be true. For example, the centerpiece of contemporary UN reform is the integration of its core agencies—such that, for example, a national government might in the future deal with one UN office and source technical expertise there (the reform is labeled "One UN"). MDGs provide the common denominator, which makes at least feasible the integration of what, in reality, are diverse organizational cultures. Another rationale is contextual—that international organizations are characterized by geographical distance (e.g., headquarters from field office) and that a common denominator (a goal or a result) allows central authorities to predict and control action at the periphery. This further strengthens the universalist side of the paradox.

A prominent critique of the programming-by-results approach suggests that it embodies a confusion between consistency and coherence (i.e., that the price of creating and sustaining a good pattern at the level of global/corporate aims is disorder at the level of action), something we know less about in the development field given the shortage of critical evaluation (see, e.g., Baser & Morgan, 2008, who argue that results-based management is, at best, appropriate for stable and predictable contexts: "Once the playing field became more uncertain, more informal, more contested, more intangible and more long term, RBM quickly lost traction and relevance" [p. 92]—that is, RBM tends to be unsuited to development contexts). The localist side of our paradox is, that is to say, correspondingly underdeveloped.

To take an example here, we might think of the instability of an MDG indicator. MDG2 seeks universal primary education; the target is stated as by "2015, children everywhere, boys and girls alike, will be able to complete a full course of primary schooling," and the official UN website states the indicator as the net enrollment ratio in primary education. The first observation to make is that the indicator does not match the goal (i.e., the goal talks about completion, whereas the indicator focuses on enrollment). A key issue in local development settings is that it is easier to put a child on a school register than to ensure that the child attends school on a regular basis. Here, too, we hear an echo of our paradox. Enrollment is a more stable measure and allows for cross-country comparison; completion requires local verification and analysis and is so contextualized as to defy comparison (it was easier to enroll girls under the Taliban than to guarantee attendance). The goal, target, and indicator have other unstable aspects when played out at the local level, where context and idiosyncrasy overwhelm universalist ambition, such as:

- Many countries require children to repeat years of schooling, so completion of a course of primary schooling may mean a significant and prejudicial diversity in age and experience;
- What we define as a "course of primary schooling" is, obviously, ambiguous and likely to frustrate comparison, as is the term *full*, which varies from country to country and from family to family;
- "Boys and girls alike" may stretch comparability to the breaking point because the challenge of enrolling and then guaranteeing the attendance of girls is, in many places, significantly higher than that facing boys—and vice versa in other places;
- Enrollment, attendance, and completion can be measured in diverse ways;
- Enrollment, attendance, and completion are minimum expectations and contain no indicators as to quality of local educational experience; and
- Baselines are the key to measuring progress, given that MDGs are measured, almost exclusively, in an interrupted time-series approach. Because countries develop (and regress) in their own pattern, baselines are likely to be incomparable in themselves.

This is not to undermine the millennium aspiration, but to bring into question its articulation as a goal, its evaluation, and how we account for context—the other side of the paradox. What I also want to highlight, because this is the theme of the later stages of this chapter, is the impact of universalist comparators on democracy and participation—in short, who owns these goals? It is often the case that an indicator may be written in ways that are more or less useful to mothers, families, and communities, say, and more or less inviting of them to join the development push. For example, a community or municipality seeking to take control of its own educational development will find local comparisons (i.e., with proximal contexts and/or within the same culture and conditions) more meaningful than cross-country comparisons, whereas a national government setting broad policy parameters might find other country data more informative. A community will find attendance measures more useful in solving exclusion, just as national governments may find enrollment more useful in resolving international accountability demands.

Let me take one other example from the area of early childhood development. How do we measure chronic malnutrition in pursuit of MDG7? In practice, this is measured either by wasting (calculating weight for height) or stunting (calculating height for age) and the decision that to opt for is made by an agency or a government or, indeed, an agency's regional office. It is then applied in a uniform way to communities and families and the measures used as a basis for policy advocacy and institutional development. For mothers on the ground, the choice of method is significant because one (stunting) is more observable to her than the other and allows her to participate in the monitoring process, whereas the other (wasting) requires weighing technology and measurements over time. Choice of one indicator over the other may be consistent with methodological policy and useful in policy contexts, but less useful and less inclusive for a mother. All such indicators are unstable in one way or another.

Strengths and Weaknesses of the Universalist Project

Nonetheless, this MDG framework is the glue that holds together many, if not all, international development efforts in such a way that (a) all efforts are bent to internationally agreed priorities, and (b) all efforts across international agencies and NGOs are comparable and complementary. The strengths of this program are:

1. that its goals have a democratic warrant, in that they were verified by (broadly) elected governments;

2. they represent an international consensus on a moral framework and priorities for development—a unique political accomplishment;

3. they have measurable indicators of progress that give rise to a transparent accountability system, consolidating the political gain;

4. they permit country-by-country and region-by-region comparisons (for the purposes, principally, of resource distribution); and

5. they reflect in their substantive content the broad range of specialist and sectoral interests in international agencies that allows for immediate engagement with them (e.g., poverty reduction specialists, nutrition experts, education advisers, etc.).

These are undeniable strengths valued by international aid agencies and made good sense in action. MDGs also have their weaknesses, of course. Some are familiar from critiques of results-based programs (see, e.g., Franklin, 2008) and the general case of the NPM (Kushner & Norris, 2007)—for example, that prespecification of results has a tendency to lead to (a) risk aversion (i.e., setting low-level goals to ensure attainment), (b) resistance to learning and adaptation to context, (c) limited opportunities for participation (priorities are inflexible), and (d) centralization of control. Hence, we may consider weaknesses of the MDG program that correspond to the obvious strengths given earlier and that highlight, once again, the other side of that paradox:

- *MDGs have a democratic warrant*: although qualifying as a democratic

warrant, this is possibly the weakest available (i.e., it binds citizens and professional institutions into the preferences of their political elites). Contemporary democratic theory is tending toward "deliberative democracy" (i.e., subsidiarization of policy with high levels of participation; Dryzek, 2000).

- *They represent an international consensus on a moral framework*: The moral framework derives from the deliberations of international elites, not from those who are intended beneficiaries. In any event, there is a logical and a rights-based inconsistency to the concept of "international" morality—moral systems are always culturally, even locally, embedded. Concentrating the moral center of gravity at global and international levels has a tendency to leave national and local levels to concentrate on its applications (i.e., on technical aspects of development).

- *They provide measurable indicators of progress—a transparent accountability system*: Quite apart from the instability of both indicators and their measurements (just hinted at in the examples of primary education and chronic malnutrition), this ignores the impact of methodological choices on possibilities of participation and inclusion. The more we focus on technical measurement, the less we make programs and interventions accessible (or meaningful) to civil society and the more we ignore the politics of knowledge internal to a country.

- *They are universal*: A universal social context can be little more than a theoretical construct looking for grounding—an answer looking for a question. Many (not all) aspects of poverty, for example, are contextualized in local circumstances and expectations. But MDGs suffer from a key weakness in all goal-based programs—that the price of universal application is generalization to a point of abstraction. If we want a goal to be responsive to context or a concrete guide to action, it must be written in such a way as not to appeal to all.

- *They reflect the range of specialist and sectoral interests in international agencies*: Insofar as MDGs are a 15-year program, the structure of the demands they make on attainment has the tendency to reinforce and freeze that same structure on organization, making UN agencies less able to respond to changing roles and changing contexts (including UN reform). For example, we may have less need for nutrition and pediatric and education specialists and more need for multidisciplinary specialists in policy shaping, institutional development, and professional change. That is, MDGs potentially distort the nature of organization in development agencies toward greater responsiveness to global goals than to local contexts.

These weaknesses do not mitigate the strengths, nor do they imply that MDGs are without merit. However, we do have to treat as problematic how MDGs are realized in contexts of local action and cultural diversity—how, while honoring the universalist side of our paradox, they do not violate localism. We also have to balance the extensive effort and resources put into measuring progress in indicators-based ways toward meeting these goals. A great deal of local experience, diversity, and complexity is being lost. The weight of resources is dedicated to measuring progress toward meeting the goals, and so the rhetoric is one of striving and achievement, not reflection and learning. By the year 2015, attention will shift to a justificatory rhetoric for having met or otherwise a particular goal. MDGs have no change strategy specifically attached to them, and insufficient work is being done to develop evidence-based understandings of change. The risk is that we reach 2015 probably with partial success, but with little or no understanding of why certain goals were met and others not, of what were the local mechanisms of change.

Above all, with the dominance of universalism, too little work has been done to ensure ownership of the MDG effort in local, civil society (it is too late to ensure socially embedded democratic ownership of the goals—the program is well underway). It would be a betrayal on a universal scale if, having pursued these priorities over a 15-year period and bent all efforts and resources to the task, to discover that the society created by this program is not one found to be desirable by those citizens who are required to live in it. Access to primary education, birthing resources, clean drinking water, the Internet, and so on are notable and desirable technical accomplishments of the MDGs—but we are not collecting data on their social and political spinoffs and consequences—on the kind of society their accomplishment implies.

The final critique of the MDGs, then, is to point out that they make no mention of democracy and governance and so lose an essential grounding in localism. The goals may be pursued through authoritarian, bureaucratic, democratic, or any other means. In fact, they represent a set of ends divorced from means, whereas in democratic terms, ends can only be justified by means—that, for example, there are threats to democracy in imposing liberal goals through autocratic, paternalistic, or coercive procedures. This is, perhaps, a casualty of universalism.

I turn now to the localist view of the paradox with which this chapter started. I want to resolve the question of how we democratize MDGs—because this is still possible to an extent. I do this by restating the argument for democratic evaluation—or, indeed, with its sibling, rights-based evaluation.

Democratic Evaluation

"What goes around comes around," as they say. As international agencies intensify their advocacy of citizen rights, it is not unlikely that citizens of those countries in which they work will come back asking to exercise their rights. One of the places in which we may expect rights to be asserted is over the creation of social programs that are designed to shape new futures for citizens. Women and children are asked to participate in development programs that are frequently designed and managed by others and to inhabit new futures promoted by these programs. At what point may they assert their right to make judgments about the kinds of futures being envisaged—how such programs are judged, against what criteria, and for what purposes? At what point may we expect people and communities in developing countries to demand the right to information about MDG programs?

As we pursue the MDGs, we envision societies with reasonable life expectancies among women and children; the alleviation of, at least extreme, poverty; broad educational coverage, including gender balances; easy access to clean water; and so on. From these goals flow attempts to reduce disease, enhance medical care, give children the right to a birth registration, and enroll children in school. These are the technical accomplishments for which we aim. What underlies them, however, is a vision of society radically different from that which many developing countries currently enjoy—with different power relations, different institutional structures, and cultural adaptations—societies in which democracy and authority bite in different ways.

To take one minor but significant example, a key strategy in the promotion of children's rights is birth registration—the official acknowledgment of a child's existence with which that child can then assert their right to health care, education, and participation. Of course, what we are also doing is expanding and reshaping the electoral base of a country. In the case, for example, of Andean countries with large indigenous populations, we are contributing to the reshaping of geopolitics by bringing into the citizenry hitherto excluded groups who will enjoy rights previously denied to them—a project with historic implications, as we have seen in Bolivia, which recently elected an Indigenous man (*originario*) as president. The question of democratic rights concerns who has direct access to judgment about our attempts to induce and manage social

change. This, indeed, is the real promise of development interventions. The democratic evaluator asks "Who has the right to know about these things?" and concludes that all do.

In the advanced industrial countries of Europe, Australasia, and the United States, there is a lively debate around the merits of democratic evaluation—an approach that recognizes that program evaluation is a form of (at best, impartial) political action. This is not to say that evaluators are party political activists, but that we recognize that knowledge and information are exchanged and applied in political contexts, and that this demands that evaluation has a political strategy. Just as we live in an age that is broadly skeptical about the possibility of value-free social science, so we are developing skepticism about politics-free social science. Insofar as we recognize that, although we are conducting evaluation, we are acting politically, we look around for appropriate guides to action and to an appropriate warrant. Why? Because it does not take long in a program evaluation for evaluators to be challenged to justify their actions—for example, in providing or withholding knowledge to one or more groups.

One of the early solutions to the dilemma was to link evaluation to democratic precepts. The proposal was not to assert representative democracy in evaluation—for example, that evaluators become or serve exclusively elected representatives—but that what stands as due democratic process should govern the conduct and transactions of evaluation. In fact, in the earliest expression of democratic evaluation, MacDonald (1976) specifically excluded the definition of *evaluation* as a privileged service to elected representatives (he labelled this *bureaucratic evaluation*).

The kind of democracy envisaged by evaluation theorists and tested by them in practice is the kind of civic democracy found at municipal levels of society (i.e., the pursuit of collective rights at the community level). Here is an approach designed for localism and to combat universalism. Civic democracy is intimate and often face to face, and so involves argument and direct exchange. Because civic relations are so close, it is essential to make decisions by negotiation, and this goes for evaluators, too. What the evaluator is prepared or free to negotiate will vary according to their confidence and their contract. Another implication of the civic model to democratic evaluation is the role of common sense. Science is expensive, and it is rarely available to municipal-level actors—but in any event, local politicians and administrators live close to their constituents and have to rely on personal persuasion more than on scientific demonstration. Argument and persuasion, therefore, tend to happen on the basis of day-to-day language and concepts, and so it is in democratic evaluation. The democratic evaluator tries to collect data and report it in ways that reflect how program people think and talk—ideally, in the language of persuasion, rather than proof.

But the main implication of this civic politics understanding of democratic evaluation is that, as in municipal governance, political structures are defined less as sites for the determination and dissemination of policy and more as sites that allow for argumentation and the shaping of policy—there tends to be a shift of emphasis from policy outcomes to policy processes. Those who govern are within touching distance of the governed and so have to negotiate their way. So it is with democratic approaches to evaluation, which seek out that same proximity and intimacy. Hence, these are good instruments for resolving paradoxes and dilemmas created for local communities by distant national and international elites. Evaluation is not a process for arriving at unblemished truths (outcomes), but for the interplay of competing values in defining what a reasonable outcome is.

What follow are some basic dimensions of democratic evaluation practice around which there has grown some agreement. Look carefully for echoes of localism—for it is only through (institutionally) intimate forms of interaction that these can be feasibly guides to action:

- All people own the data over their own lives and work—evaluators need permission to use it. Some people use

protocols—ethical agreements—that govern the conduct of the evaluation and that are explicit about the rights of all respondents to negotiate their data;

- Key evaluation questions and methodological principles—like ethics procedures—should be negotiated and agreed on with program stakeholders;[7]

- Program stakeholders, including program managers, program workers, and recipients, have the right to contribute to the criteria against which their work is to be judged;

- Evaluation should adopt methodologies that permit and do not deter participation and exclusion, and that capture the lived experience of program stakeholders;

- Evaluators have no warrant to grant privileged access to any stakeholder—they must serve all equally. For example, that one party has the resources and the warrant to sponsor an evaluation gives them no proprietary rights over it—they take their place along with all others as respondents and stakeholders;

- Program stakeholders have the right to know about the views and interests of those who influence their work in whatever way. Ministers and mothers each have the right to know of the others insofar as they one way or another impact on their lives and aspirations. Evaluators have the obligation to support open information exchange;

- Evaluation should be inclusive, seeking out a *range* of views, including those that may be highly valued as well as views that may be controversial—disreputable, even. Evaluators have no warrant to censor or select views; and

- Evaluators have no warrant to make their own judgment—their job is to help articulate and feed into other people's judgments. This means that the evaluator must be, at the least, reserved about making recommendations. (This is most probably subject to less of a consensus than the others.)

Together, these define the localist project for the evaluator—the obligation to inform civil society and its professional institutions. Here are the links between democratic evaluation and good governance.

Rights-Based Evaluation

We can invoke the concept of *information poverty* (i.e., a parallel to material poverty with the same effect of reducing the capacity for self-determination). Under information poverty, people have insufficient information about social arrangements that determine their lives to be able to make decisions and judgments about them. This is the case with MDGs. For the most part, monitoring and evaluating MDG progress is locked in reports that are fed back to international organizations, government, and the administrative system (i.e., the information wealthy). There are few established mechanisms for communities—or even their representatives—to receive that information and act on it. Think, for example, of professional practitioners—the nurses, police officers, social workers, and teachers who generate the results that international agencies claim. Where they do receive feedback on programs that envelop them it will tend to be framed as advocacy and may not often represent their immediate dilemmas. (This has often been represented in the development field as the denial of local knowledge in favor of Western science; see Long & Long [1992] for one of the early expressions of this.)

In any program of intervention, those who are expected to live with the consequences of the program (i.e., living with them or working with them) have the right to know about it: its accomplishments, its flaws, its logic, and its history. Just as with material poverty, the solution to information poverty is redistribution (i.e., from the information wealthy to the information poor). This has a range of procedural implications: providing access to the framing and sponsoring of enquiries, making reports publicly available, adopting methodologies that represent the real dilemmas people live with, and sharing information across stakeholder groups in such a way as to allow for informed public accountability. This is about public conversation more than management information.

The principle of rights provides the conceptual leverage for redistribution and for arriving at these procedural imperatives: Some people have rights over information, whereas others have obligations to provide it. Evaluation, as the generator and broker of information, is the redistributive mechanism.

The international commitment to rights-based approaches goes further than the claim people make to individual rights. Indeed, the principal (among many) critique of the rights approach is that aimed at the various UN declarations of rights: that they individualize action rather than collectivize it (Uvin, 2004; but see the counterargument, e.g., by Howard, 1995). The practice, however, is more complex. The human rights-based approach to programming (HRBP) focuses development interventions on policy-shaping processes, withdrawing from direct, field-based action so as to gain purchase on broader determining factors of poverty and exclusion. The aim is to take on the challenge of structural change in developing societies, redefining poverty, for example, less as an issue of economic pathology and more as the structural failure of society (i.e., a failure of rights and a failure of those in power to meet both their social and economic obligations). A rights-based approach to child protection, for example, might involve direct action to rescue particular children from sexual and economic exploitation, but, more important, would see collaborative action with municipal authorities to establish child protection commissions as principal duty-bearers and then to ring-fence budgetary allocations to guarantee their sustainability. In terms of the rights vocabulary, HRBP goes beyond the conventional differentiation of rights into civil/political rights, on the one hand, and economic, social, and cultural rights, on the other hand. This is, at best, an integrating framework.

This, too, is directly translatable into evaluation. Any program evaluation addresses both the politics and economics of social innovation because the program commands resources as well as the power structures that give rise to the pattern of resource allocation. Within a rights-based approach, it becomes imperative, then, to build democratic evaluation processes into local political structures on the principle of inclusion. This implies, for example, public observatories, a political facilitation role for universities, evaluative forums, and mobilizing schools to support community evaluative enquiry (of the kind developed in the OECD/ENSI program; see, e.g., Posch, 2001). The other principal objection to human rights—that it tends to subvert democratic structures (see Gould, 2005)—also is resolved in HRBP where the two can interlock.

Rights are not taken in terms of simple individualism (i.e., the conceding of discrete rights to attributed individuals). As part of the shift of development intervention to the social policy sphere, the rights agenda addresses collectivist values. The rights activist cannot fail to come up against democratic structures: parliaments and senates, ministries, regulatory bodies, accountability systems, and professional institutions. These are the structures that create the space within which rights are realized, and the question of whether rights are realized in individualistic or collective ways is an important debate. Indeed, a rights-based approach would almost inevitably lead to advocating a subsidiarity of policy shaping coinciding with deliberative democratic evaluation (House & Howe, 1999) because individual or collective rights may be protected and resourced at international and national levels, but can only be realized at local levels. A rights-based approach to evaluation sees evaluation providing information in a place, at a time, and in a way that supports this local realization of rights, as well as the shaping of the policy umbrella to support it (what Uvin [2004] describes as the "empiricist strategy" to rights implementation; i.e., piecemeal, locally defined, nonuniversalist).

In the context of rights-based evaluation, and in the international language of rights, this defines the evaluator as a duty bearer. Indeed, we might go so far as to say that the evaluator enjoys no rights at all (other than those held in trust for their respondents), but that the role is defined exclusively and uniquely in terms of obligations—obligations, that is, to allow for the redistribution of information goods. The rights-based evaluator in a democratic setup is the servant of all rights bearers and is warranted to grant no privileges to any. The agency that commissions an evaluation shares, by complicity, the same set of obligations and can be held, in the same way, to enjoy no privileged rights. Their role is defined as *sponsor* not *purchaser*. This goes for those agencies—including the United Nations—that commission evaluations of MDG progress.

Evaluation sensitive to rights issues is an instrument for working on the issue of how to translate universalist rhetorical statements of rights (such as international conventions) into local action, taking account of local complexities. There has to be a dynamic tension between international agreements such as MDGs and local preferences because human rights conventions cannot ignore contexts, nor can local authorities declare immunity from them. Similarly, we can ignore neither collective nor individual rights, and we have to be able to cope with the reality of people being rights holders and duty holders at the same time. Solutions, as always, are case made at the local level and regulated by decent, democratic, and fair accountability systems—evaluation provides the resources and opportunity to theorize solutions at the local level, and without it such resolutions are not available. In the end, international agreements and treaties—including MDGs—should be judged for their relevance to local contexts.

Conclusion: Evaluation for Social Consensus

All societies are characterized by fragmentation over purposes and values. Professional practitioners, program managers, and ministers, little understanding each other's challenges and accountabilities, frequently differ over how best to secure social change. The citizen, distant from exchanges between these groups, is rarely even party to them. If participation meant sometimes overturning the aspirations of the political and administrative elites, it would not happen—or be advocated—as often as it is. There is no need to be sentimental.

Most serious of all are breaches of communication and understanding between practitioner and government because it is that relationship that is most potent in generating development gains and ensuring that social investment is both utilized and utilized well. Democracy may fall as a result of political corruption, but it can only stand on the basis of well-founded, publicly accountable, and responsive social institutions. The most democratically aspirational government without a consent-based, efficient police service and school system will come to nothing.

Social fragmentation is corrosive of understanding between these two groups. Program evaluation is potentially nurturing of such understanding. Evaluation that is motivated by an ideology of rights and focused on democratic approaches to their deliberation and realization offers a site in which differences can be made transparent, legitimated, discussed, and resolved. It is important to say that the resolution of differences and the forging of consensus over, for example, MDG action need not be a permanent state and need not launder fundamental differences of approach and ideal. We are talking about overlapping consensus (Rawls, 1996; Umphres, 2008) based on common moral principles and temporary agreements focused on immediate priorities—both of which allow for continuing differences of purpose and value, but allow for immediate and concerted action. The mechanism for arriving at an overlapping/temporary consensus through informed argumentation is evaluation. For example, House and Howe (1999) lift program evaluation out of the realms of technical action and into the realms of the political.

In terms of our opening paradox, a rights-based approach to evaluation, set within a commitment to democratic structures and processes, helps to shape that mechanism. The challenge for MDGs is to have them owned at the level of community (i.e., by those who have to live with their consequences). That ownership has to be negotiated and can neither be assumed nor imposed because the question of whether programs of intervention that are motivated by MDGs are appropriate or desirable is entirely empirical and tested in local action. The only legitimate party to facilitate that negotiation for ownership—legitimate by virtue of being independent and impartial—is the evaluator. Whose rights is she or he championing?

Notes

1. http://www.unicef.org/lifeskills/index_7260 .html#A%20Framework%20for%20Rights-Based,%20Child-Friendly

2. The Program for International Student Assessment (PISA; www.pisa.oecd.org) describes itself as an "internationally standardized assessment" of pupil performance, currently across 57 countries. The International Association for Educational Assessment (IAEA; www.iaea.info) is a global NGO whose aims are to share experience of assessment as a driver for improving educational achievement.

3. "At one time a conclusion describes the existing situation well, at a later time it accounts for rather little variance . . . the half-life of an empirical proposition may be great or small" (p. 121).

4. See the official UN website (http://www.un .org/millenniumgoals/).

5. See the website http://www.un.org/millenni umgoals/

6. See the website http://www.unicef.org/evaluation/ files/RBM_Guide_20September2003.pdf

7. I am aware that I use the term *stakeholder* frequently, and I now need to say that the term can be tendentious. It too easily implies, for example, that all who may be termed *stakeholder* have equal status in evaluation. As House and Howe (1999) have previously reminded us, not all stakeholders are equal, and we may have to do something more than treat them all equally. A government minister is a stakeholder in a social program just as may be a pupil or a nurse, but the former is more skilled, robust, and better positioned to advocate for him- or herself than are the latter.

References

Baser, H., & Morgan, P. (2008). *Capacity, change and performance*. Maastricht: European Centre for Development Policy Management.

Black, M. (2008). *The no nonsense guide to the United Nations*. Oxford: New Internationalist.

Cameron, J., & Ojha, H. (2007). A deliberative ethic for development: A Nepalese journey from Bourdieu through Kant to Dewey and Habermas. *International Journal of Social Economics, 34*(1/2), 66–87.

Cronbach, L. J. (1975). Beyond the two disciplines of scientific psychology. *American Psychologist, 30*(2), 116–127.

Dryzek, J. (2000). *Deliberative democracy and beyond: Liberals, critics and contestations*. Oxford: Oxford University Press.

Franklin, T. (2008). Reaching the Millennium Development Goals: Equality and justice as well as results. *Development in Practice, 18*(3), 420–423.

Gage, N. L. (1996). Confronting counsels of despair for the behavioural sciences. *Educational Researcher, 25*(3), 5–15.

Gould, C. C. (2005). Democracy and human rights. In R. K. M. Smith & C. Van den Anker (Eds.), *The essentials of human rights* (pp. 84–86). London: Hodder Arnold.

House, E. (1974). *The politics of educational innovation*. Berkeley, CA: McCutchan.

House, E., & Howe, K. (1999). *Values in social research and evaluation*. London: Sage.

Howard, R. E. (1995). *Human rights and the search for community*. Oxford: Westview.

Jonsson, U. (2003). *Human rights approach to development programming*. Kenya: UNICEF.

Kushner, S., & Norris, N. (Eds.). (2007). Dilemmas of engagement: Evaluation and the New Public

Management. *Advances in Program Evaluation 10*. Oxford: Elsevier.

Long, N., & Long, A. (Eds.). (1992). *Battlefields of knowledge*. London: Routledge.

MacDonald, B. (1976). Evaluation and the control of education. In D. Tawney (Ed.), *Curriculum evaluation today: Trends and implications* (pp. 125–136). London: Macmillan.

Norris, N., & Kushner, S. (2007). The New Public Management and evaluation. In S. Kushner & N. Norris (Eds.), *Dilemmas of engagement: Evaluation and the new public management. Advances in Program Evaluation 10* (pp. 1–16). Oxford: Elsevier.

Posch, P. (2001). School development and education for sustainable development. In CERI, *What schools for the future?* Paris: OECD.

Rawls, J. (1996) *Political liberalism*. New York: Columbia University Press.

Ryan, K., & DeStefano, L. (Eds.). (2000). Evaluation as a democratic process: Inclusion, dialogue and deliberation. *New Directions in Evaluation 85*. San Francisco, CA: Jossey-Bass.

Segone, M. (Ed.). (2006). *New trends in development evaluation* (Evaluation Working Papers No. 5). Regional Office for CEE/CIS. Geneva: UNICEF.

Stenhouse, L. (1967). *Culture and education*. London: Nelson.

Umphres, W. P. (2008, April). *In defense of overlapping consensus: Stability, legitimacy and disagreement*. Paper presented to the Midwest Political Science Association annual national conference, Chicago, IL. Available at http://www.allacademic.com/meta/p267283_index.html.

Uvin, P. (2004). *Human rights and development*. Bloomfield, CT: Kumarian Press.

CHAPTER 24

Reclaiming Knowledge at the Margins

Culturally Responsive Evaluation in the Current Evaluation Moment

Rodney K. Hopson

If there is no contradictory impression, there is nothing to awaken reflection.

—Plato (*The Republic*, cited in Allen, 1991)

Few Americans have ever considered the idea that African-Americans are extremely knowledgeable about whites and whiteness. In the mainstream of American culture, and certainly in intellectual circles, a rough and unproductive division of labor exists where the claiming of expert knowledge and commonsense wisdom on race are concerned. White writers have long been positioned as the leading and most dispassionate investigators of the lives, values, and abilities of people of color. White writing about whiteness is rarer, with discussions of what it means to be human standing in for considerations of how racial identity influences white lives. Writers of color, and most notably African-American writers, are cast as providing insight, often presumed to be highly subjective, of what it is like to be "a minority." Lost in this destructive shuffle is the fact that from folktales onward African Americans have been among the nation's keenest students of white consciousness and white behavior.

—Roediger (1998, p. 8)

AUTHOR'S NOTE: I would like to acknowledge Terry Denny, Fiona Cram, Stafford Hood, Karen Kirkhart, Katherine E. Ryan, and an anonymous reviewer for their critiques to earlier drafts of the chapter. Additionally, thanks to the National Science Foundation for their support of commissioned work on cultural context in evaluation, which helped plant the seeds on this topic several years ago.

Introduction and Layout

The title of this chapter is inspired by a lecture and an excerpt from a book, both of which made references to an interview of Toni Morrison, recipient of the Nobel Prize in Literature in 1993, with Bill Moyers. In the interview, Moyers is quoted as asking Morrison when she would start writing about White people.[1] Her reply would serve as testament to those nascent and seasoned scholars who identify with the understanding and contributions of culturally responsive evaluation (CRE) and other standpoint theoretical reflections, extrapolations, and applications that privilege the indigenous, the minoritized, and the traditionally marginalized. In both testaments, they indicate that "she pledged to 'stay out here at the margin and let the center come looking for me.'" Although Morrison's response was hardly direct (i.e., either her response warranted a time in which she would start writing, or not in this case), it was revealing, paradoxical, and symbolic. Why would Morrison acknowledge or insist on staying at the margins? What is it about the margins that attracts Morrison (and her literary work) and implies a redefinition, redirection, or a "contradictory impression" as Plato echoes?

In the book, *Black on White: Black Writers on What it Means to Be White* (Roediger, 1998), in the dialogue between Morrison and Moyer, David Roediger opines that Morrison's statement is more than about whether, if, or when she will start including White characters in her literary work. Instead, Morrison's reply both acknowledges the expert knowledge and commonsense wisdom of people of color and challenges knowledge claims that delegitimize the lives, values, and abilities of these same people of color. The Roediger quote at the outset of the chapter and the Morrison reply reposition what counts as knowledge, who has the right to make knowledge claims, and what can be learned from redefining knowledge about people of color, their institutions, communities, and individual lives. The admonition from Morrison resonates within a proud tradition of scholars and writers in humanities, liberal arts, and the social sciences captured in John Stanfield's (1999) similar stance when he claimed that "the racialist and paternalistic traditions of social scientific work reproduce dominance and subordination relations in the academy and in the worlds we study and evaluate" (p. 424).

This chapter reviews the conceptual underpinnings and contributions of CRE by situating it within larger sociocultural knowledge productions and in the current historical moment of evaluation. That is, in tying into the larger theme of the edited volume, this chapter situates and legitimizes CRE in contemporary society through examples that illustrate and reflect on its ongoing challenges and directions for evaluation.

The implications of this chapter for social programs and policies suggest that considerations should be made in initially legitimizing the lived experiences of and building and implementing efforts aimed at traditionally underrepresented and underserved groups. Amid the continued discussions at the national and local levels around the need for nonprofit, philanthropic, and governmental agencies and educational settings to be more responsive to communities of color, indigenous communities, and those historically underserved and underrepresented, more attempts are being made to ensure that strategies align the needs and sensitivities of these particular populations (Lee, 2007).

In framing CRE, this chapter reflects on the complex dynamics and turns of indigenous, racialized, and minoritized knowledge productions in today's global context and intends to make way for CRE within existing, assumed, and validated evaluation knowledges. By proposing a way of understanding CRE beside and within other linkages that legitimate indigenous and subjugated groups, the chapter ultimately raises tensions, questions, and claims in evaluation (theory, method, practice, and profession) where minoritized, racialized, and indigenous groups are concerned. In raising these tensions, questions, and claims, the chapter also intends to speculate about how to achieve CRE theory in use in ways that move the conversations onward. Ultimately, in providing a definitional, historical, and conceptual discussion of CRE, this chapter intersperses practical examples that further illustrate and situate CRE in this 21st-century moment.

The chapter is divided into several sections aimed at tying CRE to a larger theoretical underpinning in transforming mainstream frameworks. Beginning with a definition and major theses of CRE, along with similarity and alignment of other social agenda/advocacy approaches in evaluation, this chapter draws on indigenous, decolonizing, and critical race theories and epistemologies to conceptually frame the emerging study, practice, and theory of CRE.

Defining CRE in This 21st-Century Evaluation Moment

The last decade has witnessed considerable growth in the attention paid to culture in evaluation as evidenced by the number of professional workshops, conferences, and (invited and funded) meetings on related topics.[2] When the first set of papers began to emerge and be defined as CRE (cf. Frierson, Hood, & Hughes, 2002; Hood, 1998, 2001), it was clear than an awakening moment of reflection was on the field led by earlier contributions that paved the way (in particular, refer to Kirkhart, 1995; Madison, 1992) in this 21st-century moment.

Although newly recognized in the field of evaluation, CRE is multidimensional and has multiple perspectives. On the one hand, CRE is emerging as an evaluation approach or model in a Stufflebeamian (2001) sense used by evaluators and researchers to guide the quality and principles of evaluation. On the other hand, CRE is a system or culmination of practical strategies and frameworks that attend to culture during the various stages and phases of an evaluation, from preparing for the evaluation to disseminating and using the results of study (Frierson et al., 2002). Parekh (2006) defines *culture* as "an historically created system of meaning and significance" (p. 143) and distinguishes its nature, structure, dynamics, and characteristics. When adjectivized (i.e., culturally) to precede another

approach or method of evaluation (i.e., responsive evaluation), the new word conjoins qualities and features unique to systems of beliefs and practices of unique groups, most often perceived outside or alternative to mainstream, with the social and technical practice of evaluation.

As this chapter intends to advance even more, CRE is a theoretical, conceptual, and inherently political position that includes the centrality of and attunedness to culture in the theory and practice of evaluation. That is, CRE recognizes that demographic, sociopolitical, and contextual dimensions, locations, perspectives, and characteristics of culture matter fundamentally in evaluation. Those who use CRE understand and value lived experiences that help to (re)define, (re)interpret, and make sense in everyday life. By privileging notions of lived experiences and especially regarding communities and populations of color or indigenous groups, new explanations and understandings of evaluands, programs, and phenomena of study emerge.

Notions of *lived experiences*, and in particular shared lived experiences, are foundational to CRE. In articulating these notions, evaluators and researchers redefine how CRE can be done and by whom. In findings that reveal epistemological tensions in a study of Mäori health, Cram, McCreanor, Smith, Nairn, and Johnstone (2006) illustrate where two different kinds of "lived ideologies"—namely, Päkehä (or European New Zealanders) and Mäori—resulted in competing struggles between patients and physicians "over power and over whose ideology inform and control the interactions." Lived experiences, as the study shows, mark historical and contemporary battles and competing explanations in the disparities of treatment and health care between indigenous and settler groups. In much the same way that Laura Nader (1999) and Linda T. Smith (1999) warned in anthropology and indigenous studies, respectively, about the tendency for researchers to study "down" or the process of engaging in patronizing partnerships and relationships with individuals, groups, and the agencies or institutions that serve traditionally marginalized or indigenous groups, those who espouse CRE notions warn against "evaluating down." For instance, efforts should be taken to prevent pathologizing or delegitimatizing viewpoints and experiences of communities of color in deficit perspectives at any point in the practice and process of evaluation. As the next section illustrates, CRE's legacy has roots both within evaluation "mainstream" and standpoint perspectives in the social sciences.

Historical Roots and Contemporary Branches of CRE

The historical antecedents of CRE emerged from and within a larger but loosely coupled network of social agenda/advocacy approaches in evaluation that have resonated with social justice, democratic practice, and use. Additionally, CRE has not developed in isolation from other social science and transdisciplinary fields of study; that CRE's historical development and roots resemble those of other disciplines and practices is an observation that does not go unnoticed. In fact, as the following subsections show, the influences of CRE are both within and beyond evaluation, and its branches extend to other subfields of education, psychology, and even more fields that have gone underexplored by the transdisciplinary evaluation community.

Influences Within Evaluation

Social agenda/advocacy approaches are defined as models that make a difference by addressing issues of access, opportunity, and power and have become more prevalent in the field of evaluation. Stufflebeam (2001) describes four evaluation models that are characterized as social agenda/advocacy approaches that are particularly relevant for evaluation in the 21st century: responsive evaluation, constructivist evaluation, deliberative democratic evaluation, and utilization focused evaluation. Greene (2006) links CRE with other approaches in and beyond the United States that have focused on

democracy and social change and the concomitant attention to power, differential access, and other related issues that emerge in an evaluation context. Greene situates and juxtaposes culturally and contextually responsive evaluation with evaluation by and for indigenous peoples as a contemporary development of ideologically oriented theories in the making, which both "attend directly to issues of culture and, relatedly, race and ethnicity, and both seek to supersede historical legacies of enslavement and colonization with theories rooted in once-dominated cultures" (p. 114). What CRE finds compatible with these social agenda/advocacy approaches is hardly idiosyncratic; the pursuit of democratic principles in evaluation like those addressed in deliberative democratic evaluation and its related branches (Hood, 2000; House, 2006) resonates with CRE in ways that raise questions about participation by and with groups and communities who have been and continue to be on the margins of society.

In much the same way that CRE blends democratic tenets in evaluation, it also is influenced by responsive evaluation. *Responsive evaluation*, as coined by Stake (1975, 1991) and others (Greene & Abma, 2001), is a continuously interactive, reflectively dynamic, and participatory approach that intends to be particularly oriented to clients' needs, experiences, and conflicts without surrendering design and authority of the evaluation to those same stakeholders. Where responsive evaluation implies being in touch with multiple but particular positions, interests, and perspectives, this notion of responsive evaluation resonates with CRE. To CRE theorists, knowledge is situational and context-bound, and CRE extends responsive evaluation to matters of power, race, equity, and culture.

The description of African-American evaluators, as initially chronicled by Hood (2001) and subsequently known as the Nobody Knows My Name Project, tapped some of the early history of CRE in the context of African-American education, history, and evaluation (Hopson & Hood, 2005).[3] That these evaluators existed in the shadows of the emerging field, giants in the field such as Ralph Tyler, and in the first generation of evaluation is noteworthy in and of itself. Perhaps most important, as Hood argues, these CRE pioneers were being socially responsible in attempting to ameliorate the social and educational conditions of African Americans in a pre-*Brown v. Board* (1954) era. These pre-*Brown* educational evaluators and researchers, armed with knowledge of technical applied survey and naturalistic approaches, were responsive and responsible to their segregated and marginalized community in their pursuit of equity and in countering the legacy of racial and ethnic discrimination and apartheid in educational and social life in the United States. As is demonstrated in the following section, evaluation has not been the only field to recently undergo a culturally responsive turn. These historical references help to situate CRE both by providing historical context to current developments and linking the work in CRE in the last decade or so to similar evaluation roots and branches.

Influences Other Than Cultural Responsiveness

Like other inter- and transdisciplines, evaluation was especially ripe for the emergence of CRE and for lifting the centrality of culture in evaluation theory and practice. There were similar turns that preceded or are concurrently being developed in fields such as educational research (Fuller & Clarke, 1994; Lee, 2008; Tillman, 2002), teacher education (Foster, 1995; Hollins & Oliver, 1999; Ladson-Billings, 1990; McAllister & Irvine, 2000; Ogbu, 1982; Pewewardy, 1999), learning styles (Boutte & DeFlorimonte, 1998; Irvine & York, 1995), early childhood education (Lubeck, Jessup, deVries, & Post, 2001), human development (Slaughter-Defoe, Nakagawa, Takanishi, & Johnson, 1990), counseling (Arredondo, 1999), assessment (Solano-Flores & Nelson-Barber, 2001), educational anthropology/ethnography (Au, 1980; Eisenhart, 2001; Leacock, 1977, Ogbu, 1982;

Watson-Gegeo, 1988), and community and counseling psychology (Sue, 1998).

Culturally relevant and responsive teaching and pedagogy have considerable currency in current multicultural education reform in schools, used as a way of teaching and educating cultural diversity in classrooms. At its basic level, a culturally relevant/responsive teaching and pedagogy orientation helps teachers attend to the needs of each learner; it encourages a connectedness of classroom content to student cultural and experiential backgrounds in the support of learning and academic achievement, especially for ethnically and linguistically diverse students. Pewewardy's (1999) definition of *culturally responsive teaching* incorporates cultural pluralism and is dynamic, particularly in the context of educating and teaching American Indian students when he writes:

> to be "culturally responsive" is to be sensitive, aware, and capable of employing cultural learning patterns, perspectives, family structure, multiple worldviews, tribal languages, and Indian English in the teaching, learning, and mental ecology of the classroom. It is important to think multiculturally, rather than monoculturally, and to be aware of one's own development as a teacher within a culturally diverse society. (p. 91)

Similar threads of CRE are noted about how the need for evaluators to be aware of their own personal selves is integral to the practice of evaluators (Hopson, 2004; Symonette, 2004).

Foster's (1995) discussion of excellent African-American teachers and her focus on culturally relevant pedagogy extends the understanding of this approach in her use of educational ethnography and anthropology literature (e.g., Au, 1980; Dumont, 1972; Heath, 1983; Philips, 1972, 1983) to suggest how and why incorporating culturally compatible communicative patterns and recognizing familial cultural patterns are helpful aids toward culturally relevant pedagogy. To address the often-cited cultural mismatch, conflict, and discontinuity hypotheses that exist in schooling (e.g., Ogbu, 1982; Trumbull, Rothstein-Fisch, & Greenfield, 2000), Foster contends that cultural solidarity and connectedness are important beliefs and practices that resonate among effective African-American teachers who develop strong intergenerational attachments to the Black community through caring relationships, use fictive kin relationships to promote parental social roles, and simultaneously command respect and require students to meet high academic and behavioral standards.

The emphasis on the cultural context has been recognized as a vital orientation and perspective in teaching and learning. Irvine and York (1995) suggest, in learning styles research for instance, how cultural variables might be powerful explanatory factors in the failure of children of color. The tendency to overlook variables such as cultural forms, behaviors, a group's history, language, values, norms, rituals, and symbols, all inclusive of the notion of cultural context, in learning styles research is not uncommon. Effective teachers of these students attend to individual students' learning styles and are self-reflective and critical of "their own actions, instructional goals, methods, and materials as they relate to their students' cultural experiences and preferred learning environment" (Irvine & York, 1995, p. 494). This work extends others' work that identifies unique learning patterns among various ethnic and cultural groups (Gay, 1988; Hale-Benson, 1986) and helps safeguard the mislabeling, misplacement, misassessment, and mistreatment of these children in schooling settings (Hilliard, 1992; Ladson-Billings, 1994; Solano-Flores & Nelson-Barber, 2001) or the misappropriation of theoretical and conceptual models that explain academic achievement and failure of children of color (Gordon, Miller, & Rollock, 1990; Leacock, 1977; Slaughter-Defoe et al., 1990).

Inherent in the discussion of culture in educational subfields that address teaching, learning, and school or program improvement is an inevitable discussion of how particular forms of knowledge are privileged over local and cultural forms. Few scholars review how dominant cultural productions manifest in the study of education and reify themselves in classroom practices. Hilliard (1997), for one, suggests that beneath a discussion of cultural context in education is a need to look deeper at illuminating hidden problems and questioning fundamental assumptions in the field. He contends, "instead of confining our analyses of classroom processes to student behavior alone . . . we must look for evidence of conscious or unconscious reinforcement of patterns of domination within the educational institution as a whole" (Hilliard, 1977, p. 120). The call by Fuller and Clarke (1994) toward a "culturally situated model of school/ program effectiveness," in the context of their understanding school effectiveness and student achievement in developing country contexts, reveals the complicated nature of local and cultural contexts within broader global processes, norms, and standards (Lubeck et al., 2001). Current topics around the role of culture in educational program, policy, and teaching efforts do not neglect a discussion and consideration of the wider processes of stratification, power, and globalization (Eisenhart, 2001).

An additional term that has emerged in recent years in the psychological and public health arenas is *cultural competence*. Mario Orlandi's (1992) definition of cultural competence as a set of skills (academic and interpersonal) recognizes the importance of cultural differences and similarities within, among, and between groups and inevitable reliance on community, local, and indigenous-based cultural contexts to develop appropriate supports, interventions, and other mechanisms. As a commonly discussed term among scholars and practitioners interested in ethnic minority issues, cultural competence is replete in community psychology and health, cross-cultural and ethnic psychology, counseling psychology, and psychotherapy. Like the introduction of cultural competence and cultural context in other disciplines, scholars in psychology and health point to the ever-increasing multiethnic and demographic changes taking place in the United States, as well as the important philosophical and paradigm shifts that signal the growth of subfields (Nguyen, Kagawa-Singer, & Kar, 2003; Sue, 1998).

From this body of work around cultural responsiveness from other disciplines, theorists and practitioners in evaluation raise important issues to consider. First, evaluators who concentrate on CRE, despite a limited amount of scholarship in the field, have both historical and interdisciplinary scholarship in topics around cultural responsiveness that adds to the understanding in the context of evaluation. Second, the topics around the role of culture in education, public health, psychology, and other related fields require understanding of the dynamics and role of race, power, and privilege in globalized contexts so as not to consider notions of culture in a societal vacuum. Finally, the body of literature that situates cultural responsiveness suggests a particular role for the reflective evaluator who makes sense of one's own development and location as an evaluator sensitive to the context of the evaluand and program in which one works.

The following section, having now explored the historical and interdisciplinary relationships of cultural responsiveness, provides two standpoint frameworks—decolonizing/indigenous and critical race—to expand the understanding of CRE and its theoretical understandings and contributions.

Theoretical Roots of Cultural Responsiveness

The theoretical roots of cultural responsiveness, at least in evaluation, tend to be associated with indigenous, minoritized, and subjugated ways of knowing, appropriating, collecting, and interpreting knowledges that challenge the dominant, Western, and colonizing information and knowledges. CRE rests at the theoretical nexus between certain cultural ways of knowing, valuing, and judging, which are to be discussed next. Figure 24.1 illustrates this, with its aim to reclaim, reconnect, and reorder those ways of knowing, valuing, and judging, which tend to be submerged or driven underground.

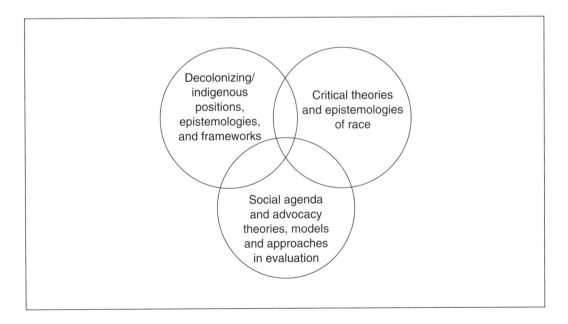

Figure 24.1 Visualizing Indigenous, Critical Race, and Social Agenda/Advocacy Evaluation Approaches With CRE

NOTE: At the intersection of the union of decolonizing/indigenous positions, critical race theories, and social agenda and advocacy approaches rests CRE.

Decolonizing/Indigenous Positions, Epistemologies, and Frameworks

Decolonizing or indigenous positions, epistemologies, and frameworks form important theoretical threads of CRE. In describing the decolonizing framework, L. T. Smith (1999) describes its aim as twofold. One significant part of these positions, epistemologies, and frameworks involves deconstructing Western scholarship and discourse. Part of a larger intent of the decolonizing framework, *deconstruction* involves taking stories apart, revealing underlying texts, and giving voice to experiences and realities often glossed over in traditional scholarship. This process of deconstruction problematizes and interrogates evaluation processes and practices, which, according to L. T. Smith (1999), "deny the validity of indigenous peoples' claims to existence, to land and territories, to the right of self-determination, to the survival of our language and forms of cultural knowledge, to our natural resources and systems for living within our environments" (p. 1). In much the same way that L. T. Smith describes the process of deconstruction in a decolonizing framework, Semali and Kincheloe (1999) write how students of indigenous knowledge engage in a "critique of Western epistemological tyranny and the oppressive educational practices that follow it" (p. 31). Specifically, Semali and Kincheloe challenge the denigration of indigenous knowledge, the oppression of indigenous peoples, and the concomitant role and power of Western knowledge and science as universal and imperialistic. Their own critique of epistemological hegemony of Western science, modernism, and knowledge productions through the evolution of the Scientific Revolution in the 16th and 17th centuries and the influences of René Descartes, Sir Isaac Newton, and Sir Francis Bacon problematizes the essentialist notions of neutrality and the scientific method that tend to privilege narrow ethnocentric perspectives. As Semali and Kincheloe (1999) argue,

> Western epistemological tyranny decrees that the reality constructed by Cartesian-Newtonian ways of seeing is the only reality worth discussing in academic settings. Knowledge in this context becomes centralized and the power to produce knowledge is concentrated in the hands of a limited power bloc. In this process one begins to understand that science is the most powerful cultural production of Western society. The knowledge Western science produced became the benchmark by which the productions of non-Western civilizations were measured. (p. 31)

The second important part of decolonizing and indigenous positions, epistemologies, and frameworks involves creating spaces of resistance and hope within a larger framework of self-determination, decolonizing, and social justice. The increasing demands of the international indigenous community of scholars and researchers have privileged approaches to research, protocols, and methodologies in ways that reclaim and remake indigenous communities, cultures, languages, and social practices. As a result, indigenous communities and organizations exercise means of control over research activities and the knowledge that research produces, and develop their own ethical guidelines and documents (Ormond, Cram, & Carter, 2006). For instance, it is not uncommon for researchers and evaluators to complete multiple informed consents: one for the university or agency in which they are employed, and one specific to the indigenous group or community where research or evaluation is conducted. The additional informed consent procedures at the community level are attempts to preserve the respect and dignity of ethical principles not often articulated or required in mainstream Institutional Review Boards, ethical research committees, or even principles and standards of evaluation.

This aspect of *transformation* realized in the reshaping, reclaiming, and renaming of the purpose and use of indigenous knowledges involves the deliberate study and reconstruction of academic curricula and training of repressed and subjugated knowledges. Semali and Kincheloe

(1999) suggest that, instead of being passive or reactionary about oppressive educational practices that follow Western ways of knowing indigenous peoples, students of indigenous knowledges become active as "researchers of such repressed knowledges, to search out what Western and Western-influenced academics have previously neglected, to recover materials that may often work to change our consciousness in profound ways" (p. 32). The authors contend that the process of *reconstruction* requires deconstructing. However, reconstructing and reconceptualizing academic curricula challenge the visible and invisible cultural assumptions embedded in all aspects of schooling and education, contests dominant cultural views of reality, and, more important, brings new awareness and recontextualized versions of history and education that espouse critically multicultural and critically grounded political visions of research and knowledge production.

Indigenous/Decolonizing Frameworks and CRE

The theoretical intersection of indigenous, decolonizing frameworks in evaluation adds an interesting perspective to the application of cultural responsiveness. LaFrance's (2001, 2006) work grounds evaluation in the context of tribal communities rather than tribal communities in the context of evaluation. That is, grounding evaluation in the context of tribal and indigenous communities ensures that evaluation both serves the needs of a larger indigenous community and raises fundamental questions about decolonialization, self-determination, and social justice (L. T. Smith, 1999). Serving the needs of a larger community means operating from a place where indigenous knowledge is valued and the process of coming to know or valuing is centered within indigenous epistemologies, histories, and practices and committing oneself to notions of sovereignty, self-determination, and reciprocity.

Applying Foucault's notions of *cultural archive*, defined here as the knowledges, philosophies,

and definitions of human nature particular to people who share similar historical traditions, L. T. Smith (1999) suggests that the archive reveals rules of practice and ideas about what is considered real. In a real sense, rules of evaluation practice are unassailably governed by indigenous contexts and realities and not the converse: Indigenous contexts are governed by evaluation practice, protocols, and the like. Referring to a developing community of international indigenous scholars and researchers, L. T. Smith (1999) notes where indigenous communities and organizations "have developed policies about research, are discussing issues related to control over research activities and the knowledge that research produces, and have developed ethical guidelines and discussion documents" (p. 4). This reaction from indigenous communities and organizations illustrates how culturally archived rules frame appropriate ways to situate evaluation practice and theory.

In a similar way, LaFrance (2006) draws on focus groups with and literature being written by indigenous peoples from the United States, Canada, and New Zealand to contribute to the development of an indigenous framing or scaffolding, a comprehensive effort to improve American Indian student achievement in science, technology, engineering, and mathematics (STEM) led by the American Indian Higher Education Consortium (AIHEC). What LaFrance draws on initially is the set of guiding principles, goals, and values that guide indigenous epistemologies, knowledges, and sense of knowing where holism, family, and community, living responsibly and in harmony with community, and where having a sense of place and sovereignty have significant consequences for evaluation practice in indigenous communities. Drawing on this developing work, LaFrance (2006) notes how the context of indigenous communities is critical, as well as fundamental to the framing of evaluation practice:

The holistic framing of an Indigenous world view and the extensive sense of interrelationship, community and family demand that evaluation of programs include rich descriptive narratives that set the program within its contextual situation, location and time. The notion central to empirical methodology that one can separate out factors among program variables for independent analysis is not useful when framing evaluation in an Indigenous way of viewing the world. Learning and knowledge derive from experiencing the program, and it is the subjectivity of this experience that leads to meaning and understanding. (p. 5)

Another important aspect of grounding evaluation in the context of indigenous communities inevitably includes raising important questions, discoveries, and solutions in order to avoid the continual exploitation and colonization of indigenous communities (Kawakami, Aton, Cram, Lai, & Porima, 2008). With the overwhelming nature and background of research (and, to a certain extent, evaluation) in indigenous communities being done, according to L. T. Smith (1999) "through imperial eyes," efforts such as the one described earlier by AIHEC are searching for ways to use evaluation and research responsive with community agendas for change, transformation, and sovereignty. In an earlier work, LaFrance (2001) noted how the name of an approach or tool may be inappropriate, signaling something antithetical to the indigenous ways of asking and conceptualizing. In describing how she builds conceptual pictures of programs to illustrate underlying values and assumptions in Indian country, where apparent logic modeling takes place, she contends, "I never use the term *logic model* since it connotes an intellectualism that can come across as elitist, mysterious, and Western" (LaFrance, 2001, p. 45), not as a way of diminishing the necessity for building conceptual pictures, but in respect for "fitting the program and the stakeholders' way of seeing the program" (LaFrance, 2001, p. 45). The work that LaFrance describes suggests that designs, methods, models, and other tools in the evaluation enterprise are created based on community values and indigenous ways of knowing.[4]

Critical Theories and Epistemologies of Race

Critical theories and epistemologies of race also undergird the theoretical notions of CRE. Although scholarship on race and racist epistemologies broadly defined is well known in sociology and anthropology (Harrison, 1997, 2008; Hymes, 1972/1999; Ladner, 1973; Lewis, 1973; Stanfield & Dennis, 1993), a recent surge of literatures in the social sciences contributes to the conceptual grounding and developing of CRE. In the seminal work of Stanfield and Dennis (1993), Stanfield (1993) suggested in a groundbreaking work on race and ethnicity in research methods how epistemological considerations need rethinking in the social sciences. In particular, he questioned the assumptions and identification of social groups in terms of race and ethnic categories in what he describes as race-saturated everyday society that tends to be overly simplistic and reifies mythologies and dominant cultural hegemonies that exist between groups. That the "mundane racial categories they use in their research are actually grounded in folk beliefs derived from precolonial era thinking about the inherent superiority and inferiority of populations along phenotypic and genetic lines" (Stanfield, 1993, p. 17) was rarely problematized or questioned by social scientists, according to Stanfield.

Another key consideration that opened the theoretical door of work into race theories and epistemologies is Stanfield's (1993) contributions on ethics and human values. The crux of his argument lies in the perpetuation and legitimation of cultural hegemony in the selection and rewarding of intellectual careers, especially those that speak to the realities of racial and ethnic issues. Laying out this argument and its relevance to the larger issue of epistemological considerations, Stanfield (1993) writes:

Cultural standards of data generalization are the basis of researcher presumptions regarding the racial or ethnic population source of constructing universal statements. It has always been the norm in the social sciences to assume that Eurocentric empirical realities can be generalized to explain the realities of people of color. In most presumptuous fashion, for decades, researchers steeped in Eurocentric norms have applied Eurocentric concepts of families, deviance, social movements, psychological development, organizational behavior, stratification, and even spirituality to the experiences of people of color. This has occurred to such an extent that our social science knowledge of the indigenous senses of people of color is actually quite sparse and superficial.

From his previous quote and the general thesis of this work, Stanfield argues not only that the cultural standards of data generalization tend to be Eurocentric and the very realities of people of color, either as social scientists or as communities being researched, were not considered legitimate, generalizable, nor mainstream. Furthermore, the dearth of scholarship challenging the dominant Eurocentric cultural standards led the way to the emergence of race-focused and central scholarship (cf. Zuberi & Bonilla-Silva's [2008] most recent book, which lifts this work of race-based logic and method in contemporary scholarship).

One recent and applicable body of scholarship that situates the role of race and racism in the production of inequality is that of critical race theory (CRT). Special issues, books, and presentations on CRT have been ubiquitous since its initial development in the mid-1990s (Ladson-Billings & Tate, 1995; Lopez, 2003; Parker, Deyhle, & Villenas, 1999; Tate, 1996, 2005). From its intellectual and scholarship development from legal studies to other disciplines in social sciences, humanities, and education, CRT is recognized as a vibrant theoretical proposition that asks questions about "broader notions relating structural barriers and ideological projects to the realities of access and opportunity

to learn scientific knowledge" (Tate, 2005, p. 122). Practically speaking, CRT emerged at a moment in the 20th and 21st centuries at a time ripe for "a new paradigm using a variety of methodological tools including storytelling to inform understanding of racial injustice and to provide new ways of seeing the links between race, gender and class" (Tate, 2005, p. 122).

The rapid proliferation of writings and articles associated with CRT emerged from the work of legal scholars such as Derrick Bell, Kimberle Crenshaw, Patricia Williams, Richard Delgado, and other members of the CRT movement. These scholars created intellectual spaces for focusing on understanding critical race decision making in legal and political settings. Bell's (1987) critique of legal hurdles to racial justice provided foundational CRT perspectives on civil rights legislation, voting power, segregated schools, affirmative action, and more. Crenshaw's (1988) seminal paper in the *Harvard Law Review* questioned liberal and conservative legal discourse in the post-Reagan era and contributed more insights into the lived realities and gains of racial and ethnic groups and their gains from traditional civil rights methods.

Referring to the seminal work of CRT scholars and analyzing researcher positionality of race and culture in educational research, Milner (2007) summarizes the three key tenets of CRT as (a) the ingrained nature of race and racism, (b) the importance of narrative and counternarrative perspectives told by people of color, and (c) the centrality of interest convergence.[5] The first tenet of CRT presumes that race matters and that the indelible and pervasive quality and effect of racism seeps into the everyday fabric of our lives and our laws in ways that appear normal and natural to most people. With its origins in the study of law, early progenitors of CRT situated that our American jurisprudence is inextricably shaped by the formation, development, and permanence of race matters and racism in our larger society.

The second tenet of CRT realizes the necessity of creating and naming one's own reality in the form of counterrealities and counternarratives that are captured by people and communities of color. Critical race theorists believe that the narratives name reality; in doing so, they tell stories of oppression and resilience by people on the margins of society. These stories of hope and struggle are what Duncan (2005) refers to as "the stories of people of colour as necessary to disrupt the allochronic discourses that inform racial inequality in schools and society" (p. 101). These counterpoints, as he refers to them, challenge "the existing narratives that shape how we understand the post-Civil Rights schooling experiences and outcomes of students of colour" (Duncan, 2005, p. 101) and extend Freire's (1996) idea that stories of the oppressed identify and assist in transforming pedagogy or research to represent realities of the people. In fact, the formation of narratives informs the development of new and "transgressive knowledges" (Yosso, 2005) to transform dominant paradigms such as wealth, success, achievement, and the social structures and practices that follow.

The notion of interest convergence is the third tenet of CRT. This construct, not unlike Spring's (2004) analysis of conflict of interests, more directly positions the issues of racism, privilege, power, and injustice in American education. Where Spring suggests that our educational settings are beset with competing issues and interests among a plethora of major political actors, the CRT description of interest convergence juxtaposes and centralizes the issues and interests of people of color within a larger umbrella of sociolegal, political, environmental, public health, and educational contexts (Donnor, 2005). Chapman's (2005) analysis of the conflicting patterns and events in northern and southern states, especially in light of the Rockford, Illinois, court case (*People Who Care v. Rockford Board of Education, School District 205*, 1997), illustrates how the converging of interests are at play in issues related to desegregation and parental involvement and activism. The narrative that Chapman weaves inextricably links the tenets of CRT into an illuminating story of changing and converging interests around *de jure* and *de facto* segregation systems in northern cities and the battles among courts, parents, school boards, and

students that began with *Brown v. Board of Education of Topeka* (1954). More than simply telling a story, Chapman (2005) explains how the interests converged around a number of key issues, including "the changing political climate, the attack on social science research, the inability to measure racism and its eradication, the pervasive deficit model of students of colour and their families, and the economic deterioration of the urban city" (p. 31). Taken together, the tenets are mutually exclusive, but they also integrate in ways that magnify the issues that argue the primacy of race and racism in schooling and society.

CRTs and CRE

In advancing the conceptual underpinnings of cultural responsiveness beside race theories, John Stanfield's plenary address at the American Evaluation Association annual conference in Chicago in 1998 and the subsequently published article (1999) challenged the racialized conventional wisdoms, problematics, and techniques of social scientific evaluation. He directed specific questions to the evaluation profession:

> How do evaluators respond to the processes of change and transformation occurring locally, nationally, and internationally? . . . How do [social scientists] make these frameworks much more concerned with approaching anti-racism issues more from the standpoints of power and privilege, rather than from deficit models? . . . How do we make government agencies, nonprofit organizations, other agencies that fund social research, evaluation firms, and businesses that contract consulting social scientists much more forward-thinking, escaping nineteenth-century notions of America and people of color as "minorities"? (Stanfield, 1999, p. 429)

These questions and others like them, arguably, are the ones being posed by evaluators who build culture into their theoretical lenses

(Kirkhart, 2005; Nelson-Barber, LaFrance, Trumbull, & Aburto, 2005). The thesis of Stanfield's article and its implications for culturally responsive evaluation suggest that social scientific evaluation has neglected to account for issues of power, privilege, and empowerment or the pervasiveness of White privilege in disciplinary study. Instead, evaluators and social scientists tend to be overly concerned with the issues of method, technique, and/or approach. As such, Stanfield (1999) challenges the acultural and value-free notions of knowledge in the academy, which tend to view the experiences of European Americans as the normative standard (Gordon et al., 1990; Parker, 2004) and issues of relevance or the gap between "(a) what social scientists do successfully for career building and (b) how much their data and interpretations are isomorphic with the experiences with real people" (p. 418). His indictment of the relevance and adequacy of fit of social science concepts, techniques, and methods in accurately representing empirical realities of Black and other people of color is foundational to notions of validity standards espoused by others in an evaluation context (cf. Campbell & Stanley, 1966) and a fundamental contribution to the notions of cultural responsiveness. Kirkhart's (2005) recent work in multicultural validity (MCV) centers culture in conversations about validity. What she describes as the five justifications of MCV— interpersonal, consequential, experiential, theoretical, and methodological—are dimensions that direct "attention to different types of evidence to support or challenge validity" (Kirkhart, 2005, p. 22). As an example, the methodological justification of MCV is supported when measurement tools are developed for particular ethnic and cultural groups unique to their particular context or use and evaluation questions incorporate a range of perspectives, values, and interests. Methodological threats to MCV occur when research designs are in violation or conflict with cultural norms or when evaluation questions are framed within narrow perspectives that hold little or no meaning to communities or populations (Kirkhart, 2006).

Thinking Backward, Moving Forward

This chapter summarizes the theoretical framing and development of CRE by drawing on the influences of indigenous/decolonizing and critical race theories, traditions, and epistemologies. Without reducing the conceptual understandings of cultural responsiveness in evaluation to a set of simplistic themes or tenets, this final section attempts to draw on the summary of theoretical contributions that embody the CRE construct and imply ways to achieve CRE theory in use.

An important theoretical and historical development of CRE is its stance to challenge and resist dominant, mainstream thinking that pervades the tradition of scholarship that sees difference as deficit or diversity as deviant. CRE resists the "communicentric bias" that envelops narrow ethnocentric perspectives of evaluators, researchers, and the work they do. Gordon et al. (1990) refer to this notion of communicentric bias as the particular "androcentric, cultrocentric, and ethnocentric chauvinism in Euro-American and male dominated production of social science knowledge" (p. 15). Instead, Gordon et al. call for conceptual paradigms that are born of cultural, ethnic, and gender-related experiences of Black, brown, and indigenous populations. Countering hegemonic cultures, existing knowledge structures, and social experiences that constrain knowledge production is a critical position for evaluators who think culturally responsively. In fact, that CRE corresponds to other race-conscious theories and positions is noteworthy in its attempts to challenge the pervasive nature of deficit thinking in social science research (Greene, 2006).

Another important theoretical and historical achievement of CRE is in forwarding alternative epistemologies that are socially active and critical. At its core, CRE contributes to and resonates with the democratically oriented perspectives in evaluation—ones that Greene (2006) suggests is covered by a large landscape of ideas about

knowledge production, legitimacy, and ownership; about the character and role of values in evaluative knowledge generation; and about the connections between evaluation and democratic principles, practices and institutions. And it is populated today by equally important ideas related to participation and empowerment, dialog and deliberation, public spheres for communication, emancipation and social critique, cultural responsiveness, and self-determination. (p. 116)

In practical terms, CRE is much more than developing instrumentation that reflects local populations, especially those of color or traditionally underserved communities, but ask more fundamental questions that reverberate throughout the evaluation process. These questions include what and whose perspectives are represented in evaluation questions, instrument development, and/or communication of findings. Hence, the socially responsible stance of the culturally responsive evaluator and the evaluation contributes to thinking about social agendas that promote spaces of hope, praxis, and social action for indigenous, marginalized, dispossessed communities, as well as their contexts, histories, struggles, and ideals.

The challenge of achieving CRE theory in use is as much an opportunity to continue to shape the field of evaluation. Amid the attention to fundamental issues of evaluation are increasing disagreements and tensions about theory and practice, methods and tools, principles and standards, and the relevance of the profession to the larger society (Yarbrough, Shulha, Hopson, & Caruthers, in press; Smith & Brandon, 2008). In the midst of these disagreements and tensions, CRE sits at the margins, but ever present and timely, advocating for a particular kind of "practical knowledge" (Schwandt, 2008) in evaluation that is transgressive, transformative, and transdisciplinary.

This notion of CRE could be perceived as threatening to a mainstream, scientific way of thinking or post-positivist perspective about evaluation that organizes methods and practices around the scientific method, one that tends to value determinism, reductionism, and empirical observation and measurement, and where a world exists separately from the world of the evaluator (Creswell, 2009; Ryan & Schwandt, 2002; Schwandt, 1990). Then again, CRE might well be perceived by those who "speak disdainfully of advocacy and promotion" (Stake, 2003, p. 1), as if evaluators do not "have strong feelings about certain matters and which we promote those values in our work" (Stake, 2003, p. 1). In the final analysis, CRE is theoretical, practical, positional, political, and methodological, and CRE pushes the envelope of those traditionally dichotomous methods and approaches. In a Fanonian sense (i.e., in the words and thoughts of Algerian psychiatrist, philosopher, revolutionary, and author from Martinique), CRE is about tools and approaches, as well as who, why, and when these tools and approaches are used and the extent to which these notions are embedded into program and stakeholder knowledges and worldviews. Instead, as he writes, our tools and approaches serve a means toward a larger end: "I, the man of color, wish only this: that never should a man be possessed by his tools, that oppression of man by man should cease forever" (Frantz Fanon, 1967).

For now, in this global moment of evaluation ending the first decade and moving into the second decade of the 21st century, CRE is staying at the margin of the field of evaluation, critically posing questions, stances, methodologies, and ways of thinking about programs and stakeholders that are socially active and attuned to the realities of (in) difference, diversity, democracy, and hegemony (or lack thereof).

Notes

1. I have to thank Professor Jackie Jordan Irvine for introducing me and others to the Morrison quote at the June 2007 commencement address of the American Evaluation Association (AEA)/Duquesne University Graduate Education Diversity Internship Program in Atlanta, GA.

2. For example, at the annual meeting of the American Evaluation Association (www.eval.org), the main professional organization of evaluators in the United States, considerations of culture continue to be timely topics. Judging by a keyword search of

culture and *culturally* in the online program of the last 3 years at the Portland, Baltimore, and Denver conferences, at least 30 sessions each year have taken place. In addition, since the beginning of the AEA/Centers for Disease Control Summer Institute a few years ago, the topics related to culture continue to grow each year.

3. The historical perspective of CRE does not suggest that its roots lie only in the African-American experience and community, although the documentation of this historical view adds richly to the roots of CRE specifically and evaluation in general. It is worth noting that CRE extends to disability and feminist theories (Thomas, 2008), as well as indigenous frameworks (Greene, 2006).

4. Although efforts to build CRE theoretical and program logic are only recently emerging, Symonette (2004) frames a CRE spiral depiction that uses typical features of the logic model (inputs, activities, outputs, and outcomes) with an overlay of questions of relevance (For whom? So what?) in this portrayal.

5. It is important enough to note here that others have identified a different number of CRT tenets. Arguably, there are four tenets (Thomas, 2008), six tenets (Dixson & Rousseau, 2005; Matsuda, Lawrence, Delgado, & Crenshaw, 1993), or even more. Milner's (2007) three tenets most adequately overlap the broader notions of CRT.

References

Allen, R. E. (1991). *Greek philosophy: From Thales to Arisotle.* New York: Simon & Shuster.

Arredondo, P. (1999). Multicultural counseling competencies as tools to address oppression and racism. *Journal of Counseling & Development, 78,* 102–108.

Au, K. H. (1980). Participant structure in a reading lesson with Hawaiian children: Analysis of a culturally appropriate instructional event. *Anthropology & Education Quarterly, 11*(2), 91–115.

Bell, D. (1987). *And we are not saved: The elusive quest for racial justice.* New York: Basic Books.

Boutte, G. S., & DeFlorimonte, D. (1998). The complexities of valuing cultural differences without overemphasizing them: Taking it to the next level. *Equity & Excellence in Education, 31*(3), 54–62.

Brown v. Board of Education of Topeka, 347 U.S. 483 (1954).

Campbell, D. T., & Stanley, J. (1966). *Experimental and quasi-experimental designs for research.* New York: Houghton Mifflin.

Chapman, T. K. (2005). Peddling backwards: Reflections of *Plessy* and *Brown* in the Rockford public schools *de jure* desegregation efforts. *Race, Ethnicity and Education, 8*(1), 29–44.

Cram, C., McCreanor, T., Smith, L., Nairn, R., & Johnstone, W. (2006). Kaupapa Māori research and Pākehā social science: Epistemological tensions in a study of Māori health. *Hūlili, 3,* 41–68.

Crenshaw, K. W. (1988). Race, reform and retrenchment: Transformation and legitimation in antidiscrimination law. *Harvard Law Review, 101,* 1331–1387.

Creswell, J.W. (2009). *Research design: Qualitative, quantitative, and mixed methods approaches.* Thousand Oaks, CA: Sage.

Dixson, A. D., & Rousseau, C. K. (2005). And we are still not saved: Critical race theory in education ten years later. *Race, Ethnicity and Education, 8*(1), 7–27.

Donnor, J. K. (2005). Towards an interest-convergence in the education of African-American football student athletes in major college sports. *Race, Ethnicity and Education, 8*(1), 45–67.

Dumont, R. V. (1972). Learning English and how to be silent: Studies in Sioux and Cherokee classrooms. In C. B. Cazden, V. P. John, & D. Hymes (Eds.), *Functions of language in the classroom* (pp. 344–369). New York: Teacher's College Press.

Duncan, G. (2005). Critical race ethnography in education: Narrative, inequality and the problem of epistemology. *Race, Ethnicity and Education, 8*(1), 93–114.

Eisenhart, M. (2001). Changing conceptions of culture and ethnographic methodology: Recent thematic shifts and their implications for research on teaching. In V. Richardson (Ed.), *Handbook of research on teaching* (4th ed.). Washington, DC: American Educational Research Association.

Fanon, F. (1967). *Black skin, white masks.* New York: Grove Press.

Foster, M. (1995). African American teachers and culturally relevant pedagogy. In J. A. Banks & C. A. McGee-Banks (Eds.), *Handbook of research on multicultural education* (pp. 570–581). New York: Macmillan.

Freire, P. (1996). *The pedagogy of the oppressed.* New York: Continuum.

Frierson, H., Hood, S., & Hughes, G. B. (2002). Strategies that address culturally responsive evaluations. In J. Frechtling (Ed.), *The 2002 user-friendly handbook for project evaluation* (pp. 63–73). Arlington, VA: The National Science Foundation.

Fuller, B., & Clarke, P. (1994). Raising school effects while ignoring culture? Local conditions and the influence of classroom tools, rules, and pedagogy. *Review of Educational Research, 64*(1), 119–157.

Gay, G. (1988). Designing relevant curricula for diverse learners. *Education and Urban Society, 20*(4), 327–340.

Gordon, E. W., Miller, F., & Rollock, D. (1990). Coping with communicentric bias in knowledge production in the social sciences. *Educational Researcher, 19*(3), 14–19.

Greene, J. C. (2006). Evaluation, democracy, and social change. In I. Shaw, J. Greene, & M. Mark (Eds.), *Handbook of evaluation* (pp. 102–122). London: Sage.

Greene, J. C., & Abma, T. (Eds.). (2001, Winter). Reponsive evaluation. *New Direction for Evaluation, 92.*

Hale-Benson, J. (1986). *Black children: Their roots, culture, and learning.* Baltimore, MD: The Johns Hopkins University Press.

Harrison, F. V. (1997). *Decolonizing anthropology.* Washington, DC: American Anthropological Association.

Harrison, F. V. (2008). *Outsider within: Reworking anthropology in the global age.* Urbana: University of Illinois Press.

Heath, S. B. (1983). *Ways with words.* New York: Cambridge University Press.

Hilliard, A. G. (1992). The pitfalls and promises of special education practice. *Exceptional Children, 59*(2), 168–172.

Hilliard, A. G. (1997). Language, culture, and the assessment of African American children. In A. Lin Goodwin (Ed.), *Assessment for equity and inclusion: Embracing all our children* (pp. 229–240). New York: Routledge.

Hollins, E., & Oliver, E. I. (Eds.). (1999). *Pathways to success in school: Culturally responsive teaching.* Mahwah, NJ: Lawrence Erlbaum.

Hood, S. (1998). Responsive evaluation Amistad style: Perspectives of one African-American evaluator. In R. Sullivan (Ed.), *Proceedings of the Stake Symposium on Educational Evaluation.* Urbana-Champaign, IL: University of Illinois Press.

Hood, S. (2000). Commentary on deliberative democratic evaluation. *New Directions for Evaluation, 85,* 77–83.

Hood, S. (2001). Nobody knows my name: In praise of African American evaluators who were responsive. *New Directions for Evaluation, 92,* 31–43.

Hood, S., Hopson, R., & Frierson, H. (Eds.). (2005). *The role of culture and cultural context in evaluation: A mandate for inclusion, the discovery of truth, and understanding in evaluative theory and practice.* Greenwich, CT: InfoAge.

Hopson, R. (2004). *Overview of multicultural and culturally competent program evaluation: Issues, challenges, and opportunities.* Woodland Hills, CA: California Endowment.

Hopson, R., & Hood, S. (2005). An untold story in evaluation roots: Reid E. Jackson and his contributions toward culturally responsive evaluation at three quarters of a century. In S. Hood, R. Hopson, & H. Frierson (Eds.), *The role of culture and cultural context in evaluation: A mandate for inclusion, the discovery of truth, and understanding in evaluative theory and practice* (pp. 87–104). Greenwich, CT: InfoAge.

House, E. (2006). Democracy and evaluation. *Evaluation, 12*(1), 119–127.

Hymes, D. (1972/1999). *Reinventing anthropology.* Ann Arbor: University of Michigan Press.

Irvine, J. J., & York, D. E. (1995). Learning styles and culturally diverse students: A literature review. In J. A. Banks & C. A. McGee-Banks (Eds.), *Handbook of research on multicultural education* (pp. 484–497). New York: Macmillan.

Kawakami, A. J., Aton, K., Cram, F., Lai, M. K., & Porima, L. (2008). Improving the practice of evaluation through indigenous values and methods: Decolonizing evaluation practice: Returning the Gaze from Hawai'i and Aotearoa. In N. L. Smith & P. R. Brandon (Eds.), *Fundamental issues in evaluation* (pp. 219–242). New York: Guilford.

Kirkhart, K. E. (1995). Seeking multicultural validity: A postcard from the road. *Evaluation Practice, 16*(1), 1–12.

Kirkhart, K. E. (2005). Through a cultural lens: Reflections on validity and theory in evaluation. In S. Hood, R. Hopson, & H. Frierson (Eds.), *The role of culture and cultural context in evaluation: A mandate for inclusion, the discovery of truth, and understanding in evaluative theory and practice* (pp. 21–39). Greenwich, CT: InfoAge.

Kirkhart, K. E. (2006, February). *Establishing multicultural validity in evaluation.* Workshop presented to the Graduate Education Diversity Internship Program, American Evaluation Association/Duquesne University, Washington, DC.

Ladner, J. (1973). *The death of white sociology.* New York: Random House.

Ladson-Billings, G. (1990). Culturally relevant teaching: Effective instruction for Black students. *College Board Review, 155,* 20–25.

Ladson-Billings, G. (1994). *Dreamkeepers: Successful teachers of African American children.* San Francisco, CA: Jossey-Bass.

Ladson-Billings, G., & Tate, W. F. (1995). Towards a critical race theory of education. *Teachers College Record, 97,* 47–68.

LaFrance, J. (2001). Evaluation in Indian Country. In M. Thompson-Robinson, R. Hopson, & S. SenGupta (Eds.), In search of cultural competence in evaluation: Toward principles and practices. *New Directions for Evaluation* (pp. 39–50). San Francisco, CA: Jossey-Bass.

LaFrance, J. (2006, April). *Building an indigenous model for evaluation: An initiative of the American Indian Higher Education Consortium.* Paper presented at the American Educational Research Association annual meeting, San Francisco, CA.

Leacock, E. (1977). Race and the "we-they dichotomy" in culture and classroom. *Anthropology & Education Quarterly, 8*(2), 152–159.

Lee, C. (2008). The centrality of culture to the scientific study of learning and development: How an ecological framework in education research facilitates civic responsibility. *Educational Researcher, 37*(5), 267–279.

Lee, K. (2007). *The importance of culture in evaluation: A practical guide.* Denver, CO: The Colorado Trust.

Lewis, D. (1973). Anthropology and colonialism. *Current Anthropology, 14*(5), 581–591.

Lopez, G. R. (2003). The (racially neutral) politics of education: A critical race theory perspective. *Educational Administration Quarterly, 39*(1), 68–94.

Lubeck, S., Jessup, P., deVries, M., & Post, J. (2001). The role of culture in program improvement. *Early Childhood Research Quarterly, 16,* 499–523.

Madison, A.-M. (Ed.). (1992). Minority issues in program evaluation. *New Directions for Program Evaluation,* 52. San Francisco, CA: Jossey-Bass.

Matsuda, M., Lawrence, C., Delgado, R., & Crenshaw, K. (Eds.). (1993). *Words that wound: Critical race theory, assaultive speech and the first amendment.* Boulder, CO: Westview.

McAllister, G., & Irvine, J. J. (2000). Cross cultural competency and multicultural teacher education. *Review of Educational Research, 70*(1), 3–24.

Milner, H. R. (2007). Race, culture and researcher positionality: Working through dangers seen, unseen, and unforeseen. *Educational Researcher, 36*(7), 388–400.

Nader, L. (1999). Up the anthropologist—Perspectives gained from studying up. In D. Hymes (Ed.), *Reinventing anthropology.* Ann Arbor: University of Michigan Press.

Nelson-Barber, S., LaFrance, J., Trumbull, E., & Aburto, S. (2005). Promoting culturally reliable and valid evaluation practice. In S. Hood, R. Hopson, & H. Frierson (Eds.), *The role of culture and cultural context in evaluation: A mandate for inclusion, the discovery of truth, and understanding in evaluative theory and practice* (pp. 61–85). Greenwich, CT: InfoAge.

Nguyen, T.-U. N., Kagawa-Singer, M., & Kar, S. (2003). *Multicultural health evaluation: Literature review and critique.* Los Angeles, CA: UCLA School of Public Health.

Ogbu, J. U. (1982). Cultural discontinuities and schooling. *Anthropology & Education Quarterly, 13*(4), 290–307.

Orlandi, M. A. (Ed.). (1992). *Cultural competence for evaluators: A guide for alcohol and other drug abuse prevention practitioners working with ethnic/racial communities.* U.S. Department of Health and Human Services, Office for Substance Abuse Prevention. DHHS Publication No. (ADM)92-1884.

Ormond, A., Cram, F., & Carter, L. (2006). Researching our relations: Reflections on ethics. *Alternative: An International Journal of Indigenous Scholarship, Special Supplement 2006—Marginalisation,* pp. 180–198.

Parekh, B. (2006). *Rethinking multiculturalism: Cultural diversity and political theory* (2nd ed.). New York: Palgrave Macmillan.

Parker, L. (2004). Commentary: Can critical theories of or on race be used in evaluation research in education? In V. Thomas & F. Stevens (Eds.), Co-constructing a contextually responsive evaluation framework. *New Directions for Evaluation* (pp. 85–93). San Francisco, CA: Jossey-Bass.

Parker, L., Deyhle, D., & Villenas, S. (Eds.). (1999). *Race is . . . race isn't: Critical race theory and qualitative studies in education.* Boulder, CO: Westview.

People who care, et al. v. Rockford Board of Education, School District No. 205, 111F.3d 528, 1997.

Pewewardy, C. (1999). Culturally responsive teaching for American Indian students. In E. Hollins & E. I. Oliver (Eds.), *Pathways to success in school: Culturally responsive teaching* (pp. 85–100). Mahwah, NJ: Lawrence Erlbaum Associates.

Philips, S. U. (1972). Participant structures and communicative competence: Warm Springs children in community and classroom. In C. B. Cazden, V. P. John, & D. Hymes (Eds.), *Functions of language in the classroom* (pp. 370–394). New York: Teacher's College Press.

Philips, S. U. (1983). *The invisible culture: Communication in classroom and community on the Warm Springs Indian Reservation.* New York: Longman.

Roediger, D. R. (1998). *Black on White: Black writers on what it means to be white.* New York: Schocken.

Ryan, K., & Schwandt, T. (Eds.). (2002). *Exploring evaluator role and identity.* Greenwich, CT: InfoAge.

Schwandt, T. (1990). Paths to inquiry in the social disciplines: Scientific, constructivist, and critical theory methodologies. In E. Guba (Ed.), *The paradigm dialog* (pp. 258–276). Newbury Park, CA: Sage.

Schwandt, T. (2008). The relevance of practical knowledge traditions to evaluation practice. In D. L. Smith & P. R. Brandon (Eds.), *Fundamental issues in evaluation* (pp. 29–40). New York: Guilford.

Semali, L. M., & Kinchloe, J. L. (Eds.). (1999). *What is indigenous knowledge? Voices from the academy.* New York: Falmer.

Slaughter-Defoe, D., Nakagawa, K., Takanishi, R., & Johnson, D. J. (1990). Toward cultural/ecological perspectives on schooling and achievement in African- and Asian-American children. *Child Development, 61,* 363–383.

Smith, L. T. (1999). *Decolonizing methodologies: Research and indigenous peoples.* London: Zed.

Smith, N. L., & Brandon, P. R. (Eds.). (2008). *Fundamental issues in evaluation.* New York: Guilford.

Solano-Flores, G. & Nelson-Barber, S. (2001). On the cultural validity of science assessments. *International Journal of Research in Science Teaching, 38,* 553–573.

Spring, J. (2004). *Conflict of interests: Politics of American education.* New York: McGraw-Hill.

Stake, R. (1975). *Evaluating the arts in education.* Columbus, OH: Merrill.

Stake, R. (1991). Retrospective on the "The countenance of educational evaluation." In M. W. McLaughlin & D. C. Phillips (Eds.), *Evaluation and education: At quarter century* (pp. 67–88). Chicago: University of Chicago Press.

Stake, R. (2003, November 5). *How far dare an evaluator go toward saving the world?* Paper presented at the annual meeting of the American Evaluation Association, Reno, NV.

Stanfield, J. H., II. (1999). Slipping though the front door: Relevant social scientific evaluation in the people of color century. *American Journal of Evaluation, 20*(3), 415–431.

Stanfield, J. H., II. (1993). Epistemological considerations. In J. H. Stanfield II & R. M. Dennis (Eds.), *Race and ethnicity in research methods* (pp. 16–26). Newbury Park, CA: Sage.

Stanfield, J. H., II, & Dennis, R. M. (Eds.). (1993). *Race and ethnicity in research methods* (pp. 16–26). Newbury Park, CA: Sage.

Stufflebeam, D. (2001). Evaluation models. *New Directions for Evaluation, 89.*

Sue, S. (1998). In search of cultural competence in psychotherapy and counseling. *American Psychologist, 53*(4), 440–448.

Symonette, H. (2004). Walking pathways toward becoming a culturally competent evaluator: Boundaries, borderlands, and border crossings. In M. Thompson-Robinson, R. Hopson, & S. SenGupta (Eds.), In search of cultural competence in evaluation: Toward principles and practices. *New Directions for Evaluation* (pp. 95–109). San Francisco, CA: Jossey-Bass.

Tate, W. F. (1996). Critical race theory and education: History, theory, and implications. *Review of Research in Education, 22,* 195–239.

Tate, W. F. (2005). Ethics, engineering and the challenge of racial reform in education. *Race, Ethnicity, and Education, 8*(1), 121–127.

Thomas, V. G. (2008). Critical race theory: Ethics and dimensions of diversity in research. In D. Mertens & P. Ginsberg (Eds.), *International handbook of research ethics* (pp. 54–68). Thousand Oaks, CA: Sage.

Tillman, L. C. (2002). Culturally sensitive research approaches: An African-American perspective. *Educational Researcher, 31*(9), 3–12.

Trumbull, E., Rothstein-Fisch, C., & Greenfield, P.M. (2000). *Bridging cultures in our schools: New approaches that work.* San Francisco, CA: WestEd. (ERIC Document Reproduction Service No. ED440954)

Watson-Gegeo, K. A. (1988). Ethnography in ESL: Defining the essentials. *TESOL Quarterly, 22*(4), 575–592.

Yarbrough, D., Shulha, L. M., Hopson, R., & Caruthers, F. (in press). *The program evaluation standards: A guide for evaluators and evaluation users* (3rd ed.). Thousand Oaks, CA: Sage.

Yosso, T. J. (2005). Whose culture has capital? A critical race theory discussion of community cultural wealth. *Race, Ethnicity and Education, 8*(1), 69–91.

Zuberi, T., & Bonilla-Silva, E. (2008). *White method, white logic.* Lanham, MD: Rowman & Littlefield.

CHAPTER 25

Evaluation for and by Navajos

A Narrative Case of the Irrelevance of Globalization

Stafford Hood

Introduction

I am hopeful and a bit optimistic that evaluation theory and practice, as well as our evaluation community, will undergo "redefinition" in the early stages of this new millennium. Rapid demographic changes, the race toward a global economy, and continuing efforts to "reform" national educational systems have increased the intensity of the spotlight focused on education. Consequently, we expect that evaluators will feel the "heat" and share our sense of responsibility to provide helpful illumination as well. Certainly, there is much our respective national and global evaluation communities can and should do to address the major challenges already facing us today and inevitably awaiting us tomorrow. As asserted appropriately by Yarbrough, Shulha, and Caruthers (2004), "now more than ever before in our globalized villages and globalized world American evaluators are aspiring to practice in ways that recognize diversity in the evaluation setting" (p. 21). There are also an increasing number of non-American evaluators who share this aspiration because it is appropriate and necessary. We all face similar current, historical, and future challenges regarding the extent to which evaluation can/will/should contribute in efforts to improve the educational, social, political, and economic circumstances of the traditionally disenfranchised in our shared global and national societies.

AUTHOR'S NOTE: This chapter is based, in part, on work supported by the National Science Foundation under Relevance of Culture in Evaluation Institute: Implementing and Empirically Investigating Culturally Responsive Evaluation in Underperforming Schools 2004-2007 (award no. 0438482) and Relevance of Culture in Evaluation Institute: An Institute and Organizational Change Project Building Culturally Responsive Evaluation Capacity 2003-2005 (award no. 0335699).

Katherine E. Ryan and Brad Cousins, as the editors of this *International Handbook of Educational Evaluation* desire the authors to

engage in a thoughtful discussion: (a) whether and how educational evaluation is being redefined by the changing circumstances of globalization, and (b) how we might address the challenges, tensions, and issues within and across educational evaluation perspectives in response to an increasingly global society. (K. Ryan and B. Cousins, personal communication, September 7, 2006)

This chapter provides an opportunity to share one case of what Diné (Navajo) and other indigenous educators (more recently Maori colleagues in New Zealand) have taught me as a student of culture and cultural context in evaluation. Although I struggled to find positive results of globalization in my experiences at the Navajo Nation, important lessons were learned about the relevance of culture and cultural context in evaluation and education. One of the overarching lessons that has become poignantly clear from my experiences, conversations, and tutelage among Navajo teachers, administrators, and my personal "cultural liaison" (Christine Chee, PhD, Arizona State University) is the tension between the educational goals of the Navajo, those that have been prescribed by the state and federal government of the United States, and their conflicting interactions within the context of globalization. In part, this chapter provides a few (of many) of the historical and cultural antecedents to help frame this tension, but is primarily grounded in the context of the challenge to preserve, teach, and value the Navajo way of life within the context of the American educational system. The chapter also evaluates teaching within this context. Specifically, one example in Navajo economic history illustrates how engagement away from the Navajo way of life toward a more globalized orientation may indeed have negative consequences for the Navajo community.

Myriad challenges, questions, and issues face the field of evaluation and the practitioners of culturally responsive evaluation (CRE). The complexity of our task increases exponentially when considered within the context of globalization and globalized educational reform. This chapter seeks to raise questions more than provide answers for consideration by the broader evaluation community. I write particularly for evaluation colleagues in the United States and internationally who conduct evaluations in settings with pronounced cross-cultural dimensions. This chapter also has the goal of moving forward a broader conversation about CRE. The reader should be mindful that the perspectives and observations I share in engaging this chapter are filtered through the lens of a middle-age African-American man *who happens to be* a university professor and evaluator. With this caveat in mind, I present personal lessons learned from the emerging CRE literature created by a small but growing cadre of evaluators who similarly view the importance of culture in evaluation and a group of committed elementary school teachers who have participated in our Relevance of Culture in Evaluation Project (RCEP) over the past 7 years.

I begin this chapter by discussing observations titled "Globalization and Education 101" to reveal my *personal* understanding about globalization, its interconnectedness to education, and how it impacts poor and disenfranchised racial groups. Next, I offer a "Culturally Responsive Evaluation 101" discussion for readers who have not closely followed this particular conversation, and I review recent contributions to the CRE literature. The chapter then turns to our RCEP and what we learned about building evaluation capacity in American schools with high concentrations of racial minority and poor students. These lessons have enabled project participants to flesh out an incipient theoretical framework for CRE. The chapter concludes with a case study narrative of a Navajo Nation school that participated in the RCEP. The case is presented in the historical context of globalization and its current irrelevance for the school and Diné Nation.

Globalization and Education 101

To describe fully the extensive and growing body of scholarly writing on globalization, the global economy, and their interconnectedness with national educational systems requires a multivolume treatment. One can begin by saying that our economic and educational systems have become increasingly globalized (Dale, 2000; McGinn, 1996; Spring, 2008). Few would disagree that globalization has become a "dominant driving force" that gained its momentum in the 1990s and has accelerated in this new millennium. In fact, it has been suggested that globalization is the "most powerful manifestation of capitalism seen yet" ("Globalization: Lessons Learned," 2000). Globalization is an important set of ideological concepts and processes, with a lack of consensus on how it should be defined (Steger, 2005). The Carnegie Endowment for International Peace's Globalization 101.org (A Project of the Levin Institute), to "promote a greater understanding of globalization," defines *globalization* as

a process of interaction and integration among the people, companies, and governments of different nations, a process driven by international trade and investment and aided by information technology. This process has effects on the environment, on culture, on political systems, on economic development and prosperity, and on human physical well-being. (What_is_ Globalization. Retrieved September 27, 2007, from http:// www.globalization101 .org/)

Manfred Steger (2005), Professor of Global Studies and Academic Director of the Globalism Institute at RMIT University in Australia, states that globalization "refers to a multidimensional set of social processes that create, multiply, stretch,

and intensify worldwide social interdependencies and exchanges while at the same time fostering in people a growing awareness of deepening connections between the local and the distant" (p. 159). Sociologists Davies and Guppy (1997) agree, in part, with Steger and Globalization 101.org by defining the term as simply "the description and explanation of social processes that transcend national borders" (p. 436). Regardless of how one views the origin and nature of globalization (social processes or economically driven values), it is a highly controversial topic.

A major area of contention regarding the outcomes of globalization is the steadily accumulating evidence that the poor, undereducated, and certain racial groups will minimally benefit (if at all) from globalization and a global economy (Ozturk, 2007). One might argue that, in a global economy, these groups could be further ignored, neglected, and/or exploited. I explore this topic further in my concluding discussion of a Navajo school.

The Carnegie Endowment for International Peace's Globalization.org (2007) succinctly captures the arguments by the proponents and opponents of globalization and the global economy when it notes:

Proponents . . . argue that it allows poor countries and their citizens to develop economically and raise their standards of living, while opponents [claim its] creation of an unfettered international free market has benefited multinational corporations in the Western world at the expense of local enterprises, local cultures, and common people. (What_is_Globalization. Retrieved September 27, 2007, from http://www.glo balization101.org/)

Tomlinson (2003) concurs in her assessment of the current status of globalization by reporting that there is

a growing awareness that the term [globalization] refers to increased and often inequitable processes of trade and financial flows, the development of information and communications technologies, cultural convergences between countries and resistance to cultural imposition. (p. 213)

One can hear echoes of similar arguments made in the past about the effects of industrialization and colonization in the United States as well as Europe. W.E.B. DuBois made a similar observation to that of Tomlinson and Globalization 101.org more than 60 years ago in his post-World War II essay on colonialism, democracy, and capitalism when he asserted,

in most modern instances, the wealthy country is thinking in terms of profit and is obsessed with the long ingrained conviction that the needs of the weaker country are few and its capacity for development narrow or nonexistent. In that case, this economic partnership works to the distinct disadvantage of the weaker country. The terms of sale for raw materials, the prices of goods and rent of capital; even the wages of labor are dictated by the stronger partner, backed by economic pressure and military power. (Dubois, 1944/1985; cited in Aptheker, 1985, p. 234)

My reading of DuBois' 1944 observations is particularly unsettling when I view how little has changed in the economic relationships between the powerful and the less powerful nations and people.

Bales (2004) provides another disturbing picture of the exploitation of the poor and uneducated in a global economy, noting that globalization was a more profitable endeavor for the new world economy than colonization because globalization treats the poor and uneducated as "disposable people," thereby creating a new form of slavery. Disturbingly, Bales (2004) observes:

The new slavery mimics the world economy . . . it is like the shift from the "ownership" of colonies in the last century to the economic exploitation of those same countries today without the cost and trouble of maintaining colonies. Transnational companies today do what European empires did in the last century—exploit natural resources and take advantage of low cost labor but without needing to take over and govern the entire country. Similarly the new slavery appropriates the economic value of individuals while keeping them under complete coercive control but without asserting ownership or accepting responsibility for their survival. (p. 24)

First World nations and their multinational corporations will be the primary beneficiaries of increased global trade and financial redistributions of capital with Third World nations struggling to benefit from the scraps that are left (Franklin, 2003). Thus far, globalization has not benefited those who have typically been disenfranchised by the political, economic, and social systems of "developed" countries—particularly those whose histories included oppressive colonization. There is evidence that disenfranchisement has not discriminated based on race when poverty has been a major variable in the equation. Still, it remains painfully evident that in the United States, African, Hispanic, and Native Americans continue to be less likely to be successful in competing in a global or U.S. economy. Ozturk (2007) argues that "underrepresented groups" (particularly African, Hispanic, and Native Americans) will be unable to effectively compete in a global economy due to the persistence of the academic achievement gap between them and their White counterparts. Peter Drucker ably noted the shift of our economic systems from land, labor, and capital as key resources in the previous century to the production of knowledge/information and information technology becoming the key resources in this new millennium (Davies & Guppy, 1997).

Reducing labor and the cost of labor (outsourcing) has been frequently used as a viable option for increasing profits, with fewer employment opportunities for the less educated, resulting in a further increase in poverty—unless educational systems can provide a workforce with the skills and knowledge that can contribute to the prosperity of a global economy. Education must play a critical role for the global economy to prosper and also determining who will truly benefit ("Globalization: Lessons Learned," 2000). The programs and services being undertaken by Educational Testing Services (ETS) and its Global Division provide an important example of the critically important linkage between education and globalization. ETS notes that "globalization drives demand among countries, businesses, government ministries and individuals for improved education systems, tools and services and ways to measure academic achievement and workplace skills" (Educational Testing Service, 2007, p. 3). Consequently, globalization in turn can promote a convergence of institutional arrangements among nations (particularly the more powerful ones) and their education systems because it is through these systems that knowledge is organized and distributed (Davies & Guppy, 1997).

I concur with Tomlinson (2003) that educational systems designed for a White dominant society (dominant by virtue of population, power, and/or economics) perpetuate the treatment of underserved groups that "have not been able to overcome racist exclusion and inequities" (p. 214). Consequently, I ask, does this continue by accident or by design? Whatever the answer to that rhetorical question, evaluators work within the global, national, and local systems that exist and strive to improve the validity of their efforts for their clients and themselves. CRE has considerable possibilities of responding to the forces of globalization by focusing on more fully understanding how cultural context impacts the design and implementation of programs intended to assist underserved and disenfranchised populations. Such an understanding is critical for these populations to truly benefit in this context of globalization. CRE embodies the approach I follow.

CRE 101

CRE can be seen as an extension of Stake's (1975) responsive evaluation framework that fully takes the culture of the program being evaluated by providing a full description and explanation of its contextual factors (Frierson, Hood, & Hughes, 2002; Manswell Butty, Reid, & LaPoint, 2004; Thomas, 2004). As CRE embeds cultural context into the responsive evaluation framework (Mertens & Hopson 2006), it does so in an effort to:

[honor] the cultural context in which the program takes place by bringing needed shared lived experiences and understanding to the program. The lived experiences captured by the culturally responsive evaluator include individuals in positions of power in the program, as well as those who have been underrepresented or marginalized. (Ryan, Chandler, & Samuels, 2007, p. 201)

Honoring cultural context with special attention to the role of power differentials across stakeholders melds nicely with other evaluation approaches that have a social justice agenda. That cultural context, central in nearly all CRE approaches, is illustrated in the work of Thomas (2004) at Howard University, who looked beyond the philosophical and values orientation of CRE to provide an important elaboration of the core components of CRE: culture, context, and responsiveness.

Culture is at the heart of the CRE components. Culture can be described as a commonly shared set of values, traditions, norms, customs, and so on that can be observed in communication (verbal and nonverbal), clothing, art, and an endless number of other things. Culture provides critically important information to the evaluator and the evaluation regarding how a community/cultural group is socialized with respect to: governance and governmental organizations; family and social systems/organizations; spiritual/religious expressions; relationships/

interpersonal processes; and communications sets (e.g., verbal and nonverbal cues and language literacy; Hood & Hall, 2005). Clearly, the cultural background of individuals and their experiences within their respective cultures can and usually will influence how programs are designed and implemented, as well as their outcomes. At the same time, one would expect that miscommunication and misunderstanding often occurs when there is a lack of cultural understanding and sensitivity. Such obstacles can negatively impact the collection of accurate and meaningful information, as well as an accurate understanding of what this information means within the evaluative context. A lack of cultural understanding and sensitivity prevents one from understanding the culturally grounded information that is being communicated and restricts one from understanding the cultural context of the program.

Simply stated, context describes "the totality of the environment where the evaluation takes place" (Thomas, 2004, p. 13). It may be seen as the presence and interaction of factors that are associated with the implementation of the evaluation as well as the program (e.g., urban, rural, politics, economics, geographical region, racial composition, age, etc.; Manswell Butty, Reid, & LaPoint, 2004). The context of the program will impact the evaluation and is critical for evaluators to understand if they are to be responsive to the stakeholders (Ryan et al., 2007). Nelson-Barber, LaFrance, Trumbull, and Aburto (2005) provide a more forceful explanation of why understanding cultural context in an evaluation is important. They assert:

> Failure to understand how cultural context interacts with program implementation and impact jeopardizes the validity of the evaluation. . . . One can only conclude that there are both ethical and validity concerns that make it mandatory for all evaluators to learn about cultural context. . . . Without specific understandings of the cultural context in which a program is being implemented, for example, evaluators are likely

to miss important information that can shed light on why a program has particular outcomes or impact on a community. (Nelson-Barber et al., 2005, pp. 61–62)

An understanding of culture is a prerequisite for understanding cultural context, and without it the validity of the evaluation is brought into question. Having an understanding of the culture and cultural context facilitates the effectiveness of one's ability to be responsive. The third critical component of CRE is responsiveness.

Again, this concept is grounded in Stake's (1975) responsive evaluation approach and has been discussed by numerous authors elsewhere. Citing House (2001), Thomas (2004) notes that being responsive requires the evaluator to respect, honor, attend to, and represent stakeholders' perspectives. To do so, culturally responsive evaluators must have an active awareness, understanding, and appreciation of the evaluation context (SenGupta, Hopson, & Thompson-Robinson, 2004). If they are indeed sensitive to the program's cultural context, they are more likely to capture and accurately interpret the cultural nuances as part of the evaluation (Nelson-Barber et al., 2005). Hood (1998, 2001, 2004) also has argued that culturally responsive evaluators should have a "shared lived experience" with the culture they are examining (i.e., substantive and extensive experience working in the racial minority communities where they conduct their evaluations). However, it is of critical importance that the culturally responsive evaluator also is reflective about and understands his or her own cultural values (Ryan et al., 2007), with a heavy dose of humility as well (White & Hermes, 2005).

Emerging Thoughts on the Training of Culturally Responsive Evaluators

Being a culturally responsive evaluator is *not* a matter of a particular race or ethnic group having exclusive rights or insights because of a family of origin. It *is* a matter of acknowledging who is aware of what and how we can maximize our collective talent, skills, and insight to make educational evaluation as effective as possible (Hood, Hopson, & Frierson, 2005). Any "good" evaluator can be a culturally responsive evaluator or can become one if he or she is committed to making the long-term investment of his or her time and self to acquire the necessary skills and shared lived experiences to do so. Learning how to be a culturally responsive evaluator can and should be a lifelong professional endeavor for evaluators who work in culturally diverse settings. It is also imperative that some consideration be given as to how to prepare evaluators who are culturally responsive in our graduate and nondegree evaluation programs.

There is anecdotal evidence of an increase in discussions and readings regarding CRE strategies making their way into some of our graduate degree and nondegree evaluation training programs. Preliminary conversations have been undertaken to specifically address the content of a CRE training program. A culturally responsive evaluator must first be well trained as an evaluator as a result of relevant coursework and practical experiences in evaluation. At the same time, there should be little disagreement that few (if any) of our training programs have evaluation curricula and/or clinical experiences grounded in CRE strategies. One example of such a discussion being formally undertaken was Hood and Hopson's (2004) project, *Preparing a Culturally Diverse and Culturally Responsive Generation of Evaluators: A Workshop to Design a Proposal for Advanced Training* (funded by the National Science Foundation).

We turn now to an effort undertaken to design, implement, and study CRE, the 7-year RCEP.

The RCEP

The Relevance of Culture in Evaluation Institute (RCEi) Implementing and Empirically Investigating Culturally Responsive Evaluation in Under-Performing Schools Project is a collaborative effort of Stafford Hood (University of Illinois, Urbana-Champaign) and Melvin Hall (Northern Arizona University) that grew out of the RCEP initiated in 2000. RCEP evolved over a 6-year period, with funding provided by four grants from the National Science Foundation (NSF).

The first phase of the RCEP was the Relevance of Culture in Evaluation Workshops (RCEW). RCEW was designed to build evaluation capacity in schools with high concentrations of racial minority and poor students by providing a small group of teachers from these schools with a basic knowledge and understanding of educational evaluation. While the workshops provided the participants with basic knowledge and professional development activities in evaluation, its content also was grounded in the application of CRE strategies. The next phase of the RCEP was the RCEi.

The RCEi was based on the premise that, by training school personnel to conduct evaluations responsive to their schools' culture, learning gaps could be correctly identified and effectively addressed through changes in curriculum and teaching strategies. RCEi's overall goal was to produce an evaluative framework that both responded to the school's cultural context and was tailored to the needs of a multicultural school population. RCEi's three major goals were to:

1. Provide schools labeled as "underperforming" or in danger of being labeled as such with a viable opportunity to determine what is working in their curricula and which modifications are necessary;

2. Train and support teams of teachers and building administrators to design, implement, and report their own school-based evaluation; and

3. Further develop CRE through lessons learned from empirical data.

School-based evaluation teams from the Phoenix, Arizona, metropolitan area and the Navajo Nation (largest Native American tribe in the United States) were established, with each team composed of a minimum of three teachers and a senior administrator. The teams were required to meet weekly, and monthly progress meetings were held where all teams were convened. Consultants served as the primary resource to their assigned teams for technical assistance, mentoring, and guidance throughout the process, from the development of the design, implementation, and submission of the final report. They were to provide technical assistance by maintaining, at a minimum, monthly telephone conversations and two site visits—but not "do the work" for their teams.

The RCEi consultants were matched with schools by the principal investigators to enhance a "connectedness" between the schools and their evaluation teams. For example, the teams with African-American principals and several African-American team members were assigned African-American consultants. In another instance, a White female consultant with extensive experience working with indigenous tribes was assigned to the two teams at the Navajo schools.

Navajo Nation School Case

The following narrative case illuminates the issues and challenges of CRE strategies within the context of globalization. The case chosen for this purpose is a Navajo Nation school in the southwestern United States. The school was one of two schools on the Navajo reservation that participated in the earlier RCEP, the school-based evaluation team that was able to complete all requirements of the previous project. This case also was selected because it illustrates the complex issues present when evaluating schools serving indigenous students and communities and addresses how evaluative approaches can be more culturally responsive in these settings.

Nearly a decade ago, Christine Chee, a Navajo woman, began her master's and subsequent doctoral studies in Counseling Psychology at Arizona State University and ultimately played a major role in the conceptualization of the overall RCEP. Under her tutelage, I came to understand how to be more responsive to Diné culture in general and the two participating Navajo school project teams in particular. Other personal tutors include indigenous evaluators Drs. Joan LaFrance (Turtle Mountain Chippewa) and Sharon Nelson-Barber (Rappahannock), as well as Anglo educational researchers/evaluators (Drs. Guy Senese and Carolyn White), who have devoted a large fraction of their professional careers to work in indigenous settings as "insider outsiders" (White & Hermes, 2005). The narrative case that follows is largely based on the work of Christine as the lead RCEi graduate research assistant and an Anglo professor emeritus in evaluation, Terry Denny (member of the Relevance of Culture in Evaluation Advisory Board) who provided extensive technical assistance to the Navajo Nation School's (NNS') school-based evaluation team in completing their evaluation project.

Historical and Contextual Profile of Navajo Nation School (NNS). I follow the advice of Nelson-Barber et al. (2005) and LaFrance (2004), who suggest that when conducting evaluation in "Indian Country," it is critically important that evaluators learn as much as possible about the community's history, resources, governance, and composition. To accomplish this goal, one must learn to "shut up and listen."

The Navajo Nation extends into the states of Utah, Arizona, and New Mexico, covering more than 25,000 square miles of open terrain and painted dessert. The Navajo territory (also known as Diné Bikéyah: The land of the People) is larger than 10 of the 50 states in the United States (Roessel, 1995). According to the U.S. 2000 census, 298,197 individuals claimed Navajo ethnicity, 180,000 reside on the Navajo tribal land, 168,000 are Navajo enrolled members, and the remaining are nonmembers who reside and work within the Navajo Nation. Another 80,000 Navajos reside near or within "border towns" of the Navajo Nation or in metropolitan centers across the United States (U.S. 2000 Census). NNS is located in a small town on the Navajo Reservation bordering northeastern

Arizona. The "business community" of this town is comprised of a single convenience store that has two gas pumps and a public laundry facility.

According to the NNS team report on school history, NNS was formerly known as the Navajo Nation Boarding School and opened in 1960 to serve residential students in kindergarten to eighth grade. In 1986, NNS became a Contract School that negotiated funds with the U.S. Bureau of Indian Affairs (BIA) for school operations. In 1988, NNS became a Grant School, whereupon the BIA directly funded the local school board. The governing school board was then given responsibility for complete oversight of the school. Those teachers who did not obtain a State of Arizona teaching license were not allowed to continue teaching at NNS. Since 1988, NNS has been serving students in kindergarten to 12th grade, with some students residing in residential halls, while most are either bussed or walk to school. The Vision Statement for NNS is, "Learners will become successful, balanced, productive individuals in a multicultural and technical environment." In 2004, there were approximately 350 students enrolled at NNS, with 47 of these students residing in residential housing.

The NNS team noted that there had been a dramatic decrease in its student enrollment in recent years. The student enrollment has historically been overwhelmingly Navajo, with varying levels of Diné (Navajo) language fluency. During 2006, the K-12 academic staff had 23 certified teachers, 3 short-term teachers, 5 full-time teacher assistants, and 3 short-term teacher assistants. Other academic staff included a principal, an academic counselor, a home-school liaison worker, a librarian, and two secretaries/registrars. Eighteen teachers were Navajo and eight were non-Navajo. All teacher assistants and academic staff members were Navajo. The breakdown of the 211 students during the spring of 2006 was as follows: 19 kindergarten students, 12 first graders, 17 second graders, 16 third graders, 18 fourth graders, 16 fifth graders, 19 sixth graders, 15 seventh graders, 28 eighth

graders, 13 ninth graders, 12 tenth graders, 14 eleventh graders, and 12 seniors.

NNS RECi Team and Project. NNS became involved with the RCEi project as a result of the previous participation by a teacher who had been involved with the RCEP since its first project, when she was at another Navajo school. She was contacted to determine the possibility of her new school participating in the RCEi project. She expressed her enthusiasm about the project to the NNS principal, who saw the RCEi as a potential vehicle for addressing one of her long-term concerns—replacing the NNS teacher evaluation instrument (created prior to her tenure as principal). The principal then recruited a Talented and Gifted students' teacher, first grade teacher, and a seventh-/eighth-grade Language Arts teacher who had demonstrated his or her ability through participation on other NNS projects to join with the "RCEP veteran." The principal assumed the responsibilities of evaluation team leader.

The focus of the NNS RCEI evaluation project was to develop a teacher evaluation instrument specifically for NNS certified classroom teachers. The questions that drove this effort prior to the initiation of the project were: (a) Can an evaluation tool be developed that is culturally relevant and appropriate for Navajo and non-Navajo teachers? (b) Are "written" teacher evaluation instruments the only way to evaluate teachers? (c) What tensions are created between the national education mandates by the U.S. federal government and the Navajo education goals? and (d) Are current teaching practices at NNS (instructional strategies and interventions) meeting the goals and expectations of the Office of Indian Education Program (OIEP), goals of the school accreditation agency, and the goals of the federal government's No Child Left Behind (NCLB) law? The case narrative speaks volumes to the first and third questions that initially emerged from NNS. The second and fourth questions are more fully addressed in other RCEI cases, but are not reported herein.

Once the team had developed its evaluation plan, it met weekly during the following year, planning and designing the teacher evaluation instrument. The team shared its evaluation plan, goals, and activities with the NNS academic staff during its regular staff meetings to solicit feedback and input. After numerous revisions and refinement, the draft instrument was completed and ready for piloting. The NNS teacher evaluation instrument was comprised of four parts: (a) Principal's Checklist for Evaluating Teacher's Classroom Performance, (b) Teacher's Professional Self-Evaluation Inventory, (c) Teacher Professional Growth Plan, and (d) Principal's On-going Checklist. Important and extensive lessons were learned by the NNS team members, RCEi project staff, consultants, and advisory board. All this contextual information is important for readers to ground themselves in the following discussion. I now turn to a few of the lessons learned about cultural responsiveness from my RCEi experience at NNS. It was within the context of developing this teacher evaluation instrument where we would encounter the first of our *lessons learned*.

Lessons Learned

Lesson Learned #1: Challenge of Developing a Navajo Specific Teacher Evaluation Instrument. Before conducting a pilot trial testing of the new teacher evaluation procedure, three NNS team members reflected on the probable consequences of implementing their new evaluation scheme. It was here that the challenge of developing a culturally responsive instrument that focused on teaching in a Navajo school context became clearly evident. At issue was the incorporation of Navajo language and culture into the evaluation instruments. One member argued that Navajo culture would be too difficult to incorporate in several subject areas (e.g., science and higher math). Another wondered aloud whether teachers should be evaluated on skills for which they had not received training. A third saw the issue still differently: She saw it as an opportunity for her to learn more about her Diné culture and language. With these issues in

mind, the NNS team members conducted classroom observations of three teachers who volunteered to participate in the piloting of the instrument. Following the pilot, the team met with RCEi staff and teachers who participated in the pilot to discuss the results. The NNS team then made further adjustment and refinement to the instrument.[1]

Further team efforts to create a teacher evaluation instrument became increasingly difficult when its members foresaw that it also would impact the school's curriculum, culturally as well as linguistically. Although the Diné RCEi liaison to NNS felt it was a privilege to be privy to the team members' "happy moments" and "struggling situations," their struggles were not disclosed at the RCEi large group meetings with the other RCEi teams or to the project's advisory board and rarely mentioned to the principal investigators. The NNS team wanted to be perceived by RCEi in a positive light, and team member conflicts were not revealed to outsiders. At the same time, they openly expressed the challenge of trying to meet the multiple demands imposed on them from different stakeholders throughout their project.

Lesson Learned #2: The Significance of Clanship. The second lesson learned, which occurred early in our work with NNS, was the significance of clanship in all of the interactions within the evaluation team and school personnel. When NNS team members described themselves, they first said that they were a mother, sister, aunt, grandmother, and so on and then stated their relationship to one another by clan. Kinship is an aspect of the Diné culture that must be understood, acknowledged, and taken into account by those who wish to understand the story of the NNS team's project. The Diné people kinship system follows the lineage of the women. The primary clanship of all comes directly from the women's descendants and remains the same as her primary clan. In addition to the primary clan, there are three additional clans: their father's clan and the clans of the mother's father and the father's father. These are used with the primary clan in determining relationships to others. Each individual must constantly fulfill different roles based on these relationships. For example, a young woman may be a mother to some, a sister to others, and a daughter or grandmother all at the same time. Traditionally, it is polite and expected to introduce oneself by clan membership first, then your name, to establish where you fit in relation to others. Another tradition still respected by many is that individuals who share a common clan do not marry. Far more subtle nuances based on clan can be seen in everyday school life by one who knows the culture. Someone from outside the Diné culture should at least be aware of the importance and pervasiveness of clan as a central dimension of Diné life.

The principal was the primary decision maker of the evaluation team with an intimate circle of advisers. One of the cultural dimensions requiring insight was the extent to which issues of clan was a variable in decision making at the school. An evaluation team member's clan relations can have a major impact on team functioning and school dynamics, especially when it centers on "bad energy" or gossip. The challenge for an outsider is knowing when such a situation exists, although for the primary RCEi liaison (Christine Chee, a member of the same clan and that of the evaluation team leader as well), it was not always apparent even to her why team members were interacting the way they were.

Lesson Learned #3: Significance of Cultural Protocols for Initiating Evaluation Meetings. We also slowly came to understand an unstated cultural protocol for RCEi site visits and NNS evaluation team meetings. The protocol was that team members would first share personal matters and lived experiences with one another and with the Navajo RCEi liaison *before* initiating any conversation about the status of the RCEi project implementation. We learned that failure to acknowledge and accept this social protocol could negatively impact the progress of our evaluation work. It became apparent that, although NNS team members were receptive to the author

as the RCEi principal investigator and to an advisory board member, who served as their consultant, there was a noticeable difference in their heightened level of openness with the primary RCEi liaison contact (Christine Chee) regarding issues related to their team dynamics and their views about the "bigger" picture.

Lesson Learned #4: The Unique Role of Culture and Language in the NNS Project. One of the major lessons learned, to no surprise, was found in the unique role of Navajo culture and language in the NNS Project. The singularity of the NNS team's effort is at least threefold. First, the project team members and the stakeholders are bilingual. They speak Navajo and English. A two-word phrase in Navajo may require two or more sentences to express in English—if the phrase can even be translated. Hence, language proved to be a continuous and central aspect of the project. Second, the team members were attempting to be responsive to themselves (i.e., to their own multidimensional culture). Finally, project team members sometimes experienced difficulty in speaking or writing in English their Navajo thoughts about issues related to culturally responsive evaluation. Through working with the NNS team, the RCEi project consultants came to understand many of the multiple commitments to projects other than the RCEi held by the teachers and the principal. Furthermore, several other projects competed for their time. Equally important was confirmation about the critical importance of someone to serve as a cultural/language translator in conducting CRE in an indigenous setting, as was exemplified during an exit interview with the NNS evaluation team.

The exit interview with the NNS evaluation team was conducted by the RCEi advisory board member who had worked closely with the team over 2 years and the aforementioned Diné RCEi liaison. During the course of the interview, the topic turned to the role of native language in developing their teacher evaluation instruments, as well as the difficulties associated with trying to imbed the Navajo language within the school curricula. It was reported that the first 15 minutes of the interview proceeded in an unremarkable fashion with both the RCEi advisory board member and liaison questioning the team members and taking notes. The course of the conversation changed when the Navajo language began to carry the discussion, with English receding quickly. Although the RCEi advisory board member was a former professor of educational evaluation with considerable expertise in interviewing methodology and practice, he was also a White male who did not speak Navajo. Fortunately for the project, he knew enough to be still and not interfere.

After the interview, the Diné RCEi liaison explained to him that, in Navajo culture, the use of terms of endearment is heavily influenced by the age of the student and the kinship relationship of the teacher with the student(s). It was this topic that had been discussed so animatedly in the Navajo language. The three Navajos had discussed how their decision to use terms of endearment was influenced by the subtleties and nuances of gender and age while paying attention to community and family contexts, as well as the school context. The Navajo team members had argued about the appropriateness of teachers using Navajo terms of endearment with students as a vehicle for cultural preservation and daily communication in the school room. To have interrupted their conversation in an attempt to translate for the White, non-Navajo evaluator would have interrupted the flow of the discussion and might have stopped it altogether. It also may have been a fruitless interruption because the three Navajos later concurred that some of the Navajo terms they had used were not translatable.

The two Navajo teachers, the Navajo liaison, and the White advisory board member concurred that the White male evaluation specialist had neither adequate lived experience nor sufficient knowledge of Navajo culture to have warranted an attempt on their parts to have attempted to include him directly in that part of the conversation. They also knew enough about the specialist to feel comfortable about "leaving

him out" of their conversation. This serves as an illustration of how competence in standard evaluation site-visit techniques, even when accompanied by a good heart and openness to learn, can still fall far short of what it takes to be an effective evaluator in a cultural setting that is significantly different from one's own. The previously noted lessons learned during the RCEi experience at NNS illustrate some of the complexity of the issues and challenges when conducting an evaluation in a setting with indigenous people. Even when a CRE orientation has been undertaken at the initial onset of a project with evaluators who have a "shared lived" experience in that community, the challenges remain nuanced, complex, and multidimensional.

The RCEi experience at an NSNS made globalization appear to be remotely connected, if at all, to life on the reservation. But there is a historical and persistent connectedness that inevitably impacts the students, teachers, administrators, and community of NSNS. The Navajo, like many other indigenous people, have, as noted by the Maori scholar Linda Smith (1999), been denied their global citizenship. She asserts:

> Indigenous peoples have already experienced the denial of their humanity and many indigenous peoples have struggled for recognition of their citizenship within the states which colonized them. . . . It costs to belong. To refuse to pay or to pull out will effectively deny nation states and their members' citizenship status with the global world order. (Smith, 1999, p. 103)

Globalization: Another False Promise for the Navajo?

The previous sections of this chapter were devoted to the lessons learned within a CRE and training project undertaken within the community of a Navajo School on the Navajo Nation. The relevance of globalization and a global economy to the NNS appears to be minimal. This era of globalization may have too many echoes of colonization, elimination, slavery, or another generation of disposable people to serve those who have historically benefited to engage the attention of the participants in the NNS project. From the Navajo perspective, we should begin with the 1848 U.S. treaty with the Navajos, which declared:

> Said Indians do hereby acknowledge that, by virtue of a treaty . . . the said tribe was lawfully placed under the exclusive jurisdiction and protection of the Government of the said United States, and that they are now, and will forever remain, under the aforesaid jurisdiction and protection. Treaty with Navaho. (September 9, 1849)

Behind every treaty lies a goal of achieving economic advantage. Economic development has been, and remains, a vital concern for the Navajo Nation. The historical systematic expropriation of many Indian resources and decades of paternalistic, non-Indian control over Indian affairs have been two factors that worked against the economic development of the Navajo Nation.

It is important for our conversation about globalization and global economy to raise this question: What are the essential ingredients for a society to improve its economy? The next question must be: Can economic development be accomplished with social, political, and cultural outcomes that are acceptable to the members of that society? The largest question of all in this particular case is: Can the Navajo Nation accomplish a self-determined, substantive, and economic transformation without losing its character, culture, and direction? It is one thing to recognize the distinctiveness of the Navajo culture and quite another to accept and support the idea of the Navajo Nation.

For those present in the corporate and international boardrooms, the globalization wave of our future must be an exhilarating panorama. For those on the reservation of the Navajo Nation, the view must look like something between a "perfect storm" and a tsunami. With 60% unemployment and low-paying subsistence jobs for those who are employed, participation in the global economy is a distant vision at best. Similarly, the long-range view of the benefits of education is hard to bring into focus when much more pressing things are at hand.

Joseph Stiglitz won the Nobel Prize in 2001 for his work on the economics of information—how people with differing levels of knowledge interact with one another. If ever there were a lesson illustrative of Stiglitz's thesis, it would be the Navajo Nation and the global economy. His books, *Globalization and Its Discontents* (Stiglitz, 2002) and *Making Globalization Work* (Stiglitz, 2006), contain harsh analyses of how international organizations affect policy and the lives of ordinary people. Stiglitz asks how a public institution can ignore growing evidence of a flawed policy and not take action or be held accountable. Navajos (as well as other U.S. tribes) have been misused and abused by the U.S. Congress, other federal government entities, and state governments for more than 200 years. Their lives as "ordinary people" have not been fairly considered when treaties, schooling, and mineral resources have been handed down "from on high." One might pose Stiglitz's question within the context of a century of U.S. federal education policy regarding the Navajo Nation. This question remains: Can political structures be created that will allow Navajo education to flourish in a democratic way? Can the Navajo Nation's inalienable right of self-governance be achieved and their culture preserved? The growing inequality around the world, the gap between the rich and the poor, can be readily seen on the Navajo reservation.

One simple way to think about globalization is the lowering of transport and communication costs. Can this be done fairly with consistent respect for the individual and concern for the poor? To put it generously, the United States has exercised its leadership in the area of globalization and educational opportunity within the Navajo Nation in a fashion that has been inconsistent with those values. Illustrative of my assertion is the shameful story of globalization, uranium, and the Navajo Nation.

The importance of uranium to the United States is a global issue that Navajos came to understand a half-century ago. From 1920 to 1960, Navajos were those "disposable people" who worked in uranium mines (on their own land) and were met and overpowered by the U.S. industrial system. Former uranium miners subsequently developed severe health problems due to working in substandard conditions and no appropriate health care, and they sought remedy through the U.S. courts. In its ruling against the workers, a federal district argued that,

> The (U.S.) government was in need of a constant, uninterrupted and reliable flow of uranium ore from the mines to the mills for urgent national security purposes and as an emerging source in the future for the growing peacetime nuclear energy industry. (*Begay v. United States*, 1976)

The short-term benefits associated with having jobs in the uranium mines were outweighed by the long-term devastating health problems that shortened their lives and produced no lasting economic gain for the people of the Navajo Nation. Although coal and uranium resources have received the most attention, oil and gas revenues have been, by far, the more important income for the Navajo economy. By the year 2000, mineral resources remained the main source of revenue for the workings of the Navajo government—mineral wealth that stands to be depleted after a finite period of time. U.S. domestic energy needs will continue to place extreme pressure on the Navajo Nation for those sources to be utilized. A perceptive analysis of this state of affairs comes in a study by Benson (1976).

Economic development for the Navajo Nation has been studied for decades. Experts have been commissioned and reports rendered. When the studies end and the experts have filed their reports, life continues as it did before the studies began. A Harvard University project on American Indian economic development resulted in a report—*Pathways From Poverty: Economic Development and Institution-Building on American Indian Reservations* (Cornell & Kait, 1990). The report observed that contemporary Indian reservations are notable for "extreme poverty, a host of related social problems, and economies founded largely on transfer payments and government services." The Harvard study found this to be "enigmatic." Despite decades "of professed federal and public concern and a seemingly endless flow of federal and private dollars, there is as yet relatively little sign of meaningful improvement . . . or of the emergence of sustainable productive activity." Even with such a negative lesson in mind, the importance and centrality of a culturally responsive approach is made clear in the words of Dr. Iris Pretty Paint (Blackfeet),

> It was important to have planning meetings where only Indians were involved because of the common shared lived experience and common exposure to negotiating racism and western (culture). (It helped them to) recognize the strength of their health and resilience at a tribal level rather than dwell negatively on their experience of racism. It took us to our sources of knowing. We asked important questions. Why is our tribe still here? What has caused us to survive? . . . What are we in relationship to this world? What are we doing here? How will this affect the world? We value the ability of people to come in but it is how you enter into relationships. Support can come in any form. Someone must understand your vision and in order to do so you need a relationship that allows balance. Spirituality is the most important part of our resilience, strength, hope, and courage. The Source is Our Creator. (Interview with author, August 2008)

Closing Thoughts

It should be clear to the reader that I am not even remotely optimistic that the global economy will benefit the Navajo Nation in the foreseeable future. The immanent import of globalization is undeniable. But the relative importance of the promise of globalization is low indeed today for the Navajo Nation, its schools, and its children.

Globalization and the global economy will remain central to policy discussions about the conversations and policies of nations throughout the world, particularly those that are typically characterized as "developed" rather than "developing." Policy issues related to the interconnectedness and role of education in the global economy are likely to receive even more attention. The decade-old conversation (mostly between comparative education scholars) that "globalization and education" is a developing field of study, as evidenced by the founding of the journal *Globalisation, Societies, and Education* in 2003 (Spring, 2008).

Considering the central importance of evaluation to the education enterprise, one can see that the conversations of the authors in this particular *International Handbook on Evaluation* are both indeed timely and appropriate—but represent preliminary analyses of the issues related to the interconnectedness of globalization, education, and evaluation. When I consider how globalization might manifest itself in the education of non-White and poor communities, both internationally and domestically, discouragement rears its ugly head. Nevertheless, it has reaffirmed my contention that the role of culture and cultural context must be central to our conversation—even without clear answers to how one conceptualizes and implements a global education evaluation approach where culture and cultural context are honored.

Yes, globalization and the rush toward a global economy is indeed an inescapable reality. What they will look like once achieved remains unclear. If history is our teacher, the underprivileged will not benefit to the same degree in this global economy as will the already franchised. Those who have typically been the last to be asked to the table during the eras of colonization, industrialization, and/or computerization will likely be the last in line to enjoy the fruits of the

new global banquet—unless something drastically changes. Is it possible that educational evaluation could be an agent for such a change? The answer is yes, if, in our evaluation efforts to become more culturally responsive, we are willing to learn about, understand, and involve hitherto uninvolved participants as equal partners.

Note

1. However, shortly after the project was completed, the principal was replaced, and no further action has been reported regarding the implementation of the new teacher evaluation instrument.

References

Aptheker, H. (1985). *Against racism: Unpublished essays, papers, addresses, 1887-1961, by W.E.B. Du Bois* (Herbert Aptheker, Ed.). Amherst, MA: University of Massachusetts Press.

Bales, K. (2004). *Disposable people: New slavery in the global economy* (rev. ed.). Berkeley: University of California Press.

Begay v. United States, 591 F. Supp. PP 1011-12.

Benson, M. (1976). *Sovereignty: The Navajo Nation and taxation, people's legal services.* Window Rock, AZ: DNA. (ERIC document ED141019)

Cornell, S., & Kait, J. P. (1990). Pathways from poverty: Economic development and institution-building on American Indian reservations. *American Indian Culture and Research Journal, 14*(1), 89–125.

Dale, R. (2000, Fall). Globalization and education: Demonstrating a "Common World Educational Culture" or locating a "Globally Structured Educational Agenda." *Educational Theory, 50*(4), 427–448.

Davies, S., & Guppy, N. (1997, November). Globalization and educational reforms in Anglo-American democracies. *Comparative Education Review, 41*(4), 435–459.

DuBois, W. E. B. (1944/1985). Colonialism, democracy, and peace after the war. In H. Apteker (Ed.), *Against racism: Unpublished essays, papers, addresses, 1887-1961* (pp. 229–243). Amherst, MA: University of Massachusetts Press.

Educational Testing Service. (2007, Summer). A world of assessment: In the global marketplace, education and skills are passports to success. *Innovations, 4,* 3–5.

Franklin, V. P. (2003). Commentary: U.S. African Americans, Africans, and globalization. *The Journal of African American History, 88*(4), 327–329.

Frierson, T., Hood, S., & Hughes, G. (2002). A guide to conducting culturally responsive evaluations. *In the user-friendly handbook for project evaluation* (NSF publication No. 02-057). Arlington, VA: National Science Foundation.

Globalization: Lessons learned. (2000). *Business Week.* Retrieved October 14, 2006, from http://www.mywire.com/pubs/BusinessWeek/20 01/11/06/28517

Globalization101.org. What is Globalization. Globalization101.org (A Project of the Levin Institute, State University of New York). Retrieved September 27, 2007, from www .globalization101.org/[What_is_Globalization].

Hood, S. (1998). Responsive evaluation Amistad style: Perspectives of one African-American evaluator. In R. Sullivan (Ed.), *Proceedings of the Stake symposium on educational evaluation* (pp. 101–112). Urbana-Champaign, IL: University of Illinois at Urbana-Champaign.

Hood, S. (2001). Nobody knows my name: In praise of African American evaluators who were responsive. *New Directions for Evaluation, 92,* 31–43.

Hood, S. (2004, July). A journey to understand the role of culture in program evaluation: Snapshots and personal reflections of one African American evaluator. In M. Thompson-Robinson, S. SenGupta, & R. K. Hopson (Eds.), Cultural competence in evaluation. *New Directions for Evaluation.* San Francisco, CA: Jossey-Bass.

Hood, S., & Hall, M. (2005). *Relevance of Culture in Evaluation Institute: Implementing and empirically investigating culturally responsive evaluation in underperforming schools.* Unpublished manuscript, Arizona State University/Northern Arizona University.

Hood, S., & Hopson, R. K. (2004). *Preparing a culturally diverse and culturally responsive generation of evaluators: An action plan for advanced training.* Unpublished manuscript, Arizona State University/Duquesne University.

Hood, S., Hopson, R. K., & Frierson, H. T. (2005). Introduction. In. S. Hood, R. K. Hopson, & H.T. Frierson (Eds.), *The role of culture and cultural context: A mandate for inclusion, the discovery of*

truth and understanding in evaluative theory and practice (pp. 1–6). Greenwich, CT: InfoAge.

House, E. R. (2001). Responsive evaluation (and its influence on deliberative democratic evaluation). In J. C. Greene & T. A. Abma (Eds.), *Responsive evaluation: New directions for evaluation* (No. 92). San Francisco: Jossey-Bass.

LaFrance, J. (2004). Culturally competent evaluation in Indian Country. *New Directions for Evaluation, 102,* 39–50.

Manswell Butty, J. L., Reid, M. D., & LaPoint, V. (2004). A culturally responsive evaluation approach applied to the talent development school-to-career intervention program. In V. Thomas & F. Stevens (Eds.), Co-constructing a contextually responsive evaluation framework. The talent development model of school reform. *New Directions for Evaluation, 101,* 37–47. San Francisco, CA: Jossey-Bass.

McGinn, N. F. (1996, November). Education, democratization, and globalization: A challenge for comparative education. *Comparative Education Review, 40*(4), 341–357.

Mertens, D. M., & Hopson, R. K. (2006). Advancing evaluation of STEM efforts through attention to diversity and culture. *New Directions for Evaluation, 109,* 35–51.

Nelson-Barber, S., LaFrance, J., Trumbull, E., & Aburto, S. (2005). Promoting culturally reliable and valid evaluation practice. In S. Hood, R. Hopson, & H. Frierson (Eds.), *The role of culture and cultural context in evaluation: A mandate for inclusion, the discovery of truth, and understanding in evaluative theory and practice* (pp. 61–85). Greenwich, CT: InfoAge.

Ozturk, M. (2007, June 11). *Global competition: America's underrepresented minorities will be left behind.* Teacher's College Record. Available at http://www.tcrecord.org

Roessel, M. (1995). *Songs from the loom: A Navajo girl learns to weave.* North Minneapolis, MN: First Avenue Editions.

Ryan, K. E., Chandler, M., & Samuels, M. (2007). What should school-based evaluation look like? *Studies in Educational Evaluation, 33,* 197–212.

SenGupta, A., Hopson, R., & Thompson-Robinson, M. (2004). Cultural competence in evaluation: An overview. In M. Thomson-Robinson, R. Hopson, & S. SenGupta (Eds.), In search of cultural competence in evaluation:

Toward principles and practices. *New Directions for Evaluation 102*. San Francisco, CA: Jossey-Bass.

Smith, L. T. (1999). *Decolonizing methodologies: Research and indigenous peoples*. London: Zed Books.

Spring, J. (2008, June). Research on education and globalization. *Review of Educational Research, 78*(2), 330–363.

Stake, R. E. (1975, October). *Program evaluation, particularly responsive evaluation*. Paper presented at a conference on New Trends in Evaluation, Goteborg, Sweden.

Steger, M. B. (2005). *Globalism: Market ideology meets terrorism* (2nd ed.). Oxford, UK: Rowman & Littlefield.

Stiglitz, J. (2002). *Globalization and its discontents*. New York: W.W. Norton.

Stiglitz, J. (2006). *Making globalization work*. New York: W.W. Norton.

Thomas, V. (2004). Building a contextually responsive evaluation framework: Lesson from working with urban school interventions. In V. Thomas & F. Stevens (Eds.), Co-constructing a contextually responsive evaluation framework. The talent development model of school reform. *New Directions for Evaluation, 101*, 3–23. San Francisco, CA: Jossey-Bass.

Thomas, V., & Stevens, F. (Eds.). (2004). Special issue: Co-constructing a contextually responsive evaluation framework. The talent development model of school reform. *New Directions for Evaluation, 101*, 3–23. San Francisco, CA: Jossey-Bass.

Tomlinson, S. (2003). Globalization, race, and education: Continuity and change. *Journal of Educational Change, 4*, 213–230.

Treaty with Navaho. (September 9, 1849). http://www.firstpeople.us/FP-Html-Treaties/TreatyWithTheNavaho1849.html

U.S. Census Bureau. (2000). *Statistical abstract of the United States*. Washington, DC: U.S. Government Printing Office.

White, C. J., & Hermes, M. (2005). Learning to play scholarly jazz: A culturally responsive evaluation of the Hopi teachers for Hopi Schools Project. In S. Hood, R. Hopson, & H. Frierson (Eds.), *The role of culture and cultural context in evaluation: A mandate for inclusion, the discovery of truth, and understanding in evaluative theory and practice* (pp. 103–126). Greenwich, CT: InfoAge.

Yarbrough, D. B., Shulha, L. M., & Caruthers, F. (2004). Background and history of the Joint Committee's Program Evaluation Standards. *New Directions for Evaluation, 104*, 15–30. San Francisco, CA: Jossey-Bass.

CHAPTER 26

Dialogue, Deliberation, and Democracy in Educational Evaluation

Theoretical Arguments and a Case Narrative

Ove Karlsson Vestman and Christina Segerholm

T his chapter discusses problems of trying to control the contemporary process of globalization of ideas and policies. More precisely, we first discuss an attempt to introduce certain methods of implementation, such as dialogue and deliberation, in another cultural and political context than the one in which they had been developed. That is, we examine an effort to implement in Russia the idea and practice of a dialogic, democratic evaluation approach developed in Sweden. The main purpose of this project was to evoke learning among the civil servants of that new context. Thereafter, we discuss an attempt to introduce an evaluation model, the deliberative democratic model, for evaluation of the same project. First, we characterize the kind of learning that took place in the evaluated project as mainly instrumental, which implies a partial failure of implementation.

Second, in the new context, the evaluation model could only be used to fulfill one of the two purposes for which it had been introduced; it was useful for identifying learning that took place in the evaluated project, but it could not be used to evoke further learning among the civil servants who took part in the evaluation. We argue that the failure to elicit further learning in the evaluation stemmed from the contrasts between basic political and cultural conceptions in the area where the evaluation model was introduced and the corresponding ones in the area where the model was developed. Finally, we discuss our conclusions in relation to earlier research and the contemporary discussion on the globalization of ideas and policies.

This chapter is structured in three sections. In the first section, we outline our view of globalization, traveling ideas, and governing (in this chapter understood as the process to get national or state intentions carried out), and we briefly describe different evaluation paradigms developed in the so-called Western democracies. We also present some basic values in which liberal democracies are rooted. In the second section, we introduce our case narrative: an evaluation of a Swedish-Russian training program directed at developing Russian civil services. A short description of the evaluation, its epistemology, basic values, and original intentions for the Russian setting is provided, together with a more detailed account of experiences made by the evaluator in practicing this approach. The third section is an analysis of learning that took place in the evaluation process on behalf of the Russians, the Swedes, and the evaluator. Finally, we consider learning in a wider perspective: What can we learn about these kinds of evaluation approaches from this case narrative? In that vein, we discuss this and similar approaches as the globalization of values and their possibilities to become "global."

Globalization and Its Origins

Before 1989, many people understood economy and politics in relation to an East and West division. Described simply, there were basically two systems: One was based on liberal democracy, capitalism, and the supremacy of the individual, whereas the other relied on socialism, planned economy, and state/collective control. Evaluations, or systems to measure outputs and outcomes, were part of both economic systems. In the Soviet system, production was measured and compared to the goals set in the 5-year plans and used as a basis for further planning (Englund, 1999; Nove, 1989/1990). In Western societies, evaluations were performed to assess the quality of different programs and efforts in order to inform policy decisions/choices and development (compare with Wildavsky's [1979] "rational reform paradigm" concept).

After the breakdown of the Berlin Wall, a new understanding of the world economy and world

politics seems to have emerged. The idea "death of ideologies" was strongly revived by Francis Fukuyama (1989, 1992), who proclaimed the victory of Western liberal democracy. Moreover, powerful supranational organizations such as the World Bank, the Organisation for Economic Co-operation and Development (OECD), and the European Union (EU) nowadays work systematically to spread their ides of a global market and education policy (Martens & Balzer, 2004; Robertson, 2005). Most states today aspire to be part of the world/global market, be they former communist countries or Western democracies (e.g., China, Ethiopia, Laos, Singapore, and South Africa).

Crucial to the concept of globalization is that processes such as economic transactions and the transmission of ideas and lifestyles formerly based in nation-states and restricted by geographical conditions are now independent of time and space. New communication technology makes this possible. One can notice that the globalization also is a highly questioned concept, and most scholars would not accept it in this early "total" form as our description suggests.[1]

Globalization and Education

We have found three aspects of globalization to be of importance in relation to education and evaluation. These aspects are: (a) the idea of globalization as competition on a global market, (b) globalization as connected to knowledge as commodities (Ozga, Seddon, & Popkewitz, 2006), and (c) the idea of life-long learning as one of the pillars of globalization rhetoric in education.

Globalization as Competition

The production of goods and services is, to a large extent, global. Corporations and enterprises produce their merchandise where conditions are favorable for maximizing their profits by enlarging their number of customers. It is vital to produce the best products at the lowest costs and to constantly find new things to produce that are attractive on the global market. Competition is the ideological and economic driving force of this condition. Knowledge and, by extension, education and learning (life-long and organizational) have become key ingredients of this new (knowledge) economy (Ozga et al., 2006).

Globalization and Knowledge as a Commodity

Knowledge is necessary to stimulate inventions that may lead to production of goods, technology, and so on, and it also has become necessary as merchandise. Hirtt (2004) uses the concept "merchandization" of education for this process. Included in his concept is also the notion of education as encouragement of consumerism. One example of the merchandization of education and knowledge is the work of consultants and experts in specific knowledge areas (such as evaluators). Courses in all sorts of subjects, which are now offered and purchased within nations and on a global market, constitute another example. Education is both a means to changes in production and a product in itself—there is a global education and evaluation market.

Globalization and Life-Long Learning

Linked to the development of a knowledge economy is the idea of a flexible and highly educated and competent work force to be competitive. Thus, transnational organizations such as the OECD, the EU, and UNESCO promote life-long learning (see, e.g., European Commission, 2008; Organisation for Economic Co-operation and Development, 2007). Policies and work on indicators for assessing national efforts for life-long learning are developed and disseminated to member countries and other countries that are anxious to be part of this view of success.

Policy Transmission, Borrowing, Indigenization, and Traveling Policy

On a global market where competition, knowledge production, and life-long learning are promoted, education policies and strategies for governing play a vital role. Attempts are made in all kinds of states to find new ideas and imitate successful strategies—policy borrowing. Attempts are also made to disseminate ideas that are in line with the overarching values of a global competitive market to both developed and developing countries (e.g., former east European countries that aspire to enter the EU)—policy transmission (Robertson, 2005). Supranational organizations, such as the World Bank, the OECD, and the EU are key actors in this respect, albeit with slightly different agendas. The World Bank invests in an education policy that favors the market and liberalism, while the OECD is more concerned with human capital and enhancing teachers' tacit knowledge to improve student outcome/innovations (Robertson, 2005). It is also common practice to export/disseminate policy on education and evaluation in connection to foreign aid efforts.

However, as Steiner-Khamsi (2000) points out, it is naive to believe that education policies and strategies to improve education can be borrowed or transmitted from one historical and political context to another. Rather, ideas and policies are adapted to local contexts—they are indigenized. This goes for globalization of education policies, as well as for globalization of evaluation policies. Although buzzwords are the same in different national contexts, and although supranational organizations strive to implement their policies and strategies, they are tailored or reconstructed to fit the local cultural codes of the contexts in which they are to be implemented (for a theoretical model, see Phillips & Ochs, 2003). This conclusion is sustained by Alexiadou and Jones (2001) who use "traveling policy" to denote activities and ideas promoted by supranational agencies. Further, they refer to "embedded policy" (i.e., traditions, ideologies, organizational forms, and habitual behaviors developed in national and local contexts) when underscoring that local practices are still important in the mediation of global ideas. This process of indignation of ideas promoted from outside and the significance of "embedded policy" in the local context is evident in the example we refer to next.

How Policy Travels

Policy travels by consultants who bring particular expertise (evaluation) from country to country. Experts bring certain values and perceptions of how things should be to the new context, often without being aware of this. Insensitivity to cultural, historical, and ethnic differences has, for example, been noticed as a problem in evaluations of foreign aid efforts (Kulsamrit, 2004; Van der Eyken, Goulden, & Crossley, 1995). A less obvious form of policy traveling has been described by Lawn and Lingard (2002) in a European context in terms of "a 'new magistracy of influence' in the European educational policy domain: a policy elite that acts across borders, displays similar habitus" (p. 292). To this magistracy belong policymakers such as high-ranking civil servants and education experts (scholars/researchers) who are often found in task force groups and committees and are not directly part of formal national decision making. We believe similar policy spaces to exist globally concerning evaluation and that members carry certain evaluation policies around. As our case narrative shows, evaluators are bearers of policy in terms of ideas of how education and evaluation are to be performed.

Governing and Evaluation

In Sweden, the change in governing education, such as a new national curriculum based on specified goals/targets and an aligned criterion-based grading system, has for a long time been described in terms of "decentralization" (Aasen, 2004; Lindensjö & Lundgren, 2000). We understand the standards reform in the United States and the No Child Left Behind Act, with its emphasis on testing, to be experienced as centralization. However, we argue that these two examples are part of a global governing strategy. The new strategy rests on a rationale where prespecified objectives/goals/targets/standards are set, and means to measure goal fulfillment by different techniques and criteria are developed (Lindblad & Popkewitz, 1999, 2000).

Governing by setting goals/objectives and measuring results/outputs/outcomes requires activities such as follow-ups, evaluations, quality assurance/assessment systems, and so on and the possibility to compare to improve. Evaluation and evaluative activities have thereby become a central part of what constitutes the contemporary governing paradigm (Segerholm, 2007).

There is presently little consensus among evaluators in Western democracies about what evaluation should be, how it should be performed, and for what reasons. Throughout half a century, several approaches and models have been developed. In a brief overview of the history of educational evaluation, Simons (2004) says "Using evaluation evidence to inform policy and practice has been the sine qua non of evaluation practice since Cronbach (1963) and Stufflebeam et al. (1971) first defined evaluation as a process of providing information to make decisions about educational programmes" (p. 413). She maintains that what counted as evidence was based on quantitative methodologies. This is still the case considering global assessments of education such as Programme for International Student Assessment (PISA) and Trends in International Mathematics and Science Study (TIMSS)[2] and national systems for evaluation of education.

Alternative evaluation approaches were developed in opposition to this evaluation paradigm. They were designed to be more sensitive to local contexts and professional practices; to include democratic, moral, personal, and plural values; and to enhance communication, understanding, and deliberative processes (see Simons [2004] for further references). Some examples (but not an overview) include Stake (1974), who early advocated sensitivity and openness to the evaluand (responsive evaluation), an approach taken further by Abma (1999), who added the importance of using stories from different participators/groups in a learning dialogue. Karlsson (1995, 1996) argued for bringing in stakeholders in the evaluation process by dialogue to sustain learning. Schwandt (2002) enhances the moral responsibility of the evaluator while Kushner (2000) emphasizes interpersonal meetings. Other examples include House and Howe (2000), who constructed a deliberative democratic approach. This approach attracted Ryan and DeStefano (2000), who discussed it further, and the approach was tried by Greene (2000). Common to these examples is their attempt to support learning and democratic processes by dialogue, involvement of many groups and practitioners, moral reasoning, and self-scrutiny. Nonetheless, they do differ. Some approaches emphasize constructivist views and personal morality, whereas others underline the importance of material conditions and political awareness.

To summarize, contemporary evaluation theory and practice in the West is multimethodological and rests on plural values. The dominating governing strategy rests on evidence based on evaluations carried out by quantitative methodologies. Systems for local quality assurance and quality assessment are closely connected to information from national evaluations, statistics, and student tests. Educational programs, schools, municipalities, regions, and countries can thereby compare themselves to other successful ones and improve. But there are also national evaluation systems using techniques for internal assessment and self-evaluation/monitoring anchored in the idea of learning by exposing weaknesses and strengths, quite like what has been described as common features of alternative evaluation approaches. Today, as before, those who promote these approaches are critical of how evaluation is used as a governing instrument because negative influences such as window-dressing and teach-to-the-test activities

have been noticed (Segerholm & Åström, 2007). These evaluators stress the need for evaluations to be sensitive to local contexts and to be uncompromised by hegemonic power discourses.

Values in Western Evaluation

All Western evaluation approaches are based on certain values, which underpin democratic rights in Western democracies. The citizens in democratic nation-states expect the state to guarantee their protection and equality before the law—civil rights (Heater, 1990). It is also expected that individual citizens have the right to share power and/or participate in political decision making, either directly or by representatives—political rights (Dahl, 2000; Laski, 1931; O'Donnell, 2007). Finally, in most modern democracies, citizens anticipate the right to certain services, such as education, pensions, and so on—social rights. These democratic rights rest on a perception of the society as a product of the will of individuals. In turn, this means that one particularly valued idea is the right of the individual to express her or his opinion and to make decisions concerning her or his own direction in life. A belief in "a democratic decision-making process" is an additional cherished idea. The procedural aspect of democracy is still strongly debated (Macedo, 1999; O'Donnell, 2007), and different standpoints are advocated, also in the field of evaluation (see, e.g., Hanberger, 2006; House & Howe, 1999). Although these principles are said to be characteristic for democratic welfare societies, it is also noticed that they suffer from a loss of political legitimacy and trust, among other things connected to problems with governing an expanded welfare sphere (Rothstein, 1984).

We perceive the values in traveling policy, evaluation, and democracy described earlier as partly intertwined but also more or less related to prominent beliefs characterizing rational modern societies (modernism). When considering historical conditions for the former East and West, it is worth noticing that a system of production based on government by objectives and results was discarded at the end of the 1980s in the East. This is about the same time it was introduced in public sectors such as education in the Western democracies. A general understanding of evaluation and evaluative activities as means to make rational decisions and plans is an idea equally familiar to the West and to the former East.

So, what happens when an evaluation based on liberal democratic values, directed at dialogue and learning, is practiced in another political, cultural, and social context than the one in which it was developed?

Developing Social Services—A Case Narrative and Evaluation

In this section, we describe and analyze a Russian-Swedish project for development of the social services in Leningrad County and an evaluation of that same project. Thereafter, some critical incidents from the work on the evaluation are highlighted. In the third section, we discuss the implications of the incidents for the practice of a deliberative democratic evaluation.

A Project to Develop Social Services

In the Soviet Union, social problems were generally addressed from within the framework of the communist party and the trade union. With Perestrojka (reconstruction) in 1985, a reorganization of society's social services was initiated, and in 1992 a decision was made on a further reorganization. The reorganizations diminished the influence of the party and the trade union. Since then, social problems in Russian society have become even more evident and the need for new policies acute. It was against this background that the Swedish state through Swedish International Development Cooperation Agency (Sida) sought to stimulate an exchange of experiences between Swedish and Russian social services and to thereby exert an influence on the Russian development. The "Social Project in Leningrad County" could be described as an education project, a

form of in-service training or life-long learning process. It ran from 1998 to 2001 and was carried out by the social services in Södermland County, Sweden, and Leningrad County, with financial support from Sida. The overarching goal of the cooperation was to bring about a structural transformation capable of increasing the quality of social services in Russia. Four programs were prioritized in the project: (a) elderly and disabled, (b) family and child policy, (c) the problem of drugs, and (d) rehabilitation of children with limited opportunities. To be able to carry through these programs, the development of organizational forms and methods was needed, as well as an overview of the individuals requiring support and assistance. From the point of view of the project organizers, it was also necessary to disseminate to the Russians a more positive attitude toward consumers of social services.

An important method for establishing these prerequisites was to enhance learning by sharing of experiences between the Russian and the Swedish partners. The project catered to eight groups; there were 160 participants from the social services in the 29 municipalities of Leningrad County. All these participants were involved with local projects in their municipalities dealing with the four designated areas of social problems mentioned previously. About 100 of them were responsible for local projects. The remaining 60 included politicians, top decision makers of the social services in different municipalities, and representatives of the Central Bureau for Social Matters in Leningrad County. The project included a 2-week course at the university level, field studies at Swedish institutions for social services, and evaluations of social services in Russia.

The Evaluation: Its Epistemology, Design, and Methods

The evaluation of the "Social Project in Leningrad County" began in 1999, shortly after the project had started. It had two main objectives: (a) to identify what the civil servants had learned from the project, and (b) to evoke further learning by allowing these civil servants to take part in the evaluation. By involvement in the evaluation process, the civil servants were supposed to gain both instrumental knowledge and insights into the norms, beliefs, and assumptions implicit in the tacit knowledge used when judgments were made when determining what high quality is.

The Epistemology and Design

The evaluation design was outlined in accordance with the deliberative democratic evaluation model (or policy) to stimulate learning by participation, dialogue, and deliberation (Abma, 2001; House & Howe, 1999, 2000; Karlsson, 1998, 2001; Karlsson Vestman, 2004). Dialogue was supposed to take place between the civil servants taking part in the evaluation and between the evaluator and these individual civil servants. Dialogue has captured the interest of several evaluation scholars. They rely on elaborate work done in the area of stakeholder and participatory evaluation. Abma (2001) presents some of the various and central arguments stressing the relevance of dialogue for evaluation: dialogue to improve the quality of judgment, dialogue as a force and forum for democratization, dialogue to revitalize the notion of praxis (i.e., to reinstall moral-political judgments in our practices and social life), dialogue as a forum for reconsideration and reflection, and dialogue as a contribution to a more democratic society at large by involving a larger number of interests.

The deliberative democratic evaluation model relies heavily on dialogue as the mechanism for reaching the intended results. The purpose of this approach is to create deliberation and thereby new knowledge and insights. That is, the purpose of deliberative democratic evaluation is to create insights and understanding, rather than make decisions, thereby underpinning democracy. Ideally, the dialogue initiated in the evaluation is followed up in the decision-making process with a debate over the judgments of the evaluator.

From a scientific point of view, this deliberative democratic evaluation model can be placed in a critical hermeneutic tradition (see, e.g., Schwandt, 2001, 2003). Inspired by the Frankfurter school and more modern theorists such as Hans-Georg Gadamer, Jürgen Habermas, and Paul Riceur, we think a critical perspective is characterized by a reluctance to regard the dominant form of thinking and existing social situation as natural, neutral, and rational or an assertion of how things should be. To adopt a critical stance involves searching for alternative interpretations in order to see other perspectives.

The aim of using a critical perspective is to develop a deeper understanding of what the project means for different stakeholders in terms of limitations and possibilities and to reach greater insight and clarity into the foundations of one's own judgments and those of others. This entails looking toward the question of how people experience and interpret different phenomena and relations in their real life world (e.g., in terms of what learning means to a person). In evaluation, then, a critical perspective includes, for example, to question taken-for-granted or overtly stated goals and objectives for a program, to question the way a program is intended to be carried out, and intended outcomes as the only interesting or most desirable outcomes.

The Methods

The selection of respondents in the evaluation was supposed to create a good cross-sectional sample of data from different decision-making levels of the social services in Leningrad County and the different municipalities. An important source of data for the evaluation was the material collected from local municipal offices, which contains statistics describing the social conditions and the particular projects of the municipalities. To gain an impression of the social situation in the county, statistics also were collected from the Work and Social Security Committee. Moreover, literature in the form of reports and books on methodology was used to supplement the picture of Russian social development.

Several questionnaires were administered during the evaluation's formative and summary phases. Four case studies were undertaken in four local municipalities. The number was justified partly by the cost and time plan and partly by the desire to do a case study in each problem area: (a) the elderly and the disabled, (b) children with limited opportunities, (c) children and families, and (d) drug preventative initiatives for children and youth. The interviews in the four case studies included representatives from the top tier of management, middle management, and street-level bureaucrats. The interviews were carried out with individuals or with groups of staff. Observations were used to supplement the interviews.

The Project Meets the Sociopolitical Reality

The evaluation results show that the "Social Project in Leningrad County" in some respects managed to enhance learning among its participants. Instrumental knowledge and methods for solving everyday matters of the social services were disseminated to the Russian participants. Some of the participants also stated that they had developed new cultural competences by comparing the ways of working of the Swedish and the Russian social services. However, the detected new insights into the foundations of people's own judgments were not so obvious. Furthermore, it was difficult to find any new attitudes toward the rights of the consumers of social services or toward citizens taking part in the outlining of social service programs.

Ellström's (1996) notion of three types of learning can be used to structure the findings. Ellström distinguishes among reproductive learning (single-loop learning), development-oriented learning (double-loop learning), and creative and development-directed learning (meta-learning). Of the knowledge produced by the project instrumental knowledge and new methods for solving everyday matters were the products of reproductive learning. That there were only few new

insights into the foundations of people's own judgments implies that there was little development-oriented learning. The adherence to old attitudes suggests that there was no development-directed learning. But the local context also suggests that even if learning took place, change may have been seen as inappropriate.

This supports the observations of theorists of globalization of ideas and policies, who state that ideas and policies adopt to new contexts and thereby do not serve the same purposes in the new contexts as in the ones in which they have been developed.

Deliberative Democratic Evaluation Meets the Sociopolitical Reality

To show the marked contrast between the situations that were created by the practice of the deliberative democratic evaluation model in the Russian context and the situations that, according to House and Howe (2000), should be created when practicing that model, we supply some examples of puzzling situations that one of us (Karlsson Vestman) experienced while evaluating the Russian-Swedish project (see Karlsson Vestman, 2004). It may be instructive for the reader to keep in mind House and Howe's criteria for deliberate democratic evaluation when reading about the following situations. Their criteria for ideal practice of the model are structured in line with the concepts of inclusion, dialogue, and deliberation:

- *Inclusion:* All relevant interests are represented (not only the most powerful). A rough balance and equality of power should be attempted.
- *Dialogue:* Participants should be encouraged to engage in dialogues of various kinds to express their views and opinions.
- *Deliberation:* A cognitive process takes place that is founded in reason, evidence, and valid arguments. Through deliberation, stakeholders become more aware of what their own interests are and why.

They also learn about each other's conceptions and interests. This is described as a process of enlightenment.

The situations described next are retold as the evaluator Karlsson Vestman experienced them. We use a more narrative tone because we want to convey the personal encounter with an unfamiliar context.

Hospitality in Personal and Distance in Business Relationships

The evaluator tried to establish trust in relation to his Russian business partners. Because he was received with great hospitality and warmth, he believed he had succeeded. When visiting organizations that supplied social services, the evaluator was often received by children performing music or theater on an impressive level or by advanced professional musicians. His Russian business partner supplied overwhelming dinners, toasts in vodka or champagne, and delivered speeches on the friendship between their two peoples, Russians and Swedes. He received gifts on every visit and was driven both to and from the airport.

The social interaction with the evaluator's Russian business partners gave him the impression that it would be possible to discuss both strengths and weaknesses of the project in which they took part. This assumption turned out to be wrong. In the words of Shaw and Ormston (2001), the contrast "between warmth over the vodka by night and the ruthlessness by day" (p. 123) is explicit in the Russian context. The personal friendliness that the evaluator was received with at dinners and theaters did not correspond to the unwillingness to help him in his daily work, which was actually shown. There was a marked contrast between public and private in the communication with his business partners.

One example of this was when the evaluator wanted statistics on the work of the institutions supplying social services (e.g., on their economy, personnel, or clients). To receive these statistics, he had to formulate precise questions on what

he wanted to know, and he was only given exactly that for which he had asked. For example, when requesting detailed statistics, the evaluator was never told that there were corresponding summarizing statistics. When he later found out that there was such information available and he expressed surprise that he had not already received it, he was told that he had not made himself clear enough. The evaluator was assured that "there was nothing to hide" and that he "would receive anything he asked for."

However, he came to experience that the more straightforward his questions, the more avoidant and self-contradictory the answers. Because it would take some time to gather the statistics the evaluator wanted, it was agreed that they should be sent to Sweden. However, the information seldom arrived. During his next visit, the evaluator mentioned this and stressed that a promise had been given to send the information he needed. He was thereby again assured that the statistics would be sent and was told that "there must have been some misunderstanding."

Control of Information

It had been made clear that the evaluator would not be allowed to visit the municipalities that took part in the project without an accompanying officer. A representative of the central leadership in the county thereby always observed his excursions. The representative's task was "to address all the practical questions" arising in the course of the evaluator's visits. Furthermore, it was obvious that he would not be allowed to take part in the continuous communication among his different business partners. The evaluator's interpreter told him that he must keep in mind that the accompanying civil servant of the ministry every day reported to her superior on which questions he had asked and what he had found out.

During the evaluator's first visit to the municipalities, in the spring of 2000, he wanted to hold some individual interviews with staff of the activities involved in the project. His ambition was to establish a dialogue among equal partners. The county officer introduced him to the first person to be interviewed and remained in the room to, as she put it, "learn how scientific interviews were carried out." He accepted this without further thought, but soon his respondent reacted with a nervous look toward the county representative, who sometimes intervened and corrected some of the answers given by the respondent. At the next interview, the evaluator asked the county officer to leave the room. She protested and argued that her task was also to check what the staff said about their work. Her view was that it was "a waste of staff time" holding separate interviews. The evaluator refused to drop his demand, and the representative left the room under protest. This example illustrates that the presence of a supervisor was an attempt to control what information was made accessible to outsiders.

Another strategy was to arrange the context of the interview in such a way that the questions were neutralized and the hopes for an equal dialogue dashed. On one occasion, the intention was to interview the leader of an initiative. This person had taken part in the education in Sweden. The evaluator arrived at the institution, together with the interpreter and the county representative. They were met by the leader who took them to a meeting room, where she had arranged for all the staff (about 30 persons) to be present. After a presentation of all, the evaluator was to interview the leader, and it was her intention that the rest of staff should remain present to hear what was said. Surprised by the situation, the evaluator accepted, and they sat at a table with 30 people in the audience. To the evaluator's questions about the center's activity, the leader replied with well-prepared answers, which were more of a lecture for the staff, than a presentation of her personal views on the project and the education program in Sweden, which was what he had hoped for.

"We Already Know This"

In the centralized top-down Russian governance tradition, there is a need to show that every situation is under control and that no information that an evaluator or anyone else can present provides news to the top bureaucrats. When the evaluator informed them about his impressions and conclusions from the work on the evaluation of the social services in the municipalities, he was told, "We already know this." To prove this statement, he was shown books containing statistics and guidelines on how the problems should be dealt with. When asked which steps had been taken to deal with the problems, new central guidelines were referred to. This way of dealing with difficulties is the norm; implementation is considered done when central guidelines have been established.

Furthermore, the belief that the system works is never shaken no matter how wide the gap between the central decision makers and the practitioners. Every critical question is answered by referring to a rule or by stating that a rule concerning the problem is just about to be formulated.

Different Concepts of Democratic Evaluation

During one of Karlsson Vestman's visits to St. Petersburg, the vice director general accompanied him. They had not met before. She inquired about his evaluation commission, and he responded by describing the project and the work with a deliberative democratic evaluation aimed at promoting learning and development, rather than control. She said that she recognized the model and that it was in line with the kind of evaluation work already practiced in her area of responsibility in the region (i.e., child care and preschool). "This is also what we are doing. Each year, after a process of proposing candidates, the best child-care center of the year is elected." She then described that the director general and her group scrutinized the candidates by site visits, and after that the group selected the child-care center that best met the goals. The evaluator mentioned that he had heard that a similar practice was in operation under the Soviet regime concerning the best worker, and that what she described was something akin to that, but added that this was not what he meant by a democratic evaluation for learning and dialogue. The vice director general looked puzzled and responded that the process of voting for the best services in her opinion was a democratic evaluation. At that time, they arrived at the airport and their conversation ended.

Control of the Agenda for Negotiation on the Evaluation Premises

Would it be a solution to make more detailed agreements regarding under what circumstances the evaluation should be conducted? Could this be a way to establish assurances for circumstances, under which learning can be obtained and deliberative democratic evaluations can be conducted?

The questions may seem naive given the description of cultural clashes provided earlier. However, they are still justified because Western evaluation literature often stresses the importance of being clear during negotiations about under what circumstances an evaluation shall be conducted. The following descriptions of interactions with the evaluator's Russian business partners may give a picture of what such an agreement could look like.

After some introductory contacts via fax and mail to clarify the conditions for the evaluation and commission from Sida, a first meeting was arranged with Russian representatives in St. Petersburg in the autumn of 1999. The evaluator emphasized his hopes for a dialogue on how the evaluation should be carried out. Some issues that he wanted to discuss concerned which initiatives could be visited, the kind of information to which he would like to have access, as well as opportunities to make field observations and hold interviews with different local representatives.

The meeting in St. Petersburg began with the Russian representatives presenting a comprehensive list of questions they wanted to raise, which they then proceeded to ask. The agenda was formal. No opening was given for the evaluator's topics. When the evaluator remarked on this, the chairwoman answered, "We have to finish my points first." Finally, when the evaluator was given a short time to ask his questions and to present the evaluation model, it was approaching lunchtime. The Russians proposed that the evaluator's concerns and questions should be dealt with during lunch. During the meal, the Russians took turns expressing gratitude and praising the Swedish-Russian bond of friendship. This gave the conversation a different character than the formal negotiations and business meeting of the morning, when they were supposed to come to an agreement on the evaluation procedures.

The program continued with different cultural activities and study excursions. They were motivated by the desire to show the evaluator as much as possible during his short visit. In the end, he only gained the opportunity to clarify questions and claims, which enabled him to proceed to the next stage of the planned evaluation. The evaluator learned his lesson from this experience. At the next meeting in St. Petersburg some months later, he was more emphatic in demanding a say on the agenda for the visit. This strategy was not totally successful. Even if the Russian control of the meeting was toned down, they still kept the power to set the agenda.

Contrasts Between the Intended Situations and the Real Situations

In the following, we highlight the contrasts between the situations of equal dialogue and deliberation based on broad inclusion that the practice of the deliberative democratic evaluation model was supposed to create and the situations that actually were created. The practice of the model was supposed to create situations characterized by inclusion, dialogue, and deliberation. However, all the five situations described earlier show features that are not compatible with these intended characteristics.

1. The situation "Hospitality in personal and distance in business relationships" showed a sharp line between the public

and private spheres. That created difficulties in inducing deliberation at the work places because deliberation demands critical rethinking concerning *personal* basic conceptions of reality.

2. "Control of information" and the accompanying county representative created power imbalances among the different participants of the evaluation. This created hierarchical situations in which only the official opinions were expressed. That is, no dialogue took place.

3. "We already know this." There was no willingness to critically examine and question own conceptions. Thereby, deliberation could not take place, and the evaluation model was disarmed.

4. "Different concepts of democratic evaluation." This situation showed critical differences between our basic conceptions of evaluation. That is, we used the same buzzwords but (intentionally or unintentionally) interpreted them differently. Thereby, it became difficult to understand our dialogues.

5. The Russian counterpart established control of the agenda for negotiations on the premises of the evaluation. Attempts to specify how inclusion of as many interest groups as possible, equal dialogues, and deliberation should be established were silenced with assurances that there was a will to reach these goals. These assurances turned out not to be binding in the hierarchical top-down Russian practices.

Limitations of the Evaluation Model

There is no reason for us to assume that the civil servants, after having taken part in the deliberative democratic evaluation, reflect on their work and how it could be developed in a more scrutinizing way than before. That is, there is no

reason to believe that the deliberative democratic evaluation model fulfilled its second purpose—to generate further knowledge among the civil servants that took part both in the evaluated project and also in the evaluation. We even consider this unlikely because of the sharp contrast between the intended interactions characterized by dialogue and deliberation on an equal basis and the situations that were actually generated (described earlier). In this section, we offer an explanation for this failure in establishing the intended situations. That is, why were situations of only little dialogue and deliberation evoked and, consequently, no observable generation of knowledge? We discuss our conclusions in relation to earlier research. Finally, we present some theoretical implications of our findings for the discussion on globalization of ideas and policies.

Explaining the Lack of Dialogue and Deliberation

The causal factor that we offer is incompatibility between basic cultural and political conceptions inherent in the deliberative democratic evaluation model and the corresponding conceptions of the Russian civil servants that in our narrative study were supposed to practice the model.

This explanation is justified by the research of Foss Hansen and Borum (1999) on the process of development of evaluation models (in their article referred to as standards) and evaluation practices in organizations and organizational fields. They distinguish among three phases: adoption, construction, and implementation. They define these three phases in the following:

> Adoption implies that the general concept of evaluation is discussed and reflected in activities in the field. Construction implies that specific models, in the following called standards, for evaluation are developed. Finally implementation means that standards are used and evaluation activities practised and documented in reports. (p. 306)

They analyze these phases as processes of isomorphism—that is, as a "constraining process that forces a unit in a population to resemble other units facing similar environmental conditions" (p. 306). In the case narrative presented previously, an institution of the social services can be defined as such a unit captured in the process of isomorphism.

The explanation that we want to offer for the partial failure of implementation described in the case narrative is as follows. The adoption phase of the development of evaluation in the Russian social services took place in the Soviet years. The conception of evaluation that was developed in this adoption phase mirrors the bureaucratic structure of that period. The accompanying county representative indicates that evaluation is still today conceived mainly as a tool for central administration to control local levels.

Furthermore, the findings of Foss Hansen and Borum (1999) indicate that a new adoption phase—a new window of opportunity—must take place before introduction of models based on other basic conceptions of evaluation can lead to a new practice. This brings forth the question of what should characterize a new basic conception of evaluation emanating from a new adoption phase to make the introduction of the deliberative democratic evaluation model and corresponding practices possible.

Some light can be shed on this question by the study of the presented experiences from the evaluation because these experiences reflect differences between basic Swedish and Russian cultural conceptions inherent in the evaluation practices of those two countries. The differences that we want to highlight include the following:

1. The attitudes of the civil servants *as* civil servants (not as persons) toward the evaluator makes clear a marked difference between Swedish and Russian general attitudes toward insight into the work of civil servants and thereby about the *influence from society upon the work of civil servants.* As evaluators, and perhaps particularly as Swedish evaluators, we have been formed

by a society with a tradition of public access to the work of civil servants. When doing this evaluation, Karlsson Vestman was faced with a marked contrast: a society where civil servants handed out insufficient information even after he put pressure and made explicit demands.

2. The unwillingness of the civil servants to admit that an evaluator can produce anything new for them suggests a difference between the attitudes of Swedish and Russian civil servants toward *learning from persons that are not above them in the state hierarchy.*

3. The fact that the evaluator was accompanied by an officer during the visits to the suppliers of social services and the county representative seemed to supervise the referents at the interviews implies that *individualism* is more central to the Swedish public administration than the Russian one.

We think that these are important differences between Swedish and Russian cultural codes for explaining the failure of generating knowledge and insights in our case: diverging attitudes toward public influence on and insight into the work of the civil servants, the state hierarchy learning from the citizens, and individualism.

Our Findings Discussed in Relation to Earlier Research

Our findings are in line with a discussion by House and Howe (2000). They point out that "[e]valuation is tied to the larger society by democratic principles argued, debated and accepted by the evaluation community" (p. 4). That is, they imply that evaluation can only work the way the deliberative democratic evaluation model was supposed to do in a democratic context. Furthermore, Hyatt and Simons (1999) indicate that different cultures are open to a greater or lesser extent to outsiders, and cultural codes in Eastern Europe are more intricately locked than others. They explain this by reference to the "closed" histories of these countries. Information has seldom been handed out to citizens unless it has been absolutely necessary. This heritage of closedness can still be observed today when the authorities systematically deny most mistakes and problems until the truth cannot be hidden any longer. In this tradition, there is no room for participatory principles, as has been shown in our case narrative. Russian evaluation is today mainly a means for superiors to control their subordinates. However, the increase in evaluative activities that is now a common feature of education systems in many contemporary Western democracies is a similar example of control (see, e.g., Grek et al., 2009; Pollitt, 2006). Such evaluation forms a basis of governing (i.e., deciding on policy for the future and trying to realize it) or, in other words, steering the process and the subjects in the intended direction (Segerholm, 2001).

Our findings are also in line with Skott's (2001) description of transitions from hierarchical top-down rule to democracy as a long and difficult process. A characteristic of the Soviet period was that a person who reported a problem endangered his or her future and health. New principles of governance have always been dictated from the top of this hierarchy, and the willingness to question and make proposals has been repressed for many years (Skott, 2001). Still today many are afraid that showing initiative will be perceived as a threat by those in power, which could be observed in the course of the evaluation presented earlier.

At the same time, however, as Shaw and Ormston (2001) point out, the Russians are highly particularistic and emphasize the establishment of personal relationships and loyalty to individuals as more important than contracts. This is in contrast to the Swedes (and other Westerners), who "tend to operate in a more universalistic way by applying the same set of norms to all situations, having a greater faith in decisions that have been made collectively" (Shaw & Ormston, 2001, p. 124). These authors also noticed that the high degree of power distance

meant that an ideal Russian evaluation was more top-down, inspectorial, and critical (mainstream evaluation) than the self-motivated, "improve-from-within" approach they practiced. Here we face a possible explanation for the reaction to the efforts in practicing a dialogue, inclusive evaluation, and for resistance to telling "how it should be" when asked. Shaw and Ormston's Russian partners declared that "I am an expert, and therefore my job is to criticise" (p. 127). They also noticed that self-direction is a problem for Russian managers: Nothing in their formal education or afterward prepares them for it. In a similar way to Shaw and Ormston, we need to bear this in mind, given that the evaluation narrated here concerned people taking more responsibility and to be active in the dialogue also at lower levels in the organization. The reaction from the vice director on Karlsson Vestman's (2004) reaction that her description of democratic evaluation did not correspond to his view could be understood against this background. Again, as has been pointed out previously, there are differences in views on what evaluation is to accommodate also in Western societies, as well as differences in what approaches Western evaluation theorists support.

Our Findings Discussed in Relation to Globalization of Ideas and Policies

In this final section, we summarize our results and dwell on their implications for the discussion on globalization of policies and ideas.

Before starting the evaluation described earlier, the representatives of the Russian Central Administration accepted the proposed evaluation policy—a deliberative democratic evaluation. However, in the practical evaluation work, the local practitioners were put under a kind of pressure that made it impossible to conduct such an evaluation. We interpret this as a series of deliberate attempts by the central administration to disarm the deliberative democratic evaluation model. We find it likely that the local practitioners also had some problems under-standing of this kind of evaluation approach because of diverging conceptions as to why eval-uations are made.

In the literature on evaluation, this reaction to external evaluation is well known and seems to be typical for bureaucracies, which use evalua-tion primarily for control purposes. This implies that Russia is only one of many (transitional) countries in which civil servants have no experi-ences of using evaluation to advance learning, which means that Russia is probably far from the only country in which introduction of the delib-erative democratic evaluation model would turn out to be problematic. Greene (2000) gives evi-dence that there are also problems encountered when trying to use this model in other parts of the world. She struggled to use it in a local edu-cation setting in the United States, but she noted, for example, how the absence of significant stakeholders made it difficult to include values sustained by these stakeholders, making the idea of inclusion aspect hard to match. Furthermore, because bureaucracies and (national) authorities in Western countries also often use evaluations for control purposes, similar problems concern-ing this model as the ones described in this chap-ter may be expected.

Regarding globalization in the field of evalu-ation, this means that there may be an impor-tant difference concerning the potentials of globalization of economic policies and global-ization of evaluation policies. In the first part of this chapter, it was described how globalization of economic policies has been correlated with changes in economic practice. By contrast, when the Russian Central Administration agreed on the policy of democratic deliberative evaluation, a corresponding change in Russian evaluation practice did not follow. This implies a case of isomorphism on the policy level; the democratic deliberative evaluation *policy* seems to have been adopted to mirror the evaluation policies of other countries but for other reasons than a will to develop Russian evaluation practices. This also reminds us of the importance of Alexiadou and Jones' (2001) concept "embedded policy"

(i.e., the importance of local history and tradi-tions in the reception and transformation of policy from the outside).

At the same time, it seems likely that the Russian Central administrators have an interest in becoming a part of a "new magistracy of influ-ence" in the policy space of evaluation (compare with the theories of Lawn and Lingard, 2002, presented in the first section of this chapter). They wanted to be part of the training program and evaluation, and by such contacts and collab-oration they may strive to be part of the global networks that are influential in education (life-long learning), social service, and evaluation.

However, our results, supported by the theory of Steiner-Khamsi (2000) presented in the first section of the chapter, indicate that further adop-tion in Russia of internationally developed evalu-ation policies may, under current circumstances, be of little importance for the development of Russian evaluation practices, particularly if the evaluation approach is also one of those we have called "alternative." The findings rather indicate that social, political, and administrative reforms are needed before a new adoption phase can take place (i.e., before policies such as the democratic deliberative evaluation model can be dissemi-nated in Russia and Russian evaluation practices can be developed to mirror the democratic delib-erative evaluation model). Because practicing the model has encountered problems also in Western democracies, it is perhaps more likely that other global evaluation policies and practices more like the ones already in use in Russia will be received and indigenized more easily.

Pressman and Wildavsky (1984) pointed to the general problems of getting policy (decisions and intentions) implemented into local contexts and practice within the same nation. Lindensjö and Lundgren (2000), writing about education policy and governing, use the concepts of "area of formulation" and "area of realization" to make us understand that different contexts, logics, and rationales set different scenes for different levels in the policymaking, decision making, and implementation processes. In this chapter, we described an even more complicated process than implementing national policies to local contexts and practices. We presented an effort to transfer a policy that was a mix of ideas concerning life-long learning as a way to improve public service (the training program) and evaluation as a device to support democratic processes and local development, from one national and cultural context to another. The intentions were to transfer ideas/ideology and change practice, by both the training program and the evaluation as presented in our case narrative. The evaluation approach was not what could be called mainstream compared with what transnational organizations such as the OECD and the EU support. The fact that education and evaluation are by definition concerned with reproduction of values and ways to organize society, and therefore are directly connected to basic cultural codes, also may account for the problems in getting such policy to travel and be transformed into actual practice. Looking back, perhaps it makes sense that good evaluation intentions in Sweden were dashed in Leningrad County.

Questions for Future Debate and Dialogue

Of course, our objective in making this analysis is certainly not to engage in apportioning judgments about virtue or blame regarding Western and non-Western approaches to evaluation. Rather, our aim has been to bring into sharp relief the grave dangers of making easy assumptions about the translation of evaluation models from one's own cultural contexts to others. In conclusion, it is therefore appropriate that we should ask evaluators to raise these questions in their respective communities and in their evaluation work so that these problems might be dealt with constructively in the future.

Notes

1. *Globalization* has been critiqued on two main grounds: (a) in a sense, the globalization process can be seen as old history; and (b) the local mediation of

global processes seems to be massive, so if globalization is used nowadays, it is usually in terms of this mediated form (see, e.g., Hirst & Thompson 1996; Pease & Pringle 2001).

2. Programme for International Student Assessment (PISA) is an evaluation that includes about 40 countries in the Organisation for Economic Co-operation and Development (OECD). Trends in International Mathematics and Science Study (TIMSS) is an evaluation of knowledge in mathematics and natural sciences in the comprehensive school done by the International Association for the Evaluation of Educational Achievement (IEA).

References

Aasen, P. (2004). What happened to social-democratic progressivism in Scandinavia? Restructuring education in Sweden and Norway in the 1990s. In M. Apple (Ed.), *The state and the politics of knowledge* (pp. 109–149). New York: Routledge Falmer.

Abma, T. (1999). Introduction: Narrative perspectives on program evaluation. In T. Abma (Ed.), Telling tales: On evaluation and narrative. *Advances in Program Evaluation 6* (pp. 1–27). Stamford, CT: JAI Press.

Abma, T. (2001). Dialogue in evaluation. Opening thoughts. *Evaluation, 7*(2), 155–163.

Alexiadou, N., & Jones, K. (2001, September). *Travelling policy/local spaces.* Paper presented to the Congrès Marx International 111, Paris, France.

Cronbach, L. J. (1963). Course improvement through evaluation. *Teachers College Record, 64*(8), 672–683.

Dahl, R. A. (2000). *On democracy.* New Haven, CT: Yale University Press.

Ellström, P.-E. (1996). Rutin och reflektion. Förutsättningar och hinder för lärande i dagligt arbete [Routine and reflection. Pre-conditions and barriers in learning in daily life]. In P.-E. Ellström, B. Gustavsson, & S. Larsson (Eds.), *Livslångt lärande* (pp. 142–179). Lund: Studentlitteratur.

Englund, P. (1999, November). *Om Berlinmurens fall. Recension i Dagens Nyheter* [On the Berlin wall. A review]. Retrieved January 18, 2007, from http://www.peterenglund.com/textarkiv/murens fall.htm.

European Commission. (2008, February). *Education and training 2010. Main policy initiatives and outputs in education and training since the year 2000.* Coordination of Lifelong Learning Policies. Retrieved February 26, 2009, from http://ec.europa.eu/education/policies/2010/doc/compendium05_en.pdf.

Foss Hansen, H., & Borum, F. (1999). The construction and standardization of evaluation. The case of the Danish University sector. *Evaluation, 5*(3), 303–329.

Fukuyama, F. (1989, Summer). The end of history? *The National Interest.* Retrieved March 2, 2009, from http://www.wesjones.com/eoh.htm

Fukuyama, F. (1992). *The end of history and the last man.* New York: The Free Press.

Greene, J. C. (2000). Challenges in practicing deliberative democratic evaluation. In K. E. Ryan & L. DeStefano (Eds.), Evaluation as a democratic process: Promoting inclusion, dialogue, and deliberation. *New Directions in Evaluation, 85,* 13–26.

Grek, S., Lawn, M., Lingard, B., Ozga, J., Rinne, R., Segerholm, C., & Simola, H. (2009). National policy brokering and the construction of the European Education Space in England, Sweden, Finland and Scotland. *Comparative Education, 45*(1), 5–21.

Hanberger, A. (2006). Evaluation of and for democracy. *Evaluation, 12*(1), 17–37.

Heater, D. (1990). *Citizenship. The civic ideal in world history, politics and education.* London: Longman.

Hirst, P., & Thompson, G. (1996). *Globalisation in question.* Cambridge: Cambridge Polity.

Hirtt, N. (2004). The three axes of school merchandization. *European Educational Research Journal, 3*(2), 442–453.

House, E. R., & Howe, K. (1999). *Values in evaluation and social research.* Thousand Oaks, CA: Sage.

House, E. R., & Howe, K. R. (2000). Deliberative democratic evaluation. *New Directions for Evaluation, 85,* 3–12.

Hyatt, J., & Simons, H. (1999). Cultural codes—Who holds the key? The concept and conduct of evaluation in Central and Eastern Europe. *Evaluation, 5*(1), 23–41.

Karlsson, O. (1995). *Att utvärdera—mot vad? Om kriterieproblemet vid intressentutvärdering* [To evaluate—with what criteria? The problem of criteria in stakeholder based evaluation]. Stockholm: HLS Förlag.

Karlsson, O. (1996). A critical dialogue in evaluation. *Evaluation, 2*(4), 405–416.

Karlsson, O. (1998). Socratic dialogue in the Swedish political context. In T. A. Schwandt (Ed.), Scandinavian perspectives on the evaluator's role in informing social policy. *New Directions for Evaluation, 77,* 21–38.

Karlsson, O. (2001). Critical dialogue: Its value and meaning. *Evaluation, 7*(2), 211–227.

Karlsson Vestman, O. (2004). *Evaluation as learning. A study of social worker education in Leningrad County* (Research report no. 8). Eskilstuna: Mälardalen University.

Kulsamrit, W. (2004). *Evaluator cultural competence in international development evaluation practices.* Unpublished doctoral dissertation, School of Education, University of Illinois at Urbana-Champaign, Urbana-Champaign, IL.

Kushner, S. (2000). *Personalizing evaluation.* London: Sage.

Laski, H. J. (1931). Democracy. In *Encyclopaedia of the social sciences* (Vol. 5, pp. 76–85). London: Macmillan.

Lawn, M., & Lingard, B. (2002). Constructing a European policy space in educational governance: The role of transnational policy actors. *European Educational Research Journal, 1*(2), 290–307.

Lindblad, S., & Popkewitz, T. (Eds.). (1999). Education governance and social integration and exclusion: National cases of educational systems and recent reforms. *Uppsala Reports on Education 34.* Uppsala: Uppsala University.

Lindblad, S., & Popkewitz, T. (Eds.). (2000). Public discourses on education governance and social integration and exclusion: Analyses of policy texts in European contexts. *Uppsala Reports on Education 36.* Uppsala: Uppsala University.

Lindensjö, B., & Lundgren, U. P. (2000). *Utbildningsreformer och politisk styrning* [Education reforms and governing]. Stockholm: HLS Förlag.

Macedo, S. (Ed.). (1999). *Deliberative politics: Essays on democracy and disagreement.* New York: Oxford University Press.

Martens, K., & Balzer, C. (2004, April 13–18). *Comparing governance of international organisations—The EU, the OECD and educational policy.* Paper presented to the European Consortium for Political Research, Uppsala, Sweden.

Nove, A. (1989/1990). *An economic history of the U.S.S.R.* (2nd ed.). London: Penguin Books.

O'Donnell, G. (2007). The perpetual crises of democracy. *Journal of Democracy, 18*(1), 7–11.

Organisation for Economic Co-operation and Development. (2007, July). *Lifelong learning and human capital* (Policy Brief). Retrieved September 23, 2007, from http://www.oecd.org/dataoecd/43/50/38982210.pdf.

Ozga, J., Seddon, T., & Popkewitz, T. (Eds.). (2006). Introduction. In *World Yearbook of Education* (pp. 1–14). London: Routledge Falmer.

Pease, B., & Pringle, K. (Eds.). (2001). *A man's world? Challenging men's practices in a globalised world.* London: Zed Books.

Phillips, D., & Ochs, K. (2003). Process of policy borrowing in education: Some explanatory and analytical devices. *Comparative Education, 39*(4), 451–461.

Pollitt, C. (2006). Performance management in practice: A comparative study of executive agencies. *Journal of Public Administration, 16*(1), 25–44.

Pressman, J. L., & Wildavsky, A. (1984). *Implementation: How great expectations in Washington are dashed in Oakland: Or, why it's amazing that federal programs work at all, this being a saga of the Economic Development Administration as told by two sympathetic observers who seek to build morals on a foundation of ruined hopes* (3rd ed.). Berkeley: University of California Press.

Robertson, S. L. (2005). Re-imagining and rescripting the future of education: Global knowledge economy discourses and the challenge to education systems. *Comparative Education, 41*(2), 151–170.

Rothstein, B. (1984). *Vad bör staten göra? Om välfärdsstatens moraliska och politiska logic.* Stockholm: SNS Förlag [Published in 1998 in English as *Just institutions matter: The moral and political logic of the universal welfare state*]. Cambridge: Cambridge University Press.

Ryan, K. E., & DeStefano, L. (Eds.). (2000). Evaluation as a democratic process: Promoting inclusion, dialogue and deliberation. *New Directions for Evaluation 85.* San Francisco, CA: Jossey-Bass.

Schwandt, T. A. (2001). A postscript on thinking about dialogue. *Evaluation, 7*(2), 264–276.

Schwandt, T. A. (2002). *Evaluation practice reconsidered.* New York: Peter Lang.

Schwandt, T. A. (2003). Linking evaluation and education: Enlightenment and engagement. In P. Haug & T. A. Schwandt (Eds.), *Evaluating educational reform: Scandinavian perspectives* (pp. 169–188). Greenwich, CT: InfoAge.

Segerholm, C. (2001). National evaluations as governing instruments: How do they govern? *Evaluation, 7*(4), 427–438.

Segerholm, C. (2007). New public management and evaluation under decentralizing regimes in education. In S. Kushner & N. Norris (Eds.), Dilemmas of engagement and the new public management. *Advances in Program Evaluation 10* (pp. 129–138). Amsterdam: Elsevier JAI Press.

Segerholm, C., & Åström, E. (2007). Governance through institutionalised evaluation. Recentralisation and influences at local levels in higher education in Sweden. *Evaluation, 13*(1), 47–66.

Shaw, M., & Ormston, M. (2001). Values and vodka: Cross-cultural anatomy of an Anglo-Russian educational project. *International Journal of Educational Development, 21*(2), 119–133.

Simons, H. (2004). Utilizing evaluation evidence to enhance professional practice. *Evaluation, 10*(4), 410–429.

Skott, S. (2001). *Sovjetunionen och det nya Ryssland* [The Soviet Union and the New Russia]. Stockholm: Hjalmarsson & Högberg Bokförlag.

Stake, R. E. (1974). Program evaluation, particularly responsive evaluation. In *New Trends in Evaluation. Report No. 35* (pp. 1–20). Gothenburg: Institute of Education, University of Gothenburg.

Steiner-Khamsi, G. (2000). Transferring education, displacing reforms. In J. Schriwer (Ed.), *Discourse formation in comparative education* (pp. 155–187). Frankfurt am Main: Peter Lang.

Stufflebeam, D. L., Foley, W. J., Gephart, W. J., Guba, E. G., Hammond, R. I., Merriam, H. O., & Provus, M. M. (1971). *Educational evaluation and decision making.* Itasca, IL: F. E. Peacock.

Van der Eyken, W., Goulden, D., & Crossley, M. (1995). Evaluating educational reform in a small state. A case study of Belize, Central America. *Evaluation, 1*(1), 33–44.

Wildavsky, A. (1979). *Speaking truth to power: The art and craft of policy analysis.* Boston, Toronto: Little, Brown.

CHAPTER 27

Pursuing the Wrong Indicators?

The Development and Impact of Test-Based Accountability

Harry Torrance

Introduction

As evaluation has emerged as a professional practice over the last 30 to 40 years, it has largely been concerned with working at the level of individual programs or interventions: program evaluation, curriculum evaluation, and the like. Furthermore, this emergent field has increasingly acknowledged and tried to develop strategies to deal with the political dimension to and implications of evaluation. Evaluation is characterized as a political activity involving judgments about the success and failure of programs and the associated allocation and reallocation of resources, not as a neutral or technical activity. Recognizing this has often involved recourse to theories of democratic and participatory involvement.

Thus, for example, Barry MacDonald (1974) argued that evaluation should be democratic rather than bureaucratic or autocratic; that is, it should seek out and represent the (often conflicting) views of all stakeholders in an evaluation; it should be an open service to inform the understanding and decisions of the citizenry, rather than a closed (technical, bureaucratic) or an open-but-privileged (scientific, autocratic) service to government. At around the same time, Stake (1973) argued for the importance of responsive evaluation oriented "more directly to program activities than to program intents," responding to "audience requirements for information and . . . the different value-perspectives of the people at hand" (see also Stake, 2003). House (see House & Howe, 1999) developed similar ideas with respect to "deliberative, democratic evaluation," arguing that all stakeholders should be involved in the design and conduct of evaluation and emerging findings should be discussed and debated at each stage of the process. Other theorists have taken the argument further still, suggesting that all stakeholders, but particularly those most affected by social interventions—on the receiving end, as it were—should be involved in evaluation data gathering and writing. Evaluation should broaden the authorship of reports, as well as the readership and ownership of them, and build capacity for social action in local communities (e.g., Fetterman, 2001; Whitmore, 1998). Taken as a whole, this body of work has argued that the perspectives of all stakeholders, including all those participants in, and especially those most affected by, programs and interventions, should be included in evaluation design and their diverse views represented in reports and recommendations (for a full discussion of the genealogy, relationship, and development of such approaches, see Greene, 2006). The rationale for this approach is that evaluation should understand program needs and impact at local level, represent the full range of costs and benefits (not just the explicit objectives pursued by the program), and reflect different criteria of judgment about success and failure.

These arguments are well rehearsed in some of the chapters in this part of the *Handbook*, along with some of the problems encountered when evaluators attempt to implement such approaches to evaluation (e.g., Vestman & Segerholm, Chapter 26; Kushner, Chapter 23).

My concern in this chapter, however, is to examine the changing focus of government interest in evaluation, and in particular the move toward new public management (NPM) as Kushner describes it. Theories of evaluative action seem to have become more radical over the years and increasingly focused on the representation and empowerment of those groups most affected by government programs but with the least power to define, influence, or indeed resist them. However, government has become more assertive of its right to intervene. If we are to understand how educational evaluation might contribute to improved student learning in a globalized society, we have to understand the political issues that are driving changes in the focus of evaluation at the present time. Many of the approaches and strategies that have been developed to address the politics of evaluation and reflect diversity of perspective and judgment

are now at considerable variance with government attempts to build overarching universal systems of monitoring and accountability. Defining and measuring the output of educational systems has come to replace understanding of the impact of programs and interventions as the key policy problematic of educational evaluation. Managing systems certainly demands the gathering and use of evaluation data, but they are specific kinds of data that are being pursued in educational systems at the present time.

In this chapter, I treat the development of test-based accountability in England and the United States as examples of the new political demands being placed on the concept and practice of evaluation, and I review some of the problems this creates at the local level. I also explore the reasons that governments now seem so committed to NPM, and in particular to system-wide educational testing, and identify ways in which more deliberative forms of evaluation might be reinstated in our educational systems. Although the chapter focuses on the United States and England as examples, the argument has broader relevance, and I include other brief references as appropriate.

The Development of Test-Based Accountability

Recently, governments, certainly in the English-speaking world, have become increasingly interested in monitoring and managing whole systems, rather than evaluating individual programs, and various theories and practices of NPM or performance management have been adopted with respect to the development of public services, including education (Julnes, 2006; Stame, 2006). The key element in performance management is measurement of efficiency in meeting predetermined objectives rather than understanding of process, and this has involved the deployment of measurement tools and techniques across the public sector, particularly in the UK. Such developments are also apparent in international contexts (Kushner, Chapter 23, this volume) and are sponsored and disseminated internationally by agencies such as the Organisation for Economic Co-operation and Development and the World Bank (Rizvi & Lingard, 2006).

Beyond this general shift in emphasis and orientation, however, with respect to educational provision in particular, we seem to be living in a moment when governments are seeking to both evaluate the efficiency and effectiveness of educational systems, through appeals to the apparently objective measures produced by testing, and control these same systems through the mechanism of test-based accountability. Enormous reliance is being placed on test-based accountability systems to both drive up standards by influencing teaching and learning and provide evidence of output, evidence that those standards are indeed being driven up. In addition, policies of school choice have been introduced, whereby, at least in principle, parents can choose which school to send their children to, informed by the test results that those schools achieve. Such choice is seen as another pressure exerted on schools to bring about improvements in standards; parents and students can vote with their feet if standards are perceived not to be high enough. This is certainly the case in England with the National Curriculum and Testing system (Torrance, 2003, 2009) and is now the case in the United States with the impact of the No Child Left Behind (2001) legislation (see Centre on Education Policy, 2007; Hamilton et al., 2007). For evidence of similar developments elsewhere, see Cisneros-Cohernour and Grayson (Chapter 13, this volume) and Pang (2003).

The general analysis of policymakers and indeed some educational researchers seems to be that educational research in general, and program evaluation in particular, is too fragmented, too slow, and too complex to build usable knowledge of system performance for system improvement (Hargreaves, 1996; Hillage, Pearson, Anderson, & Tamkin, 1998; Julnes, 2006; Slavin, 2002). It is argued that one-off research studies, including individual program evaluations, cannot provide the regular monitoring and timely findings that system management needs or indeed provide

timely, easily accessible, and relevant information for parents at the local level. Some researchers have argued that what is needed is better educational research and evaluation based on more rigorous scientific methods, specifically randomized control trials (RCTs; Shavelson, Phillips, Towne, & Feuer, 2003; Slavin, 2002). These arguments might be characterized as a reversion to autocratic evaluation and are certainly not without their critics (e.g., Thomas & Pring, 2004). However, the key point I wish to emphasize here is that, even if the arguments in favor of such a change were to be accepted, the development of more RCTs would simply compound the problem of timeliness and utility because they take a great deal of time, resources, and organization to conduct (cf. Torrance, 2008). The outcomes of RCTs cannot provide the regular information flow that policymakers require. Rather, it increasingly seems as if policymakers are determined to develop their own solutions to such issues, particularly involving test-based evaluation and accountability systems. System-level monitoring is being put in place to provide overall information to policymakers and specific information on individual students and schools for parents, in effect to supplant previous conceptualizations and practices of educational research and evaluation.

At the same time, large-scale international studies have been developed (TIMSS, PIRLS, PISA[1]), which provide country-level comparative data for governments, placing governments in an analogous position to parents when it comes to identifying where their particular system is in relation to others in the latest international league table. Governments seem to value this information as they seek to ascertain whether the standards of their domestic system are comparable with those of other similar countries; governments quite literally buy into these studies by helping to fund them and carry them out. However, they are also trapped by them, having to respond to the latest results as they appear in the media. In this respect, they are both seduced and ensnared by the simplicity of the information provided. Although such league tables are hedged around with all sorts of methodological caveats in the full published reports, these caveats disappear when the media publish the league tables produced, and England or the United States is reportedly 4th, 14th, or whatever in the latest table. Even apparently good results are greeted with skepticism. When England was ranked seventh in Reading and fourth in Maths in the 2000 PISA study, the headline on the BBC Education News website read "Are Our Students Really This Bright?" (see Torrance, 2006, for a full discussion).

Thus, we seem to be faced with an international convergence in the use of testing in evaluation and accountability, with both international studies and national systems of testing treating a small range of quite narrow measures as proxies for the quality of the system as a whole. Why is this happening, how has it come about, and what impact does it have on schools and students? This chapter goes on to review the development of new forms of evaluation and accountability in England and the United States to explore the ways in which the economic pressure exerted on governments by globalization seems to be translated, in turn, into pressure on education systems. The chapter closes by reflecting on what possibilities there are for different forms of evaluative inquiry to reemerge.

Globalizing Policy

Globalization is a much debated and contested topic, as is its impact on education (Burbules & Torres, 2000; Lauder, Brown, Dillabough, & Halsey, 2006). For the purposes of this chapter, it is important to recognize that there is no straightforward economic determinism at work here. As Singh (2004) recently argued: "Globalisation has to be actively implemented, reproduced, serviced and financed . . . [it] is not a predetermined force that pushes and molds local contexts into uniform shapes" (p. 103).

Nevertheless, broad trends in both economic development and international policy borrowing do seem to be influencing government education policies in similar directions. Thus, education policies over the last 25 years have been increasingly linked to and justified by the need to constantly improve educational standards to improve the economic competitiveness of nation states (Goals 2000: Educate America Act, 1994; National Commission on Excellence in Education, 1983; No Child Left Behind Act, 2001). As a recent White Paper[2] on School Choice in England put it:

> Standards must keep rising in the globalised world in which we now live . . . given the scale of the global economic challenge we face there is no other choice . . . We cannot content ourselves with a schools system which, while much improved, is not universally good. (Department for Education and Skills, 2005, pp. 7 & 20)

It might be argued that the rhetoric of change always revolves around challenge and the need for improvement: For politicians and policymakers, it was ever thus. But the stakes now do seem to be higher than before as previously underdeveloped economies such as India and China enter into serious competition with Europe and the United States. Apple (2000) is convincing when he argues that, "behind the stress on higher standards, more rigorous testing . . . is the fear of losing in international competition and the loss of jobs" (p. 58).

Interestingly enough, the Foreword to the White Paper cited earlier, written by the then Prime Minister Tony Blair, quoted Florida's improved tests scores as evidence of the efficacy of school choice:

> Studies have found that schools in areas where there is more choice have improved most rapidly. In Florida, parents can choose an alternative school if their school has "failed" in two of the last four years . . . studies showed test scores improved fastest where schools knew children were free to go elsewhere. (Department for Education, and Skills 2005, p. 4)

The findings of such "studies" have been undermined by Haney's (2006) recent analysis of Florida's results, suggesting that apparent improvements are an artifact of Florida's grade retention and transition policies (cf. Linn, 2000, for longer term analyses of similar issues). However, such research does not seem to be able to undermine the logic of using test scores to indicate success or to deflect the general trend of policy borrowing as governments become ever more frantic in their efforts not to be left behind in the global knowledge economy. As Morrow and Torres (2000) note, "It is the interplay between the economic and political contexts of globalization that has driven most discussions of the need for educational reform" (p. 29). They also argue that "the new global economy requires workers with the capacity to learn quickly and to work in teams in reliable and creative ways" (p. 33).

Quite how narrow testing regimes might be thought likely to produce a creative and flexible workforce is a moot point, and one to which I return later. The main point to note for now, however, is that the imperative to improve educational standards, and in particular to use test-based accountability systems as a key mechanism for this, seems to derive from concerns over economic competitiveness, combined with a need for government to devise simple ways of identifying how the education system is performing. Thus, the effects of globalization are manifest in the policy borrowing in which governments engage. Vestman and Segerholm (Chapter 26, this volume, citing Lawn & Lingard, 2002) note this trend and refer to "a new magistracy of influence . . . a policy elite that acts across borders . . . often found in task force groups and committees . . . not directly part of formal national decision making." However, *magistracy* seems far too solemn and powerful a term to deploy in these circumstances. Task forces and committees there certainly are, but their deliberations and decisions seem to reflect an increasingly frenzied circulation of paranoia about educational standards in policy circles and apparent solutions to the

perceived problems. It is precisely because policymakers do not have a 'magisterial' level of control over such matters that short-term policy borrowing seems to triumph over longer term deliberation of the evidence. Overall, however, the impact of globalization and global policy borrowing is the reorientation and homogenization of educational goals toward the single purpose of national economic competitiveness. Individual student success and individual school success are judged in terms of test results, while national systems are judged against national test targets and international comparisons such as TIMSS and PISA. New programs and interventions are designed in the taken-for-granted context of raising test scores and judged against whether short-term test scores are indeed raised, as opposed to, for example, whether the educational experiences of students (particularly disadvantaged students) are improved and/or whether the program may have other positive or negative outcomes.

The Logic of Testing

The drive for test-based evaluation and accountability seems to derive from a strange amalgam of assessment theory combined with policy needs for performance measurement and policy assumptions about cause and effect in human systems. Thus, the measurement-driven instruction movement of the late 1980s and 1990s argued that if desired educational objectives were put into testing programs, teachers will teach these desired objectives (Airasian, 1988; Popham, 1987). As Resnick and Resnick (1992) put it, "You get what you assess; you don't get what you don't assess; you should build assessment towards what you want . . . to teach" (p. 59).

This statement seems to summarize what we might call the educational argument for standards-based education: agree on your main educational goals and objectives, put them into the curriculum, align tests with the curriculum so there is a high degree of reinforcing curriculum fidelity, and over time the system will improve as teachers and students pursue high-quality curriculum objectives through test success. Such an apparently rational linking of curriculum and assessment makes many assumptions about motivation and causality and begs many questions of empirical operation, not least of which is whether high-quality valid tests can indeed be devised and administered across large-scale national systems. At its core, however, this linking of curriculum and assessment endorses the use of testing to improve educational standards, and this clearly provides some educational legitimacy and momentum for the development of test-based evaluation and accountability systems. It is one element of the active implementation of globalization by human agents that Singh (2004) identifies.

The accountability arguments trade on a similar logic but are much simpler and more clear-cut. Here the claim is that education systems in general, and schools in particular, must have their efficiency and effectiveness measured by the outcomes produced. Tests are simply measurement instruments that can achieve this without impinging on the system. Expected standards of achievement must be prescribed and tests regularly employed to identify whether these expectations have been met. In publicly maintained school systems, which are financed out of taxation, such an argument involves governments determining what is to be taught and how it is to be tested, along with the publication of results so that government, schools, and parents can see whether standards are indeed rising and taxpayers are getting value for money from the system. The quality of teaching and learning in the classroom is assumed to rise if results improve. Essentially, testing is used as a lever to affect the system *qua* system; the detail at the classroom level is assumed to look after itself. It is still important to the logic and practice of such a system that the tests employed do indeed validly sample the curriculum and reliably measure student achievement. However, from the policy perspective, this is simply assumed to be the case. The mechanism of change is parental choice and the pressure that league table position and the

marketplace exerts on schools, not the quality of the tests. So, curriculum objectives are set, tests measure whether those objectives have been met, and students and parents have the right to change schools if the objectives are not met and if standards are not seen to be improving.

The Paradox of Test-Based Evaluation and Accountability: Evidence From England and the United States

The irony of this approach to improving educational standards, however, is that it seems to have almost the opposite effect to that for which policymakers are ostensibly aiming. All of the problems associated with focusing on too narrow a range of performance indicators, which Kushner (Chapter 23, this volume) identifies as a key issue for NPM, are manifest in test-based accountability. Empirical evidence from both sides of the Atlantic suggests that testing does indeed impact on the curriculum, but that it narrows the curriculum to that which is tested and, in so doing, probably *lowers* rather than raises educational standards.

Thus, for example, in England, the National Curriculum and Testing system focuses on testing English, Maths, and Science (designated as core subjects) at ages 11 and 14. The General Certificate of Secondary Education has been retained to assess standards at ages 16+ and to continue to provide single-subject qualifications for students at the end of the compulsory phase of schooling. Not surprisingly, this testing system has led to a narrowing of the curriculum, particularly in primary schools (ages 5–11 years). Perhaps rather more surprising is that it is the government's own school inspectors that have drawn attention to this problem, as much as independent researchers.

The English National Curriculum is set out, subject by subject, in terms of attainment targets, and these attainment targets are organized into expected levels of progress. Level 4 is the expected level to be achieved at age 11 (end of primary school). The current national target is that 85% of students should reach Level 4 in English and Maths at age 11 "as soon as possible" (Department for Education and Skills, 2004, p. 4). However, with no date attached, this is not really a target at all but rather an interesting example of a government being put under pressure by its own commitment to a flawed evaluation tool. Also, interestingly, such improvement, as has been seen in results at age 11, seems to have leveled off after initial progress (see Figure 27.1).

Not every year's results are recorded in Figure 27.1. Rather, sufficient years are recorded to indicate trends over time, along with key dates that the government has variously used and dropped as indicators of progress. Because previous targets were set but missed, the baseline for comparison is now routinely given by official

documents as 1997 when the New Labour government was first elected (Department for Education and Skills, 2005; Earl et al., 2003). At first sight, such progress seems significant. But closer scrutiny indicates significant improvements in results prior to 1997. Thus, for example, in the 2 years *before* 1997, immediately after National Testing was first introduced at age 11 (1995–1997), results improved by 15 percentage points in English (48%–63%) and 17 percentage points in Maths (44%–61%). In the 10 years *since* 1997, results have improved by 16 percentage points in English (63%–79%) and 14 percentage points in Maths (61%–75%), with most of that improvement being achieved up to 2000. The plateau effect since 2000 is particularly notable because it was previously identified by Linn (2000) in the context of U.S. developments such as minimum competency testing. Linn

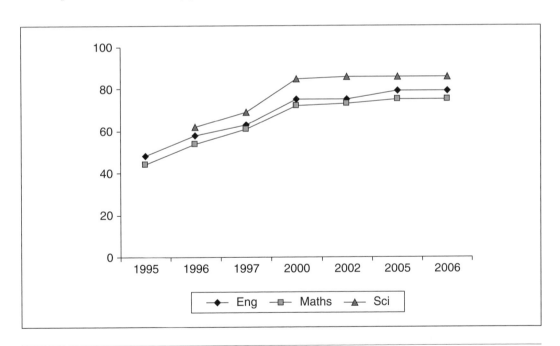

Figure 27.1 Percentage of Pupils Gaining National Curriculum Assessment Level 4 or Above at Age 11 (i.e. end of primary schooling)

SOURCE: http://www.dfes.gov.uk/rsgateway/

NOTE: 1995: First full run of English and Maths tests at age 11 (i.e., end of Key Stage 2 of the National Curriculum). 1996: First full run of Science tests at age 11. 1997: First tests under New Labour government elected in May 1997. 2002: First national target date set by New Labour government: The target was 80% of students reaching Level 4 English at age 11 and 75% reaching Level 4 Maths at age 11. Both targets were missed; 75% of students reached Level 4 or above in English and 73% reached Level 4 or above in Maths. For other sources of test results data, prior to Department for Education and Skills' online archiving, see Torrance (2003).

(2000) reports that "the pattern of early gains followed by a leveling off is typical of . . . high stakes use of tests" (p. 6). The pattern of scores starting low, improving rapidly, and then tailing off also seems to reflect something of Fullan's (2001) notion of an implementation dip: There is no initial dip in scores because there were no such scores to record previously, and the testing system constitutes the innovation. However, it is arguable that the introduction of national testing deskilled teachers, leading to initially low scores. They then learned how to engage with the innovation and scores improved, but such improvement has since leveled off.

The evidence in England suggests that "teaching to the test" is the most likely explanation for scores rising initially and then tailing off as teachers and students come to be about as efficient as they can be at scoring well on the tests within a regime of coaching and practice. Research studies have reported an increasing focus on test preparation, particularly in the final year of primary school prior to the tests being taken (cf. McNess, Triggs, Broadfoot, Osborn, & Pollard, 2001; K. Hall, Collins, Benjamin, Nind, & Sheehy, 2004). However, it is not only independent research studies that highlight such problems. A government-commissioned study of a parallel initiative to improve literacy and numeracy in the National Curriculum reported that "many teachers acknowledged considerable test preparation especially in the term leading up to the national assessments" (Earl et al., 2003, p. 7). Furthermore, school inspectors who routinely visit schools on a regular basis have reported on a narrowing of the curriculum and summaries of their inspection findings that have been included in the annual reports from the Office for Standards in Education:

> In many [primary] schools the focus of the teaching of English is on those parts of the curriculum on which there are likely to be questions in national tests. . . . History and, more so, geography continued to be marginalized. . . . In [secondary] schools . . . the experience of English had become narrower . . . as teachers focused on tests and examinations. . . . There was a similar tension in mathematics. (Office for Standards in Education, 2006, pp. 52–56)

Comparable evidence also can be identified internationally. Klein, Hamilton, McCaffrey, and Stecher (2000), Linn (2000), and Shepard (1990) report similar findings from previous studies of test-based reform in the United States, and the same issues are now beginning to emerge from studies of No Child Left Behind (NCLB). State-level NCLB test scores are rising (Centre on Education Policy, 2007), but equally "Administrators and teachers have made a concerted effort to align curriculum and instruction with state academic standards and assessments" (Centre on Education Policy, 2006, p. 1). A recently completed study by Rand Education funded by the U.S. National Science Foundation noted that:

> changes included a narrowing of the curriculum and instruction toward tested topics and even toward certain problems styles or formats. Teachers also reported focusing more on students near the proficient cutscore. (Hamilton et al., 2007, p. xix)

Thus, it is clear that rising test scores do not necessarily provide unequivocal evidence of rising educational standards. Indeed, rising scores might actually mask falling standards because students are exposed to a much restricted curriculum.

A further key issue in England is that we have learned from bitter experience that the larger the scope and scale of the testing regime, the simpler the tests must become. Our national tests employ traditional paper-and-pencil methods, and there is little opportunity for proper piloting or quality control (Daugherty, 1995; Torrance, 1995, 2003).[3] However, were the number of ages/stages of testing to be reduced, while still retaining testing at key transition points (e.g., age 11), the political imperative of producing outcome data could still be met while relieving pressure on the system and releasing resources to improve the quality of the tests/tasks designed and deployed for smaller numbers of students. The lessons for the United States as NCLB extends its reach to include Science are apparent: Annual testing in Reading and Math should be curtailed and replaced by, at most, periodic testing, with adequate yearly progress (AYP) reconceptualized to include other forms of student assessment. Research already indicates that AYP is not a constant measure that can be relied on across contexts, but rather varies according to state-level and school-level implementation policies and resourcing (Balfanz, Legters, West, & Weber, 2007), and monitoring standards across the system as a whole can still be achieved by the light sampling approach of the National Assessment of Educational Progress.

All of which is not to say that there is no validity or potential benefit in using test results in evaluation studies and international comparative studies. Good quality outcome measures are important if we can produce them. Equally, the results that we currently have in the public domain are all that we have got within and across systems and, as such, should be treated as potentially useful, if fallible, sources of evidence (cf. Torrance, 2006). The problem, of course, is that these sources of evidence are not treated as fallible in the context of current policy imperatives. There are many weaknesses and cautionary riders to be considered that do not appear to trouble policymakers (consider the unproblematic deployment of evidence from Florida in UK policy documents, noted earlier). Furthermore, the use of a narrow range of tests actually seems to be impacting negatively on the educational experience of even successful students, let alone unsuccessful ones. Successive research studies over 40 years have indicated that the vitality of teacher-student relationships and the quality of teacher-student interaction are the most important factors in improving student learning experiences and raising attainment (Galton, Simon, & Croll, 1980; Galton, Hargreaves, Comber, & Wall, 1999; Jackson, 1968; Mehan, 1979; Mercer, 1995). Yet this is precisely what is threatened by an overconcentration on testing.

So what is going on here? One argument might be that governments only cite evidence when it legitimates policy that has already been decided. Florida's apparent success is deployed to legitimate UK policy, and the Texas miracle is deployed to underpin the development of NCLB (despite the various critiques, including Haney, 2000, Klein et al., 2000). But if policymaking is so powerful and cynical, this begs questions of why evidence is needed at all. Clearly there is still some genuflecting to the need for some form of evidence to inform decision making. The development of accountability and forms of NPM also begs questions of where policy comes from in the first place and why an ideology of centrally determined standards, linked to choice and market forces, is assumed to be determining of quality in human services.

Another argument might be that detailed critical research studies rarely reach the desks of politicians and policymakers: They simply do not know what is really going on at the periphery and what impact their policies are having. This would certainly provide a new opportunity for more qualitative and exploratory forms of evaluation, although in the case of England, it does not seem plausible at the present time. As we have seen, the government's own inspection service has drawn attention to the impact that testing is having on narrowing the curriculum.

Globalizing Educational Management

So how is it that a commitment to testing outweighs the negative impact that testing has on the system under consideration? Part of the explanation seems to lie in the continuing skepticism of government about research findings, and particularly a sense that the short-term harm that testing *might* do to individual schools and children is nevertheless still outweighed by the longer term control that testing affords system management and development. System control outweighs the nebulous benefits of trying to improve quality by other means. Tests/testing is the one major lever that governments can use to reach directly into classrooms, and they are unlikely to relinquish it lightly. Tests and testing also seem to promise a tangible return on relatively low and predictable levels of expenditure when compared with other tools that might raise standards, such as increased in-service training and/or lower student-teacher ratios. In this respect, it is worth noting that the commitment to test-based evaluation and accountability spans continents and persists across administrations. New Labour continued with and indeed has intensified the previous Conservative government's commitment to a National Curriculum and Testing system. The Republican Bush administration introduced NCLB following the Democratic Clinton Educate America Act, and NCLB attracted wide bipartisan support (although less so now; Dillon, 2007a, 2007b).

The issue seems to revolve around risk management and governance. Large sums of public money are invested in education systems, and the pressure of economic globalization is intense or at least is perceived as intense. To maintain legitimacy, governments have to at least *be seen* to be doing something in response to concerns about economic competitiveness and educational standards, and testing programs and test scores are certainly visible. The urge to control, in the face of global uncertainties, seems to outweigh the collateral damage of testing. Some information about system performance, however flawed, is better than none (for parents as well as governments) especially if it involves pressure on schools to focus on the apparently core subjects of a high-tech knowledge economy: Math, Science, and Language. Equally, the act of testing, in the context of system-wide monitoring and accountability, both assumes and at one and the same time creates the managerial right-to-test, the right-to-manage the system. It is almost as if democratic governments now conceive of their role as more corporate than representative, managing systems *qua* systems irrespective of the impact of particular technologies of control on that system, or indeed on individual citizens. Citizens are treated as conscripts in the constant struggle for national economic supremacy. Rather than acting on our behalf, governments now expect us to help them in their struggle with globalization.

However, this reorientation of governance, if such it is, begs some key issues about the role of the state and the relationship among individual, community, and government. In England, the extensive testing system, especially as it applies to younger students at ages 7 and 11, has received sustained professional, public, and media criticism (see numerous stories over several years on the BBC Education News website). Nevertheless, testing continues with relatively little modification. Individual parents may be unhappy about the pressure placed on their children and may be uneasy about the overall direction of the system as a whole. However, as long as *their* children succeed, the promise of social and economic mobility in a meritocratic test-driven system seems to outweigh any consideration of the broader public good. Likewise, governments may be held hostage to test results as much as schools (viz. the UK Labour government missing the targets that it set for itself), but not to have some sort of output data about system performance as a whole would be unthinkable in the context of the contemporary managerial state. Similarly, not to take part in international comparative studies, and not to have access to some sort of comparative data, would present worse problems for government image management than occasionally having to defend apparently poor results. The media would immediately ask: If other countries are taking part, why aren't we? What has the government got to hide? Also of course, sometimes there are good results to publicize from international comparative studies.

Developing and Evaluating Educational Quality

The problem remains, however, that narrow test-driven accountability systems are unlikely to produce flexible and creative workers for the knowledge economy, far less to contribute to more general deliberation about the democratic purposes and organization of schooling. The research evidence is clear about the narrowing of the school curriculum, and, certainly in the UK, there also is an increasing perception in higher education and among employers that, despite rising test scores, the skills and capacities of school leavers and job applicants are not improving. Coaching for tests is producing learners who are too dependent on support to operate effectively in other more challenging environments (Hayward & McNicholl, 2007; Torrance, 2007). Now, again, it might be said that it was ever thus. Employers, in particular, have been complaining that educational standards are not high enough ever since compulsory schooling was first introduced. Current complaints have not stopped the UK from enjoying its longest period of economic growth (1992–2008) since World War II.[4]

Nevertheless, employers and higher education are important political lobbies. If they are skeptical about the reality of rising educational standards, their views will be taken seriously. The English government has acknowledged the criticisms to some extent by introducing specific programs to reinstate and support creativity in the school curriculum (Hall & Thomson, 2007). These efforts have been rather piecemeal and tokenistic to date. Nevertheless, they indicate both an uncertainty that simply teaching and testing Maths, Science, and English will indeed produce the creative talent that a knowledge economy needs and the first evidence that government understands that narrow forms of system management may be inadequate to the task of producing quality and flexibility, rather than standardization and compliance. Currently, however, the UK Department for Education and Science (DfES) still insists that tests and testing "are a non-negotiable part of school reform" and that "the government does not accept that our children are over-tested" (DfES spokespersons quoted on BBC Education News website, May 1, 2007, and February 29, 2008). So we must assume that criticisms will be acknowledged and

some tinkering may occur, but the edifice will still stand. Testing seems to constitute the security blanket or comforter of insecure policymakers.

Where does this leave evaluation approaches that are committed to serving democracy rather than bureaucracy; privilege stakeholder engagement and deliberation about quality and experience; and are about ends as well as means, rather than simple measures of outcome and efficiency? Furthermore, where does it leave the aspirations of the field to reflect diversity rather than pursue homogeneity, conduct more culturally sensitive and ethnically aware evaluations, and acknowledge the racism that still underpins many conceptions of social scientific inquiry (cf. Kushner, Chapter 23, this volume; Hopson, Chapter 24, this volume)?

Biesta (2004) notes that different forms of accountability both derive from and change the relationships between citizens and the state. In particular, he argues that contemporary forms of test-based accountability focus on the economic value of the service provided to consumers (especially tax-paying parents), rather than the general value of the activity and its outcomes to the community. As such, government and citizens are tied into an economic relationship revolving around choice and value for money, rather than a political one involving "deliberation and contestation" (p. 237). This is an important point, but, as we have seen, others involved in the polity, including employers and higher education who "receive and use" the products of schooling, also have a less direct but nevertheless still significant longer term interest in educational opportunities, standards, and outcomes. The managerial interests of government and the socioeconomic interests of the wider community are not yet completely synonymous; and it is within the interstices of these diverse and competing agendas and relationships that more open forms of evaluation may yet prosper. Schools, local communities, and local authorities (i.e., local/regional government) need to know more about how to improve the quality of educational processes and products, as well as how to build stronger relationships between schools and their communities, such that they are seen to work in tandem for the benefit of their children. Such work cannot be accomplished by a centrally controlled testing system, and there are clear possibilities for the further development of responsive, democratic, and participatory methods.

Furthermore, test scores are poor proxies for all the important information that parents and other stakeholders want to know: Is the school a safe and happy place to be? What is the quality of the teaching and learning? Are there vital and constructive relationships forged between teacher and student? Are a wide range of aptitudes and abilities recognized and nurtured? This more local knowledge certainly requires a different form of enquiry and reporting, be it produced by the school or in collaboration with parent groups and school district evaluation procedures. There is an obvious role for responsive and participatory approaches that can produce detailed knowledge and understanding of local problems and achievements while also addressing emergent political issues and how improvement might be engineered. Likewise, more generally, investigating why test scores always seem to be going up while standards are rarely considered to improve requires a form of evaluation that addresses the political context of the issue, as well as pursues more fine-grained evidence about its production and perception in action. Democratic evaluation approaches are absolutely central to such an undertaking because they can identify and seek to move beyond the self-interested and overly defensive political imperative of constant improvement to address the stubborn realities of partial success, partial failure, and what to do about it. Democratic approaches can once again help us to address the political project of improving the quality of schooling and building public confidence in it, rather than the managerial project of regulating schooling and rendering it more efficient.

Many potential evaluation sponsors, certainly, again, in England, have a need for and an interest in commissioning such investigations. In this respect, the state and the managerial project of regulating schooling is not monolithic. Regional development authorities, local education authorities, local health authorities, and the like are all charged with various responsibilities with respect to implementing government policy and have their targets to meet; but equally, because they have to operate at the local level and actually make a difference (pulling levers is not enough), they need to know where to make their investments and with what detailed effects. Most important of all in this context, they need local support and feedback, and responsive and participatory methods are recognized as significant in accomplishing such an agenda. Such work is being undertaken in England, although it often has to operate despite and against national policy rather than in congruence with it (Cook, Owen, & Jones, 2005).

Equally, at the classroom level, we know that the curriculum and assessment relationship can be understood and realized in different ways. Routine, informal assessment can play a key role in underpinning or undermining the quality of teaching and learning in the classroom. How teachers assess students' work, what sorts of positive or negative feedback is given, and whether advice on how to improve is provided can make a great deal of difference to what is learned and how it is learned. This is the thinking that underlies the formative assessment movement in England (Black & Wiliam, 1998; Torrance & Pryor, 1998) and has been acknowledged as potentially important for developments in the United States and elsewhere (Carless, Joughin, Liu, & Associates, 2006; Shepard, 2000). In a context that is still dominated by testing and targets, it is unlikely that an alternative vision of formative classroom assessment will gain much of a foothold in everyday teaching practices. Nevertheless, the vision exists and could develop at the local level were arguments about restricting the scope and scale of the testing regime to prove successful. Such an approach would also directly attend to the key issue of improving the vitality and quality of teacher-student interaction and provide detailed feedback about student progress for parents: effectively knitting together more responsive approaches to student assessment and school evaluation.

In pursuing such a goal, perhaps the most important piece of evidence to be deployed is the plateau effect. Certainly in England, some new spin of the policy wheel is required if the government's own rhetoric about raising standards is to continue to be credible. There is a large minority of students, usually located in poor communities, who are still not benefiting from even the apparently inflated test scores that are currently being produced (15%–20% at age 11; see Figure 27.1). It is becoming apparent that a one-size-fits-all standards agenda in educational policymaking has run its course and that what is needed going forward is a focus on diverse experiences of learning, in and for an uncertain world. Understanding and addressing issues of poverty and the disputability of knowledge and values is a key issue for education and educational evaluation, as is the development of creativity and self-confidence in the community at large, particularly those most marginalized at the present time. There is a pressing need for schools and the communities they serve to act more in tandem, as well as for schools and educational policymakers to identify the potential strengths of their communities and to better understand how to support student learning in interaction *with* schooling, rather than force it to accord with institutionalized learning *through* schooling. Integrating formative assessment with democratic and participatory evaluation approaches could provide both the evidence base and the practical context for face-to-face deliberation about the quality of local school provision and experience and how to improve it.

Potential growth points for the development of alternative visions of a more democratic and formative approach to educational evaluation and student assessment are local and relatively small scale. Precisely because testing still dominates system evaluation, such possible developments are inevitably positioned as fragmented and not capable of evaluating systemic performance overall. As such, they manifest the weaknesses that test-based accountability and performance management claims to address. Yet as we have seen, test-based accountability brings its own problems and developing high-quality educational practices, particularly with respect to the quality of teacher-student interaction, is ultimately a local, ecologically fragile activity.

Twenty years of increasing central control and regulation have produced a narrow and risk-averse education culture, which is the antithesis of the ostensible purpose of the exercise. Producing test scores is not enough for educational consumers or governments. The need for better quality information with which to make decisions has never been more acute. Responsive, democratic, and participatory approaches to evaluation offer precisely this possibility, along with the potential for capacity building at the local level. Ultimately, improvement of the system as a whole will be built up from such efforts; it cannot be imposed by regulations that employ a single measure of success or a single form of inquiry.

Notes

1. TIMSS: Trends in International Maths and Science Study involving 25 countries at fourth grade and 46 countries at eighth grade; PIRLS: Progress in International Literacy Study involving 35 countries at fourth grade; PISA: Programme for International Student Assessment involving 43 countries at ages 15+. See Torrance (2006) for a full review.

2. White Papers are the official policy statements that precede legislation in England.

3. In 2006, for instance, 2,339,313 students took tests at ages 7, 11, 14, and 16, involving an estimated 15+ million separate papers; moreover, the scale of the enterprise is now such that the 2008 procedure descended into an absolute shambles when the company that was sub-contracted to set and mark the tests (ETS) mislaid and did not mark large numbers of papers. Many schools and individual students did not receive their results, and many of those who did were skeptical of their validity and reliability (see BBC Education News website, July 16, 2008: http://news.bbc.co.uk/1/hi/education/7507113.stm). The UK government subsequently abandoned testing at age 14 with effect from 2009.

4. That such growth must be driven by school leavers of the 1970s and 1980s moving into mature adulthood and positions of economic significance in the 1990s is highly ironic, of course. The 1970s and 1980s were the period when educational standards first started to attract severe critical attention from government. This begs many questions about whether standards really were too low at that time, and if they were, what sort of linkage, if any, there really is between the education system and the economy.

References

Airasian, P. (1988). Measurement-driven instruction: A closer look. *Educational Measurement: Issues and Practice, 7*(4), 6–11.

Apple, M. (2000). Between neoliberalism and neo-conservatism: Education and conservatism in a global context. In N. Burbules & C. A. Torres (Eds.), *Globalisation and education.* New York: Routledge.

Balfanz, R., Legters, N., West, T., & Weber, L. (2007). Are NCLB's measures, incentives and improvement strategies the right ones for the nation's low-performing high schools? *American Educational Research Journal, 44*(3), 559–593.

Biesta, G. (2004). Education, accountability and the ethical demand: Can the democratic potential of accountability be regained? *Educational Theory, 54*(3), 233–250.

Black, P., & Wiliam, D. (1998). Assessment and classroom learning. *Assessment in Education, 5*(1), 7–74.

Burbules, N., & Torres, C. A. (Eds.). (2000). *Globalisation and education.* New York: Routledge.

Carless, D., Joughin, G., Liu, N.-F., & Associates. (2006). *How assessment supports learning.* Hong Kong: Hong Kong University Press.

Centre on Education Policy. (2006). *From the capital to the classroom: Year 4 of the No Child Left Behind Act: Summary and recommendations.* Available at http://www.cep-dc.org/.

Centre on Education Policy. (2007). *Has student achievement increased since No Child Left Behind?* Available at http://www.cep-dc.org/.

Cook, T., Owen, J., & Jones, E. (2005). Evaluating the early excellence initiative: The relationship between evaluation, performance management and practitioner participation. *Evaluation, 11*(3), 331–349.

Daugherty, R. (1995). *National curriculum assessment: A review of policy 1987-1994.* London: Falmer Press.

Department for Education and Skills. (2004). *Excellence and enjoyment: A strategy for primary schools.* London: DfES. Available at http://www.standards.dfes.gov.uk/primary/publications/literacy/63553/pns_excell_enjoy037703v2.pdf

Department for Education and Skills. (2005). *Higher standards, better schools for all.* Available at http://www.dfes.gov.uk/publications/schoolswhitepaper/index.shtml

Dillon, S. (2007a, November 6). For an education law, reauthorisation stalls. *New York Times.*

Dillon, S. (2007b, December 23). Democrats make Bush School Act an election issue. *New York Times.*

Earl, L., Watson, N., Levin, B., Leithwood, K., Fullan, M., Torrance, H., et al. (2003). *Watching and Learning 3: Final report of the external evaluation of England's literacy and numeracy strategies; executive summary.* Nottingham: DfES Publications.

Fetterman, D. (2001). *Foundations of empowerment evaluation.* Thousand Oaks, CA: Sage.

Fullan, M. (2001). *Leading in a culture of change.* San Francisco, CA: Jossey-Bass.

Galton, M., Hargreaves, L., Comber, C., & Wall, D. (1999). *Inside the primary classroom: 20 years on.* London: Routledge.

Galton, M., Simon, B., & Croll, P. (1980). *Inside the primary classroom.* London: Routledge and Kegan Paul.

Goals 2000: Educate America Act. (1994). P.L. 103-227.

Greene, J. (2006). Evaluation, democracy and social change. In I. Shaw, J. Greene, & M. Mark (Eds.), *Handbook of evaluation policies, programs and practices.* London: Sage.

Hall, C., & Thomson, P. (2007). Creative partnerships? Cultural policy and inclusive arts practice in one primary school. *British Educational Research Journal, 33*(3), 315–330.

Hall, K., Collins, J., Benjamin, S., Nind, M., & Sheehy, K. (2004). SATurated models of pupildom: Assessment and inclusion/exclusion. *British Educational Research Journal, 30*(6), 801–881.

Hamilton, L. S., Stecher, B. M., Marsh, J., McCombs, J. S., Robyn, A., Russell, J., Naftel, S., & Barney, H. (2007). *Standards-based accountability under No Child Left Behind.* Santa Monica, CA: RAND Education.

Haney, W. (2000). The myth of the Texas miracle in Education. *Education Policy Analysis Archives*, *8*, 41.

Haney, W. (2006, September 8–10). *Evidence on education under NCLB (and how Florida boosted NAEP scores and reduced the race gap)*. Paper presented at Hechinger Institute "Seminar for K-12 Reporters," Teachers College, New York.

Hargreaves, D. (1996). Teaching as research-based profession: Possibilities and prospects. *TTA Annual Lecture*. London: TTA.

Hayward, G., & McNicholl, J. (2007). Modular mayhem? A case study of the development of the A level science curriculum in England. *Assessment in Education*, *14*(3), 335–351.

Hillage, J., Pearson, R., Anderson, A., & Tamkin, P. (1998). *Excellence in research on schools* (DfEE Research Report 74). London: DfEE.

House, E., & Howe, K. (1999). *Values in evaluation and social research*. Thousand Oaks, CA: Sage.

Jackson, P. (1968). *Life in classrooms*. New York: Holt, Reinhart & Winston.

Julnes, P. L. (2006). Performance measurement: An effective tool for government accountability? *Evaluation*, *12*(2), 219–235.

Klein, S., Hamilton, L., McCaffrey, D., & Stecher, B. (2000). What do test scores in Texas tell us? *Education Policy Analysis Archives*, *8*, 49. Available at http://epaa.asu.edu/epaa/v8n49.

Lauder, H., Brown, P., Dillabough, J., & Halsey, A. H. (Eds.). (2006). *Education, globalisation and social change*. Oxford: Oxford University Press.

Linn, R. (2000). Assessments and accountability. *Educational Researcher*, *29*, 4–16.

MacDonald, B. (1974). Evaluation and the control of education. In R. Murphy & H. Torrance (Eds.), *Evaluating education: Issues and methods*. London: Harper & Row.

McNess, E., Triggs, P., Broadfoot, P., Osborn, M., & Pollard, A. (2001). The changing nature of assessment in English primary schools: Findings from the PACE Project 1989-1997. *Education 3-13*, *29*(3), 9–16.

Mehan, H. (1979). *Learning lessons: Social organization in the classroom*. Cambridge, MA: Harvard University Press.

Mercer, N. (1995). *The guided construction of knowledge*. Clevedon: Multi-Lingual Matters.

Morrow, R., & Torres, C. A. (2000). The state, globalisation and education policy. In N. Burbules &

C. A. Torres (Eds.), *Globalisation and education*. New York: Routledge.

National Commission on Excellence in Education. (1983). *A nation at risk*. Washington, DC: Author.

No Child Left Behind Act. (2001). Public Law 107-110; see: http://www.ed.gov/nclb/landing.jhtml

Office for Standards in Education. (2002). *The annual report of her majesty's chief inspector of schools 2000/01*. London: Author. Available at http://www.ofsted.gov.uk.

Office for Standards in Education. (2006). *The annual report of her majesty's chief inspector of schools 2005/06*. London: Author. Available at http://www.ofsted.gov.uk.

Pang, S.-K. N. (2003). Initiating organization change through school self-evaluation. *International Journal of Knowledge, Culture and Change Management*, *3*, 245–256.

Popham, J. (1987). The merits of measurement-driven instruction. *Phi Delta Kappan*, *68*, 679–682.

Resnick, L., & Resnick, D. (1992). Assessing the thinking curriculum. In B. Gifford & M. O'Connor (Eds.), *Future assessments: Changing views of aptitude, achievement and instruction*. Boston, MA: Kluwer.

Rizvi, F., & Lingard, B. (2006). Globalisation and the changing nature of the OECD's educational work. In H. Lauder, P. Brown, J. Dillabough, & A. H. Halsey (Eds.), *Education, globalisation and social change*. Oxford: Oxford University Press.

Shavelson, R., Phillips, D., Towne, L., & Feuer, M. (2003). On the science of education design studies. *Educational Researcher*, *32*(1), 25–28.

Shepard, L. (1990). Inflated test score gains: Is the problem old norms or teaching to the test? *Educational Measurement: Issues and Practice*, *9*(3), 15–22.

Shepard, L. (2000). The role of assessment in a learning culture. *Educational Researcher*, *29*(7), 4–14.

Singh, P. (2004). Globalisation and education. *Educational Theory*, *54*(1), 103–115.

Slavin, R. (2002). Evidence-based education policies: Transforming educational practice and research. *Educational Researcher*, *31*(7), 15–21.

Stake, R. (1973). *Program evaluation, particularly responsive evaluation*. Paper presented to "New Trends in Evaluation" conference, Goteborg University. Reprinted in W. Dockrell & D. Hamilton (Eds.). (1980). *Rethinking educational research*. London: Hodder & Stoughton.

Stake, R. (2003). *Standards-based and responsive evaluation*. Thousand Oaks, CA: Sage.

Stame, N. (2006). Governance, democracy and evaluation. *Evaluation, 12*(1), 7–16.

Thomas, G., & Pring, R. (Eds.). (2004). *Evidence-based practice in education.* Maidenhead, UK: Open University Press.

Torrance, H. (Ed.). (1995). *Evaluating authentic assessment: Issues, problems and future possibilities.* Buckingham, UK: Open University Press.

Torrance, H. (2003). Assessment of the national curriculum in England. In T. Kellaghan & D. Stufflebeam (Eds.), *International handbook of educational evaluation.* Dordrecht: Kluwer.

Torrance, H. (2006). Globalising empiricism: What, if anything, can be learned from international comparisons of educational achievement? In H. Lauder, P. Brown, J. Dillabough, & A. H. Halsey (Eds.), *Education, globalisation and social change.* Oxford: Oxford University Press.

Torrance, H. (2007). Assessment *as* learning? How the use of explicit learning objectives, assessment criteria and feedback in post-secondary education and training can come to dominate learning. *Assessment in Education, 14*(3), 281–294.

Torrance, H. (2008). Building confidence in qualitative research: Engaging the demands of policy. *Qualitative Inquiry, 14*(4), 507–527.

Torrance, H. (2009). Using assessment in education reform: Policy, practice and future possibilities. In H. Daniels, H. Lauder, & J. Porter (Eds.), *Critical perspectives in education.* London: Routledge.

Torrance, H., & Pryor, J. (1998). *Investigating formative assessment: Teaching, learning and assessment in the classroom.* Buckingham, UK: Open University Press.

Whitmore, E. (Ed.). (1998). Understanding and practicing participatory evaluation. *New Directions for Evaluation 80.* San Francisco, CA: Jossey-Bass.

PART VI

Educational Evaluation

Opportunities and New Dilemmas

The chapters in Part VI assess the future of educational evaluation, focusing on the challenges, tensions, and issues within and across educational evaluation perspectives in contemporary society. Taken together, these chapters define and elaborate new opportunities for educational evaluation and consider what answers there may be for foundational dilemmas, evaluation dilemmas with a new face, or new dilemmas. These dilemmas included issues such as addressing power relations in the evaluation context, relations between educational policy and evaluation, how to include stakeholders' perspectives, and providing useful information to programs.

Working within a Western framework, Lundgren (Chapter 28) examines the relations between educational evaluation and policymaking, highlighting shifts throughout the modern period including globalization effects on and within contemporary society. Among other claims, he contends that current political governance and the creation of markets are producing an "evaluating state" that is focused on developing competences instead of knowledge. Scriven (Chapter 29) considers the intersection between educational evaluation and technology. He catalogues in detail how recent and potential technological advances such as communications devices like simulcasts are likely to profoundly influence the future conduct of evaluation. After an in-depth analysis of globalism effects on education, Mathison (Chapter 30) considers how to counter prevailing educational evaluations characterized by efficiency, rational management, and performance-based accountability. Defining evaluation as critical to the heart of democracy, she makes the case for participatory, collaborative, and democratically oriented evaluation approaches as the vehicles for educational evaluation in service to the public interest. Using the volume chapters as the background, Cousins and Ryan (Chapter 31) provide a first step toward synthesizing relations within and across globalization and educational evaluation. In this final volume chapter, they identify and elaborate educational evaluation tensions in contemporary society that are reframing evaluation dilemmas such as evaluation purpose (e.g., improvement and accountability as dual purposes in evaluation). Closing on an optimistic note, Cousins and Ryan propose that diverse educational evaluation families are essential for discerning both important educational commonalities and local variations in making judgments about educational program quality in contemporary society.

CHAPTER 28

Evaluation and Educational Policymaking

Ulf P. Lundgren

The focus of this chapter is on how the relations between evaluation of education and policymaking have changed character over time. These changes are illustrated by concrete examples from both Europe and the United States. Hence, the interplay between evaluation and policymaking is discussed as part of educational history in general.

The concept of evaluation is a part of modernization (cf. House, 1980) and was formed as a mode to value alternative ways for school development. With the modernization of school systems, evaluation developed as an instrument for the political decisions on choice of alternative ways to organize education (Lundgren, 2003). With the expansion of education after the Second World War, evaluation became an element within educational planning systems to increase efficiency. Later, the efficiency motif for evaluations also included the need for control. With increasing globalization and international competition in the era of the cold war, new international instruments for evaluation were established within organizations such as the

International Association for the Evaluation of Educational Achievement (IEA) and later in the 1990s by the Organisation for Economic Co-operation and Development (OECD). The future history of evaluation is open, but tendencies point in a direction of using evaluations for increased control as a means to improve national competitiveness and bench-marking.

Evaluation and Modernity

Modernity grew out of the Enlightenment. Fundamental was the idea that economy and society will prosper if grounded on rational decisions. Perhaps the most condensed expression for this credo is the motto for the 1933 World Exhibition in Chicago: "Sciences explore; Technology executes; Mankind conforms." One essential feature of the modern society is the change from being chosen to make choices. The modern citizen was not born to a position in society. Each could create her or his own future and choose a life career. Rational choices demanded reliable grounds. Evaluations gave information for choice. To be able to compare and decide how well goals and criteria were achieved became with time a process of knowledge production. The concept of evaluation is, hence, deeply rooted in the paradigm of modernity.

With industrialization, with an expanding infrastructure, and with urbanization, a labor market was established. The values on this market were, to a substantial degree, given by education. The forming of democracies called for an education of the new citizens. It was in these transformations of ideas, thoughts, economies, and societies that a progressive conception of education was formed. In this new progressive thinking, the main purpose of education was perceived to produce the future, not to solely reproduce the past. Evaluation became a vital part of the progressive ideas. If education was to be developed by rational means, the results of education had to be evaluated. If the best methods were to be chosen, then alternative educational programs had to be evaluated.

With the progressive stream of thinking, shaped at the end of the 19th century and the beginning of the 20th century by philosophers such as John Dewey in the United States and Georg Kerschensteiner, Ellen Key, and Elsa Köhler in Europe, evaluations came to be of importance for the development of education generally and for each school specifically.

Together with his wife, Alice Chipman Dewey, John Dewey started an experimental school in 1896 at the University of Chicago, where 2 years earlier he was inaugurated as a professor of philosophy. The idea behind the experimental school was to both develop the school by evaluating various alternative ways to form curricula and methods of teaching and gain knowledge through the process of experimenting—*learning by doing*. Köhler, to take another example, created methods for classroom observations in order to construct systematic knowledge and experiences as a basis for school development (Köhler, 1936). Hence, evaluation became important as a method to value alternatives and to shape knowledge for school development.

Even if the progressive movements in the United States did not develop exactly in the same direction as progressivism in Europe, the interaction between the European movements and the American movement is clear:

> Progressivism in the U.S. began as a part of a vast humanitarian effort to apply the promise of American life—the ideal of government by, of, and for the people—to the puzzling new urban-industrial civilization that came into being during the latter half of the 19th century. (Cremin, 1964, p. viii)

The American progressive movement can be described as centered around the concept of community (Feinberg, 1985), whereas the European progressive movement was more related to the question of how to create a school in which the ethic and skills of work and civic life were to be taught—or to express it in the same way with slogans formed within the French progressive movement: "École active (The active school)" and "École par la vie pour la vie (Schools through life for life)."

The progressive ideas in practice developed in various ways depending on the soil in which it was planted. The political development of Europe after the depression—during the 1930s and 1940s—changed the direction of the development of education. The ideas of the progressive movement had no longer a ground. The authoritarian pedagogy was reinforced in many places, and the parallel school system strengthened. With fascism, the progressive ideas were oppressed. Köhler disappeared in one of the concentration camps. In the United States, the school tradition developed along other lines than the corresponding school systems in Europe. During the 1920s and 1930s, methods were developed for describing curriculum content and societal demands on curricula (Bobbitt, 1925). These ideas were further developed by constructing curricula where the goals were expressed in terms possible to evaluate (Tyler, 1950). The next step was then to develop taxonomies of objectives (Bloom, 1956). The consequence was that goals were expressed in test items.

After the Second World War, many European countries had to reconstruct and build new societal structures. New educational systems had to be formed and developed. Once again, a new citizen was to be educated, and for this education had to be democratic—not only fostering democratic citizens, but be democratic in the daily life of schooling. Education became a cornerstone in the building of the welfare society. It was a construction based on rational choices and thus evaluation.

Evaluation for Development of Educational System

Sweden provides a concrete example of how evaluation became an integrated part of the politics of education and the forming of educational policies.

At the beginning of the 20th century, there were in Sweden, as in many European countries, two parallel school systems: one public system and one academic system. There was no connection between these two systems. In practice, the academic line was chosen by the parents from educated and affluent homes. With the forming of the modern society, the main political question on education was how to construct a link between these two systems (i.e., the possibility of moving from lower to higher education). A solution was decided on in the 1930s, and after fourth or sixth grade, it was possible to move to a 5- or a 4-year-long academic line. However, the students who moved to the academic line were still children of families from the upper classes. The arguments for a common comprehensive school were raised with the argument that it would provide all children with the same opportunities. The argument against a comprehensive school was that the existing school constructed for ability grouping gave the best outcomes for individuals as well as for society. This discussion on the pro and cons of a comprehensive school system was not unique for Sweden.

Swedish school planning was centralized. The reform processes followed a well-established procedure. Parliament appointed school committees and commissions that investigated the current school situation and proposed reforms. The reports of these committees were published as official documents; remitted to various interested groups, institutions, and organizations; and presented for public debate. Using both the reports and reactions as a base, the Ministry of Education submitted a government bill.

The reforming of the school system started with the School Committee of 1940. The purpose of the School Committee was to get an overall view of future school planning and to suggest a 9-year compulsory and comprehensive school. Before the Committee had ended its work, a parliamentary Commission was called for in 1946.

The questions about a comprehensive school reform were intensely discussed. One way to solve the political problem, it was argued, was to have a period of experimentation during which various alternatives including new methods for teaching could be evaluated. A scientific answer would bridge the political opinions. This rational idea was expressed in the report from the 1946 School Commission in the following way: "Instruction must not be authoritarian, as it would be if it served a particular political doctrine, even if this doctrine were democracy's own. Quite the contrary, democratic instruction must be based on a scientific foundation." (SOU, 1948, p. 3; my translation)

An experimentation period started in 1950, and in 1962, the decision on a 9-year comprehensive school was taken. A series of small evaluations were carried out, but there was only one larger study—the Stockholm study—that showed small differences between a parallel school system and a comprehensive one (Svensson, 1962). This study was later followed up by a similar one—the Gothenburg study

(Bengtsson & Lundgren, 1969)—delivering more or less the same results. However, Dahllöf (1971) later showed in a reanalyses of the data from the Stockholm study that there were considerable differences between the systems. It took more time in the comprehensive system, compared with the parallel system, to reach the same results. This study by Dahllöf was the beginning of a theoretical development of models for evaluations and educational policymaking (Lundgren, 1985).

In the 1960s and 1970s, governmental bodies or programs for evaluation and the development of systems, including curricula and instruction, were developed. In Sweden, the central administrative agency, the National Board of Education, was instructed by the government that

> it shall see to it that education, as far as content and methods are concerned, continuously is renewed, developed and improved, keeping pace with the findings of research and with the developments within official and private administration, in the country's economic life and the labour market as well as in other areas of society. (His Royal Majesty's instruction; SFS, 1965:737 § 37, p. 4; my translation)

The prior example could have been Norway as well as Finland, where the reforming of the educational systems in the 1960s and 1970s followed the same pattern.

It is to be noted that this pattern for reforms was a movement from evaluation as a base for school development to evaluation as a base for system development (i.e., from policy programs in a context of micropolitics to policy programs in a context of macropolitics). This change seems to be linked to two lines of arguments. One was the development of the human capital theory as a way of planning and making education more effective and productive. The other was an insight about the growing globalization, even if the term *globalization* in the first phase was not used. This tendency is perhaps better labelled as *internationalism*. The cold war and education as an instrument to strengthen research capacity in science is another part of this new international context.

Human Capital and Investments in Education

The public sector that has expanded the most during the latter half of this century (leaving aside defense) is the educational sector. Behind this expansion, we can identify at least three factors: an increase in demand for education and thus for educated manpower, an increase in the level of aspiration, and the population growth.

Educational systems in the Western world have only partly been able to cope with this expansion. Traditions and various types of system factors have delayed the adaptation of the educational systems to the new demands and challenges. To explain that statement, it is necessary to see the alterations of education behind this development. During the last two centuries, the goals of education have increasingly been to reproduce knowledge of importance for production and for one's preparation as a citizen. Education has developed in such a way that it has been an investment for the individual as well as for society.

Besides the objective fact of population growth, there are two basic changes in society that have been of decisive importance. One is ideological and the other is economic in nature.

The ideological factor refers to ideas and ways of thinking that move toward a change in social structure. These ideas are expressed by those who demand education, as well as by those who decide about the dimension and direction of education. The argument is that education is perceived as being something valuable in itself and a democratic right to receive.

The economic factor refers to the relationships among a given economic structure, the progress of production, and investments in education. After the Second World War, the economic factor was given increasing importance in planning and expanding educational systems.

The rationale behind such an approach was the economic-political goal of rapid economic progress. During the 1950s and 1960s, several economists could show correlations between investment in education and economic growth. It can be assumed that the ideological factor, in the last instance, is to be understood as shaped by economic circumstances.

In educational economics, two main theories were formulated. The first is the theory of human capital, which was formulated during the 1950s and 1960s and became one of the foundations for educational expansion (Mellander & Håkansson, 2006; Waldow, 2007). This assumed that it was possible to show that the share of economic growth, which did not result from manpower, capital, and tools, could be explained by the level of education (i.e., it provided the means of explaining the so-called rest factor of the GNP). To quote one of its founders: "Truly, the most distinctive feature of our economic system is the growth in human capital" (Schultz, 1961, p. 17).

The other theory can be labelled the filter— or sorting theory. According to this view, the aim of education is not, first and foremost, to refine manpower but to sort subjects. At the risk of oversimplifying, this theory can be expressed in the following way: Education aims at sorting students according to their ability. An education system is, then, a "filter" for sorting and an information system for those who receive the products (Arrow, 1974).

The first of these two theories can be seen as an important tool that had an influence on the planning of education during the expansion period. The expansion was an effect of new demands and new expectations voiced about education. Economic development in the post-war period allowed for rapid expansion. The second type of theory had a bearing on the question of ability grouping and comprehensive school systems.

The economics of education gave a theoretical frame for interpretations of results from system evaluations. In the beginning of the reform period, the questions of interest for policy decisions were: Is organization A better than organization B? In other words: Does a comprehensive school system produce better or equal results than a parallel school system? The last question is now again in focus in, for example, Germany (Artelt et al., 2001). This time the question is raised as a consequence of the results from international tests (Meghir & Palme, 2005).

When the decisions on forms for organization were taken, the political questions became much more complicated. It was no more a question of better or worse, but rather what measures have to be taken to increase productivity and effectiveness and what are the consequences of changes in curricula and instruction? In the first phase, economic theories took a role in giving explanations.

Political Governing and Evaluation

On October 4, 1957, the first satellite—Sputnik 1—was launched by the Soviet Union. In April 1961, the first satellite with a man on board—Gagarin—was sent into space. In May of that year, President Kennedy promised that, by the end of the decade, the United States would land a person on the moon. This space war had consequences for education. The productivity and efficiency of the educational systems in the United States and most countries in the Western world were criticized. Especially in mathematics and science, the search for new teaching methods was intensive. Cognitive theories got a renaissance as a ground for curricula and instruction. New demands on evaluation were articulated. We can see it evident in Senator Robert Kennedy's arguments, in the beginning of the 1960s, that all federal reforms had to be evaluated. The background was the launching of the "Great Society" by President Johnson. The consequences were the hectic expansion of evaluation technology. In 1964, the first international comparison of school results was carried out. It concerned 13-year-old children, and the subject was mathematics. The result of this study was demands on curriculum reform and evaluation in many countries. An association for international achievement studies was constituted (International Educational Achievement).

To evaluate and monitor national educational systems, the methods used needed to be adapted to large-scale data surveys. To evaluate entire systems, the questions in the next phase became more complicated than the question of whether A is better than B. The new questions needed broader theoretical frames for formulating policy strategies than what economic models delivered. They could not build on studies of the relation between goals and outcomes alone. To deliver explanations, they had to build on more complicated theoretical models relating the conditions or frames for the process, the teaching and learning processes, and the outcomes (i.e., explanations to be used in monitoring educational systems; Granheim, Kogan, & Lundgren, 1990).

During the expansion period, political administration of reforms was relatively straightforward. Decision makers ascribed to the system well-articulated goals defined according to priority and provided resources that, it was assumed, would guarantee their attainment. The various sectors appeared as possible instruments for reaching political goals. If administration failed, the blame was often ascribed to shortcomings in the original plan. These problems, it was felt, could be solved at the next stage. Moreover, by systematic use of evaluations and research, an accumulation of knowledge was assumed to prevent such failures.

During the 1970s, new models for evaluation were born, and there was a heated debate on methods. Existing methods were criticized for being limited to quantitative techniques, and new qualitative methods were used in evaluation. However, systematic evaluations of entire educational systems were not carried out even if statistical studies directed toward the overarching goals of reforms showed that their effects on equality and equal opportunities had not been reached. There are, of course, many reasons for this state of affairs. One explanation may be found in the changes of methodological approaches. It is difficult to use qualitative methods alone in evaluations of national education systems.

During the 1980s, the quality of education came into focus. In the 1990s, it seems that the earlier dominating concept in educational policy—equality—lost the prefix "e." Now quality and quality assurance became the focus of educational policy programs. The quality notion is linked to evaluation, which expanded the evaluation field. It has its background in changes of educational systems in the 1980s with a change in political governing (Goldsmith & Newton, 1988). Choice of schools demands more visibility concerning the quality of schools. Decentralization increases the central control by means of evaluation and quality assurance (Haug & Schwandt, 2003).

In the 1980s, the demand on comparability of national educational systems was discernable. Within the Organisation for Economic Co-operation and Development (2007), an indicator project was initiated. This project has incorporated tests (PISA) now used in more than 50 nations. These and other international comparisons also have brought in a scent of national pride.

Problems in political governing visible in the late 1970s and 1980s were responded to by decentralization reforms and/or reforms intending to create an educational market. These changes have meant that the instruments for political governing have changed focus from governing the frames for education and schooling to governing by demands on results—thus, governing by evaluation and quality assurance. This, in its turn, means that tests and large-scale surveys are in focus. To some extent, this has been stimulated by the expansion of systems for international comparisons. To once again return to Sweden as a case, we can see that the national evaluation that has been built during the 1990s yields a quantity and quality of information never before seen. In its turn, education has been more transparent and open for public discussions. Results from international comparisons get space in media and influenced the political agenda.

France and Germany are two examples. In France in 2000, a committee was established on national evaluation (Haut Conseil de l'évaluation de l'école [High Council for evaluation of schools]), and in 2003 the president gave the task to a commission to organize a national debate on education (Commission du Débat national sur l'avinir de l'École, 2004). The results of these works have placed educational policies in general, and evaluation policy in particular, high on the political agenda (Forestier & Thélot, 2007). In Germany, the results of the first PISA survey have been striking. The national debate and the criticism of the school system have been heavy. The impact on the financing of educational research and evaluations is clearly visible (Artelt et al., 2001; Bonnet, 2002).

It can be argued that the consequence of changed policies has been a return to centralization through exercising political governing by assessment instruments and evaluations (Waldow, 2007; Weiler, 1990). One consequence is that tests limit outcomes by narrowing goals for education, and thus in the long run they inhibit new developments in the systems.

Within this frame of national evaluation and quality assurance is a space for direct central political governing in the form of earmarked resources. To the extent that earmarked resources are linked to results, the centralization of governing has a much better efficiency than ever before. The use of evaluations and quality assurance makes the systems transparent and opens it up for public pressure on reforms.

Consequently, the traditional models for political governing of education have changed character—the politics of education is the politics of evaluation, and the reforming state has been transformed to an evaluating state (Kellaghan & Greaney, 2001).

The Evaluating State

At the beginning of the last century, the demands on education were evident. The new modern world called for new and pragmatic knowledge. Education was linked to value in the labor market. We are in a similar situation today,

but the demands are, of course, different in character. Human capital theories are renewed (Organisation for Economic Co-operation and Development, 2000). Even so, we have to confess that there is little knowledge of what exactly brings quality to education and how these qualities enhance societal development. Life-long learning is, for large groups, a necessity, but we still have limited knowledge of how to construct the content and processes for life-long learning. To develop education in a new economic context calls for new knowledge and new modalities of political governing. One important change concerns the relationship between national policymaking and the control of the national economy. Production has changed character. Capital is moving from being located in tools and machinery to focusing on human knowledge and competence. To move enterprises in which the main substance is human competence is easier than moving tools and machinery. With this increasing dependence on the international economy, the possibilities of managing the national economy and the incentives for growth have changed in nature.

The transformation from a labor market structured by industrial production to a labor market structured by service production, circulation of products, reproduction, and above all the new information technology creates new demands on reforms. It can be argued that the traditional organizations constructed to handle the economy and the political economy of modern industrialized society is no longer suited to handling a late-modern society. These organizations could not mobilize support for action. Accordingly, state institutions such as schools could not attract and build on the interests of the clients or users. Governance has to take other paths.

Globalization gives new arguments for reforms. Curricula must be changed to promote competitive values on an intentional knowledge market. In a rapidly changing world, where the structure and access to knowledge is constantly altering, the content of curricula is difficult to identify and decide on. The question of what the content of education should be is moved over to the question of what competencies should be promoted.

It is to be noted that this is a change in terminology. What was in the 1960s discussed in terms of *knowledge* is today discussed in terms of *competencies*. The latter term indicates more of an ability than acquired knowledge. This change in terminology is also to be understood in relation to the development of tests, where the measurement of various forms of literacy is focused. The development of tests within the PISA project of OECD has here been of importance. The indicator project within the OECD to work out educational indicators initially used the results from IEA studies as outcome indicators. The problem that arose was the late access to outcome data. The IEA came to include more and more nations, and before data could be used by the OECD, the time between collection of data and the publication of results became rather long. This was one of the reasons for the OECD to run its own test system—PISA. The criticism against the IEA studies was that it favored some national curricula. In 1994, the OECD had conducted a survey concerning adult literacy. The experiences of this test development were used within PISA by focusing competencies and thus use curriculum neutral tests as much as possible.

The international impact of the PISA studies has been striking. This impact is visible in the national policies of those countries involved. In several countries, the aim for national educational reforms has been to be one of the best on PISA (Schriewer & Martinez, 2003). The change of evaluation directed toward competencies also is seen in the change of perspectives of learning, with a focus on situated learning and contextual competencies.

In summary, the interplay between evaluation and policymaking over a century is a change from evaluation as valuation of alternatives directed toward local policy and local school development. With the expansion of education and the reforming of modern society, evaluation became a part of national reform policy. A criticism of statistical methods for evaluation

reinforced the development of qualitative methods and a new relationship to school development and local policy programs. With the dilemmas of governing, the institutions of modern societies' decentralizations and/or the creation of markets with privatizations came to occupy the politics of education. These changes promoted evaluations related to control. Changes in production toward more knowledge production and globalizations came to focus on international competitiveness. International surveys and comparisons among national systems meant that evaluations took the role of delivering the objectives for education. The concept of competence and literacy came in focus as instruments for political governing. The history of the future seems to be a history in which educational reforms are more and more alike over nations driven by comparative studies of outcomes.

References

Arrow, T. (1974). Higher education as a filter. In K. G. Lumsden (Ed.), *Efficiency in universities*. New York: Elsevier.

Artelt, C., Baumert, J., Klieme, E., Neubrand, M., Prenzel, M., Schiefele, U., et al. (2001). *PISA 2000 Zusammenfassung zentraler Befunde: Schüler-leistungen im internationalen Vergleich* (PISA 2000 Summary of central findings: Pupil achievements in international comparison). Berlin: Max-Planck-Institut für Bildungsforschung.

Bengtsson, J., & Lundgren, U. P. (1969). *Utbild-ningsplanering och jämförelser av skolsystem* [Educational planning and comparisons between school systems]. Lund: Studentlitteratur.

Bloom, B. S. (1956). *Taxonomy of educational objectives: Handbook 1. Cognitive domain.* New York: David McKay Company.

Bobbitt, F. (1925). *How to make a curriculum.* Boston: Houghton Mifflin.

Bonnet, G. (2002). Reflections in a critical eye (1): On the pitfalls of international assessment. Knowledge and skills for life: First results from PISA 2000. *Assessment in Education, 9*(3).

Commission du Débat national sur l'avinir de l'École. (2004). *Les Francais et leur École. Le miroir du débat* [The French and their school. The mirror of the debate]. Paris: Donod.

Cremin, L. A. (1964). *The transformation of the school. Progressivism in American education 1876-1957.* New York: Vintage Books.

Dahllöf, U. (1971). *Ability grouping, content validity and curriculum process analysis.* New York: Teacher's College Press.

Feinberg, W. (1985). *Reason and rhetoric: The intellectual foundations of twentieth century liberal educational policy.* New York: Wiley.

Forestier, C., & Thélot, C. (2007). *Que vaut l'ensignement en France?* [Where is education in France going?]. Paris: Éditions Stock.

Goldsmith, M., & Newton, K. (1988). Centralization and decentralization. Changing patterns of intergovernmental relations in advanced western societies. *European Journal of Political Research, 16*(4).

Granheim, M., Kogan, M., & Lundgren, U. P. (1990). *Evaluation as policy making. Introducing evaluation into a national decentralised educational system.* London: Jessica Kingsley Publishing Company.

Haug, P., & Schwandt, T. A. (2003). *Evaluating educational reforms. Scandinavian perspectives.* Greenwich, CT: InfoAge.

House, E. (1980). *Evaluating with validity.* London: Sage.

Kellaghan, T., & Greaney, V. (2001). The globalisation of assessment in the 20th century. *Assessment in Education, 8*(1).

Köhler, E. (1936). *Aktivitetspedagogik* [Active pedagogy]. Stockholm: Natur och Kultur.

Lundgren, U. P. (1985). Frame factors and the teaching process. In T. Husén & T. Neville Postlethwaite (Eds.), *The international encyclopaedia of education. Research and studies* (Vol. 4, pp. 1957–1962). Oxford: Pergamon Press.

Lundgren, U. P. (2003). The political governing (governance) of education and evaluation. In P. Haug & T. A. Schwandt (Eds.), *Evaluating educational reforms. Scandinavian perspectives.* Greenwich, CT: InfoAge.

Meghir, C., & Palme, M. (2005). Educational reform, ability and parental background. *American Economic Review, 95*, 414–424.

Mellander, E., & Håkanson, C. (2006). Transparency in human capital policy: A prerequisite for European economic growth. In L. Oxelheim (Ed.), *Corporate and institutional transparency for economic growth in Europe* (pp. 117–153). Amsterdam: Elsevier.

Organisation for Economic Co-operation and Development. (2000). *Knowledge management in the learning society.* Paris: Author.

Organisation for Economic Co-operation and Development. (2007). *Education at a glance.* Paris: Author.

Schriewer, J., & Martinez, C. (2003). *World-level ideology or nation-specific system reflection? Reference horizons in educational discourse. Cadernos Prestige* (Final Series 3/7). Educa: Lissabon.

Schultz, T. W. (1961). Investment in human capital. *American Economic Review, 51*, 1–17.

SOU. (1948). *1946 års skolkommissions betänkande med förslag till riktlinjer för det svenska skolväsendets utveckling* [Report of 1946 School Commission with suggestions for the main lines for the development of the Swedish school system]. Stockholm: Ecklesiastik Departementet.

Svensson, N.-E. (1962). *Ability grouping and scholastic achievement.* Stockholm: Almqvist & Wiksell.

Tyler, R. W. (1950). *Basic principles of curriculum and instruction.* Chicago: The University of Chicago Press.

Waldow, F. (2007). *Ökonomische Strukturzyklen und internationale Diskurskonjunkturen: Zur Entwicklung der schwedischen Bildungsprogrammatik, 1930–2000* [Economic structure cycles and situation-discourses: The development of the Swedish programs for education 1930–2000]. Frankfurt am Main: Peter Lang.

Weiler, H. (1988). *Education and power: The politics of educational decentralization in comparative perspective.* Stanford, CA: Stanford University, CERAS School of Education.

Weiler, H. (1990). Decentralisation in educational governance: An exercise in contradiction? In M. Granheim, M. Kogan, & U. P. Lundgren (Eds.), *Evaluation as policymaking.* London: Jessica Kingsley Publishers.

CHAPTER 29

Technology and Educational Evaluation

Michael Scriven

Introduction

The original version of this chapter discussed three ways in which the volume themes of educational evaluation and globalization were related to technology. The three topics were: (a) an evaluation of education about technology, (b) an evaluation of educational technology, and (c) a survey of evaluation technology. That exercise took this author—an enthusiast about all three—25,000 words, nearly three times the allotted space. After serious but unsuccessful efforts by the editors and myself to condense that effort to a manageable size, the editors felt that the part they most needed from me was the third one in that list, and it takes up almost all that follows. But they also allowed me a few pages to set this in the original context because that has some effect on the reader's understanding of the topic presented, and to mention that the original paper is now available online for those interested.[1] So there follows a short synopsis of the sections on technology education and educational technology—without the detailed supporting argument. These two brief sections

can be skipped by those simply interested in the current and emerging ways in which technology assists or can assist evaluation, which are found in the third section.

Education About Technology

A technology is commonly understood to be the body of artifacts in use by a society, including all functional artifacts and usually—although these are sometimes excluded—aesthetic creations (i.e., art objects), and the skills and knowledge for producing and maintaining them. Artifacts are generally defined as made objects, although selected found objects put to practical use (e.g., the often treasured anvil and pounding stones used for cracking nuts and grains) presumably qualify as tools and so should probably be included (fire and branch nests are other examples).

Technology has been around since long before the Stone Age, although the artifacts from that period are the earliest ones that survived in any numbers until now, unlike most of their wooden and unfired clay predecessors.[2]

It follows that technology antedates science by more than 2 million years, and hence defining it as applied science—the definition in the *Oxford American Dictionary* and many others—is absurd.

There are other reasons besides history for rejecting this definition and the point of view it reflects. Technology is an *essentially* different enterprise from science in aims, products, and methods. Its aim is to produce or improve *things and the ways to make and maintain them* and its method is *physical construction*; the aim of science is to increase and refine our information about and understanding of the world, so its products are new *facts, classifications, explanations, predictions, and theories*; and so its method is *thinking/writing/calculating*. Technology antedates and includes spoken language, and science is virtually impossible without a written one. Most science is impossible without instruments (i.e., technology). Most technology, even now, even in the space program or the computer industry, required no scientific knowledge to develop. The atomic bomb is just one type of case, not the paradigm.

The failure to understand these and other radical differences between science and technology has been fostered, in the United States and many societies influenced by it, by those pushing science education as the way to develop a technologically competent society. The result is the complete absence of any serious education about technology in the general education curriculum. (In the UK, by contrast, there is a well-developed technology curriculum in the general secondary education curriculum; see http://www.dcsf.gov.uk/index.htm.) Competent curriculum evaluation would have exposed this blunder 70 years ago and would at least be fighting to change it now. But it has been silent on this disaster perhaps because its experts have not had any serious education about technology.

In the historical eye blink when science and technology have both existed—one fifth of 1% of technology's history—each has made substantial contributions to the other, but even in this era, major breakthroughs in technology (e.g., steam engine, car, phone, radio, electric lighting, personal computer, spreadsheet, giant online databases, etc.) have all been produced or mainly developed by people with no scientific (or engineering) training. Hence, the idea that a science- and mathematics-based education is essential for developing new technologists is not only ill-based, but has been a major factor in deterring young women from going into technology, which is a huge handicap to its development and to their options and earnings.

General education about technology has virtually nothing to do with technician training, which we do have, generally treated as a low-status path for those not smart enough for the science/mathematics track. This attitude is not only stupid snobbery but close to suicidal for a society that achieved its high economic status—and can only hope to maintain it—through technology, not science. A society whose citizens have to vote on many crucial issues about technology (e.g., funding alternative energy sources) and one that desperately needs to grow next-generation technologists (especially, e.g., in the United States, with its restrictive immigration policies) must educate its citizenry to understand the nature of the beast on whose back it rides.

Specifically, we need three types of education about technology: (a) general education for all students to provide the citizen with the ability to *use* consumer-oriented technology (e.g., computers) and to *know* enough about general technology to *vote* intelligently on issues that affect the support and development of current and future technologies (e.g., the space program, solar/wind/hydro/wave energy alternatives), (b) specialized training of technicians to maintain sophisticated artifacts (e.g., automobiles, medical equipment), and (c) specialized education for technologists (i.e., those who wish to or are working at refining or inventing technologies) that parallels but does not duplicate training for scientists. Now we look at some of the consequences when that education is absent.

Educational Technology

To illustrate the serious consequences of technological illiteracy, and exactly what it is about technology that most people lack understanding of, I provide several examples, of which one is a case study in educational technology—the development of computer-assisted instruction (CAI). This is a participant observer report on 50 years of development from B. F. Skinner's (1958) teaching machines to the publication of *Oversold and Underused: Computers in the Classroom*, the recent negative evaluation by Cuban (2002). Cuban is entirely correct in arguing that CAI was oversold (i.e., prematurely claimed to be a cure-all) and that most of its classroom use has had little payoff. I argue that the latter culminates half a century of unsound technology assessment by evaluators as such, as well as almost everyone else in education, comprising a major tragedy. For it misses the main point, which is that CAI is probably a major breakthrough, although still needing intensive further development to become a great educational technology. This is a tragedy for many students in the United States, those not well served by the present schools, but even more for those in many other countries where CAI offers the best hope for achieving general literacy because they cannot now and probably never will be able to afford the traditional schools and teacher corps.

The mistake was, at its heart, the mistake of thinking that a technological invention works like a scientific discovery. That is, once announced and published, the big event has occurred, and we can stand back and evaluate its consequences. That is not how technology works. When Hero of Alexander got the idea for a steam engine in the first century AD and made a working model, it had zero practical utility. It took 1,600 years to get to industrial payoffs. With Skinner's teaching machines and its descendants, we had a working model with good payoff from the beginning, but that does not mean we had something that would pay off where big gains were most needed, in the weakest

public schools. There were barriers to that payoff in the form of resistance by teachers, parents, and administrators for specific reasons—and some further materials development costs (nothing that could not be overcome, but there had to be leadership, and work done, and funding, to overcome them).

To someone familiar with technological development in the medical, biological, or computer fields, these were routine types of problems, and not tough ones. But in education, the leadership was working on the wrong paradigm; it thought, implicitly at least, that good inventions would prove themselves. This is a sad story and, of course, a controversial version of it. My hope is that we will take another look at it. In my view, doing so can save thousands and perhaps millions of lives, in this and other countries, from the deadly doom of known failure to be what they could have been.

Evaluation Technology

Now we come to the much less controversial—but not entirely uncontroversial—topic of what technology has done and, more interesting, what new technology might do for evaluation, particularly educational evaluation. Of course, evaluators are just professionals working like millions of others at their desks and computers and black or white boards or projection screens, so all the hardware and software technologies that have transformed those activities apply. But there are one or two items, even there, that in my view are somewhat underappreciated, so some of what follows will not be news, only highlighting of the news. For those of you who are well informed about what is new in technology, there will not be many surprises. But perhaps putting it all together will jog your thinking in one way or another and get you started in a slightly new and worthwhile direction, so here we go.

The great technologies that transformed education are, of course, above all the spoken and written languages. In educational evaluation, local knowledge means understanding these technologies and their contemporary embodiments and their use where appropriate. Today this includes understanding the means for storing and distributing (in the limit, globalizing) what is said or written with an educational function (intended or not)—that is, the book and other print media, discs and memory chips, tape, data warehouses, sound systems and intercom systems, phone, radio, television, and the Internet (e-mail, texting, podcasting, posting, etc.). So one aspect of educational evaluation, the local knowledge aspect, involves understanding—at the level required for being able to evaluate the educational use of—these technologies (the store and forward technologies). Another involves a similar level of understanding of education-specific technologies such as CAI, language labs, school of the air, Sesame Street, and programmed texts; and a third involves understanding curricular treatments—actual or ideal—of technology in general, as discussed earlier. Now, let us be more specific.

Evaluation is a complex process and one that is challenging for evaluators and anxiety-provoking for evaluees, and there are many different accounts and varieties of it. But the aim of this chapter is not to advance a particular account of it; it is simply to talk about how technology affects and might affect it. Even professional evaluation, some of which we hope was provided in the preceding section, is not a new practice, only a new profession. It is no more than *systematic critical appraisal using specialized tools and knowledge*—of facts, methods, and relevant standards—appropriate to the category of entity being evaluated.

"Critical appraisal," although a loose description, does not cover all varieties of professional analysis, such as purely statistical analysis or content analysis. It refers to analysis aimed at *determining the merit, worth, or significance* of the entity appraised (here called the evaluand). The need for specific professional training in evaluation emerged when the need for a specialized level of training became clear in order to deal with an increasing number of difficult

areas, such as large-scale program evaluation and quality control in manufacturing, and the increasing number of demands for detailed answers in those areas.

Evaluation as a profession began 1,000 years ago, with the emergence of the Japanese proto-guild of sword evaluators (www.wikipedia.com)—a category of product evaluation—but only became self-conscious in the mid-20th century when program evaluators in the United States formed the first association, a process since replicated in more than 50 other countries.

Of course, there were many people doing professional-level evaluation before then, even in the limited field of education, both in specialized areas such as student testing and in book reviews in educational journals. But evaluation of that kind was seen, correctly, as part of all professional approaches, not recognized—as was also true—as part of an extensive network of activities that had a substantial common logic, and much shareable practical wisdom. Rendering that logic and wisdom explicit has created the possibility of substantial improvement through self-critical study, the same process that had previously led to the emergence of science and technology as professional fields from anecdotal and artisanal activities. The development of evaluation from a profession into a discipline, as it is today, has in fact resulted from continued application of that self-appraisal and self-improvement process.

The questions of present interest that naturally arise at this point are: What effect has technology had on this newborn discipline? What effects might emerge in the future? How does this relate to globalization? A list of suggestions follows, some explained here and some without detailed explanations when these can be found in appropriate references.

Analytic Tools

Technology has provided many *quantitative* analytic tools for the social sciences that are often of great importance in evaluation, especially software tools for computers used in statistical analysis (SPSS, SAS, etc.), and in financial analysis (Excel, etc.). These have become part of most professional evaluators' toolkits, and their existence is part of what justifies talking about a profession of evaluation.

Many analogous tools for so-called *qualitative* data analysis exist, although most of them are tools for converting certain kinds of data (often text or interview notes) into quantitative form, and dealing with it thereafter, and so might better be called hybrid or conversion software. They have a cadre of enthusiastic users and developers, but their net benefits are less easily demonstrated than is the case with the quantitative software. This is because the skill required for coding is still considerable, and the resultant data do not easily lead to firmly establishing significant conclusions not suggested by an equally skilled pass at the original material. Still, the results do sometimes turn up and confirm new hypotheses. A related example has come up in the multiyear Heifer International external evaluation project, where we have recently developed some customized tools in Excel that integrate qualitative and quantitative data and that facilitate conversion of the combined data into graphical format (Scriven, 2009).

Much more is to be hoped for in this category as the logic of qualitative data and pattern recognition software is further developed. For example, recent work on refining the modus operandi approach to causal analysis suggests that this kind of approach might be programmable (see Scriven, 2008). Various attempts are also being made to facilitate causal analysis by sophisticated statistical techniques that may move us farther along that path.

Searchable Storage

Technology has provided ways to store project data in electronic databases that are easily and quickly searchable and can be designed to facilitate the production of useful types of reports, including graphical reports. Some tools assist in

suggesting novel implications of data (e.g., programs that automatically run randomized selection of variables for interaction testing). The most interesting future possibilities here are perhaps the three-dimensional databases that exploit the human brain's high sensitivity to pattern recognition. Simple examples display data points' clustering as spatial density in three dimensions selected from a dozen or more options. This approach also has been applied to concept mapping and to mapping searchers' choices in Google information space (www.google.com).

Data Display

Taking the last suggestions further in their own right, programming technology facilitates the use of graphical representation that can improve presentations (PowerPoint, etc.) as well as facilitate understanding and the perception of significance and implications of data. Although pseudo-three-dimensional (3D) graphics are common enough, and can be illuminating (as well as sometimes confusing), it is easy enough to make true 3D, if that repays the trouble of distributing special glasses. We are still about 2 years from true 3D with lenticular screens (no glasses) for home video; it may appear in movie theaters by mid-2009. Possibly more promising is the creation of videographics—showing 5- or 10-second videos to illustrate trends in a fourth dimension (time), which can be done with present technology. Although this has only speculative payoff for report presentation, its value is immense in another context, which is discussed next.

Photographic Advances

Photographic techniques for presentation of case study content and contexts, including video interviews, are important because qualitative methodology has convincingly made the case for the importance of visual context in interpreting oral exchanges, through seeing both body language and environmental characteristics.

There are more exotic evaluation tasks where this kind of equipment is invaluable (e.g., with infrared filters and motion sensors for detecting night visitors or guard movements).

Camera technology has taken several recent quantum jumps, each with some payoff for evaluators using or considering photographic media:

1. Several shirt pocket digital cameras in the low hundreds of dollars range were released in 2008 that take good short video clips with up to 5x telephoto lenses, excellent for portraits and also for making contextual vistas possible as backgrounds to audio records, which some of these cameras also can make. For example, the Canon SD 890IS (released 7/08) runs 6.5 oz, is the size of a pack of cigarettes, but with 10MP resolution, and it has a 5x (optical, not digital) stabilized telephoto lens.

2. The current small camcorders, in the same price range, will fit in a jacket pocket, can do high definition (HD), and record in stereo. They won't give you high-quality stills, but they make it possible to be unobtrusive and unassisted in getting motion records of service delivery or customer activity at a program site.

3. If you want a camcorder that is for the *shirt* pocket, simple to operate (e.g., fixed focus 1m to infinity), cheap ($100 or $150),[3] low-quality video (okay for e-mailing, looks poor on your TV screen), but remarkably good in poor light, there is currently just one: the Flip Mino. For crisis/disaster assistance evaluation, a growing specialty with its new topical interest group in The American Evaluation Association (AEA), or for our Heifer Project evaluations in remote villages from the Tibetan mountains to the arid forests of Peru, this will be invaluable for documenting claims of excellent or defective practices, shelters, animals, or supplies.

4. In another performance category, the latest Casio camcorder (the Exilim EX-F1) enables you to take ultra-high-speed video at a previously impossible price point (under $1,000),

critical for some kinds of evaluation (e.g., evaluating athletic performance for judging or training purposes, evaluating self-defense skill training, or evaluating high-speed machinery/ordnance).

5. The Nikon D90, released in mid-August 2008 at around $1,000, is a rather bulky digital single lens reflex (DSLR) with a number of firsts for qualitative evaluators using photographic equipment: It is the first SLR with full video—it allows 80-minute HD videos with interchangeable lenses, something you can't get on a camcorder under $20,000. It has auto focus and extreme low-light capabilities (up to ISO6400) for still photography, with professional quality detail in the shots.

6. A week or two earlier, another breakthrough was announced by Microsoft, and it is free. This is software called Photosynth, and it allows anyone with any digital camera to do something that can be of great importance immediately in product and property evaluation, and of some importance immediately in personnel and some program evaluation; of great value in training evaluators when used for situation simulation and testing; and other applications will quickly suggest themselves. What it allows is spherical panoramas with unlimited detail. For example, a real estate agent could stand in front of a property on the Kona coast in Hawaii and take about 300 pictures with any ordinary DSLR, using tele, normal, and macro lenses, and send them to Microsoft, which will "photosynth" them for you. Then you—the prospective buyer, in Manhattan—can project the result on a screen and zoom in to almost any level of detail on the garden, the façade of the house, the birds in the coconut palms overhead, the ants in the turf at your agent's feet, the surfboards on the distant beach, or the whales spouting miles out to sea. If you want the closest thing to being there (with your binoculars), you can have it in depth. It beats the heck out of a postcard—especially in the Sistine Chapel.

Text Processing

We should not fail to acknowledge the benefits for evaluation report writing of word processing programs, with the attendant spelling and grammar correction options plus instant dictionary/thesaurus/encyclopedia lookup and near-instant translation of short passages in foreign languages, already in Word 08. The use of hypertext—cross-references built into documents so that one can link any point instantly to other locations relevant to the same point such as definitions, encyclopedias, photos, or fast-breaking news sites on the Web—is still rare but can be useful especially in text and reference works. Voice annotation is available now, and voice recognition software, with the release in summer 2008 of Dragon Naturally Speaking version 10, is now at an extremely high level, far ahead of any of the three or four available competitors. It will now work quite well with accented voices, even without the speaker reading some training passages as previously required, and it can handle editing commands easily so that users with limited manual dexterity are able to dictate faster than anyone can type and with low error rates—one error per page is a common report from users after some experience, and that is well under the error rate of good typists. It must be noted that it will not work for recording interviews—it can only handle one speaker at a session because it heavily relies on an individualized database of their pronunciation. Interview and focus group transcription will probably first arrive with a rotary switch that the operator uses to indicate who is talking, but eventually will replace that with faster identification via intonation.

The holy grail of development here, for the evaluator working overseas, is the multilingual simultaneous translator; a simple version is available now, with a vocabulary of a couple of thousand words and phrases in 12 languages. However, handling continuous speech will require at least 5 more years, even with the heavy military funding currently said to be available

(justified as avoiding the use of foreigners as translators and the attendant security risk). It is a great value to have at the moment—online translation of nonsecure documents and tapes at moderate prices, with fast turnaround for an extra charge.

Checklists

A key tool for evaluators is the humble checklist (e.g., the Program Evaluation Standards). Its logic is not trivial,[4] but its utility is almost universal across evaluation fields of application. The software for formulating and improving checklists, originally an extension of word processing software, is worth a moment's attention. This is an area of special interest for me as the author of a book on word processing software and hardware (Word Magic), and the source of the inspiration—so he says—that led a student of mine, Ted Holm, to invent hypertext.

Idea Processors

It may seem odd to suggest that something now seen as passé be reconsidered seriously, but I want to recommend it partly because it is useful far beyond the domain of checklists. I think we should not accept the commercial abandonment of what used to be called "idea processors." Some remnants of these are still available as outliners (e.g., in Microsoft Word) and as stand-alone applications from many sources (search on concept processors or "reviews of outlining software" for up-to-date references), but the one most people know about, in Word, lacks several features found in some of the full-blown idea processing software when it was popular. One of these is available in some of the independent products: graphical representation of the outline. This, especially the spoke-and-hub design, has some advantages over the linear design of standard outliners because it gives subheadings equal status (as spokes all starting from the same hub; i.e., the main heading) instead of the usual convention of placing them in a hierarchical list, whose order suggests but does not normally represent their relative importance. Another feature, perhaps dropped because no one wanted to admit that it was useful, was the shuffling option that, without losing the original arrangement, would randomly reallocate subheadings under headings, which quite often suggests new connections.

Informational Search

On the pure fact-hunting issue, there are now vast informational databases and repositories containing multiple databases that are instantly available and make access to comparative and baseline educational data either feasible or at least much faster and easier.[5] There are also general knowledge databases (Google, Yahoo, Wikipedia, etc.), specialized educational databases (nces.ed.gov, etc.), and—still underused by evaluators—the huge image databases, of which PicLens is by far the most spectacular and versatile. These are now rapidly acquiring general question-answering capability (ask.com is slightly in the lead here), and we may expect better voice-driven interfaces shortly, although some human-serviced ones are currently available without charge (e.g., from Google). In the text or voice version, the big new advantage we are looking to get by summer 2009 is having the computer capable of being interactively interrogated to focus search questions quickly. The big gain here is expected to come from enabling the computer to ask the requestor for specific types of clarification in the disambiguation process.

Communications Technology

There have been, and continue to be, frequent large jumps in communications ("comms") technology beyond the telephone—which today means the cell phone (or, for remote field work, the satellite phone)—and radio that now make it possible to reach anyone who does not block access (and many who think they *have* blocked access) almost instantly and almost without cost (i.e., Skype and its six imitators). They can be reached with voice contact and video, so important in serious efforts to benefit from face-to-face (F2F) verbal exchanges. Developments in comms technologies carry with them many implications for evaluation practice:

1. They make it possible to use online interviewing—and hence detailed case studies—to expand the F2F accessible population as an alternative to traveling to visit the interviewees, at much lower cost, thereby facilitating cross-cultural representation (and, to some degree, expanding it to different linguistic groups with simultaneous translation).

2. They also make it possible for the evaluator to confirm, expand, and refine reports and accounts to a degree not previously possible and still not fully exploited. For example, in doing international aid evaluations, in 2010 we will be able to send illustrated draft reports to country field staff for checking *and* round-table online video discussion without appreciable delay in delivering the final report and with a significant increase in validity.

3. Webinar and many competing brands of software also make possible group meetings with consultants and focus groups with participants from all global locations, an almost certain way to improve critical dialogue and information/perception collection, hence many evaluations. It also seems likely that evaluators will be able to create some useful improvements in Delphi technique by using new comms capabilities. For example, we might develop something we could call "fast Delphi" with a spatially extended group, meeting several times within a day, to avoid the slow speed of traditional Delphi.

4. Online surveys are, of course, now frequent and becoming a subspecialty with almost as much known about good and bad practices as in classical focus group methodology; upgrading

these to video status will be a natural extension, useful in special circumstances.

5. The addition of true 3D to the video presentations possible over the Internet or via satellite will make truly competitive something that is currently only marginally effective—the use of distance consulting and interviewing and small-group conferencing at a level of realism that will make it hard to justify real travel to meetings or consultations, especially in view of the carbon footprint dimension of evaluation. Of even greater importance in personnel evaluation, the addition of 3D will make it possible to avoid the cost of travel (and the handicap, for candidates, of not traveling) to interviews for jobs. It will also significantly enhance an approach that is already fairly functional—online teaching, which is covered in the next item. For example, teaching an evaluation approach such as Appreciative Inquiry or Participatory Evaluation via text or lecture is, students report from analogous cases, *hugely* improved if HD, life-size demonstrations by leading exponents can be added (with no-glasses 3D in 2010 and beyond). The ultimate instructional version of these, to anticipate the next main section, will be fully interactive (i.e., will feature Q&A sessions where avatars [graphical simulations of the experts] answer free-form questions).[6]

6. Looking once more into the near future, a reasonable bet is that the next large payoff from technology in the comms area is already in place in some of the large phone survey shops or at least an approximation to it. This is the extension of the call waiting feature already available for domestic phone service, which now shows you a picture of the person calling as well as their name. The extension will provide every professional interviewer with a screen full of details about the person being interviewed in a survey, along with customized prompts for the next questions.

7. With regard to the list of comms-based technological jumps for evaluation, it is now becoming clear that we could come close to running shadow conferences in which at least the main speakers and a selection of others at the big professional conventions could be put online as simulcasts for access by those unable to attend. Because these annual meetings in evaluation are of great importance in keeping up with the field, it seems clear that making an effort to narrowcast a slice of them would show an appropriate concern to globalize evaluation; we presumably believe this would be a benefit to those who are interested but unable to afford the trip.

8. We are also approaching the era of Web 2.0, the mythical redesign of the Internet of which some tendrils are beginning to appear (e.g., cloud computing—the use of online applications instead of software located in each computer). This will inevitably involve highly personalized sample selection, where the pattern of Web and phone use by subjects will be used to select them. Integrated into cell phones, as is already the case, and given that we are now approaching the point where 50% of the world's population has a cell phone, the Web will clearly become the primary vehicle for survey work, including F2F phone interviewing.

Online Instruction/E-Learning

It seems fair to say that we have now reached the point with online teaching where we can claim "parity on balance" with onsite teaching, of evaluation in particular. That is, there are enough advantages to the online approach to offset the undeniable loss of some advantages pointing in the other direction, such as the greater inspiration of direct contact with the instructor and with classmates, at least for many students.[7] Advantages for the online mode include:

1. access to instructors who cannot be afforded in person or who are unwilling to travel;

2. access to the instructional process by students who cannot afford the time or travel costs, or physical difficulties, of attending a lecture in person;

3. those who cannot schedule the times the instructor is available in person;

4. the ability to delay, replay, or slow down/speed up the presentation to suit the learner's preferences;

5. the ability to pull together a wider range of students, where diversity of occupation, income, or age is important for the student and class discussions; and

6. the ability for the presenter to edit and improve a presentation, piece by piece, until it becomes the best possible production by that presenter.

This one use of educational technology today (i.e., "e-learning" or remote instruction), which will be further enhanced—for many people—as we move into true 3D, means that we now have a genuine alternative to classroom and campus-based education, from pre-kindergarten (for some children at least) to the professional development domain. (A later section of this chapter discusses the ramifications of this for instruction at all levels in all subjects.) Here we just stress that the globalization of evaluation is made possible by this single aspect of technology because fast updating of remote countries' professionals is now possible in a way not previously done during decades of slow percolation. A new twist in authoring instructional materials will be viewable on commercial TV in late 2008: Using a technology from a cutting-edge video game designer (Electronic Arts), it will be possible for instructors to interact with 3D simulations of leading thinkers or players in professional fields (e.g., Socrates, Deming, Michael Phelps), who can answer questions from a phone line and have their avatar speak the lines—or demonstrate the move—on screen.

Spatial/Graphical Analysis

Graphical information systems (GIS), 3D global positioning systems (a.k.a. GPS/WAAS), and radio-frequency identification (RFID) are now available and beginning to be used in evaluation. They make spatial/geographical analysis possible, which in cases such as evaluations of crime-control programs (e.g., random patrol patterns) can be helpful in locating success and failure areas. The third dimension can also be valuable in dealing with high-rise crime in housing developments, fire in office buildings, and rescue efforts in mountainous areas. Working in central Africa, on both coastal and central countries, the application that occurs to a technophile evaluator is the control of illicit logging and poaching of game animals by using a combination of GPS, GIS, and RFID. Tagging a substantial random sample of trees and animals would make tracing their movements as easy as using LoJack with cars in big cities. It would be an easy application of a mid-priced technology with high potential for monitoring and arresting criminals as well as its deterrent effects.

Portable Computers

Almost everything mentioned so far depends on the computer, especially the personal computer. It is the tool that uses the software and, for that matter, is often used to create it. The evaluator almost has to have one or, increasingly these days—especially if he or she does any field work—more than one. On this front, the latest breakthrough is the emergence of what is now being called the "netbook," the ultraportable successor to the notebook computer. These were inspired by the quest for the $100 computer by the One Laptop per Child project initiated by Nicholas Negroponte at the Massachusetts Institute of Technology, culminating in an advanced solar-powered small computer at around $200 (with price reductions to come). These are now also available commercially for $200 to $400 from Acer (the Aspire), Dell (the Mini Series), and the first of the commercial entries, the Asus PC. They all have 9- to 12-inch screens, and most have (sometimes optional) small RAM (magnetic memory) drives instead of hard disks, hence no moving parts to break down or wear out. They either omit Windows/Mac operating systems, keeping the price down by using an open-access operating system and browser to access the Internet (hence, netbook), or the fairly cheap Windows XP. With a weight under 3 pounds (1.5 kg), they provide the evaluator with a real computer in the field with almost negligible portability problems. Current smartphones also have keyboards, but the keyboards are so small they cannot be used extensively. Eventually, voice input will make the keyboard less important, but one cannot—or does not always want to—speak out loud what one is inputting, and the smartphones are not much good for spreadsheet or graphics work.

The future here lies with nanotechnology, and it is clear that it is only a matter of time before the computer will be the size of a pack of cigarettes or, using a thinner form factor, be stitched into a hat lining or a shirt collar, with the optional keyboard being printed on electrophoretic paper, folded to 3 × 5 inches, and unrolled when needed. The step beyond that, already in the planning stage, means implanting the computer subcutaneously behind the ear and learning to type on a keyboard projected as a transparent film in the field of sight by injection into the optic nerve on (eventually mental) request. Hence, the computer eventually becomes integrated with and simply an augmentation of the human brain (i.e., an artifact working to provide virtual enlargement of cranial capacity; the "prosthetic computer").

Maintenance Applications

For everything that has been mentioned so far, including all the payoffs for evaluation, there is always the shadow hanging over them of possible breakdown, maintenance, and the need for upgrading. Here, many of the software applications mentioned can come to their own rescue—to some extent at least. Not only do we now have full-scale remote control of our computers so that we can allow the remote online

technician to take over its operation and do the trouble-shooting directly, but when a part has to be installed—which cannot be done remotely—or diagnosis requires actions outside the control of the computer, or the computer will not work at all, then the phone line and a laptop, personal digital assistant (PDA), or mobile phone is increasingly able to transmit video of the problem machine or screen to the distant technician. Thus, using these computerized enhancements to evaluation is not as risky as it used to be—not that it is 100% bulletproof.

Publication Access

Finally, we come to publications. It is still the case that scholarly discourse and research is much more influenced by what is published in scholarly journals and books than by material that is online. Additions to these influential media are still largely inaccessible to most of the educated people in the world, including—to an increasing extent, as evaluation expertise is globalized—professional evaluators in other countries because neither they nor their libraries can afford more than a small sample of relevant professional publications. This is especially important to new disciplines such as evaluation because the regular educational system, worldwide, is not yet geared up to provide evaluation skills and tools to its mainstream students. For some time, access to these new tools, with their increased powers of resistance to economic exploitation and inappropriate cultural globalization, was an elite privilege. This situation with respect to *current research and discussions* was in marked contrast to the situation with respect to knowledge at a more general and slightly less current level, where Wikipedia and its imitators, as well as Google/Yahoo and so on, have made access to much of the corpus available without charge. The traditional repository of such knowledge, exemplified by the Encyclopedia Britannica, now takes a back seat—not to be entirely dismissed, but clearly much less important because so often out of date in the accelerating world of research, and so expensive. Two new approaches—one from Google—hybridize with classical encyclopedias by using referees, experts, and volunteers, and some hybrid eventually may be the best option for the scholar.

The economic justification of the old system in the professional area has vanished and could swiftly change still more toward open access. Technology has removed the original cost barriers to access to evaluation publications, for example, by introducing high-speed scanners and copiers, online publication, and the commercially workable, publishing-on-demand (POD) model, which almost completely eliminates inventory and overrun costs. However, social inertia, commercialism, vested interests, lack of sensitivity to overseas needs in the professional associations, or a combination of these has delayed anything like the maximum possible helpful response for an inexcusable period.

The difference between the professional associations is, however, perhaps more notable than the average situation. Close to the bad end of the scale, we would have to list the American Educational Research Association (AERA), where:

1. the recent increase in membership fees has put them well over the average annual income in many countries ($120);

2. their key publication in the methodological area, the third edition of *Complementary Methods*, has recently been issued in hardbound at $175, paperback at $90; and

3. access to their online discussion forums has now been restricted to members.

In other words, this is a fairly complete closeout of most professionals in poorer nations from discussions and developments in educational research, an important lifeline to improving their own quality of education and standard of living. Not incidentally, this cost barrier discriminates sharply against students, despite some discounts for them, and against less well-funded college faculty and libraries in the United States and elsewhere.

It should be noted that an important exception to this situation in educational research has been created by the *pro bono* work of Gene Glass, who started a free online journal 15 years ago[8] and later added a free online journal of reviews in the same field.[9] (His example was part of the stimulus for me to do something similar in evaluation.)

The AEA has done much better. Its hyperactive online discussion forum is open to all, and it has supported a small effort at low-cost book publishing. It is now easy to publish useful books in evaluation for sales in the low hundreds at about $12 per copy,[10] but they are still usually made available at about 5 times that price and sometimes 10 times that price. Similarly, it is not too hard to make journals available free online with minor subsidies,[11] but they are commonly only available at about the same multiple, either via expensive memberships or via high subscription or per-article charges. It is true that the low-cost versions are sometimes not up to the highest commercial or university press standards in terms of copyediting, but the content is widely thought to be comparable, on balance, in quality and utility, which is arguably a defensible trade-off at the price. It seems clear that a thoughtful strategy would require most professional associations to employ something such as these options.

But there is a gap in the professional publications offerings, and it is an important one. We would greatly benefit from a library of minipresentations by leading proponents of particular approaches to our subject—in our case, evaluation, but the point is equally valid in political education or woodturning—and minidemonstrations by their choice of actors and subjects. Done for a big screen with HD and stereo sound, perhaps adding 3D in a couple of years, this library would make possible a huge jump in the effectiveness of teaching and training. Ideally, the professional associations should assume responsibility for assembling these and managing them as a nonprofit effort, with rental/sales fees for CDs (and perhaps online access via Amazon/Apple/Audible) just covering the administrative costs and grants and association membership fees covering start-up and add-ons.

Public Participatory Evaluation

Finally, we come to a technological phenomenon that is both important and highly evaluation-specific. I call this public participatory evaluation (PPE), and it was never predicted. Indeed, when it appeared, its failure was predicted with an equal lack of validity. The term refers to a range of phenomena exemplified by Wikipedia (and its many imitators) and the online feedback ratings offered by many large retailer and news services (e.g., Amazon, BBC, CNet, TravelMole). It involves three factors: (a) near-zero supervision; (b) online reporting, often highly evaluative, on a highly publicized website with million-plus daily hits (there are now many websites that were set up for and are devoted entirely to this kind of amateur evaluation) and (c) dealing with both controversial factual issues and often controversial estimates of merit. The recent highly credible run-off between Wikipedia and the Encyclopedia Britannica,[12] which resulted in a tie, is a fair indicator of the general level of success of PPE. Established evaluation sources (e.g., Consumers Union) have been slow to respond to PPE, with consequent loss of credibility, validity, and utility, and the relevant evaluation associations will need to respond or risk the same consequences. PPE has a wider political range than conventional evaluation, as is discussed next.

Conclusion

The preceding list is not claimed to be complete, but it is perhaps enough to indicate that, taken in conjunction with what was said earlier about online teaching, technology has produced a huge accelerant to the facilitation, extension, application, and internationalization of evaluation, if not to globalization in its less attractive aspects.

The main conclusion for our purposes in this chapter is this: Technology is as crucial to evaluation as it is to education, and hence doubly crucial to educational evaluation. Understanding its importance requires understanding technology, and understanding its potentiality for evaluation is arguably a professional duty in evaluation, as it is in teaching, and indeed in any profession. In particular, understanding its potential importance for giving the world a high level of expertise in evaluation is a mirror of the main theme of the chapter—a case of largely unfulfilled potential. Our country has done marvels in donating food to help meet global needs, and it has done considerable damage in blundering efforts to give them (or withhold) technology. The reforms due to the appropriate technology movement have corrected much of that tendency,[13] but the errors of omission now need to be addressed, and using technology to improve access to professional evaluation materials should be a top priority.

Notes

1. "The Decline of the Best" is available at http://homepages.wmich.edu/~mscriven

2. Allowing for bone and wood tools, and shaped gourds in use before there were any handmade (as opposed to found) flint or stone tools, probably pushes the birth of technology back beyond 2.5 million years, not just the 2 million years since the earliest hominid, *homo habilis*, used stone tools. Including skilled collection and manipulation of found objects (stones, bones, branches, fire, and snow) would push it further (www.wikipedia.com).

3. All dollar figures henceforth are in US$.

4. See the collection of checklists for evaluators in specific fields, and papers on checklist methodology, at wmich.edu/evalctr/checklists.

5. NCES.com, the National Center for Education Statistics, is the key location for these.

6. The first version of this was seen on ESPN beginning in mid-September 2008. It uses an ingenious slice of the latest video game technology (i.e., Electronic Arts' Sports Virtual Playbook) to place commentators in the same space as virtual simulations of real football players to illustrate plays.

7. One problem with distance education for credit purposes has not been surmounted in any of the commercial packages, although I have now developed a solution. This is the "authentication problem," a.k.a. control of the widespread problem of cheating by the use of surrogates to take the tests and do the term papers. (The extent of this is often denied, but all the hard evidence available points the other way. In evaluating this situation, keep in mind that the use of ringers at the leading onsite universities [in the United States, at least] also appears to be extensive in large classes, so this is not a ground for condemning online college degrees as inferior.) The solution is a little complex, but it uses video and randomly timed online visits by Skype to ask the students questions about their tests and papers with a government-verified photo on a split screen next to the direct feed on the instructor's desk.

8. *Educational Policy Analysis Archives* (epaa.asu.edu).

9. *Education Review* (edrev.asu.edu).

10. I produce the Monograph Series for the AEA at $16 (paperback edition), but that includes $4 for AEA publications funding (and $4 for the author). By choosing titles for saleability rather than disciplinary importance, as most publishers do, one could do break-even publishing at $12. This is economically possible because AEA announces the books (i.e., free advertising), and the editor donates his time as manager, editor in chief, and so on, and no doubt others would be willing to do this.

11. I established and publish the *Journal of MultiDisciplinary Evaluation* online, free (jmde.com),

with the only subsidy being the small cost to the Evaluation Center at Western Michigan for hosting the website. All labor is donated, which is a valuable experience for the students who provide most of it. This journal joins many others (there are now more than 1,000 refereed journals) in the open publishing movement and is further facilitated by useful software funded by the Canadian government and made available without charge to all free online refereed scholarly journals.

12. This competition was set up and run by *Nature*, and a typical report is at Silicon.com, dated 12.16.05. This and other reports on the same event are on Google (search on Wikipedia vs. Encyclopaedia Britannica).

13. See Wikipedia and thefarm.org.

References

Cuban, L. (2002). *Oversold and underused: Computers in the classroom.* Cambridge, MA: Harvard University Press.

Scriven, M. (2008). A summative evaluation of RCT methodology and an alternative approach to causal research. *Journal of MultiDisciplinary Evaluation, 5*(9), 11–24. Available at www.jmde.com

Scriven, M. (2009). *Journal of MultiDisciplinary Evaluation.* Available at www.jmde.com

Skinner, B. F. (1958). Teaching machines. *Science, 128,* 91–102.

CHAPTER 30

Serving the Public Interest Through Educational Evaluation

Salvaging Democracy by Rejecting Neoliberalism

Sandra Mathison

The public's interest is manifest in many contexts, but one that touches almost every member of society is schooling. Therefore, the institution of schooling is a key context for serving the public's interest, but schools are a complex and contested venue for both special and public interests. Simultaneously, schools are opportunities to create passive, docile workers *and* to create critical, independent-minded thinkers and doers.

The public interest (or common good, as it is sometimes called) is something most people agree is worthy, but the devil is in the details. For some, the public interest is served when there is the greatest good for the greatest number, a classic utilitarian perspective. For some, the public interest is served when all individuals are free to do as they please as long as they do no harm to others, a libertarian perspective. For some, the public interest is the elevation of every member of a group, a communitarian perspective.

In this chapter, I argue that globalism, and neoliberalism particularly, is a primary influence on conceptualizations of schooling and education; as a consequence, it influences what we consider to be quality schooling and education, including the means we employ to discern quality in education. This chapter analyzes the impact of globalism on education and thus on the evaluation of education. I suggest how evaluation of and in schooling might alternatively challenge or resist the values inherent in neoliberal conceptions of schooling and thus promote democratic values, including education for the benefit of all and a governmental role that arises from the interests of the people rather than capital.

Understanding the Global Context

When we speak of global contexts, we may invoke a common worldwide concern with say the environment—a common collective concern that we care for the natural resources on earth. This is what Nye (2002) refers to as globalism—that is, that the world is characterized by economic, military, environmental, and social connections across nations and continents. These connections are manifest in mutual relationships such as, for example, the dependence on low labor costs in Asia to provide affordable goods for U.S. and European markets. Often the term *globalism* connotes a mutually satisfying interconnected relationship—Asian workers are gainfully employed, and a desire for affordable consumer goods in other parts of the world is satisfied.

The political theory underlying economic globalism is neoliberalism. To bring stability to the unstable and conflict-riddled world after the Second World War, organizations with global reach (the United Nations, the International Monetary Fund, and the World Bank) were created. Many nations experienced affluence and economic growth during this period, but a global increase in unemployment and inflation during the 1970s disrupted this sense of progress resulting in increases in political power for socialist and communist parties in Europe and even the United States (Harvey, 2005). It is this populist threat to the economic elites in both capitalist and developing countries that is commonly understood to have ushered in neoliberalism, a theory of political economic practices that promotes individual entrepreneurial freedom, frees capital to move across time and space by eliminating regulations, and assigns the state the role of facilitating competitiveness and privatization (Harvey, 2005). The cover of David Harvey's book, *A Brief History of Neoliberalism*, shows portraits of Ronald Reagan, Deng Xiaoping, Augusto Pinochet, and Margaret Thatcher. This book cover signals the worldwide reach of neoliberalism, a set of economic practices that have simultaneously taken hold in a wide range of contexts, including developed and imperialist countries such as Britain and the United States, emerging democracies such as Chile, and communist countries such as China.

Neoliberalism is suspicious of democracy, in either a majoritarian or populist sense. In either sense of democracy, the collective good is viewed as potentially inconsistent with individual rights and liberties, and thus neoliberals favor governance by experts and elites, usually elites with capital. In practice, neoliberalism looks different in different regions of the world and is in large part not effective at achieving its outcomes—both the U.S. and Chinese governments have had to use deficit financing to support their militarism, consumerism, and infrastructure development (Harvey, 2005). Neoliberalists would claim that neoliberalism has been imperfectly applied, but others might suggest that the free market ideology has run up against the resistance of other ideologies. Still, the rhetoric of neoliberalism underlies many educational reforms around the world, including how we determine whether education is effective and efficacious.

Educational Reforms Driven by Neoliberalism

Although this chapter deals most especially with the manifestation of globalization on evaluation in elementary and secondary education in the United States, there are similar educational reforms around the world that are provoked by neoliberalism and have seen a focusing of evaluation on single measures, standardization, and breaking down of the sanctity of national boundaries for the sake of the global economy (Ross & Gibson, 2007). The following examples illustrate the common thread of neoliberalism in educational reform around the world and across educational levels.

The Reinvention of European (and Latin American) Higher Education

Higher education in Europe and Central and South America is being reinvented to be more competitive in the global market (in both attracting students and producing graduates) and to increase the mobility of labor across national boundaries. The Bologna Declaration of 1999 was signed by the European ministers of education to facilitate this intent and called for the development of "comparable criteria and methodologies" to promote quality assurance. The objectives of these higher education reforms are: "1) to facilitate the speedy entrance of educated professionals into the job market through shortened degrees; 2) to enhance the cross-border mobility of students and job seekers; and 3) to increase the competitiveness of European higher education internationally" (Sedgewick, 2003). Two key features of the Bologna Process are the creation of a common two-tiered degree structure (bachelor's and master's degrees) already typical in Britain, the United States, Australia, and Canada, as well as the introduction of tuition fees, the latter change contributing significantly to a conception of education as a private good (Altbach, 2008).

This sort of universal accreditation movement promotes individual accomplishment, mobility, and economic benefit, the student and graduate as commodities that can be attracted for the mutual benefit of individuals, regions, and nations.

International Comparisons of Achievement

All evaluation involves comparisons, and so the fascination with international comparisons of educational achievement makes some inherent sense. Studies that make such comparisons (e.g., Program of International Student Assessment [PISA], Trends in International Mathematics and Science Study [TIMSS], Progress in International Reading Literacy Study [PIRLS], and the International Assessment of Educational Progress [IAEP]) are also motivated by the perception that schooling plays a critical role in global economic competitiveness, and so we need these indicators to take the pulse of national economic competitiveness (Bracey, 2008).

The neoliberalist claim is that the availability of data about schooling practices and outcomes around the world will result in the adoption of approaches from around the globe that "work" (Puryear, 1999). Such cross-national comparisons are meant to motivate political action at the national level:

> Convinced that poor-quality schools are a major bottleneck to economic growth and social advancement, [heads of state] are charging ministers of education with reform agendas and providing them with political support. Often, they are aided by technocrats from sectors of government other than education, particularly ministries of finance and planning, or from nongovernmental think tanks, whose views of educational policy are based firmly on modern economic theory. (Puryear, 1999)

No Child Left Behind

No Child Left Behind (NCLB), the manifesto for educational reform in the United States, is always described as bipartisan, but it is a substantial collaboration among politicians, at the federal and state levels, and coalitions representing corporate interests (Mathison, Ross, & Vinson, 2006). The rhetoric of NCLB suggests that schools will finally be held accountable for the success of each and every child, but the legislation also supports privatization (through tutoring provided by for-profit businesses and by encouraging parents to take their children elsewhere if their school is "failing") and the standardization of teaching and curriculum. This 2001 reauthorization of the previous *Elementary and Secondary Education Act* focuses on a number of required outcome measures, including testing of all third through eighth graders in reading and mathematics and the disaggregation of test scores by subgroups of students (e.g., by ethnicity, race, gender, and special needs). For the first time, federal funding to local educational authorities is tied to participation in the mandates of NCLB and clear demonstrations of academic progress.

Neoliberalism and the State's New Evaluative Role

It is important to understand that neoliberalism defines a role for government—it is not an ideology that rejects governmental intervention. Whereas classical liberalism simply rejects the state, neoliberalism accepts and fosters a role for the state.[1] Corporate CEOs, politicians, and bureaucrats work together to promote and sustain the ideology's core values.

> [N]eo-liberalism has come to represent a positive conception of the state's role in creating the appropriate market by providing the conditions, laws and institutions necessary for its operation.
>
> In the shift from classical liberalism to neo-liberalism, then, there is a further element added, for such a shift involves a change in subject position from "homo economicus," who naturally behaves out of self-interest and is relatively detached from the state, to "manipulatable man," who is created by the state and who is continually encouraged to be "perpetually responsive." It is not that the conception of the self-interested subject is replaced or done away with by the new ideals of "neo-liberalism," but that in an age of universal welfare, the perceived possibilities of slothful indolence create necessities for new forms of vigilance, surveillance, "performance appraisal"

and of forms of control generally. In this model the state has taken it upon itself to keep us all up to the mark. The state will see to it that each one makes a "continual enterprise of ourselves" . . . in what seems to be a process of "governing without governing." (Olssen, 1996, p. 340)

The New Evaluative Role of the State

In part, the state is assigned the responsibility of constructing and sustaining the rhetoric that fosters the neoagenda. DeJarnatt's (2003) analysis of the rhetoric of school reform in Philadelphia illustrates how a set of values that suggest limited government intervention can best be manifest with specific and strong government intervention:

> The reform forces use the rhetoric of choice and parental empowerment dear to the authoritarian populists and the privateers but the reforms themselves have been imposed with minimal choice or input by parents, students, or teachers and the market has been imposed by the state not chosen by any parent or student. Instead the changes have been dictated by the neoconservative[2] state bureaucracy, guided by an unquestioned belief in the value of uniformity and high-stakes standardized testing. (p. 33)

Gutmann (1999) defines three models of the state's role in education: a "family state" model, where the state controls education; a "state of families" model, where parents are vested with responsibility for education; and a "state of individuals" model, where individual choices are made possible without prejudice for any perspective. Although the neoliberal rhetoric of educational reform suggests a "state of families" perspective, for example, with the claim that parents are a child's first teacher and will be empowered by accountability, in reality the implementation of this agenda employs a "family state" theory through the construction of an image of failing schools that can only be saved by state-controlled accountability primarily based on student assessment.

Education may be a local prerogative, but often the regional or federal government is uniquely positioned to demand compliance through particular approaches to evaluation by threatening to withhold funding or support from those who do not comply and succeed. In the United States, the withholding of Title I money (i.e., money meant to support those who are academically disadvantaged because of poverty) is the federal government's leverage. The neoliberal agenda depends on this state intervention to support the rhetoric of choice and quality. Without the governmental power to demand common indicators for making choices, the neoliberal preference for private, charter, and other school choice options simply does not work.

Additionally, the state, through its power of surveillance and specialized knowledge, has taken on a role of providing evaluative information to the public about what is good and right. This is sometimes confined to programs the government funds, such as the U.S. Office of Management and Budget's system for evaluating and publicizing whether government-funded programs work. *Expect More* (http://www.expectmore.gov) offers to tell the public which programs are performing effectively and ineffectively, as well as those about which the jury is still out. Other government resources reach beyond government-funded programs to let the citizenry know what works. The best example of this is the *What Works Clearinghouse* (http://ies.ed.gov/ncee/wwc/), created in 2002 by the U.S. Department of Education's Institute for Educational Science "to provide educators, policymakers, researchers, and the public with a central and trusted source of scientific evidence of what works in education." In both cases, the government assumes the role of telling the public what the best choices are.

There are, of course, private nongovernmental agencies that offer similar services to the public, such as SchoolMatters, a product of Standard

and Poors, which is owned by McGraw-Hill Companies—one of the biggest producers of educational tests. "SchoolMatters gives policymakers, educators, and parents the tools they need to make better-informed decisions that improve student performance. SchoolMatters will educate, empower, and engage education stakeholders." In Canada, the Fraser Institute publishes school rankings for half of the country's provinces based on provincially mandated student achievement tests based on their contention that, "An educational market, one in which parents choose their children's schools and schools compete more freely for students, will produce better educational results for more students." CanWest Global Communications, the company that owns many Canadian daily newspapers, implicitly supports this contention by publishing newspaper inserts with these "reports" of the quality of schools prepared by the Fraser Institute and relegating alternative views to the op-ed pages.

The New Role of Evaluator as Technician

This government as evaluator role coheres with neoliberalism's governance by experts and Chomsky's (1997) "spectator democracy," a society in which a specialized class of experts identifies what is good and manufactures consent for the populace. Educational evaluators become technicians in this environment, carrying out the tasks associated with managing, administering, and reporting student assessment data. For some evaluators this is a positive sign of focus and unity, whereas for others it is stepping away from true evaluation—that is, using multiple criteria, indicators of performance, with an eye to all consequences of education (Mathison & Muñoz, 2008).

This technician role carries over to what are accepted as appropriate evaluation methodologies. Although there is much debate, the U.S. government has indicated a preference for funding randomized clinical trials or regression discontinuity designs. This expectation is outlined in the *Identifying and Implementing Educational Practices Supported by Rigorous Evidence: A User Friendly Guide*, published by the U.S. Department of Education (2003).

> Well-designed and implemented randomized controlled trials are considered the "gold standard" for evaluating an intervention's effectiveness, in fields such as medicine, welfare and employment policy, and psychology. This section discusses what a randomized controlled trial is, and outlines evidence indicating that such trials should play a similar role in education.

Few, if any, educational evaluations have been of the sort suggested by the U.S. government, and indeed much of the theoretical and practical work in educational evaluation since the 1960s has been directed to creating different evaluation methods and models of evaluative inquiry (not just borrowed research methods) that answer evaluative questions—questions about feasibility, practicability, needs, costs, intended and unintended outcomes, ethics, and justifiability (Mathison, 2008). The methodological mandates described earlier put aside the unique contributions evaluation can make and demand compliance with particular methodologies driven by particular epistemologies.

The professional evaluation community is not of a single mind about the claim that randomized clinical trials are the gold standard for educational evaluation (Donaldson & Christie, 2005). Although this is simplistically portrayed as revival of the quantitative-qualitative debates in evaluation, the situation is more complex. The methodology of choice is a reflection of underlying values (House & Mathison, 1984). Just as progressivism was the value context up to the late 1970s and even early 1980s, neoliberalism has been the value context that brings educational evaluation to where we are today in the United States and, indeed, in most parts of the world. Schools are a business, education is a product, products should be created efficiently, and one should look to the bottom line in making decisions. Implicit in this neoliberal perspective are values (and rhetoric) that motivate action. The most obvious of these values is that accountability is good, that simple parsimonious means for holding schools accountable are also good, that choice or competition will increase quality, and that it is morally superior to seek employability over other purposes of education. Econometrics drives thinking about what these simple parsimonious means are—thus the appeal of single indicators such as standardized tests.

Neoliberalism relies on specialized knowledge and silencing or at least muting the voices of the populace. Unlike many approaches to evaluation that are built on the inclusion of stakeholders in directing and conducting the evaluation, experimental design is controlled by experts and stakeholders (especially service providers and recipients) are conceived of more as anonymous subjects and less as moral, sociopolitical actors.

Educational Evaluation Simplified to Student Assessment

The educational reform package promoted within a globalized world is large and complex, but often evaluation of education is simplified to a single outcome and a single measure, often the assessment of student learning in a few academic areas. This key element is controlled by the government and thus is a means for controlling the institution of schooling. Tests are therefore a government-mandated intervention that creates, even if primarily rhetorically, market conditions and focuses the content of schooling on certain knowledge and values.

But the question is: How does the assessment of students cohere with neoliberal ideology? The idea of assessment-based accountability is deceptively simple:

Students take tests that measure their academic performance in various subject areas. The results trigger certain consequences for students and schools—rewards, in the case of high performance, and sanctions for poor performance. . . . If students, teachers, or schools are chronically low performing, presumably something more must be done: students must be denied diplomas or held back a grade; teachers or principals must be sanctioned or dismissed; and failing schools must be fixed or simply closed. (Elmore, 2002)

The assumption is that the threat of failure will motivate students to learn more, teachers to teach better, educational institutions to be better, and the level of achievement to continue to rise.

Neoliberalism, more generally, is

the desire to intensify and expand the market, by increasing the number, frequency, repeatability, and formalization of transactions. Market forces are also intensified by intensifying assessment, a development especially visible on the labor market. The use of specialized software in call centers has provided some extreme examples: the time employees spend at the toilet is measured in seconds: this information is used to pressure the employee to spend less time away from the terminal. Firms with contracts are also increasingly subject to continuous assessment procedures, made possible by information technology. For instance, courier services use tracking software and GPS technology, to allow customers to locate their packages in transit. (Treanor, n.d.)

To make rational choices, as one is presumed to do within the neoliberal framework, it is necessary to have comparative indices about the performance of alternatives. Because the focus is on individual choice, it is critical to have individual-level performance data. Although the matrix sampling procedure used by the National Assessment of Educational Progress (NAEP), and in the past by some state departments of education, provides sound evidence about the performance at an aggregate level, these approaches provide no data at the individual student, teacher, school, or even district level. The assessment promoted by the neoliberal agenda emphasizes individual choice and therefore requires data at every unit of analysis, from the individual student to whole schooling systems. So, as suggested by Treanor the intensification of assessment in schools reflects neoliberalism's increased surveillance.

Indeed the intensification of assessment takes a number of forms: standardized assessment at legislated grade levels and the narrowing of teaching and learning to conform to the test content and format. The census assessment of, for example, every third- through eighth-grade student in the United States is an obvious form of intensification. In many classrooms, what is taught and learned at all grade levels reflects the substance and form of knowledge on standardized assessments. Research demonstrates that teachers adopt generic forms of content and presentation, develop a test-based curriculum, separate content for the test from "real" content, and fragment knowledge even more than is already the case in schools (Mathison & Freeman, 2003; McNeil, 2000).

The benefit of this intensified assessment is portrayed as necessary to provide information about the quality of schools that parents need to make rational choices about the best educational options for their children. If a school "fails" to educate all of its students, parents are advised to take their business elsewhere. This rhetoric communicates a promise that there are high-quality educational experiences available for all children, and parents must actively make choices to move their children into succeeding schools. That this rhetoric is hollow only minimally diminishes the suggestion that a market of educational options exists and can be chosen if individuals just select the options that produce the highest test scores.

The value of standardized test scores within the neoliberal rhetoric is fortified by values of modernity. There is a predominant view that we truly know something is valuable when it can be objectively measured and statistically manipulated. This view conspires with preoccupations with individualism, competitiveness, the indispensable role of hard work to success, and the equating of equity with sameness.

The Business of Assessment

Neoliberalism's free market exchange encourages the creation of derivative professions and submarkets. In the United States, assessment, especially high-stakes assessment, has created roles for tutors and testing coaches to increase the likelihood of success. The demand for assessment is big business. The U.S. General Accounting Office estimates that, between 2002 and 2008, states spent somewhere between $1.9 and $5.3 billion to develop tests and then score and prepare reports of the test results (Metcalf, 2002). Private, multinational companies that are not accountable to the public are major players in the accountability promises of the neoagendas. The connections between at least McGraw-Hill and the Bush government are not secret. Indeed, the Bush and McGraw families have had close ties for three generations (Metcalf, 2002).

In addition, these same companies score standardized tests, warehouse and report test results, provide tutoring services, create test preparation materials, and sell a plethora of services that promise to increase test scores. For example, NCLB fosters the expansion of tutoring businesses by at least initially requiring that failing schools use federal funds to contract out extraschool tutoring for students. The need for tutoring has therefore created businesses that assist with the development of tutoring businesses. As one website suggests,

Tutoring is great for entrepreneurs and home based business opportunity seekers! College students find tutoring to be an excellent part time, flexible job! Homeschooling moms and other homeschoolers are naturals as tutors! Dads can tutor too! Teachers often do tutoring on the side! Tutoring is the perfect job for stay-at-home moms who want to work from home and earn extra money to add to the family income without daycare hassles. (see http://www.cleverapple.com/)

In addition to providing help with setting up one's business, this quote illustrates a coming together of this business opportunity with other values that are often consistent with neoliberalism, such as reinforcing stay-at-home moms, emphasizing the importance of employment, portraying child-care issues as hassles, and supporting nonpublic school options such as home schooling.

The Rhetoric of Assessment-Based Reform

The rhetoric of accountability—leaving no child behind, closing the achievement gap, high expectations, personal effort, and so on seems sensible. The idea of education as a commodity has been naturalized, and the concomitant business language of control, regulation, bottom lines, profits, quality control, and maximized benefits also come to seem sensible. This is especially true for politicians, but many school and university administrators, teachers, parents, and even students are drawn into and live this rhetoric.

However, the rhetoric of assessment and accountability hides a deep-seated advantage of privilege and agendas that undermine educating the populace. By centering the success and failure of schools in children's test scores, attention is diverted away from such issues as reasonable and adequate resources for education and equitable and even free access to educational opportunities. By adopting market perspectives on schooling, families and schools that value positive social development and happiness over competitiveness and progress over achievement find themselves displaced, floundering to sustain an alternate rhetoric, one that is not shared by those with privilege and capital. Understanding how neoliberalism works against strong schools for all is a necessary step in developing an alternative rhetoric that recaptures schooling as a necessity in a democratic society, one where there are common public interests that will not be served by private interests.

Educational Evaluation in the Public Interest

What the best and wisest parent wants for his own child, that must the community want for all of its children. Any other ideal for our schools is narrow and unlovely; acted upon, it destroys our democracy. (Dewey, 1907)

What Is the Purpose of Schooling?

Vocationalism and democratic citizenship have long competed as the main purpose of schooling. Taylorism came to U.S. schools early in the 20th century, an approach to schooling that emphasized efficiency of production but developed alongside progressivism's focus on the effectiveness of schools to promote democratic principles. A rationalized system of degrees and credentials has come much later to European universities. Education has always been conceived as an institution that serves the public interest by preparing young people for work and citizenship, promoting a common culture (especially in nations of immigrants), and reducing race, ethnic, and class inequalities. What is critical about these purposes is whether they are conceived in the interest of individuals or the collective, public interest. The current emphasis is on the private and economic benefits (vocational purpose or schooling for the market that serves individual and corporate economic interests), rather than the public benefits (schooling for democratic citizenship with attention to

mediating special interests for the common good). (For a discussion of the purpose of public schools, see the Center on Education Policy report, *Why We Still Need Public Schools: Public Education for the Common Good* [Kober, 2007]). Neoliberal values currently capture the public attention regarding the purpose of schooling and, consequently, how education is evaluated. As politicians, corporate CEOs, and free marketeers continue to dominant the public rhetoric about the quality (or lack of quality) of schools, so too will the strategies for educational evaluation reflect those values. There is, of course, a debate about whether in the United States, for example, the quality of schools has actually declined (Berliner & Biddle, 1996; Jennings & Hamilton, 2004).

Evaluation as a Democratizing Force in Schooling

The practice of evaluation is typically conceived of as following the lead of the interventions it is meant to judge. Evaluators are seen and see themselves as serving decision-making masters. Evaluators have special methodological expertise, which is employed to answer the questions set by those who control the intervention. For educational evaluation to serve the public interest, this relationship and purpose of evaluation must be disrupted. Such a disruption can occur when evaluators work with all stakeholders in schools and communities, with much greater attention paid to parents, children, and local community perspectives on what counts as good schooling.

An example that illustrates a different rhetoric and methodology for educational evaluation is the Massachusetts Coalition for the Authentic Reform in Education (MassCARE) platform. MassCARE is a statewide organization of primarily parents, but also educators, students, and researchers, who through grassroots organizing are pushing back on the neoliberal agenda for schooling and its purposes. Their goal is to replace the single high-stakes indicator (the Massachusetts Comprehensive Assessment System or MCAS as it is more commonly called) with an accountability system that defines the quality of schools in fairer and necessarily more complex ways. The MassCARE plan consists of four integrated components:

1. Local authentic assessments that are gateways to graduation, approved by regional boards and based on the Common Core of Learning and a streamlined set of competencies

2. A school quality review model to assess the effectiveness of school practices, based on the models in Britain, Boston Pilot Schools, Rhode Island, and Massachusetts' own process for reviewing charter schools

3. Standardized testing solely in literacy and numeracy, to provide one method for tracking progress of schools from year to year

4. Required annual local reporting by schools to their communities, using a defined set of indicators that also focuses on equal opportunity and access to knowledge for all students. (MassCARE, n.d.)

The MassCARE plan suggests what professional evaluators would typically agree is good evaluation practice: the use of multiple and agreed-on indicators, attention to context, genuine involvement of stakeholders, focusing on improvement given the fundamental formative nature of educational evaluation, and appropriate reporting to schools' stakeholders. This approach to school evaluation is meant to place judgments about the quality of schools and plans for improvement in the hands of local communities, with the state playing an oversight and technical support role, a plan that MassCARE asserts focuses on high standards and allows local innovation and improvement. This is a decidedly New England plan, but it suggests key features of how educational evaluation can serve the public interest. If educational evaluation is to

make a contribution in the public interest, then evaluation must be done in ways that permit education's various publics to be involved in determining what is right and good and what is not. Participatory, collaborative approaches to evaluation suit this intention best (Mathison, 2000). An approach such as the MassCARE plan has a particular formative purpose, genuinely involves multiple stakeholders, and does so through democratic deliberative processes.

Current educational evaluation is in some senses a backlash against what is seen as too much focus on process, a softhearted approach that looks primarily at intentions but not results. While looking only at what are often called input variables, one certainly has only a partial basis for determining the quality of an educational intervention. The pendulum has, however, swung too far in the other direction, with a focus on a single outcome (student scores on state-mandated achievement tests or international assessments of student achievement). Rethinking educational evaluation as a fundamentally formative task does not diminish the importance of accountability but focuses on forms of accountability other than bureaucratic outcomes-based accountability. The fundamental ameliorative intent of evaluation may be most palpable in public institutions like schooling, where the moral obligation to get things as right as possible is simply what it is about. Getting things as right as possible in such a context is making a commitment to doing evaluation in the public service (i.e., evaluation that contributes the best information possible about how things are working and how to make them better).

Such evaluation requires evaluators to assume leadership roles, ones in keeping with the American Evaluation Association (AEA) guiding principle of "responsibility to the general and public welfare." MacNeil (2002) suggests that evaluators should be stewards of citizen deliberation, and Greene (1996) calls on evaluators to be scientific citizens who accept "the assumption of public accountability and social responsibility for the political, moral and value consequences of one's work as a scientist" (p. 278). There are two contexts in which adherence to this guiding principle must occur—in the doing of a specific evaluation and as a professional evaluation community.

In a particular educational evaluation, evaluators cannot be technicians serving the interests of decision makers, but instead they must accept responsibility for creating an evaluation process that is in the public interest. House and Howe's (1999) deliberative democratic evaluation provides a set of principles for this process: inclusion (considering the interests, values, and perspectives of stakeholders), dialogue (with and among stakeholders), and deliberation (publicly engaged reasoning toward evaluative conclusions). Any participatory, collaborative approach to evaluation will suggest procedures for how to do educational evaluation in the public interest, but Cousins and Whitmore's (1998) transformative participatory evaluation and Guba and Lincoln's (1989) fourth-generation evaluation are two good examples. The extent to which educational evaluation is done in the public service might be judged by using the Deliberative Democratic Evaluation Checklist developed by House and Howe (2000).

But in addition to doing evaluation as a public service, collectively, as a profession, evaluators also need to act like MacNeil's stewards and Greene's scientific citizens. How educational evaluation is done is a matter of both local practice and public policy, and, as such, educational evaluators' participation in the public discourse about the matter is an obligation. The AEA offers some examples of this, including their statements on high-stakes testing and on educational accountability. This is not a straightforward matter (as illustrated by the dissension within AEA over its response to the U.S. Department of Education's endorsement of randomized clinical trials as the gold standard for educational evaluation; see Donaldson & Christie, 2005) and will inevitably create conflict and discomfort. But as Linda Mabry (personal communication, January 31, 2007) characterized evaluators' responsibility: "I doubt we would deserve more arrows for doing something that might excite debate than we would deserve

for fearful disengagement." Such is an essential stance for educational evaluators working in the public interest.

As already mentioned, serving the public interest through educational evaluation needs to recognize that education has multiple stakeholders and that all need to be included in authentic ways. The MassCARE plan illustrates the many stakeholder groups that should be involved in the evaluation of schools. The refrain of parent, teacher, student, guardian, and grandparent voices must be as loud as, or louder than, those of the state, politicians, and corporate CEOs. All of these stakeholders are necessary for a fair and democratic evaluation, but the power of money (such as in the corporate-backed NCLB legislation) will not satisfy the need to work in the public interest. The interests of "Voltaire's bastards," as Saul (1992) called the ruling elite so contemptuous of the citizenry, must be balanced by the interests of the populace.

Incorporating multiple stakeholders in a dialogue will inevitably lead away from a single criterion (such as student academic achievement in limited areas) and a single indicator (such as state-mandated test scores). It is not common sense that schools or the quality of the education provided should be judged based on test scores alone. Student achievement in literacy and numeracy is important, but not at the expense of other indicators, such as the academic, social, and physical opportunities and achievements of students; the adequacy of curricular and instructional resources; the opportunities offered to teachers; safety; tolerance; and so on. Whatever the criteria, and given the likelihood many of the same criteria will be invoked in whatever context, there is still the need to respect and include the perspectives of all stakeholders.

Dialogue and deliberation are key for identifying education's stakeholders, engaging them in a process that identifies what the good-making attributes of schools are, identifying how best to capture those attributes, making sense of information, and concluding with a forward-looking deliberation about how to make things better.

Conclusion

Participatory, collaborative evaluation approaches that rely on deliberation are fundamental to educational evaluation in the public interest. The current neoliberalism reflects elite, corporate interests that are disdainful of the populace's ability to understand and promote their own interests. Importantly, the kind of educational evaluation suggested here does not guarantee a clear resolution, and indeed many aspects of schooling have been contentious from the common school era to the present (Mathison & Ross, 2008). The role of evaluation is not to settle a matter, make a decision, or take an action that is definitive and immutable. To serve the public interest, we must see evaluation as a continuous process of assessing the particulars to move toward betterment with the implicit expectation that an ideal state or a single solution cannot be attained and does not exist. Evaluation, in this deliberative way, contributes to the heart of democracy because it is the means by which a democratic community maintains its intent and identity, given an indeterminate future.

Notes

1. The term *state* here refers to a geographically bounded, economically organized, and dependent entity that has the power to provide social (e.g., education and police services) and material (e.g., transportation and currency) services and goods for its polity.

2. I have avoided the use of the term *neoconservatism* in this discussion because this term means somewhat different things in different parts of the world. In general, neoconservatism is a political philosophy that rejects liberalism and implies certain roles for the state. In the United States, this means a governmental focus on foreign policy and maintenance of superpower status and the implicit adoption of certain values such as Christianity and heterosexuality. In the Middle East, this political philosophy focuses on the legitimacy of religious authority for governments. Neoconservatism and neoliberalism are not the same, but they often co-exist, and this is especially so in the United States.

References

Altbach, P. (2008). Globalization and the forces of change in higher education. *International Higher Education, 50*. Retrieved on March 3, 2008, from http://www.bc.edu/bc_org/avp/soe/cihe/newsletter/Number50/p2_Altbach.htm.

Berliner, D., & Biddle, B. (1996). *The manufactured crisis: Myths, fraud, and attack on America's public schools*. Addison Wesley.

Bracey, G. (2008). International comparisons: Worth the cost? In S. Mathison & E. W. Ross (Eds.), *The nature and limits of standards-based reform and assessment* (pp. 35–48). New York: Teacher's College Press.

Chomsky, N. (1997). *Media control*. New York: Seven Stories Press.

Cousins, J. B., & Whitmore, E. (1998). Framing participatory evaluation. *New Directions for Evaluation, 80*, 5–23.

DeJarnatt, S. (2003). *The Philadelphia story: The rhetoric of school reform* (ExpressO Preprint Series, Paper No. 71). Available at http://law.bepress.com/expresso/eps/71

Dewey, J. (1907). *School and society*. Carbondale, IL: Southern Illinois University Press.

Donaldson, S., & Christie, C. (2005). Determining causality in program evaluation and applied research: Should experimental evidence be the gold standard? *Journal of Multidisciplinary Evaluation, 3*. Retrieved on March 3, 2007, from http://www.wmich.edu/evalctr/jmde/content/JMDE%20Num%203_files/Webpages%20JMDE%20003/JMDE_003_Part_I.htm#_Toc116196689

Elmore, R. F. (2002). An unwarranted intrusion. *Education Next, 2*(1). Available at http://www.hoover.org/publications/ednext/3398996.html

Greene, J. C. (1996). Qualitative evaluation and scientific citizenship: Reflections and refractions. *Evaluation, 2*(3), 277–289.

Guba, E. G., & Lincoln, Y. (1989). *Fourth generation evaluation*. Newbury Park, CA: Sage Publications.

Gutmann, A. (1999). *Democratic education*. Princeton, NJ: Princeton University Press.

Harvey, D. (2005). *A brief history of neoliberalism*. New York: Oxford University Press.

House, E., & Howe, K. R. (1999). *Values in evaluation and social research*. Thousand Oaks, CA: Sage.

House, E., & Howe, K. R. (2000). *Deliberative democratic evaluation checklist*. Retrieved April 25, 2007, from http://www.wmich.edu/evalctr/checklists/dd_checklist.htm

House, E. R., & Mathison, S. (1984). Methodology and values in evaluation. *Educational Theory*, *17*(2), 151–152.

Jennings, J., & Hamilton, M. (2004). What's good about public schools? *Our Children*, *29*(6), 4–6.

Kober, N. (2007). *Why we still need public schools: Public education for the common good*. Washington, DC: Center on Education Policy. Retrieved March 3, 2007, from http://www.cep-dc.org/PublicSchoolFacts/why/

MacNeil, C. (2002). Evaluator as steward of citizen deliberation. *American Journal of Evaluation*, *23*(1), 45–54.

MassCARE. (n.d.) *CARE Plan*. Retrieved on March 12, 2007. Available from http://www.parentscare.org/AuthenticAccount/Authentic_Home.htm

Mathison, S. (2000). Promoting democracy through evaluation. In D. W. Hursh & E. W. Ross (Eds.), *Democratic social education* (pp. 229–241). New York: Falmer Press.

Mathison, S. (2008). A short history of assessment and the standards based movement. In S. Mathison & E. W. Ross (Eds.), *The nature and limits of assessment and standards based educational reform* (pp. 3–14). New York: Teachers College Record.

Mathison, S. (2008). Public good and private interest: A history of educational evaluation. In W. C. Ayers (Ed.), *The handbook of social justice in education*. London: Taylor & Francis.

Mathison, S., & Freeman, M. (2003, September 24). Constraining elementary teachers' work: Dilemmas and paradoxes created by state mandated testing. *Education Policy Analysis Archives*, *11*(34). Retrieved February 1, 2006, from http://epaa.asu.edu/epaa/v11n34/.

Mathison, S., & Muñoz, M. (2008). Evaluation of schools and education: Bad practice, limited knowledge. In S. Mathison & E. W. Ross (Eds.), *The nature and limits of assessment and standards based educational reform* (pp. 71–81). New York: Praeger.

Mathison, S., & Ross, E. W. (Eds.). (2008). *Battleground schools: An encyclopedia of conflict and controversy*. New York: Greenwood Publishers.

Mathison, S., Ross, E. W., & Vinson, K. D. (2006). Defining the social studies curriculum: Influence of and resistance to curriculum standards and testing in social studies. In E. W. Ross (Ed.), *The social studies curriculum: Purposes, problems, and possibilities* (pp. 99-115). Albany, NY: SUNY Press.

McNeil, L. (2000). *Contradictions of school reform: Educational costs of standardized testing*. New York: Routledge.

Metcalf, S. (2002, January 28). Reading between the lines. *The Nation*, pp. 12–15.

Nye, J. (2002). Globalism versus globalization. *The Globalist*. Retrieved March 1, 2008, from http://www.theglobalist.com/StoryId.aspx?StoryId=2392.

Olssen, M. (1996). In defense of the welfare state and of publicly provided education. *Journal of Education Policy*, *11*, 337–362.

Puryear, J. M. (1999). The Americas: Educational reforms, external forces, and internal challenges. In D. Morales-Gomez (Ed.), *Transnational social policies*. Ottawa: The International Development Research Centre. Available at http://www.idrc.ca/en/ev-85585-201-1-DO_TOPIC.html

Ross, E. W., & Gibson, R. (Eds.). (2007). *Neoliberalism and education reform*. Cresskill, NJ: Hampton Press.

Saul, J. R. (1992). *Voltaire's bastards: The dictatorship of reason in the west*. New York: The Free Press.

Sedgewick, R. (2003). The Bologna process as seen from the outside. *World Education News & Review*, *16*(5). Retrieved March 2, 2008, from http://www.wes.org/ewenr/03Sept/Feature.htm

Treanor, P. (n.d.). *Neo-liberalism: Origins, theory, definitions*. Available at http://web.inter.nl.net/users/Paul.Treanor/neoliberalism.html

U.S. Department of Education. (2003). *Identifying and implementing educational practices supported by rigorous evidence: A user friendly guide*. Available at http://www.ed.gov/rschstat/research/pubs/rigorousevid/index.html

CHAPTER 31

Dilemmas for Educational Evaluation in a Globalized Society

J. Bradley Cousins and Katherine E. Ryan

Introduction

The notion that the ends of evaluation serve progress or play a part in "moving forward" is not new. The role of evaluation in policy implementation and program intervention is an illustration of how evaluation has hoped to contribute to social or educational progress or advancement. Nevertheless, there are longstanding tensions about what kinds of evaluation approaches are best for accomplishing this goal. Today, like most aspects of modern life (e.g., culture, employment), the notions of progress and evaluation are both being "globalized" by the circulation of ideas, ideologies, technologies and techniques, and people across national boundaries. Globalization is often characterized by values such as efficiency, entrepreneurship, market-based reform, rational management, and performance-based accountability (Burbules, 2002), although there are a variety of perspectives (Spring, 2008).

The tensions and contradictions within evaluation that are emerging or recurring coterminous with these political and social changes require further study. We emphasize these contradictions and tensions in relation to the role of evaluation in policy implementation and program intervention from a variety of evaluation perspectives. Although several contributors to advancement of evaluation theory and practice have embraced globalization as a force shaping policy and practice (e.g., Bhola, 2003; Lundgren, 2003; Stern, 2006), we are unaware of any treatises that centralize this construct for focus and debate. We are therefore in the fortuitous position of being able to look across a wide spectrum of educational evaluation perspectives to deepen understanding of the interrelationships between globalization and educational evaluation. In this chapter, we want to look across chapters in the *Handbook* to pull out some interesting ongoing dilemmas and challenges for educational evaluation both within and among various evaluation genres or families: role of science in educational evaluation, capacity building, and monitoring; educational evaluation as learning and discovery; and educational evaluation in a political world. To do so, we begin by looking at globalization. How is it defined? How is it manifest in contemporary society generally and within the educational policy and practice arena specifically? We then turn to a summation of the kinds of direct and mediated relationships and influences globalization is purported to have on educational evaluation theory and practice. Finally, we arrive at a listing of what we see as the main lingering dilemmas, issues, and challenges to be addressed within and between evaluation genres.

Educational Evaluation in a Globalized Society

Globalization, as we have described it, is an amorphous, complex, and contentious psychosocial phenomenon. For some it is characterized by expansionism, the concentration and acceleration of worldwide relations, and the compression of time and space. Innovation in technology and communications has in many ways made the world a smaller place, yet at the same time it is becoming larger because horizons have never been so broad (Osterhammel & Peterson, 2003). The rapid and sudden appearance of new technologies is concomitant with exponential, potentially overwhelming increases in the quantity of information (Adams & Carfagna, 2006). For others globalization implicates the decline of the nation-state and the deterritorialization or liberalization of markets. It has meant an increasing scale, rate, variety, and extent of cross-border economic, military, political, social, and cultural interaction (Krieger, 2006), the consequences of which are exceptionally difficult to predict and enormously challenging to even track. So how can we make sense of these complexities? What do we need to know? What do we need to do?

We ask these questions in the context of educational evaluation. Our intention with the *Handbook* project was to open wide the dialogue about globalization forces and their implications for evaluation theory and practice. To begin to understand the impact of globalization influences on educational evaluation, we believe, it is essential to think of them as either direct effects or those mediated by educational policy and practice. We represent these effects in Figure 31.1 while showing evaluation as a force for understanding, monitoring, and leveraging educational productivity, as well as change in policy and practice. The extent to which evaluation has become integrated into the discourses of educational policy and practice is debatable and sure to vary over global contexts, yet we understand evaluation to be a force for change and a mode of "assisted sensemaking" (see Mark, Chapter 4) in the complex domain of educational policy- and decision making.

So we challenged authors to think about globalization forces and how they serve to shape evaluation theory and practice. Depending on their charge and their own perspectives, understandings, and analyses, we observed variation in the extent to which direct or mediated influences on educational evaluation were addressed, including how policy and practices were mediated or moderated by globalization or changes in contemporary society. In this section, we highlight some of the globalization influences that were identified. In the next, we list emergent dilemmas and challenges for consideration in the context of the theory and practice of educational evaluation. But first we turn to an overview of just how authors actually conceptualized globalization.

How Is Globalization Represented?

Authors described globalization in many different ways, but four themes seem to be particularly noteworthy: interconnections, drivers and accelerants, homogenization, and consequences.

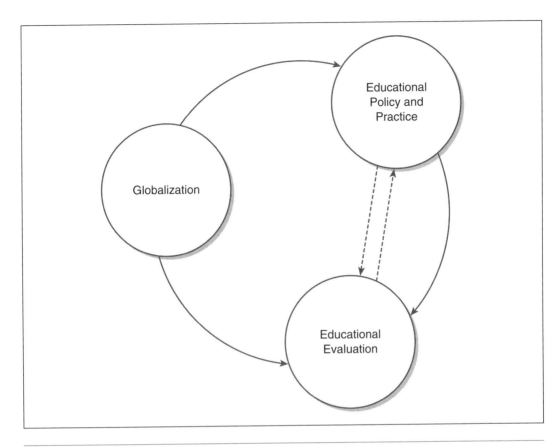

Figure 31.1   Educational Evaluation in a Globalized Society

Interconnections. Most authors represented globalization in terms of interconnections at different levels and on different dimensions—such as economic, military, environmental, and social—independent of time and space. Such interconnections are across national/regional and cultural borders and boundaries and include the spontaneous and reciprocal cross-fertilization of ideas and ideologies, lifestyles, people and goods, and images and messages (Greene, Chapter 18; Karlsson Vestman & Segerholm, Chapter 26; Marszalek & Bragg, Chapter 8; Mathison, Chapter 30; Nevo, Chapter 16; Rizvi, Chapter 1; Schwandt, Chapter 2; Smith, Chapter 3). As Friedman (2000) puts it, globalization reflects an

> inexorable integration of markets, nation-states, and technologies to a degree never

witnessed before—in a way that is enabling individuals, corporations, and nation-states to reach round the world farther, faster, deeper, and cheaper than ever before. (p. 7; quoted in Rizvi, Chapter 1, this volume)

Lundgren (Chapter 28) observes that, within the policy arena, globalization is best thought of as internationalism; its influence has been around for a while even though it has not always been called globalization. Nevertheless, most agree that globalization has led to "exposure to and contact with" differences on an increasing scale (Greene, Chapter 18, p. 328) and that the term can be taken as a shorthand for what is happening to individuals, community, and society as a result of flows of information and ideas (Schwandt, Chapter 2).

Drivers and Accelerants. A second theme that emerged was the role of economic forces and communication technologies as drivers of globalization. Several authors argued that globalization is driven by international trade and investment and fueled by information technology (e.g., Dahler-Larsen, Chapter 17; Hood, Chapter 25; Schwandt, Chapter 2). In this sense, it can be argued that traditional organizations constructed to handle the political economy of modern industrialized society are no longer suited to handle late-modern society (Lundgren, Chapter 28) or reflexive modernity (Dahler-Larsen, Chapter 17). Henry and Rickman (Chapter 7) refer to increased international trade, the internationalization of production and financial markets, and the internationalization of a "commodity culture." Torrance (Chapter 27) observes that globalization does not just happen; it has to be actively implemented, reproduced, serviced, and financed. In this sense, it is not a predetermined force that molds local contexts into uniform shapes.

Homogenization. Several authors highlighted the homogenizing influences of globalization. For example, Elliott (Chapter 22) describes a pervasive theory of globalization implicating free enterprise and movement toward a single commodity world; diverse market economies are integrated into a single global free market freed from social and political restraint. Terms such as *McDonaldization, Americanization, Westernization, imperialism,* and *neocolonialism* were often used (e.g., Elliott, Chapter 22; Nevo, Chapter 16) to characterize the homogenization trend. The terms most often imply the cross-cultural blending of markets and production, governance and human rights, ideas and inspirations (Greene, Chapter 18). Transactions, ideas, and lifestyles are not restricted by geography or traditional political structures such as nation-states (Karlsson Vestman & Segerholm, Chapter 26).

Yet the homogenization theory is not the only explanation offered. For example, Elliott (Chapter 22) refers to an alternative perspective, one that has significantly different implications

for a global society. Specifically, he refers to multiple indigenous capitalisms coming together in transnational space. Integral to this perspective is the notion of dependency on diversity of culture and the concept of "glocalization" as a replacement for globalization because local and global are not best understood as exclusive categories (Hood, Chapter 25). In this theory, "*globalization* is the bringing together of *clashing localities* in transnational space in the process of redefining and integrating them into a larger whole" (Elliott, Chapter 22, p. 403).

Consequences. A range of societal impacts of globalization were identified by various contributors (Henry & Rickman, Chapter 7; Hood, Chapter 25). Many of these were structural, including the spawning of multinational political organizations, multinational corporations, and political alliances that bring together nations for political, economic, and cultural purposes. Globalization is seen as breaking down boundaries and borders and reconfiguring demographic profiles of nation-states in dramatic ways (e.g., Christie & Klein, Chapter 20; Rallis & Militello, Chapter 14). But with increasing idea and information flows, individuals, communities, and institutions are more exposed to how things are done in different contexts; as a result, expanded opportunities for action and new arenas for competition emerge (Dahler-Larsen, Chapter 17; Greene, Chapter 18). For example, changing the educational system is one potential consequence (Cisneros-Cohernour & Grayson, Chapter 13; Rallis & Militello, Chapter 14).

On the flip side, some authors argue that globalization has led to increasing marginalization of historically oppressed groups (Cisneros-Cohernour & Grayson, Chapter 13; Hood, Chapter 25; Hopson, Chapter 24; Mathison, Chapter 30). As Hood (Chapter 25) puts it,

One of the major areas of contention regarding the outcomes of globalization is the steadily accumulating evidence that the poor, undereducated, and certain racial groups will minimally benefit (if at all) from globalization and a global economy. (p. 544)

What Are the Implications of Globalization for Educational Policy and Practice?

In a globalized society, education systems need to emphasize new and more complex skills to meet the demands of technological labor markets to compete globally. Educational evaluation is assigned an important part to play in changing educational systems to meet these demands. Information from educational outcomes-based performance systems is used to see whether educational actors and organizations are meeting performance standards. Further, to improve education, knowledge from science-based educational evaluations is used for educational planning and evidence-based educational policy.

Several authors acknowledged this pervasive implication of globalization for education and educational systems (Chatterji, Chapter 6; Elliott, Chapter 22; Ryan & Feller, Chapter 10; Rizvi, Chapter 1; Tamassia & Adams, Chapter 12). A corollary, according to Rizvi (Chapter 1), is a market-friendly education policy that is designed to meet the demands of a global knowledge economy. Rizvi adds that the nature and source of authority underlying public policy in education is changing because globalization has destabilized the traditional conception of policy research as territorially bounded. Nations are looking beyond their borders for input on educational content, standards, and implementation policies (Tamassia & Adams, Chapter 12). Yet Mark (Chapter 4) notes globalization can be characterized by content (currently neoliberalism) and processes (e.g., information technology). He points out that globalization defined by a different content might be much different than the current notion of globalization dominated by this kind political ideology.

Market-based notions are widely identified as a pervasive force influencing educational policy and governance (Elliott, Chapter 22; Greene, Chapter 18; Lundgren, Chapter 28; Mathison, Chapter 30; Rizvi, Chapter 1; Ryan & Feller, Chapter 10; Schwandt, Chapter 2; Torrance, Chapter 27).

Decentralization for increased flexibility and competition are cast as prevailing ideas and practices endorsed by dominant current economic and political elites (Schwandt, Chapter 2). These foundational notions are reflected in the recent emergence of new public management (NPM), an approach to governance that is designed to restore public trust in government, enhance efficiency, and anchor policy and management decision making in evidence (Greene, Chapter 18; Mathison, Chapter 30; McNamara & O'Hara, Chapter 15; Ryan & Feller, Chapter 10; Schwandt, Chapter 2). The approach is centered on principles of accountability and transparency through ongoing measurement and monitoring of educational outcomes. Within this framework, education is conceived of as a mechanism through which human capital is built with a significant focus on human performativity in a rapidly changing world (Elliott, Chapter 22; Lundgren, Chapter 28). At the same time, evidence-based policy is central to educational policy. Evidence-based educational evaluation that is based on science-based evaluation is proposed as key to producing generalizable knowledge that will maximize educational resources (e.g., financial, human).

Yet NPM with a significant emphasis on performance measurement and outcome-focused management is framed as being problematic in many respects. For one thing, it flies in the face of alternative theories of globalization, such as those that embrace the notion (mentioned earlier) of the bringing together of clashing localities in transnational space (Elliott, Chapter 22). The implications of this perspective for educational policy and practice are significant:

Capabilities should not be confused with hollowed-out generic skills that will tend to constitute human capital from the standpoint of global free market capitalism. They are bound to particular functional contexts and depend on the accumulation of appreciative experience in these contexts. (Elliott, Chapter 22, p. 405)

Greene (Chapter 18) and Chatterji (Chapter 6) resist this kind of standardization in proposing mixed methods. Greene proposes that performance measurement misses the point in such simplifications. Chatterji argues that implementing elaborate interventions in complex contexts such as developing countries needs to be systematically rolled out in an extended timeframe to be successful. Mathison (Chapter 30) provides an alternative critique that is grounded in a moral-political orientation focused on the public interests. She argues that, by centering the evaluation of educational policy and management on performance measurement and test scores, attention is diverted from essential issues such as the adequacy of resources and equitable access to educational opportunity. Further, Torrance (Chapter 27) describes test-based accountability regimes designed in the name of improving student learning as paradoxically serving to lower standards, this the result of the need for government to devise simple ways of monitoring system performance and the concomitant narrowing of the curriculum. Finally, Rizvi (Chapter 1) holds that a new social imaginary of education predicated on a range of neoliberal assumptions is neither spontaneous nor deterministic.

What Are the Implications of Globalization for Educational Evaluation?

Schwandt (Chapter 2) nicely represents the complexities of educational evaluation and why it is almost impossible to define: (a) it encompasses a broad range of objects; (b) there exists considerable variation in unit of analysis or location (public, private, higher, training); (c) it is practiced from different social locations (individual contractors, evaluation institutes, national systems); (d) it embraces different and conflicting schools of thought on how to do it—psychometrics

(assessment, measurement, testing), case and context tradition, managerial decision making approach (e.g., CIPP), and experimentalist tradition; (e) it is not a professionalized or credentialed practice; and (f) there exists wide-ranging evaluation discourse (Thorndike, Dewey, etc.). Yet evaluation is represented by a set of regularities, principles, and a coherent evaluator identity. This is what Schwandt (Chapter 2) refers to as the "Western evaluation imaginary." He suggests that evaluation has currency because it is oriented toward the corporate and public management elites, but it is also aligned with the moral-political orientation focused on the masses. In this section, we consider globalization effects on evaluation mediated by educational policy and practice and, subsequently, direct effects on evaluation.

Globalization, Educational Policy, and Evaluation. In the previous section, we observed the pervasive acknowledgment that contemporary educational policy and practice is predicated on a range of assumptions associated with a neoliberalism as a political ideology and NPM. What are the attendant implications for evaluation? Several authors described the privileging of technical-rationalist approaches to evaluation, including those associated with performance measurement and scientific evaluation including the use of randomized control trial designs (Henry & Rickman, Chapter 7; Mark, Chapter 4; Ryan & Feller, Chapter 10; Schwandt, Chapter 2; Steiner, Wroblewski, & Cook, Chapter 5; Tamassia & Adams, Chapter 12). International comparisons and accountability-, consumer-, and performance-oriented approaches to evaluation align well with NPM. Several strengths and weaknesses were identified.

Tamassia and Adams (Chapter 12) describe the benefits of international testing comparisons: (a) system monitoring, (b) assessment anchoring, (c) international ranking, (d) international agreement on standards, (e) expansion into more complex domains, and (f) measurement-driven research in education. Mark (Chapter 4) argues that evaluation as assisted sensemaking provides ample justification for scientific evaluation as a viable and valued approach. He suggests that "fork-in-the-road" evaluation problems are best suited for such evaluation. Datta (Chapter 9) also acknowledges the role of scientific evaluation but cautions that alternative approaches have emerged with good reason.

Several authors identified important caveats associated with evaluation approaches that align with the market-based framework. Generally, concerns were grounded in moral-political critiques—specifically, in concerns about the inadequacies of technical-rational approaches in serving democracy and the public interests. Some argued that test-based accountability systems associate well with public educational choice and value-for-money determinations but tend to rely on simplistic representations of knowledge and skills and do not promote public deliberation and contestation (Elliott, Chapter 22; Greene, Chapter 18; Mathison, Chapter 30). The proper role for evaluation is to raise contradictions and involve the public in determining what is educationally right and good (Mathison, Chapter 30; Rizvi, Chapter 1; Schwandt, Chapter 2).

Kushner (Chapter 23), writing within the context of global education initiatives, describes the existence of a paradox between local and global standards. He pushes a rights-based approach to evaluation with adaptation appropriate to global programs in international contexts. He describes the paradox of "situated generalization": "How can it be that we pretend to such cross-cultural knowledge while still cherishing the view that our cultural traditions confirm our uniqueness?" (p. 417). Kushner argues that the implications of the paradox are far reaching and challenge the heart of NPM. He details a localist view of the paradox, one that privileges context and stakeholders' right to know views and interests of those who influence their work. This perspective aligns well with Elliott's (Chapter 22) assertion that evaluation needs to move from "quality as measured" to "quality as experienced" and the methodological alternatives that attend to context: case study (Mabry, Chapter 19); mixed methods (Greene, Chapter 18); extended-term,

mixed methods approach (ETMM; Chatterji, Chapter 6); and culturally responsive evaluation (Hopson, Chapter 24).

Other authors grounded concerns in practical and technical realities, rather than moral-political discourse. Steiner et al. (Chapter 5) provide an excellent overview of challenges to comparative group designs, including randomized control trials, and they provide a response to each. They conclude that such approaches are essential to educational policy and practice. Ryan and Feller (Chapter 10) call for the systematic, preferably longitudinal evaluation of performance measurement regimes. They observe that seemingly similar performance measurement systems across nations can lead to differentiated effects depending on the relative share of public and private interests. Marszalek and Bragg (Chapter 8) argue that outcome data should necessarily be interpreted in the light of process data, an assertion that is consistent with Chatterji's (Chapter 6) ETMM approach. Rallis and Militello (Chapter 14) acknowledge that accountability implies feedback on results. They provide a case example of engagement with district-level personnel in ongoing and iterative evaluation but show that sustainable influence within schools remains a significant challenge. Similarly, McNamara and O'Hara (Chapter 15) examined the benefits and challenges of implementing school-based, consensus-driven evaluation and observed several drawbacks associated with quality of evidence, benign reporting, and sketchy stakeholder involvement.

Direct Globalization Influences on Evaluation. Direct influences on evaluation theory and practice were addressed by several authors. Perhaps the most expansive and comprehensive treatment of the topic was provided by Scriven (Chapter 29). He listed several ways in which evaluation has benefited or otherwise evolved as a consequence of globalizing influences. These include: analytic tools for quantitative and qualitative analysis, database storage that facilitates searches, graphical representations of data for better understanding, word processing advances, establishment of vast informational databases, and repositories containing multiple databases that make access to comparative and baseline data feasible and easier. Additionally, the jump in communications technology now makes it possible to: (a) reach anyone almost instantly and cheaply; (b) confirm, expand, and refine reports and accounts to a degree not previously possible; (c) hold group meetings from a distance (e.g., video conferences); (d) conduct online surveys; (e) use true 3D video presentations; (f) take advantage of extensions to the call waiting feature of telephones; and, last, (g) hold shadow conferences, which are simulcasts for access by those unable to attend.

Smith (Chapter 3) describes three possible impacts on evaluation of globalization: spread, interaction, and ecological transformation. He makes the case that the impact of spread and interaction has been considerable to date. Datta (Chapter 9) concurs, citing the establishment of national and regional associations, capacity-building initiatives, journals (traditional and open source), conferences, and similar developments.

Finally, by way of setting up his treatment of the topic of learning in evaluation, Dahler-Larsen (Chapter 17) advanced the epistemological construct of "reflexive modernity" as a way of thinking about contemporary global society: "modernity is not giving up, but [is] marred by doubt, side effects, contingency, and reflexivity" (p. 312). He suggests that different forms and manifestations of educational evaluation can be understood as being relevant within this view, including technical-rational approaches mentioned earlier, as well as learning-oriented approaches. He argues that tensions between learning and accountability functions of evaluation must be addressed if learning is to be achieved. We now turn to a discussion of this and other tensions, challenges, and dilemmas arising from author contributions to the *Handbook*.

Ongoing Dilemmas, Issues, and Challenges

We represented educational evaluation according to four genres or families: scientific evaluation with an emphasis on evidence-based policy and programming (EBP) and premised on the identification of what works; performance measurement and auditing, monitoring and evaluation capacity building (ECB); learning and discovery-oriented evaluation; and political- or values-oriented evaluation. These families represent a reasonable way to understand educational evaluation in the context of globalizing forces, yet they are highly interconnected and interdependent. In considering the identification of ongoing dilemmas, issues, and challenges for educational evaluation, such interdependency is highlighted. Figure 31.2 represents this interconnectedness.

Some of the challenges that we identified are new. They represent the product of changing contexts in educational policy and practice. Many, however, are not new, yet they take on new meaning and significance in the face of globalizing forces. Smith's (2008) identification of fundamental issues in evaluation provides a suitable lens for thinking about evaluation challenges and dilemmas. This is the case for at least two reasons. First, fundamental issues are by definition recurrent; they are "the underlying problems or choices that continually resurface in different guises" (p. 2). Second, they provide a useful frame of reference for considering evaluation in a state of flux in the global context. Evaluation as a profession, according to Smith, will have to learn to accommodate considerable and rapid redefinitions of theory, methods, and practice in a global society. Attention to fundamental issues can help to respond to this changing context.

Smith (2008, Chapter 3) identified selected fundamental issues in his commentary about evaluation in a changing society. We adapt these for our present purpose as a way to organize thinking about ongoing evaluation challenges and dilemmas (see Figure 31.2). They are:

- What are the proper *purposes* for evaluation?
- What *roles* should evaluators play?
- What *evidence* should count in evaluation? What are the appropriate bases for deciding?

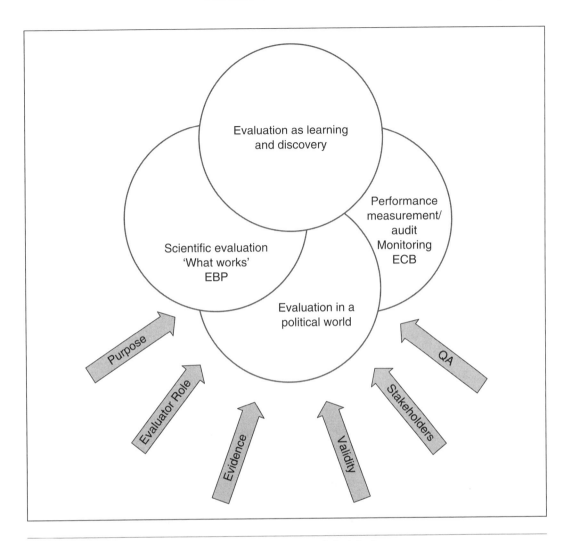

Figure 31.2   Fundamental Issues in Evaluation in a Global Society

- How should evaluation be carried out to ensure the *validity* of inferences from findings?
- How and when should *stakeholders* be involved in evaluation? What roles should they play?
- How should evaluators meet demands for quality assurance (QA)?

Just as interconnections exist among evaluation genres or families, so too are fundamental issues in evaluation necessarily interdependent.

What Are the Proper Purposes for Evaluation?

The emergence of NPM as a public service management framework and the pervasiveness of neoliberalism as the overarching political theory framing contemporary educational policy discourse has generated several questions about evaluation purposes. Several authors have argued that evaluation in this context best serves a technical rationalist agenda directed toward meeting accountability demands and providing evidence about what works as the basis for policy and decision making. At least two major tensions have been identified under this scenario.

First, in addition to accountability demands, the learning function of evaluation has come to be understood as a powerful contribution that evaluation can make. Dahler-Larsen (Chapter 17) makes the case that learning should not be limited by the information needs of the management function (e.g., program strengths and weaknesses, improvement of program functioning), but that evaluation can foster learning about policy functions and professional practices. He suggests that learning and accountability are not functional alternatives and that under reflexive modernity the use of data to handle contingency is appropriate. Nevo (Chapter 16) agrees that evaluation must be seen as a means for understanding rather than judgment alone. He calls for increased dialogue between internal and external evaluation.

A second scenario is that moral-political discourse in evaluation is undervalued and underplayed. Yet several would argue that stimulating such discussion and debate is the true and proper function for evaluation in contemporary times. Privileging scientific evaluation implies that there exists no sanctioned place for evaluators to debate and engage with the values of policies and programs. According to some, evaluation's purpose should be to provide meaningful enlightenment of policy and inform on the appropriateness of programs as responses to unmet social and educational needs (Elliott, Chapter 22; Greene, Chapter 18) and to raise contradictions if policy discourse is not aligned with democratic forces or national best interests. Evaluation should find its proper place as a vehicle for social critique—for raising questions about what is right. In this regard, several authors identified dynamic tensions and ongoing debates. Consider the following examples:

- Serve government versus serve governance (Kushner, Chapter 23; Schwandt, Chapter 2)
- Consistency-oriented versus diversity-oriented evaluation (Datta, Chapter 9)

- Customer-service oriented versus public-service oriented (Mathison, Chapter 30; Schwandt, Chapter 2)
- Apolitical assurance and accountability versus social critique (Schwandt, Chapter 2)
- Educational choice and value for money versus deliberation and contestation (Torrance, Chapter 27)
- Evaluation of learning systems versus evaluation of the learning that has taken place (Dahler-Larsen, Chapter 17)
- Improvement versus innovation (Dahler-Larsen, Chapter 17)
- Local versus global standards (Elliott, Chapter 22; Kushner, Chapter 23)
- Conflation between evaluation (programs and policies) and performance measurement (including individuals and organizations; Ryan & Feller, Chapter 10)
- Evaluation for control or evaluation for improvement (Lundgren, Chapter 28)

What Roles Should Evaluators Play?

The diversification of evaluator roles appears to be increasing. The traditional role of evaluator as researcher takes on new meaning and understanding in the context of increasing demands for scientific evaluation and support for sophisticated approaches to systematic inquiry (Chatterji, Chapter 6; Datta, Chapter 9; Steiner et al., Chapter 5). With the challenges of implementing sophisticated indicator systems and managing complex large-scale comparative evaluation designs (Chatterji, Chapter 6; Marszalek & Bragg, Chapter 8), the development of evaluator competencies in the principles and logic of inquiry are underscored. But globalizing forces have shaped the role in several other ways. Educational performance measurement and management systems can limit the evaluator role to measurement technician and/or performance auditor (Ryan & Feller, Chapter 10).

Several authors have argued for responsive, participatory, and collaborative approaches to evaluation to understand programs in context and to privilege the concept of localness as being integral to such understanding (Elliott, Chapter 22; Kushner, Chapter 23; Mabry, Chapter 19; Niessen, Abma, Widdershoven, & van der Vleuten, Chapter 21). This line of argument heightens the need for diversification of evaluator roles. Evaluators increasingly will be called on as teachers, developers, and capacity builders (Levin-Rozalis, Rosenstein, & Cousins, Chapter 11); advocates of diversity and democracy through dialogue (Greene, Chapter 18; Niessen et al., Chapter 21); and facilitator. In making the case for a rights-based approach to evaluation, Kushner (Chapter 23) eschews the role of evaluator as judge, suggesting that evaluators have no warrant to make judgments but rather have an obligation to inform. Yet judgment remains central to scientific approaches to evaluation in the context of supporting evidence-based decision making.

What Evidence Should Count in Evaluation? What Are the Appropriate Bases for Deciding?

As we have discussed, the NPM framework privileges a technical-rationalist approach to evaluation, one that relies heavily on quantitative performance measurement and indicator systems and designs that support evidence-based decision making through the generation of valid data and defensible causal arguments (Henry & Rickman, Chapter 7; Steiner et al., Chapter 5). Although the call to develop a solid evidence base of what works enjoys support on many fronts, challenges remain. First, although the case for privileging randomized control trials as a superior method for establishing causal arguments is strong (Steiner et al., Chapter 5), it may be limited to particular types of evaluation questions. Mark (Chapter 4) refers to these as "fork-in-the-road" questions, answers to which assist in policy direction and decision making. But how frequent are these sorts of questions

that evaluation can and should address? Both Mark (Chapter 4) and Datta (Chapter 9) suggest there may be some limits worthy of consideration here.

Increasingly, policymakers look to international comparisons as a basis for judging national productivity toward identified goals (Greene, Chapter 18; Ryan & Feller, Chapter 10). Such systems allow countries to monitor on an ongoing basis and to be no longer isolated in meeting requirements for accountability (Tamassia & Adams, Chapter 12). Yet several challenges continue to confront international comparison systems. These include choices about what to assess, how to identify the range of content, the feasibility of using methodologically desirable longitudinal designs, and comparability and fairness across cultural contexts (Tamassia & Adams, Chapter 12). Many of these concerns are cost-intensive, and their resolution depends heavily on the availability of resources.

A significant problem associated with outcome-oriented performance indicator systems is that they tend to oversimplify the complexity of student learning. What gets measured is relatively simplistic knowledge and skill because measures of more complex cognitive skills are simply not feasible on a large scale (Ryan & Feller, Chapter 10; Tamassia & Adams, Chapter 12). This implies that progress toward identified targets becomes the focus rather than meaningful student learning (Greene, Chapter 18; Mathison, Chapter 30; Torrance, Chapter 27). Additionally, as Ryan and Feller (Chapter 10) observe, performance measurement systems across nations can lead to differentiated effects. Examples of deleterious impact are provided by Cisneros-Cohernour and Grayson (Chapter 13) in their case examining test-based educational reform in the context of a developing country.

Calls for mixed methods approaches and for reliance on epistemologically appropriate qualitative data (Chatterji, Chapter 6; Greene, Chapter 18; Mabry, Chapter 19) provide justified responses to several challenges, not the least of which are cross-cultural appropriateness

(Cisneros-Cohernour & Grayson, Chapter 13; Hood, Chapter 25; Hopson, Chapter 24). Yet in addition to associated cost and feasibility issues, policymaker preferences for quantitative data need to be addressed. Mabry (Chapter 19) argues that the problem of catalytic validity should be a central concern for evaluators who seek to represent program quality in alternative ways. Policymakers need to be persuaded of the value and utility of quality as experienced, as opposed to quality as measured (Mabry, Chapter 19). Yet this will undoubtedly provide significant challenges. Torrance (Chapter 27) casts testing systems as the security blanket or comforter of policymakers.

How Should Evaluation Be Carried Out to Ensure the Validity of Inferences From Findings?

Rizvi (Chapter 1) argues that globalization has destabilized the policy community and authority for policy decision making, and, as such, the objectivist focus for evaluation is no longer relevant. He suggests that evaluation does not look at the question of how policies and programs have become deeply implicated in transnational processes. As such, methodological territorialism is no longer appropriate. Additionally, Rizvi (Chapter 1) argues that transnationalization is affected by the extent to which there is connection between local and national. Therefore, differential effects can be expected in different locations. These sentiments, specifically those concerning the essentiality of localness, are echoed by others as serious tensions to be addressed (Datta, Chapter 9; Elliott, Chapter 22; Kushner, Chapter 23; Marszalek & Bragg, Chapter 8; Ryan & Feller, Chapter 10). The implications for evaluation are significant. Evaluation needs to connect local realities to evaluation idealities (Datta, Chapter 9) to accommodate disparity across schools. According to Ryan and Feller (Chapter 10),

performance measurement systems need to think globally and analyze locally.

Kushner (Chapter 23), in making the case for rights-based evaluation of international educational initiatives (or universalist projects), argues that evaluation needs to deal with the paradox of situated generalization, noting "schools and classrooms are identical and different at one and the same time." Kushner suggests that the implications of the paradox are far-reaching and challenge the heart of NPM. He goes on to critique the universalist project as having democratic warrant but catering to the policy elite, valuing transparency through indicators yet technical complexity renders them inaccessible to the public, promoting comparison to the point of abstraction, and achieving international consensus while at the same time failing to recognize that moral systems are always culturally embedded.

Another issue related to the validity of indicator systems and outcome measures is that such systems do not privilege process data collection, analysis, and interpretation. Chatterji (Chapter 6) identified this as a significant shortcoming in extolling the virtues of the ETMM approach. Marszalek and Bragg (Chapter 8) also acknowledged the importance of gathering process data in comparative designs. Process data can and should help to support the interpretation of outcome findings and ultimately the validity of conclusions. Yet such data add complexity and costs to evaluation, a tension that will need to be addressed.

How and When Should Stakeholders Be Involved in Evaluation? What Roles Should They Play?

The complexity of this issue is grounded in fairly direct ways to the issue of the connectedness of local interests to national and even transnational ones. Values, assumptions, and perspectives need to be understood at the local level for evaluation to accommodate disparity among schools and communities (Datta, Chapter 9). Yet large-scale assessment and indicator systems and universalist projects of the sort discussed by Kushner (Chapter 23) are quite limited in the extent to which they take into account such information. To what extent, for example, are adjustments to school-level indicator data made on the basis of socioeconomic status of communities, access to resources, and the like? To what extent are the voices of the community represented in aggregated comparisons? School-based evaluation and approaches that link internal and external evaluation forces have the potential to accommodate such variation (McNamara & O'Hara, Chapter 15; Nevo, Chapter 16), yet developing meaningful systems is not without its challenges. McNamara and O'Hara's (Chapter 15) study of such reform in the Irish school system, for example, revealed mixed results and observations of evidence-free evaluation, superficial feedback, benign reporting by the inspectorate, and sketchy stakeholder involvement.

Stakeholder involvement in evaluation is generally taken to imply something more than merely serving as a source of data. At one level, stakeholders can be involved in the production of evaluation knowledge by virtue of participating on evaluation teams and projects and engaging with technical aspects of evaluation, such as planning and framing; data collection, analysis, and interpretation; and reporting and use. Yet such participation, particularly in practical participatory contexts where stakeholder selection for involvement may be limited to primary users—those who are in a position to actually act on findings—may be completely associated with a technical rationalist approach to evaluation, which ultimately may enhance use while serving the interests only of policy elites (Dahler-Larsen, Chapter 17; Schwandt, Chapter 2).

However, stakeholder involvement may serve the interests of democratically fair accountability systems (Greene, Chapter 18; Mathison, Chapter 30). Evaluation provides the resources and opportunity to theorize solutions to community problems at the local level. Kushner (Chapter 23) argues that democratic resolutions to problems are not possible without such participation at the local level, and that international agreements and treaties, in the end, should be judged by their relevance to local contexts. Similarly, Mathison (Chapter 30) asserts that the purposes of test-based accountability systems must be disrupted if educational evaluation is to serve the public interests. Greater attention must be paid to parents, children, and local community perspectives on what counts as good schooling. Evaluation must be done in ways that permit education's various publics to be involved in determining what is right and good and what is not (Elliott, Chapter 22; Mathison, Chapter 30).

Of course such moral-political discourse represents the essence of cross-cultural approaches to evaluation, including culturally responsive evaluation (CRE) described by Hopson (Chapter 24). In his words,

> Hence, the socially responsible stance of the culturally responsive evaluator and the evaluation contributes to thinking about social agendas that promote spaces of hope, praxis, and social action for indigenous, marginalized, dispossessed communities and their contexts, histories, struggles, and ideals. (p. 444)

Yet the theoretical elegance of CRE is tempered by practical realities, as revealed in the case exemplar provided by Hood (Chapter 25) in the context of engagement in CRE by Navajo peoples. Finally, Karlsson Vestman and Segerholm (Chapter 26) showed how power imbalances resulting from information control and entrenched power structures and traditions served to compromise a Scandinavian-Russian cross-cultural evaluation.

How Should Evaluators Meet Demands for Quality Assurance?

As we described earlier, method-driven approaches to evaluation, particularly those with scientific warrant, are part and parcel of NPM management framework. Yet the complexities of scientific evaluation and sophisticated cross-national indicators systems are daunting and continue to pose many challenges for evaluators (Marszalek & Bragg, Chapter 8; Ryan & Feller, Chapter 10; Steiner et al., Chapter 5; Tamassia & Adams, Chapter 12) particularly in terms of quality assurance (QA). Practical challenges occur in mounting randomized controlled trial studies, especially in ensuring that planned treatment contrasts are not compromised and nontrivial. Steiner et al. (Chapter 5) identify several trade-offs and tensions that should be taken into account, including concomitant decreases in external validity (generalizability) in the face of pressure to increase internal validity (attribution), and scientific purity as a priority over utility, particularly with respect to decentralized decision makers. Dahler-Larsen (Chapter 17) also acknowledges the trade-off between technical quality in evaluation and responsiveness.

In the face of such complexity, misunderstandings and inconsistencies in understanding limit the ability to employ rigorous scientific methods as originally planned (Marszalek & Bragg, Chapter 8). Datta (Chapter 9) identifies other dilemmas with which scientific evaluators must grapple, including the conditions under which such approaches are appropriate (e.g., mature programs; ethical considerations; favorable, high salience of contrasting approaches) and the availability of evaluation personnel skilled in managing and administering such approaches. Tamassia and Adams (Chapter 12) describe state-of-the-art, international, indicator-based accountability systems and steps that have been taken to ensure quality. The bourgeoning industry of international testing and assessment organizations has created an international culture of data collection of educational outcomes. These collaborations have ensured state-of-the-art expertise, innovative methodologies, and, notwithstanding limits on the range and scope of what gets measured, have gone a long way toward the generation of high-quality outcomes. Yet to what extent have such systems been evaluated? Ryan and Feller (Chapter 10) argue for the systematic, preferably longitudinal evaluation of the impact of performance measurement systems.

Technical training in evaluation based on a well-developed and coherent set of evaluator competencies would be one approach to evaluation QA. Yet as we have seen, evaluation in a global society is increasingly diverse with a plethora of alternative approaches emerging in response to challenges of the inadequacies of traditionalistic approaches. It seems likely that, despite the existence of a Western evaluation imaginary (Schwandt, Chapter 2) and the ascendancy of evaluator identity, systems of competencies-based training would favor the agenda of NPM and its penchant for technical-rationalist approaches. How then can QA in an increasingly diversified evaluation community be satisfied? Can the soft skills associated with participatory and collaborative approaches (e.g., Christie & Klein, Chapter 20), culturally responsive approaches (Hopson, Chapter 24), and dialogic approaches (e.g., Niessen et al., Chapter 21) actually be captured, codified, and otherwise serve as the basis for training and professional development?

Concluding Remarks

Educational evaluators are living in interesting times. Today, education is being influenced and changed by a "world culture of values that sometimes mixes with (and other times flattens) national and local cultures on a massive scale" (Baker & LeTendre, 2005, p. 5). On the one hand, this world culture of values is making educational experiences, including both teaching and learning highly similar from one locale to another. At the same, there are dissimilarities and uniquenesses from place to place within and across global boundaries.

Moreover, with futures thinking on the horizon, schools are going to be asked to educate students for occupations, trades, and careers that do not exist. Likewise, schools, teachers, and students will teach and learn with technologies that are not yet developed so they can solve problems that have not been identified (Theisens, 2008). Today, life-long learning is a central feature of education, where life-long students of any age are to develop skills for a more flexible career trajectory and life involving formal and informal learning (Organisation for Economic Co-operation and Development, 2008).

Evaluation has the capability to respond to these challenges and opportunities in contemporary society. Understanding, disentangling, disaggregating, and hypothesizing about educational similarities and differences as well as judging the quality and effectiveness of these educational experiences are all essential for improved educational programs and policies. Educational evaluation theories and practices offer the kind of wide-ranging knowledges and resources to aid in this effort. Capturing the important processes and products of an improving global education characterized by important local variations will require the multiplicity of educational evaluation families rather than restricting the kinds of evaluations that might contribute to the improvement of educational policies and programs.

What is the history of the future of evaluation and globalization (Lundgren, Chapter 28)? In a paper session at the 2008 European Evaluation Society, Saville Kushner, Peter Dahler-Larsen, and a friendly audience proposed turning the notion of globalization and evaluation upside down to consider the globalizing influences of evaluation. Is it the case that evaluation has a role in this set of complex processes? Certainly much of evaluation is located within or near the administration and institutional structures, practices, and discourses that support and maintain governance. As House (1993) notes, "Governments use evaluation to legitimate,

inform, and control . . . evaluation is an alternative means of achieving guidance and compliance" (p. 32). Moreover, Lundgren (Chapter 28) characterizes the evaluating state as part of the history of the future. We concur and look forward to seeing a critical examination of these relations and their connections to the globalizing influences of evaluation charted as a next step.

References

Adams, J. M., & Carfagna, A. (2006). *Coming of age in a globalized world: The next generation.* Bloomfield, CT: Kumarian.

Baker, D. P., & LeTendre, G. K. (2005). *National differences, global similarities: World culture and the future of schooling.* Stanford, CA: Stanford Social Sciences Press.

Bhola, H. S. (2003). Social and cultural contexts of educational evaluation: A global perspective. In T. Kellaghan & D. L. Stufflebeam (Eds.), *International handbook of educational evaluation* (pp. 397–416). Boston: Kluwer.

Burbules, N. C. (2002). The global context of educational research. In L. Bresler & A. Ardichvili (Eds.), *Research in international education: Experience, theory, and practice* (pp. 157–170). New York: Peter Lang.

Friedman, T. (2000). *Lexus and the olive tree.* New York: First Anchor Press.

House, E. R. (1993). *Professional evaluation: Social impact and political consequences.* Newbury Park, CA: Sage.

Krieger, J. (Ed.). (2006). *Globalization and state power: A reader.* New York: Pearson.

Lundgren, U. P. (2003). The political governing (governance) of education and evaluation. In P. Haug & T. A. Schwandt (Eds.), *Evaluating educational reforms: Scandinavia perspectives* (pp. 99–110). Greenwich, CT: InfoAge.

Organisation for Economic Co-operation and Development. (2008). *Trends shaping education.* Paris: Author.

Osterhammel, J., & Peterson, N. P. (2003). *Globalization: A short history.* Princeton, NJ: Princeton University Press.

Smith, N. L. (2008). Fundamental issues in evaluation. In N. L. Smith & P. R. Brandon (Eds.), *Fundamental issues in evaluation* (pp. 1–23). New York: Guilford Press.

Spring, J. (2008). Research on globalization and education. *Review of Educational Research, 78*(2), 330–363.

Stern, E. (2006). Contextual challenges for evaluation practice. In I. Shaw, M. M. Mark, & J. Greene (Eds.), *The Sage handbook of evaluation* (pp. 292–314). Thousand Oaks, CA: Sage.

Theisens, H. (2008, September). *Futures thinking in action: Lessons learned.* Paper presented at the Schooling for Tomorrow conference, Centre for Educational Research and Innovation, Organisation for Economic Co-operation and Development, Helsinki, Finland.

Author Index

Subject Index

About the Editors

Katherine E. Ryan is a faculty member in the Educational Psychology Department at the University of Illinois in Urbana-Champaign (UIUC). After receiving a PhD in 1988, she worked as an evaluator for a decade before joining the UIUC faculty in 1999. Her research interests focus on educational evaluation and the intersection of educational accountability issues and high-stakes assessment. She has served as Associate Editor for the *American Journal of Evaluation* and *New Directions for Evaluation*. Her work has examined both evaluative capacity building and monitoring issues involved in test-based educational accountability. Her current research includes an evaluation of the intended and unintended consequences of a state-wide assessment and accountability system in relationship to students, instruction, and educational outcomes.

J. Bradley Cousins is Professor of Educational Administration at the Faculty of Education, University of Ottawa. Cousins' main interests in program evaluation include participatory and collaborative approaches, use, and capacity building. He received his PhD in educational measurement and evaluation from the University of Toronto in 1988. Throughout his career, he has received several awards for his work in evaluation, including the Contribution to Evaluation in Canada award (CES, 1999) and the Karl Boudreau award for leadership in evaluation (CES-NCC, 2007) and the Paul F. Lazarsfeld award for theory in evaluation (AEA, 2008). He has been Editor of the *Canadian Journal of Program Evaluation* since January 2002.

About the Contributors

Tineke A. Abma is Associate Professor and Program Leader of "Autonomy and Participation in Chronic Care" at VU Medical Centre, EMGO Institute, Department of Medical Humanities, Amsterdam. Her scholarly work concentrates on participatory and responsive evaluation approaches, dialogue and moral deliberation, narrative and storytelling, and patient participation in health research. She has conducted many evaluation projects in the fields of healthcare (psychiatry, elderly care, intellectual disabilities, rehabilitative medicine, palliative care), social welfare, and higher education.

Raymond J. Adams, BSc (Hons), DipEd, MEd(Melb), PhD (Chicago), FACE, is Professorial Fellow of the University of Melbourne and an independent consultant specializing in psychometrics, educational statistics, large-scale testing, and international comparative studies. He has led the OECD PISA Programme since its inception. Ray has published widely on the technical aspects of educational measurement, and his item response modeling software packages are among the most widely used in educational and psychological measurement. He has served as chair of the technical advisory committee for the International Association for the Evaluation of Educational Achievement and as Head of Measurement at the Australian Council for Educational Research.

Debra D. Bragg is Professor of the Department of Educational Organization and Leadership in the College of Education at the University of Illinois. She is responsible for coordinating the College of Education's Higher Education and Community College Executive Leadership programs, and she is the principal investigator for research and evaluation studies funded by the U.S. Department of Education, state agencies, and the Lumina Foundation for Education. Her research focuses on P-16 policy issues, with special interest in high school-to-college transition and various policies and practices focused on addressing the educational needs of underserved students.

Madhabi Chatterji, PhD, is Associate Professor of Measurement and Evaluation and Codirector of the Assessment and Evaluation Research Initiative, Teachers College, Columbia University. Her research, currently focusing on diagnostic classroom assessment, evidence standards, and educational equity, has been recognized by the Fulbright Commission (2007–2008), the American Educational Research Association (2004), and the Florida Educational Research Association (1993). Refereed publications have appeared in the *American Journal of Evaluation, Journal of Educational Psychology, Review of Educational Research, Educational and Psychological Measurement,* and *Educational Researcher.* Her book, *Designing and Using Tools for Educational Assessment* (Allyn & Bacon, 2003) offers an integrated model for designing and validating measures accounting for user contexts; the model is being applied to develop a national assessment for graduate medical education programs. She is presently serving on an evidence frameworks committee at the Institute of Medicine of the National Academies.

Christina A. Christie, PhD, is Associate Professor in the School of Behavioral and Organizational Sciences at Claremont Graduate University. Christie cofounded the Southern California Evaluation Association, is former Chair of the Theories of Evaluation Division, and is current Chair of the Research on Evaluation Division of the American Evaluation Association. She received the 2004 American Evaluation Association's Marcia Guttentag Early Career Achievement Award. She is also Section Editor of the *American Journal of Evaluation* and Editor of two recent books: *Exemplars of Evaluation Practice* (with Fitzpatrick & Mark) and *What Counts as Credible Evidence in Evaluation and Applied Research?* (with Donaldson & Mark).

Edith J. Cisneros-Cohernour, PhD, is Professor and Research Coordinator of the College of Education at the Universidad Autónoma de Yucatan, Mexico. A former Fulbright fellow, she received her PhD in Higher Education Administration and Evaluation from the University of Illinois at Urbana-Champaign in 2001. From 1994 to 2001, she was also affiliated with the National Transition Alliance for Youth with Disabilities and the Center for Instructional Research and Curriculum Evaluation of the University of Illinois at Urbana-Champaign. Her areas of research interest are evaluation, professional development, organizational learning, and the ethical aspects of research and evaluation. Among her recent publications are *Academic Freedom, Tenure, and Student Evaluations of Faculty: Galloping Polls in the 21st Century* (2005), *Validity and Evaluations of Teaching in Higher Education Institutions Under Positivistic Paradigm* (2005), and *An Interpretive Proposal for the Evaluation of Teaching in Higher Education* (2008). Further, she has made numerous presentations of her work at professional conferences in México, the United States, and Europe.

Thomas D. Cook is the Sarepta and Joan Harrison Professor of Ethics and Justice at Northwestern University where he is also a professor in the Departments of Sociology, Psychology, Education, and Social Policy as well as being a Faculty Fellow of the Institute for Policy Research. His professional interests are in research methodology, particularly methods that can be applied to the evaluation of social programs in education and health. He is a Fellow of the American Academy of Arts and Sciences and has won prizes from many professional organizations, most recently the Sells Prize of the Society for Multivariate Experimental Psychology.

Peter Dahler-Larsen, PhD, is Professor of Evaluation at the Department of Political Science and Public Management, University of Southern Denmark, where he is coordinating the Master Program in Evaluation. His main research interests include cultural, sociological, and institutional perspectives on evaluation. His publications include contributions to *The Sage Handbook of Evaluation* and *The Oxford Handbook of Public Management*. With Jonathan Breul and Richard Boyle, he co-edited "Open to the Public. Evaluation in the Public Arena" (Transaction 2008). He has also published extensively in Danish on evaluation and the concept of quality. He was President of the European Evaluation Society 2006–2007.

Lois-ellin Datta, PhD, Comparative and Physiological Psychology, has been a National Institutes of Health Fellow, National Director of Head Start Evaluation, National Institute of Education Director for Teaching, Learning, and Assessment, and General Accountability Office Director for Evaluation in Human Services. A Past-President of the American Evaluation Association (ERS) and Editor-in-Chief of New Directions for Evaluation, she is an editorial board member of the *American Journal of Evaluation, New Directions for Evaluation,* and the *Journal of MultiDisciplinary Evaluation.* Recipient of both Myrdal and Ingle Awards, Datta has written more than 100 articles, chapters, and books on evaluation.

John Elliott is Emeritus Professor of Education in the Centre for Applied Research in Education at the University of East Anglia, UK. He is well known internationally for his roles in developing, in the education field, the theory and practice of action research, and the development of democratic approaches to programme evaluation. UEA awarded him a DLitt degree for his published work (2003), and he has received Doctorates, *honoris causa*, from the Hong Kong Institute of Education (2002) and the Autonomous University of Barcelona (2003). His selected works, titled "Reflecting Where the Action Is," are published in the Routledge World Library of Educationalists (2007).

Irwin Feller is Senior Visiting Scientist at the American Association for the Advancement of Science. He is also Emeritus Professor of Economics at The Pennsylvania State University, where he served on the faculty for 39 years, including 24 years as Director of the Institute for Policy Research and Evaluation. His current research interests include the economics of science and technology, the evaluation of federal and state technology programs, the university's role in technology-based economic development, and the adoption and impacts of performance measurement systems. He has a BBA in economics from the City University of New York and a PhD in economics from the University of Minnesota.

Thomas E. Grayson, PhD, is Director of Evaluation and Assessment in the Office of the Vice Chancellor for Student Affairs and adjunct professor in the College of Education at the University of Illinois at Urbana-Champaign. Dr. Grayson's expertise is in program evaluation with an emphasis on strategies for conducting performance-based assessment. He helps organizations build their capacity to conceptualize and implement evaluations that enable them to strengthen their programs and services. He has published articles and written book chapters on educational policy and practice regarding youth at risk of school failure and individuals with learning disabilities. His publications also include areas on concept mapping technology and appreciative inquiry. Further, he has made numerous presentations on evaluation policy and practice at professional conferences and training seminars.

Jennifer C. Greene has been an evaluation scholar-practitioner for more than 30 years and is currently Professor of Educational Psychology at the University of Illinois at Urbana-Champaign. Her evaluation scholarship focuses on analyzing the intersections of social science method with policy discourse and program decision making, with the intent of making evaluation useful and socially responsible. Greene has concentrated on advancing qualitative, mixed methods, and democratic approaches to evaluation. Her evaluation practice has spanned multiple domains of practice, including education, community-based family services, and youth development. In 2003, Greene received the American Evaluation Association's Lazarsfeld award for contributions to evaluation theory.

Gary T. Henry holds the Duncan MacRae '09 and Rebecca Kyle MacRae Professorship of Public Policy in the Department of Public Policy and directs the Carolina Institute for Public Policy at the University of North Carolina at Chapel Hill. Also, he holds the appointment as Senior Fellow in the Frank Porter Graham Institute for Child Development at UNC-Chapel Hill. Henry has evaluated a variety of policies and programs, including North Carolina's Disadvantaged Student Supplemental Fund, Georgia's Universal Pre-K, public information campaigns, and the HOPE Scholarship, and published extensively in the fields of evaluation, policy research, and education policy.

Stafford Hood is the Sheila M. Miller Professor of Education and Head of the Department of Curriculum and Instruction at the University of Illinois at Urbana-Champaign, where he also holds an appointment as Professor of Educational Psychology in the College of Education. His research and scholarly activities focus primarily on the role of culture in educational assessment and culturally responsive approaches in program evaluation. He has also served as a program evaluation and testing consultant internationally and in the U.S. to the federal government, state departments of education, school districts, universities, foundations, and regional educational laboratories. He was selected as a Fellow of the American Council on Education in 2001.

Rodney K. Hopson holds the Hillman Distinguished Professorship in the Department of Educational Foundations and Leadership, School of Education, Duquesne University. With postdoctoral and visiting research and teaching experiences from the Johns Hopkins Bloomberg School of Hygiene and Public Health, the University of Namibia Faculty of Education, and Cambridge University Centre of African Studies, his general research interests lie in ethnography, evaluation, and sociolinguistics. His publications raise questions about the differential impact of education and schooling in comparative and international contexts and seek solutions to social and educational conditions in the promotion of alternative paradigms, epistemologies, and methods for the way the oppressed and marginalized succeed in global societies.

Ove Karlsson Vestman is Professor of Education at Mälardalen University, Sweden, where he directs the Mälardalen Evaluation Academy. He has been appointed Visiting Professor in the Department for Applied Social Science at London Metropolitan University and Visiting Professor in Social Work at Övebro University, Sweden. He was one of the founders and the first vice president of the Swedish Evaluation Society. His work concentrates on building evluation capacity. In this work, he typically uses participatory and mixed-method approaches. He has published on dialogue methods and critical theory, as well as the role of values and politics in evaluation.

Brock M. Klein, EdD, is Director of Pasadena City College's Teaching and Learning Center (TLC), which is committed to helping underprepared, first-generation college students move successfully from basic skills to transfer-level courses. Dr. Klein developed the TLC in 2000 with funds from a U.S. Department of Education Title V grant and currently manages several private and federal grants. In addition to his work with basic skills instructors and students, he serves on the advisory board for California's Basic Skills Resource Network and is Associate Professor of ESL.

Saville Kushner is Professor of Applied Research in Education and Professor of Public Evaluation at the University of the West of England. He is an advocate of both the theory and practice of Democratic and Rights-Based Evaluation. Between 2005 and 2007, he served as Regional Officer for Monitoring and Evaluation in UNICEF (Latin America and the Caribbean) and continues to serve as a consultant. For many years, he worked at the Centre for Applied Research in Education at the University of East Anglia, which was prominent in the early advocacy and development of case-based approaches to program evaluation. His evaluation work covers diverse areas of professional enquiry, including schooling, police training, nurse and medical education, and the performing arts. Saville serves in editorial positions for the *American Journal of Evaluation* and the AEA monograph series, *Advances in Program Evaluation*.

Miri Levin-Rozalis, PhD, Sociologist and Psychologist, is a faculty member of the Department of Education at the Ben-Gurion University, the head of the track for Education Management and Policy, and the head of the Graduate and Post Graduate Program in Evaluation. In the Mofet Institute, she is the co-head of the qualification program in evaluation for teachers' trainers. She is the cofounder and the former president of IAPE (the Israeli Association for Program Evaluation) and has practiced evaluation for almost 30 years. Her current research interest is the sociology of evaluation in Israel and in the world.

Ulf P. Lundgren, Professor, took his doctorate degree in Göteborg, Sweden, in 1972. He became Professor of Psychology and Education in Denmark and in 1975 at Stockholm Institute of Education, Sweden. Later he was Vice Chancellor of the Institute. In 1990, he became Director General for the Swedish National Agency for Education. He has served as a chairman for several committees, including the committee for a national curriculum, and the committee for an educational act. Lundgren has been an expert in various positions within educational ministries in Sweden, Norway, France, and Portugal, as well as within the European Union, OECD, and UNESCO. He served in the steering group that formed the PISA evaluations at OECD. Today, Lundgren has a personal chair at Uppsala University, where he is leading a research group working with studies on educational policy and evaluation.

Linda Mabry is Professor of Educational Psychology at Washington State University Vancouver, specializing in research methodology, program evaluation, and the assessment of K-12 student achievement. She has served on the Board of Directors of the American Evaluation Association and on the Board of Trustees of the National Center for the Improvement of Educational Assessment. She practices case study methodology in research and program evaluation and publishes empirical examples as well as methodological texts such as the one in this volume.

Melvin M. Mark is Professor and Head of Psychology at Penn State University. A past president of the American Evaluation Association, he has also served as Editor of the *American Journal of Evaluation*, where he is now Editor Emeritus. Among his books are *Evaluation: An Integrated Framework for Understanding, Guiding, and Improving Policies and Programs* (with Gary Henry and George Julnes), the *SAGE Handbook of Evaluation* (with Ian Shaw and Jennifer Greene), *What Counts As Credible Evidence in Applied Research and Evaluation Practice* (with Stewart Donaldson and Tina Christie), *Evaluation in Action: Interviews With Expert Evaluators* (with Jody Fitzpatrick and Tina Christie), and the forthcoming *Social Psychology and Evaluation* (with Stewart Donaldson and Bernadette Campbell).

Jacob Marszalek is Assistant Professor of Counseling and Educational Psychology in the School of Education at the University of Missouri-Kansas City. His research interests include applying new quantitative techniques to address research questions in education, program evaluation, testing, and psychology. As a student at the University of Illinois, he assisted with several program evaluations funded at the local, state, and national levels. He consults regularly on the design and implementation of grant evaluations in the Midwest.

Sandra Mathison is Professor of Education at the University of British Columbia. Her research focuses on educational evaluation and especially on the potential and limits of evaluation to support democratic ideals and promote justice. She has conducted national large- and small-scale evaluations of K-12, postsecondary, and informal educational programs and curricula; published articles in the leading evaluation journals; and edited and authored a number of books. She is editor of the *Encyclopedia of Evaluation* and co-editor (with E. Wayne Ross) of *The Nature and Limits of Standards Based Reform and Assessment* and *Battleground Schools*; she is co-author (with Melissa Freeman) of *Researching Children's Experiences*; and she is Editor-in-Chief of the journal *New Directions for Evaluation*.

Gerry McNamara, PhD, is Professor of Education at the School of Education Studies, Dublin City University. His research interests include educational evaluation and practitioner research. He is an active member of both the European Evaluation Society and the Irish Evaluation Network, and he is a member of the Council of the British Educational Leadership, Management and Administration Society. Their (see O'Hara) most recent publications include *Trusting Schools and Teachers: Developing*

Educational Professionalism Through Self-Evaluation (Peter Lang, 2008) and "The Importance of the Concept of Self-Evaluation in the Changing Landscape of Educational Policy," *Studies in Educational Evaluation*, 34, 173–179.

Matthew Militello is Assistant Professor in Educational Leadership and Policy Studies at North Carolina State University and has taught at University of Massachusetts, Amherst. Prior to his academic career, Militello was a middle and high school teacher and administrator. His current research centers on preparing school leaders. Most recently, Militello coauthored *Leading With Inquiry and Action: How Principals Improve Teaching and Learning*, a book that provides explicit examples of how principals enact collaborative inquiry-action cycles to increase student achievement. He has published in *Education and Urban Society, Harvard Educational Review, Journal of School Leadership*, and *Qualitative Inquiry*.

David Nevo, Tel Aviv University, Israel, is Professor Emeritus at the School of Education, Tel Aviv University. His professional interests include evaluation theory, program evaluation, school-based evaluation, and student assessment. His current research is focused on dialogue evaluation, combining internal and external evaluation and working with schools and teachers to improve their evaluation capabilities and their ability to cope with external evaluation requirements and accountability. Dr. Nevo is the author of *Evaluation in Decision Making* (with Glasman, Kluwer, 1988) and *School-Based Evaluation: A Dialogue for School Improvement* (Pergamon, 1995), the editor of *School-Based Evaluation: An International Perspective* (Elsevier, 2002) and a past editor-in-chief of *Studies in Educational Evaluation*. He served as Head of School of Education, Tel Aviv University, and Chief Scientist of the Israeli Ministry of Education.

Theo J. H. Niessen, PhD, is a senior researcher and lecturer at Fontys University of Applied Sciences-Faculty of Nursing. He is also appointed as the head of an ethics committee at a home for elderly people. Within his PhD, he developed an enactivist epistemological framework to understand teachers' learning processes during responsive evaluation. Currently his research is concentrating on ethics and moral deliberation and practice improvement.

Joe O'Hara, PhD, is Senior Lecturer at the School of Education Studies, Dublin City University, with responsibility for Initial Teacher Education. His research interests include educational evaluation and initial teacher education. He is an active member of the Irish Evaluation Network and European Evaluation Society. He is currently a member of the General Council of the European Educational Research Association and is Vice President of the Educational Studies Association of Ireland. Their (see McNamara) most recent publications include *Trusting Schools and Teachers: Developing Educational Professionalism Through Self-Evaluation* (Peter Lang, 2008) and "Importance of the Concept of Self-Evaluation in the Changing Landscape of Educational Policy," *Studies in Educational Evaluation*, 34, 173–179.

Sharon F. Rallis is Dwight W. Allen Distinguished Professor of Education Policy and Reform at the University of Massachusetts, Amherst. A past president of the American Evaluation Association, Rallis has worked with evaluation for over three decades and has published extensively in evaluation journals. Her research focuses on local implementation of policy-driven programs. She has taught on education leadership and policy faculties at University of Connecticut, Harvard, and Vanderbilt. Rallis' doctorate is from Harvard University. Her books include *Learning in the Field: An Introduction to Qualitative Research* (with Gretchen Rossman) and *Leading with Inquiry and Action: How Principals Improve Teaching and Learning* (with Matthew Militello).

Dana K. Rickman was recently named the Director for Research and Policy at the Annie E. Casey Foundation, Atlanta Civic Site. Before then, she was a Senior Research Associate at Georgia State University, Andrew Young School for Policy Studies. Rickman has participated in a variety of public policy evaluations including North Carolina's Disadvantaged Student Supplemental Fund, Georgia's Universal Pre-K, and Georgia's TANF system. Rickman has published in the fields of evaluation, and education policy.

Fazal Rizvi has been a Professor in the Department of Educational Policy Studies at the University of Illinois since 2001, having previously held academic and administrative appointments at a number of universities in Australia. His new book, *Globalizing Education Policy* (Routledge), will appear in 2009. He has written widely on theories of globalization, educational, and cultural policy and the internationalization of higher education. He is currently researching higher education in India, especially with respect to the ways in which Indian universities are engaging with issues of globalization and the knowledge economy. At Illinois, he directs an online program for teachers around the world in Global Studies in Education. See gse.ed.uiuc.edu.

Barbara Rosenstein, PhD, grew up in New York and studied at Brooklyn College of the City University of New York, the University of Chicago, and Ben Gurion University of the Negev. After 2 years in the Peace Corps in Tunisia and several years of teaching ESL and French in Connecticut, she moved to Israel. In 1984, she was introduced to the field of evaluation through work with the Bernard van Leer Foundation and has studied, taught, and practiced evaluation ever since. She developed a method of using video for evaluation and has given talks and workshops on the subject. Her main focus has been on community-based programs concerned with education, empowerment, and co-existence. She is a founding member and now chairperson of the Israeli Association for Program Evaluation and was on the first board of the International Organization for Cooperation in Evaluation. Barbara teaches Theory of Evaluation and Ethics in Evaluation at Ben Gurion University of the Negev.

Thomas A. Schwandt is Professor and Chair, Department of Educational Psychology, at the University of Illinois at Urbana-Champaign, where he also holds an appointment in the Department of Educational Policy Studies. He is the author of *Evaluation Practice Reconsidered*; *Evaluating Holistic Rehabilitation Practice*; *Dictionary of Qualitative Inquiry*; and, with Edward Halpern, *Linking Auditing and Meta-Evaluation*. In 2002, he received the Paul F. Lazarsfeld Award from the American Evaluation Association for his contributions to evaluation theory. He is currently a member of the Standing Committee on Research and Evidentiary Standards, National Research Council, Division of Behavioral and Social Sciences and Education.

Michael Scriven is Professor of Psychology at Claremont Graduate University and Senior Research Associate at the Evaluation Center, Western Michigan University. He took two degrees in mathematics from Melbourne University in Australia and then a doctorate in philosophy at Oxford. His 400+ publications are in four fields: computer studies, philosophy of technology, historiography, and educational research. He was on the faculty at the University of California/Berkeley for 12 years, as well as at Swarthmore and the Universities of Minnesota, Indiana, Western Australia, and Auckland. He has held fellowships at Harvard and the Center for Advanced Study in the Behavioral Sciences at Stanford, among others; has served as president of the American Educational Research Association and the American Evaluation Association; and is on the editorial or review boards of 42 journals.

Christina Segerholm is Senior Lecturer at MidSweden University, Sweden. Her research interest is mainly directed toward critical studies of evaluation impact in education. A more recent interest is evaluation as global policy and governance. Some of her studies include National Evaluations as Governing Instruments: How Do They Govern?, *Evaluation*, 7(4); Governance Through Institutionalized Evaluation: Recentralization and Influences at Local Levels in Higher Education in Sweden (co-author Eva Åström), *Evaluation*, 13(1); and *New Public Management and Evaluation under Decentralizing Regimes in Education Dilemmas of Engagement: Evaluation and the New Public Management* (Saville Kushner & Nigel Norris, Eds.).

Nick L. Smith (PhD, University of Illinois, 1975) is Professor and Chairperson in the Instructional Design, Development and Evaluation Department, School of Education, at Syracuse University. He has served on numerous editorial boards, including as Editor of *New Directions for Evaluation*. Professor Smith has received distinguished awards from the Association of Teacher Educators, the American Psychological Association, and the American Evaluation Association. He is a Fellow in the American Educational Research Association and the American Psychological Association, and is a 2004 President of the American Evaluation Association. His primary research interests concern the theory and methods of evaluation and applied research.

Peter M. Steiner is Assistant Professor in the Department of Sociology at the Institute for Advanced Studies in Vienna and Visiting Assistant Professor at Northwestern University. He holds a master's degree and a doctorate in statistics from the University of Vienna, as well as a master's degree in economics from the Vienna University of Economics and Business Administration. His research interests are in the methodology of causal inference, particularly quasi-experimental designs in education and experimental vignette designs in survey research.

Claudia V. Tamassia, MEd (Columbia, MO), PhD (Champaign, IL), works at the Educational Testing Service coordinating the OECD Programme for the International Assessment of Adult Competencies (PIAAC). Her primary interests are international education and comparative and international assessment. She has worked at the Ministry of Education in Brazil, at the OECD in Paris in managing the Programme for International Student Assessment, and at the Chicago Public Schools. As a consultant, she has worked with UNESCO and taught at the University of Illinois. She completed her undergraduate studies in Brazil and her graduate work at the University of Missouri-Columbia and at the University of Illinois at Urbana-Champaign.

Harry Torrance is Professor of Education and Director of the Education and Social Research Institute, Manchester Metropolitan University, UK. He has conducted many empirical studies of student assessment and has published widely in the fields of assessment, program evaluation, and education reform. He is an elected member of the UK Academy of Social Sciences.

Cees P. M. van der Vleuten is Professor in Education at the department of Education, Maastricht University. He is appointed as Professor of Education at the Faculty of Health, Medicine, and Life Sciences; Chair of the Department of Educational Development and Research; and Scientific Director of the School of Health Professions Education (www.she.unimaas.nl). His area of expertise lies in evaluation and assessment. He has published widely on these topics and holds several academic awards for this work. He has frequently served as an educational consultant internationally.

Guy A. M. Widdershoven is Professor in Philosophy and Ethics of Medicine at the VU University Medical Centre, EMGO Institute, Department of Medical Humanities, Amsterdam. His work concentrates on the development of contextual approaches to ethics (hermeneutic ethics, dialogical ethics, narrative ethics, ethics of care) in chronic care (psychiatry, care for the elderly, care for persons with an intellectual disability).

Angela Wroblewski is Assistant Professor in the Department of Sociology at the Institute for Advanced Studies in Vienna and Lecturer at the Vienna University of Economics and Business Administration and the University of Vienna. She teaches research methods to students at the BA, MA, and PhD levels. Her research interests are in evaluation research (especially of education and labor market programs with a gender focus) and equal opportunities in education and labor markets.